Victorian Poetry Now

Victorian Poetry Now
Poets, Poems, Poetics

Valentine Cunningham

WILEY-BLACKWELL

A John Wiley & Sons, Ltd., Publication

This edition first published 2011
© 2011 Valentine Cunningham

Blackwell Publishing was acquired by John Wiley & Sons in February 2007. Blackwell's publishing program has been merged with Wiley's global Scientific, Technical, and Medical business to form Wiley-Blackwell.

Registered Office
John Wiley & Sons Ltd, The Atrium, Southern Gate, Chichester, West Sussex, PO19 8SQ, United Kingdom

Editorial Offices
350 Main Street, Malden, MA 02148-5020, USA
9600 Garsington Road, Oxford, OX4 2DQ, UK
The Atrium, Southern Gate, Chichester, West Sussex, PO19 8SQ, UK

For details of our global editorial offices, for customer services, and for information about how to apply for permission to reuse the copyright material in this book please see our website at www.wiley.com/wiley-blackwell.

The right of Valentine Cunningham to be identified as the author of this work has been asserted in accordance with the UK Copyright, Designs and Patents Act 1988.

Library of Congress Cataloging-in-Publication Data

Cunningham, Valentine.
   Victorian poetry now : poets, poems, poetics / Valentine Cunningham.
     p.   cm.
   Includes bibliographical references and index.
   ISBN 978-0-631-20826-6 (hardback)
  1. English poetry–19th century–History and criticism.   2. Poetics–History–19th century. 3. Poetry–Authorship–History–19th century.   4. Literature and society–Great Britain–History–19th century. I. Title.
  PR591.C86 2011
  821'.809–dc22

                  2010049294

A catalogue record for this book is available from the British Library.

This book is published in the following electronic formats: ePDFs [9781444340419]; Wiley Online Library [9781444340440]; ePub [9781444340426]

Set in 10/12 pt Sabon by SPi Publisher Services, Pondicherry, India
Printed in Malaysia by Ho Printing (M) Sdn Bhd

1 2011

Contents

Preface

This critical-historical account of Victorian poetry attempts to give some sense – to *make* some sense – of the productions of the most aweingly productive period of poetry there's ever been, in any language. Just how many 'Victorian' poets and poems there were really came home to me in compiling my Blackwells collection *The Victorians: An Anthology of Poetry and Poetics* (2000), with its 158 named poets (and a ghostly band of not-all-that-bad poets excluded for reasons only of space). Most of the discussion in this book has grown out of lectures and classes at Oxford and elsewhere seeking to arm undergraduates and graduates – and still more grown-up readers too – with some map through this densely matted overgrowth and undergrowth. How to see the wood for the trees, and the trees for the wood. To make out the figures in this very large carpet. To see, in Matthew Arnold's phrase, the poetic object 'as in itself it really is' – though reckoning the poetic object, the text, not as some neatly bounded, autotelic, done and dusted, perfectly finished thing (did Arnold ever really think that?), but as it indeed is, a messy, fluid scene or drama of language, its 'final' words never unconscious of their precedent try-outs (many of them now handily, and always eye-openingly, available in major editions), and in many cases bearing the traces of its as it were evolutionary ancestors in earlier poems (what we now think of as its intertextual forebears); its words slippery to grip, given as they are more to connotation than denotation, to multivalence rather than singleness of mind; its grammar happily *fuzzy* (as modern grammarians have it); its referentiality so difficult to pin down because this writing is so utterly receptive to the world of things outside it. These texts are deictic alright, but pointing all over the place. This textuality is so porous: all at once also intertextual and contextual.

Every genre, said Derrida on a wise occasion, overflows all boundaries assigned to it. And so it is with every item in consideration by my title: *poem, poetics, poet* even, certainly *poetry*, and of course *Victorian*.

They're all of them hazy and blurry as would-be knowable 'objects'; though in practice we do have to keep talking about them as such: Victorian, poetry, poet, poem, poetics.

A multi-pronged complexity then. My prime critical business is with 'poems', those complex utterances. Poems in their great Victorian multiplicity. High canonical ones, of course, but backed of necessity by reference to the great mass of second-division and also obviously minor ones. As well as merely citing lots, I do keep dwelling at some length on individual poems – there's much close reading here – singletons which have to stand (as is the inevitable way of criticism) synecdochically, and I hope convincingly, for the always greater numbers of their authors' production, and the literary production of their era, the very very large Victorian poetic oeuvre. My sub-title puts 'poets' first, because I'm not afraid of the fact that poems are produced by poets, actual men and women, living in the real world, who are the actual thinking, feeling, writing channels for all the contents and discontents which poems evince. It's not writing that writes – to reverse Roland Barthes's notorious formula – but writers. So, no Death of the Author here, but rather constant biographical name-checking and a constant eye out for what have been called 'biographemes', the textualizing of authorial concerns. Poets, then; and my mission is to show how poets, and so their poems, come marinaded in politics and economics, the wars of contemporary ideas, and how they're utterly conscious of their times. And poets, and so their poems, also, in the main, highly self-conscious poetically, aesthetically. These writers are nothing if not readers, who keep positioning themselves and their work in relation to other writers and writings, and other aesthetic practices like painting, practising intertextuality and intermediality (as we say nowadays). Hence the constant stress in my analyses on the 'poetics' of my title – on the contemporary theorizing of poetry and the poetic; on the constant discussion within poems about poeticity and aesthetic function (metatextuality: poems about poems; poems self-reflecting by proxy in ekphrastic engagements with surrogate made-objects such as paintings); my constant hearkening to what's done with the Bible and Shakespeare and Dante and the Classics (especially the Roman); and my interest in the debate for and against medievalism and classicism. I persistently position my poets and their poems around large nodes of contemporary theoretical/critical discussion – about rhyme, onomatopeia, Ruskinian 'pathetic fallacy', Arnoldian 'modernity', the so-called 'Fleshly School', Mrs Browning's 'sort of novel-poem', and so on – because that's what contemporary poets and their poems and their readers did.

Much of what reading the poetic objects as in themselves they really are must take in is, of course, given: the particular words on the page (and/or in the footnotes of good editions), and so words and word-issues occupy prime place in my critical narratives; as also the available, legible, statements from the poets about what they think and mean and intend; and the poetic concerns and topics of my authors and of their times; and the contemporary Victorian critical agenda which foreground the current questions of form, rhetoric, content, style. But reading in the 'Now' of my title – *Victorian Poetry Now* – is always contingent on the modern reader's contemporary reading agenda. Which is constantly shifting the textual and critical emphases and directions, refocussing response, refocalizing it (as we say now, borrowing from film-theory). No modern reader's contemporary critical agenda can utterly ignore, let alone displace or erase the givens perceived to be importantly in play in whatever old poetic object, whenever. But current critical thought about how words and so poems work and mean, and the possibilities for interpretation, for hermeneutics, and the importance or otherwise of this or the other issue of belief, thought, action, politics economics, class, gender, race, and so forth, will inevitability inflect the modern reader's approaches. However retro, however hostile to modern theory, you want to be, you will inevitably be affected by it. And since we all now come After Theory, we all now read, more or less, some of us enthusiastically, some of us distantly, under the fashionable twin, hegemonic flags of (post) structuralism and post-Marxist materialism. We're inevitably commanded on the one hand by the so-called Linguistic Turn, stressing textuality (and intertextuality and metatextuality), a sort of neo-formalism, with a prominent stake in aporia, abysmality, endless difference rather than reference, that is something like Derridean deconstruction, certainly an epistemological and hermeneutic scepticism about readability and knowability which scoops in Freud, courtesty of Lacan, and thus applies to persons as well as texts. And on the other, rather contradictorily, commanded by deep and wide contextualism – politically concerned, ideologically curious and furious, concerned to discuss the 'construction' of gender, race and class, the self, the body in literature – travelling variously under the names of Cultural Materialism, New Historicism, third-generation Feminism, Gender Studies, especially Q, that is Queer, Studies, and Post-Colonialism (with its mighty subset Edward Saidian Orientalism), all mightily animated by Michel Foucault and his studies of institutionalized power and its assorted discourses. This is the modernist critical recipe book which has made Victorianists all more or less a spotty, opportunistic blend of a sort of Derrideanism and Focauldianism. And so it is inevitably here. I try to write as plainly and unjargonizingly as possible – William Empson is my favoured model – but it should be clear just how much I accept how much Theory and Theorized reading have affected our sense of what's up, and what's important, in Victorian poetry.

Introducing a characteristically of-now Tennyson-centennial number of *Victorian Poetry* (Vol 30, iii–iv, Autumn-Winter 1992), the volume's editor, the openly deconstructionist Tennysonian Gerhard Joseph, imagines the

Shade of Tennyson complaining about 'All this talk about "repression", "sexual confusion", "patriarchal functions", cultural formation of masculinities, ... "deconstruction" of one binary opposition or another, "colonial discourse", ideological moments and disruptions'. Tennyson's ghost is not placated, but Gerhard's point that all this sort of reading is inevitable is not to be gainsaid. Of course Joseph concedes that there is a possible danger of current readers 'imputing' (he uses Tennyson's own word) our contemporary concerns in the old writings, that is forcing in such considerations, even imagining some issues and practices to be present when they're not. But what's arresting is just how little false imputing of values and meaning has gone on through the critical agenda Gerhard Joseph is so receptive to. I myself believe, in fact, that nothing critically useful (to paraphrase King Lear) comes out of nothing; critical somethings only come from things actually present – however previously invisible they might have been. The falsely imputed doesn't stick long – if it sticks at all. And, in fact, what I hope I keep showing is the way *Now* reading is actually only reworking what Victorian poets and poems have already worked with, whether consciously or not – an emphasis culminating in my final chapter on 'Victorian Modernismus'.

What's striking in recent times is how post-Theory reading has opened up Victorian poetry so convincingly, and (in the best sense) as never before. With palpable gains of all sorts. In terms, not least, of expanding the ranks of considerable clientele. Theorized rereadings of the canon have brought in from the cold many otherwise neglected men and women, including regional and proletarian writers, who are given their now due weight in my account: Christina Rossetti and Elizabeth Barrett Browning, now in the Top Team, jostling hard against the Top Three of Tennyson, Robert Browning, and Hopkins (though I do think some of the feminist praise-singing on behalf of LEL, Felicia Hemans, and Michael Field a *parti-pris* advocacy too far); Swinburne, happily promoted by Gender Studies; Oscar Wilde, convincingly placed now as the most considerable end-of-century British writer through the efforts of Queer theorists. And so forth. There have been massive conceptual, hermeneutic gains too, notably the queering of Hopkins (and Tennyson), but with accesses of new meaning all over the shop – about the poets' anxieties for language, form and genre (the post-structuralist linguistic, epistemological, deconstructionist challenge), about how selfhood, belief, history, politics, empire, the real, play. Issues, to repeat, rarely imputed; but animated and, of course re-animated, for our greater advisement.

My own now reading – *Victorian Poetry Now* – falls into two, I think necessary rather than contingent, and I hope critically useful, parts. Part I, 'So Far as the Words Are Concerned', foregrounds basic verbal, textual issues; Part II, 'Contents and Discontents of the Forms' tackles major issues of content, the subject-matters of the poetic forms, and inspects the interactions of form

and content (branching out from the demonstrations in Part I, Chapter 4 of
the way poems' merely verbal practices (in this case rhyming/repetition) sustain the extra-verbal meanings – are rhymings with reasons beyond what's
merely aural. 'Words, Words, Words, and More Words', Chapter 1, dwells on
the aweingly large scope of Victorian poetry, its numerosity, its big poems, its
multivalence; how (contrary to myths of Victorian repression and narrowness –
which lasted well into the twentieth century) and the allegation that formal
prowess over-rode close attention to the choice and arrangement of the words,
the Victorians lavished great care on their verbal doings – in the unstoppable
critical conversation going on in the extended Victorian poetic family (examples from the Rossettis and their chums, Tennyson and the Reviewers, and
Ruskin and Browning toughing it out *mano a mano*, hard and personally).
'Rhyming/Repeating', Chapter 2, sets out my theory of essential poetic (how
to tell a poem when you see one), offering rhyme, 'bound words', that is repetition (anaphora, doubling, iteration, dittography; rhyme as the repetition of
any and every possible verbal item) as the hard core of (Victorian) poeticity.
(Victorian) poetry as a set of repetition machines. (No such thing as free verse;
no refraining from refraining, from the burden of the burden.) 'Making Noise/
Noising Truths', Chapter 3, suggests mere noise, the mere 'ring of rhyme', as
prime (Tennyson the Auriculate Laureate leading the noisy way), and exam-
ines varieties of poetic noise-making, the lure of *onomatopoeia* (with special
reference to Hopkins: God's rhymester), Tennyson and noise as horrible vital-
ity, Hardyesque stillicide, the noisiness of Browning and his marginalized ilk
that's so offensive to the elitist and the posh (Arnold's 'tone of the centre'),
and noise-making as a kind of truthfulness to the real. 'These Rhyming/
Repeating Games are Serious', Chapter 4, expands the idea of repeated noise,
the poems' noise-making – poetry's *jouissance* in the repetition/rhyming
games it indulges so much, its delighted response to the abysmality of nonsense and Nonsense (helter-skelter 'Goblin Market', and all that) – as nonetheless the bearer of meanings beyond mere aurality: by the way repetitions,
doublings, returns, echoings sustain and make fulness of meaning, work the
question of meaning, in particular in representative main poems by Hood,
Christina G Rossetti ('Goblin Market', 'Winter: My Secret' (aka 'Nonsense'),
'Echo' and 'A Christmas Carol'), Dante Gabriel Rossetti ('Troy Town'),
Clough ('Dipsychus'), Tennyson ('The Charge of the Light Brigade'), Robert
Browning ('Two in the Campagna'), and Hopkins ('Spelt from Sibyl's
Leaves').

Part II is besotted by content, the contents (and discontents) in, and made
by and through, the poetic forms, the verbal containers. Chapter 5, 'Down-
Sizing' makes a methodological segue into the critical ways of Part II.
Offering an antithesis to the massivity, the bigness heroic, of the period it
investigates the way the forms and contents of *smallness* interact – the small
poem (exemplarily the sonnet, a main production of this *sonnettomaniac*

time, especially Charles Tennyson Turner's sonneteering); the child subject and children's literature; the fetish of *dollanity*, of the small subject, the small text (little girls, dolls, toys, photographs, postage-stamps); the metonymic, synecdochic force of the small poeticized item (the 'flower in the crannied wall' syndrome); the overwhelming powers of reductionism ('Letty's Globe', Browning's Duke); the menace and horrors of smallness (poetry's shop of little horrors); *fairyology* (fairies, fairy poems, fairy paintings); the convergence of these tropes, subjects, objects in particular in Lewis Carroll; the shock, menace, madness, neurosis of such fetishizing (black-handed Carroll, mad Richard Dadd, the exemplarily fearful Dong-ish nose of Edward Lear). Chapters 6, 7, and 8 in Part II are large umbrellas under which are instructively clustered what seem to me the most prominent and far-reaching anxieties of Victorian poetry (with much side-glancing, here as elsewhere, at parallel pictorial work). 'Selving', Chapter 6, exposes the massive self-preoccupation of Victorian poetry, thinks much about the going problems with personification (*prosopopoeia*, the making of *prosopa*), feels the force of Ruskin's 'pathetic fallacy' charges, focusses a lot on the dramatic monologue, on deceiving self-presentation (slippery characters), on variously distraught persons – people in poetry's *madhouse cells*, the wildly spasmodic 'Maud' very important here), selves on edge (especially on the beach, where they're threatened with disselving, self-dissolution under the real and allegorical threat of incoming tides), with much about poets and poetry taking on the destructive element of water (Swinburne not least); all of which wateriness leads into the gender perturbations (the massive Queer-dilemma mongering) typically allegorized in and around water (Hopkins's 'Epithalamium', Clough's swimming holes, Symonds's blue Venetian lagoon, Swinburne's Hermaphroditus fantasy), and to the frustrations of hermaphroditism and 'Contralto' parts, and the problematic of garbled and garbling poetic identity (the truth/untruth of pronouns) especially in the gay aesthetic practices of Michael Field, Symonds, and Pater. Which selfhood considerations and consternations turn into bodily questions in Chapter 7, 'Fleshly Feelings', where the poetry's faith in the body as the most reliable signifying system of personal meaning (body truth) is inspected, beginning with the large issue of the sexualized body as prompted by Buchanan/Maitland's revealing attacks on 'The Fleshly School' of poetry; going on to look at how the poetry handles all sorts and conditions of body, the desired and the undesirable, the good, the bad and the ugly; and climaxing with an extended discussion of poetry's (and painting's) troubling body synecdoches for the person – mouths, of course, but above all hair (fetishistically alluring, frighteningly demonic, genderized (straight, gay), religious – religiose hair starring 'Mary Magdalene', the composite fantasy woman from the Gospels so enticing to poets (and painters). 'Mourning and Melancholia', Chapter 8, the longest chapter because these are Victorian poetry's biggest subject-matters, deals with the ubiquitous sadness, grieving, mournfulness, melancholy, ghostedness, death-consciousness, death-wishing, death-antici- pating (the direct inheritance of Albrecht Dürer's Protestant 'Melencolia' and Shakespeare's Melancholy Protestant Man Prince Hamlet); its tone set by 'The City of Dreadful Night' by James Thompson the Victorian Dürer-ite known as the 'Laureate of Pessimism'; the period when elegy is the prevail- ing mode (with 'In Memoriam' as exemplary poem, and Tennyson's Hallam- grieving ouevre as exemplary poetic career). A typology of the period's huge roster of elegies, the poetry that remembers the dead, is offered: elegy the genre of grieving which has so many prompting causes – ruins of all sorts: civilizations, cities and empires (Timbuctoo, Babylon, Nineveh, Pompeii, Rome; British imperialism), Italian culture, fallen leaves (the large glum poetry of autumn and winter); the fallen trees of Hopkins and Barnes; the death of God and allied Recessionals; all an extensive poetry of apocalypse, ending-up, endedness which provokes much poetic wondering about the possible cheating of death, of doing something 'ere the end', the poetry of 'penultimateness' and possible living-on, of survival, of resurrection (hence the great poetic interest in the Gospel's Lazarus). Elegy, then, as memorial, *mnemotechnik*, an art of aesthetic life after death. The chapter ends with the cravings to make, at the least, a good end, massively illustrated by the cultic construction of the 'Last Chapter' of Tennyson's life, and with what the exhumation of Dante Gabriel Rossetti's poems from Lizzie Siddall's tomb might mean.

My final two chapters are a connected pair, about how modernity incites, infects, and affects Victorian poetry. 'Modernizing the Subject', Chapter 9, looks at how poets braced up (or not) to the challenges of the modern sub- ject in the sense of the realist issues of society, economics, politics which were commonly thought rather the prerogative of the novel; and 'Victorian Modernismus', Chapter 10, shows how modernist, even (post-modernist), Victorian poetic practices actually were. 'Modernizing the Subject' is about how the period's genre wars between the realist, modern, outward-looking, publicly-minded claims and tendencies of the novel and the private, anti- modern, backward-looking inclinations of much poetry worked out. A class warfare, on the whole, with the aesthetic gents, Anglican Christians, Oxonian posh or posh-ish poets (and painters), tending to retreat Arnoldianly into classicizing, pastoral and the medieval, shunning the modern world of urbanism, mechanism, the factory, democracy; and, on the other side, with the aesthetic proletarians and provincials, the truculent underclass of poetry (including many women), the religious Dissenters (in particular the Uni- tarians, and notably the Congregationalist Brownings) being steeped in urban, regional, technological and industrial matters, the movement of masses at home and abroad, the Carlylean stuff of the period's novels. This conflict of genre and matter is focussed in the terrifically important *Aurora*

Leigh, Elizabeth Barrett Browning's Carlylean 'Poetry of theWorld', her 'sort of novel-poem'. That this was by no means a simple of matter class and background alignments, though, is shown variously in the exemplary conflict between pastoralizing, classicizing, urban-provincial-Dissenter-averse Arnold and Oxonian 'Citizen Clough', in the two-way street up which fairyologist socialist Dissenter George Macdonald and the medievalizing Oxonian socialist William Morris travel, and in the fraught, unresolved, dualisms of Tennyson: his medievalism, pastoralism and classicism on the one hand, and his (*Aurora Leigh*-admiring) urban-conscious, machine-age, political, imperialist (and orientalist) preoccupations on the other. The chapter closes with Arnold and Tennyson fighting over who is the truest classicist, Virgilian, Horation, and with Tennyson acing Arnold in revising the classical subject as truly modern – releasing Lucretius's inner modern, rewriting him as a Roman Hamlet, melancholy mad like the narrator of 'Maud', or Tennyson himself.

Tennyson's modern Lucretius: signpost into 'Victorian Modernismus', which argues that so much of the linguistics, poetics, hermeneutics, narrativity, characterologies which have emerged in precedent chapters is in fact so proto-modernistically sceptical and relativist, even deconstructionist, as to be reckoned actually modernist, even post-modernist. Proof is offered in the great Victorian indebtedness of the great modernists, especially Pound and Eliot, and the way modernist Henry James could read *The Ring and the Book* as a Jamesian novel. The modernism of *The Ring and the Book* brings home the case, as, amply, does the great array of Victorian ekphrastic poems (by the Brownings and Swinburne and Dante Gabriel Rossetti), which the chapter ends by reading – powerful, metatextually modernist inspections of art-objects as surrogates for poems, poised in classic deconstructionist fashion at the aporetic borders of fulness-emptiness, presence-absence, meaning-unmeaning. Here's the challenging textuality of (post)modernism well before its time. Or, as one might well think, well within it.

Part I

So Far as The Words
Are Concerned

*'Whitman was ... a poet of the greatest and utmost delicacy, and
sensitivity, so far as words are concerned.' 'So Far as Words are
Concerned' might almost be the title of this book; every page brings
out the forgotten truism that words are what poems are made of.*
Louis MacNeice, quoting Randall Jarrell's *Poetry
and the Age* (1955) on the subject
of Walt Whitman's poems.[1]

[1]   *London Magazine* 2:9 (Sept 1955), 71–74; *Selected Literary Criticism of Louis MacNeice*,
ed Alan Heuser (Clarendon Press, Oxford, 1987), 205.

1

Words, Words, Words and More Words

> Polonius: *What do you read, my lord?*
> Hamlet: *Words, words, words.*
>
> *Hamlet*, 2.ii.190–191

The instantly striking feature of Victorian poetry is just how many poets there were and how much they wrote. (There are 122 named poets in Christopher Ricks's *Oxford Book of Victorian Verse* (1990), 145 in Danny Karlin's *Penguin Book of Victorian Verse* (1997) and 158 in my *The Victorians: An Anthology of Poetry and Poetics* (Blackwell, 2000).) Copiousness, bigness, magnitude are the order of the Victorian textual day. It's a muchness of poetic activity and production which manifestly mirrors the stupendous bigness of the times. This was the age of the colossal, of a numerical and physical largesse as never before experienced anywhere. It was, for instance, 'The Age of Great Cities', as it was dubbed in 1843, and how, according to Asa Briggs' classic study of Victorian urbanism, 'most Victorian writers on society thought of their age'.[2] Cities, those vast man-made objects – acres of bricks and mortar on a scale never before imagined let alone constructed – great because packed with people doing and making and consuming, selling and buying more things than anybody had ever done before in a single place. Inflatedness, inflation were on the up and up. Large cities were growing across the 'civilised world'– New York, Chicago, Paris – but above all in Britain: Glasgow, Liverpool, Birmingham, Manchester, London. And the greatest of these was London. The sheer

---

[2] Robert Vaughan, *The Age of Great Cities* (1843); Asa Briggs, *Victorian Cities* (Odhams Books, London, 1963), 57.

Victorian Poetry Now: Poets, Poems, Poetics, First Edition. Valentine Cunningham.
© 2011 Valentine Cunningham. Published 2011 by Blackwell Publishing Ltd.

'numerosity' of London, its 'senseless bigness', quite bowled over the American incomer Henry James in 1876. He'd never seen so much or so many as this 'enchanting' 'great city' offered: 'the biggest aggregation of human life – the most complete compendium of the world'. It was, of course, the 'right place' for a writer to be.[3] London was the centre of world consciousness. Everything and everybody, so to say, came to it. It was the economic epicentre of the world, the market-place of the globe, centre of the largest empire and colonial enterprise the world had ever known. For their part, Manchester and Birmingham were the factories – or manufactories, as the word then was – of the world. Everything, indeed, came from them. There was nowhere on earth that Manchester stuff – literally stuff, cotton goods – did not travel to: the product of the hands of the immigrant Irish machine-operatives, or 'hands', packed as never before into that city's grotesquely overcrowded slums.

So many people; so many things; so much for writers to reflect and reflect on; and so many poets (and novelists) to say it. Which is how it immediately came home to Tennyson when he was appointed Poet Laureate in November 1850. 'I get such shoals of poems that I am almost crazed with them; the two hundred million poets of Great Britain deluge me daily with poems: truly the Laureateship is no sinecure.'[4]

There was indeed much to say; and the poets did say it. Victorian poets can say almost anything, and about almost anything. They kept quiet about next to nothing. Only sex, the flesh, the functions of the lower parts of the body, which were, and are, busy writerly obsessions as they were, and are, busy human ones, had to be approached with some caution, but even then with not much caution, and certainly not with caution among friends. Of course there was plenty of public and private censorship. Podsnappery flourished – fathers suppressing anything likely to 'bring a blush into the cheek of the young person', like Dickens's Mr Podsnap, pompously protective of his daughter (*Our Mutual Friend* (1864–1865), I.i.11). The Bowdler Family's *Family Shakespeare* (1818), which edited out anything 'which cannot with propriety be read aloud in a family', was a huge nineteenth-century best-seller.[5] Characteristically of much current reader sensitivity, Mrs Richard Burton burnt a lot of her husband's erotically charged papers, and filled his posthumous translation of Catullus's poems (1894) with expurgatory dots. Verbally blunt, uneuphemizing versions of sexually explicit

---

[3]   Henry James, 1881 notebook entries, *The Notebooks of Henry James*, edd FO Matthiessen and Kenneth B Murdock (Galaxy, and Oxford University Press, NY, 1961), 25–28.
[4]   Hallam Lord Tennyson, *Alfred Lord Tennyson: A Memoir, By His Son*, 2 vols (Macmillan, London and New York, 1897), I. 337. Known as *Memoir* hereafter.
[5]   For the cleaning-up of Shakespeare by Dr Thomas Bowdler and his sister Fanny, see Noel Perrin, *Dr Bowdler's Legacy: A History of Expurgated Books in England and America* (Macmillan, London, 1970).

Petronius, Apuleius, Martial and Catullus texts appeared only in limited editions for posh private subscribers. Schoolboys were brought up on expurgated texts of the classical poets, as of Shakespeare. Some printers would draw the line at printing materials they thought too filthy – Swinburne's poems, Richard Burton's *Kama Sutra*, and so on. The Nonconformist consciences of William Henry Smith (a Methodist) and Charles Edward Mudie (a Congregationalist) kept their hugely influential subscription libraries free of 'immoral' books. (Smith, who started in railways bookstalls on the London and Northwestern Railways out of London's Euston Station was known as the 'North Western Missionary'.) There was much legal repression. An Obscene Publications Act came in, 1857. The Society for the Suppression of Vice reported in 1868 that since 1834 it had caused to be destroyed 16,220 books and pamphlets, and 129,681 prints, tons of print in fact. Henry Richard Vizetelly went to prison in 1889 for defiantly publishing Zola's novels – thought *bestial* and *obscene* by his prosecutors. Notoriously Swinburne's publisher Moxon withdrew *Poems and Ballads* within weeks of its publication in April 1866 because of the outcry over its sado-masochism and necrophilia. 'Swine-born' Swinburne, people called him. ('There is assuredly something wrong with you', Ruskin told Swinburne; 'you are rose graftings set in dung'.) And so the Victorian hostilities went.[6] And yet, literature, and poetry not least, abounded in what was called 'fleshliness' (see 'Fleshly Feelings' Chapter, below), in explicit eroticism, gruesome sexual gothicity, violence, perversity, fetishism, as well as blasphemy and heresy of every sort. Ekbert Faas is quite right to suggest that 'the Victorian reading public was surprisingly open-minded'.[7] (Hotton, the notorious specialist publisher of flagellation fantasy fiction, who stepped in to rescue *Poems and Ballads* for the public, was never prosecuted for issuing that 'filth'.)

Plainly, Victorian poems offered a more or less open door to the whole wide world of things and ideas, thoughts and events, feelings and actions. Victorian poetry is not just deictic, it's omni-deictic. *Deixis*, the linguistic action of pointing towards, pointing out, things in the non-verbal world (things of all sorts, not just objects and items, but events, persons, feelings), *this*, *that*, *there*, is what this poetry luxuriates in. Victorian poetry refers. It is ostensive, ostentatiously assuming a world, and worlds outside of

---

[6] *Letters of Charles Algernon Swinburne*, ed Cecil Y Lang, I, 1854–1869 (Yale University Press, New Haven, and Oxford University Press, London, 1959), 182. Much historical detail in Donald Thomas, *A Long Time Burning: The History of Literary Censorship in England* (Routledge Kegan Paul, London, 1969).

[7] He's thinking of how 'readers clamoured for more' revelations about the kind of morbid sadistic satisfactions Robert Browning paraded in 'Porphyria's Lover': 'Swinburne, or the Psychopathology of Poetic Creation', Ch X, *Retreat Into the Mind: Victorian Poetry and the Rise of Psychiatry* (Princeton University Press, Princeton, NJ, 1988), 184.

language. It is by no means as autotelic as some bad post-structuralist theorists and theorizing have suggested poetry and poetic language automatically are. Of course there's much self-reference in Victorian poetry – poems taking language, poeticity, textuality and their ways as subject. And, as we shall see again and again, poems do keep registering the difficulties of language, discourse, art; the problematics of reference, of telling the real, of, precisely, the deictic endeavour; registering the appeals of silence and the honesty of stymied utterance, all in a (at first blush) rather startling pre-post-modernist, ur-deconstructionist way (the large subject of my chapter 'Victorian Modernismus', Chapter 10, below). But what's nonetheless arresting and exciting is that, for all of their manifest doubtings, the poets do keep taking on as subject what's outside and beyond the poem, determined to finger, grasp, grip, mawl the world, the worldly subject, in all its apparent plenitude. And to do so plenitudinously.[8]

'The world was all before them', says Milton of Adam and Eve as they leave the Garden of Eden for ordinary fallen life at the end of *Paradise Lost*. And Victorian poets eagerly embraced that plenitude. And, commonly, at great length, unstoppably, on and on. Of course there was a reverse habit and cult of the small poem and the sequence of small poems (especially the sonnet) – as we shall see later (Chapter 6, 'Selving'). But it is great length that is the first most noticeable thing about Victorian poetic form. Textual hypertrophy is a nineteenth-century problem. It's no surprise that *metromania* and *metromanie*, meaning a mania for producing poetry, enter the English language in the 1790s. The Victorians were *metromaniacs* (*metromaniac*: first recorded in English in 1830), with a mania for producing large poems. What Coleridge approved of as *the Vast*.[9] Victorian readers remarked, and not always with pleasure, that Elizabeth Barrett Browning's *Aurora Leigh* (1856) had more lines than the *Odyssey* or *Paradise Lost* – 2,000 more than Milton's great epic, gnashed Coventry Patmore.[10] There are 21,116 lines in Robert Browning's *The Ring and the Book* (1868–1869), with even more added in subsequent editions.

---

[8]   Deixis of course features in (famed deconstruction sceptic) Raymond Tallis's fine meditation on pointing, *Michelangelo's Finger: An Exploration of Everyday Transcendence* (Atlantic Books, London, 2010). 'Pointing is the most blatant example of "deixis", a property that connects signs with the material circumstances in which they occur. ... Pointing silently utters "That ... that thing ... that state of affairs" and links that local explicitness with the massively elaborated explicitness that is made possible through language'. Tallis, 76.

[9]   See Adam Roberts, *Romantic and Victorian Long Poems: A Guide* (Ashgate, Aldershot, 1999), a big lexicon for Romantic and Victorian poems of 1,000 words or more, with a few smaller ones let in, e.g. Tennyson's 'Enoch Arden' (941 lines) and Matthew Arnold's 'Sohrab and Rustum' (892).

[10]   *Westminster Review* 68 (October 1857). Quoted in *Aurora Leigh*, ed Margaret Reynolds (WW Norton & Co, NY & London, 1996), 424.

> It takes up about eighty thousand lines,
> A thing imagination boggles at:
> And might, odds-bobs, sir! in judicious hands,
> Extend from here to Mesopotamy.

That's Charles Stuart Calverley, the ace Victorian parodist, who couldn't stand Browning's bulging effort, and mocked it rigid in his 'The Cock and the Bull', 129 lines of rich parody Browning-ese. Tennyson told Browning that 'Mr Sludge, the Medium' (sic) was 'two thirds too long'.[11] Browning's 'new poem has 15,000 lines: there's copiousness!', the Irish poet William Allingham reports Tennyson as declaring with some wonderment in October 1863 – before he sloped abruptly off to bed (overwhelmed, perhaps, by the thought of all those words).[12] Actually Browning did not produce a poem of 15,000 words in 1863, so it's not easy to tell which poem Tennyson might have been referring to. But the point of the report is clear: Browning had, from the start of his career, become a by-word as the poet of many words. And in truth. His *Paracelsus* (1835) has 4,152 lines; his *Sordello* (1840) some 5,000 lines. '[A] nother jet from his full fountain', said Tennyson when Browning's *Aristophanes Apology* (1875) turned up (Memoir, II, 231). Indeed it was. 'Cannot your task have end here, Euthukles?', the character Aristophanes asks at line 2,709 of his poem. Well, no, there are another 3,002 lines to go.

Browning just loves bulking out, raising the rhetorical stake, shifting up through the verbal gears, relishing the sheer energy of the rapid verbal ride, the mere accumulation of verbal material: 'the world of words I had to say', as Browning's Count Guido Franceschini puts it at the end of his second address in Book XI of *The Ring and the Book* (by far the longest Book in the *Book*). It's a relish for excessive verbal acquisition and expression nicely illustrated in the story Browning told Elizabeth Barrett about a friend who was asked to annotate a third-party's sonnets and just kept on upping the verbal ante. *Bad, worse, worst*, was his friend's note against the first three lines. The next three were designated *badder, badderer, badderest*. The next three were *worster, worsterer, worsterest*. By which stage there was nothing for it but to label the final couplet *worsterestest and worsterestest*.[13] This is only Robert Browning's second joke, very early on in his wonderful epistolary wooing of Miss Barrett. Part of the fun of creativity for Browning is that only the *most* words possible, or the *mostest*, the *mostestest* even, as we might say, will do. And what's true for him is true for lots of others – for Elizabeth Barrett Browning, for Christina G Rossetti, for Tennyson himself (if his *In Memoriam* and *The Idylls of the King* are anything

[11]   Hallam Tennyson, *Memoir*, II.285.
[12]   Allingham is quoted in the Appendix, Hallam's *Memoir*, I. 514.
[13]   Robert Browning to Elizabeth Barrett Barrett, January 28, 1845, *The Letters of Robert Browning and Elizabeth Barrett Barrett 1845–1846*, 2 vols (Smith, Elder, & Co, Fourth Impression, 1900), I. 10.

to go by), for John Addington Symonds, it might be, for Swinburne, of course, and for many another. Like the 'curse' of Tennyson's Lady of Shalott, the epic urge, or something like it, is come heavily upon them. They enjoy too much writing too much. They simply can't resist setting down yet another line of iambic pentameters, that favourite building block of the English poet. And another line. And another. The great length of the Biblical-classical epic *The Fall of Nineveh* (1828–1868), the aweing *chef d'oeuvre* of Edwin Atherstone, all 30 Books and around 24,420 lines of it – he was a close friend of the great apoca-lyptic painter John Martin and like Martin needed a broad canvas – does not make it outstandingly bulky for its time, though the plodding sameness of its thousands upon thousands of entirely flat iambic pentameter lines does rather grant it First Prize for utter numbing boredom, albeit in a close-run competition where it's pressed close by others (in the not kind words of Virginia Woolf about the talk in *Aurora Leigh*) going 'on and on', with the reader's mind stiffening and glazing 'under the monotony of the rhythm'.[14]

It's small wonder that TS Eliot should open his famous essay on Swinburne by asking how much of a poet you *have* to read. The question has real force for these Victorians. '[A]lmost no-one, to-day, will wish to read the whole of Swinburne'.[15] The deterring size of some Victorian poems and oeuvres was a keynote of Eliot's criticism. 'One can get on very well in life without having read all the later poems of Browning or Swinburne.' 'What about Mrs Browning's *Aurora Leigh*, which I have never read, or that long poem by George Eliot of which I don't remember the name?'[16] And Eliot's prefer-ence for necessary skimming and overlooking has been rather widely felt. It is why the canon of commonly read Robert Browning poems is so small.

---

[14]   Virginia Woolf, 'Aurora Leigh', *The Second Common Reader* (1932). Edwin Atherstone, *The Fall of Nineveh: A Poem*, In Two Volumes (William Pickering, London, 1847). He brought out another great epic, *Israel in Egypt* (1861). A revised edition of *The Fall of Nineveh* appeared in 1868, four years before Atherstone's death. 'His works did not sell well, and he gained', says the DNB with feeling, 'a reputation for verbosity.' The ancient-looking approving pencil-marks in my 1847 copy of *The Fall of Nineveh* run out on page 3 of Volume One. Monique R Morgan makes too light work of the heaviness of the long work, *Don Juan*, *The Prelude*, *Aurora Leigh*, *The Ring and the Book*, all read through their epicities as sets of smaller lyric encounters: *Narrative Means, Lyric Ends: Temporality in the Nineteenth-Century British Long Poem* (Ohio State University Press, Columbus OH, 2009).

[15]   TS Eliot, 'Swinburne as Poet", *Selected Essays*, 3rd, enlarged edn (Faber & Faber, London, 1951), 323.

[16]   TS Eliot, 'What is Minor Poetry' (1944), *On Poetry and Poets* (Faber & Faber, London, 1957). Some of this was bluff, the put-down of somebody who had only felt the muchness of, say, Browning, by actually munching through it. More revealing even than Eliot's profound respect for *In Memoriam*, evidently based on much re-reading, is that moment in 'The Three Voices of Poetry', where he applies two wonderful lines of Thomas Lovell Beddoes' *Death's Jest-Book* (1851) – 'bodiless childful of life in the gloom / Crying with frog voice, "what shall I be?"' – to a poet's embryo-poems: lines at Act II.sc iii.line 294, i.e. over 1700 lines of verse into Beddoes's deterringly vast poetic drama.

(In the customary style of Oxford examination papers, I recently set a whole lot of Browning questions using quotations from the wonderfully satirical and literary-critical later poems, 'Of Pacchiarotto, and How He worked in Distemper' (1876), *Parleyings With Certain People of Importance in Their Day* (1887), and the like: 'Nobody reads those poems', protested my fellow-examiner, the poet and critic Tom Paulin; and he was right – *hélas*.) Philip Larkin professed to love 'reading up and down of an evening' in the brick-sized *Collected Poems* of Thomas Hardy (that volume which Hardy's Will stipulated should be available as cheaply as possible for the benefit of the poor, Jude the Obscure-like, reader's pocket, and which thus got reprinted and reprinted from the same old plates whose type got more and more wonderfully nicked and dinged as time went by). You were sure, Larkin said, to come across poetic gem after gem. But still, happening upon such linguistic treasure trove required persistent reading up and down, an extending acquaintance with the brick-like collection. It's such protracted encounters the Victorian author typically demands.

Of course, as the jeers at Robert Browning's expense indicate, many Victorian readers did not take at all to this intense contemporary plenitude, this stunning copiousness and variety. Henry James patently gets less pleasure from being stunned by the hugeness of Robert Browning ('one of the most copious of our poets') than he does from London's vastness. *The Ring and the Book*, 'the most voluminous of his works', is 'so vast and so ... gothic a structure, spreading and soaring and branching at such a rate, like a mad cathedral', all 'brave excrescences ... clustered hugeness ... inordinate muchness', a 'monstrous magnificence'.[17] Many of the cavillers were, ironically, producers of great muchnesses for their own part – like Tennyson, declaring (of Robert Browning) that he much preferred 'A small vessel' to 'a big raft', when his own poetic barque often hove to quite loaded to the gunwales.[18] The not particularly quiet Dante Gabriel Rossetti was keen to quieten the young musician-poet Théophile Marzials by getting him to 'refrain from contributions ... in voluminousness to the poetry of the day': a 'perfect' poem of six lines was worth far more than an 'imperfect' one of 6,000.[19] Rossetti told Swinburne that William Morris was simply over-productive: 'The fact is Topsy writes too much both for his own sake and for that of his appreciators'.[20] What the very mouthy Swinburne thought of this is not known. He certainly thought Robert Browning impossibly wordy, with an

[17]   'The Novel in the *The Ring and the Book*', lecture of 1912; in James's *Notes on Novelists* (1914) – much discussed in Ch 9, 'Modernizing the Subject', below.
[18]   Hallam's *Memoir*, II, 230.
[19]   Letter of 20 April 1873, *Letters of Dante Gabriel Rossetti*, eds Oswald Doughty and John Robert Wahl, III, *1871–1876* (Clarendon Press, Oxford, 1967), 1163.
[20]   Letter of 12 December 1869, *Letters of Dante Gabriel Rossetti*, edn cit, II, *1861–1870* (1965), 773.

unstoppability he parodied in 'The Last Words of a Seventh-Rate Poet' (it's fifth in Swinburne's package of parodies called *The Heptalogia*):

> I don't like to break off, any more than you wish me to stop: but my fate is
> Not to vent half a million such rhymes without blockheads exclaiming –
> Iam Satis.[21]

Iam satis: Latin for *enough already*. Enough is never enough for the disliked Browning. One of the most vicious assaults Swinburne, past-master at critical abuse, ever made is on Browning for not being able to stop talking, stop afflicting his audience with his inarticulate noise – his 'windy gamut of inharmonious sound … shrieks of violated English, groans of grammar undergoing vivisection, gasps of expiring sense and moans of tormented metre'. He's much like the missionary Swinburne has heard of 'somewhere' whose 'savage' converts had suffered his preachments to 'such a sensibly insufferable degree' that they 'cut off exactly one half of his tongue and sent him back with the other half unextracted'. And still he wouldn't shut up – 'being quite unable to hold the tongue which remained to him he went on talking in a dialect of which no mortal could make anything.' Peculiar surgical help – 'judicious extirpation of the tongue' – enabled him 'to speak thenceforward in an audible intelligible manner, by a select use of guttural and labials': a 'memorable though mournful example of strenuous human perseverance' who 'has now been uttering for the last twenty or thirty years the inarticulate vocal appeal of a tongueless though verbose eloquence.' 'For a man with organs unimpaired' this 'would indeed be unpardonable; 'in the case of Mr Browning, it is more than pitiable – it is commendable'.[22] For one poet cheerfully to wish such a two-part excision of tongue upon another poet is about as sick as criticism gets – even for sado-masochistic pain-worshipping Swinburne. But it does at least point to how extreme the aversion to the period's protractednesses could get.

Matthew Arnold is, happily, less vicious in his hostility to Browning's 'confused multitudinousness'. It comes, Arnold thinks, from being 'prevailed over by the world's multitudinousness'. (This is in a letter of Arnold's to his friend Arthur Hugh Clough, September 1848, attacking Keats for the same fault: 'What a brute you were to tell me to read Keats's letters'.[23]) Browning was trying to get too much in; to say too much. Walter Pater was

---

[21]   Swinburne, *Specimens of Modern Poets: The Heptalogia or the Seven against Sense; A Cap With Seven Bells* (Chatto & Windus, London, 1880).

[22]   Algernon Charles Swinburne, 'The Chaotic School', written circa 1863–1864; not published until 1964, in *New Writings by Swinburne*, ed Cecil Y Lang: in *Browning: The Critical Heritage*, edd Boyd Litzinger and Donald Smalley (Routledge & Kegan Paul, London, 1970), 214–215.

[23]   *Letters of Matthew Arnold to Arthur Hugh Clough*, ed HF Lowry (Oxford University Press, Oxford, 1932), 97.

rather inclined to approve of Browning's generously absorbent response to an age whose overcrowdedness Pater couldn't himself quite celebrate. The 'complex, perhaps too matterful, soul of our century has found in Mr Browning ... the capacity for dealing masterfully with it' – the link of *matterful* and *masterful* is wonderfully contrived (and, actually, Pater thought the Decadent poet Arthur Symons, in many ways Browning's poetic disciple, was even better than Browning in his 1889 *Days and Nights* volume at 'concentrations, powerful, dramatic, of what we might call the light and shadow of life').[24] Arnold was, of course, hidebound by the classical literary theory he'd been schooled in, and was evidently attracted to the old Aristotelian idea that the most important poetry – epics and tragedies – were 'imitations' of *actions*, and nothing else. Arnold publicized the notion in the – very important – Preface to the first edition of his *Poems* (1853). The 'eternal objects of poetry', he alleged, are 'actions; human actions'. But every reader of contemporary poetry could see not just how constraining Aristotle's formula was, but also how it failed to fit what the poets were actually doing. WC Roscoe objected with the truth about contemporary literary production. 'We have poems to the Lesser Celandine, to a Mouse, to the Skylark ... which ... are purely descriptive of natural objects', and by no means imitations of human actions. Arnold wisely conceded his mistake in his Preface to the second edition of his *Poems* (1854). If he'd been concentrating, he said, he would have recognized from the first that Aristotle's formula didn't even fit the great poetic classics, Virgil and Dante and Shakespeare, let alone the poets of his own time.

Victorian poetry is indeed mouthy about almost anything under the sun:

> about cod-liver oil, railway-lines and railway trains, chairs, soup, soap, paintings, omnibuses, going to the dentist, Grimm's Law, weather in the suburbs, dead dogs, cricket players, a cabbage leaf, Missing Links, tobacco, booze, snow, sadomasochism, Psychical Research, leeks, onions, genitalia, war, New Woman, fairies, love, death, God, pain, poverty, poems, faith, doubt, science, poets, poetry.[25]

The Words to Say It

What, though, about the words in which these almost anythings are said? Across the ages, poeticity has been taken to consist in the selection of the words used to say things – the *words* in which *to say it* (I'm thinking of the title of Marie Cardinal's momentous memoir-novel of 1975, *Les Mots pour le dire*, translated into English as *The Words to Say It* (1984)) – and the way

[24] Pater, 'A Poet With Something to Say', review of Symons's *Days and Nights* (Macmillan & Co., London, 1889), in, e.g., *Uncollected Essays* by Walter Pater (Portland, Maine, 1903), 80.
[25] Valentine Cunningham, 'Introduction', *Victorian Poetry and Poetics* (Blackwell, Oxford, 1999).

ey're arranged. Jonathan Swift talked up the importance of finding
er words'. to be put in 'their proper places', stressing *propriety* of
ce and deployment, a kind of verbal contract with conventionally agreed
p~ tic goods.[26] Coleridge went bestingly further, stressing a sort of absolute
quality to be arrived at by the poeticizing subject's individual sense of what's
good: 'the best words in the best order'.[27] TS Eliot adapted Coleridge: 'an
arrangement of the right words in the right order' – the poet 'finding the
right words or, anyhow, the least wrong words' and arranging them in 'the
right way – or in what he comes to accept as the best arrangement'.[28] Always,
though, considered words and considered deployment of those words. The
dual hard-word front, on which you can still find it suggested that the
Victorians flopped and failed.

There's still a travestying cliché around that Victorian poetry fails to
measure up in word-choice and word-arrangement, that it is verbally slack,
casual, trite, carelessly chosen, prosey, full of doggerel, too hummy and
hymny, nursery-rhyme stuff, and carelessly arranged – somehow a bad and
verbally inattentive parenthesis between the great force and forces of preceding times (however they're defined) and the tighter, alerter powers of the
modernists. Ezra Pound's harshly discriminatory line on Swinburne sums up
much long continuing twentieth-century hostility. Swinburne's libertarian
politics, his 'paganism' were good, and his 'verbal music', his 'melopoeia'
(that's the art of making melodies) were unsurpassable ('No one else has
made such music in English'), but his choice and use of words were awful.
'He neglected the value of words as words, and was intent on their value as
sound'. 'The word-selecting word-castigating faculty was nearly absent'
(*castigating*: correcting, revising, amending). All his 'defects can be summed
up in one – that is, inaccurate writing'.[29] Which was Yeats's line in the
notorious Introduction to his *Oxford Book of Modern Verse 1892–1935*

---

[26] 'To find out proper words': 'Directions for a Birthday-day Song', 232; '... when I wanted
proper words': Gulliver in Houhynhym land, *Gulliver's Travels*, Part IV; 'I have put the several
Explanations in their proper places', Swift tells the reader about the annotations to 'The Grand
Question debated WHETHER *Hamilton's Bawn* should be turned into a *Barrack* or a Malt-
House'.

[27] *Specimens of the Table-Talk*, Vol I (1835), 84.

[28] TS Eliot, 'The Three Voices of Poetry' (1953), *On Poetry and Poets*, edn cit, 97–98.

[29] Ezra Pound, 'Swinburne Versus His Biographers', Poetry, XI, 6 (March 1918), reprinted in
Literary Essays of Ezra Pound, ed and intro TS Eliot (Faber & Faber, London [1944], 1960),
290–294. 'Swinburne has long been out of fashion', said Cecil Y Lang in 1959, opening the
Introduction to the first volume of what would become the great six-volume Swinburne *Letters*,
one of the first of the publishing scholarly endeavours turning the back the anti-Victorian tide,
and helping initiate the sixties canonizing of Victorian poets. (Graham Storey's edition of
Hopkins's *Journals and Papers* also appeared in 1959; Gordon Haight's George Eliot *Letters*
started to appear in 1954; Madeline House and Graham Storey's Pilgrim Edition of Dickens's
Letters in 1965.)

(1936) when he described 'the revolt against Victorianism' as a rejection of a 'poetic diction' which had less interest in the quality of the words and their organization than in 'irrelevant descriptions of nature, the scientific and moral discursiveness of *In Memoriam* ... the political eloquence of Swinburne, the psychological curiosity of Robert Browning'. 'We must purify poetry of all that is not poetry', Yeats has his young ones say, implying that the Victorians were poetically contaminated. Oscar Wilde's dismissiveness – 'Meredith was a prose Browning and so was Browning' – catches this still not banished mood. Speaking with 'brutal frankness' in 1934, in his often admirably word-history conscious *English Poetry and the English Language*, FW Bateson put the 'faults' of Victorian poetry, its 'diffuseness' and 'vagueness', down to its desire 'to write poetry as prose'. A charge not altered a jot in his polemic's second edition of 1961 (almost, interestingly, on the eve of the revolution in poetry publication brought about by the great Longman's Annotated English Poets series which Bateson initiated and masterminded, which included Kenneth Allott's ground-breaking *Matthew Arnold* (1965) and Christopher Ricks's revolutionizing *Tennyson* (1969)). The weakness of Victorian poetry was history's fault, Bateson alleged; the language the Victorians inherited had turned all prosaically prolix; but the poets were also to blame for linguistic spinelessness, with only a few exceptions – Tennyson's rare awareness of 'the condition of the language he was compelled to use'; Dante Gabriel Rossetti's and Swinburne's 'love of words for their own sake'. Hopkins was poetically tough, but no help to his contemporaries because hidden way. Housman was verbally attentive but came too late to be of contemporary use. Otherwise the poets were 'language proof'.[30] Bateson's repeatedly referred-to critical helpmeet was TS Eliot, Ezra Pound's great critical ally and publicist, whose loud pronouncements (Swinburne's 'meaning is merely the hallucination of meaning'; his 'adjectives are practically blanks';[31] Tennyson's 'Idylls of the King are hardly more important than a parody, or a "Chaucer retold for children"'[32]), echoed forcibly though the critical jungle for a long time. Eliot's Victorian suspicions were rooted in his influential conviction that a corrupting break occurred in the middle of the seventeenth century, 'the dissociation of sensibility' (his momentous slogan of 1921),[33] a collapse in intellectual and aesthetic force, cognate with the killing of the King and the abolition of the Established Church, which the Restoration never restored and which went

---

[30]   FW Bateson, *English Poetry and the English Language* (1934; 2nd edn, Russell and Russell, NY, 1961), Ch IV, 'The Nineteenth Century', 86–111.

[31]   'Swinburne as Poet' (1951), 327.

[32]   In *Ezra Pound: His Metric and Poetry* (Alfred A Knopf, NY, 1917), reprinted in *To Criticize the Critic, and Other Writings* (Faber & Faber, London, 1965), 166.

[33]   'The Metaphysical Poets', *TLS*, 20 October 1921, 669; reprinted in *Selected Essays* (Faber & Faber, London, 1932; 1934; 3rd edn, 1951), 288.

on impoverishing English poetry right through the Romantic period and beyond. It was fed strongly in the twentieth century as a matter of modern – and modernist – contempt for the likes of 'Alfred Lawn Tennyson, Gentleman Poet', as James Joyce notoriously dismissed the Victorian Laureate when he appeared in the nightmare of the Nighttown episode of *Ulysses* (1921). Tennyson the favourite poet of Mr Ramsay, absurd representative of old-fashioned patriarchy and lamedog Cambridge philosophy in Virginia Woolf's *To the Lighthouse* (1927), who charges about the lawn of his Cornish holiday home reciting 'The Charge of the Light Brigade' to himself. Nobody reads Elizabeth Barrett Browning, poetic star of her day, said Virginia Woolf in 1932 in her 'Aurora Leigh' essay; 'nobody discusses her'. 'The primers dismiss her with contumely' for never having learned 'the value of words and a sense of form'. She's aesthetically uncouth – a poetic uncouthness registered in Woolf's pert, snooty social allegory of Barrett Browning's low poetic place with a crew of like aesthetically impoverished ones: 'downstairs in the servants' quarters, where, in company with Mrs Hemans, Eliza Cook, Jean Ingelow, Alexander Smith, Edwin Arnold, and Robert Montgomery, she bangs the crockery about and eats vast handfuls of peas on the point of her knife'.[34]

One trouble for much serious modern criticism was that Victorian poetry had entered the popular consciousness – as whole poems, bits of poems, opening lines, titles. People knew these poems, knew them 'off by heart' – Browning's 'Home-Thoughts, from Abroad' ('Oh, to be in England / Now that April's there'), his 'How They Brought the Good News from Ghent to Aix' ('I sprang to the stirrup, and Joris, and he, / I galloped, Dirck galloped, we galloped all three'); Tennyson's 'The Charge of the Light Brigade' ('Half a league, half a league, / Half a league onward / All in the valley of Death / Rode the six hundred'); Thomas Hood's 'The Song of the Shirt'; Clough's 'Say not the struggle nought availeth'; Macaulay's 'Horatius' ('Lars Porsena of Clusium / By the Nine Gods he swore'); William Allingham's 'The Fairies' ('Up the airy mountain / Down the rushy glen'); TE Brown's 'A garden is a lovesome thing, God wot' ('My Garden'); Lewis Carroll's 'Jabberwocky' ("Twas brillig, and the slithy toves'); Edward Lear's 'The Dong With a Luminous Nose'; Kipling's 'Mandalay', Newbolt's 'There's a breathless hush in the Close Tonight' ('Vitaï Lampada'); Housman's 'Home is the sailor, home from the sea' ('RLS'); Hardy's 'Darkling Thrush'; and so on and on.

Here was a body of utterly memorable stuff – remembered of course because of the attractive sentiment, and sentimentalism, the human touches,

---

[34]   For Woolf's quarrelsome and frequently farcical relationships with her female domestics, her very own pea-puzzled bangers of crockery, see Alison Light, *Mrs Woolf and the Servants: The Hidden Heart of Domestic Service* (Penguin Figtree, London, 2007).

the patriotism, the religiosity, but memorable not least because so many of these rhymes and rhythms were easy on the ear. Lots of Victorian poems caught on because they were indeed catchy. Children took to them. They were pleasing to chant, and they were indeed chanted in school, as a key part of an unofficial national syllabus. They had lilt, in fact; they were singable (that great criterion of poetic merit according to the wise and happily old-fashioned Philip Larkin). Many of them caught on precisely because they were set to music – like 'Come into the garden, Maud' from Tennyson's 'Maud'; and Adelaide Anne Procter's 'A Lost Chord' ('Seated one day at the Organ'); and Kathleen Tynan's 'Sheep and Lambs' ('All in the April evening'); John Henry Newman's 'Lead kindly light, amid the encircling gloom' ('perhaps the most popular modern hymn in the language', Newman's biographer thought in 1912)[35]; and Christina G Rossetti's 'In the bleak mid-winter', her 'A Christmas Carol', perhaps the most famous Christmas Carol in the English language ever. Many of the best known memorable Victorian poems indeed began their life as hymns – as Henry Francis Lyte's 'Abide with me! fast falls the eventide' (favourite of English Football Association Cup Final crowds), and Sarah Flower Adams's 'Nearer, my God, to thee (famous not least for having allegedly been played by the ship's orchestra as the *Titanic* went down), and Charlotte Elliott's 'Just as I am Without One Plea' (the best-selling anthem of worldwide Evangelical Christianity).

Pish-Posh?

Here was precisely what patrons of the modern and modernist, the so-called New Poetic, jeered and fleered at as the badness of the Old Poetic – its terribly pleasing plangencies and emotional accessibilities, its words and ideas requiring (it was said) little effort from either poet or reader (what Ezra Pound thought of as a deteriorated and ossified linguisticity; an inauthentic speech according to Arthur Symons, champion of late nineteenth-century symbolism), the tones and rhythms of a terribly popular poetic. (The negative critique is most revealingly set out and endorsed in CK Stead's still standard work of literary history, *The New Poetic: Yeats to Eliot*.[36]) Lots of educated critics, especially the ones in the very new University Schools of English Literature, critical cannon-fodder for the new professionalized ways of doing reading, were for other poetic measures, other canons of taste and poeticity. The reaction to Victorian poets by IA Richards's Cambridge audience of the 1920s – the whole of the embryonic Cambridge English faculty,

---

[35]   Wilfrid Ward, *The Life of John Henry Cardinal Newman: Based on his Private Journals and Correspondence*, 2 Vols (Longmans, Green & Co, London and NY, 1912), II.357.
[36]   CK Stead, *The New Poetic: Yeats to Eliot* (Hutchinson, London, 1964).

students and teachers, gathered by Richards to find out experimentally just how poems were being read in practice, and so suggest how they might be read better, and lay down some bases for how English could be turned into a more empirical and so examinable discipline – is characteristic of the dismissive post-Victorian response. The poems chosen by Richards for lecture-audience comment were issued anonymously and without dates, but the educated audience's anti-Victorian instincts were pretty sure. The rhymes of Christina Rossetti's 'Spring Quiet' – 'Gone were but the Winter' – were found *poor* and scarcely *bearable* ('I laughed at the rhyming of thrush and bush; and boughs and house. *Reminds one quite pleasantly of the "poetry" one wrote when aged ten'*). 'Sentiment ... utterly absurd'; metre 'a jingle', 'sing-songy'; 'slight in thought and hideously worded'. 'This poem might have been pleasing to the reading public a few hundred years ago, but *today I can see little reason why it should be read, except for historical interest*. It is simple, almost childish ... rambling, discursive ... *says nothing that matters'*. Gerard Hopkins's 'Margaret, are you grieving' fared a lot better (his poems, only recently published in 1918 by his friend Robert Bridges, were already enjoying the status of ur-modernistic verses among the likes of IA Richards, whose pioneering appraisal appeared in the *Dial* magazine in September 1926).[37] But even so there were lots of complaints and gibes at this Hopkins poem as merely old poetic rubbish. 'Trite thought, somewhat incoherently and badly expressed'; 'extraordinarily bad poetry ... trite philosophy.' 'Pish-posh!' 'Sentamental' [sic]. Richards was clearly grimly amused by that particular Cambridge English student who couldn't even spell the common denigratory charge of sentimentality, but he was also plainly taken aback by what was passing for critical reasonableness among so many of these bright and clever pioneering students of English literature. The book *Practical Criticism: A Study of Literary Judgement* (1929) in which his findings are analysed keeps pointing out how simply *bad* his readers' responses were ('bad reading ... reading that prevents the reader himself from entering into the poem'). The repeated allegations of *simplicity*

---

[37]   IA Richards, 'Gerard Hopkins', *Dial*, 81:3 (September 1926), 195–203. Richard's best pupil William Empson never forgot Richards's 'pioneering' criticism which got him on to Hopkins's merits in 'one of the earliest bits of his criticism that I read', which picked 'out the good things even when he might have been out of sympathy' with Hopkins's Christianity: letter (Jan 1980) of Empson quoted in John Haffenden, *William Empson*, Vol II: *Against the Christians* (Oxford University Press, Oxford, 2006), 637. The sales of the *Poems of Gerard Manley Hopkins: Now First Published*, ed and annotated by Robert Bridges (Humphrey Milford, London, 1918) were small; the sales of the second edition (Oxford University Press, 1930), with a celebratory introduction by Charles Williams, were large and steady; helped on, no doubt, by Richards's publicity, and Empson's interest in *Seven Types of Ambiguity* (Chatto & Windus, 1930), but of course mainly by Oxford University Press's publicity and some superior reviews. Standard account: Elgin W Mellown, 'The Reception of Gerard Manley Hopkins's *Poems*, 1918–1930', *Modern Philology*, 63:1 (August 1965), 38–51.

and *sentimentality* were thoughtless and unhistorical.[38] But for all that he doesn't do much actually to defend Christina Rossetti from her detractors; and adding to one's gloom over these modern poetry readers' difficulty in taking Victorian poetry seriously is a sense that Richards himself feels the really good stuff is being produced by others than Christina Rossetti.

What emerged from Richards's work was the canonization of Shakespeare, the Metaphysicals and Milton as the very best English poets because verbally the most complex, especially in and through the great foundational practical-critical work of Richards's best pupil William Empson, first manifest in his *Seven Types of Ambiguity* (1930), and in the polemics of another of the outstanding members of Richards's Cambridge audience FR Leavis, who became the grand critical guru of Downing College, Cambridge, and, in turn, of Leavis's disciples spreading the critical word especially in British schools. Leavis's extremely influential *New Bearings in English Poetry* (1932) was dutifully IA Ricardian in its rock-jawed dismissals of the big Victorians. Tennyson, Arnold, Morris are all poets of withdrawal from modern life. Meredith's *Modern Love* 'seems to me the flashy product of unusual but vulgar cleverness working upon cheap emotion: it could serve later poets, if at all, only as a warning.' Browning is 'concerned merely with simple emotions and sentiments'; his 'sensibility' is superficial; it's 'possible to consider him as a philosophical or psychological poet only by confusing intelligence with delight in the exercise of certain grosser cerebral muscles'. So inferior a mind and spirit as Browning's 'could not provide the impulse needed to bring back into poetry the adult intelligence'. Victorian poetry was 'anaemic'.[39] English poetry had to wait for its twin saviours in the persons of American TS Eliot and Ezra Pound.[40] There was one great Victorian poet, namely Gerard Manley Hopkins – 'one of the most remarkable technical inventors who ever wrote … a major poet' – but, alas, unknown to his poetic contemporaries except for his friends Robert Bridges, Coventry Patmore, and RW Dixon; a poetic king locked away in Jesuit exile; only let out in 1918; 'likely to prove, for our time and the future, the only influential poet of the Victorian age'.[41] Leavis was pleased, and rightly, at the pioneering of his chapter on Hopkins – major critical first-fruits of the Hopkins approval coming out of the Richards world, and possibly the best critical discussion ever of Hopkins's techniques. But still this clear-eyed espousal of Hopkins's greatness is founded in a critically distorted faith in Hopkins's

---

[38]   IA Richards, *Practical Criticism: A Study of Literary Judgement* (Kegan Paul, Trench, Trubner & Co., London, [1929] 3rd Impression, 1935), 'Poem II', 33–41; 'Poem VI', 81–90'; 'Sentimentality and Inhibition', 254–270.

[39]   FR Leavis, *New Bearings in English Poetry: A Study of the Contemporary Situation* (Chatto & Windus, London, 1932), 20, 49.

[40]   Leavis (1932), 47, 49–50.

[41]   Leavis (1932), 159, 193.

absolute qualitative difference from the surrounding waste and trash. A polemical faith pushed hard in the 1934 Chatto practical-critical textbook for schools and school-teachers, *Reading and Discrimination* by Leavis's close aide and English school-teacher of English, Denys Thompson.[42]

Here was a set of narrow critical-historical assumptions being set in stone for student readers, at school and university.[43] An ossification affirmed in the massively influential (and utterly Richards- and Empson-influenced) New Critical movement in the United States. The slighting of Victorian poets at the expense of Donne and Marvell and Co. was certainly vivid from the start in that student guide-book *Understanding Poetry* by New Critical gurus Cleanth Brooks and Robert Penn Warren (1938) – and maintained in the revisions that have kept this great piece of practical-critical First Aid for the American student going steady ever since. 'Where it [alliteration] occurs frequently as in the work of Swinburne, it often impresses the reader as a mechanical and monotonous mannerism or a too gaudy decoration.'

---

[42]   Modelled on Richards's Cambridge experiments, *Reading and Discrimination* provided unassigned passages of writing for school-kid analysis and comparison. The passages are identified for the benefit of teachers, who are busily advised what they (and so their pupils) should think. The book's historical and critical 'Commentary' is steered by repeated references to Richards, and Leavis, and Eliot. What's on offer is the whole Cambridge package. Shakespeare, the Metaphysicals, Blake are supreme (Milton's a bit dodgy). The Victorian texts on offer are embarrassing (Henry Newbolt), emotionally narrow (Housman, Tennyson), trite and shallow (Adelaide Anne Procter), unctuous (Robert Browning), imprecise in the use of assonance and alliteration (Swinburne – whose 'flow of words and haze of emotion' are excused only because he mocks his own verbally slack mode in his *Heptalogia*). Pater's famous discussion of Leonardo's *Mona Lisa* is affected, 'pretentious "fine writing"', hypnotic merely, a lot like the criticism of Ruskin and Wilde (contrast, Thompson suggests, the extract from TS Eliot on Blake for 'an exemplary piece of explication, precise and consecutive'). 'Which is the more interesting of the two?', the student is asked: Shakespeare's 'Noe longer mourn for me when I am dead', or Christina G Rossetti's 'Remember me when I am gone away'? The implied answer is clear. Of the Victorians, only Hopkins is any good. Thompson is speaking loud in His Master's Voice. In the sonnet 'No worst, there is none. Pitched past pitch of grief', Hopkins 'knows what he is doing, and uses language precisely, to invite a particular response from the reader' – unlike Swinburne. Hopkins is Shakespearian in his ' "imagery, and his way of using the body and movement of the language" ' – 'As Mr Leavis observes in his *New Bearings*'.

[43]   *Reading and Discrimination* was last reprinted in 1959, and only rewritten and stripped of its anti-Victorian hostilities in 1973, after heavy revision by Thompson in collaboration with another long-time schoolteacher of English, and prominent national leader in English studies for schools, Stephen Tunnicliffe, reflecting the impossibility of carrying on the old prejudices in the light of the recent canonizing of Victorian poetry, the great 1960s revolution in the reception of Victorian writing. The 1973 *Reading and Discrimination* has no slanted literary history or jeering at Victorian inadequacies. Hopkins's 'Binsey Poplars' remains more or less prominent. The implied discrediting of Christina G at the expense of Shakespeare has gone (this volume's pairings are 'not done in order to praise one at the expense of the other'). But still it is noticeable that the Victorian poetic presence is much depleted. Only five Victorian poets survived – with one poem each by Hopkins, Tennyson, Arnold, Emily Brontë and Christina G. Something of the old prejudice remained, it would seem, in this criticism done by sending-to-Coventry.

Tennyson's 'Tears, Idle Tears' 'at first reading may appear to have little in common with the vigorous thinking through images that we associate with poets like Marvell and Donne. We find here no witty turns or plays on the meaning of certain words, and certainly no bold leaping from image to image or involved elaborations of some central analogy. ... There are no sharply disparate materials, no images that clash violently in their association.' Tennyson's patent weakness is that he's not a verbally potent Metaphysical. The reader is invited to 'look deeper' into the poem. Which is good. But what this deeper inspection might unearth is only a half-hearted allowance. 'At any rate, the reader must not conclude in advance that the strategy of poets so different as Tennyson and Marvell are in complete opposition. They need not be. Tennyson's attempt to define what overcame him as a fit of unmotivated melancholy may in fact exhibit a real thinking through images.'[44] It may; but it need not. The second-rate nature of Victorian poetry had got itself embedded as a key bit of English Studies' founding doctrine. Samuel Beckett's cheerful mockery of the Victorian poetic heritage in his traducing of Tennyson's 'A Dream of Fair Women' as *Dream of Fair to Middling Women* (eventually published in 1992) sums up a common feeling: Victorian poetry was at best middling.

More Form Than Content?

Justification and rationalizations for this critical downgrading of Victorian poetry were of course to be found – like that allegation by TS Eliot of an ongoing mid-seventeenth-century failure of English *mentalité* and aesthetic. It was fashionable in twentieth-century criticism to believe that the real creative energy of the Victorians had moved into the Novel. If their poems were any good (Browning's say), it was because they were managing to be like short stories, were really novellas or novels *manqués*. Henry James's reading in his 'Novel in the Ring and Book' lecture of Browning's *The Ring and the Book* as a modernist novel along Jamesian lines is a superior example of this

---

[44] Cleanth Brooks and Robert Penn Warren, *Understanding Poetry*, Fourth Edition (Holt, Rinehart and Winston, New York, 1976), 524, 242–243. The New Critical way of damning the Victorians through close reading is well illustrated in Paull F Baum's one-time influential *Tennyson Sixty Years After* (University of North Carolina Press, Chapel Hill NC, 1948, in which Tennyson is granted some good things, but all tarnished by the dross of carelessness, mediocrity, vapidity: illustrated by three New Critical 'Notes' on 'Ulysses', 'In Memoriam' and 'Maud'. 'The Charge of the Light Brigade' was, Baum's analysis leads him to fancy, dashed off in a few minutes (p.134). 'Maud' is '*Balder*-dash' (Baum likes Matthew Arnold, author of 'Balder Dead'). And so on. Kathy Alexis Psomaides refers to the assumption of Victorian poetic badness in *Understanding Poetry*, and also Richards's *Principles of Literary Criticism* (1924): 'The Critical Fortunes of Victorian Poetry', *The Cambridge Companion to Victorian Poetry*, ed Joseph Bristow (Cambridge University Press, Cambridge, 2000), 37.

line of thought. (See its role in 'Victorian Modernismus', Chapter 10, below.) WH Auden had an even more interesting (and more soundly based) theory about the second-rate nature of Victorian poetry, working from the nature of nineteenth-century middle-class education and the idea of poetry and the poetic it put across to its young male partakers. Classical literature, Latin and Greek, was the basis of the Public School curriculum (vernacular literature was peripheral to the syllabus), and boys spent a lot of their time, every school-day, translating Greek and Latin poetry into English. But translation is always inexact, always approximate, so that these little translators grew up, Auden alleged, with the feeling that verbal exactitude in a poem did not, after all, matter greatly: poems meant, but elastically. Form, though, the large poetic shape, was not something translation affected; form was something as it were inviolate; so the idea that form was more important than verbal meaning set in. Hence, Auden suggests in the Introduction to his anthology *Nineteenth-Century Minor Poets* (1967), the way that Victorian poets are particularly good at form, but are less strong on, are not specially interested in, verbal precision.

Now the Victorians are undoubtedly attracted to form as such, and to formal variety; they like showing off formally, showing that they know their way around hexameters, hendecasyllabics, epillyons, double sonnets, anacreontics, alcaics, odes, epodes. They like demonstrating that they can do the metres of Virgil and Homer, and Catullus and Horace, can play with all the old varieties of rhyme and meter. They're dab hands with the available array of different metrical feet and different kinds of line-length and line arrangement; nobody has to remind them where the break, the caesura, should come; and so on and so forth. These are the mere custom and practice of the well-brought-up gentleman with a classical education. And so it is that Hopkins, say, can translate Shakespeare into Latin, into Catullan hendecasyllabics in fact, as it were on demand.[45] For his part, Tennyson, according to his son Hallam, 'confessed that he believed he knew the quantity of every word in the English language except "scissors"' (an arresting as well as amusing exception: does *scissors* consist of two heavy beats, or two light ones, or a heavy one and a light one, or a light one and a heavy one? It can be all of these). Upon which boasting the Tennyson family (and Browning) demanded 'a Sapphic stanza in quantity, with the Greek cadence', and Tennyson produced one at the drop of a hat.[46] It was the easiest game for the classically brought-up poet to play.

Swinburne wonderfully proves this part of Auden's point. Kenneth Haynes, Swinburne's Penguin editor, thinks Auden's 'generalisation applies with par-

---

[45]   For this see Norman Vance, *The Victorians and Ancient Rome* (Blackwell, Oxford, 1997), 125. Vance's story of Victorian Latinism is superbly detailed.

[46]   *Memoir*, II, 231.

ticular force to Swinburne', and he's right.[47] Swinburne is *the* Victorian master of form, *the* Victorian expert in varieties of poetic shape, because he's a product of the Eton system. Brought up on daily translation from Latin and Greek, on regular imitation of the ancient masters, he sports a metrical expertise that was beaten into him daily, bloodily, on the Eton flogging-horse. (Yoppie Prins rightly ascribes his 'metrical virtuosity' to the 'horror of strange metres' beaten into him at school – though she rather confuses the impetus got from all that school-time 'swishing' by putting his – undoubtedly influential – submission, his bondage, to Sappho's verbally dominatrix role too much into this pedagogic picture.[48]) No wonder he's so good at poetic beat, at poetic din: the regular din of verse was so regularly dinned in.

> I'll give you more to cry for, you young dog, you!
> I'll flog you – flog you – flog, flog, flog, flog you.

That's the Master in 'Reginald's Flogging', by 'Etonensis', aka Swinburne, in his *The Whippingham Papers*, published anonymously in a very limited edition in about 1888.[49] Swinburne knows all about how to do beat, or rhythm – knowledges so painfully acquired. Hexameters for instance – like the flogging ones just quoted. This was the rhythm the Victorians were most anxious to try their hand at – because, it's been suggested, the poets were conscious of how tired-out the English staple of iambic pentameters had got through overuse in the tradition.[50] Matthew Arnold famously had a go at hexameters in Englishing four passages of the Iliad in his Oxford lectures 'On Translating Homer' (1861). He made the mistake of repudiating Tennyson's blank verse on that occasion (it was no good for translating Homer, Arnold said), a repudiation expanded in his 1862 lecture 'On Translating Homer: Last Words.' Incensed, Tennyson responded with a 'Specimen of a Translation of the Iliad in Blank Verse' in the *Cornhill Magazine* (Dec 1863), doing a version of Iliad VII, 524–561, a passage Arnold had himself attempted, and adding a few feisty lines dismissing English providers of 'lame' and 'barbarous' hexameters ('On Translations of

---

[47]   Swinburne, *Poems and Ballads and Atalanta in Calydon*, ed Kenneth Haynes (Penguin, Harmondsworth, 200), xv. I usually quote this edition.

[48]   Especially insightful is the 'Suffering Metre' section of Prins's *Victorian Sappho* (Princeton University Press, Princeton NJ, 1999), 140ff.

[49]   Lucy Binding is greatly informative about Victorian flogging practices in 'The Pleasures and Pains of Flogging' chapter of her *The Representation of Bodily Pain in Late Nineteenth-Century English Culture* (Clarendon Press, Oxford, 2000), 240–274.

[50]   Elisabeth W Schneider's wonderfully informative article on Victorian form, especially Hopkins's, 'Sprung Rhythm: A Chapter in the Evolution of Nineteenth-Century Verse', describes 'something like a stampede of anapaestic verse after about 1850': *PMLA*, 80, no. 3 (1965), 238.

Homer. Hexameters and Pentameters'). Arnold rightly guessed that he was the target.[51] Swinburne also thought Arnold's hexameters were terrible, and guessed why. The Rugbeian Arnold (and Clough) could have done with more of the Eton educational treatment.

> They look like nothing on earth, and sound like anapaests broken up and driven wrong; neither by ear nor by finger can I bring them to any reckoning. ... And at best what ugly bastards of verse are these self-styled hexameters! ... burlesque improvisation. ... Once only, as far as I know, in Dr Hawtrey's delicate and fluent verse, has the riddle been resolved; the verses are faultless, are English; are hexametric; but this is simply a graceful interlude of pastime, a well-played stroke in a game of skill played with language. Such as pass elsewhere for English hexameters I do hope and suppose impossible at Eton. Mr Clough's I will not presume to be serious attempts or studies in any manner of metre; they are admirable studies in graduated prose....[52]

Impossible at Eton. Especially under the strong tutelary hand of the Reverend Doctor Edward Craven Hawtrey, bit-part translator of Homer, successively Headmaster and Provost of Eton College in Swinburne's time there. About hexameters they were never wrong the Old Etonians. In fact, Old Etonian Swinburne can do anything at all in the formal line, and he shows off this formal versatility all the time. He has a formal flamboyance and perfectionism that the classicizing poetic establishment naturally applauded. The great Latinist professor and poet AE Housman of course greatly admired Swinburne's formal powers. Of the characteristically elaborate stanzaic patterning used in 'Dolores' Housman said that Swinburne had 'dignified and strengthened' it 'till it yielded a combination of speed and magnificence which nothing in English had possessed before'.[53] ('The metre combines iambs and anapaests in seven trimeter lines concluded by the dimeter eighth line, which always consists of an iamb followed by an anapaest; in every other stanza, the refrain is "Our Lady of Pain". The rhyme scheme is

---

[51] Arnold's translations, including Iliad VII, 560–565, are in the standard edition of his *Poems*, ed Kenneth Allott (Longmans, 1965), 467–468. The Arnold-Tennyson encounter is dwelt on in more detail in the discussion of Tennyson's classicizing in 'Modernizing the Subject', Ch 9, below.

[52] *Essays and Studies* (1867), quoted in *Poems & Ballads and Atalanta in Calydon*, ed Kenneth Haynes (Penguin, Harmonsdworth, 2000), 357.

[53] 1910 lecture, quoted *Poems and Ballads...*, Penguin edn cit, 352. Haynes suggests, loc cit, correctly, that the metre and stanza of 'Dolores' are very close to what the poet Winthrop Mackworth Praed, another Etonian and a protégé of Hawtrey, favoured. Haynes's sharp point about the location of 'Dolores' in the feminine rhymes is a good case of the 'rhyming with reason' I discuss in Ch 4, 'These Rhyming/Repeating Games are Serious', below.

ababcdcd; where *a* and *c* are regularly feminine'; "Dolores" appears nine
times in this position': thus the metrically enthusiastic Kenneth Haynes.[54])

Perfection of form indeed. But does it follow that training in and expertise at and ingrained fascination for form necessarily entail what Auden
suggests as radical lack of interest in verbal precision? Auden's educational
suggestion certainly holds a bit of water. Being brought up on poetry in
foreign tongues whose verbal meanings and verbal play you will never get
absolutely close to, and can never hope to reproduce exactly, such being
the nature of poetic words and of the translating act, might well give you
a funny idea about the way words work in poetry. (Every examiner of
school and university translation-papers is regularly filled with wonder
at what candidates seem to believe a poet is saying: can this student really
think this poem might really be saying *that*, believe that poetry is really *that*
daft?) And Swinburne, the perfect form-maker, is indeed commonly
accused of a too unheeding rush and gush, of producing endlessly flowing
streams of verse, lines foaming along liquidly in poems not accidentally
obsessed with the foaming waves of the sea: a hypnotically accumulating
throb and pulse that do get to seem rather like verbal masturbation – so
that all that foam and foaming, the spume of the sea, are easily suspectable
of being code for ejaculate. (And it's perhaps not too fanciful hereabouts
to think of the poetico-paedogogical syndrome Auden is arrested by as it
impinges on the arguments and case of the Reverend John Conington and
his circle, he the Corpus Christi College, Oxford, Professor of Latin who
strongly defended the Public School and University practice of classical
verse composition as being precisely a most helpful initiation into poeticity –
in his essay on 'A Liberal Education', published in his *Miscellaneous*
Writings, edited (of course) by his lifelong chum John Addington Symonds,
the Balliol classicist and poet, and fellow 'Arcadian', that is 'paiderast', or
classically-inspired boy-lover, as Symonds has it; he Symonds for whom
the *poetic* is indeed what got dinned in at Public Schools and was practised
in dormitory masturbation groups, as well as, in Symonds's case, in the
arms of handsome young Viennese gondoliers and other 'strong young
men of the lower-classes', as EM Forster would later put it.[55]) But still

---

[54]   Haynes, edn cit, 354.

[55]   'We take Latin and Greek ... as typical languages, and apply to them a minuteness of study
which we cannot afford to apply to others; and part of this minute study is the practice of
verse-composition. And we choose verse-composition in particular, because as a matter of fact
we find that verse-composition is suited to the capacities of young boys. ... but further, I believe
that a man ... will appreciate the artistic part of poetry better if he tries to write verses himself.'
John Conington, 'A Liberal Education', *Contemporary Review* (January 1868); in *Miscellaneous*
Writings, ed John Addington Symonds (2 vols, Longmans, Green, London, 1872), I. 449–478.
For Symonds, see *The Memoirs of John Addington Symonds*, ed and intro Phyllis Grosskurth
(Hutchinson, London, 1984), and the discussion in 'Selving', Ch 6, below.

what Auden thinks follows from all that boyish classicizing clearly does not. Not even in the case of Swinburne. His wonderful fluency is purchased, as the manuscripts prove, by extremely hard work in mounting those fluencies.

Swinburne's starring role in Empson's *Seven Types of Ambiguity* (1930) is telling – and not just because it is clearly part of Empson's polemical mission to counter the casual assumptions about Victorian verbal slackness knocking about noisily in the Cambridge of his day, assumptions riding on the back of what Empson later described as 'the newly discovered merits of Donne, Marvell, and Dryden', the new critical Zeitgeist driven in particular by TS Eliot's criticism.[56] Empson had loved Swinburne's poems as a boy at Winchester – 'intoxicated' by the 'drug' of Swinburne's verse, 'a slave' to that orgasmic fluidity, the poeticity of pain and painfully acquired adeptness. Swinburne's 'paeans of perversity answered to his own distress', thinks his biographer John Haffenden, providing 'a song for his pains', when, as Empson put it, he was (like Swinburne himself) ' being beaten rather too often'.[57] But in the *Seven Types* it's Swinburne the cannily adept word-chooser and arranger who's celebrated for working through his usual and persistent throb and swoon and foam to an engaged and engaging puzzlement of the reader's imagination in an intellectually sharp eliding run of metaphors.

> Night falls like fire; the heavy lights run low,
> And as they drop, my blood and body so
> Shake as the flame shakes, full of days and hours
> That sleep not neither weep they as they go.
>
> Ah yet would God this flesh of mine might be
> Where air might wash and long leaves cover me,
> Where tides of grass break into foam of flowers,
> Or where the wind's feet shine along the sea.

These two stanzas from Swinburne's 'Laus Veneris' (49–56) are offered by Empson as examples of his fifth type of ambiguity, the one occurring 'when the author is discovering his idea in the act of writing, or not holding it all in his mind at once, so that, for instance, there is a simile which applies to nothing exactly, but lies half-way between two things when the author is moving from one to the other'. ('Shakespeare continually does it'.)

[56]   William Empson, Preface to Second Edition of *Seven Types of Ambiguity* (Chatto and Windus, 1946; 3rd edn, Peregrine Books, Harmondsworth, 1961), viii.
[57]   John Haffenden, *William Empson*, Vol I, *Among the Mandarins* (Oxford University Press, Oxford), 87. John Haffenden, ed, *Selected Letters of William Empson* (Oxford University Press, Oxford), 468–469.

When Swinburne comes off he is a very full and direct writer; it is no use saying these verses show interest in mere sound, or pattern of verbal cadence. It would be true, perhaps, to say that he feels it more important to keep up his effect of texture than that, in any particular case, the meanings, the chord of associations, should come through. But in a literary, not perhaps in a stage, sense, this hypnotised detachment is a powerful dramatic weapon.[58]

And Empson goes on to praise passages of like rich mixing in *Atalanta in Calydon* and 'Dolores' as well as 'Laus Veneris'. '[T]he famous chorus of *Atalanta in Calydon*' – 'Time, with a gift of tears; / Grief, with a glass that ran' – 'pretends to be two elements of a list with their attributes muddled, but is in fact a mutual comparison between the water-clock and the tearbottle'. 'People', Empson says, 'are oddly determined to regard Swinburne as an exponent of Pure Sound with no intellectual content. As a matter of technique, his work is full of such dissolved and contrasted reminiscences as need to be understood; as a matter of content, his sensibility was of the intellectual sort which proceeds from a process of analysis'. Swinburne is capable repeatedly of 'a perfectly solid metaphysical conceit', and so is later nineteenth- century poetry, even if its plentiful 'conceits and ambiguities' are so subdued as to be thought 'sleeping' and thus truly described as 'decadent',

---

[58] '"The coming of night is like the falling of fire"'; the sun becomes a red, glowing, exhausted ball on the horizon, day is going out, the fire, as it burns down, glows hotter, and all the heat natural to the firmament is being brought down (as if the ceiling was weighing on me) and crushed into my temples. But when the *flame shakes* our attention is transferred to a lamp; it is lighting-up time; the indoor Victorian-furnished Venusberg becomes hotter, stuffier and more enclosed, more irritating to sick head-ache and nervous exhaustion, and the gas-jet will have to be popping from now on. Or the *flame* may be a symbolical candle; it gutters in its socket which, low in its last struggles, it scorches, and rises and falls in popping and jerking disorder, like the throbbing and swooning of headache, and casts leaping and threatening shadows on the walls. *Full*, because it has ended the time it is capable of, and because in its shaking it seems to be measuring seconds, magnified by a sickbed fixity of attention into *hours*; not *sleeping* or *weeping*, because of the poet's insomnia and emotional exhaustion, because of its contrast with, and indifference to, his *weeping* and the approaching *sleep* of his death, and because, in the story, this mood is fixed into an eternity outside the human order, in which tears are pointless, and the peace even of death unattainable.

'In the next verse, *air might wash*, like water, and *leaves might cover*, like the sea or the grave; then by direct implication *grass* and *flowers* are compared to waves; then the *wind's feet shining along the sea*, whitening the tops of the waves, is compared, the other way round, to *grass* and *flowers*, and, as a fainter implication, to grassy mounds with white tombstones on them. The sea, in Swinburne, shares with earth the position of great sweet mother, is cleaner, fresher, and more definitely dead. Nor must one forget the feet, so beautiful upon the mountains, of him that brings good tidings of the Lord.'

William Empson, *Seven Types of Ambiguity* (3rd edn, Peregrine Books, Harmondsworth, 1961), 163–166.

or even (marvellous phrase) as 'in part the metaphysical tradition dug up when rotten'.[59]

Empson's defence of the Victorian poet's verbal adroitness and astuteness was going on even as his tutor's audience were denying it. It was a defence continued and affirmed when Hopkins's 'The Windhover, to Christ our Lord' was called in evidence alongside George Herbert's already canonical Metaphysical poem 'The Sacrifice' to illustrate the Seventh Type of Ambiguity, 'the most ambiguous that can be conceived', occurring 'when the two meanings of the word, the two values of the ambiguity, are the two opposite meanings of the word defined by the context, so that the total effect is to show a fundamental division in the writer's mind'. Admittedly, granting Hopkins this elevated, if highly fraught, place of verbal work was easier than polemicizing for complexities in Swinburne, because Hopkins was already emerging as an accepted exception to the conventional low estimate of the Victorians' work (even in Cambridge, as the *Practical Criticism* audience showed; and Empson pays tribute to Richards for putting him on to this case of Hopkins and writing 'excellently' about it, presumably in his 1926 *Dial* article). Still, you can hear Empson rather gritting his teeth and forcing his admiration for this Jesuit priest's Christian poem about a Christ-like Falcon whose subject prompts this militant atheist's dislike from the start – the poem is 'strong' and 'beautiful' but its triumphant ambiguity is 'precarious' and even on occasion ludicrous. The poem's now notorious exhortation 'Buckle!' is rich in meaning, Empson can tell, but for him rather disagreeably so. It 'admits of two tenses and two meanings: "they ['Brute beauty and valour and ... pride' and so forth] do buckle here", or "come, and buckle yourself here"; *buckle* like a military belt, for the discipline of heroic action, and *buckle* like a bicycle wheel, "made useless, distorted, and incapable of its natural motion." *Here* may mean "in the case of the bird", or "in the case of the Jesuit"; and so "when you have become like the bird", or "when you have become like the Jesuit".' Empson admits in a footnote that 'the test' for his reading is *buckle*. 'What would Hopkins have said if he could have been shown this analysis? It is, perhaps, the only really disagreeable case in the book. If I am right, I am afraid he would have denied with anger that he had meant "like a bicycle wheel", and then after much conscientious self-torture would have suppressed the whole poem'. Notably, what's actually *disagreeable* in Empson's statement remains highly ambiguous: is it the poem as a whole, the alleged dividedness of Hopkins as a Christian and Jesuit and poet, the analysis as a whole, the local ambiguity of *buckle*, or even Empson's way with this particular poem? It's by no means clear. And the fuzz adds to the sense that Empson is less happy about proposing Hopkins's verbal forces than about advertising Swinburne's; his

---

[59]   William Empson, ibid.

praise for Hopkins's verbal achievements evidently comes more grudgingly. But the fact is that, grudging or not, Empson is offering it. And Hopkins is taking his rightful place alongside Metaphysical Herbert. (Empson admitted in the Preface to the Second Edition of *Seven Types* that along with TS Eliot's propagandizing for Donne and Co. he'd been influenced by Freud. He had, it seems, in particular, been inspired by reading Freud's review of a pamphlet by the German philologist Karl Abel on the contrary meanings of early words, namely Freud's article 'The Antithetical Structure of Primal Words', which celebrates the way certain ancient Egyptian words could simultaneously carry precisely opposite meanings, and how that was rather like the way 'slips of the tongue' happened and like the multivalent and over-determined way Freud found dream images working. This was a philological inspiration that, clearly, carries over into Empson's bravura follow-up to *Seven Types*, his *The Structure of Complex Words* (1951), in which, once again, Swinburne stars, this time in the matter of the rich oppositional complexities of the word *delicate* and what it contradictorily conveys about human work, aesthetics, behaviour and selfhood (now fine, refined, sensitive, pleasing and delightful in the best senses, now sickly, inclined to debilitation, pleasurable and delightful in bad ways, perverse even) in 'Hymn to Proserpine', 'The Leper' and 'Dolores'.[60]

And of course Hopkins's earliest poetic education was, like Swinburne's, all in the classics. Auden's suggestion just won't hold, not even in the notorious case of foaming Swinburne. Historically, it's a washout. Auden might have paused over the fact that the authors of the most verbally tight poetry in English, the poets whose verbal strengths nobody has ever disputed, Shakespeare and The Metaphysicals and so on, the great poetic subjects who fall off the tree straight into Empson's analytic hand in the *Seven Types*, were all brought up translating the classics, and that their education didn't have the alleged verbal impoverishing effect on them. What is more, many of the Victorians Auden's poetic net is presumably gathering in as alleged verbal slackers were not educated in the classics nor brought up on translation from ancient poets. The education he is interested in was limited to men of a certain class, the clientele of Public Schools and Oxford and Cambridge; it excluded the poor, who if they went to school at all went to elementary and practical schools which didn't have Latin and Greek as main staples, and bourgeois women

---

[60] Sigmund Freud, 'The Antithetical Structure of Primal Words' (1910), *Collected Papers*, Volume IV (Hogarth Press, London, 1925), 184–191. William Empson, *The Structure of Complex Words* (Chatto & Windus, London, 1951), 76–79. Empson's case about the ambivalences of *Buckle!* and *Here* in 'The Windhover' was rehearsed, in more or less the same words as in *Seven Types*, including the vexed buckled bicycle-wheel analogy, and drawing support from Freudian dream-work, jokes, and 'primitive languages', in letters in 1928 to his Cambridge English contemporary Elsie Phare (Elsie Duncan-Jones to be): *Selected Letters of William Empson*, ed John Haffenden (Oxford University Press, Oxford, 2006), 3–6.

o were educated at small girls' schools, or at home with private tutors, and were excluded from Oxford and Cambridge), and religious Dissenters (like Robert Browning) whose Dissenting Academies were less classics-obsessed and who were also debarred from Oxford and Cambridge. So the verbal ways – whatever they are – of the hordes of Victorian working-class and female and Dissenting poets must be ascribed to other causes than Auden's.

And, on the face of it, it would be a distinct historical oddity, would it not, if suddenly writing were to collapse, fall away, go to the dogs, turn into pish-posh at the beginning of Victoria's reign and then suddenly recover again sixty or so years later. As if a nicely running engine were to suddenly stutter and die and then just as suddenly rev up again after sixty years lying in the garage. As if the poets were doing rather well, paying close attention to words and their ways, thinking hard about their language, wrestling with it, striving like Jonathan Swift for 'proper words in proper places' or, like Coleridge, for 'the best words in the best order', and then suddenly there's an end of the old poetic order (Coleridge happening to die 25 July 1834), followed by nothing much, a period of riding along on buckled bicycle wheels, until, just as abruptly, there arrive on the scene Joyce and Pound and Eliot and the rest, poetic bicycle wheels miraculously unbuckled, all verbally attentive and strong again and (remarkably) speaking, and acting on, the old language of care and attention once more ('What I am seeking is the perfect order of words in the sentence': that's James Joyce to his friend Frank Budgen about the poeticizing word-manoeuvres of *Ulysses*).

The Mythic Victorian Gap

And of course this notion of the Victorian gap, a dire parenthesis for real poetry, is a complete myth. Victorian poetry can be weak and strong just as the poetry of other ages is both bad and good; it can be extraordinarily strong, both verbally and formally, whether the poet spent his youth translating from the Classics (as Tennyson, and Matthew Arnold, and Clough, and Housman did), or did not (like Browning, and Christina G. Rossetti, and Emily Brontë, and Hardy). The good Victorian poets are highly alert to their verbal doings, as all good poets have been. Wilde, the author of that double sneer at Meredith and Browning, was, of course, himself a Victorian. For their part, many Modernists, Eliot and Pound especially, greatly respect and are inspired by certain Victorian poets (it's one of the themes of my final chapter, 'Victorian Modernismus'). After Robert Bridges published his friend Gerard Hopkins's poetry posthumously in 1918, Hopkins was quickly embraced as a missing father in the modern poetic faith. Cecil Day Lewis's *A Hope for Poetry* (1934) acknowledges three inspirations, a trinity of powerful parents for the new Auden generation: TS Eliot, Wilfred Owen, and Hopkins.

The phenomenon of Hopkins should be taken as symptomatic of the intense self-consciousness of Victorian poets about their art (and, not incidentally, it was self-consciousness fuelled and fired in Hopkins's case by immersion in, and evident admiration for, the formal power, the swaggering formal mastery of Swinburne's *Atalanta in Calydon* and *Poems and Ballads*).[61] Self-consciousness: that high Wildean criterion of poetic and critical merit. Hopkins is only the most spectacular example of the way Victorian poets are completely preoccupied with verbal quality, verbal truth, verbal experiment – their own, and other people's. His diaries and letters in which he hammers out a poetic, theorizing form and poetic language and the responsibilities of the poet, are only special in intensity, not in kind. Hopkins's discussion with himself and his friends RW Dixon, Coventry Patmore, and Robert Bridges is just one small segment of the large, loud, and continuous Victorian critical conversation and argument going on in private and in public. This unstopping discussion is what generates the heat, the emotionality, hostility and scepticism of the reviews; and the great squabble over the rival merits of Tennyson and Browning; and the even bloodier bloody poetic wars, like the one over Browningesque Realism, or the Spasmodics, or the School of Fleshliness; and that extraordinary level of discussion about writing going on within poems, the frequent metatextuality of verse (what Schlegel labelled the 'Poesie der Poesie'), which includes the great mass of pastiche, parody, mockery, the jeering undoing of others (and, as in the case of Swinburne's 'Heptalogia', the undoing of oneself).

Family Critical Business Inc.

It was in a great measure all in the family, family business, family networking, family squabbling, a huge family conversation and argument. For in large part Victorian poets comprise a huge intellectually incestuous cousinhood, a tribe, or at least a closely interrelated and overlapping set of tribes. (Incest didn't worry them: 'if Byron fucked his sister he fucked her and there an end,' as Dante Gabriel Rossetti put it dismissingly to his brother William Michael.[62]) There are three poetic Rossetti siblings, Dante Gabriel, William Michael, and young Christina Georgina (one reason, I think, why Christina wanted to be known as Christina G was so she would patently rival big brother Dante G – he who changed his name from Gabriel Dante to Dante Gabriel: CGR wasn't going to be outshone by DGR).

---

[61]   As Elizabeth W Schneider nicely shows in her 'Sprung Rhythm' article, *PMLA*, 80, iii (1965), 237–253.

[62]   Letter of 15 September 1869, *Letters of Dante Gabriel Rossetti*, II, 1861–1870, eds Oswald Doughty and John Robert Wahl (Clarendon Press, Oxford, 1965), 743.

Father Gabriele was a poet and Dante-translator. There are three poetic Tennyson brothers, Frederick, Alfred, and young Charles Tennyson Turner. And four poetic Brontë siblings, Charlotte, Branwell, Emily and Anne. Rugbeian Matthew Arnold has Rugbeian Arthur Hugh Clough forced on him as a kind of adopted brother – his headmaster-father Dr Thomas Arnold's more favoured son. Elizabeth Barrett Barrett marries Robert Browning, after a long fan-mail correspondence – the published poet EBB, Elizabeth Barrett Barrett, eliding easily into the published poet EBB, Elizabeth Barrett Browning. It was a partnership of poets in which he played George Henry Lewes to her George Eliot, as his wife's agent and promoter – her 'church-organ-bellows blower', as he put it.[63] The poet 'Michael Field' was a pair of lesbian lovers, Katherine Harris Bradley and her sixteen years younger niece Edith Emma Cooper. The male poets ganged up – at school and university. So many of them were at Balliol College, Oxford – Swinburne and Hopkins, and Clough and Arnold and JA Symonds (and FT Palgrave, promoter of the Pre-Raphaelites, friend of Tennyson, and the age's greatest poetry publicist through his 1861 *Golden Treasury of the Best Songs and Lyrical Poems in the English Language*) – or at Magdalen College, Oxford (Symonds and Wilde), or Trinity College, Cambridge (Bulwer Lytton, the Tennysons, Edward FitzGerald). Ted Jones (Edward Burne-Jones to be) meets William Morris at Exeter College, Oxford.

Bedding, or at least would-be bedding, was by no means confined to the heterosexuals. Hopkins adores Digby Mackworth Dolben (Eton-Balliol) who adores John Henry Newman. The Old Etonians and the Balliol and Magdalen men all fancy each other – smiled on by Jowett the Greek-translating Master of Balliol (Hopkins's tutor as well as Swinburne's and Symonds's), and by the aesthetic high-priest of Brasenose College, Walter Pater, and John Conington the Latin Professor of Corpus Christi College, Oxford, that hot-bed of paiderastic longings (Robert Bridges was at Corpus, which is where Hopkins met him). Buggery and Balliol went, proverbially, together. Aesthetic life was for brothers, and brotherhoods. The career of the ritualist poet RW Dixon is quite symptomatic. A friend of Ted Jones at King Edward's School Birmingham, he joins the Birmingham Group of Oxford aesthetes when he arrives at Pembroke College, Oxford, and through Ted Jones gets into the PreRaphaelite Brotherhood, which stars the Exeter Boys, Ted Jones and William Morris. Ordained into the Church of England ministry, he officiates at the marriage in Oxford of Morris and Janey, the daughter of a livery-stable owner a stone's throw from Exeter College. Poor, as well as poor in spirit, he teaches at Highgate School, where one of his pupils is Gerard Hopkins. In June 1878 Hopkins, now a Roman Catholic

---

[63] Letter to his and her publisher Edward Chapman, 2 Dec 1856: quoted in Margaret Reynolds's Norton edn of *Aurora Leigh* (1996), 337.

priest, sends his old schoolmaster a fan-letter praising his 1861 volume *Christ's Company*; Dixon replies, flattered, moved, and his career as Hopkins's close poetic consultant and confidant (alongside Hopkins's old Oxford friend Bridges and his co-religionist Coventry Patmore) takes off.[64]

Group consulting and advising like that is more the norm than not. Rich Ruskin (Christ Church, Oxford) takes Dante Gabriel Rossetti under his wing, is a great friend of Browning, keeps dispensing critical advice along with his financial largesse. Rossetti is intimate with Swinburne, who not only advises him about his poems, but also how to dig up his notebook from Lizzie Siddal's grave. When Tennyson needs someone to try and find the lost manuscript book of *In Memoriam* verses he sends Coventry Patmore round to his old Mornington Street lodgings – and the book is discovered in the food cupboard. The Irish poet William Allingham fixes a relocation of his job as a customs officer from Ballyshannon to England so he can be near Tennyson on an almost daily basis. And an awful lot of reading to fellow poets went on. Tennyson read his poems to everybody who would listen (including the Queen). On one characteristic occasion he reads 'Maud' to Browning, while Rossetti sketches him, before Browning reads 'Fra Lippo Lippi' in return. Clough weeps 'like a child' whilst reading 'Mari Magno' to Tennyson in 1861. (George Eliot wept as Tennyson read 'Guenevere' from *Idylls of the King* – at the request of George Henry Lewes.) And mutual eating and drinking were as common as mutual reading. The widowed Browning dined out with everybody. Meanwhile, the London Celts and 'decadent' Francophiles – Yeats, Lionel Johnson, Victor Plarr, AE Dowson, Richard LeGallienne, John Davidson, Arthur Symons – clubbed together in the Rhymers' Club. And the women had their groups too, like the allied Portfolio Society and Langham Place Group (Barbara Leigh Smith, Bessie Rayner Parkes, Jean Ingelow, Isa Knox, Adelaide Anne Procter). This group set up the Victoria Press to make women's poetry more available.

And so it went. Victorian poets comprised a field of insiders, a set of mutually profitable societies. Being on the outside, continuing as an outsider, being a real loner, working mainly on your own, not being part of some critical support group, was, evidently, the exception. It was, naturally enough, the melancholy plight of just a few working-class poets, self-taught people, cobbling together an idea of how verses might go from bits of private and random reading. Like John Clare, the Northamptonshire plough-boy who was indeed taken up by literary London but remained more or less

---

[64] See *The Correspondence of Gerard Manley Hopkins and Richard Watson Dixon*, ed CC Abbott (Oxford University Press, London, 1935; revised, 1955); *The Letters of Gerard Manley Hopkins to Robert Bridges*, ed CC Abbott (Oxford University Press, London, 1935; revised. 1955); *Further Letters of Gerard Manley Hopkins, Including His Correspondence with Coventry Patmore*, ed CC Abbott (Oxford University Press, London, 1938; revised 1956).

entirely shut away inside his own richly fantasizing head and in his various lunatic asylums (he probably never exchanged a single poetic word with Alfred Tennyson when they were both ensconced in Dr Matthew Allen's asylum at High Beech in Epping Forest). Or Janet Hamilton, the blind Scottish Calvinist poet, perhaps Victorian Britain's most famous working-class author, much visited by celebs, who came, though, rather to stare at a writing phenomenon than to consult in any way. Or Ebenezer Elliott, the famous 'Corn-law Rhymer', a Sheffield iron-master, entirely self-schooled on the poems of Crabbe and Mrs Hemans. Or Thomas Cooper, Leicester cobbler and famous rhymester in the Chartist cause (he wrote his *The Purgatory of Suicides* in Stafford Gaol), who came to literature in the way of so many provincial working-class children by reading Bunyan's *The Pilgrim's Progress*, taught himself Latin and Greek and Hebrew and memorized all of *Hamlet*, but never mixed in any of the contemporary literary circles (Carlyle gave him the brush-off when he was sent *The Purgatory*: 'I always grudge to see any portion of a man's *musical talent* ... expended on making *words* rhyme'.) But these isolates (part of the crowd of provincial, working-class poets featured in 'Modernizing the Subject', Chapter 9, below) are rare. Strikingly, the culture was rather eager to take in and help along the promising working-class poet. Like Gerald Massey, son of illiterate bargee parents who went to work at the age of eight, but was given literary shelter under several literary wings – Sidney Dobell's, Charles Dickens's, John Chapman's (Chapman edited the *Westminster Review*: many people thought Massey the original of the working-class intellectual Felix Holt in the novel of that name by Chapman's assistant editor George Eliot). Or Ellen Johnston, the Scottish mill-worker, known as 'The Factory-Girl' poet, who was picked out by Glasgow newspaper editor Alex Campbell and given her own regular column for her poems and rhymed discussions with fellow contributors.[65] It was simply hard at this time not be related to other poets, or not to have such relationships thrust upon one.

Take the unpromising Gloucester Grammar School-boy WE Henley, the one-legged poet (original, it was thought, of Long John Silver in Robert Louis Stevenson's novel *Treasure Island*). Hospitalized for months in Edinburgh Infirmary, he sends his 'In Hospital' sequence to Leslie Stephen at the *Cornhill Magazine* and is immediately encouraged and published (not without contention: Stephen wouldn't take the poems lacking end-rhymes). And he ends up as snugly embedded as anyone could be in the London literary world, becoming the great promoter of Hardy and Kipling and Yeats

[65]   For Ellen Johnston, see H Gustav Klaus, *Ellen Johnston and Working-Class Poetry in Victorian Scotland* (Peter Lang, Frankfurt am Main, 1998). Some of her poems are in the copious anthology *Working-Class Women Poets in Victorian Britain*, informatively edited by Florence S Boos (Broadview Press, Toronto, 2008).

and HG Wells and Robert Louis Stevenson and JM Barrie in his *National Observer* magazine of the early 1890s. (His daughter Margaret was thought to be the inspiration for Wendy in Barrie's *Peter Pan*.) Even if you had certain trademarks of the outsider, the appearance could be deceptive. The London Jewish poet Amy Levy was rumoured to live in a garret and work in an East End factory, whereas she had been briefly a student at Newnham, the college for women at Cambridge (the first Jew to be admitted), got published in Oscar Wilde's *Woman's World*, and was a close friend of the suffragist Clementina Black (sister of Constance Garnett the great translator of Dostoevsky) and of Eleanor Marx (who translated one of Levy's novels into German, was a chum of the Christian Socialist poet and novelist E Nesbit, whose sister Mary was the one-time fiancée of the blind poet Philip Bourke Marston). She died in a botched suicide pact with the novelist Olive Schreiner. (All these 'outsider' poets are featured, with some others, in 'Modernizing the Subject'.)

It was simply rather hard in this culture not to be close to some literary person or other with whom to discuss your work. Even if you were a poet who upset almost everybody you rubbed shoulders with. Like the terrifying down-and-out Scottish wino James Thomson (author of the desolate urban nightmare 'The City of Dreadful Night'), a violent, quarrelsome, falling-over drunkard, who went to prison for setting a landlady's kitchen on fire, hung out stinkily in the British Museum Reading Room for want of a home to go to, but still managed to be great friends with the novelist and poet George Meredith and with Philip Bourke Marston (in whose room Thomson collapsed and died of a stomach haemorrhage).

The Big Critical Conversation

And the great critical conversation went on. Unconcerned about their intimate verbal proceedings these writers certainly were not. Pound was simply wrong about Swinburne's lack of verbal heed. Writing is an almost frantic preoccupation which Victorian writers' diaries, notebooks, letters and manuscripts, and the reminiscences of their friends and enemies, almost over amply witness. In the first place poets discuss things with themselves. TS Eliot famously suggested that the First of the poet's Three Voices is of the poet talking to himself (and, we should add, herself).[66] And you hear that self-debate and argument going on on every page of poets' work-sheets, manuscripts, and printed proofs available to us. You see its traces in the deletions and insertions, in the marks and re-marks witnessing second- and third-thoughts

[66] TS Eliot, 'The Three Voices of Poetry' (1953), in *On Poetry and Poets* (Faber & Faber, 1957), 89–102.

and more, in the dense scribblings up and down and around the page, in the repeated harsh scrubbings-out and emphatic writings-in. The manuscript page often comes quite blackened, polluted with ink, a self-obscured mess, close to illegibility. No wonder authors' manuscripts are called their *foul papers*. ('[W]rite verse, / Burnt in disgust, then ill-restored, and left / Half-made, in pencil scrawl illegible': Clough, 'Dipsychus', X.131–133.[67]) And when the clean page-proofs come back from the printers they're frequently subject to the same kind of restless correcting and nagging alteration all over again. Poets patently can't stop this verbal contention with themselves.

> All delicate days and pleasant, all spirits and sorrows are cast
> Far out with the foam of the present that sweeps to the surf of the past:
> Where beyond the extreme sea-wall, and between the remote sea-gates,
> Waste water washes, and tall ships founder, and deep death waits.

That's Swinburne once more at the sea-side in lines 47–50 of his 'Hymn to Proserpine' as published in *Poems and Ballads* (July 1866). And what an effort it took to get there! At first the 'spirits and sorrows' of line 47 were *whirled*, and the *past* of 48 that now rhymes with *cast* of line 47 was instead the audio-auto rhyming *world*, for 'the present that sweeps to the surf of the past' started off as 'the present that cast[s] on the wake of the world'. It's impossible to tell whether or not it was worry about rhyming *whirled* and *world* that sparked off the wholesale rewriting of line 48. Line 49 at first ran 'Where beyond the extreme sea-rocks & beyond the reach & the reef' (where that second & – a mere squiggle – reads like a slip of the pen for *of*). At any rate Swinburne altered *sea-wall* to *sea-rocks*, and crossed out 'beyond the reach &' writing 'the black bare fangs of' over it. But much as he is perennially drawn to what fangs do, that alteration didn't last and it got crossed out in turn, and 'between the remote sea gates' got written below the whole original phrase 'beyond the reach & the reef' – with '& the reef' now also being crossed out. How to go on then clearly gives the poet even more pause. He writes *In*, and crosses it out. Starts again with *Aphrodite*, and crosses that out. Starts yet again with *Like*, but like what is unclear: there's the beginning of an illegible capital letter, which is in turn crossed out. And he starts again with *The*, and crosses that out too. And begins yet once more with 'Waste water washes, & locks up', or maybe 'looks up' (the word is hard to make out). Then he crosses out the *locks*, or *looks*, *up*, and writes underneath the line, 'tall ships founder, & deep death waits'. And line 50 is now very impressive. 'Waste water washes' is wonderfully contradictory – this water *washes*, even though it's *waste* water, in an

---

[67]   *The Poems of Arthur Hugh Clough*, edd HF Lowry, ALP Norrington and FL Mulhauser (Clarendon Press, Oxford, 1951), 279. This is the edn of Clough which I normally quote.

oxymoron that's as good as any of the Swinburnean contradictions Empson celebrated. And the threat of this watery *waste* – the sea's vasty wastes are notoriously scary and dangerous: a set of worrying associations, inescapable because the rhyming, alliterative, initial letters bind the water and the washing and the wasting tightly together – gets endorsed by *deep death*: *deep* because the oceans in which ships *founder* are *deep*, and *deep* enough easily to engulf even the tallest of ships whose height might be thought to challenge those depths.[68]

The poet will consult with himself, like this. It's what poets do. He might also bring his brother and his sister and his friends into the process of revision. Dante Gabriel Rossetti, that intense scrutineer of others (he copied out all of Robert Browning's *Pauline* in the British Museum Reading Room), is not only hyper-critical of his own verses, but ropes in the family to aid the inspection. He sends the proofs of what will become *Poems* (1870) to his brother William Michael for comment.[69] There are detailed notes and questions, 21 August 1869. William Michael responds on the 23rd August 1869. He's 'been reading' the poems 'all the evening with intense pleasure: they are most splendid and ought to be published without any not seriously motived delay'. He's corrected a few misprints. There are, though, some serious problems with, for instance, 'The Burden of Nineveh', the poem whose narrator stands outside the British Museum as a great effigy of a winged God arrives from Nineveh and reflects on the fate of deities ancient and modern, including the Christian God. One of the mummified persons now upstairs in the Museum, said the text, could well have travelled to Nineveh and seen this particular deity: for 'even to some / Of these thou wert antiquity'. Which is true, William Michael agrees, 'literally accepted', 'but you know Egyptian civilisation and art are far *older* than Ninevite, and I think the *impression* from your passage runs counter to this fact.'

Other poems require thought of a different kind. There's a sonnet about two lovers parting after sex called 'Placatâ Venere' (which means something like: When Love Has Been Appeased), and beginning 'At length their long kiss severed, with sweet smart'. That should go into the volume 'by all means – at any rate, so long as the collection remains private. I must re-read the poem before expressing a distinct opinion as to publication'. And meanwhile that supposed Egyptian visitor to Nineveh is still a worry. He's called 'A pilgrim', which William Michael now thinks won't do. So he adds

---

[68] Detail from the photographed and transcribed and much worked-over work-sheets, in Robert Peters, 'AC Swinburne's "Hymn to Prosperpine": The Work Sheets', *PMLA*, 83 (October 1968), 1400–1406.

[69] Jerome McGann sets Rossetti's extreme anxiety over this volume in the context of his turn to poetry as an authentication of what he felt was his true aesthetic integrity after years of selling out – making lots of 'tin' by his pot-boiling painting: 'Dante Gabriel Rossetti and the Betrayal of Truth', *Victorian Poetry* 26, no. 4 (Winter 1988), 339–361. It's a thought.

a PS: 'I also rather doubt the phrase "a pilgrim" as applied to these Egyptians. I understand it to mean what we should call "an art-pilgrim" – a tourist with an archaeological object. I suspect these mummies were innocent of such purposes – or at the extreme utmost would have "done" Egypt. Nineveh is very distant, and alien too. If it is a *religious* pilgrim – as a consulter of the Oracle at Delphi, for instance – I believe it is equally or more untenable'. He's not yet finished with the proofs but posts off these interim suggestions.

On 26 August Dante Gabriel thanks him for his 'valuable letter. I am attending to it, and will do so further when I get your concluding admonitions'. On 24 August, William Michael finishes going through the proofs and fires off a second letter full of his further thoughts. *Placatâ Venere* is still nagging. William Michael now thinks it should be published, but 'you might *perhaps* reconsider the title, which appears to me a nearer approach to indecorum than anything in the sonnet itself'. On 27 August Dante Gabriel replies to this, and extremely fully. He'd already thought, he said, of that difficulty with the mummies, and been 'troubled' by it. He offers *traveller* instead of *pilgrim*, and a juggle with the antiquity line: 'Nay, but were not some / Of these even then antiquity?' But he's still not satisfied. Perhaps 'thine own' antiquity would be better: 'Which is the best?' And 'The word *traveller* I do not quite like… I meant no more by *pilgrim*. Do you think the change desirable?' And apparently William Michael did not. The poem finally has *alien*, and a still further caution about *antiquity*, presumably at the insistence of the brother, who also plumped for *thine own* over *even then*.

> Why, of those mummies in the room
> Above, there might indeed have come
> One out of Egypt to thy home,
> An alien. Nay but were not some
> Of these thine own 'antiquity?'

'What say you?' He needs his brother's opinion on many points. In 'The Blessed Damozel', for instance, is the 'sound awkward' in line 11, 'Her hair that lay upon her back'? 'Is "And her hair laid upon" etc. better?' (The final decision went to 'Her hair that lay upon her back / Was yellow like ripe corn'.) How should the sea in the poem 'Ave' have 'Sighed further off eternally' for the Virgin Mary in Nazareth? Is it to be *As heavy*, or *human*, or *ancient, sorrow sighs in sleep*, or *Like ancient sorrow or sad sleep*? (The vote went to 'As human sorrow sighs in sleep'.) And so the poet goes on, in deep and deepening detail. Which includes a return to the clearly inescapable 'Burden of Nineveh'. 'It occurs' to Dante

Gabriel 'to go back and ask your opinion' about the stanzas beginning at
what is now line 41.

> On London stones our sun anew
> The beast's recovered shadow threw.
> (No shade that plague of darkness knew,
> No light, no shade, while older grew
> By ages the old earth and sea.)
> How much Heaven's thunder – how much else
> Man's puny roar? what cry of shells
> Cleft – amid leagured citadels –
> How many lordships loud with bells
> Heardst thou in secret Nineveh?
>
> O when upon each sculptured court
> Where even the wind might not resort
> Oe'r which time passed, of like import
> With the wild Arab boys at sport,
> A living face looked in to see, –
> And seemed it not etc ...

He's already condensed these lines once. 'Is there anything lost by it?' Does
that make the poem too abrupt? He's just read aloud the longer version (as
above in his letter) to William Bell Scott, who 'thinks the second half of the
first stanza rather extraneous but the first half of the second a great gain'.
Dante Gabriel has 'some idea' that Brown – presumably Madox Brown –
'once suggested difficulties about the shells, bells, etc. Could they be heard
under the earth? Were there any to be heard? etc.' If William Michael thinks
the first half of the second stanza '*very* desirable and the previous omitted
lines objectionable', he is to 'try and suggest some point or idea to fill the
gap'. And one assumes that the five lines now following 'the old earth and
sea' are William Michael's suggestion:

> Lo thou! could all thy priests have shown
> Such proof to make thy godhead known?
> From their dead Past thou liv'st alone;
> And still thy shadow is thine own,
> Even as of yore in Nineveh.

Dante Gabriel's list of queries is rather large (about 'Hand and Soul' and
'Plighted Promise' and 'Our Lady of the Rocks' and 'A Venetian Pastoral'
and so on and so forth), but he still wants a quick response: 'post your set
of proofs to me *at once* on getting this letter, as I have other changes to make
in them before sending back to the printers and can more shortly do them

myself than explain them to you. Please answer questions here asked as soon as possible'.[70]

And the business of family consultation isn't over yet. When the next set of cleaned-up proofs comes back from the printer he'll give probably give Christina another look: 'I will probably apply again for Christina's views with the *next* revise'.[71] He finds himself on 2 September writing again to William Michael to say he has 'benefited much by your labours as you will see':

> Your last line to the *Satan* sonnet ['"Retro me, Sathana"!'] I adopted with a slight change but am rather uncertain whether I may not change back again. What you said of the foggy opening of *Nocturn* ['Love's Nocturne'] induced me to restore a second stanza which I had cut out in printing it, in case this might make things any clearer. I have also added three stanzas towards the close of this poem to develop the sudden flight of the bogy on finding another bogy by the girl's bed, which seemed funkyish though of course the right thing if she was already in love. I have also added three new stanzas at the point I referred to in *Stratton Water* and made the proposed restoration (with addition) to the *Nineveh*. Also added a further useful stanza in the middle of *Sister Helen*.

He's changed the worrying title of 'Placatâ Venere' to 'Nuptial Sleep' – so that it might appear to be about a married couple rather than love out of wedlock, 'which I think will help it to stand fire'. He has 'improved some lines in it'. But he's still concerned about lines 1 and 5: he wants William Michael 'to say if you think one can say "their long kiss *severed*" and "their bosoms *sundered*" or whether "*was* severed" and "*were* sundered" are necessary' (brother William evidently thought the former). And the naggings go on and on. On 14 September he's writing to William Michael again about the new proofs: 'You will see much that is due to your labours in them. However I have been at work on them still further now and have done various things'. He's tinkered further with the third stanza of 'Nocturn' ('I think you will agree with me that this is preferable'), but is still 'worrying about what you said of the obscurity of the opening of this poem' and has changed it some more. And what about the fourth stanza? He's altered it to 'flow better', but he's 'just noticed that in the present version there is "whisperings" rhyming with "rings" which is bad. But on the other hand I like the new meaning best. What is your view?'

---

[70]   Joseph Bristow is interested in the genderized imperialism of the finalized 'Burden of Nineveh': ' "He and I": Dante Gabriel Rossetti's Other Man', *Victorian Poetry* 39, iii (Fall 2001), 365–388.
[71]   Alison Chapman's feminist attack on the Rossetti brothers for flattening out Christina's 'metric jolt', her 'queer rhymes' and 'groans', and on her for being complicit in a 'dis-figuring' of the feminine subject, takes too little note of her part in editorially helping out Dante Gabriel's poems: 'Defining the Feminine Subject: Dante Gabriel Rossetti's Revisions to Christina Rossetti's Poetry', *Victorian Poetry* 35, iii (Summer 1997), 139–156.

'Nuptial Sleep' is still a bother. How should the lovers mouths act after love: 'yet still their mouths, burnt red,' and *did what* to 'each other where they lay apart"? One possibility is 'chirped at each other', which 'is expressive of the lips kissing *at* each other as they lie apart. But is it clear, or if clear is it pleasant? Would it be better "kissed at each other" or more likely "moaned to each other? Or does any other phrase occur to you? Or do you like it as it stands?' *Chirped at* is certainly unpleasant – these lovers are not birds. *Kissed at* is not much better, suggesting the rather violent pecking of antagonists or the mere air-kissing of friends and acquaintances rather than lovers. The moaning of *moaned to* is erotically expressive enough, but *moaned to* suggests whingeing and complaining. The final choice was 'Fawned on' – much more realistic, and physically and erotically vivid.

> At length their long kiss severed, with sweet smart:
> And as the last slow sudden drops are shed
> From sparkling eaves when all the storm has fled,
> So singly flagged the pulses of each heart.
> Their bosoms sundered with the opening start
> Of married flowers to either side outspread
> From the knit stem; yet still their mouths, burnt red,
> Fawned on each other where they lay apart.

These lines from 'Nuptial Sleep' were singled out by Robert Buchanan in his notorious attack on Rossetti in 'The Fleshly School of Poetry' essay (*The Contemporary Review*, October 1871) as 'simply nasty', and characteristic of Rossetti's lack of privateness and decorum. (My Chapter, 'Fleshly Feelings', Chapter 7, below, begins with this egregious attack.) But at least Buchanan was right to note the apparent pains taken over the writing: 'so careful a choice of epithet to convey mere animal sensations'. A care going right down to the smallest items, even to the choice of prepositions: chirped *at*, kissed *at*, moaned *to*, fawned *on*; *at*, *at*, *to*, *on* – so expressive in their variety of possible degrees of relationship, ending with the close-up positioning of intense intimacy.

Brotherly consultation and criticism had this way of paying off poetically. And not just from natural brothers. Dante Gabriel got immense help from his friend Swinburne, to whom, of course, he sent his proofs for comment. Swinburne was most useful, for instance, over Rossetti's 'Jenny', that extraordinarily strong, satirical dramatic monologue about a fallen woman, uttered by the man who has used her and who assuages his guilty concern for her by paying her off, leaving some golden coins in her golden hair as she sleeps.

> Why, Jenny, waking here alone
> May help you to remember one,
> Though all the memory's long outworn

Of many a double-bedded morn.
I think I see you when you wake,
And rub your eyes for me, and shake
My gold, in rising, from your hair,
A Danaë for a moment there.

(372–379)

Having the paying lover turn himself for a moment self-mythicizingly into the God Zeus who seduced the human woman Danaë in a shower of gold coins is a shrewd thrust by the poet. But it was the possible weakness of *double-bedded* that attracted Swinburne's critical gaze. 'Surely it can only mean', he wrote on 10 December 1869, 'that there were two beds, implying separate sleepers; which is chaste but startling, as a suggestion – proper but improbable. Also it sounds to me to have just a shade or breath of coarseness – escaped so exquisitely elsewhere in the most familiar parts of the poem; *double-pillowed*, now, would evade this, and give better the idea of two heads waking together, as nobody can sleep on two pillows at once'. Actually *double-bedded*, as in *double-bedded room*, could, apparently, indicate either a bed for two persons or two single beds, and what is coarse about a *double-bedded morn* in Swinburne's limited sense of double-bedded is not too apparent, unless he has in mind the classical idea of the dawn arising from night-time sleep, and the dawn is never thought of as sleeping ludicrously in two single beds. But the *double-pillowed* suggestion is in any case very good for the reasons of intimated intimacy that Swinburne indicates (and if Swinburne was thinking of Keats's 'Pillowed upon my fair love's ripening breast' in his 'Bright star' sonnet, so much the better). And *double-pillowed* it became.[72]

Rossetti's dedicated team-work evidently pays off like this, again and again. This way his poems just get better and better. Tennyson's poems improved too, though not because of any asked-for attention from family and friends, but because of the unwanted attentions of the critics – the sort of interfering critical lecture the Victorians were so manifestly good at, whether the poets liked it or not. Tennyson never got to actually like it. As he matured he did, of course, get more thick-skinned, shrugging off certain critics' unwanted attentions. 'No', 'Not so', '!!!!', and so on, run his annotations of John Churton Collins's suggestions about classical sources for so many of his lines (there's more about this encounter in Chapter 9, 'Modernizing the Subject'). Later on Tennyson could bad-mouth back ('Friswell, Pisswell – a liar and a twaddler – / Pisswell, Friswell – a clown

---

[72]   Details of all this critical ping-pong are in William Michael's letters to his brother in *Rossetti Papers 1862 to 1870*, compiled by William Michael Rossetti (Sands & Co, London, 1903), 453–457, 461–462, 465–469; and in *Letters of Dante Gabriel Rossetti*, eds Oswald Doughty and Robert Wahl, Vol II 1861–1870 (Clarendon Press, Oxford, 1965), 714–715, 721–722; 723–727; 733–735; 738–741; 772 & n.

beyond redemption', was his vigorous response to JH Friswell's 1870 criticisms), but early on he was easier prey.[73]

He was deeply shocked, quite knocked off his poetic perch, by the critical mauling given his 1832 *Poems* by JW Croker, the fierce, and Tory, but also sharp-eyed and canny *Quarterly Review* critic – he whose rough handlings were thought to have contributed to the death of Keats. Tennyson was 'almost crushed' by Croker, he said; he was minded to give up poetry entirely; and it took him ten whole years before he felt able to face the public again. But the hard knock was good for his verse. He clearly had been verbally too complacent (his poetic enemies thought he'd been carried away by the flattery of friends like Arthur Hallam who praised up Tennyson's first (1830) volume, *Poems, Chiefly Lyrical*). Tennyson would never be complacent again. He furiously reconsidered and rehashed his 1832 poems for their reappearance in *Poems* (1842), rewriting and rewriting them massively, fearful of some Tory 'fop' getting his hands on his verses again – 'I have had abuse enough'. According to Edgar Shannon's calculations, Tennyson corrected or suppressed an enormous 70% of the passages Croker criticized.[74]

Croker's *Quarterly* piece (April 1833) was full of sarcastically ironic praise for 'Mr Tennyson's singular genius, and … the peculiar brilliancy of the sense of the gems that irradiate his poetical crown'. These best, that is worst, bits Croker picked out with italics in his lengthy quotations from the poems. His play with 'The Lady of Shalott' and Tennyson's response are characteristic of the whole encounter. In that poem, the merry song and the mirrored vision of the passing-by Sir Lancelot mightily attract the poem's walled-in Lady:

> From the bank, and from the river
> He flashed into the crystal mirror
> 'Tirra lirra, tirra lirra'
> Sang Sir Lancelot.

[73]   For Tennyson pissing well on the hostile Friswell, see 'The Gentle Life' and Christopher Ricks's headnote, *The Poems of Tennyson*, ed Christopher Ricks (Longmans, London and Harlow, 1969), 1230. This is the very big one-volume edition I customarily quote from. Sometimes I refer to its great and necessary supplement, Ricks's 3 volume *Poems of Tennyson* (2nd edn, Longman, Harlow, 1987), which makes some corrections (though not all that it might), adds more poetry, updates the criticism, and above all includes manuscript materials from the great Trinity College, Cambridge, archive that nobody, including Ricks, was still in 1969 allowed to quote. These new materials are included in Ricks's student-handy one-volume *Selected Edition* (Pearson Longman, Harlow, 2007) but only in relation to the poems it includes – it hasn't space for a lot of the poems published in the 3-volume edn, nor in the (pretty complete) 1969 edition. 'The Gentle Life', for instance, is not in the *Selected Edition*. I do occasionally refer to the *Selected*. It's the edition my students use.

[74]   Edgar Finley Shannon, Jr, *Tennyson and the Reviewers: A Study of His Literary Reputation and of the the Influence of the Critics upon His Poetry 1827–1851* (Harvard University Press, Cambridge, MA, 1952), 41.

That's the 1832 version. Croker underlined '*from* the river', '*into* the crystal *mirror*', and the second '*lirra*', adding a derisive '(*lirrar?*)'. How, the implication was, could Sir Lancelot be both on the bank and also on or in the river; and shouldn't *lirra* be spelt *lirrar* to rhyme more closely with *river* and *mirror*? And Tennyson took the point, cutting the second *tirra lirra*, bringing in a purer rhyme *river* (even though this meant *river* self-rhyming with *river*), and meeting the position objection by now telling us Sir Lancelot is singing *by the river*, that is is on the bank and not on or in the water.

Croker's italics also poked sneeringly at the Lady's facial changes:

> Till her eyes were darkened *wholly*
> And her smooth face *sharpened slowly.*

The objection would seem to be about whether a face can all at once darken and sharpen. And Tennyson carefully took the point:

> Till her blood was frozen slowly
> And her eyes were darkened wholly.

(Later on, Tennyson noted that George Eliot 'liked my first the best'. And he would presumably have liked John Stuart Mill's liking of the first version and Mill's waspishness towards Croker's judgement: 'This exquisite line, the egregious critic of the *Quarterly* distinguishes by italics as specially absurd! proving thereby what is his test of the truth of a description, even of a physical fact. He does not ask himself, Is the fact so? but, have I ever seen the expression in the verses of any former poet of celebrity?'[75])

Croker was critical about boats as well. Tennyson had his dying Lady write her name 'below the stern' of her boat, which is where people read it as she floats by.

> Knight and burgher, lord and dame
> To the plankèd wharfage came
> Below *the stern* they read her name,
> *The Lady of Shalott.*

By underlining *stern*, Croker indicates the case that the names of boats are normally displayed at the front, the prow, and also that something written *below the stern* might be at or below the waterline and so difficult or even impossible to read. And again Tennyson has a rethink, getting the Lady to write her name at the prow and 'round about' it, not below it, which is where the Camelot citizens now read it.

---

[75]   John Stuart Mill, *London Review* (July 1835), i. 402–24; quoted, *Tennyson: The Critical Heritage*, ed John D Jump (Routledge & Kegan Paul, London, 1967), 89.

> Out upon the wharfs they came,
> Knight and burgher, lord and dame,
> And round the prow they read her name,
> *The Lady of Shalott.*

One notices too that the 'plankèd wharfage' of 1832 became merely the 'wharfs' – presumably because Croker had been sarcastic about Tennyson's use of the kind of emphasis *plankèd* got ('This use of the grave accent is, as our readers may have already perceived, so habitual with Mr Tennyson, and is so obvious an improvement, that we really wonder how the language has hitherto done without it. We are tempted to suggest, that if analogy to the accented languages is to be thought of, it is rather the acute (´) than the grave (`) which should be employed on such occasions; but we speak with profound diffidence; and as Mr Tennyson is the inventor of the system, we shall bow with respect to whatever his final determination may be').

And so it went, on and on, the critic carping and jeering and the poet nervously amending – and improving. In the pastoral 'Oenone', for example, the deserted woman Oenone (deserted by Paris) tells her 'mother Ida' (a lovely Greek mountain adorned with fountains) how the three naked goddesses arrive for the Judgement of Paris. There 'follows' – this is Croker – 'a description, long, rich, and luscious – Of the three naked goddesses? Fye for shame – no – of the "lily flower violet eyed" and the "singing pine", and the "overwandering ivy and vine", "festoons", and "gnarlèd boughs", and "tree tops", and "berries", and "flowers", and all the inanimate beauties of the scene. It would be unjust to the *ingenuus pudor* of the author not to observe the art with which he has veiled this ticklish interview behind such luxuriant trellis-work, and it is obvious that it is for our special sakes he has entered into these local details, because if there was one thing "mother Ida" knew better than another, it must have been her own bushes and brakes'. And, sure enough, in 1842, though 'many a wild festoon' and 'berry and flower' and 'the gnarlèd boughs' stayed in, lines 94–97 were completely rewritten to eliminate 'Lustrous with lilyflower, violet eyed' and the 'singing pine' and 'the overwandering ivy and vine'.

Tennyson takes the aggressive reviewer's point, however hurtful – compelled to respond to the intense and detailed critical discussion that publication thrust him into (Victorian reviews were, by modern standards, extremely long). He rewrote the last stanza of 'The Lady of Shalott' presumably because John Stuart Mill thought the original 'lame and impotent'. Mill's objection no doubt made Tennyson worry about how the Camelot onlookers were supposed to be able to read the dead Lady's parchment note lying on her breast in the boat, standing as they were on the river-bank. Having instead Sir Lancelot pay his tribute to her lovely face and wish her God's grace makes far more sense.[76] It is also clear, though, that Tennyson's revising, tinkering, amending, are going some way beyond the critics' pushes, as if the adverse voices are waking him up to the large verbal obligations good poets perennially feel themselves to be under. Tennyson's revisings of the 1832 verses also show him thinking for himself and not just for the reviewer. The way he ignores many of Croker's gibes indicates this ('gnarlèd', for instance, gets to stay). As does the way, too, that he'll sometimes wait a good while to respond. In 'A Dream of Fair Women' the ghost of Iphigeneia describes her murder:

> 'The tall masts quivered as they lay afloat,
> The temples and the people and the shore,
> One drew a sharp knife through my tender throat
> Slowly, – and nothing more.'

'What touching simplicity', enthused Croker mockingly, 'what pathetic resignation – he cut my throat "*nothing more!*" One might indeed ask, "what *more*" she would have?' This time Tennyson let the point mulch, only responding to it for the 1853 reprint.

> 'The high masts flickered as they lay afloat;
> The crowds, the temples, wavered, and the shore;
> The bright death quivered at the victim's throat;
> Touched; and I knew no more.'[77]

It's also characteristic of Tennyson, now that he's been prompted by the critic to think again, that he has actually gone beyond Croker, and made more sense of the stanza's second, apparently uncriticized, line: he's put in a verb, *wavered*, because it has evidently struck him that it wasn't clear what the people, the temples and the shore were supposed to be doing. He's made it clear: their reflections are shimmering in the water. Evidently the reviser is also his own man, and not simply the reviewer's dummy. And *Oenone* is only one of Tennyson's poems to get revised massively, way beyond any reviewer's nigglings, because the poet himself now felt the, so to say, raw poetic need and the fundamental obligation to keep scrutinizing. As Tennyson told his friend Spedding in 1835: he'd been going over his 'old poems, most of which I have so corrected (particularly *Oenone*) as to make them much less imperfect'. And Tennyson would never abandon the revising habit. He became the intensest of self-revisers

---

[76]   John Stuart Mill, in *Tennyson: The Critical Heritage*, 88–89.
[77]   Croker's review, *Critical Quarterly*, vol xlix (April 1833), 81–96, is reprinted in John Jump's *Tennyson: The Critical Heritage*, 66–83. The footnotes in all the Ricks editions nicely reveal the story of Tennyson's revisions.

and self-scrutineers. (How amusing to find him having rather got the hang
of Croker's kind of aggressive close reading – as in 1869 when Hallam
records him gibing in Croker-like terms at Dr Johnson's famous lines from
'The Vanity of Human Wishes':

> Let Observation with extensive View
> Survey Mankind from *China* to *Peru.*

'Why did he not say "Let observation, with extended observation, observe
extensively"?'[78])

Pushed by the critics, Tennyson had joined the ranks of the most verbally careful and astute Victorians. For his part, Robert Browning thought
Tennyson had given in too easily. Critics were swine, Browning thought,
a 'whole sty of grunters'. He cared little for their conduct of the large
national critical conversation, especially as it affected him and Mrs
Browning. Critics were like night-soil men, the city's domestic excrement-
collectors, 'always emptying their cart at my door'. Adverse reviews meant
loss of sales and so of money – of 'bread'. Those shitty reviewers touch
'our bread with their beastly hands'; Browning will 'rub their noses in
their own filth some fine day' (he was feeling especially sore about the
trashing his volume *Men and Women* (1855) had received).[79] Tennyson
should not have submitted to Croker. He 'reads the *Quarterly* and does as
they bid him, with the most solemn face in the world – out goes this, in
goes that, all is changed and ranged. Oh me'. This to Elizabeth Barrett
(11 February 1845); and she agreed (17 February: 'anybody is qualified,
according to everybody, for giving opinions upon poetry') – but only up
to a point: 'I do not say that suggestions from without may not be accepted
with discrimination sometimes, to the benefit of the acceptor'.[80] This was
a benefit Browning found hard to accept. Though there was a benefit,
even to him.

Browning's reactions to John Stuart Mill's annotations of the early *Pauline*
(1833) in the review-copy that Mill sent back to WJ Fox, editor of *The
Monthly Repository* and which Browning saw, show his annoyance, hostility, and deep reluctance to listen to any critic, but also a begrudging acceptance of improving points. *Pauline*'s I-narrator talks of his imitative beginnings
as a poet; he

---

[78]   *Memoir*, II. 73.

[79]   Letters to his and Elizabeth Barrett's publisher Edward Chapman, April and December
1856, *New Letters of Robert Browning*, edd WC DeVane and KL Knickerbocker (John Murray,
London, 1951), 92–93; 97.

[80]   *Letters of Robert Browning and Elizabeth Barrett Barrett 1845–1846*, Impression cit,
I. 20, 24.

> rather sought
> To rival what I wondered at than form
> Creations of my own; so much was light
> Lent by the others, much was yet my own. (390–393)

Mill thought the *so*, meaning *therefore, accordingly*, a 'colloquial vulgarism', and anyway it caused confusion as it always did in that position (should the line be read as *so* [*therefore*] *much*, or quantitatively as *so much?*). Browning took the confusion point, adding a comma after *so* in the 1868 edition, but with a bad grace. His notes responding to Mill's notes grouch fiercely: 'The recurrence of "so" thus employed is as vulgar as you please: but the usage "*so* in the sense of accordingly" is perfectly authorized, – take an instance or two from Milton'. And, really vexed and on the defensive, he listed a whole ten examples from *Paradise Lost*. But still the criticism went on rankling, so that for his 1888 text he dropped *so* altogether, altering it to *if*: 'if much was light': thus cutting out the confusion, and dropping the contended sense of *therefore*. Goaded by Mill's critical fire he amended a lot of *Pauline* like this; and soon turned quite against the poem as amateurish work. It's even been traditionally assumed that Browning went out of his way after *Pauline* to try and make quite clear the merely dramatic nature of his later personae as a result of Mill's assuming that Pauline's speaker was Browning himself ('This writer seems to me possessed with a more intense and morbid self-consciousness than I ever knew in any sane human person'). Whatever the truth of this large career-move allegation, it's clear that, for all Browning's reluctance to admit it, Mill was landing many good punches in this critic-poet grudge match. The critical conversation Browning so loathed was nonetheless keeping him on his mettle.[81]

Ruskin and Browning Go Head to Head

As when Browning received a long letter from Ruskin in response to the new volume *Men and Women* (10 November 1855), which Browning had sent him. Ruskin sat up all night with Dante Gabriel Rossetti, 'laying siege', as Rossetti put it, to Browning's 'mass of conundrums', and then wrote 'a bulky letter' containing his critical responses for Rossetti to pass on to Browning.

Ruskin has 'found some great things' in the volume, he says; Browning is like 'a wonderful mine' which Ruskin will set to work digging in when he

---

[81]   See WS Peterson and FL Standley, 'The JS Mill Marginalia in Robert Browning's *Pauline*: A History and Transcription', *Papers of the Bibliographical Society of America*, LXVI, 1972, 135–170.

has 'real time & strength' – admiration immediately undermined by Ruskin especially praising 'That bit about the Bishop & St Praxed ... very glorious', given that 'The Bishop Orders His Tomb at Saint Praxed's Church' appeared in *Dramatic Romances and Lyrics* ten years earlier ('Rossetti showed it me'). And Ruskin must speak out negatively: for 'a good many more' people are like him – they 'ought to admire more and learn from you, but can't because you are so difficult.' Browning's poems have more truths in them than anybody else's but Shakespeare's, but their opacity is awful. Ruskin feels like Rosencrantz in *Hamlet* who can't make Hamlet out: ' "I understand you not, my Lord" '. 'I look at you everyday as a monkey does a cocoanut, having great faith in the milk – hearing it rattle indeed – inside – but quite beside myself for the Fibres'. And this common allegation against Browning is afforced by three particular charges. First, Browning's rhythms do damage to pronunciation, playing fast and loose with the normal rhythms of English. Ruskin refers to some lines from Stanza III of Browning's dramatic poem 'Saul' where David describes entering King Saul's tent:

> I groped my way on
> Till I felt where the foldskirts fly open. Then once more I prayed,
> And opened the foldskirts and entered, and was not afraid.

This is harsh, and really prose, Ruskin thinks, and full of heavy monosyllables and what would normally be spondees – poetic feet of two heavy-stresses each – *once more / I prayed / foldskirts* – which Ruskin resents finding are turned unnaturally into 'dactylic verse', that is feet of three stresses, a heavy followed by two lights: -vv: *once more I*; *foldskirts fly*. 'I entirely deny & refuse the right of any poet to require me to pronounce words short and long, exactly as he likes'. Then there's a problem with Browning's characters, people like the speakers of 'Saul': they're too often mere mouthpieces for their author. It's the old JS Mill allegation: 'I entirely deny that a poet of your real dramatic power ought to let himself come up, as you constantly do, through all manner of characters, so that every now and then poor Pippa herself shall speak a long piece of Robert Browning'. (Pippa is the main character of the early piece *Pippa Passes: A Drama* (1841).) And third, Browning's verse is too elliptical, too gappy: 'your Ellipses are quite Unconscionable: before one can get through ten lines, one has to patch you up in twenty places, wrong or right, and if one hasn't much stuff of one's own to spare to patch with! You are worse than the worst Alpine Glacier I ever crossed. Bright, & deep enough truly, but so full of Clefts that half the journey has to be done with ladder & hatchet.'

These observations are telling, but it's the local verbal obscurities which are Ruskin's main problem – the poor 'Presentation' which is smothering the 'Power'. For every line Ruskin can 'make out' there are two he cannot. He has no time amidst his day's work to read poetry, he says, but 'when I take up these poems in the evening I find them absolutely and literally a set of the most amazing Conundrums that ever were proposed to me.' And he takes the poem 'Popularity' – one of Browning's many poems about being a poet, an artist, a painter, and no doubt immediately attractive to Ruskin the poet and painter and aesthete and critic for that reason – and simply takes it apart.

I

Stand still, true poet that you are!
    I know you; let me try and draw you.
Some night you'll fail us: when afar
    You rise, remember one man saw you,
Knew you, and named a star!

II

My star, God's glow-worm! Why extend
    That loving hand of his which leads you,
Yet locks you safe from end to end
    Of this dark world, unless he needs you,
Just saves your light to spend?

III

His clenched hand shall unclose at last,
    I know, and let out all the beauty:
My poet holds the future fast,
    Accepts the coming ages' duty,
Their present for this past.

IV

That day, the earth's feast-master's brow
    Shall clear, to God the chalice raising;
'Others give best at first, but thou
    Forever set'st our table praising,
Keep'st the good wine till now!'

V

Meantime, I'll draw you as you stand,
    With few or none to watch and wonder:
I'll say – a fisher, on the sand
    By Tyre the old, with ocean-plunder,
A netful, brought to land.

VI

Who has not heard how Tyrian shells
    Enclosed the blue, that dye of dyes
Whereof one drop worked miracles,
    And coloured like Astarte's eyes
Raw silk the merchant sells?

VII
And each bystander of them all
    Could criticize, and quote tradition
How depths of blue sublimed some pall
    – To get which, pricked a king's ambition;
Worth sceptre, crown and ball.

VIII
Yet there's the dye, in that rough mesh,
    The sea has only just o'erwhispered!
Live whelks, each lip's beard dripping fresh,
    As if they still the water's lisp heard
Through foam the rock-weeds thresh.

IX
Enough to furnish Solomon
    Such hangings for his cedar-house,
That, when gold-robed he took the throne
    In that abyss of blue, the Spouse
Might swear his presence shone

X
Most like the centre-spike of gold
    Which burns deep in the blue-bell's womb,
What time, with ardours manifold,
    The bee goes singing to her groom,
Drunken and overbold.

XI
Mere conchs! not fit for warp or woof!
    Till cunning come to pound and squeeze
And clarify, – refine to proof
    The liquor filtered by degrees,
While the world stands aloof.

XII
And there's the extract, flasked and fine,
    And priced and salable at last!
And Hobbs, Nobbs, Stokes and Nokes combine
    To paint the future from the past,
Put blue into their line.

XIII
Hobbs hints blue, – straight he turtle eats:
    Nobbs prints blue, – claret crowns his cup:
Nokes outdares Stokes in azure feats, –
    Both gorge. Who fished the murex up?
What porridge had John Keats?

'Popularity' is really not a terribly obscure poem, but it is a characteristically jumpy one – jumpy as a flea – skittering rapidly from thought to thought, across aesthetic history and politics and practices, fired by Browning's resentments about how some poets, like himself and John Keats, don't get the recognition they deserve and even go hungry while other poets and artists become famous and well-rewarded, and, in the case of some painters very ironically so – through using the humble materials of their craft, in this case the colour purple which comes from a mere lowly sea-creature, the whelk, the *murex*, which made the Phoenicians, or Tyrians, famous for the purple dye which dyed the silks that made Solomon's Temple so glorious, a whelk fished up by a fisherman who stays poor and anonymous while the silk-merchants and certain artists (Hobbs, Nobbs, Stokes and Nokes) prosper on the back of his efforts. 'Who fished the murex up? / What porridge had John Keats?': the bitter ending encapsulates the poem's large bitterness about the way all art, as Browning sees it, uses humble materials, the stuff of the mere world, to bring prosperity to some but not, alas, to all. Not least annoying are the poem's bystanders, the public know-it-alls who think they have a right to criticize other people's made (the dyed) work – a most irritating thought in the Browning household. A thought which must have made Ruskin's extended running criticisms of this very poem all the more irking.

> Stand still, true poet that you are
> I know you; – let me try and draw you:

(Does this mean: literally – stand still? or where was the poet figuratively going – and why couldn't he be drawn as he went?) Some night you'll fail us? (Why some *night*? – rather than some day? – 'Fail us.' Now? Die?) When afar you Rise – (Where? – Now?) remember &c. (Very good – I understand.) My star, God's glowworm. (Very fine. I understand and like that.) 'Why ^ extend that loving hand.' (Grammatically, this applies to the Poet. The ellipsis of 'Should He' at ^ throws one quite out – like a step in a floor which one doesn't expect.) Yet locks you safe. How does God's hand lock him; do you mean – keeps him from being seen? – and how does it make him safe. Why is a poet safer or more locked up than anybody else? I go on – in hope. 'His clenched hand – – beauty' – very good – but I don't understand why the hand should have held close so long – which is just the point I wanted to be explained. Why the poet *had to be* locked up.

'My poet holds the future fast'. How? Do you mean he anticipates it in his mind – trusts in it – I *don't* know if you mean that, because I don't know if poets *do* that. If you mean that – I wish you had said so plainly.

That day the earths feastmaster's brow. Who is the earths F.? An Angel? – a Everybody?

The chalice *raising*. This, grammatically, agrees with '*brow*,' and makes me uncomfortable. Others, &c. very pretty I like that. 'Meantime I'll draw you'. Do you mean – his Cork? – we have not had anything about painting for ever so long – very well. *Do* draw him then: I should like to have him drawn very much.

I'll say – 'a fisher – &c.'

Now, where *are* you going to – this is, I believe pure malice against *me*, for having said that painters should always grind their own colours.

Who has not heard – – merchant sells. Do you mean – the silk that the merchant sells Raw – or what do you want with the merchant at all.

'And each bystander.' Who are these bystanders – I didn't hear of any before – Are they people who have gone to see the fishing?

'Could criticise, & quote tradition.'

Criticise what? the fishing? – and why should they – what was wrong in it? – Quote tradition. Do you mean about purple? But if they made purple at the time, it wasn't tradition merely – but experience. – You might as well tell me you heard the colourmen in Long-Acre, quote tradition touching their next cargo of Indigo, or cochineal.[82]

'Depths – sublimed.' I don't know what you mean by 'sublimed'. Made sublime? – if so – it is not English. To sublime means to to evaporate dryly, I believe and as participle 'Sublimated'.[83]

'Worth scepter, crown and ball' – Indeed. Was there ever such a fool of a King? – You ought to have put a note saying who.

'Yet there's', &c. Well. I understand that, & it's very pretty

Enough to furnish Solomon, &c.

I don't think Solomons spouse swore. – at least not about blue-bells. I understand this bit, but fear most people won't. How many have noticed a blue-bells stamen?

'Bee to her groom' I don't understand. I thought there was only one Queen-bee and *she* never was out o'nights – nor came home drunk or disorderly. Besides if she does, unless you had told me what o'clock in the morning she comes home at, the simile is of no use to me.

'Mere conchs – [art?].' Well, but what has this to do with the Poet. Who 'Pounds' *him*? – I don't understand –

World stand[s] aloof – yes – from the purple manufactory, but from Pounding of Poets? – does it? – and if so – who distils – or fines, & bottles them.

'Flasked & fine' Now is that what you call painting a poet? Under the whole & sole image of a bottle of Blue, with a bladder over the cork? The Arabian fisherman with his genie was nothing to this.

Hobbs, Nobbs, &c. paint the future. Why the future. Do you mean *in* the future?

Blue into their line? I don't understand; – do you mean Quote the Poet, or write articles upon him – or in his style? And if so – was this what God kept

---

[82] Long Acre, Covent Garden, London, street of artists' workshops and shops.

[83] *Sublimed = made sublime* was just old-fashioned English, common in the sixteenth and seventeenth centuries.

him *safe* for? To feed Nobbs with Turtle. Is this what you call Accepting the future ages duty. – I don't understand.

'What porridge'? Porridge is a Scotch dish, I believe; typical of bad fare. Do you mean that Keats had bad fare? But if he had – how was he kept safe to the worlds end? I don't understand at all!!!!!!!

Written fast, clearly, and as unpolished as can be, these annotations none-theless drive right to the heart of the opacities of the poem – even if Ruskin's occasional stubborn obtusenesses and his heavy-handed jocu-larities about corks and drunken queen-bees and porridge distract from the critical force. What the letter illustrates is just how wonderfully close-up a Victorian reader and reading could get: Ruskin's method of attentive reading makes him sound positively Empsonian. Any idea of a period of writer-readers not being concerned with how the words are working simply vanishes in the presence of such probings. Ruskin ends up dissatisfied, but that's a danger obviously implicit in the method's scruti-nizing scrupulosity.

Now, that is the way I read, as well as I can, poem after poem, picking up a little bit here & there & enjoying it, but wholly unable to put anything together. I can't say I have really made out any one yet, except the epistle from the Arabian physician ['An Epistle Containing the Strange Medical Experience of Karshish, the Arab Physician'], which I like immensely, and I am only a stanza or so out with one or two others – in by the fireside ['By the Fire-Side'] for instance I am only *dead* beat by the 41–43, and in Fra Lippo – I am only fast at the grated orris root ['Fra Lippo Lippi', line 351], which I looked for in the Encyclopaedia and couldn't find: and at the There's for you ['Lippi' line 345] – give me six months – because I don't know *What's* for you.

He's tried to fish the murex up, but is unsure how much purple the terrible shell of Browning's poems really conceals.

There is a stuff and fancy in your work which assuredly is in no other living writer's, and how far this purple of it *must* be within this terrible shell; and only to be fished for among threshing of foam & slippery rocks, I don't know.

And he begs Browning to make himself clearer. 'I would pray you, faith, heartily, to consider with yourself, how far you can amend matters, & make the real virtue of your work acceptable & profitable to more people.[84]

All of which annoys Browning no end, prompts him, clearly, to furious self-inspection, and to stout defence in his reply of 10 December.

---

[84]   John Ruskin, Letter December 2nd 1855, published with valuable context, in David J de Laura, 'Ruskin and the Brownings: Twenty-Five Unpublished Letters', *Bulletin of the John Rylands Library*, 54 (1971–1972), 314–356.

For the deepnesses you think you discern, – may they be more than black-nesses! For the hopes you entertain of what may come of subsequent readings, – all success to them! For your bewilderment more especially noted – how shall I help *that*? ... I cannot begin writing poetry till my imaginary reader has con-ceded licences to me which you demur at altogether. I *know* that I don't make out my conception by my language; all poetry being a putting the infinite within the finite. You would have me paint it all plain out, which can't be; but by various artifices I try to make shift with touches and bits of outlines which *succeed* if they bear the conception from me to you. You ought, I think, to keep pace with the thought tripping from ledge to ledge of my 'glaciers', as you call them; not stand poking your alpen-stock into the holes, and demon-strating that no foot could have stood there; suppose it sprang over there? In *prose* you may criticise so – because that is the absolute representation of por-tions of truth, what chronicling is to history ... Why, you look at my little song as if it were Hobbs' or Nobbs' lease of his house, or testament of his devisings, wherein, I grant you, not a 'then and there', 'to him and his heirs', 'to have and to hold', and so on, would be superfluous; and so you begin:- 'Stand still, – why?' For the reason indicated in the verse, to be sure – to let me draw him – and because he is present going his way, and fancying nobody notices him, – and moreover, 'going on' (as we say) against the injustice of that, – and lastly, inasmuch as one night he'll fail us, as a star is apt to drop out of heaven, in authentic astronomic records, and I want to make the most of my time. So much may be in 'stand still'. And how much more was (for instance) in that 'stay!' of Samuel's (I.xv.16.) So could I twit you through the whole series of your objurgations, but the declaring my own notion of the law on the subject will do. And why, – I prithee, friend and fellow-student, – why, having told the Poet what you read, – may I not turn to the bystanders, and tell them a bit of my own mind about their own stupid thanklessness and mistaking? Is the jump too much there? ...

The other hard measure you deal me I won't bear – about my requiring you to pronounce words short and long, exactly as I like. Nay, but exactly as the language likes, in this case. A spondee possible in English? Two of the 'longest monosyllables' continuing to be each of the old length when in junction? Sentence: let the delinquent be forced to supply the stone-cutter with a thou-sand companions to 'Affliction sore – long time he bore', after the fashion of 'He lost his life – by a pen-knife' – 'He turned to clay – last Friday', 'Departed hence – nor owed six-pence', and so on – so would a jury accustomed from the nipple to say lord and landlord, bridge and Cambridge, Gog and Magog, man and woman, house and workhouse, coal and charcoal, cloth and broadcloth, skirts and fold-skirts, more and once more, – in short! ...

The last charge I cannot answer, for you may be right in preferring it, how-ever I am unwitting of the fact. I may put Robert Browning into Pippa and other men and maids. If so, *peccavi*: but I don't see myself in them, at all events.

Do you think poetry was ever generally understood – or can be? Is the busi-ness of it to tell people what they know already, as they know it, and so pre-cisely that they shall be able to cry out – 'Here you should supply *this* –, you evidently pass over, and I'll help you from my own stock'? It is all teaching, on the contrary, and the people hate to be taught. They say otherwise, – make foolish fables about Orpheus enchanting stocks and stones, poets standing up and being worshipped, – all nonsense and impossible dreaming. A poet's affair is with God, to whom he is accountable, and of whom is his reward: look elsewhere, and find misery enough. Do you believe people understand *Hamlet?* ...

Don't let me lose *my* lord [i.e. Ruskin] by any seeming self-sufficience or petulance: I look upon my own shortcomings too sorrowfully, try to remedy them too earnestly: but I shall never change my point of sight, or feel other than disconcerted and apprehensive when the public, critics and all, begin to understand and approve me. But what right have *you* to disconcert me in the other way? Why don't you ask the next perfumer for a packet of *orris*-root? Don't everybody know 'tis a corruption of *iris*-root – the Florentine lily, the *giaggolo*, of world-wide fame as a good savour? And because 'iris' means so many objects already, and I use the word, you blame me! But I write in the blind-dark and bitter cold, and past post-time I fear. Take my truest thanks, and understand at least this rough writing, and, at all events, the real affection with which I venture to regard you. And 'I' means my wife as well as yours ever faithfully,
Robert Browning.[85]

Thus Browning, cornered, refuses to be knocked to the canvas, punches tellingly back. He's absolutely clear about what his formal gappiness is for, and confident in his use of words and rhythms and his knowledge of real things like orris root and his not kowtowing to the needs of stupid 'mistaking' readers; confident too of his place in the canon, comparing his texts happily with *Hamlet,* and lining himself up with the young poet-prophet David in the Biblical Book of Samuel (since Ruskin has dragged David into the discussion), who tells the older man to 'Stay and I will tell thee what the Lord hath said to me this night', and all in that lovely potently punning colloquialism which Browning has made his own and which he offers as the match for any one of Ruskin's jokey gibes (the poem 'goes on' in ways Ruskin has failed to appreciate, and Browning will 'go on' about it).

So much, as I say, for the utterly unsustainable libel, that Victorian poets – and Victorian readers – gave too little heed to getting hold of the right words and putting them in the right order.

[85]   WG Collingwood, ed, *The Life and Work of John Ruskin* (Methuen & Co, London, 1893), Vol I, 199–202. Letter summarized, in Cook and Wedderburn, 36, xxxiv–vi. 'Popularity' is quoted from the edition of Browning and used throughout this book, *The poems,* ed. John Pettigrew, completed Thomas J. Collins, 2 vols (Penguin, Harmondsworth, 1981).

2

Rhyming/Repeating

How to tell a Victorian poem when you see one? It's a subset of the very large question, how to tell a poem when you see one – that good old question of poetics. Traditional poetics are, of course, resolute that what makes the poetic comes down to what's done with the words, both in and for, the 'poem' – the selection and the arranging. And naturally enough – for this is a long discussion, 2,400 or so years old, going back at least to Aristotle – many verbal features have been claimed as the main ones that are constitutive of a 'poem'. But three verbal features do keep recurring in this long debate to such an extent that we can think of them as the three main ingredients of poetic language. Poetic words, it's widely agreed, are inevitably (i) *heightened*, (ii) *compressed*, and (iii) *bound*.[1]

They're *heightened* because they're loaded with meaning above the ordinary. They come loaded, even overloaded, with meaning, especially through their figurality, their metaphoricity, and their preference for connotation (over and above their denotation), and their ambiguity, indeed not just their ambivalence but their multivalence – what modern linguists like to label their fuzziness. They're *compressed*, that is compact, tighter than the usual, going about their business of communication fast rather than slowly, happy to be gappy, to leave verbal bits out, eschewing the looseness and bagginess of ordinary speech And so, in particular, poems defy, resist, the order of the sentence (sentences can spread and spread more or less endlessly), preferring

---

[1] See *The New Princeton Encyclopedia of Poetry and Poetics*, eds Alex Preminger and TVF Brogan (Princeton University Press, Princeton, New Jersey, 1993). Astoundingly compendious and ultra-informative 'must have' volume. Especially entries on Poetics; Poetry; Poetry, Theories of; Verse and Prose; Versification; Anaphora; Line; Metaphor; Meter; Rhyme.

Victorian Poetry Now: Poets, Poems, Poetics, First Edition. Valentine Cunningham.
© 2011 Valentine Cunningham. Published 2011 by Blackwell Publishing Ltd.

rather the order of the line, the poetic line which even at its longest (such as the so-called *fourteeners*, those lines of seven *heptameters*, fourteen beats of 7 × 2-beat iambic feet, which Kipling used in his 'Tommy' – 'An' Tommy ain't a bloomin 'fool – you bet that Tommy sees!', or the *sesquiheptameters*, 7 iambic feet plus a beat, of Tennyson's 'Locksley Hall' – 'Comrades, leave me here a little, while as yet 'tis early morn') is still a rather short grouping of words. It is a dominant of poetic form, poetic arrangement, that the words are organized first in lines of words, rather than in sentences. The complete line might actually be a sentence, but it need not be, and very often is not. Lines. It's no accident that a traditional synonym for *poem* is *Lines* – as, say, Anne Brontë's 'Lines Written at Thorp Green' – because poems consist of lines. Naturally enough, poems are traditionally identified not just by their titles but by their first lines. (*Line*, from *linen*, of course: *line*, and its equivalents in other European languages, started their linguistic life as the thread of flax, linen thread, before they got applied to words arranged in sets like lines of thread, and so got launched on their path as the basic (metaphoric) stuff of the aesthetic weave, or text. Follow the *thread*!)

And, third, poetic words are *bound* words – words tied together, held together, by the repetition of verbal components. By repetition, that is by rhyme. What the Greek rhetoricians called *anaphora*. Which is, I suggest, out of these three poetic fundamentals, the most fundamental of all.

Poetry is repetition; saying it again. Well recognized in practice by most poets, and in theory by lots. By Victorian Gerard Hopkins, notably. Repetition, he noted in his lecture notes on 'Poetry and Verse' is the mark of poetry, if the repetition 'is meant to be heard for its own sake': the verbal 'oftening, over-and-overing, aftering', which his own poems go in for so massively. If the repetition is just a mnemonic device, to assist memory merely, as 'Thirty days hath September, April June and November', or is choric 'nonsense', as 'Hey nonny nonny', then that's the lower poetic level Hopkins would categorize as 'verse'. Poetry, though, can be 'high or low'; even the 'poor or low' rhyming you might dismiss as 'doggrel' (sic) can be poetry by dint of its verbal repeating.[2] Seamus Perry, dwelling (rightly) on Tennyson as a poet of intense repetivity, garners opinion from the beginnings of English poetic theorizing to modern and post-modern European times to support Hopkins: from George Puttenham in his influential *Arte of English Poesie* (1589) asserting that poetry 'worketh by iteration or repetition of one word or clause' (poetry is the rhetoric of *Eccho sound*; it's *the doubler*), to the great structural linguist Roman Jakobson arguing that parallelism is a fundamental element of poetry, and the post-structuralist critic Stamos Metzidakis claiming that the 'iterative process is constitutive of the

---

[2] *The Journals and Papers of Gerard Manley Hopkins*, edd Humphrey House and Graham Storey (Oxford University Press, London, 1959), 289–290.

artistic work'.[3] The eighteenth-century word *repetend*, meaning numbers circulating in arithmetical problems, got borrowed in late Victorian times to denote the way words and phrases recur with such plenitude in the poetry, and it has got into (post)modern critical discussion as a key term to denote the linguistic repetivity post-structuralist theory is so interested in.[4] (A modern appreciation founded in and greatly overshadowed by Jacques Derrida's argument that repeatability/iterability is the mark of all communication *in writing*, and that the texts of stage plays and poems are key kinds of iterable statements.[5])

Iteration. Or dittography. ('Ditto', says Tweedledum. 'Ditto, ditto!' says Tweedledee in Lewis Carroll's *Through the Looking Glass* – and they are indeed experts on poetry.) Saying it again and again.

> Say over again, and yet once over again,
> That thou dost love me. Though the word repeated
> Should seem 'a cuckoo-song', as thou dost treat it,
> Remember, never to the hill or plain,
> Valley and wood, without her cuckoo-strain
> Comes the fresh Spring in all her green completed.
> Belovèd, I, amid the darkness greeted
> By a doubtful spirit-voice, in that doubt's pain
> Cry, 'Speak once more – thou lovest!' Who can fear
> Too many stars, though each in heaven shall roll,
> Too many flowers, though each shall crown the year?
> Say thou dost love me, love me, love me – toll
> The silver iterance! – only minding, Dear,
> To love me also in silence with thy soul.[6]

---

[3] Seamus Perry, in 'Returns', Ch 1, *Alfred Tennyson* (Writers and their Work, Northcote House/British Council, Tavistock, Devon, 2005), 21–23. Roman Jakobson, 'Closing Statement: Linguistics and Poetics' in Thomas A Sebeok, ed, *Style in Language* (Technology Press of MIT, Cambridge MA, New York, London, 1960); S Metzidakis, 'Formal Repetition and the Perception of Literature', *L'Esprit créateur*, 24 (11984), 49–61. (See also Metzidakis, *Repetition and Semiotics: Interpreting Prose Poems* (Summa, Birmingham AL, 1986.)

[4] Perry refers to, e.g., Laury Magnus, *The Track of the Repetend: Syntactic and Lexical Repetition in Modern Poetry* (AMS Press, New York and London, 1989). Perry (2005), 22.

[5] 'Signature, Event, Context', *Glyph* 1 (1977), trans Samuel Weber and Jeffrey Mehlman; retrans Alan Bass, in Derrida, *Margins of Philosophy* (Harvester, Brighton, 1986), 307–330. Contested from the start by John R Searle in 'Reiterating the Difference: A Reply to Jacques Derrida', *Glyph*, 1 (1977), 198–208, grumpily pointing out that nobody ever thought otherwise than that repeatability was an essence of language (but oral as well as written), and objecting very strongly to Derrida's fundamentalist deconstructionist allegation that iterability applied only to the written, and only in the absence of the utterer.

[6] Written in 1846; only shown to Robert after their marriage; published at his insistence ('the finest sonnets written in any language since Shakespeare's'), and as if translated, in her *Poems* (1850) (she wanted to call them 'Sonnets from the Bosnian', but he preferred 'From the Portuguese' because of her repeated celebration of the sixteenth-century Portuguese poet

Iterance. It is – according to this highly iterating Sonnet XXI *From the Portuguese* of Elizabeth Barrett Browning (a courtship poem for her husband-to-be) – the very nature of Nature, of lovers' utterances, of love poems, of poetry itself. Repetition is necessary and inevitable, even at the risk of sounding like a cuckoo, the echo bird, its call always a repeated one, 'cuckoo cuckoo', the noise and the name of the silly and mad (what Puttenham called the *cuckowspell*). It is, after all, *silver iterance*: lovely and valuable ; a gift of treasure to be treasured by the hearer.

Poets, and Victorian poets not least, know the basic poetic equations: poetry = repetition; repetition = rhyme; and rhyme = poetry. Rhyme: repetition: *anaphora*. 'I love to rhyme' as the Gershwins' song of 1938 has it. Poets (and song-writers) love to rhyme. Victorian poets especially. The only thing wrong with Seamus Perry's bravura stress on repetition as poeticity *per se* is his suggestion that this 'has special pertinence to the case of Tennyson, for no other great English poets seems drawn quite so powerfully, so repeatedly, to the poetic resource of repetitiveness' (Perry, *Tennyson* (2005), 22). Tell that, one wants to riposte, to Hopkins or Christina G Rossetti, or many another. They're all hard at it. A poet, the poets recognized, is precisely someone who does repetition, because he/she writes in rhyme. As that lively Irish Virgilian scholar and poet James Henry well knew – in his little poem about versifying, 'I am a versemaker by trade'. How he employs his 'idle time' is in ' "stringing blethers up in rhyme" / For you and other fools to sing'.[7] Poets are rhymesters – Tennyson's word for poet ('Authors – essayist, atheists, novelists, realist, rhymester, play your part': 'Locksley Hall Sixty Years After', 139). It's no accident that 'Rhyme' is a standard synonym for poem. 'Nursery rhymes'. 'My rhymes.' The Poet of Tennyson's 'Epilogue [The Charge of the Heavy Brigade]' knows that poets have rhymed in all ages: the poets of the past, a Horace it might be, had an easier time of it than those 'who rhyme today'. They rhymed; Tennyson rhymes. (Ruskin writes to Tennyson that *In Memoriam*, *Maud*, and 'The Miller's Daughter' are 'my own pet rhymes'.[8]) What makes *poetic* squabblers, as opposed to ordinary ones, according to Tennyson, is that they do their squabbling in rhyme ('Ah, God! the petty fools of rhyme': 'After-Thought', his poem of 1846 later retitled 'Literary Squabbles'). The aptly repetitious refrain of poet and art-critic

---

Camoëns, celebrator of his beloved's eyes – as in her 'Caterina to Camoëns' – which reminded Browning, it is thought, of her dark 'Creole' eyes). The editors of the (valuable) Penguin volume *Aurora Leigh and other Poems*, John Robert Glorney Bolton and Julia Bolton Holloway (1995), prefer the British Museum Notebook text to the 1850 version, beginning 'Beloved, say again and yet again' – which is less repetitive, less emphatic on the command 'say', and thus less forceful. In fact, they print only the 1846 ms versions.

[7]   In *Poems Chiefly Philosophical* (CC Meinhold & Sons, Dresden, 1854). Available now in James Henry, *Selected Poems*, ed Christopher Ricks (Lilliput Press, Dublin, 2002).

[8]   *Memoir*, I.453.

Cosmo Monkhouse's 'Recollections of Alfred Tennyson: *A Day Dream* (1869)' (in his *Corn and Poppies* volume, 1890), tells how he was *full of*, and *steeped in*, and *borne upon*, and *lived in*, 'the golden rhyme / Of Tennyson, the Laureate'. Tennyson *is* rhyme.

Rhyme: repetition, the repeating of verbal items of any and every kind. Of everything commonly included in 'rhyme' – phrases, words, bits of words, the sounds repeated at the ends of lines – but also what's ordinarily separated out as alliteration (front-rhyme) and assonance (middle-rhyme), as well as what Perry rightly lists among poetry's repeatables: metre, stanzas, refrains, burdens, Puttenham's 'wheels'.[9] All rhymes. Which make what Austin Dobson thought of as poetry's necessary *rippling* effect. Prose, he says, in 'The Ballad of Prose and Rhyme (*Ballade à Double Refrain*)', in his *Old World Idylls and Other Verses* (1883), is short on rhyme's ripple effect, which might be suitable for wintry thoughts, dry brains and quarrelling pedants, but not for springtime and loving, 'Then hey! – for the ripple of laughing rhyme!' And this line, repeated four times, a refrain at the end of every stanza of the poem, demonstrates this rippling. For his part, Coventry Patmore thought of rhyming, poetic repetition, as an affair of intimacy, as *kissing*, the loving joining of verbal partners, physical copular of the mouth – apt locale for rhyme's copulation since poetry's rhymes are indeed mouth-work. They're noises made in and for the mouth: nicely metaphoricized as kissing – mouth action that makes a noise, represented by the noise-word itself: *kiss* – onomatopoeic, for sure, as young Stephen Dedalus thought in Joyce's *A Portrait of the Artist as a Young Man* when he reflected on the kisses his mother gave him. Patmore wants, he says in 'The Paragon' section of *The Angel in the House* (1854, 1879), to write a hymn to his wife, to womankind:

> Arousing these song-sleepy times
> With rhapsodies of perfect word
> Ruled by returning kiss of rhymes.

Poetic perfection: rhapsodies effected under the law of verbal repetition, by verbal returning as kissing. In this sense James Thomson was wrong in his

---

[9]   Perry (2005), 21. Cannily, FW Bateson offered repetivity as Victorian poetry's main rhetorical strategy (deplored, naturally for the time of his writing in the early 1930s, as 'diffuseness'), cannily illustrated with reference to William (Johnson) Cory's 'Heraclitus', his very 'popular' translation from the Greek Anthology ('They told me Heraclitus, they told me you were dead / They brought me bitter news to hear and bitter tears to shed'), after earlier making a powerful 'codification', 'a sort of elementary poetic grammar', 'under which the technical devices of poetry can all be subsumed': all a matter of repetitions – 'repetitions of sound (rhythm, metre, rhyme, assonance, alliteration)'; of 'sense (refrains, puns, "ambiguities")'; of 'context (quotations, the use of proper names, or specialized words from a particular literary tradition)'; and 'variations of the prose order (hypallages, inversions, zeugmas)'. *English Poetry and the English Language*, edn cit, fn 1 pp222–223; 122–124.

art-deprecating poem 'Art' (1865; originally titled 'Elementary Philosophy of Love Poems': in *The City of Dreadful Night* volume (1880)), to separate 'singing', making poems, from kissing: 'Singing is sweet, but be sure of this, / Lips only sing when they cannot kiss'. For what engages the lips of the true singer is the kiss of rhyme. This singing *is* a kissing.[10]

Effecting these verbal unions is the main business of poems. 'How shall I be a poet?' asks the would-be young poet of an old adviser in Lewis Carroll's mocking 1883 poem 'Poeta Fit, Non Nascitur' (the Latin title means: a poet is made, not born), and he adds 'How shall I write in rhyme?' Writing in rhyme is what poets do, by definition. Poems are zones of repetition; poets are repetition merchants. (Poets also, according to Carroll's 'old man', and rightly, 'chop' sentences into 'small' bits, ie lines, in which 'The order of the phrases makes / No difference at all'. But then lines are one of the commonest repeated items in poems.)

Don Juan, the apparent narrator of Browning's *Fifine at the Fair* (1872) – he's one of Browning's more obvious mouthpieces – talks about how to renew poems and the poetic tradition. The contemporary audience's old teeth and gums can't chew, can't take, the old poetic foodstuffs simply as they are, dished up straight from the old poets' ovens; they must 'needs be cooked again':

> Dished up anew in paint, sauce-smothered fresh in sound,
> To suit the wisdom-tooth, just cut, of the age, that's found
> With gums obtuse to gust and smack which relished so
> The meat o' the meal folk made some fifty years ago.

And what does this cooking again, this repeating with a difference, consist of? It's a cooking again 'in rhyme' (*Fifine at the Fair*, 1632ff). Poems are texts of repetition performed in acts of keen repetitivity. (What they're about, in the words of the American Wallace Stevens' poem 'The Plain Sense of Things', is 'a repetition / In a repetitiousness'.) What poets have to do is cook, and cook again, in rhyme. They do their verbal repetitions over and over again. The poet, according to Monsieur Miranda of Browning's *Red Cotton Night-Cap Country, or Turf and Towers* (1873), is one who is 'rapt / In rhyming wholly' (2126–2127). He's *rapt* in rhyming: caught up in it, enraptured by it, enrapt by the prospect and activity of doing the rhymes. And *wholly rapt in rhyming*: enrapt in and by the business of rhyming to the exclusion of other poetic features. And *rapt in rhyming wholly*: enrapt in making the rhymes whole, that is as good as can be. What enraptures the

---

[10]   TS Eliot movingly reprises Thomson's thought at the very end of his 1930s Harvard lectures: ' "Lips only sing when they cannot kiss" ', it may be that poets only talk when they cannot sing' – one more Victorian poem in Eliot's memory. 'Conclusion', *The Use of Poetry and the Use of Criticism* (Faber & Faber, London, 1933; 1964), 156.

poet on this reckoning is not just getting down any old rhymes, but getting the rhymes right. Repetition with attitude.

Which is clearly what Arthur Hugh Clough had in mind in his remarkable poem about being a poet (it's a private meditation on the task of getting the right words into the right order, in one of his '1851' notebooks):[11]

> If to write, rewrite, and write again,
> Bite now the lip and now the pen,
> Gnash in a fury the teeth, and tear
> Innocent paper or it may be hair,
> In endless chases to pursue
> That swift escaping word that would do,
> Inside and out turn a phrase, and o'er,
> Till all the little sense goes, it had before, –
> If it be these things make one a poet,
> I am one – Come and all the world may know it.
>
> If to look over old poems and detest
> What one once hugged as a child to one's breast,
> Find the things nothing that once had been so much,
> The old noble forms gone into dust at a touch:
> If to see oneself of one's fancied plumage stript,
> If by one's faults as by furies to be whipt;
> If to become cool and, casting for good away
> All the old implements, take 'em up the next day;
> If to be sane to-night and insane again to-morrow,
> And salve up past pains with the cause of future sorrow, –
> If to do these things make a man a poet,
> I am one – Come and all the world may know it.
>
> If neverthless no other peace of mind,
> No inward unity ever to find,
> No calm, well-being, sureness or rest
> Save when by that strange temper possest,
> Out of whose kind sources in pure rhythm-flow
> The easy melodious verse-currents go;
> If to sit still while the world goes by,
> Find old friends dull and new friends dry,
> Dinners a bore and dancing worse,
> Compared to the tagging of verse onto verse, –
> If it be these things make one a poet,
> I am one – Come and all the word may know it.

[11]   The verses were not published until a century later in *The Poems of Arthur Hugh Clough*, edited by HF Lowry, ALP Norrington, and FL Mulhauser (Oxford University Press, Oxford, 1951), 435.

Most striking about this poem of Clough's about writing is its stress on repetition. The first activity that's claimed to denote a poet is writing, re-writing and writing again. The poet repeats himself. Poets repeat themselves to the extent of risking verbal death – turning phrases inside out and over and over 'Till all the little sense goes, it had before'. Risking, as that Elizabeth Barrett Browning sonnet 'Say over again, and yet once over again' had it, sounding like a mere cuckoo, even becoming cuckoo. Is Clough thinking of the poets who pay homage to the Goddess Dulness in Alexander Pope's *Dunciad* (1743), IV. 251–252: 'For thee explain a thing till all men doubt it / And write about it, Goddess, and about it'? The extinction of meaning, and so of self, which Tennyson, in almost the most famous statement about language he ever made, said was brought on by repeating his name to himself.[12] The practice of *echolalia*, the meaningless repetition of words and phrases – what little children do in learning to talk; a sign too, psychiatrists think, of schizophrenia. For all the possible satisfactions of such emptying through verbal repetition – and Tennyson described (*Letters*, cit, 78–79) a consequent state of bliss, 'not a confused state but the clearest of the clearest, the surest of the surest, utterly beyond words – where Death was an almost laughable impossibility – the loss of personality (if so it were) seeming no extinction but the only true life' (what the Ancient Sage, in the poem of that name, describing the same experience, calls 'The gain of such large life as matched with ours /Were sun to spark, 'The Ancient Sage', 237–238, a 'loosing' of 'The mortal limit of the self' (232): a *loosing*: recalling the out-of-the body ecstasies of Milton's 'Il Penseroso') – such repetition was for Freud and the Freudians a mental plight, a sign of hysteria (as in the case of Dora, the founding case of psychiatry, stuck in her poetry-like repeated dream tropes and narratives, in Freud and Breuer's classic studies of hysteria, 1893, 1895, 1905). A psychopathology (puns and slips of the tongue, verbal rhymes and half-rhymes are central to what Freud called *The Psychopathology of Everyday Life*). Freud is perplexed, dismayed even, in his *Beyond the Pleasure Principle* (1920) by his small grandson's repeated to-and-fro play (*Spiel*: game, drama) with a bobbin on a string, allegedly repeatedly miming his mother's absence from the room and his father's at the Great War: allegorizing, grandad thought, the perplexing way we get pleasure

---

[12] '..."a kind of waking trance" (for want of a better word) I have frequently had quite up from boyhood when I have been all alone. This has often come upon me through repeating my own name to myself silently, till all at once as it were out of the intensity of the consciousness of individuality the individuality itself seemed to dissolve & fade away into boundless being'. Letter to Benjamin Paul Blood, 7 May 1874, *The Letters of Alfred Lord Tennyson*, edd Cecil Y Lang and Edgar F Shannon Jr, III, 1871–1892 (Clarendon Press, Oxford, 1990), 78.

from repeated performances of painful aesthetic experience, the repetitions of *Theaterspiel*, of tragedies and such.[13]

Poetry, on this view, is a curse, the 'curse' of 'the compulsion to repeat', as exemplified by echolalics, helpless stutterers, 'ticqueurs' (people with repeated tics – muscular twitches), 'coprolalics' (compulsive swearers), Tourette's syndrome, sundry aping and parrotting compulsions, as graphically examined by Hillel Schwartz.[14] *Dittography* was, in fact, a pejorative Victorian term, coined to describe scribal error, the deplorably mistaken repetition of letters and words. Dittographing was what scribal copyists should avoid in the name of textual purity. A painful mistake; repetition as pain; the pain of repetition, of doing and saying it again and again, which repetitive Clough knew as a very painful case:

> To spend uncounted years of pain,
> Again, again, and yet again,
> In working out in heart and brain
> The problem of our being here;
> To gather facts from far and near,
> Upon the mind to hold them clear,
> And, knowing more may yet appear,
> Unto one's latest breath to fear,
> The premature result to draw –
> Is this the object, end and law,
> And purpose of our being here?[15]

(A poem that haunted, it so happens, Chester Carlson, the inventor of xerography, the foundation of modern photocopying.[16])

But herein lies the enraptment, the pleasure no less, that Browning talked about in *Red Cotton Night-Cap Country*, and for what? For 'the tagging of

[13]   Joseph Breuer and Sigmund Freud, *Studien über Hysterie* (Leipzig and Vienna, 1893), trans as *Studies in Hysteria* by James and Alix Strachey (Hogarth Press, London, 1953); Freud, 'Fragment of an Analysis of a Case of Hysteria,' trans J and A Strachey (1925; *Standard Edition of the Complete Works of Sigmund Freud*, Vol VII (Hogarth Press and the Institute of Psychoanalysis, London, 1953); *The Psychopathology of Everyday Life: Forgetting, Slips of the Tongue, Bungled Actions, Superstitions and Errors*, trans by AA Brill (Fisher Unwin, London, 1914) of *Zur Psychopathologie des Alltagsleben* (Karger, Berlin, 1907); *Beyond the Pleasure Principle*, trans by DJM Hubback (London, Vienna, 1922) of 2nd edn of *Jenseits des Lustprinzips* (Vienna, 1920).

[14]   *The Culture of the Copy: Striking Likenesses, Unreasonable Facsimiles* (Zone Books, NY, 1996).

[15]   *The Poems of Arthur Hugh Clough*, edn cit, 90. Originally in *Putnam's Magazine*, II (1 July 1853); titled 'PERCHÈ PENSA? PENSANDO S'INVECCHIA' in the 1869 edition of *The Poems and Prose Remains*.

[16]   As noted by Hillel Schwarz in his 'Ditto' chapter, op cit, 231.

verse onto verse' – *tagging*, tying, binding, 'verse onto verse', verbal item onto verbal item. The poem precisely as repetition, as an act of repeated rhyming. And Clough's 'If to write' registers its insistence on the primacy of the activity of repeating by its own intense practice of repetition. Repetitions dominate his poem. In the very first line, the one about poetic writing as repeating, the word *write* occurs three times – *write*, re*write*, *write* again. The poem's own practice of rhyming tells the story of the poetic writing trade's investment in repetition, by publicizing it in the blatant rhyming of its own announcement. Demonstrative word-tagging starts in this poem as early as possible. Poeticity, the art of the poet, the sign of a poet at work, is alleged by the poet to consist in the practice of repetition, and the poem's pronounced use of rhyme sharply illustrates the claim. The poem's practice, in other words, answers to its theory. (And, of course, *answering* is another word for rhyming. Rhyming is verbal answering ; and quick answering. The answerings of rhyme come, and follow, quickly in poems. 'You are wont to answer, prompt as rhyme', Robert Browning tells his wife in his 'By the Fire-Side' (*Men and Women*, 1855). Poems are verbal quick-answer machines.)

In Clough's poem, the *write* rhymes – *write*, re*write*, *write* – are *median* rhymes, that is rhymes occurring in the middle of the line. The term *median rhyme* is sometimes used to describe the rhyming of vowels when they come between consonants, as in *write: write*. Here, of course, the consonantal beginnings and endings and the vocalic middles of these words are all rhyming: and there's a great deal of this kind of mixed- or multi-rhyming in the poem, words rhyming among themselves in more than one way. The rhyming of vowels is usually called *assonance*: as in *now: now*, and *paper: chases*; and *poet: know it* in stanza one. *Poet: know it* occurs three times, no less. Assonance is plentiful like this. The rhymes in *poet: know it* also involve end-rhyming: the *it* sound comes at the end of the two words, which are sited at the end of lines. *End-rhymes*, rhymes at the end of words and of lines like these are what people usually mean when *rhyme* is talked about, and they're obviously a staple of this poem. End-rhymes do indeed greatly abound in the poems of the English tradition, which no doubt has helped end-rhyme to be so commonly taken as the limit-case or type of rhyme. Clough's end-rhymes bind together each pair of his poem's lines into *rhyming couplets*. The couplet at the end of each stanza is identical in the first and third and third stanzas, and almost identical in the second. These lines make a *refrain* or *burden* – the repeated line or lines that come at the end of every verse in a poem: what's also known as a *chorus* at the end of a ballad, or song, or hymn. Arrestingly, *burden* is another synonym for poem: as in Dante Gabriel Rossetti's 'The Burden of Nineveh' or Swinburne's 'A Burden of Burdens'. (And burdens, as the name implies, are a burden, a task and responsibility that can weigh heavily: the burden of having to keep doing burdens, refrains, the repetitions ; the burden of the poetic refrainer, the one who cannot refrain from refraining because poetry demands repetition. Necessary repetition, a matter of life, the life of the poem, but also the chore, the load the poet has to bear, that's a matter of pain, even mortal pain – a doubling preciously captured by John Greenleaf Whittier, the nineteenth-century American Quaker abolitionist poet, in his hymn about namings of Jesus, 'Immortal love for ever full': 'Through him the first fond prayers are said / Our lips of childhood frame; / The last low murmurs of our dead / Are burdened with his name'.)

For its part, *front-rhyme*, the rhyming of the initial parts of words – what's usually known as *alliteration* – is almost ridiculously plentiful. *Write: write: rewrite* (this last with a doubled *r* sound, a doubling not uncommon in the poem); *now: now: gnash: know: nothing: noble: No: No; to: teeth: tear: turn: till: to-night: to-morrow: temper: tagging; pen: paper: pursue: poet: poems: past pains: poet: peace: possesst; fury: phrase: forms: fancied: faults: furies: for: future: flow: friends: friends; one: once: oneself: one's; word: would: world: world: while: world; verse: verse: verse; dull: dry: dinners: dancing.* And so on. Many whole words are made to rhyme with themselves on the *write, poet, world, know it* pattern – what's sometimes known as *auto-rhyme.* A noticeable whole flight of repeated little whole words – *if,* and *one* and it and *no* – adds to this tight auto-rhythmic lacing. These little words and the smallest parts of speech add up potently. The least significant-seeming parts of speech, definite articles and demonstratives, make themselves heard by their shared repetition – all those initial *th* sounds of the poem: *the lip, the pen, That, that, things* (in the first stanza alone). One thing poems like this do is make you conscious of the way the little words and little bits of words matter, certainly of the way mere grammatical features build rhyming into the very bone-structure of the language: we not only get the *th* sounds of *this* and *that* and *the* (the little *deictic* words), but the repeated *-ing* ending of the so-called *gerund* or *gerundive*: *escaping, casting, dancing, tagging.* (These bits of words, such as the initial *th* and the final *ing* are known as *phonemes*; and *phonemic repetition* is, of course, the fundamental element of all this repetition.) It's all a setting up of echoes, a matter of noise repetition (similarity of sound: strictly *assonance*), and those are the ties that do the poetic binding – not least in certain very tightly bound adjacent words: *write: bite; one once; things nothing; sane … insane … pains.* Alliances are formed like this among physical near-neighbours in the poem, but also among quite far-flung ones, ones spread out across the space of the poem. Rhyming makes neighbours, and neighbours of all sorts of verbal items, all kinds of 'parts of speech' – and not just in the obvious fashion of whole words being united, but in the neighbouring activity of similar sounding phonemic bits being brought together: *In*nocent and *In*side; *In*nocent: *n*othing: *n*oble: *N*o: *N*o; *If* and swi*ft.*

Such repetitions involve, in the main, and in their way, *full rhymes*. But the poem's ample full rhyming is closely supported by so-called *half-rhymes*, or *para-rhymes*: *word*: *would*; *implements*: *take 'em*; *by*: *be*; *inward*: *unity*. Such unitings are neighbourly, but only, as it were, near-neighbourly. And para-rhyming can be as versatile as full rhyming: just as there are fully and half-rhyming words, so there are fully and half-rhyming phrases. The refrains of Clough's stanzas one and two, for instance, are full rhymes; whereas *old friends dull*: *new friends dry*; or *sane to-night*: *insane ... tomorrow*, are para-rhymes. When a rhyme returns, like these last paired phrases, with a difference, the action is sometimes known as *incremental repetition*. But whatever the nature of the repeat, of the return, it is all – to keep insisting – rhyme. Tagging of like onto like. The tag-wrestling match of the poetic.

And – to repeat – poems can and do rhyme, that is repeat, any part at all of the verbal structure. The anaphoric work is not limited, certainly not to just words and phrases (as in the case of the Biblical Psalms, the usual example of poetic anaphora, whose verses are built of repetitive two-line segments). Anything and everything is up for anaphora: phonemes, words, phrases, part-lines, whole lines, groups of lines (choruses, burdens, and refrains); the sounds at the beginnings, the middles, the ends of words (the repeats too commonly known as alliteration, assonance, and rhyme). Poems can do front-rhyme, median rhyme, end-rhyme, auto-rhyme, full-rhyme, para-rhyme. Poems regularly practice the repetition of line-lengths and stanza shapes. Puns work their rhyming trade somewhere between full-rhyme and para-rhyme. Poems can also – and frequently do – repeat the beat, the rhythm, the metre, the so-called *metrical feet* (most of the lines of Clough's poem enjoy a steady four beats). Repeating the beat, as successive poetic lines tend to, is one of the commonest forms of rhyming. In other words, rhythm should be thought of as a function of rhyme. Anything verbal in a poem is repeatable, and does get repeated; anything verbal you can think of is the poem's repeat material. And it is all, properly considered, *rhyme*. A fact that our rich vocabulary for varieties of rhyming unfortunately tends to obscure.

The most alert poetic theorists have, of course, realized that one should indeed think of all the repetitive devices as rhyme. As Clough implies, by having the character Spirit attack poetic Dipsychus for spoiling his hexameters with redundant 'rhyme', where the rhyming in question operates across the line and is not a matter of end-rhyming (*Dipsychus*, Scene IV, lines 63–72). The lecture notes on Rhythm for the Rhetoric lectures that Gerard Hopkins (Victorian poetry's rhyming supremo) gave to his students are wonderfully clear about this. He very cannily reflects on rhyme in numerous varieties – alliteration and assonance, half-rhyme (what he knows is known in Icelandic verse as 'skothending'), 'imperfect rhyme', 'eye-rhyme' (words that look alike but don't sound alike: Hopkins lists *plough, though, cough, rough, enough*), what he calls 'unlawful rhymes' (rhymes that 'are like enough roughly to satisfy the ear' but 'offend the mind,' like *m* and *n*; syllables ending in mute *r* (like Clough's *tear: hair* and *o'er: before*)), and poets who take rhyming liberties or 'licence' (bringing together words that Hopkins thinks are not real rhymes 'as *glory* and *for thee*: Mrs Browning and Miss Rossetti' do this). And then he pauses to as it were sum up: 'It will be seen that all these verse figures ... are reducible to the principle of rhyme, to rhyme or partial rhyme. Alliteration is initial half-rhyme, "shothending" [sic] is final half-rhyme, assonance is vowel rhyme'. And Hopkins's marginal note reads: '*Alliteration, assonance, etc all reducible to rhyme in a wide sense*'.[17] It's a recognition largely unshared by modern critics. The usual critical assumption is the casual one that 'rhyme' means end-rhyme. Denys Thompson and Stephen Tunnicliffe think *rhyme* is 'the identity of sound in the final syllable of words, normally occurring at the end of verse lines', and *alliteration* is 'the repetition of a consonant at the beginning of successive words'.[18] No, not, nohow, no way, nowhere: to put it rhymingly. Happily, the glorious *New Princeton Ecyclopedia of Poetry and Poetics* (1993) is clued-up and knows that rhyme is repetition and that every repeated element in a poem is rhyme. But among other modern commentators on rhyme only John Lennard sees rhyme this largely, and so properly.[19] How dismaying it is of the excellent and greatly useful Isobel Armstrong's *Victorian Poetry: Poetry, Poetics and Politics* (Routledge, 1993) that in her otherwise seriously good Chapter 14, 'Hopkins: Agonistic Reactionary', she distinguishes his parallelism from his rhyme, before talking of his 'insistent parallelism of alliteration and rhyme' – as if parallelism and alliteration and 'rhyme', by which she means end-rhyme, were not all rhyme by virtue of their repetivity. In her biddably sympathetic celebration of the special voice, noise, music of Victorian women's poetry in her Chapter 12, 'A Music of Thine Own', Armstrong notices especially the enormous role of repetition in Christina G Rossetti's verses. 'All her work is adamantly locked in repetition. Doubling of words, phrases, patterned iteration and duplication, create the spareness of her lyrics.' Which is true, indeed wonderfully true – even if

---

[17] 'Rhythm and the other structural parts of Rhetoric', *The Journals and Papers of Gerard Manley Hopkins*, edn cit, 283–287.

[18] Denys Thompson and Stephen Tunnicliffe, *Reading and Discrimination*, New Edition Completely Rewritten (Chatto & Windus, 1979), 'Useful Terms', 173, 175.

[19] In his superb *The Poetry Handbook: A Guide to Reading Poetry for Pleasure and Practical Criticism* (Oxford University Press 1966; 2nd edn, 2005). Even the sharply revolutionary and overturning Nigel Fabb and Morris Halle in their *Meter in Poetry: A New Theory* (Cambridge University Press, Cambridge, 2008) believe that 'In most types of rhyming poetry, rhyme is either line-final or on the final stressed syllable in the line' (260). And the good poet and critic Philip Hobsbaum (in his often useful *Metre, Rhythm and Verse Form* in the Routledge New Critical Idiom series (1996)), bows to the conventional mistake of taking end-rhyme for rhyme as such: 'the exact echoing of a sound at the end of one line by the sound at the end of another line'. No, it's the echoing of sounds and groups of sounds all over the place in poems.

spareness hardly seems the *mot juste* for a practice of repetivity that looks and sounds like the opposite of spare (it's certainly unsparing). Hopkins talked of the *grace* of alliteration, and he seems to have meant not only poetic gracefulness, or even divine blessing, but also something like a verbal equivalent of the musical *grace-note* – extras added in by the player or singer, gratuitous repeat notes, trills and the like.[20] And all of the senses of *grace* fit Ms Rossetti well, but not least the sense of overdoing, for her habit of repetition is indeed extreme. What's wrong, though, is to assume that it's her amplitudes of repetition which mark her out as singular among Victorian poets. Hopkins himself is her very close rival in striving for the 'grace' of repetition, in all its senses. Wrong, too, is the notion that being 'locked in repetition' is not something shared by all poetry as such, since all poetry, and not least all Victorian poetry, is 'locked in repetition', because it is locked in rhyming. Which is the crucial equation Isobel Armstrong doesn't at all recognize, for she goes on to distinguish rhyme from repetition. The 'formal constraint', as she puts it, of Christina G Rossetti's repetivity works *like* rhyme, works *as* rhyme does. So repetivity isn't, in her view, rhyme as such; rhyme is something else. Having mentioned rhyme, she adds that the favourite Rossetti family pastime of *bouts rimés* (the game of extemporizing verses whose lines end in rhymes based on a rhyming word suggested by others in the group of players), was a formative exercise fundamental to Christina G's poetry. And indeed we can believe it was. The observation only serves, though, to underline the usual casual assumption that only end-rhyming is rhyme, the failure to see that repetition as such is rhyme.[21]

'Writing poetry is an unnatural act,' observed the great American poet Elizabeth Bishop.[22] Poetic language is, by definition, not natural language. And a key part of this defining unnaturalness is precisely its repetivity, its rhyming. Which is to say there is no such thing as blank verse, if by blank verse is meant verse that eschews rhyming. 'Blank verse' is sometimes specialized to mean 'Unrhyming iambic pentameter verse', that is five-footed lines without end-rhymes. This is the assumption of John Addington Symonds's more or less classic study *Blank Verse* (1895). But, as I keep saying, rhyme is not just end-rhyme; and, as a matter of fact, to repeat iambic feet within the line and across a poem is itself a sort of rhyming. (And, of course, for how could it not be, the examples of 'blank verse' Symonds

---

[20]   Hopkins, op cit, 284.

[21]   Isobel Armstrong, *Victorian Poetry: Poetry, Poetics and Politics* (Routledge, London and New York, 1993), 352, 426.

[22]   Elizabeth Bishop, 'Writing poetry is an unnatural act …', *Edgar Allan Poe and the Juke-Box, Uncollected Poems, Drafts, and Fragments*, ed and annotated Alice Quinn (Farrar, Strauss and Giroux, New York, 2006), 207. Her three 'favorite' poets, she says in the piece, p.208, are Herbert, Hopkins and Baudelaire. Poetic discourse doesn't come any more unnatural than Hopkins's.

adduces, come inevitably jammed with every kind of repetition – to such an extent that realization of the critical *cul de sac* he's backed himself into does occasionally dawn, as when in talking of the 'blank verse' songs interpolated in Tennyson's 'The Princess', and in particular the way each stanza of 'Tears, idle tears' ends with the words 'days that are no more', he concedes that 'This recurrence of sound and meaning is a substitute for rhyme, and suggests rhyme so persuasively that it is impossible to call the poem mere blank verse'.[23]) 'Free verse', that unfortunate Englishing of the French *vers libre*, is also a contradiction in terms. As no verse is blank of rhyming, so no verse is free of the bindings of rhyme. Modernist versifiers and their explicators are deluded in their belief in 'free verse'. Eliot was absolutely right to say that 'no verse is really free'. Every case discussed in the best account of 'free verse', HT Kirby-Smith's *The Origins of Free Verse* (1996) proves Eliot's point.[24] 'Free verse' is a misnomer. So is 'prose poem'.[25]

The most notorious 'prose poem' in all of Victorian literature, the 'Towards Democracy' of Edward Carpenter, makes the point massively. Carpenter was Walt Whitman's intensest English admirer. He sought deliberately to imitate Whitman's apparently free and easy conversational style, in verses throwing off conventional short line-lengths, end-rhymes and regular stanzas – ostensibly unshackled verses whose deliberately loose, even louche, form would perhaps reflect the undoing sexual-convention work of the male poet's homoerotic gaze which Carpenter, of course, shared with Whitman. Here's Section LXXII from the First Edition of *Towards Democracy* (1883) – it became Section LXIV in the subsequently expanding versions of this long poem, ending up in the final version of this forever growing poem (1905) as Part I, LXIV.

> Beautiful is the figure of the lusty full-grown groom on his superb horse:
> the skin of the animal is saturated with love.
> Radiant health!

---

[23] John Addington Symonds, *Blank Verse* (John C Nimmo, London, 1895).

[24] HT Kirby-Smith, *The Origins of Free Verse* (University of Michigan Press, Ann Arbor, 1996). See, not least, Ch 8, ' "No Verse is Really Free" ', 179–209.

[25] 'I regard' *Vers Libre* 'as only our old friend, Prose Poetry, broken up in convenient lengths', said Robert Graves, with force, in his cranky but always spot-on *On English Poetry: Being an Irregular Approach to the Psychology of This Art, Mainly Subjective* (William Heinemann, London, 1922), 45. Revealingly, every case of the 'prose poem' in the best account of French 'prose poetry', *The Prose Poem in France: Theory and Practice*, eds Mary Ann Caws and Hermine Riffaterre (Columbia University Press, New York, 1983), shows how unprosily packed with verbal repetitions, i.e. rhymes, the 'prose poem' is. For all its combative refusal of the 'order of the line', this mode's insistent rhyming announces a traditional poeticity. Mallarmé's 'prose poem' version of Tennyson's 'Mariana', (referred to in 'Victorian Modernismus', Ch 10, below), shows just how much that's the case.

O kisses of sun and wind, tall fir-trees and moss-covered rocks! O boundless joy of Nature on the mountain tops – coming back at last to you!

Wild songs in sight of the sea, wild dances along the sands, glances of the risen moon, echoes of old old refrains coming down from unimagined times!

O rolling through the air superb prophetic spirit of Man, pulse of divine health equalising the universe, vast over all the world expanding spirit!

O joy of the liberated soul (finished purpose and acquittal of civilisation), daring all things – light step, life held in the palm of the hand! O swift and eager delight of battle, fierce passion of love destroying and destroying the body!

Eternal and glorious War! Liberation! the soul like an eagle – from gaping wounds and death – rushing forth screaming into its vast and eternal heaven.

See! the divine mother goes forth with her babe (all creation circles round) – God dwells once in a woman's womb; friend goes with friend, flesh cleaves to flesh, the path that rounds the universe.

O every day sweet and delicious food! Kisses to the lips of sweet-smelling fruit and bread, milk and green herbs. Strong well-knit muscles, quick-healing glossy skin, body for kisses all over!

Radiant health! to breathe, O joy!, ah!, never enough to be expressed!

For the taste of fruit ripening warm in the sun, for the distant sight of the deep liquid sea!

For the sight of the naked bodies of the bathers, bathing by the hot sea-banks, the pleasant consciousness of those who are unashamed, the glance of their eyes, the beautiful proud step of the human animal on the sand;

For the touch of the air on my face or creeping over my unclothed body, for the rustling sound of it in the trees, and the appearance of their tall stems springing so lightly from the earth!

Joy, joy and thanks for ever.

And how triumphantly repetitive, that is to say how intensely rhyming this is! It's a bustling word-hoard of massively accumulating repetitions. Sticking out is the repeated set of phrases joining two nouns – nouns that might or might not have a definite article and an adjective, or two, appended to them. The root of these phrases is a *noun* plus the small connector of: *figure of, skin of, kisses of, joy of, sight of, glances of, echoes of, spirit of, pulse of, acquittal of, joy of, palm of, delight of, passion of, lips of, taste of, sight of, consciousness of, glance of, step of, touch of, sound of, appearance of*: a potent run of full-rhyming phrases, around which definite articles (and an occasional other deictic in *th*, a *those* or a *their*) and adjectives get arrayed in a partly full-rhyming, partly para-rhyming way: *the figure of the lusty full-grown groom; the skin of the animal; kisses of sun and wind; boundless joy of Nature; sight of the sea; glances of the risen moon; echoes of old old refrains; superb prophetic spirit of Man; pulse of divine health; joy of the liberated soul; finished purpose and acquittal of civilisation; the palm of the hand; swift and eager delight of battle; fierce passion of love; the lips of sweet-smelling fruit; the taste of fruit; the distant sight of the deep liquid sea; the sight of the naked bodies; the pleasant consciousness of those who are unashamed; the glance of their eyes; the beautiful proud step of the human animal; the touch of the air; the rustling sound of it; the appearance of all their tall stems.* (The inescapable presence of these *noun of the noun*, and *[the] [adjective] noun of [the] [adjective] noun* phrases is oddly proleptic of the repeated verbal craving for such phrases in Thirties Auden – 'the beautiful loneliness of the banks', that sort of phrase from 'August for the people and their favourite islands' – for which the American poet and novelist Randall Jarrell so severely castigated him.[26]) Prominent too are positioning words, prepositions, adverbs – *on, with, on, back, to, in, along, down from, through, over, into, forth, into, with, round, in, with, to. to, all over, in, by, on, over* – and the prepositional and adverbial phrases they're positioned in. Gerunds are not as prominent as that but they still occur a lot: *coming, coming, equalizing, expanding, destroying, destroying, gaping, rushing, screaming, sweet-smelling, ripening, bathing.* Carpenter likes apostrophizing too; so exclamatory O is everywhere: *O kisses of sun, O boundless joy of Nature, O rolling ... spirit of Man, O joy of the liberated soul, O swift and eager delight of battle, O every day ... food, O joy!* The O's generate an exclamatory *Ah!*: *O joy! to sleep, ah! never enough to be expressed.* All those o's chime in with the other long rolling o's of the poem (as in *O rolling*): *old, old, over, over.* There are several chiming couplets of words of the *old old* kind: *destroying and destroying; friend ... friend; flesh ... flesh; Joy, joy.* (Carpenter likes verbal copulation: *sun and wind, trees and ... rocks, purpose and acquittal, swift and eager, destroying and destroying, eternal and glorious, wounds and death, fruit and bread,* and so on and so on.) And the repeated couplets are afforced by the repeated triplets (or quartets): *For the taste of, For the sight of, For the touch of.* As the poem has it, *friend goes with friend, flesh cleaves to flesh,* and this is no mere matter of semantics: the *word* friend goes with the *word* friend, and the *word* flesh cleaves to the *word.* flesh. Rhyming is indeed a verbal *going with* and *cleaving to*.

The former clergyman Carpenter is well aware of the two great Biblical uses of *cleaving*: the marriage injunction of Genesis 2 ('Therefore shall a man leave his father and his mother, and shall cleave unto his wife: and they shall be one flesh'), and the inseparable friendship of Jewish Ruth and her Moabite mother-in-law Naomi in *Ruth* ('but Ruth clave unto her'). And this poem is exemplarily full of verbal cleaving, is intent on making huge numbers of verbal marriages and verbal kinship affinities. How they cleave to each other, the assonances and alliterations (those pouring forth sibilants for

[26] Randall Jarrell, 'Changes of Attitude and Rhetoric in Auden's Poetry', *Southern Review* (Autumn 1941); collected in *The Third Book of Criticism* (Faber and Faber, London, 1975), 115–150.

instance – *lusty, superb, skin, is saturated*, in line one alone), and the end-rhymes (as *kisses, trees, moss, rocks, boundless, tops* in line 3), and the phonemes and words and phrases, and grammatical bits and parts of speech, full-rhymes, half-rhymes, echoes. The cleavings might be sited, text-topographically, near or nearish – as *sea: sands; dances: glances: echoes; refrains: times; light: life: love; death: forth: forth: with: with; rocks: tops; sweet: sweet; trees: stems; bathers: bathing; bodies: banks*; and so on – or they might be more long-distance: *beautiful: beautiful; groom: moon: womb: warm; skin: skin; animal: animal; love: love; kisses: kisses: kisses; body: bodies: body.* But they're all, in their particular placings and spacings, the binding ties.

And how tight this binding-by-repetition is. Think, or rather hear, the murmur of all the *m*'s across the poem: *groom: animal: moss: mountain: coming: moon: coming: from: unimagined: Man: palm: woman's: womb: milk: muscles: warm; unashamed: animal: my: my: from.* Blank, or free, verse this poem is not. Small wonder then, you might think, that the poet should be thinking of *echoes* and *refrains*, and *echoes of old old refrains*, at that. For his poem comes packed with echoes and refrains, and for all his apparent up-to-datedness (his Whitmanesque loyalties, the style which has made some people think of him as an ur-modernist and preludic of modernist 'free verse' poets such as DH Lawrence), it is dense with echoes and refrains in the old, old way. Carpenter's intense (and traditional) investment in repetivity reminds one, in fact, of the fact that Walt Whitman deeply admired and tried to imitate the 'anaphoric repetition' method of the Psalms (which Hopkins was also drawn to). And, of course, to bring home this poem's real resistance to any throwing off of old-fashioned formal restraints, it's clear that behind the curtain, as it were, of its play with short lines and long-lines and grossly spreading line-groups lies a sort of sonnet. There are fourteen verbal blocks of verse, and when you look into the way the verbal density lightens up after six of these blocks, they're evidently broken into two of the most traditional sonnet-formation groups of six and eight lines apiece: a sestet and an octet. Which is, of course, an inversion of customary sonnet order, which has the octet first (the order followed ostentatiously by Dante Gabriel Rossetti, who makes a pronounced break after the first-part octet). So, here's an *inverted* sonnet, to go with its subject of what used to be called sexual inversion.

Echoing, refraining: they're what poems do, Victorian poets especially.[27] The anaphoric density of these Clough and Whitman verses is what one should expect of the Victorian poet; and it is, *mutatis mutandis*, what one does get.

---

[27]   The most insightful reader of echoes and refrains is John Hollander: *The Figure of Echo: A Mode of Allusion in Milton and After* (University of California Press, Berkeley, Los Angeles and London, 1981), and *Melodious Guile: Fictive Pattern in Poetic Language* (Yale University Press, New Haven, 1988).

3

Making Noise/Noising Truths

Victorian poets just cannot refrain from refrains, from taking up the burden of the burden. But why? All this rhyming, this repeating, these manifold anaphoric gestures, do they have a reason? A reason, or reasons, good or bad? Any reason at all? It's a question for poetry, the rhyming mode as such, at any time, and not just in its Victorian manifestations; though these particularly heavy rhymesters do make the issue an especially stark one for them in particular.[1]

Lewis Carroll, great Victorian Nonsense poet, suggested by the question marks of his 1883 volume's title – *Rhyme? And Reason?* – that the period's rhyming, his own and other people's, might have no reason beyond itself. (A scepticism backed up by the absence of REASON, announced in his little poem also called 'Rhyme? and Reason?', 'To Miss Emmie Drury', as the missing element in her smart rhymings on her name: ' "I'm EMInent in RHYME!" she said. / "I make WRY Mouths of RYE-Meal gruel!" / The Poet smiled, and shook his head: / "Is REASON, then, the missing jewel?".'[2]) Certainly there's a strong sense around that the period's strong practice of rhyming – the repeated noise-making of the poem – is in the first place there for its own sake; that mere noise, repeated noise, rhythmic noise, is attractive *per se*, and offered as a poem's core attraction. An attraction of sound which captivates the ear, granting a certain pleasure of emotion and body, before anything like the imaginary, the semantic, the intellectual (the mentally appealing loads that poetic words usually come laden with) kicks in. Aural

---

[1] See John Hollander, *Rhyme's Reason: A Guide to English Verse* (Yale University Press, New Haven, 1981), and Gillian Beer, 'The End of the Line', *Saturday Guardian Review*, 13.01.07, p21.

[2] In the 'Acrostics...' section of *The Complete Works of Lewis Carroll*, ed and intro Alexander Woollcott (Nonesuch, 1939; Penguin, 1988). Handiest Carroll source.

Victorian Poetry Now: Poets, Poems, Poetics, First Edition. Valentine Cunningham.
© 2011 Valentine Cunningham. Published 2011 by Blackwell Publishing Ltd.

appeal first. Where words mean or signify – as the (admittedly linguistically and critically provocative) formula derived from Saussurean linguistics has it – as *signifiers* first, mere aural events, before any issue of their meaning as *signifieds* arises, their semantics, their expression of meaning in relation to the human world of intellect and thought and event, their properties of referring to things. The meaning of the mere noise, or, as some would have it, the mere music of words. (Not quite the same as WK Wimsatt's important suggestion that the rhyme words in a poem comprise their own sets of meanings which run counter to the 'logical' meanings of the poems they bind together: imposing 'upon the logical pattern of expressed argument a kind of fixative counterpattern of alogical implication'; but close.[3]) In his important book *The Printed Voice of Victorian Poetry*, Eric Griffiths worries, as one should, about how the printed poetic words might be voiced. He dwells on the real difficulty there is about our getting a sense of the tone, rhythm, cadence, and so forth, from the mere printed words, at hearing what Browning drew attention to as the 'printed voice' of the Fisc in *The Ring and the Book*, I.165–167. The Fisc is like most Victorian poets, and like all poets who wrote before the modern age of recording. His voice exists only as words on the page, as print. '[A]nd since he only spoke in print / The printed voice of him lives now as then', Browning declares. But how precisely, Griffiths wonders, can the printed voice 'live' for us as it was when the (pre-recording) poet spoke it, when it is simply unavailable to us?[4] It's an abiding question. But of course there is no doubt that we hear *something* – if we are not, unluckily, physically deaf – when we read, at least read aloud, so many of Browning's lines: in the first place mere noise, and a great deal of it. Everything about Victorian theory and practice suggests that this – the as it were degree zero of poetry's attraction – is what's afoot.

The Ring of Rhyme

Plainly, it's the mere noise of words, the utterness of mere uttering (*uttering*: *outering*, getting the sheer verbal noise out), that in the first place compels Victorian poets, as, perhaps, all poets. Tennyson, the Brownings, the Rossettis, Hopkins, Arnold, Swinburne, all of them, are infatuated by the noise their verses are making. They keep displaying what's been labelled as

---

[3]   William K Wimsatt, Jr, 'One Relation of Rhyme to Reason', in *The Verbal Icon: Studies in the Meaning of Poetry* (University of Kentucky Press, Lexington, 1954); discussed by Michael Holquist, 'What is a Boojum? Nonsense and Modernism', *Yale French Studies*, no. 43, *The Child's Part* (1969), 145–164; no. 96, *Yale French Studies: A Commemorative Anthology, Part 1: 1948–1979* (1999),114–115.
[4]   Eric Griffiths, *The Printed Voice of English Poetry* (Clarendon Press, Oxford, 1989), especially Ch 1, 'The Printed Voice'.

'sonic intelligence.'[5] They're known, and judged, by the noises they make. By their noise shall ye know them. Here's a poetry for the ear. '[R]ead it with the ears', as Hopkins advised Robert Bridges, 'as I always wish to be read, and my verse becomes all right.'[6] It's no accident that in the greatest of the period's critical wars, the one over the relative merits of Tennyson and Browning, it's their poems' noise that's the criterion of value. (Browning's 'monstrous noise', as Oscar Wilde labelled it in 'The Critic as Artist' (in his *Intentions*, 1891), is what gets him the lower rank in the refined critics' books). We the readers are driven to be as compelled as the poets by what Swinburne called the 'ring of rhyme'. The 'ring of rhyme' *is* poetry in Swinburne's reckoning – as he says in his poem 'Rococo', where he hopes that 'Remembrance may recover ... / The ring of my first rhyme'. (He eulogizes Victor Hugo in 'To Victor Hugo' for the way Hugo has fired up people by making their ears ring: 'and sang / Till with the tune men's ears took fire and rang'; and Swinburne's own rhyme – *sang*: *rang* – aptly achieves its own rather fine ring as it celebrates that ringing.) This is indeed a performative utterance. Swinburne is adept at this complex double trick of celebrating poetic noise whilst also doing it – through the narrator knight of his 'Laus Veneris', for instance, singing along to the chiming of his horse's bridle: an intense collaboration of repeating noise between noise-making persona, poem, and poet

> And heard the chiming bridle smite and smite,
> And gave each rhyme thereof some rhyme again.
> (239–340)[7]

(It's been the fate of this wonderfully and utterly self-consciously noisy poet to be repaid for his aural pains with the dispraise that he was 'all sound and no sense' – a remark properly rebuked by Bonamy Dobrée for the 'crass impercipience that cannot feel that sound is itself sense; otherwise, what is the virtue of music'.[8])

---

[5] By Matthew Campbell, *Rhythm and Will in Victorian Poetry* (Cambridge University Press, Cambridge, 1999).

[6] '[W]hen on somebody returning me the *Eurydice* ([his 'The Loss of the Eurydice'], I opened and read some lines, as one commonly reads whether prose or verse, with the eyes, so to say, only, it struck me aghast with a kind of raw nakedness and unmitigated violence I was unprepared for: but take breath and read it with the ears, as I always wish to read, and my verse becomes allright'. Quoted by Bridges in his Preface to his Notes in the 1918 edition. See ' "Read With the Ear": Patterns of Sound', Ch 5 of James Milroy, *The Language of Gerard Manley Hopkins* (André Deutsch, 1977), 114–153.

[7] All these poems appeared in *Poems and Ballads* (1866).

[8] Bonamy Dobrée, 'Introduction', The Penguin Poets' *Swinburne*, ed Dobrée (Penguin, Harmondsworth, 1961), 12.

Having the sound of words ringing, chiming, rhyming in their ears – and so ringing, chiming, rhyming in their readers' – is what Victorian poets must have. Several poets in fact perform that Swinburnean trick – talking of ringing and performing ringing at the same time. Hopkins is such another adept. As in his 'As kingfishers catch fire':

> As kingfishers catch fire, dragonflies dráw fláme;
> As tumbled over rim in roundy wells
> Stones ring; like each tucked string tells, each hung bell's
> Bow swung finds tongue to fling out broad its name;
> Each mortal thing does one thing and the same.

(What a ringing that talking of ringing makes: *ring, string, hung, swung, tongue, fling, thing, thing* – to list no more of the noisy repetitions hanging on the ringing -ing words of these lines.[9]) Tennyson can be heard doing the ringing business in the 'Ring out, wild bells' section of *In Memoriam* (CVI). *Ring out, Ring out, Ring out,* the lines command, ringing out themselves as they do so.

Tennyson became, in time, the Poet Laureate; he was never not the Poet Auriculate, the poet of and for the ear. He gives you an ear-full, because he has his own ears full.[10] Like his spokesman Ulysses, Tennyson's ears are bombarded with sounds. '[T]he deep / Moans round with many voices' declares the old man of 'Ulysses'. And for Tennyson's verses they are voices of all sorts – of nature, of actions, of his characters' speaking, of other poets' lines.[11] But the point is their many-ness, their multitude. A noisy multitudinousness transmitted by the poems – which now moan around us with their multiplied noisiness: filling our ears as they filled the poet's. And so, *mutatis mutandis*, is it with them all. Tennyson is utterly representative in the way that noise is, for him, life – the life of the subject, lover, hero, warrior, and of course of the poet and poem. No noise, no poem. Tennyson had to keep reading his poems aloud, with those great rolling Lincolnshire vowels, because that's what guaranteed their life. You can hear him giving his poems

---

[9]   James Milroy intriguingly thinks that Hopkins was mindful here of Max Müller's *ding-dong* theory of language-origins in his second volume of *Lectures on the Science of Language*, and his 'law' of nature 'that every thing which is struck rings. Each substance has a peculiar ring'. Milroy (1977), 65.

[10]   For a pleasing account of Tennyson's ear-fulls, see Angela Leighton, 'Tennyson, by Ear', in *Tennyson Among the Poets: Bicentenary Essays*, eds Robert Douglas-Fairhurst and Seamus Perry (Oxford University Press, Oxford, 2009), 336–355.

[11]   Robert Douglas-Fairhurst begins *Victorian Afterlives: The Shaping of Influence in Nineteenth-Century Literature* (Oxford University Press, Oxford, 2002), his telling book on the literary voices, of predecessors, contemporaries, even of themselves, resounding in nineteenth-century writers' ears, with a far-reaching meditation on the far-reach of Tennyson's moaning voices.

that necessary mouth on the extant sound-recordings of main poems such as 'The Charge of the Light Brigade' and 'Come into the garden, Maud' (made courtesy of the wax-cylinder recording machines the Edison Company sent to well-known writers, which made Tennyson's almost the first English poet's voice to be captured for posterity).[12] It's the voice of the poet Everard Hall in Tennyson's 'The Epic [Morte d'Arthur]', reciter of 'Morte d'Arthur', who 'Read, mouthing out his hollow oes and aes / Deep-chested music'. ('This is something as A.T. read', said his friend Edward FitzGerald.)

Characteristically, in Tennyson's medievalizing fragment 'Sir Launcelot and Queen Guinevere', the fetchingly lovely Guinevere (for 'one kiss / Upon her perfect lips' a man would give up 'all other bliss') rides along in a blend of natural and magical noises:

> Now by some tinkling rivulet,
> In mosses mixt with violet
> Her cream-white mule his pastern set:
>   And fleeter now she skimmed the plains
> Than she whose elfin prancer springs
> By night to eery warblings,
> When all the glimmering moorland rings
>   With jingling bridle-reins.
>   (29–36)

Guinevere lives within, through and as noise – the noise, the noises, that the poem is recording and making. It's the only way with Tennyson. To be silent is to be dead, for person and for poem. It's noise – in the first place any noise, any old noise – which defies the silence of death. Nothing is more consternating than environmental silence, such as the dark forest of Tennyson's 'A Dream of Fair Women':

> There was no motion in the dumb dead air,
> Not any song of bird or sound of rill;
> Gross darkness of the inner sepulchre
> Is not so deadly still
>
> As that wide forest.
>   (65–69)

---

[12]   Tennyson recorded 10 poems on 23 wax cylinders. Some appeared (famously crackly) on a vinyl LP, *Alfred Lord Tennyson Reads from His Own Poems*, Intro Sir Charles Tennyson (Craighill, Edinburgh Recordings, JEF/TD 6593): 'The Charge of the Light Brigade', 'Come Into the Garden Maud', parts of 'Song of Elaine', 'Charge of the Heavy Brigade', 'The Northern Farmer'. 'The Charge of the Light Brigade' has been re-mastered (and thus wonderfully cleaned up) on the British Library CD, *The Spoken Word: Poets*, NSA CD13 – which also includes a fragment of Browning, failing to 'remember me own poem' [sic], as he stumbles over the beginning of 'How They Brought the Good News' into a recording device stuck in his face at some dinner.

Dumb dead air: being dumb is as bad as being dead; to be dead is to be dumb. If the dead Duke of Wellington is to live on it will only be because he's become the noise Tennyson wishes on him in his 'Ode on the Death of the Duke of Wellington' (1852): a heroic 'name', to resound down the 'ever-echoing avenues of song'; a hero acclaimed by 'a people's voice' – for centuries to come. In the great despair of his private loss Tennyson cannot imagine for his dead friend Arthur Hallam any such public noising. To be sure, he'll hear an imaginary private passing-bell tolling on in Hallam's memory, speaking its 'sad words' of farewell:

> Yet in these ears, till hearing dies,
> One set slow bell will seem to toll
> The passing of the sweetest soul
> That ever looked with human eyes
>
> I hear it now, and o'er and o'er,
> Eternal greetings to the dead;
> And 'Ave, Ave, Ave', said,
> 'Adieu, adieu', for evermore.
> (*In Memoriam*, LVII)

And there'll be those church bells ringing out, again and again, in *In Memoriam* CVI, ringing out the old year, ringing in the new; the noise that paradoxically affirms, in fact, a very silent future for the dead friend. 'Ring out, wild bells, and let him die'. Ring out being wonderfully poised between the loudness of a ringing *out loud*, and a ringing *out* to a nothing, the point of extinction, until it can be heard no longer.

'How dull it is to pause, to make an end', thinks old Ulysses. How dull to be in the quietness of a retired old-age on the threshold of the great silence of the tomb. He harks back yearningly to the old noisy 'delight of battle', 'Far on the ringing plains of windy Troy'. The only way to live again would be to join in again with such noisy delights, out on the noisy sea which 'Moans round with many voices'. Ulysses and his comrades should row off once more; epic exploits await across that noisy sea-scape: 'Push off, and sitting well in order smite / The sounding furrows'. Heroic action is undoubtedly terrible, but its noises animate; they are life for soldiers and for poems about soldiers. War-noises certainly animate Tiresias, the blind seer and his eponymous poem, as he imagines the sound of the enemy attacking the city of Thebes (and the wailing of the fearful women inside):

> I can hear
> Too plainly what full tides of onset sap
> Our seven high gates, and what a weight of war
> Rides on those ringing axles! jingle of bits,
> Shouts, arrows, tramp of the hornfooted horse   92

That grind the glebe to powder! Stony showers
Of that ear-stunning hail of Arês crash
Along the sounding walls. Above, below,
Shock after shock, the song-built towers and gates
Reel, bruised and butted with the shuddering
War-thunder of iron rams; and from within
The city comes a murmur void of joy,
Lest she be taken captive – maidens, wives,
And mothers with their babblers of the dawn

    ...

Falling about their shrines before their Gods,
And wailing 'Save us.'

                      ('Tiresias', 88–104)

That 'tramp of the hornfooted horse' in line 92 is lifted from a passage in Virgil's *Aeneid* VI. 590–591 where the Sibyl tells Aeneas of Salmoneus, who was mad (*demens*) enough to drive about in a bronze chariot pulled by horny-hooved horses in an effort to emulate Zeus's inimitable thunder and lightning. Virgil presents this failed imitation: only a really foolish person would imagine he could simulate Zeus's thunder by the noise of a bronze chariot and the 'beat of the horny-footed horses' ('demens qui ... non imitabile fulmen / aere et cornipedum pulsu simularet equorum'). Tennyson liked quoting the Virgil lines for their 'descriptive beauty and fine sound'.[13] Fine sound. It's what Tennyson likes Virgil for; it's what he wants for his own poem. War may be un-fine, but its noise makes for very fine lines. Virgil's Salmoneus is mad to think he could imitate Jove's chariot, but Tennyson will capture some of that Virgilian noise of the chariot, will imitate Virgil whose poem simulates the noise of the *cornipedum pulso* : 'tramp of the hornfooted horse / That grind the glebe to powder'. And how Tennyson's lines ring and jingle and throb with the sounds of the conflict they describe! What a noise of that tramping and grinding!

When at the end of 'Maud' the protagonist-monologuist sails away from England for a kind of selfhood-cleansing and healing at the Crimean War, it is a joining in with the very noise of battle that's uppermost in his project of heroic self-redemption. 'And I stood on a giant deck and mixed my breath / With a loyal people shouting a battle cry'. The quiet pastoralism of peacetime-quiet fields and herds – a few 'languid notes' on a shepherd's pipe – is, happily for the poem's hero, disturbed by the shouts of battle. It's an odd and shocking kind of redemption, as every modern reader has supposed, but one utterly in keeping with the noise-obsessions of this poem and poet.

Aurality, they all recognized, is the key. Hopkins, one of the sharpest thinkers about poeticity ever, knew that the aural had been fundamental to poetry

---

13 Hallam Tennyson's *Memoir*, II.12–13.

right from the start, and thought it should be so now. Reflecting in his Rhythm lecture-notes on the commonness in the tradition of the 'grace' of alliteration, the repeated noise of letters, of words – it 'was an essential element in Anglo-Saxon or old English verse, as Piers the Plowman, also in Icelandic ... it is often used ... very thickly in Latin verse, more sparingly in Greek, thickly in modern English verse. ... It is common in proverbs of course (Faint heart never won fair lady)' – he concludes that 'one may indeed doubt whether a good ear is satisfied with our verse without it.'[14] Impact on the ear was poetry's archaic power. It was to be found, Hopkins realized, not just in Anglo-Saxon and medieval English verse, but in the highly alliterative Welsh *cynghanned* (full of 'consonant chime') as well as in the intensely anaphoric Psalms of the Bible; and he would seek to replicate and imitate these modes to acquire, if he could, such primitive force for his own verses.[15] He knew such merely noisy repetition as the basis of the attraction too of nursery rhymes, playground stuff, the force of unthinking and un-thought-out material for the young ear and mouth, the most primitive of living poetic audiences. 'Ding Dong Bell, Pussy's in the Well': in the first place it's not a story of bells and pussy-cats in wells that's at issue but the mere sound of the piece, the mere noisy run of the rhymes, the repetitions. Ding Dong Bell: it's childish nonsense verse: and it's Hopkins's basic example of what his so-called 'Sprung Rhythm' is after.[16] Here's a chiming that, naturally, flirts with the hollowing echolalic effects of echoing, but which thinks the risk worth taking, because noise, and mere noise repeated, rhyming, is accepted as having its own fundamental rationale, the merely aural one.

Onomatopoeia

And in Victorian poem after poem what's at stake is rhyming in its most fundamental poetic form, the form most beguiling not just to Hopkins, but to numerous of his contemporaries, namely *onomatopoeia*.

[14] *The Journals and Papers of Gerard Manley Hopkins*, ed Humphrey House and Graham Storey (Oxford University Press, London, 1959), 284.

[15] DH Lawrence knew the attraction of the Psalms' anaphorically double-line practice: 'How truly beautiful the Psalms, many of them ... Even the Jewish form of poetry that they call "parallelism", because the second line re-echoes the first in a parallel image, how curiously satisfying it can be, once one enters the image-rhythm of it!' 'Apocalypse, Fragment I', *Apocalypse and the Writings on Revelation*, ed Mara Kalnins (Penguin, Harmondsworth, 1995), 153.

[16] '... scanning by accents or stresses alone, without any account of the number of syllables ... there are hints of it in music, in nursery rhymes and popular jingles ... here are instances – Díng, dóng, béll, Pússy's ín the wéll: Whó pút her ín? Little Jóhnny Thín. Whó púlled her óut? Little Jóhnny Stóut ... So too "One, twó, Buckle my shóe".' Letter to RW Dixon (October 5, 1878), *The Correspondence of Gerard Manley Hopkins and Richard Watson Dixon*, ed CC Abbott (Oxford University Press, London, 1935), 14.

Onomatopoiea is the ancient Greek word brought into English in the middle of the sixteenth century, and familiar to rhetoricians and philologists from then on, to describe the forming of words by imitation of the sounds of the things and actions they describe. Onomatopoeia labels the making of words by doubling, repeating, rhyming with natural (and unnatural) noise, the noise of the world. It became a matter of intense interest to the Victorians, especially in the 1860s when the idea really took hold that languages begin by imitating sounds in nature, and also that this process is fundamental to poetic language, is what poems do, and should do. Here was the rhyming business at its most basic, the idea of poems as rhyming machines that were, among their other rhyming functions, echoing noisy reality, resounding with the sounding truth of the world – the noisy way, truth, and life (if you were a Christian, as were most Victorian poets) of God's creation, God's world. Derivates of *onomatopoeia* spawned busily in Victoria's reign. *Onomatopoetic* is first recorded in English in 1847, according to the OED. *Onomatopoeic* comes in in 1860, in Frederic Farrar's *Essay on the Origin of Language*. Farrar was a key contributor to the large Victorian philological movement, whose greatest achievement, of course, is the Oxford English Dictionary – that extraordinary project, begun in 1857 when members of the newish Philological Society – founded 1842 – called for a complete re-examination of English from Anglo-Saxon times on. Hopkins was steeped in the philologists' writings, which stimulated his writing and thoughts about language, and so his poetic practice, to such an extent that James Milroy, in the best account of Hopkins and language, wants to claim him as part of the philological movement.[17] Hopkins read Farrar, as well as the onomatopoeia-friendly tenth edition of Richard Chenevix Trench's *On the Study of Words* (1861). Chenevix Trench's influential *On the Study of Words* first appeared in 1851, and his *English Past and Present* in 1854: he was another important member of the Philological Society.) Hopkins also read Max Müller's hugely popular *Lectures on the Science of Language* (1861), big on etymology but scathing about onomatopoeia. Müller's Lecture XI, 'The Theoretical Stage, and the Origin of Language' is very scornful of the onomatopoetic notion of word-creation, and especially of onomatopoetic theories of language origin. He joyfully sneers at what he dubs the Bow-Bow Theory (that language began with imitations of animal noises) and the Pooh-Pooh Theory (that language began in human interjections, cries of emotion, *oohs* and *ahs*, the grunts and groans of fear, pain, joy, and such: the traditional 'Three F's' of human-emotion studies; what emotions-analysts like to list as fearing; fleeing; and sexual intercourse). Hopkins seems to have been persuaded by much in Müller's lectures, for instance the stress on the monosyllabic roots

---

[17]   In the extremely informative 'The Wonder of Language: Hopkins and Victorian Philology' chapter of *The Language of Gerard Manley Hopkins* (André Deutsch, London, 1977), 39.

of language, but was plainly less than persuaded by Müller's jeers against onomatopoeia; on onomatopoeia he was much more taken by Farrar and Trench.[18] He may also have read Richard Burton's travel-book *Abeokuta and the Cameroons Mountains* (1863), in which (again according to the OED) *onomatopoetic* makes only its second recorded appearance in English, a book happy to think of African horns and tom-toms as expressing a 'good compilation of ideas by onomatopoetic language'.

The direct results of such readings appear in those Hopkins diary entries which assemble words from the Indo-European pot in rhyming groups: words apparently united by origin in shared sense (an origin in nature of the sort which Max Müller, who liked the idea of linguistic Natural Selection, might have approved), but also by sound, by alliteration, that is by verbal rhyming, which, Hopkins thought, might well arise onomatopoetically, that is by rhyming with the natural source, the natural object-reference of the word. Hopkins began with the *horn* group

> The various lights under which a horn may be looked at have given rise to a vast number of words in language. It may be regarded as a projection, a climax, a badge of strength, power or vigour, a tapering body, a spiral, a wavy object, a bow, a vessel to hold withal or to drink from, a smooth hard material not brittle, stony, metallic or wooden, something sprouting up, something to thrust or push with, a sign of honour or pride, an instrument of music, etc. From the shape, *kernel* and *granum*, *grain*, *corn*. From the curve of a horn, *koronis*, *corona*, *crown*. From the spiral *crinis*, meaning ringlets, locks. From its being the highest point comes our *crown* perhaps, in the sense of the top of the head, and the Greek *kéras*, horn, and *kára*, head, were evidently identical; then for its sprouting up and growing, compare *keren*, *cornu*, *kéras*, horn with grow, *cresco*, *grandis*, grass, great, *groot*. For its curving, *curvus* is probably from the root *horn* in one of its forms. *korone* in Greek and *corvus*, *cornix* in Latin and *crow* (perhaps also *raven*, which may have been *craven* originally) in English bear a striking resemblance to *cornu*, *curvus*. So also *kéranos*, *crane*, *heron*, *herne*. Why these birds should derive their names from *horn* I cannot presume to say. The tree *cornel*, Latin *cornus* is said to derive its name from the hard horn-like nature of its wood, and the *corns* of the foot perhaps for the

---

[18]   Isobel Armstrong discusses at some length Max Müller's Lectures and also what Hopkins might have learned from him about language in her *Victorian Poetry: Poetry, Poetics and Politics* (1993), especially in the excellent Hopkins discussion, Ch 14 – though not about rhyme as I'm arguing it, and not at all about onomatopoeia. Proof, if proof were needed, of Müller's wide readership among poets comes in the lovely satirical poem (February 1862) of Charles Lord Neaves, 'The Origin of Language', beginning 'Tis not very easy to say / How language had first a beginning', and merrily jeering at the 'Pooh! Pooh!' and 'Bow, wow' advocates. There's a good detail about Hopkins's drawing on Farrar and Trench (neither mentioned by Armstrong) in Alan Ward's indispensable 'Philological Notes' appended to *The Journals and Papers of Gerard Manley Hopkins*, eds Humphrey House and Graham Storey (OUP, London, 1959), Appendix iii, 499–527, which James Milroy of course draws on.

same reason. *Corner* is so called from its shape, indeed the Latin is *cornu*. Possibly (though this is rather ingenious than likely, I think) *grin* may mean to curve up the ends of the mouth like *horns*. Mountains are called *horn* in Switzerland ...

These words rhyme in every sense: they rhymed at origin with nature in terms of both sense and sound, as they rhyme now with each other, their cohesion of sound confirming their sense cohesion. And so it goes with list upon list of such ingenious gatherings and speculations:

> *slip, slipper, slop, slabby* (muddy), *slide*, perhaps *slope*, but if slope is thus con-
> nected what are we to say of *slant*?
>> *Drill, trill, thrill, nostril, nese*-thirl (Wiclif etc.)
> Common idea of piercing. To *drill*, in sense of discipline, is to wear down,
> work upon. Cf. to *bore* in slang sense, *wear, grind*. So *tire* connected with *tero*.

> *Shear, shred, potsherd, shard*.
>> The *ploughshare* that which divides the soil. *Share* probably = divide.
>> *Shrad* also, with is same as shred.
>> *Shire*, a division of land? *Shore*, where the land is cut by the water?
>> *Shower*, cf. shred, a fall of water in little shreds or divisions? *Short*, cut off,
> curtailed.

> *Skim, scum, squama, scale, keel*, (i.e. skeel) – *squama* and *scale* being the top-
> most flake what may be skimmed from the surface of a thing.

> *Gulf, golf*. If this game has its name from the holes into which the ball is put,
> they may be connected, both being from the root meaning hollow. *Gulp, gula,
> hollow, hold, hilt, koilos, caelare* (to make hollow, to make grooves in, to
> grave) *caelum*, which there same as though it were what it once was supposed
> to a translation of *koilon*, hole, hell, ('The hollow hell') *skull, shell, hull* (of
> ships and beans).

> *skill*, originally I believe to divide, discriminate. From same word or root *shell*
> (in a school), *shilling* (division of a pound), and they say *school* (both of boys
> and whales), *shoal, scale* (of fish), *keel*, etc. *Skill* is of course connected with
> *scindere* and other words meaning to cut, divide – schizein.

> *Flick, fillip, flip, fleck, flake*

Flick means to touch or strike lightly as with the end of a whip, a finger, etc. To *fleck* is the next tone above flick, still meaning to touch or strike lightly (and leave a mark of the touch or stroke) but in a broader less slight manner. Hence substantively a *fleck* is a piece of light, colour, substance, etc. looking as though shaped or produced by such touches. *Flake* is a broad and decided *fleck*, a thin plate of something, the tone above it. Their connection is more clearly seen in the applications of the words to natural objects than in expla-nations. It would seem that *fillip* generally pronounced *flip* is a variation of *flick*, which however seem connected with *fly, flee, flit*, meaning to make fly off. Key to meaning of *flick, fleck* and *flake* is that of striking or cutting off the surface of a thing; in *flick* (as to flick off a fly) something little or light from the surface, while *flake* is a thin scale of surface. *Flay* is therefore connected, perhaps *flitch*.

Flag, (droop etc), *flaccere*, notion that of waving instead of rigidity, flowing (as we say of drapery). Hence *flag* the substantive. *Fledge* to furnish with wings with which to *fly, fled* ...
   With *fillip, flip*, cf. *flap, flob*.
   Cf. the connection between *flag* and *flabby* with that between *flick* and *flip, flog* and *flap, flop*.

Grind, gride, gird, grit, groat, grate, greet, kroúein, crush, crash, kroteîn, etc.
   Original meaning to *strike, rub*, particularly together. That which is produced by such means is the *grit*, the *groats* or crumbs, like *fragmentum* from *frangere, bit* from *bite. Crumb, crumble* perhaps akin. To *greet*, to strike the hands together (?). *Greet*, grief, wearing, *tribulation. Grief* possibly connected. *Gruff*, with a sound as of two things rubbing together. I believe these words to be onomatopoetic. *Gr* common to them all representing a particular sound. In fact I think the onomatopoetic theory has not had a fair chance. Cf. *Crack, creak, croak, crake, graculus, crackle*. These must be onomatopoetic.

Crook, crank, kranke, crick, cranky. Original meaning crooked, not straight or right, wrong, awry. A crank in England is a piece of mechanism which turns a wheel or shaft at one end, at the other receiving a rectilinear force. Knife-grinders, velocipedes, steam-engines, etc. have them. *Crick* in the neck is when some muscle, tendon or something of that sort in the neck is twisted or goes wrong in some way.
   Cranky, provincial, out of sorts, wrong. The original meaning *crooked*, cf. *curvus* and for derivation see under *horn*.[19]

And so on. They're extraordinarily precocious these notes by a mere undergraduate (beginning 24 September 1863 when the 19-year old Hopkins had just gone up to Balliol). He's up on the very latest philological speculations. He evidently shares Max Müller's assumptions about etymology and the 'predicative' roots of words. His *grind* list echoes Müller's first (1861) series of lectures.[20] It seems that he might have read the 1862 polemic about the fifty basic Germanic roots and 15,000 root-forms of English by the Dorset dialect poet William Barnes (whose poetry Hopkins liked), *Tiw; or A View of the Roots and Stems of the English as a Teutonic Tongue*. Hopkins's lists certainly share Barnes's assumption about the monosyllabism of roots; and

[19]   'Early Diaries' 1863–1864, beginning September 24 1863. Hopkins, *Journals and Papers*, edn cit, 4–5, 9–12, 16. I've omitted some of the entries, rearranged the order, and romanized Hopkins's Greek lettering.
[20]   Milroy (1977), 50–53.

his *fl* list coincides with Barnes's.[21] And he's in the forefront of contemporary *onomatopoeic* speculation: his use of that word coinciding, more or less, with the OED's second published recording in Burton's *Abeokula* of 1863. What young Hopkins is doing is making a map of key items in the grand Indo-European language group, Greek, Latin, English, German (the language group dominating European philological thought at the time; the language, as Isobel Armstrong's discussion of Max Müller rightly stresses, of Müller's 'Aryan' master-race[22]), tightly bound by manifold internal rhyming, massively alliterative, but also assonantal and end-rhymed: a poetic system arising apparently naturally, as language arises. It's the intrinsic poetic of Aryan man's language *per se*. (Small wonder Hopkins's lists sound like his poetry's lexicon-in-waiting.) They're words bound by rhyme in groups, and tied, too, onomatopoetically, to their referents. So here are sets of verbal rhymings announcing, and confirming, the poetic coherence of the world that the words refer to: the world as natural poem, comprising a natural poetic of *things*. Things in their unique thisness – or *haecceitas*, in the word borrowed from Duns Scotus which Hopkins was very fond of. Nature's poeticity, as proclaimed, for example, in Hopkins's (Balliol third-year) note made some time after Easter 1866:

> Drops of rain hanging on rails etc seen with only the lower rim lighted like nails (of fingers). Screws of brooks and twines. Soft chalky look with more shadowy middles of the globes of clouds on a night with a moon faint or concealed. Mealy clouds with a not brilliant moon. Blunt buds of the ash. Pencil buds of the beech. Lobes of the trees. Cups of the eyes. Gathering back the lightly hinged eyelids. Bows of the eyelids. Pencil of eyelashes. Juices of the eyeball. Eyelids like leaves, petals, caps, tufted hats, handkerchiefs, sleeves, gloves. Also of the bones sleeved in flesh. Juices of the sunrise. Joins and veins of the same. Vermilion look of the hand held against a candle with the darker parts as the middles of the fingers and especially the knuckles covered with ash.[23]

Here is a natural coherence, a rhyming, a poetic, which of course arises in Hopkins's view not in the Darwinian sense of nature working along all by itself, but of nature as God's instrument and means, His creation. The things and the words, and the words for things: all a poem. '[A]ll beauty may by a metaphor be called rhyme'. God's rhyming, in fact, His 'workmanship', His

---

[21] Milroy (1977), 56–58.
[22] Armstrong, op cit, 396–397.
[23] *Journals and Papers*, 72. Hopkins's eye for the natural object, revealed in the unstoppable word-pictures of his journals and poems and his numerous sketches are a main subject of Catherine Phillips, *Gerard Manley Hopkins and the Victorian Visual World* (Oxford University Press, Oxford, 2007).

poiema, or poem, as St Paul put it (Romans 1.20), which it is the obligation of the Christian sub-creator, the junior rhymester, as it were, to register, and to make his poems, and his readers, experience.[24]

An awareness and experience whose grace and blessing are shot through with necessary agonies but which, however burdening they might become, are mightily energizing for poems. 'The world is charged with the grandeur of God', as Hopkins's sonnet of 1877 starts off. Despite humankind's destructive efforts, nature will never be totally spoilt, 'Because the Holy Ghost over the bent / World broods with warm breast and with ah! bright wings', as on the first day of Creation in Genesis Chapter One. A new dawn is promised; there will be one day a 'new heaven and a new earth', as the Book of Revelation predicts, but meanwhile nature is, in Hopkins's favourite imagery of oppression, downtrodden, stressed, pressed under insensitive feet and foot-ware:

> Generations have trod, have trod, have trod;
> And all is seared with trade; bleared, smeared with toil;
> And wears man's smudge, and shares man's smell: the soil
> Is bare now, nor can foot feel, being shod.

God's lovely rhyming world has been done down by man's counter-rhymes: *trod, trod, trod, shod; seared, bleared, smeared; wears man's smudge, shares man's smell*. And, arrestingly, these hard, filthying, foul smelling, bad rhymings also chime in with God's allegedly grander rhymings. Man's *trod* and *shod* follow rhymingly on from *God* and his *rod* which precede them: 'Why do men then now not reck his rod?' The regrettably abusive human treading and trading are inextricably linked in this anguished socio-theological mapping – Hopkins's Green protest, so to say – with God's allegedly beneficent crushing: the grandeur that 'gathers to a greatness, like the ooze of oil / Crushed'. That's the Bible's oil of divine blessing, anointing, gladness, which usually goes with wine as an absolute good – 'wine and oil': oil from crushed nuts, wine from crushed grapes. Crushed grapes which, as Hopkins is so well aware, also denoted God's anger for sinners. God's grandeur, God's crushing, man's treading: God and men, then, united in a violence which, for all its terrors, makes the poem's crackle and sizzle with verbal energy.[25]

---

[24]   '[A]ll beauty may ... be called rhyme': Hopkins 'On the Origin of Beauty', *Journals and Papers*, 102. Quoted by J Hillis Miller in his rather good Hopkins chapter – the best in his book – in *The Disappearance of God: Five Nineteenth Century Writers* ([1963]; 1965), 277, in a discussion of Hopkins and rhyme and etymology which misses, though, the point about *God's* rhyming.

[25]   Paul S Fiddes ably puts Hopkins's obsessive treading, crushing, striking into their Biblical contexts, chapter cited in *The Blackwell Companion to the Bible in Literature*, 555–556 – though he's too easily satisfied that the notoriously difficult 'Buckle!' of 'The Windhover' refers plainly to the crucified Christ, 'buckled and crumpled'. All Hopkins quotes from *Poems*, ed. WH Gardner (Oxford University Press, 1956).

The two-way harshness here, the hardness, hurtfulness (and filth), are peculiarly prominent in Hopkins's word-hoard of rhyming things and activities, the onomatopoetic lexicon-in-waiting, his verbal current account, which his poems so freely draw on. Bite; crush, crash, crack, creak, crank, crick, cranky; drill, thrill; flick, flip, flitch, flay, flog, flap, flop; flee, fled, flag, flight, fluster; grind, gird, grate, grit, grief, gruff, gulp; hole, Hell, hold, halt; mucus, muck; scum, squama, scale; shear, shred, potsherd, shard; skull, skill, shell; spit, spittle, spatter, spot, sputter; twig, tweak, twitch, twit, twist; weak, wicked. How noisy they are, this massively consonantal and monosyllabic lot: glottal, fricative, plosive; words hard (as horn) in the mouth, banging and bashing there like brittle lumps, pebbles, rocks – sounding aggressive, denoting aggression, and doing tongue aggression to the buccal cavity, teeth, lips. We are never not reminded of that advice to Bridges to 'read with the ears'.

Here's the native consonantal, northern-European dialectal strain, of course, a modality quite other than the soft, southern, vocalic strain characteristic of Italianate verse imported at the Renaissance. It's what was deplored as 'our old English monosyllables' by Renaissance detractors, Edmund Spenser and Co., who earnestly lengthened and softened their poetic words to make them more like the admired southern-European strain. It's what Matthew Arnold castigated as the un-poetic ugliness of 'Anglo-Saxon' names, in that notorious passage in 'The Function of Criticism at the Present Time' where he makes an example of a newspaper report of a Nottingham 'girl' who has killed her illegitimate child: 'Wragg is in custody'. '[W]hat a touch of grossness in our race, what an original shortcoming in the more delicate spiritual perceptions, is shown by the natural growth amongst us of such hideous names, – Higginbottom, Stiggins, Bugg'. Ancient Greece knew nothing of such hard monosyllabic consonantalisms as Bugg or Wragg. Only in an England of ugly northern factories and workhouses, of provincial 'grimness, bareness, and hideousness', where narrow religious Dissent and democratic values have triumphed, could so many people be tagged by such ugly nomenclature.[26]

What Arnold was thus sweeping aside as too ugly for poetry was the verbal mode characteristic of so much English poetry flourishing in his day: the fundamental nursery rhyme mode revived so exemplarily by the Nonsense practitioners, the mode of Dissenting Browning, of Dorset's Hardy and the Dorset dialect poems of William Barnes; the kind of vocabulary passed on from Browning to Ezra Pound, and massively used by Midlander Wilfred Owen, who became with Hopkins the poetic mentor of the young twentieth-century poets C Day Lewis and (nursery adoring) WH Auden; the vital verbal ingredient for Hardy- and Barnes- and Owen-admiring Midlander Philip

---

[26] Matthew Arnold, 'The Function of Criticism at the Present Time', *Essays in Criticism* (Macmillan, London, 1865), 23–24.

Larkin; the essence of later poets from the old Dane-law, Northumbrian Quaker Basil Bunting (celebrator of the Yorkshire village of Briggflats, editor of the Northumbrian Victorian 'collier poet' Joseph Skipsey), the Yorkshiremen Ted Hughes and Tony Harrison.[27] It's the tone and mode Northern Ireland's Seamus Heaney, ace practitioner and celebrator of it, has called 'Guttural'[28]: the verbal toughness that's the poetically nourishing essence of the Victorian onomatopoeticists. What Tennyson, lecturing his son Hallam as a Marlborough schoolboy, praised in *Paradise Lost* (II, 879–883) as 'A good instance of onomatopoeia':

> ... On a sudden open fly
> With impetuous recoil and jarring sound
> The infernal doors, and on their hinges grate
> Harsh thunder, that the lowest bottom shook
> Of Erebus.[29]

In the gloriously jarring and grating noise of this northern vocabulary-set Hopkins found his ear's satisfactions. This was his word-hoard's chosen material. He packs his poems with that word-hoard's sort of word, with many in fact of those actually listed words, or compounds starring them. Here, for Hopkins, was poetry as such, a natural, native poetic that was also God-given – hard and harsh, as when Hopkins is being *trod* by God and kissing God's *rod*, the *fan* that's thrashing and threshing his grain, in God's toil and coil, and when he's thinking of the *hornlight* sinking in the West and hearing the *groans* of the judged-ones as God *grinds* them on the Last Day. But necessary. A 'necessary conjunction', as TS Eliot has it in his 'East Coker', of the union of male and female in marriage (quoting his ancestor, the Tudor Thomas Elyot and his *Boke of the Governour* (1537)). Well recognized by the poet and critic of an allied religio-poetic disposition, namely Charles Williams, in what must be the best celebration of the merger in Hopkins between the poetically energizing extremes of hard rhyming and Hopkins's experience of God the rod-wielder: Williams's (oddly critically underrated) Introduction to the (best-selling) Second Edition of Bridges's collection which Williams brought

[27]   John Lucas rightly throws Hughes and Bunting back into Arnold's Wragg-grinding teeth in 'Two *ggs* Bad Two *ggs* Good', *PN Review* 174, Vol 33, no. 4 (March-April 2007), 8–9.

[28]   'The Guttural Muse', in Seamus Heaney's *Field Work* volume (Faber & Faber, 1979), 28. It's what Heaney warms to, early and late, in early Auden – and which Geoffrey Grigson had the word for: 'Grigson ... spoke of "assonances and alliterations coming together to make a new verbal actuality as it might be of rock or quartz', which is precisely what this slab of verse felt like to me when I first encountered it, and why I still rejoice in it.' Heaney, 'Sounding Auden', *The Government of the Tongue: The TS Eliot Memorial Lectures and Other Critical Writings* (Faber & Faber, 1988), 120.

[29]   In May 1866: *Memoir*, II.519' and 34–37. The OED cites this as in 1860: a bad mistake ; Tennyson's mind was clearly on the discussion of onomatopoeia which flourished after 1860.

out in 1931, where the poetic usefulness of alliterations like 'the gnarl of the nails' is contrasted with what Williams considers the 'uselessness' of Swinburne's heavy alliterativeness, and the last line of 'Felix Randal' is taken as standing for Hopkins himself, 'at his poetry's "grim forge, powerful amid peers"', turning out his poems as 'precisely bright and battering sandals'.[30]

Of course, none of Hopkins's contemporaries came to their noise-making with his particular religious sense of what animated the noise of the world and thus his hard-mouthing rhymings. (Swinburne's noisy repetitions might owe a lot to the beatings he got at Eton and from flagellant dominatrices in St John's Wood brothels, but they were different, all at once more physical, less spiritual and so less serious than what Hopkins got under God's rod.) But what is striking is how widespread is something like Hopkins's sense that poetry makes noise, not just for its own sake, but to replicate the aurality of the world, to make a realistic job of rendering the natural – that this is what poetry is about – and, more, the sense that the natural the poets feel obliged to render is so greatly hard and harsh that only a punchy consonantalism of the sort we've come to associate with Hopkins will best register it.

The *drips* of rain *drop* in the poem called 'A Tragedy: DEATH!' (in Theo Marzial's *The Gallery of Pigeons* (1873)). Marzials – the poet whom Dante Gabriel Rossetti warned against voluminousness (in my Chapter 1) – was a musician with an ear for such rain-falling, and for the onomatopoetic tradition of registering it – Milton's 'minute drops from off the eaves' (in 'Il Penseroso'), it might be. (Marzials set poems of noisy Swinburne to music – which James Joyce, another musician-poet with a good ear, liked very much.) The rain's *drop* rhymes with the very realistic *flop* and *plop* of the river Thames caused by passing barges. The poem's narrator *stands* and *starts* 'At the water that oozes up, plop and plop, / On the barges that flop'. But this repeated *plop* and *flop* of the water 'dizzy me dead'. And this dementing onomatopoetic water-effect chimes in with everything else that's miserable in this scene, all rendered in a wonderfully harsh *mélange* of rhyming consonants:

> From the shiny branches the grey drips drop,
> As they scraggle black on the thin grey sky,
> Where the black cloud rack-hackles drizzle and fly
> To the oozy waters, that lounge and flop
> On the black scrag piles, where the loose cords plop
> As the raw wind whines in the thin tree-top.

Scraggle black; black cloud rack-hackles drizzle; black scrag piles; and those punchy triplets – *grey drips drop; thin grey sky; cloud rack hackles; black*

---

[30] Williams, of course, was the member of the Anglo-Saxon recuperating CS Lewis and JRR Tolkien Inklings group who was a great one for administering beatings to his own female religious disciples.

scrag piles; *loose cords plop*; *thin tree top*: it's hard not to hear Hopkins in these rhyming groups. Surely, here's a poet, you think, who has got Hopkins in his ear. But he can't have, for Hopkins wasn't published in Marzials's time. And, lo and behold, it turns out that Hopkins – remarkably *au fait* with the contemporary poetic world – read this poem and was clearly overwhelmed by it. Well, 'astonished'.[31] Can it be that Theo Marzials, this unduly neglected Victorian poet, egged Hopkins on in his rhyming way, the way of the *perittotatos* (Robert Bridge's affectionate label for his friend – meaning 'very clever in expression, but also very excessive and odd', as Bridges explained in his Preface to his Notes in his 1918 edition), by doing as it were a Hopkins, three years before the innovative Hopkinsese of 'The Wreck of the Deutschland', four whole years before the great run of Hopkins's 1877 poems, 'God's Grandeur', 'The Windhover', 'Pied Beauty', 'Binsey Poplars', and so on? Indeed it can. Hopkins is verbally extreme, all right, but his extremism is not out of touch with other poets' verbal renderings of the harshnesses of life and the world.

Prompted by the natural misery of the too-too watery Thames, Marzials's narrator is minded to kill himself by jumping into the river; he thinks of the noise his body, any body, would make as it hit the water:

> Drop
> Dead.
> Plop, flop
> Plop.

What the hard monosyllabic onomatopoeias of Marzials' 'A Tragedy: DEATH!' pronounce is a truly profound sadness. As they do in Tennyson's *In Memoriam*, where the poet's echoing sad words of farewell to Hallam fall like slow drops of water in gloomily echoing sepulchral chambers:

> In those sad words I took farewell:
> Like echoes in sepulchral halls,
> As drop by drop the water falls
> In vaults and catacombs, they fell[.]
> (LVIII)

---

[31]   Hopkins has read 'a rondeau or rondel' by Marzials in the *Athenaeum* (23 March 1878), 'shewing an art and finish rare in English verse. This makes me the more astonished about *Flop flop*'. Is the name Marzials 'Spanish, Provençal, or what?'. Hopkins is utterly intrigued. He'd like to see a letter of Marzials. He'd quite like to meet him. Did Bridges tell him, 'or is it my fancy that Marzials looks like a Jew?' The 'rondeau or rondel' in question, densely repetitive, built on two basic rhymes, and using the words of its opening line, 'When I see you my heart sings', twice as a refrain, as rondeaux are supposed to, and celebrating this *echo*, is reproduced in the Additional Notes of *Letters* 'Volume One'. *The Letters of Gerard Manley Hopkins to Robert Bridges* [known as Volume One], ed CC Abbott (Oxford University Press, London, 1935; 2nd revised impression 1955), 49–50 (13 May 1878), 162 (26 Nov 1882), 309 (Additional Notes).

Or in the 'Spasmodic' poet Sidney Dobell's onomatopoeically noise-crammed Crimean War-time poem 'Desolate':

> From the sad eaves the drip-drop of the rain!
> The water washing at the latchel door;
> A slow step plashing by upon the moor;
> A single bleat far from the famished fold;
> The clicking of an embered hearth and cold;
> The rainy Robin tic-tac at the pane.

The last line becomes a refrain; and so does 'the drip-drop of the rain': 'And alas, alas, the drip-drop of the rain'. Here are the onomatopoeias of an English melancholy brought on by war (the poem appeared in Dobell's *England in Time of War* (1856))![32] It's a mournfulness infecting, too, the deceptively pastoral lyricism of the harvesting men in 'The Barley-Mowers' Song' of Mary Howitt (that multi-denominational Christian: Quaker, turned Unitarian, turned spiritualist follower of Robert Browning's hate-object the crooked medium Daniel Dunglas Home, turned finally Roman Catholic). Repeatedly 'blithe', Howitt's mowers sing repeatedly of whetting 'the scythe', 'the ringing scythe'. 'Rink-a-tink, rink-a-tink, rink-a-tink-a-tink!': every stanza ends with this refrain attempting to register the sound of a whetstone hitting the blade of a scythe in the act of sharpening. A sharpening scythe which turns out finally to be in the hands of death-dealing Time – 'Time's whetted scythe. / Rink-a-tink, rink-a tink, rink-a-tink-a-tink'. 'Whish – rush – whish – rush ...' goes H Cholmondeley Pennell's onomatopoetic 'The Night Mail North' (in his *From Grave to Gay* volume, 1884), building on the train-journey sound-effects in Dickens's *Dombey and Son*, and oddly anticipatory of the train-rhythms of Auden's 1930s 'Night Mail'. The mail train from London to Glasgow carries a last-minute reprieve for the man condemned for the Canongate Murder: 'A mile a minute for life or death'; will the wrong man die? And so it goes with Victorian onomatopoeia. 'Half a league, half a league, / Half a league onward': Tennyson attempts, and with some success, to make audible the drumming of the horses' hooves as the Light Brigade gallops into the jaws of Death, the mouth of Hell. Onomatopoeia's mouth is often deadly like that, reporting back from 'the jaws of Death': onomatopoetic verse sounding out deadly noises.

---

[32] Did Marzials know the song that Echo sings over the 'watrie hearse' of Narcissus in Ben Jonson's *Cynthia's Revels* (1600), Act I.sc ii: 'Woe weepes out his division, when shee sings ... / O, I could still / (Like melting snow upon some craggie hill) / Drop, drop, drop, drop, / Since natures pride is, now, a withered daffodil'? Quoting these verses in *The Figure of Echo*, 105, John Hollander suggests Eliot's 'Drip drop drip drop drop drop drop', *The Waste Land*, 358, echoes the Johnson. It's just possible Eliot is echoing the Marzials.

Stillicide

What, for his part, Thomas Hardy hears and repeats is the voices of the dead villagers now lying in Mellstock churchyard, in the wonderful elegy 'Friends Beyond' (*Wessex Poems* (1898)). These dead friends speak Wessex consonantal. 'Ye mid zell my favourite heifer, ye mid let the charlock grow', says Farmer Lodlow, 'Foul the grinterns, give up thrift.' *Grinterns*: Dorset dialect for a compartment in a granary. And the poem which hears these local tones defines them in a momentous consonantal onomatopoeia:

> They've a way of whispering to me – fellow-wight who yet abide –
> In the muted, measured note
> Of a ripple under archways, or a lone cave's stillicide.

Stillicide: arrestingly awkward in the mouth, just like *grinterns*. (You never forget, when within the sound of Hardy's poetry, his belief that artistic realism always involves distortion: 'Art is a disproportioning – (*i.e.* distorting, throwing out of proportion) – of realities, to show more clearly the features that matter in those realities'.[33]) *Stillicide* is an ancient word meaning the falling of liquid in drips or drops. In Scottish housing law it's the offence of letting rain drip from your property onto a neighbour's. In pathology it's the word for morbid drips or drops from eyes, or penis, or vagina. It's another piece of verbal treasure-trove for Hardy, the keen rummager in the dictionary's by-ways, and, of course, it's an onomatopoetic triumph. *Stillicide*: you can almost hear the steady drip (and plop) in that metaphorical lone cave: sounding the note of dead people, with echoes of transgression and pathology, as well as of, for good measure, the *suicide* that you can hear rhyming so insistently in the word's hinterland. The word that dins into your ear the awfulness it refers to.

What these onomatopoetic noise-masters are about is a recreated resounding that indeed amounts to a kind of terrorism of the ear. Their verses abound in wonderfully skilful replications of reality's sounds, which make a quite terrible noise. Read Tennyson, or Browning, or Hardy, or Hopkins with your ears, as Hopkins said you must read him, and it hurts. Listen to all that shouting, shrieking, thundering, banging, roaring, clanging, clinking – the clangour – that Tennyson, for example, characteristically goes in for: it's poetry as hammering. The poet's a hammer; he's armed with a 'rhyme-hammer':

---

[33]   Note of 5 August 1890. *The Life of Thomas Hardy, 1840–1928*, by 'Florence Emily Hardy' (actually mainly by Hardy himself) (Macmillan, London, 1962), 229. (One volume version of *The Life of Thomas Hardy*, 2 vols (Macmillan, 1933); originally *The Early Life of Thomas Hardy: 1840–1891* (Macmillan, 1928) and *The Later Years of Thomas Hardy: 1892–1928* (Macmillan, 1930).)

Wherever evil customs thicken
Break through with the hammer of iron rhyme,
Till priest-craft and king-craft sicken,
But pap-meat-pamper not the time
With the flock of the thunder-stricken.
If the world caterwaul, lay harder upon her
Till she clapperclaw no longer
Bang thy stithy stronger and stronger,
Thy rhyme-hammer *shall* have honour.

Be not fairspoken neither stammer,
Nail her, knuckle her, thou swinge-buckler!
Spare not: ribroast gaffer and gammer.
Be no shuffler, wear no muffler,
But on thine anvil hammer and hammer!
If she call out lay harder upon her,
This way and that, nail
Tagrag and bobtail,
Thy rhyme-hammer *shall* have honour.

On squire and parson, broker and banker,
Down let fall thine iron spanker,
Spare not king or duke or critic,
Dealing out cross-buttock and flanker
With thy clanging analytic!
If she call out lay harder upon her,
Stun her, stagger her,
Care not for swaggerer,
Thy rhyme-hammer *shall* have honour.

This is 'What Thor Said to the Bard Before Dinner', written in 1833 after Tennyson's hammering by the *Quarterly Review* for *Poems* 1832. And what a hard-hitting onomatopoetic rhyming flurry of self-defensive blows from a poet on the ropes! Abusive noises which are, as Tennyson well recognizes, dementing. What maddens the hero of 'Maud' is precisely the failure of what should be pleasantly pastoral noises. The garden of the poem is filled with the noise of 'rapine', of a nature that's 'red in tooth and claw': 'the sparrow speared by the shrike' (a bird whose shrieking name has 'shriek' audible in it, echoing the 'shrill-edged shriek' of the narrator's mother upon hearing of her husband's murder). Now our hero listens to the 'shipwreck-ing roar' of the tide, 'Now to the scream of a maddened beach dragged down by the wave' (I.III.98–99). 'Maud the delight of the village, the ringing joy of the Hall' is now only a memory – the sad change in her ringing remi-niscent perhaps of the skewed effect of the Christmas bells of *In Memoriam*, as ever ringing out and resounding, repeating their ringing ('from hill to hill / Answer each other in the mist'), but sorrowfully now to the narrator: no longer the 'merry bells of Yule' as Section XXVIII, so packed with rhyming phrases, has it, because of the intervening death of Hallam. And the city, the zone of modernity, gets the blame for working instrusively, like the death of Hallam, to make a terrible difference to aural experience. The village may still appear 'quiet', but actually it 'bubbles o'er like a city, with gossip, scandal and spite'. The narrator's lovely pastoral dream of Maud – 'My bird with the shining head, / My own dove with the tender eye' singing, and the woodland echoing her song and the rivulet rippling in time to her ballad (II.IV.vi) – is shattered by London's dreadful wakening noises, the threatening urban tumult:

> But there rings on a sudden a passionate cry,
> There is some one dying or dead,
> And a sullen thunder is rolled;
> For a tumult shakes the city,
> And I wake, my dream is fled.
>
> (II.IV.vii)

The city is defined by inescapable noise ('And the yellow vapours choke / The great city sounding wide: II.IV.ix) which signifies badness of many kinds. All the troubles of the poem, the death of the narrator's father, the murderous wickednesses of the men of Maud's family, the financial and commercial malpractices of the time which are ascribed to them and their kind (we're probably meant to think of them as stereotypical Jewish traders and money-men, given all the exotic and Eastern / Middle-Eastern associations they're loaded with) are linked to city evil which gets felt as dementing (once again, consonantal, onomatopoetically registered) noise – 'the hubbub of the market' (II.IV.x); 'the clamour of liars belied in the hubbub of lies' (I.IV.ix); 'idiot gabble!', 'babble … babble' (II.V.iv). It's a world of moral death, evidenced in the bad noises listed and sounding loudly in the stanza preceding the 'idiot gabble' summary: the person, 'one of us', sobbing ('No limit to his distress'); the 'lord of all things, praying / To his own great self'; the fool of a statesman 'betraying / His party-secret … to the press'; the physician 'blabbing / The case of his patient' (II.V.iii). Here's a death by dementingly bad city noises and noise-makers which the narrator imagines has overwhelmed him – in perhaps the most melancholic of the poem's many melancholic passages, reaching back into the Biblical Psalms for its imagery of grievous immolation ('De Profundis…'; 'Out of the depths…'); rehearsing the pre-apocalyptic heedlessness of the citizens before Noah's Flood, 'marrying and giving in marriage' (Matthew 24.37); reaching forward to Wilde's 'The Ballad of Reading Gaol' (in which the prisoners, and their rhymes, go round and round the prison yard, like the Londoners and their rhymes here), and to TS Eliot's preoccupation with the self as a handful of dust in a city of the walking dead (Eliot's 'The Waste Land' owes much to Tennyson, and to 'Maud' in particular):

> Dead, long dead,
> Long dead!
> And my heart is a handful of dust,
> And the wheels go over my head,
> And my bones are shaken with pain,
> For into a shallow grave they are thrust,
> Only a yard beneath the street,
> And the hooves of the horses beat, beat,
> The hoofs of the horses beat,
> Beat into my scalp and my brain,   248
> With never an end to the stream of passing feet,
> Driving, hurrying, marrying, burying,
> Clamour and rumble, and ringing and clatter,   251
> And here beneath it is all as bad,
> For I thought the dead had peace, but it is not so;
> To have no peace in the grave, is that not sad?
> But up and down and to and fro,
> Ever about me the dead men go;
> And then to hear a dead man chatter
> Is enough to drive one mad.
>
> (II.V.i)

(Getting the street-noise right took care: the manuscript has a deleted line, 'All the roar of the street', line 248; Tennyson's first version of line 251 was 'Clamour and gabble, and cackle and clatter'.) Beat, beat, beat, beat; clamour and rumble; on and on: the repeating onomatopoetic consonants and beating monosyllables; the maddening rhyme of the world, rhyming on, repeating without cease through the poem. The city affirming the narrator's country plight, repeating for him, and for us, the scared beat of his heart that we hear as he anticipates Maud coming into the garden on her ever-so light feet: 'My heart would hear her and beat, / Were it earth in an earthy bed; / My dust would hear her and beat, / Had I lain for a century dead' (I.XXII.xi).

Unpleasant in the extreme. Not that Tennyson was not eager to have pleasing noises in his poems – like other poets who would rather render the noise of the natural as a pleasure for the ear, the poet's and the reader's, as a set of what John Clare called 'Pleasant Sounds':

> The rustling of leaves under the feet in woods and under hedges. The crumping of cat-ice and snow down wood rides, narrow lanes and every street causeways. Rustling through a wood, or rather rushing while the wind hallows in the oak tops like thunder. The rustles of birds wings startled from their nests, or flying unseen into the bushes.
>   The whizzing of larger birds over head in a wood, such as crows, puddocks, buzzards, &c

The tramp of roburst [sic] wood larks on the brown leaves, and the patter of Squirrels on the green moss. The fall of an acorn on the ground, the pattering of nuts on the hazel branches, ere they fall from ripeness. The flirt of the ground-larks wing from the stubbles, how sweet such pictures on dewy mornings when the dew flashes from its brown feathers.

The peasant Clare was, in the words of Hardy's poem 'Afterwards', 'a man who used to notice such things', and with delight. 'There's music in the songs of birds / There's music in the bee / There's music in a woman's voice'. Clare's delight in the constant collusion of these musical sweetnesses was to be passed on in his own delighting and delightful replicatory words.[34] *Crumping* and *whizzing* in 'Pleasant Sounds' are wonderful onomatopoetic reproductions – and obviously pleasant members of the consonantal register. Tennyson, too, would claim, and seek to pass on, such aural pleasures. 'Now rings the woodland loud and long', as the 'happy birds' fly about in Spring, singing and piping, and the grieving Tennyson's heart revives – 'and in my breast / Spring wakens too' (*In Memoriam*, CXV). The way that the brook *murmurs* and *chatters* (especially *chatters)* in 'The Brook' is indeed lovely. Tennyson was especially proud of the onomatopoetic loveliness achieved in the pastoral song 'Come down, O maid, from yonder mountain height', loveliest of the inset poems in *The Princess* (VII, 177ff):

> and I
> Thy shepherd pipe, and sweet is every sound,
> Sweeter thy voice, but every sound is sweet;
> Myriads of rivulets hurrying through the lawn,
> The moan of doves in immemorial elms,
> And murmuring of innumerable bees.
>
> (202–207)

Tennyson was surely right to think that this song had caught the 'Idyllic feeling' of Theocritus, of ancient Greek pastoral, and, more, was 'among his most successful work' for 'simple rhythm and vowel music.' Those doves really do moan in his *moan* – especially if the vowels are extended in the way of Tennyson's Lincolnshire accent; and those two last lines really do *murmur* in the large company of rhyming *m*'s.

Vowel music is right, and lovely it is. But in how short a supply it is. One of Tennyson's greatest early fans, the psychologist Dr Robert James Mann,

---

[34] 'Pleasant Sounds' and the untitled 'There's music ...' are quoted from Volume One of the standard *Later Poems of John Clare 1837–1864*, eds Eric Robinson, David Powell, and Margaret Grainger, 2 vols (Clarendon Press, Oxford, 1984). They are, like so many of the known Clare texts, tidied-up transcripts made by WF Knight, house steward at Northampton Asylum where Clare spent the last years of his life, 1841–1864, the manuscript originals of which have disappeared.

pulling every string in his booklet *Tennyson's 'Maud' Vindicated* (1856) to defend 'Maud' against its adversaries, puts very great stress on Tennyson's 'word-painting' and 'word-music' – what Mann calls his 'sound-symbolizing' – as a key to Tennyson's power. Tennyson's 'remarkable precision and truthfulness to nature' are the 'never-failing quality of his genius'. And Mann is evidently delighted when the poem 'slides from ruggedness into exquisite smoothness' to render the narrator's temporary pastoral happiness. But strikingly, most of the word-music in Mann's – and the poet's, and our – ear is distinctly cacophonous: the *scream* of the shingle on a 'maddened beach' (which you can indeed hear, he says, on Tennyson's Isle of Wight); the filthy lane's ringing 'to the yell' of a 'trampled wife'; the 'shrill-edged shriek' of the mother in the 'shuddering night'; the thump of the narrator's heart as he hears that shriek ('And *my pulses closed their gates with a shock* as I heard'); the work of the crooked pharmacist 'as he sits / To *pestle a poisoned poison* behind his crimson lights' ('how clearly the pestle of the druggist beats – lump – lump – lump – upon the poison!').[35] And 'Ruggedness' rather has it over 'exquisite sweetness' in Tennyson's onomatopoeic excursions. The Welsh slate-quarry blasting with which his 'The Golden Year' (1846) ends is symptomatic:

> and, high above, I heard them blast
> The steep slate-quarry, and the great echo flap
> And buffet round the hills, from bluff to bluff.

This hard consonantal rhyming was 'Onomatopoeic', said Tennyson, and so it is, and wonderfully. It was true to what he'd heard in the Welsh hills: ' "Bluff to bluff" gives the echo of the blasting as I heard it from the mountain on the counter side, opposite to Snowdon'. And what the buffeting, flapping, echoing of the poem are registering is violence being done with dynamite to nature. The blasting confirms the prophet-poet speaker's extreme dyspepsia with the idea of a soon-to-arrive pastoral millennium. The Virgilian Golden Year of peace and plenty is a myth; Theocritan Idyll is unlikely to return; Welsh dynamite is sounding their death knell.

By the same sort of token, the lovely murmurings of 'Come down, O maid' are accompanied by the 'yelp' of eagles in the romantic but horrid sublimity of the Swiss Alps, whose 'monstrous ledges' spill fearful waterfalls: 'thousand wreaths of dangling water-smoke / That like a broken purpose waste in air'. Tennyson's brook *chatters* and *murmurs*, but also *bickers* and *babbles* in onomatopoeias registering consternating talk. When Tennyson revisits the old landscapes in search of reminders of the former

---

[35] Robert James Mann, *Tennyson 'Maud' Vindicated: An Explanatory Essay* (Jarrold & Sons, London, 1856), 13–17. Mann's italics.

pastorals he shared with Hallam, and finds 'no place that does not breathe / Some gracious memory of my friend', and hears 'the latest linnet trill', and again 'the whispering reed' and 'the runlet tinkling from the rock', it's only characteristic that he (and we) should also hear 'the wrangling daw' (*In Memoriam*, C). Tennyson wanted his return to be an emphatically auditory event – the *tinkling* runlet was originally only a *sparkling* one – and to make a very strong auditory contrast (*wrangling* replaced an earlier *jangling*: the mere noise would acquire an aggressive moral content). And Tennyson *passes away* from the scene, mimicking Hallam's passing away, making that death happen all over again: 'And, leaving these, to pass away, / I think once more he seems to die'. Pastoral delight never keeps grief and sadness at bay; the pleasant sounds of the Tennysonian garden never remain unencroached on for long by unpleasant ones. And even so it is with Clare.

Clare's bean field yields a sweet fragrance as its blossoms are trodden on by passing feet. But this is how the *battered footpaths* of his poem 'The Bean Field' get created. And batterings never fail to hurt – even when caused by the 'bright' but 'battering sandal' of Felix Randal's great (Christ-like?) drayhorse in Hopkins's 'Felix Randal'. The *crumping* of Clare's 'Pleasant Sounds' fails to entirely keep out the sound of heavy artillery; the wind *hallows* like *thunder*, threatening rain. And who would be trampled under foot (even by wood larks), or flirted with (even by ground-larks)? And what price the *pattering* of hazel nuts, embraced as that is by two menacing occurrences of *fall*. 'The hurly-burly wind' 'Whirls the wheat about' repetitively in Clare's 'Song', and 'The billows swab behind / And the headaches scrail without.' *Swab*, mop up, as in the nautical 'swab the decks'. *Headaches* are wild poppies with a sickly smell. *Scrail* isn't known to the Oxford English Dictionary, but it's close in sound to dialect *screigh*, to screech or shriek, and neighbour of *scream*, *screak*, *skrike*, *screed* (tear up), *scrash* (crash), *scrat*, *scraw* (clearing the throat noisily) – a list Hopkins did not make, but could have. To *scrail* sounds as nasty as the adjacent *swab*. This is the vocabulary of a fallen Eden.

There's always some sort of fall going on in these gardens, and a disagreeably noisy one. The 'splendour' indeed 'falls', and loudly so. As in one more of the astonishing inset poems of *The Princess*, 'The splendour falls on castle walls', whose refrain returns, echoingly, with variants (as natural echoes return), but always with a repeated insistence on echoic death, on the echo as a persistence, but also a dying:

> Blow, bugle, blow, set the wild echoes flying,
> And answer, echoes, answer, dying, dying, dying.[36]

---

[36]   Tennyson was compelled, he said, by the fading echoes of a bugle he heard at Killarney in Ireland: 'eight distinct echoes'. This poem is subject of yet one more of John Hollander's

'And Echo there, whatever is asked her, answers "Death"': it's Echo's only work amid the blood-dabbled pastoral that *Maud* opens with. The discordant echoes of rhyming.

Unsmoothing

For his part, discordant notes are Robert Browning's *métier*, his *forte*, and, of course, the grounds of a widespread rejection by posh critics, the arrayed ranks of aesthetic smoothies. Browning's verse is patently not the product of a smooth man. If Hopkins's poems make a hard mouthful, Browning's are even harder in the mouth, even more punchily consonantal. His rhymings are unremittingly rock hard. This verse growls and grunts and grinds and girds, on and on, in its truly cacophonous way, as Browning gives voice, again and again, to his uncouth speakers, the ones whose tones he just loves to assume. 'Gr-r-r – you swine!' The speaker of 'Soliloquy of a Spanish Cloister' (in the *Dramatic Lyrics*, 1842) has the unwavering downright forcefulness his author relishes. 'What's the Greek name for Swine's Snout?' Here there will be no soft-tongued lexis. And the vocal roughness and toughness are clearly the audible aspect of Browning's realist subject. He is keeping faith with the uncouth noises of the world, which means above all keeping faith with its uncouthest talkers. He will put them on record, and do so with the matching vocal harshness his poems never stop revelling in. The voice, it might be, of the litigants in *The Ring and the Book* (1868–1869), who 'wrangled, brangled, jangled'. You never heard 'More noise by word of mouth than you hear now' – hear now in the poem (*The Ring and the Book*, I.241–244). Those janglers are as bad-mouthy, it would seem, as Browning himself, who, according to Gladstone's daughter Mary, 'talks everybody down with his dreadful voice, and places his person in such disagreeable proximity with yours and puffs and blows and spits in yr face'[37] – an unconscious verbal offending, no doubt, but matched by the deliberate sort Browning could give vent to. Spitting in Edward FitzGerald's face for expressing relief that Elizabeth Barrett was dead ('no more Aurora Leighs, thank God!'), would be, Browning wrote, too good for him ('Surely to spit there glorifies your face – / Spitting – from lips once sanctified by Hers').[38]

---

bravura treatments, in *The Figure of Echo: A Mode of Allusion in Milton And After* (University of California Press, Berkeley, Los Angeles, and London, 1981), 129–132.

[37] Mary Gladstone, 9 March 1877, *Her Letters and Diaries*, ed Lucy Marserman (1930), 116–117.

[38] 'To Edward FitzGerald', in the *Athenaeum* (13 July 1889): prompted by accidentally coming across the late Edward FitzGerald's awful remarks in the *Letters and Remains of Edward FitzGerald* (1889). FitzGerald died in 1883. Five and a bit months after writing the squib on 8 July 1889 Browning was dead, 12 December 1889. Some have thought his end was hastened by this upset.

Browning spat. He often belabours his enemies, and enemies of his wife, with offensive mouth-weaponry. He relishes doing such words; his own and other people's.[39] Like the voice of murderous Guido's lawyer in *The Ring and the Book*, who 'Wheezes out law and whiffles Latin forth'. Guido 'inchoates', that is begins, 'the argument', but with a full sense of inchoate as *making chaos*. This 'Procurator of the Poor' makes noisy rhetorical chaos:

> Sprinkling each flower [of rhetoric] appropriate to the time,
> – Ovidian quip or Ciceronian crank,
> A-bubble in the larynx while he laughs,
> As he had fritters deep down frying there.

> (I.1151–1161)

You hear that chuckling larynx, the bubbling voice of the lawyer, which is, at the same time, the voice of the poem, the voice of this wonderfully ventriloquial poet – as you hear the deep-frying fritters that his larynx work is likened to. Deep-fried fritters; deep-fried words. Here, in triumph, are the vocal rhymings, the keen onomatopoeias of a very down-to-earth naturalism, the wonderfully coarse realism of a potently rough mouth. A realism of voice and the voiced thing and person that the posh and the bourgeois did not take at all kindly to.

Notoriously in 1864 Walter Bagehot attacked Browning's verse as 'grotesque'. Wordsworth was 'pure', Poet Laureate Tennyson is 'ornate', but Browning, exemplified especially by his *Dramatis Personae* volume of that year, is grotesque. Browning is a 'great author', Bagehot allows, and his poems are 'a sort of quarry of ideas, but ... in such a jagged, ugly, useless shape that [one] can hardly bear them.' This is a 'defect, partly of subject, partly of style'. Browning has 'a taste for ugly reality'. He's too realistic; voices a too 'grotesque realism'. The poem 'Caliban upon Setebos' is, characteristically, not only *difficult*, but *unpleasant*. And it's no excuse to say that 'grotesque objects exist in real life, and therefore they ought to be, at least may be, described in art. ... though pleasure is not the end of poetry, pleasing is a condition of poetry. An exceptional monstrosity of horrid ugliness cannot be made pleasing ... .' And so on.[40] Swinburne's sadistic thought around the same time (referred to in Chapter 1) was that Browning's 'discord' – 'these audible syllables which do hiss and grind, clash and shriek', 'mere inarticulations jerked up by painful fits out of the noisy verbal whirlpools of a clamorous chaos',

---

[39]   The words Danny Karlin writes about so well in his *Browning's Hatreds* (Clarendon Press, Oxford, 1993).

[40]   Walter Bagehot, 'Wordsworth, Tennyson, and Browning; or Pure, Ornate, and Grotesque Art in English Poetry', *The National Review* (Nov 1864). *Collected Works of Walter Bagehot*, ed N St John Stevas, 8 vols (The Economist, London, 1965): *Literary Essays* (2 vols), I.318–366.

'shrieks groans ... gasps ... moans' – sounded like someone trying to talk after his tongue had been cut out and managing to communicate only 'by a select use of gutturals and labials.'[41] The same critical tune was played by Oscar Wilde in the long run-up to the charge of 'monstrous music' referred to earlier. Wilde, too, thinks Browning is great but

> he despised language ... Rhyme, that exquisite echo which in the Muse's hollow hill creates and answers its own voice; rhyme, which in the hands of the real artists becomes not merely a material element of metrical beauty, but a spiritual element of thought and passion also, waking a new mood, it may be, or stirring a fresh train of ideas, or opening by mere sweetness and suggestion of sound some golden door at which the Imagination itself had knocked in vain; rhyme, which can turn man's utterance to the speech of gods; rhyme, the one chord we have added to the Greek lyre, became in Robert Browning's hands a grotesque, misshapen thing, which at times made him masquerade in poetry as a low comedian ... There are moments when he wounds us by monstrous music....[42]

Hopkins himself chimed in with this charge in a letter to this old schoolmaster, the poet and Canon of the Church of England, RW Dixon:

> he has got a great deal of what came in with Kingsley and the Broad Church school, a way of talking (and making his people talk) with the air and spirit of a man bouncing up from table with his mouth full of bread and cheese and saying that he meant to stand no blasted nonsense ... all a kind of munch ... a frigid bluster ... not really a poet ... has all the gifts but the one needful and the pearls without the string; rather one should say raw nuggets and rough diamonds.[43]

Browning's tone is all wrong. What he lacks, according to Wilde of Magdalen, Oxford, and Swinburne and Hopkins of Balliol (and Dixon of Pembroke, Oxford), is what Matthew Arnold (also of Balliol) called 'the tone of the centre'.[44] The boy from the social margins of South London, not posh, not a gentleman, not part of any establishment, especially the Established Church of England, excluded as a Nonconformist from the Anglican preserves of

---

41   'The Chaotic School', circa 1863–1864, published in *New Writings by Swinburne*, ed Cecil Y Lang (964), 40–60. Extracts in *Browning:The Critical Heritage* eds Boyd Litzinger and Donald Smalley (Routledge & Kegan Paul, London, 1970), 214–218.
42   'The Critic as Artist', *Nineteenth Century* (July and September 1890); collected in *Intentions* (James R Osgood McIlvaine & Co, London, 1891).
43   Letter to RW Dixon (12 October 1881), *The Correspondence of Gerard Manley Hopkins and RW Dixon*, ed CC Abbott (1955), 74–75.
44   Matthew Arnold, attacking (once more) the 'provincial spirit' for its lack of 'graciousness', of 'urbanity, the tone of the city, of the centre', in 'The Literary Influence of Academies', *Essays in Criticism* (Macmillan, London, 1865; 3rd edn, revised and enlarged, 1875), 77.

Oxford and Cambridge, is thus, on the reckoning of the Oxford Boys, not educated at all, because he's not privy to the tradition, the classics, of that system, and so lacks the tonal refinement that is assumed to come with that territory. Not one of Arnold's gang of the 'cultured', the non-'provincial', Anglican, Oxford and Cambridge, anti-liberal 'centre'. Dixon thought the poems of Browning's *Dramatic Idyls* ('monstrous name') were 'very bad'. They didn't scan. He found 'every kind of monstrosity' in *The Ring and the Book*. All because Browning was 'not thoroughly educated':

> he had not taken poetry at the highest point at which it had been left by others, and was, as it were, off the track.[45]

It is no accident at all that the poet and critic who approved of Browning as breathing a 'sanative', 'bracing', 'breath of new life' into 'modern verse' with 'the strongest rhymes on record' and a love of 'a gnarly character, or a knotty problem' (nicely catching the Browning tone with that 'gnarly'), should have been the autodidact proletarian poet Gerald Massey.[46]

The Arnoldian criticism going on here is precisely what was to come from TS Eliot in the notorious *After Strange Gods: A Primer in Modern Heresy* (1933), which excludes Thomas Hardy and DH Lawrence from the ranks of the aesthetically orthodox (Hardy who never went to any university and broke with the Anglican orthodoxy, he grew up in; Lawrence the Congregationalist, 'uneducated' because he was only a graduate of University College, Nottingham). It is shocking that Walter Bagehot, scion of an old Unitarian family who thus only went to University College, London, the Nonconformist University (the one Browning briefly attended), should share in the chorus of Establishment disapproval. It's arresting that noisy Hopkins should be able to separate his own grinding and girding from Browning's merely on snobbish grounds, a classist resistance to the other man's alleged vulgarity, his lack of table-manners. (Being vulgar, a man of the crowd, is, apparently, alright with Hopkins if you're one of the big Scandinavian sailors he so admired on the streets of Liverpool, or his big parishioner the Blacksmith 'Felix Randal', or the lovely bugler-boy of 'The Bugler's First Communion', but not if you should attempt to write poems in what Hopkins has ruled out of court as an ear- and good manners-offending demotic.) Utterly interesting, too, is how this line of discrimination allowed Tennyson's gruff notes not to hurt the polite ear – his Lincolnshire growl, his particular beat of hard realistic onomatopoeia getting tuned out by dint, it would

[45]   RW Dixon, Letter to Hopkins, *Correspondence*, edn cit, 70.
[46]   *Quarterly Review* (July 1865). Quoted in *Browning: the Critical Heritage* (1970), 270–272.

appear, of his Establishment position as Laureate, his Anglican orthodoxy and the classicism he absorbed at Trinity College, Cambridge. Hopkins can complain to Dixon that Tennyson's opinions 'sink into vulgarity', that *Locksley Hall, Maud, Aylmer's Field* and *The Princess* each make 'an ungentlemanly row', that the *Idylls* are 'trumpery charades from the Middle Ages', and that Tennyson's 'later works' have been carried away with the 'dissumulation' of the Browning-Kingsley munchers (*Lady Clara Vere de Vere* is 'pure haberdasher': 'coarse' like *The Ring and The Book*, which Hopkins has had to stop reading). But still 'at his best', Tennyson is divine, as in the inspired *In Memoriam, The Lady of Shalott, Sir Galahad, The Dream of Fair Women* and *The Palace of Art* ('when he is rhyming pure and simple imagination'). He's 'a glorious poet', 'one of our greatest poets', 'chryselephantine' (that's a precious metal); 'each verse a work of art, no botchy places ... no ... low-toned ones, no drab, no brown-holland' (drab and brown holland were cheap cloths for making cheap clothes).[47] Everything is forgivable to a real gentleman and scholar of Trinity, Cambridge.

And of course Browning was very low-toned and full of drab and brown-holland, the textures and textuality of very low *Stoff* – busily eschewing, in a combination of inclination and necessity, anything like a Tennysonian subject or style. Browning was scraping around in the pages of his father's encyclopedias and art-history books for the contingent pleasures provided by out-of-the-way persons and voices from the margins of Europe and history and culture, while Tennyson was processing his fictions from the books of the great tradition, from Homer and Dante and their sort. 'This low-pulsed forthright craftsman's hand of mine' is Browning's boast through the mouth of Andrea del Sarto ('Andrea del Sarto', 82): 'The better the uncouther', Browning thinks, rhyming *uncouther* with 'Grand rough old Martin Luther' (in 'The Twins'), to get his tradition of Protestant, Nonconformist, radical demoticism clear in his antagonists' mind and ear. Browning liked recalling Biblical Moses, with his 'Right-arm's rod-sweep, tongue's imperial fiat' ('One Word More', stanza X), getting water by striking the rock 'awkwardly' (*Sordello*, III.826–827) – a very effective awkwardness, even if it cost Moses the Promised Land.

But for the likes of Hopkins and Dixon and Wilde (and Arnold), some truths and traditions, some realisms, some voices, were evidently less acceptable than others, even if the poetic noises conveying them could in practice have their similarities. The question of what was really real was at stake. Revealingly, Hopkins blamed Browning's 'munch', his 'raw nuggets and rough diamonds' on his poems' Balzacian detailism – what Dixon had labelled as *The Ring and The Book*'s 'impotent collection of particulars': 'a

---

[47] Letters to Dixon, 27 February 1879 and 12 October 1881, *Correspondence*, edn cit, 24–25, 74–75.

pointless photograph of life, such as I remember in Balzac, minute upholstery description'.[48] Hopkins might well have been thinking of George Henry Lewes's robust denigration of the '*detailism*' (his italics) of contemporary painting and literature: a 'Realism' focussing on a subject's waistcoat and the upholstery of the chair he sits in rather than on the tragedy in his face.[49] This was an attack aimed as much as anything at the practice of Lewes' life-partner George Eliot's novels. How differently she felt is very clear from her review of the third volume of Ruskin's *Modern Painters* (in the *Westminster Review*, April 1856):

> The truth of infinite value that he [Ruskin] teaches is *realism* – the doctrine that all truth and beauty are to be attained by a humble and faithful study of nature, and not by substituting vague forms, bred by imagination on the mists of feeling, in place of definite, substantial reality ... Very correct singing of very fine music will avail little without a *voice* that can thrill the audience and take possession of their souls. Now, Mr Ruskin has a voice.[50]

George Eliot, setting herself up at this time to become the period's most effective voice of realism, of the humble realism the gentlemen critics deplored in Browning, might well have been thinking of Browning, whose *Men and Women* volume she had reviewed only three months earlier in January 1856. Certainly, Mr Browning has a voice; he speaks in and dramatizes the unsmooth, even harsh tones the gents dislike. In *Men and Women* there is no 'melodious commonplace, but freshness, originality, sometimes eccentricity of expression ... dramatic inclination ... the underground stream of thought that jets out in elliptical and pithy verse ... genius ... nothing sickly or dreamy in him ... a clear eye, a vigorous grasp, and courage to utter what he sees and handles ... robust energy ... rough piquancy ... keen glance ... dramatic painting ... no soothing strains'. George Eliot singles out for lengthy quotation 'Fra Lippo Lippi', the dramatic monologue of the low-tongued, fleshly-minded outsider artist-monk, child of the gutter, bred on 'Refuse and rubbish', now a wonderfully realist painter and a briskly no-nonsense talker:

> While sharing the wine with which he makes amends to the Dogberrys [the local constabulary who have stopped him, out late] for the roughness of his tongue, he pours forth the story of his life and his art with the racy conversational vigour of a brawny genius under the influence of the Care-dispeller.[51]

---

[48]   Hopkins's letter of 12 October 1881 replies to Dixon's of 11 October, accusing *The Ring and The Book* of 'the impatient *remaking* of particulars'.

[49]   'The Principles of Success in Literature', Ch 3, 'Of Vision in Art', *Fortnightly Review*, I (July 15 1865), 562–589.

[50]   George Eliot, *Selected Essays, Poems and Other Writings*, eds AS Byatt and Nicholas Warren (Penguin, Harmondsworth, 1990), 368–369.

[51]   *Selected Essays* (1990), 349–357.

The *Care-dispeller* must be Lippi's wine: George Eliot imagines him as a big strong uncouth workman out on the booze, with lingo to match. For her he's the kind of rough male character Hopkins is excited by in life and in poetry – soldier, ploughman, farrier, tramp – but who is never allowed to speak in any of Hopkins's poems, his voice being, as Canon Dixon would aver, too ungentlemanly for the halls of verse. But for George Eliot the 'conversational vigour of a brawny genius' is the essence of an approvable truth-telling, and good in its very rough-mouthedness. This outsider-critic from the English Midlands, not posh, renegade from evangelical Anglican Christianity, herself excluded form Oxford and Cambridge as a woman, was here evincing the critical-theoretical assumptions which would within months be inspiring her beginning career as the leading provincial novelist of the day. Browning was her kind of writer. No gentlemanly critical criteria coming from the established social and critical centre would put her off him. Nor, happily, would they deter her great successor as fictionist, the Dorset 'autodidact' Thomas Hardy, neither in his novels nor his poems. Compromising with the 'tone of the centre' was not Hardy's style – even though pressure to do so was so strong it made Hardy's fellow Dorset poet (and philologist) William Barnes issue his verses in two kinds – local Dorset dialect in the *Dorset County Chronicle* and *Poems of Rural Life in the Dorset Dialect* (1844 and 1862) and *Hwomely Rhymes* (1859), and standard English in *Poems, Partly of Rural Life (In National English)* (1846) and *Poems of Rural Life in Common English* (1868).

Barnes's Dorset dialect poems are made of a vocabulary full of the 'pure and simple Saxon features' Barnes advertises in his prefatory 'Dissertation on the Dorset Dialect of the English Language' in the 1844 volume, a vocabulary notably hard, consonantal, and greatly monosyllabic. It chimes away harshly in the hard-rhyming consonantal groups that Hardy praised in his Preface to his Barnes *Selection* of 1906, as 'kindred lippings' – itself a lovely awkward consonantal rhyming phrase quite in the spirit of what Hardy was celebrating.

> Ees, the girt elem tree out in the little huome groun'
> Wer a-stannen this marnen, an' now's a-cut down.
> Aye, the girt elem so big roun' an' so high,
> Where the mowers did goo to ther drink, an' did lie
> A-yeazen ther lims, var a zultery hour.
> When the zun did strick down wi' his girtest o' pow'r.
> Wher the hâymiakers put up ther picks an' ther riakes,
> An' did squot down to snabble ther cheese an' ther kiakes,
> An' did vill vrom ther flaggons ther cups wi' ther yale,
> An' did miake therzelves merry wi' joke an' wi' tiale.

That's the first stanza of 'Vellen the Tree' (in the *Dorset County Chronicle*, 14 June 1840, and Barnes's 1844 volume). *Ees, yeazen, snabble, yale (yes, easing, gobble, ale*): as with so much of the volume's vocabulary, the standard English speaker has to consult the glossary Barnes appended to the 1844 book. Alien semantics, alien rhyming sounds, from an alien language pot, for alien activities. Genteel readers did not 'squot down to snabble ther cheese an' ther kiakes', nor talk like that.

> Here oonce did sound sweet words, a-spoke
> In wind that swum
> Where ivy clomb,
> About the ribby woak;
> An' still the words, though now a-gone,
> Be dear to me, that linger on.
>
> . . . .
>
> O ashèn poles, a sheenèn tall!
> You be too young
> To have a-sprung
> In days when I wer small;
> But you, broad woak, wi' ribby rind,
> Wer here so long as I can mind.

That's Barnes's 'The Vield Path' from the *Dorset County Chronicle*, 26 December 1867. *Spoke, wind, swum, clomb, ribby, rind*: sharp, rocky, noisy little vocables, hard in the mouth and on the ear of the non-dialect speaker, who wouldn't find their sounds 'sweet', and greatly smoothed out in the 'Common English' version, 'The Field Path' in Barnes's 1868 volume. It sounds a gentler tune, in softer tones.

> Here sounded words of dear old folk,
> Of this dear ground
> Where ivy wound
> About this ribbèd oak.
> And still their words, their words now gone
> Are dear to me that linger on.
>
> . . . .
>
> These ashen poles that shine so tall
> Are still too young
> To have upsrung
> In days when I was small;
> But you stout oak, you, oak so stout
> Were here when my first moon ran out.

Ribby survives in *ribbèd*, *wind* in *wound*, *spoke* in *folk*; but there's no *swum*, *clomb* or *rind*. 'But you stout oak, you, oak so stout' is a merely clichéed replacement for 'But you, broad woak, wi' ribby rind': a conventionalism only confirmed by the repeated half-rhyme of *you stout oak*: *you, oak so stout*. Not at all so strong as the strong front-rhyming of *ribby rind*. And how much weaker is open-vowelled *oak* than the consonantalized *woak*. And, of course, as is so often the way when poets are stuck for a rhyme word they did not want in the first place, the line ending in the 'Common English' version *oak so stout* gets a truly silly answering rhyme-line: 'Were here when my first moon ran out'. Only someone desperate for a rhyme would make the end of his first month of life a significant date and describe it in such a far-fetched way as 'when my first moon ran out'. In English of any kind, money, and time, and patience run out; but not not moons. That is simply daft. Like the loss of the old 'kindred lippings', it's enough make your patience run out. What a relief – and what a gain for poetic force – that Thomas Hardy never heeded the genteelling linguistic pressures of the Oxford Boys and their kind. And that, thankfully, Robert Browning didn't either.[52]

[52]   The handiest place to find Barnes's dialect poems and compare the Standard English versions is in the *Selected Poems of William Barnes*, ed Andrew Motion (Penguin, Harmondsworth, 1994).

4

These Rhyming/Repeating Games Are Serious

The Victorian poets' love of rhyming-games such as the Rossettis' *bouts-rimés* well indicates the basic poetic attraction of mere repeated noise, despite the patent perils of it in of writing merely nonsense. '[C]lever things of their kind', said William Michael Rossetti of his and his brother's dashed-off *bouts-rimés* sonnets, 'But ... a mere tour de force ... slapdash at a moment's notice'.[1] Tennyson and Browning, reports Hallam Tennyson,

> would laugh heartily together at Browning's faculty for absurd and abstruse rhymes. I remember a dinner where Jebb, Miss Thackeray, and Browning were present. Browning said he thought he could make a rhyme for every word in the English language. We gave him 'rhinoceros'. Without a pause he said:
>
> > O, if you should see a rhinoceros
> > And a tree be in sight,
> > Climb quick, for his might
> > Is a match for the Gods, he can toss Eros.[2]

(Getting a rhyme can be 'hard', said Browning on another occasion, in an early letter to Elizabeth Barrett, unless you're prepared to use the odd 'foolish phrase'.[3]) But rhyming for its own sake doesn't drive the verse along only in poetic games or merely kiddy stuff, whether of the traditional nursery rhyme

---

[1] *The Works of Dante Gabriel Rossetti*, ed with Preface and Notes, by William M Rossetti, revised and enlarged (Ellis, London, 1911), Note p673. William Michael collected fourteen of these sonnets in the volume's 'Juvenilia and Grotesques' section, ibid., 263–237.
[2] Hallam Tennyson's *Memoir*, II. 230.
[3] *Letters of Robert Browning and Elizabeth Barrett Barrett*, I.29.

Victorian Poetry Now: Poets, Poems, Poetics, First Edition. Valentine Cunningham.
© 2011 Valentine Cunningham. Published 2011 by Blackwell Publishing Ltd.

kind, or in the modern pseudo-Nursery rhymes, the limericks, and so forth, which the Victorians, and we, know as Nonsense. Christina G Rossetti's 'Goblin Market' (written April 1859, published in *Goblin Market* (1862)) is a very grown-up and serious poem that's a case of rather extreme rhyming, much of it for its own mere sake. What a good illustration it is of the sheer propelling power of mere verbal repetition, of the memorable, anaphoric attractions of the accidentally rhyming cluster, the mere accumulating energy of the rhyming list, with ordinary semantics and regular logic left to follow as they may a long way behind. The poem is in many places plainly far less interested in what follows logically in the sequences of words than in what follows simply by way of noise possibility. With uncanny effect, no doubt: the uncanniness of new, estranged logics, even the unsettling logics, as Freud would have it, of the textuality of dreams and nightmares. Effects that are not at all consciously sought, being results of the poet's raw echolalic indulgence – though critics have, of course, rightly pondered, Freudian-style, their unconscious, sexually repressed hintings.

> Laughed every goblin
> When they spied her peeping:
> Came towards her hobbling,
> Flying, running, leaping,
> Puffing and blowing,
> Chuckling, clapping, crowing,
> Clucking and gobbling,
> Mopping and mowing,
> Full of airs and graces,
> Pulling wry faces,
> Demure grimaces,
> Cat-like and rat-like,
> Ratel- and wombat-like,
> Snail-paced in a hurry,
> Parrot-voiced and whistler,
> Helter-skelter, hurry skurry,
> Chattering like magpies,
> Fluttering like pigeons,
> Gliding like fishes, –
> Hugged and kissed her:
> Squeezed and caressed her:
> Stretched up their dishes,
> Panniers, and plates:
> 'Look at our apples
> Russet and dun,
> Bob at our cherries,
> Bite at our peaches,
> Citrons and dates,

> Grapes for the asking,
> Pears red with basking
> Out in the sun,
> Plums on their twigs;
> Pluck them and suck them,
> Pomegranates, figs.
> (329–362)[4]

This is helter skelter, hurrying scurrying, Christina G. An utterly compelling
Victorian version of the Tudor Skeltonic – the nonce-rhyming poetry of the
early Renaissance poet whom Robert Graves dubbed 'Helter-skelter' John
Skelton.[5] Plums don't grow on twigs, but *twigs* certainly rhymes attractively
with *figs*. What's *mopping and mowing*? *Mopping* was a rare old word
meaning, apparently, grimacing; and *mowing* meant something similar.
They got paired up at the beginning of Victoria's reign, it would seem, less
for their sense repetition, than for the noise their rhyming made. And the
rhyme, as soon as instated, became unforgettable; Christina Rossetti couldn't
forget it; and the English language has never been able to forget it since she
gave it such publicity. But the sense didn't matter to start with; only the
rhyme did. That a kind of sense soon kicked in, so that the pairing *mop and
mow* got into the language as something more or less understood (Oscar
Wilde deploys it in 'The Ballad of Reading Gaol', line 295, of the 'crooked
shapes of Terror' haunting the Gaol on the night before his fellow-convict's
execution: 'With mop and mow, we saw them go' – confidently glossed as
'grimaces' by Wilde's latest editor[6]) is not in the first place relevant. The mere
rhyming is the immediate thing. 'This thing, that thing is the rage, / Helter-
skelter runs the age', was Tennyson's annoyed thought about the critics of
1832 and their heaped up varieties of objections to his poems, as he puts it
in his poem 'Poets and Critics'. And the headlong rush of this thing, that
thing, is what comprises the helter-skelter of Miss Rossetti's poem. Except
that it's an array, in the first place, of merely verbal thises and thats. Here,

---

[4]   Quoted, like all the Christina G poems in my discussions, from *The Complete Poems*, ed
RW Crump, with Notes and Introduction by Betty S Flowers (Penguin Books, Harmondsworth,
2001).
[5]   In a lovely tribute poem 'John Skelton' in *Fairies and Fusiliers* (1917), affectionately parodying
the Skeltonic – 'thoroughly irresponsible & delightful jingles' Graves told Siegfried Sassoon – and
perhaps not incidentally pastiching the 'Goblin Market' mode: 'What could be dafter / Than John
Skelton's laughter? ... But oh, Colin Clout! / How his pen flies about, / Twiddling and turning, /
Scorching and burning, / Thrusting and thrumming, / How it hurries with humming, / Leaping and
running, / At the tipsy-topsy tunning / Of Mistress Eleanor Rumming! ... But angrily, wittily. /
Tenderly, prettily, / Laughingly, learnedly, / Sadly, madly, / Helter-skelter John / Rhymes serenely
on, / As English poets should. / Old John you do me good'.
[6]   *Complete Poetry*, ed Isobel Murray (Oxford World's Classics, Oxford University Press,
Oxford, 1997), Notes, p205.

should one ever be in doubt about the possibility, is the actuality of Saussurean verbal *difference* without *reference*.[7] It can be no accident that *-ing* words are crowding in so densely here: the good old gerundive essence of *fuzzy*. Verbal gobbling (*Gobbling* Market) as delicious incoherence.

But when the rhymes are in the driving seat, as here, across and between Rossetti's lines, and all across her poem, the poetic vehicle can be felt drifting alarmingly all over the road. The semantic Highway Code, so to say, makes itself felt as counter-presence to the desiderata, as it were, of the word-music. A criticism implied by Christina G's great admirer and imitator George MacDonald in that passage in his 'Goblin Market' *hommage* novel *The Princess and the Goblin* (1872), where the boy Curdie is attacked by goblins and tries fending them off with an insulting 'rhyme' in something close to Rossetti's helter-skeltering:

> Ten, twenty, thirty –
> You're all so very dirty!
> Twenty, thirty, forty –
> You're all so thick and snorty!
>
> Thirty, forty, fifty –
> You're all so puff-and-snifty!
> Forty, fifty, sixty –
> Beast and man so mixty!
>
> Fifty, sixty, seventy –
> Mixty, maxty, leaventy!
> Sixty, seventy, eighty –
> All your cheeks so slaty!
>
> Seventy, eighty, ninety,
> All your hands so flinty!
> Eighty, ninety, hundred,
> Altogether dundred!

It's a rhyme which initially works by taking them aback, setting their teeth on edge (as it might do any hearer or repeater of these grating words). 'The goblins fell back a little when he began, and made horrible grimaces all through the rhyme, as if eating something so disagreeable that it set their teeth on edge and gave them the creeps'. But the power of the words quickly flags, perhaps, the narrative suggests, because 'the rhyming words were

---

[7]   The point about the nonce-rhyming effect made by that wonderful rhymester Ira Gershwin in 'I Love to rhyme': 'I love to rhyme, / Mountaineers love to climb, / Criminals love to crime, / But I love to rhyme. // I love to say / Gay, day, may, hey, hey! /Chuckle, knuckle, nickel, fickle, pickle! / I love to rhyme! // Variety, society, propriety, /There's no stopping when you've begun; / Capacity, veracity, audacity, / Did you ever know such fun?'

most of them no words at all, for, a new rhyme being considered the more efficacious, Curdie had made it on the spur of the moment'.[8] Driving a poem only by nonce rhyming is, clearly, a risky recipe.

And it is indeed the rhyming that frequently drives Christina G's poems, and many another Victorian poem, if not always so extravagantly as in her case. And in particular it's the line-driving force of end-rhymes that's commonly in place. What characteristically animates Dante Gabriel Rossetti as he wrestles with a passage of his poem 'Ave', about the sea sighing like sorrowful sleep at the time of the impregnation of the Blessed Virgin Mary by the Holy Ghost and the announcement of this to her, the 'Annunciation', is not just how to describe that sorrow – *heavy? human? ancient?* – but how to find a rhyme for *sleep* at the end of a line. He's not satisfied with any of his attempts. He needs 'one comprehensive line of some sort rhyming to *sleep.*' What does William Michael think? The end-rhyme-word will command the line. It often did, for Rossetti, as for many a poet before and since. And being commanded by the rhyming led easily, if not to actual nonsense, at least to deficiencies of sense.

> the sea
> Sighed further off eternally
> As human sorrow sighs in sleep.
> Then suddenly the awe grew deep [.]
> (20–23)[9]

That's what the Rossettis came up with in 'Ave', and it's simply terrible. The rhyme *deep* for *sleep* is sound enough, if rather desperately conventional and lazy, but its arrival compelled the poet to cast about for something that's deep or that might become deep in the rest of the line. The *sea* is already present; he'd like something else. In any case it would be redundant, if the sea were kept as subject, to remind us that it can be deep (we don't need a poem to tell us that). And it would be rather unusual to have the sea *growing suddenly* deep: the sea can be suddenly deep (there might be a rocky shelf falling suddenly away), but *growing* implies gradual rather than sudden change. So something else is called for. Rossetti settles for *awe* – and, to be sure, to the Christian mind the Annunciation is an aweing event. But there was no thought of awe in the narrative and the poem before this, its

---

[8]   'Curdie's Clue', Ch XVIII, *The Princess and the Goblin*: first published in *Good Words for the Young*, ed MacDonald, 3 (Nov 1870–June 1871); in book form (Strahan & Co., London, 1872); *The Princess and the Goblin and the Princess and the Curdie*, ed and intro Roderick McGillis (World's Classics, Oxford University Press, Oxford and NY, 1990).

[9]   Quoted from the *Collected Poetry and Prose*, ed Jerome McGann, the doyen of Rossetti editors (Yale University Press, New Haven and London, 2003), which has very useful notes, and is the collection I mainly use.

presence is new, so how can it be said to *grow*? Growth is only enjoyed by things already in existence. What's more the problem of the contradiction implied in sudden growth remains. And has anyone else ever thought of *awe* having depth (or shallowness): *awe* is not something with depths (or shallows). The line sticks out as simply daft – a daftness promoted by a rhyme-first practice.[10] And easily parodied – as Robert Buchanan showed in the nicely comic part of his otherwise nasty assault on Rossetti and Swinburne in his 'Fleshly Feelings' (with which Chapter 7 below, opens), where he claims that the Pre-Raphaelites take up the rhyming burden with senseless and irrelevant 'burthens', repeated rhyming groups at the ends of lines and stanzas, which has them speaking the English of 'raving madmen'. Without naming their titles, he guns for a couple of heavily end-rhymed pastiche Border Ballads, Rossetti's forty-two stanzas long dialogue poem 'Sister Helen', with its repeated refrain invoking 'Mother, Mary Mother' and something or another 'between Hell and Heaven' (a poem Buchanan had probably read Swinburne as admiring[11]), and Swinburne's 'The King's Daughter', fourteen four-line stanzas, regularly end-rhyming, with the second and fourth lines always describing something or another 'in the mill-water' and offering something or another 'for the king's daughter'. The suggestion is that these incremental repetitions add nothing to any meaning, commanded as they are by mere repetivity. Buchanan quotes Rossetti's first verse (sic):

> 'Why did you melt your waxen man,
>   Sister Helen?
> To-day is the third since you began.
> The time was long, yet the time ran,
>   Little brother.
>   (*O mother, Mary mother,*
> *Three days to-day between Heaven and Hell.*)'

And travesties it rigid. 'This burthen is repeated, with little or no alteration, through thirty-four verses, and might with as much music, and far more point, run as follows:

> 'Why did you melt your waxen man,
>   Sister Helen?
> To-day is the third since you began.
> The time was long, yet the time ran,
>   Little brother.

[10]   DGR to William Michael Rossetti, 27 August 1869, *Letters of Dante Gabriel Rossetti*, eds Oswald Doughty and Robert Wahl, II, 1861–1870 (Clarendon Press, Oxford, 1965), 723–724.
[11]   1870 essay, collected in Swinburne's *Essays and Studies* (Chatto & Windus, London, 1875), 86.

> (*O Mr Dante Rossetti,*
> *What stuff is this about Heaven and Hell?*)'

(Buchanan's point about empty repeated rhyming would have been sharper still if he had got Rossetti's end-rhyming 'Hell and Heaven' the right way around. Still, the 'thirty-four verses' works as a good joke about too much.) As for Swinburne's 'The King's Daughter', its 'burthen' is 'about as much to the point' as Rossetti's, and to prove this Buchanan pastiches it with a couple of utterly nonsensical second and fourth lines: he's quoting from memory, he says, and so is 'not quite certain of the words', but they're 'quite as expressive' as the original, and 'something to the following effect':

> 'We were three maidens in the green corn,
> *Hey chickaleerie, the red cock and gray,*
> Fairer maidens were never born,
> *One o'clock, two o'clock, off and away.*'

'Productions of this sort are "silly sooth" in good earnest, though they delight some newspaper critics of the day, and are copied by young gentlemen with animal faculties morbidly developed by too much tobacco and too little exercise'.[12]

Did You Ever Know Such Fun?

What Buchanan was jeering at was the way poets knuckled under to the felt demand for rhyme, especially end-rhymes, however patently silly, or just empty, the result might be. Of course the propensity for comedy in such linguistic silliness was exploited again and again by the comic writers, as Buchanan is exploiting it to make his readers laugh. Daft rhymes, rhyming nonsense, are the stock-in-trade of the many comic Victorian verses and versifiers. Edward Lear and Lewis Carroll, Thomas Hood, WS Gilbert, and the rest, including any old producer of those multiplying rhyme-dominated verses known as limericks: they all rely for their amusement value precisely on absurd rhyming, the delighting shock of unexpected verbal collocations, some verbal-doubling zaniness.

> There's a combative Artist named Whistler
> Who is, like his own hog-hairs, a bristler:
> A tube of white lead
> And a punch on the head
> Offer varied attractions to Whistler.

[12] 'Thomas Maitland', 'The Fleshly School of Poetry: Mr DG Rossetti', *The Contemporary Review*, XVIII (October 1871), 348–349.

(Not any old limerick producer here, in fact, but Dante Gabriel Rossetti, a dab hand at the comic rhyme, as the numerous limericks in the Uncollected section of Jerome McGann's *Collected Poetry and Prose* amply reveal.)

> Then a sentimental passion of a vegetable fashion must excite your languid spleen,
> An attachment *à la* Plato for a bashful young potato, or a not-too-French French bean!

That's a representative couple of astonishingly inventive rhyming lines from the song of the Fleshly Poet Bunthorne in the comic opera *Patience* (1881) by comic-rhyming master WS Gilbert, whose *Bab Ballads* (several series) and Savoy Operas are built on an unstoppable torrent of such wonderfully sharp rhyming nonsense. Rather like Thomas Hood's huge rhyme-steeped out-put, whose comic-rhyming virtuosity he can, however, turn to sharply serious critical use. Which, as it happens, keeps occurring even at the daftest rhyming moments. After all, Rossetti is making rather serious points about Whistler the bristler, and Gilbert's satire of Victorian aesthetes is in fact hitting them seriously hard. Bunthorne's self-image hinges on a pair of rhyming labels. Bunthorne would be thought a 'Francesca di Rimini, miminy, piminy / *Je-ne-sais quoi* young man', and 'A greenery-yallery, Grosvenor Gallery / Foot-in-the-grave young man'. *Greenery-yallery* is a characteristic Gilbertian invention, a nonce-rhyming couplet, a bit of pleasantly meaningless rhyming noise. It's modelled on, and rhymes with, the attractive older bit of rhyming nonsense *miminy-piminy* which went back to the rich parvenue Miss Alscrip in the 1786 satirical play *The Heiress* by General John Burgoyne, advised by Lady Emily to acquire a fashionable 'paphian mimp' by sitting in front of her mirror and repeating the nonce-rhyming phrase 'nimini primini'. She, though, can only stutter a poor babelic version, multiplying the rhyming babelically as she goes: 'Nimini-pimini-imini, mimini – oh it's delightfully enfantine'. Nonsense upon nonsense in the vain effort to acquire an affected 'cast of the lips', the so-called 'paphian mimp' – whose meaning is only guessable-at (*paphian* means prostitute, and *mimp*, well, something pretentious you do with your lips). *Greenery-yallery* is a pretty empty but nicely sounding rhyming jingle, built on a long back-story, a linguistic *mise en abîme*, of rhyming nonsense, there to suggest in verbal practice, and with a certain satirical relish, the empty verbalism of the Aesthetic Movement. Miminy piminy, *je ne sais quoi* indeed. But how quickly *greenery-yallery* entered the English language as a meaningful label for affectedness and over-refinement – just as *miminy piminy* and *mimping* had earlier done. The Oxford English Dictionary sounds pretty firm about them all, even whilst announcing their etymological murks. Clearly the language, and language users, cannot stand a meaning vacuum for long; we're really desperate to fill up the empty semantic spaces we so enjoy rhyming-nonsense sounding out for us, eagerly gleaning seeming meanings from contexts – which it is the way of contexts, of course, to yield.

Hood's serio-comic rhyming lesson comes in a cod anonymous letter to his own *Comic Annual* of 1832. Ace-rhymster Hood turns the tables in effect on himself as he mocks the popular taste for end-rhyme (which his own verses busily pander to), especially the notion that poems without rhyme are not poems at all. He upbraids the people who dislike 'blank verse' because its lines lack 'that harmony which makes the close of one line chime with the end of another'. To help them he offers 'A Plan for Writing Blank Verse in Rhyme' – illustrated by 'A Nocturnal Sketch', which transforms the standard 'heroic' iambic pentameter 'blank verse' line by means of silly multiple end-rhymes:

> Even is come; and from the dark Park, hark,
> The signal of the setting sun – one gun!
> And six is sounding from the chime, prime time
> To go and see the Drury-Lane Dane slain, –
> Or hear Othello's jealous doubt spout out, –
> Or Macbeth raving at that shade-made blade,
> Denying to his clutch much touch ...

In a follow-up letter headed 'Rhyme and Reason', one John Dryden Grubb, that is Hood himself again, meditates on the (clearly very real) problem of finding apt end-rhymes.

> The great difficulty in verse is avowedly the Rhyme ... The merest versifer that ever attempted a Valentine must have met with this Orson, some untameable savage syllable that refused to chime in with society. For instance, what poetical Fox-hunter – a contributor to the Sporting Magazine – has not drawn all the covers of Beynard, Ceynard, Deynard, Feynard, Geynard, Heynard, Keynard, Leynard, Meynard, Neynard, Peynard, Queynard, to find a rhyme for Reynard?

The previous correspondent's end-rhyming model hasn't helped; it certainly hasn't caught on in 'the literary world'. Grubb's scheme 'to obviate this hardship' is to 'take the bull by the horns' and *begin* with the rhymes, 'in short, to try at first what words will chime, before you go further and fare worse'. He illustrates with 'The Double Knock', lovely farcical verses about a young woman sending her maid downstairs to answer the door-knocker and admit what she hopes is an admirer:

> Rat-tat it went upon the lion's chin;
> 'That hat, I know it!' cried the joyful girl;
> 'Summer's it is, I know him by his knock;

Comers like him are welcome as the day!
Lizzy! go down and open the street-door;
Busy I am to any one but *him*.
Know him you must – he has been often here;
Show him upstairs, and tell him I'm alone'.[13]

Beginning, like this, with the rhymes, says Grubb, will at least 'correct the erroneous notion of the would-be poets and poetesses of the present day, that the great *end* of poetry is rhyme.' But it would take more than Hood's whimsical pastiches to drive out the impression. The end-rhyme urge would be obeyed, however silly the results. Even if it meant resorting to that good old crib for verse-makers, the rhyming dictionary.

FT Palgrave, editor of the famous and influential *Golden Treasury of the Best Songs and Lyrical Poems in the English Language* (1861), and for many years Tennyson's dog-like follower, once asked Tennyson whether he ever used a rhyming dictionary. 'He had tried in earlier days', Tennyson owned up, 'but found it of little use: "There was no natural congruity between the rhymes alphabetically grouped together".'[14] So, immature poets, as TS Eliot might have put it, use rhyming dictionaries, and mature poets all make up their own rhymes as they go along? Not quite. Of course Tennyson made considerable use of John Walker's *Rhyming Dictionary* (1800) as a youthful poet. But he dropped the habit only slowly – if at all. His sharp reply to the critical John Wilson ('Christopher North') in 'To Christopher North' – Crusty, Rusty, Musty, Fusty Christopher – used a run of pejorative rhymes selected from Walker's long entry under *Dusty*. And that was written in 1832, after the not terribly juvenile 1832 volume's poems, 'The Lady of Shalott', 'The Palace of Art', and the rest. When Tennyson mocked the incongruous associations set up by the rhyming dictionary's groupings in the little poem 'The Skipping-Rope' inscribed at the end of his copy of John Walker's *Rhyming Dictionary* (1800), it was with affection as well as the mere bravura of a word-gamer showing what he could do with the randomness of Walker's rhyming list under *ope*:

Sure never yet the Antelope
Could skip so lightly by.
Stand off, or else my skipping-rope
Will hit you in the eye.
How lightly whirls the skipping-rope!

[13]   There is no modern edition of the works of this enormously popular Victorian. I'm quoting from my copy of the once popular 'Lansdowne Poets' edition – you used to find them in every jumble sale – of *The Poetical Works of Thomas Hood, Reprinted from Early Editions, With Memoir, Explanatory Notes, &c* (Frederick Warne and Co., London, nd), 436–438; 448–450.
[14]   'Personal Recollections by FT Palgrave (including Some Criticisms By Tennyson). 1849–1892)', Hallam Tennyson's *Memoir*, II. 496.

How fairy-like you fly!
Go, get you gone, you muse and mope –
I hate that silly sigh.
Nay, dearest, teach me how to hope,
Or tell me how to die.
There, take it, take my skipping rope,
And hang yourself thereby.

Nonsense Not Nonsensical Though

It is silly, of course; as childish as any of that great Victorian invention, the light verse we know as Nonsense – pleasing rhyming nonsense made for kiddies with their perennial love of nonce words and incongruous rhymes. But this is a poem of 1836, and published in Tennyson's very serious and mature 1842 volume, with no indication that it is not be taken seriously. And, plainly, it can't be taken as just a *plaisanterie*; just as, plainly, neither can the great comic-rhyming greenery-yallery merchants of the period, the Hoods and Gilberts and the rest. 'The Skipping-Rope' itself skips terribly briskly, this apparent bit of playful bantering with the random resources of the Rhyming Dictionary, right across the border of playfulness into a dark place where the poet want to learn how to die, and the skipping-rope turns into a noose that he, and/or the child (depending upon who is thought to be addressing whom) can go and hang themselves with. As if there's a potential in the lovely contagious exhilarations of the poet's, and his Rhyme Book's, mere rhyming, not just for extra-verbal meaning as such (the general miminy piminy, greenery-yallery effect), but for a particularly nightmarish awfulness of signification. There's a terrible sense here that the mere play of signifiers is already an uncanny potentia of frightening signifieds and referents.[15] How easily, one might reflect, does Christina Rossetti's mopping and mowing end up in the Wildean nightmare of Reading Gaol: that place, and its poem, which are a nightmare of rhyming, of repetitiousness. Round and round go the rhymes in 'The Ballad of Reading Gaol', repeatedly repeating, returning incrementally in the high rhyming manner of the ancient border ballads that Wilde is imitating. And round and round go the prisoners. Wilde's endlessly repeating rhymes – small and great, words, phrases, lines, stanzas – are the echoic verbal equivalents of the repetitious circularity of the prison day, of its inmates' repetitious life.

---

[15]   Matthew Rowlinson makes (almost) proper play, in his discussion of 'The Skipping-Rope', with what he thinks, in a Freudain/Lacanian/Derrideanized way, of the sexual tension and anxieties implicit in the differential displacement of rhyming: in 'The Place of Voice', Ch 2 of *Tennyson's Fixations: Psychoanalysis and the Topics of the Early Poetry* (University Press of Virginia, Charlottesville and London, 1994), 60–62.

We rubbed the doors, and scrubbed the floors,
And cleaned the shining rails:
And, rank by rank, we soaped the plank,
And clattered with the pails.

We sewed the sacks, we broke the stones,
We turned the dusty drill:
We banged the tins, and bawled the hymns,
And sweated on the mill.

(219–226)

'Round and round' the exercise yard go the prisoners, repeatedly, in that phrase which gets repeated, like all the poem's rhymings, round and round. The yard is named, repeatedly, as 'the ring' (it rhymes, horribly, with 'swing', the word for hanging). And thus what Swinburne called the 'ring of rhyme' loudly announces prison reality, rings the note of the prison exercise ring. So the poem is thus a large ring, or prison-like container, of rhyme, about its subject the prison ring. A story of moral and physical rotting, the prisoners in their enclosing ring, the body of the hanged-man rotting in its quicklime vest in his prison grave, announced, like everything else in the poem, in an act of rhyming – 'we rot and rot' (599). So Wilde's rhymings, his repetitions, have their meanings beyond the mere noise-level. There's nothing redundant, nothing non-sensical in these rhymings. Nor is there in what might seem the most patently nonsensical, the most obviously non-referential, there-for-its-own-mere-verbal-sake rhyming mode of the period, namely Nonsense.

'Nonsense' poetry, best practised in the poems of Lewis Carroll and Edward Lear, does of course keep sounding like a practice of merely verbal stuff. Edward Lear's 'Twenty-Six Nonsense Rhymes and Pictures' (subset of his *More Nonsense, Pictures, Rhymes, Botany, Etc* volume of 1872), for instance, are an abecadarium, an A to Z, of verses, and creatures, existing only by courtesy of word-stuff, the alphabet, all of them entirely creatures of the alphabet which has sponsored not only them themselves but their attached alliterative, that is rhymed, attributes and doings. Like 'The Perpendicular Purple Polly', or 'The Visibly Vicious Vulture / Who wrote some Verses to a Veal-cutlet in a / Volume bound in Vellum'. The poems in Carroll's *Alice's Adventures in Wonderland* (1865) are mainly pastiche, commanded by the deftly punning, that is half-rhyming, substitution of new, in many cases dafter, words for the old sensible ones. 'Twinkle, twinkle, little star, / How I wonder what you are! / Up above the world so high, / Like a diamond in the sky', ran Jane Taylor's 'The Star' (in her *Rhymes for the Nursery*, 1806). The Mad Hatter gives Alice 'Twinkle, twinkle, little bat! How I wonder what you're at! / Up above the world you fly, / Like a tea-tray in the sky'. At the core of this poeticity is Carroll's 'Jabberwocky', the poem

Alice finds in *Through the Looking-Glass and What Alice Found There* (1871) and has to read in a mirror because it's printed in reverse.

> 'Twas brillig, and the slithy toves
> Did gyre and gimble in the wabe:
> All mimsy were the borogoves,
> And the mome raths outgrabe.

This characteristically echoic opening stanza of Carroll's, a great jumble of repeating consonants, is repeated intact as the poem's last verse. The two gatherings of rhyming signifiers with their truly enigmatic signifieds – *slithy toves*: *borogoves* – echo their mere echoings. The heavy consonantalism, all those b's, g's, and m's, is not unreminiscent of the consonantal Anglo-Saxon verse that so entranced Gerard Hopkins – and indeed these lines started life in 1855 in Carroll's last home-made family magazine, the *Mischmasch*, as a 'Stanza of Anglo-Saxon Poetry', written out in pseudo-runic lettering.[16] What Carroll was keener still to advertise was his poem's heavy investment in *portmanteau words*, explained by Humpty Dumpty to Alice as 'two meanings packed up into one' – but actually in the first place two separate phonemic sets, two sets of different sonics, combined: *slithy* made out of 'lithe and slimy', *mimsy* out of 'flimsy and miserable' – nonce doublings that make a kind of phonic pun, a pair of words forced to rhyme, jammed into one, each parasitic, as rhymes always are, on the other (*parasite*: radio interference, in French). And they're very noisy doublings – Dumpty explains *outgrabe* as related to *outgribing*, 'something between bellowing and whistling, with a kind of sneeze in the middle'; in the *Mischmash* explanation it's 'connected with the old verb to GRIKE or SHRIKE, from which are derived "shriek" and "creak"' – which are the stage-setting for the double-named Jubjub bird and the Tumtum tree. And out of this nonce-rhyming jabber of 'Jabberwocky' comes the word-play gaming of 'The Hunting of the Snark'. Here, again, come the 'frumious Bandersnatch' and the 'beamish boy', in an enigmatic chase registered in a welter of repeated 'Jabberwocky' gibberish – *uffish, galumphing, outgrabe, mimsiest*. 'The Hunting of the Snark' stars a rhyming cast of B-Men – Bellman, Barrister, Banker, Baker, Butcher, a Beaver, a Billiard-marker, a Boots, 'A Maker of Bonnets and Hoods' – in a hunt for the mysterious Boojum. Here's more Lear-like extremist alphabeticist rhyming. And lots and lots of the poem's verbal material gets repeated like those alliterative B's (and the abnormally large number of ordinary b-words scattered like verbal confetti through the text). This poem keeps saying it again – as the Bellman and the Baker do:

---

[16] In *The Rectory Umbrella; and Mischmasch*, with Foreword by Florence Milner (Cassell, London, 1932). All the Lear, in *The Complete Nonsense and Other Verse*, ed. Vivien Noakes (Penguin, Harmondsworth, 2002).

'It is this, it is this –' 'We have had that before!'
The Bellman indignantly said.
And the Baker replied 'Let me say it once more.
It is this, it is this that I dread!'
(Fit the Third. The Baker's Tale, 45–48)

One repeated stanza makes six appearances (and is echoed in a seventh):

They sought it with thimbles, they sought it with care;
They pursued it with forks and hope;
They threatened its life with a railway-share;
They charmed it with smiles and soap.

This is a self-cancelling jumble of possible and improbable. Hunting with care, pursuing with hope, charming your victim with smiles are all likely and plausible; pursuing with forks would be a waste of time, charming with soap unlikely, and hunting with thimbles ridiculous (a comical prospect not helped by knowing that Carroll seems to have had an obsession with thimbles). A railway-share is a non-life-threatening piece of paper. These are empty words, on paper as empty (in body-harming weapon terms) as a share-certificate – empty pairings, empty rhymes: *sought it with thimbles: sought it with hope*; *forks and hope: smiles and soap*. Emptinesses multiplied by six – or seven. And $0 \times X = (\text{still})\ 0$. Emptinesses affirmed by the end of the hunt as the Baker (unnameable now, known only as Thingumbob) is heard crying that he's found the Snark, which he's discovered to be a Boojum (except that the party only hears 'Boo-' with '-jum' only a passing breeze); and he has disappeared, like the Snark / Boojum, 'In the midst of the word he was trying to say'. The poem ends 'For the Snark *was* a Boojum, you see'. Which seems to offer the non-reference of those names as the reason for their being able to vanish with the Baker: empty words come and go, they're just air. (A reading affirmed by Carroll's airy confession that the poem began when that meaningless last line came to him ('I knew not what it meant, then; I know not what it means now'), that he gradually built the poem around an it whose meaning he still didn't know. It's not an allegory, has no hidden moral, is not a political satire.[17]) The Bellman's blank map, one showing all sea and no land, seems peculiarly revealing. The crew likes this map which signifies nothing, which doesn't refer, because, as they say, conventional cartographical markings, 'Mercator's North Poles and Equators, / Tropics, Zones, and Meridian Lines', are 'merely conventional signs' (Fit the Second. The Bellman's

---

[17]   Carroll, ' "Alice" on the Stage', *The Theatre* (April, 1887); 'A Wonderland Miscellany', in *The Works of Lewis Carroll*, ed. Roger Lancelyn Green (Hamlyn, Feltham, 1965), 235–236.

Speech, 5–12). Conventional signs: arbitrary signs, as Saussure called them, to the excitement of modernist linguists and critics. One way or another we're being told that these words, these rhymes refer, not, in the first place, to the world, but to themselves only; and the poet knows it, as do the poem's eager (post)modernist critics ('Nonsense, like gibberish, is a violence practiced on semantics').[18] And this self-reference is the assumed prerogative of Nonsense. And it's exemplary for poetry as such, as it is for Victorian poetry in particular.

But, of course, this story, Nonsense's nonsense story, of what poetry, what rhyming, are up to is, manifestly, not all. What's striking about Dumpty's explanations of 'Jabberwocky' is how he packs meanings into the poem's plainly non-sensical words. The doubled self-rhyming sonics of the portmanteau words can indeed, as he says, also carry a doubled semantic: *slithy* can be plausibly thought of as simultaneously meaning *lithe* and *slimy;* and so forth. Some of Dumpty's meanings are indeed arbitrary – *toves* 'are something like badgers – they're something like lizards – and they're something like corkscrews' – to make us aware, no doubt, of the mere conventionality of signs. But what's striking is the high density of threat, menace, pain and suffering implicit in this set as explicated by Dumpty, and Carroll. *Gimble* is to bore holes in things like a gimlet; *mimsy* is miserable as well as flimsy; it doesn't take much of a Freudian to know what part of the male anatomy is often both lithe and slimy. *Frumious,* Carroll explained in his Preface to 'The Hunting of the Snark', is a blend of fuming and furious. These doublets are as hurtful as the doubling rhyming action of the beamish boy's killing and beheading of the Jabbberwock.

> One, two! One, two! And through and through
> The vorpal blade went snicker-snack!
> He left it dead, and with its head
> He went galumphing back.

One two; one two; through and through; snicker-snack. The rhymes of Victorian Nonsense enthusiastically share the taste for the violent and macabre that's usual in 'nursery rhymes'. Darkness is highly visible like this through the apparent silly rhymings of Victorian Nonsense. There's not

---

[18]   Michael Holquist, 'What is a Boojum? Nonsense and Modernism', *Yale French Studies*, no. 43, *The Child's Part* (1969), 145–164; no. 96, *50 Years of Yale French Studies: A Commemorative Anthology, Part 1: 1948–1979* (1999), 114. The best account of Victorian Nonsense is Jean-Jacques Lecercle, *Philosophy of Nonsense: The Intuitions of Victorian Nonsense Literature* (Routledge, London and New York, 1994), which not only compellingly discusses the linguisticity of Jabberwocky, and such, but places it in contemporary linguistic-philosophical context, as well as indicating how it uncannily anticipates so much of modernist and post-modernist linguistics.

much truly laughable in Lear's *Laughable Lyrics*. And their murks are deepened rather than lightened by the apparent domestication, the familiarity of so many of the offered doings. Edward Lear's Wasp 'stood on a Table, and played sweetly on a / Flute with a Morning Cap', but he's still 'The Worrying Whizzing Wasp'. The Vulture may write his Verses to a Veal-cutlet in a Volume bound in Vellum, as any gentleman-poet might; but he's still 'The Visibly Vicious Vulture'. The Dolomphious Duck needs her dinner, but dines off lovely 'Spotted Frogs'.

The Frogs are harmless creatures which the Duck catches in a *runcible* spoon. *Runcible*: it's Lear's favourite adjective. It echoes, repeatingly, across his oeuvre. The Dolomphious Duck's alphabetical companion in the 1872 *More Nonsense* volume is 'The Rural Runcible Raven'. The eponymous Owl and Pussy-cat, who 'went to sea in a beautiful pea-green boat', 'dined on mince and slices of quince, / Which they ate with a runcible spoon' (in *Nonsense Songs, Stories, Botany, and Alphabet*s, 1871). The Pobble who has no toes and swims the Bristol Channel (in *Laughable Lyrics: A Fourth Book of Nonsense poems, Songs, Botany, Music Etc*,1876) is thought by passing sailors to be fishing 'for his Aunt Jobiska's / Runcible Cat with crimson whiskers'. In the same volume's 'Mr and Mrs Discobolos', the Discobolos sisters are labelled 'a runcible goose' by their terrible father before he tries to kill them all by dynamiting an 'ancient runcible wall'. In the Prefatory poem to the 1888 edition of *Nonsense Songs and Stories* Lear casts himself as the 'pleasant' Mr Lear whose 'body is perfectly spherical' and who 'weareth a runcible hat'. And what *runcible*, this teasing signifier whose identity as a piece of mere alphabeticism was loudly announced in 1872, might mean, has remained teasingly elusive. A pickle fork with three tines, one of which is very sharp and curved like a spoon, got itself jokily named as a *runcible spoon* in the early twentieth century. The great lexicographer Eric Partridge speculated that *runcible* suggested a blend of Roncevaux and fencible, something defendable, hence the sharp edge of the pickle fork, and perhaps of Lear's top hat 'with a sharp rim'.[19] The Trinity College, Cambridge philosopher John McTaggart deduced that *runcible* meant *tortoiseshell*, on the grounds that tortoiseshell was the only adjective applicable to both spoons and cats. This specifying was easily dismissed by TS Eliot in his 1950 'The Aims of Education' lectures: even a well-known eccentric like Edward Lear was unlikely to have worn a tortoiseshell *hat*. But Eliot intended more in what he called his 'Notes Towards the Definition of Runcibility', or 'McTaggart Refuted'. He wanted to advertise 'the wobbliness of words', the way words (like *culture* and *education*) resisted limitation to one sense. And especially a nonce word like *runcible* – spoon, cat, goose, wall, hat. As Eliot

[19] See TS Eliot's discussion in *To Criticize the Critic, And Other Writings* (Faber & Faber, 1978), 63–67.

says, *runcible* is more multivalent than a portmanteau word made of two semantically recognizable bits. This sign is patently arbitrary, and in its utter guessability, its utter openness to the reader's feelings, is the acme of Nonsense's semantic vagueness, its merely suggestive noisiness. And yet, as ever hereabouts, the contexts of its occurrence do keep feeding us with strong suggestions of the terrible. The runcibility of the wall portends murderous death; the runcible cat is drowned and dead, and not to be fished up by the Pobble with no toes and the nose that can't get warm even with the aid of a piece of scarlet flannel; the poet in the runcible hat with the 'remarkably big' nose weeps and weeps, and is jeered at by children as 'that crazy old Englishman'. Which portendings of awfulness were rightly rightly picked up in twentieth-century tradings in *runcible*: in Agatha Runcible, Jazz Age anti-heroine of Evelyn Waugh's *Vile Bodies* (1930), her body smashed up in a racing-car accident; and in Runcieballs, the satirical magazine *Private Eye*'s mocking version of onetime Archbishop of Canterbury, Lord Runcie. 'Long ago', says Lear of himself the 'runcible hat' wearer, 'he was one of the singers, / But now he is one of the dumbs'. Lear was awfully eloquent about dumbness – eloquently dumb: like *runcible*, whose terrible readability stands for the way these mere rhymes, these mere nonsensical noisinesses, belie the mere verbalism they pronounce.

How Rhymes Have Their Reasons Beyond The Merely Aural

Nonsense, sharpest case of poetry's noisy blankness, stands sharply for the way that the rhyming of poems can actually create meanings, conveying plenitudes of meaning beyond just the aural ones. Take, for example, the way Thomas Hood, the period's most obsessive and daftest punster, turns his mock-epic celebration of Miss Kilmansegg and her artificial golden leg, *Miss Kilmansegg and Her Precious Leg*, into a critique of the dehumanizing acquisitiveness and greed of Victorian money culture, worthy of anything by Dickens, by working with, not against, the grain of what might seem mere heaps of rhyming words present primarily for the sound.[20] The poem's long riff on *double*, for instance, which appears when rich Miss Kilmansegg (with her prosthetic leg of solid gold) marries her crooked suitor, the fortune-hunting bogus Count, making a couple, or double, and leading to a great and in many ways greatly silly list of double things – Swans in *Swan Lake*, dahlias, rainbows, coats (double-breasted), doors, windows, pipes,

[20] *Miss Kilmansegg and Her Precious Leg: A Golden Legend*, first published in *New Monthly Magazine* (1841); in book form, with 60 illustrations by Thomas S Seccombe, engraved by F Joubert (E Moxon, Son & Co., London, 1870).

barrels, locks, teeth, chins (chins become double through 'chucking'). A relentlessly punning list, as ever with Hood (double Wisdom teeth: double wisdom): the doubling of the pun layered onto the mere doubledness of the term. But, as you soon realize, this massive doubling is pointing to the large moral and immoral doubling going forward: the suitor doubling as the aristocratic he isn't; *double-crossing* his wife (that 19thc term for cheating on a gambling partner), whom he murders for her gold, beating her to death with her golden leg, an event doubling as the suicide the Jury decides her death is, the leg a single piece of metal, not jointed, let alone double-jointed. Further, and most tellingly, this repeated doubling is made the occasion for a defence by our relentlessly punning, verbal-doubling author, of double meanings (lines 1881–1882). Though critics might 'take offence', 'A double meaning shows double sense': a doubling manifest in the massive doubling the poet is currently going in for. 'There's a double sweetness in double rhymes'. It's no accident, I think, that Tennyson seems to have been as keen on reciting Hood's poems as he was on his own. Keener, in fact, on the occasion of taking his son Hallam to Marlborough College, in 1866, when he was readier to read four poems out of Hood's *Whims and Oddities* volume than his own 'The Grandmother' and 'The Northern Farmer' – namely, Hood's 'Faithless Nelly Gray', 'Faithless Sally Brown', 'Tim Turpin' and 'Ben Battle'. 'He explained the play on words to Mdlle. [sic; Stapps, a Belgian governess] who was "excessivement enchantée." He laughed till the tears came at some things he read'.[21]

The *sweetness* of doubling, of rhyming: multiple sweetness in the case of helter-skeltering 'Goblin Market' – the sweet pleasures purchased from the awful goblin men by Christina G Rossetti's 'sweet-tooth Laura' with a lock of her golden hair; pleasures brought home to us in her repeated sucking of the forbidden fruit, and the repetition of the word for it:

> She clipped a precious golden lock,
> She dropped a tear more rare than pearl,
> Then sucked their fruit globes fair or red:
> Sweeter than honey from the rock,
> Stronger than man-rejoicing wine,
> Clearer than water flowed that juice;
> She never tasted such before,
> How should it cloy with length of use?
> She sucked and sucked and sucked the more
> Fruits which that unknown orchard bore;
> She sucked until her lips were sore[.]
>
> (126–136)

[21]   *Miss Kilmansegg*, 'Her Honeymoon', Moxon edn, 119–120. Hallam, *Memoir*, II 37.

Gobbling Laura *sucked, sucked, sucked and sucked and sucked.* The repetition makes what the poem knows as an *iterated jingle.* ' "Come buy, come buy" ' is the repetitious sales-pitch of the 'brisk fruit-merchant men' – their 'iterated jingle / Of sugar-baited words' (232–234). The *sucked* run is one of those potentially self-emptying verbal sequences the poem knows so well, but it is one that's also full of terrible consequence for Laura, sucking and sucking her own damnation (like one of St Paul's Corinthian Christians, 'eating and drinking damnation to themselves', as they turn sacramental meals into occasions for gormandizing, I Corinthians 11.29). This very desirous Eve is utterly overpowered by bodily cravings, the need for oral-erotic satisfaction, for the transgressive 'sweets of sin' (as Joyce calls them in *Ulysses*). There's certainly no mere jingling here.[22] At least, that's a charge that Christina G, this compulsive repeater ('Dissi e ridissi con perenne sete, / E lo ridico e vo'ridirlo ancora, / Qual usignol che canta e si ripete / Fino all'aurora'[23]) is not at all willing to take, so to say, lying down. As, momentously, in her 'Winter: My Secret' (in the *Goblin Market and Other Poems* volume of 1862).

The repetitivity of this characteristically rhyme-driven Rossetti poem takes it very close to the Nonsense ways of 'Goblin Market'. In fact it was originally entitled 'Nonsense'. And what it wants to know is whether its agreed Nonsense ways actually amount to nonsense.

> I tell my secret? No indeed, not I:
> Perhaps some day, who knows?
> But not today; it froze, and blows, and snows,
> And you're too curious: fie!
> You want to hear it? well:
> Only, my secret's mine, and I won't tell.
>
> Or, after all, perhaps there's none:
> Suppose there is no secret after all,

[22]   Mary Wilson Carpenter is good on female sexuality and edibility in 'Goblin Market': ' "Eat Me, Drink Me, Love Me"; The Consumable Female Body in Christina Rossetti's Goblin Market', *Victorian Poetry* 29 (1991), 415–435. Reprinted in the useful *Victorian Women Poets*, ed and intro Tess Conslett (Longman Critical Readers, London and New York), 1996. Christina G's repetivity is, of course, frequently noted and lauded – as in Isobel Armstrong's 'A Music of Thine Own' chapter in her *Victorian Poetry: Poetry, Poetics and Politics* (1993), referred to in my Ch.2 above; and by, e.g. Steven Connor in his sharp piece, ' "Speaking Likenesses": Language and Repetition in Christina Rossetti's "Goblin Market" ', *Victorian Poetry* 22, iv (Winter 1984), 439–448 – but without enough thought given to the way repetitions make meanings beyond merely aural ones.

[23]   'Ripetizione' [Repetition]: 'I said it [the word *when*] and said it again with perpetual thirst./ And I say it and I still want to say it again, / Like a nightingale that sings and repeats itself/ Until the dawn'. One of the sequence of 21 poems of unhappy love in Italian addressed to her quondam suitor Charles Cayley, secreted in her desk-drawers, never translated by her and not published in her lifetime. English translation by Betty S Flowers in the *Complete Poems*, ed RW Crump (Penguin, edn cit), 1153.

But only just my fun.
Today's a nipping day, a biting day;
In which one wants a shawl,
A veil, a cloak, and other wraps:
I cannot ope to every one who taps,
And let the draughts come whistling thro' my hall;
Come bounding and surrounding me,
Come buffeting, astounding me,
Nipping and clipping through my wraps and all.
I wear my mask for warmth: who ever shows
His nose to Russian snows
To be pecked at by every wind that blows?
You would not peck? I thank you for good will,
Believe, but leave that truth untested still.

Spring's an expansive time: yet I don't trust
March with its peck of dust,
Nor April with its rainbow-crowned brief showers,
Nor even May, whose flowers
One frost may wither thro' sunless hours.

Perhaps some languid summer day,
When drowsy birds sing less and less,
And golden fruit is ripening to excess,
If there's not too much sun nor too much cloud,
And the warm wind is neither still nor loud,
Perhaps my secret I may say,
Or you may guess.

The poem's own question is whether its hectic practice of rhyme – repeating, echoing, doubling and redoubling, saying things twice over, and more than twice over – has a content. Is there something secreted in there, or is it all *just my fun*: an amusing but emptily rattling run of *froze, blows, snows; bounding, surrounding, astounding; nipping* and *clipping; showers, lowers, hours*? Is the poem, this repetition machine, mere verbal repetition, or more than just that? Is it like that hugely nonsensical, nonce-rhyming nursery rhyme which it invokes, 'Peter Piper picked a peck of pickled peppers';[24] or is there more? Well, yes there is. For this is a poem about the poet and her readers. Rossetti thanks the reader who would desist from pecking, that is biting, her nose – which is what critics (*every wind that blows*) do to any nose the poet might show to *Russian snows*. Poets endure icy wintry conditions and cool

---

[24]   Peter Piper picked a peck of pickled peppers;
     A peck of pickled peppers Peter Piper picked.
     If Peter Piper picked a peck of pickled peppers,
     Where's the peck of pickled peppers Peter Piper picked?

eceptions. And Spring's conditions aren't much better. When March comes this poet gets a 'peck of dust' up the nose she shows to the public. A peck: a great quantity (a quarter of a bushel, nearly ten kilos worth), admittedly of dust, but still a whole peck. The doubling of *peck* (a tripling, if *pecked* is included) affirms the menace and threat coming from the sensitive poet's exposure to the world. Under their shadow, the terrorizing offered by the gerunds – *nipping, bounding, buffeting, nipping, clipping* – comes pressingly home. There's evidently rather more, it would seem, to any play and replay of Peter Piper-esque nursery techniques. One's reminded of how in the kiddy verses of Ms Rossetti's *Sing-Song: A Nursery Rhyme Book* (1872), the nursery jingles keep filling up with serious meanings as they turn morbid and melancholic:

> Tell me a tale –
> What shall I tell? –
> Two mournful sisters,
> And a tolling knell,
> Tolling ding and tolling dong
> Ding dong bell.

What's told by these rhymes? What's to tell? 'Winter: My Secret' keeps to the verbal ways of the 'Nonsense' its discarded title announced, but it might have serious things to disclose. Will it tell? No, it won't ('my secret's mine, and I won't tell'); but, yes, it might ('Perhaps my secret I may say'), if the summery conditions are right. Either way, there's potential meaning in these rhymes which the reader 'may guess'. As poem after poem of Christina G, overt about its doublings and echoings and repetitions, keeps showing.[25]

'From the Antique', for instance (that one of the two unpublished poems with this title which begins 'It's a weary life, it is; she said'), takes on the notion that *doubling* is *blanking*. A female speaker announces the double blankness of 'a woman's lot'. ('Doubly blank' because she's not a man, and would rather be dead, a nothing, a set of *nots*: 'Not a body … not a soul; / Not so much as a grain of dust'; a condition in which 'None' would miss the dead as a 'nothing'). The announcement is made in an intense Rossettian set of repeatings ('I wish and I wish I were a man', and all those *nots* and *nothings*).

---

[25]   By far the best single discussion of repetivity in her poetry, Eric Griffiths, 'The Disappointment of Christina G Rossetti', *Essays in Criticism*, 47:2 (April 1997), 107–142, moves quickly on from dwelling on her 'disappointing' tic of redundant and banal repeatings to some fine analyses of some of those poems of hers which not only repeat a lot but make repeating their aesthetically serious subject – poems fulfilling Griffiths' creed (adopted from Valéry) that poetry begins with poets hearing their own lips repeat a phrase, and ones living up to Wordsworth's suggestion, culled from his 'Note' to 'The Thorn', that 'repetition and apparent tautology are frequent beauties of the highest kind'.

But the blankings of woman's condition and the desire for extinction are defied in the notion of somehow continuing that's conveyed in the repeated *still*: 'Still the world would wag on the same, / Still the seasons go and come.' There's evidently stillness and stillness, contained in the doubling of *still*: the *still*, or silence of death and the grave; the *still* of worldly and seasonal continuance.

Or there's 'Echo' (in the *Goblin Market* volume), a poem about echoing: urging happy memories to return in dreams, as echoes, or repetitions. As faded echoes, to be sure, coming back 'in the silence of the night', 'in the speaking silence of a dream', but still, for all their silence, just audible. The old lover's voice is to echo faintly ('Speak low, lean low, / As long ago, my love, how long ago') but still audibly. And this is a set of echoic returns substantiated in the many, many echoic returns of the poem's multi-rhymings (*Come, Come, Come, Come, come, Come*; *Come back, Come back*; *Come to me, come to me*; *Come back to me*: all in a mere fifteen lines). The wished-for return of the lover ('Pulse for pulse, breath for breath') is made audibly present to us, as it were, in the echoing words which announce the desire. This substantiating echoic practice should remind us of that Swinburne poem 'Rococo' about the possibility of memory: 'Remembrance may recover / And time bring back to time / The name of your first lover' – and also 'The ring of my first rhyme'. The work of remembering former lovers is linked intimately with the undying ring of rhyme. The ring, of course, as the mere noise, the ding dong of bells, but also the ring on the Hamletian model of poetic writing as engravings on the inside of a ring, a circumscription of an emptiness but also a writing against the blankness it surrounds ('Is this a prologue, or the posy of a ring?' *Hamlet* II.ii.147). It's the challenge, no less, of the apostrophes in Rossetti's 'Echo' which invite the remembered lover to return: 'O memory, hope, love of fin-ished years'; 'Oh dream how sweet, too sweet, too bitter sweet.' Which is the challenge of all apostrophe, of course – the invocation to an absent one (the trope of prayer: the address to an absent, not visible, deity); the statement of hope that the absent one will make him- or her-self present, to appear in the poem, or on stage as a manifested presence and person: apostrophe as the rhetoric of desire for a prosopopoeia or personification. The apostrophic O is a nought that's both a mark of an absence, an emptiness, a naught-ness, a no-thing, and also a sign of noughtness, absence contained, and made present. So the mark of absence is also a very potent signifier of presence, like the multi-plier 0 of mathematics which makes ordinary numbers more potent. So the apostrophic O is fellow of all the *o*'s in Rossetti's poem: the voice speaking, low, as long ago and long ago, the *o* of Echo itself, coming back, 'Breath for breath', a slight something, to be sure (echoes always return more faintly than the original sound), but not yet a nothing. (Apostrophic thoughts, bearing in on what the poet and critic JH Prynne cannily analyses as the 'quite uncertain' 'mood-content' of the 'sub-articulate outcry' of *O* and *Oh* all across the

English poetic tradition, and applicable to other apostrophe-dense Victorian poems, Tennyson's 'Oenone', for example, and not least, of course, to the heavily apostrophizing Gerard Hopkins.[26])

Returning then as by no means an emptying, a noughting of meaning. The 'oes and aes' mouthed out by the poet in those vocalically repetitious lines of the so repetitious Tennyson's 'The Epic' are, of course, 'hollow', but they're not nothings. Just so in the fading echoings Tennyson's poems keep attending to, the 'fading, fading, fading' and 'dying, dying, dying' moves which so excite critics keen on spotting a postmodernist silencing retreat into abysmality. For the very announcement of those fadings ensures their continued audibility (up to three times on those occasions). Tennyson was strangely charmed, he said, by the words 'far, far away'. He gave them to his 'Ancient Sage' recalling boyhood's 'desolate sweetness', and used them of evening bells in the poem 'Far–Far–Away (For Music)': 'What sound was dearest in his native dells? / The mellow lin-lan-lone of evening bells / Far-far-away'. And though distant, the fainting noises are still audible. What Tennyson relishes in 'The Silent Voices' is the paradox of the persistent audibility of the 'Silent Voices of the dead'. And hereabouts one's mindful of the assertion of his poem 'Reticence' that he would make his verse a shrine not to Silence, but 'to one of finer sense, / Her half-sister, Reticence'.[27] And so it goes in all the poetic turnings and returnings of Christina G. In her 'Twice' (in *The Prince's Progress and Other Poems* (1866)), to take another marvellous example of the work of rhyming: that wonderful, repeating, doubling, self-mirroring poem about the heart of the poet being taken in hand, now her own hand, now her beloved's, now her God's.[28] In the first half, Rossetti apostrophizes her lover, twice, in a twiceness twice over, '(O my love, O my love)', '(O my love)', and gives her heart away to him, in a giving that's also a taking, is doubled in a taking: 'I took my heart in my hand'; 'You took my heart in your hand'. But the beloved rejects the gift ('With a critical eye you scanned'), puts it down, so that it breaks. Apostrophe

[26]   '[T]he word O is one of the most difficult and exacting in the language of emphatical speech': JH Prynne, 'English Poetry and Emphatical Language', *Proceedings of the British Academy*, 74 (1988), 135–169.

[27]   Gerard Joseph is far too hasty in recruiting these poems into a deconstructive Tennysonian scene of utter verbal wipe-out and abysmality: 'The Mirror and the Echo *en abyme* in Victorian Poetry', Ch 5 of *Tennyson and the Text: The Weaver's Shuttle* (Cambridge University Press, Cambridge, 1992), 88ff.

[28]   Eric Griffiths is particularly telling in his reading of 'Twice' – whose title prompts him to quote Samuel Beckett on the loveliness of repetition in music. This poem's 'intense recapitulation suggests that the title may have the further sense of a musical instruction to repeat a piece, so "Twice" obeys what Beckett called "the beautiful convention of the 'da capo'" ['from the beginning']'. 'The Disappointment of Christina G Rossetti', article cit, 124.

as failure: the failure of invocation, the plea that returns a blank. So the poet turns, heartbroken, to God, the mirrored beloved, in a repeated act of taking and giving, in the mirrored, mirroring, second half of the poem. This is a giving in a renewed, different, but repeated apostrophizing, the old apostrophic twiceness over again, though all in the open, not enclosed like the other in parenthetical brackets – 'O my God, O my God'; 'O my God, O my God'. It's a giving that's a doubled taking by the poet – 'I take my heart in my hand'; 'I take my heart in my hand'. A taking that is not reciprocated for certain (not in the poem anyway) by the divine beloved, but a giving done in high faith that there is indeed a divine taking – a taking more sure and lasting than the first lover's taking, even if, at first, it appears to repeat that harshness. God is to scan the heart the lover scanned: 'This heart take Thou to scan'. But this scanning is to be conducted according to the metaphors of purposeful taking drawn from Christina G's favoured Authorised Version of the Bible. 'Refine with fire its gold, / Purge Thou its dross away.' Which is a secure taking and holding (a kind of marriage: 'to have and to hold') that the first taking and holding only parodied. 'Yea, hold it in Thy hand, /Whence none can pluck it out'. It's an almost Calvinist faith in the security of salvation – God's double hold – based, like everything else good in the poem, in the AV text of John 10.28–29: a scriptural affirmation that is, with high appropriateness for this poem, made twice. 'And I give unto them eternal life; and they shall never perish, neither shall any man pluck them out of my hand. My Father, which gave them me, is greater than all; and no man is able to pluck them out of my Father's hand'. The broken-hearted poet had stopped smiling and singing by the end of the poem's first half; at the end of this second half renewed smiling and singing are anticipated: 'Smile Thou and I shall sing'. Back then, she abandoned her questioning (of God's purposes? in despair?); now she'll be able to question again: 'But shall not question much' (because she's more secure in God's providence?). Formerly she gave her heart to a treacherous lover; now she's giving it to a faithful divine one. A repeated giving of her all now to God: a giving granted the greater finality for being stated twice, in a highly repetitive rhyming doublet of lines

> All that I have I bring
> All that I am I give.

Which should, of course, remind us of Rossetti's most famous poem, 'A Christmas Carol' (in *Goblin Market, The Prince's Progress and Other Poems* (1875)) – yet one more highly repetitive poem about repeats. 'In the bleak mid-winter' (three times) long ago Jesus Christ was born, in a plethora of repeating snow-falls: 'Snow has fallen, snow on snow / Snow on snow.' Now that He comes again, what can the poet give Him: a repeated interrogative in a multiplicity of repeated gifting possibilities; how can she match the gifts of the Magi, let alone reciprocate the gift of Himself?

> What can I give Him
> Poor as I am?
> If I were a shepherd
> I would bring a lamb,
> If I were a wise man
> I would do my part, –
> Yet what I can I give Him,
> Give my heart.

What can I give? ... what I can I give. If I were; If I were. I would bring; I would do. But what can I give Him? What suffices? What's 'Enough for Him whom Cherubim' worship; what's 'Enough for Him Whom angels' adore? A woman's gift of breast-milk and the inn-keeper's hay, were once enough. A *breastful* and a *mangerful*. Repeated sufficiences of once upon a time. This Victorian woman has no money, but her heart might suffice. *Poor as I am*; *what I can I* : the repeated poor sufficiences of now will have to suffice.

'A Christmas Carol' is an amazing performance of tight verbal binding, one that reflects, of course the theological and relational bindings the poem reflects on. Here, clearly, is rhyming for a reason, and reasons, a rhyming with very good reason. And, in fact, there's reason in the rhyming, rhyming for good reasons, all across the scene of Victorian poetic production. Alongside the very real possibility and fear that to repeat is to drain meaning away, is the counter possibility that repetition is a tactic of enforcing and endorsing meaning, of making emphasis, drawing attention to the important things by saying them twice (or more). A method of meaning that Victorian poets consciously, and very regularly, went in for. They happily confront the potential for emptiedness, for nonsense, in the kept-up ringing of the ding-dong bell, challenging the reader to accept rhyme's counter potential for meaning-fulnesses. A challenge especially strong in the case of Scene V of Clough's Venetian poem 'Dipsychus' (in his *Letters and Remains* (1869)), where the meaning that fills the repeated chiming of the bell is the absence of God: the (ironic) fulness of a ringing emptiness.

> I dreamt a dream; till morning light
> A bell rang in my head all night,
> Tinkling and tinkling first, and then
> Tolling; and tinkling; tolling again.
> So brisk and gay, and then so slow!

O joy, and terror! mirth, and woe!
Ting, ting, there is no God; ting, ting –
Dong, there is no God; dong,
There is no God; dong, dong!

Ting, ting, there is no God; ting, ting;
Come dance and play, and merrily sing –
Ting, ting a ding; ting, ting a ding!
O pretty girl who trippest along,
Come to my bed – it isn't wrong.
Uncork the bottle, sing the song!
Ting, ting a ding; dong, dong.
Wine has dregs; the song an end;
A silly girl is a poor friend
And age and weakness who shall mend?
Dong, there is no God; Dong!

Ting, Dong, Bell. It's clear to Clough for whom, and what, the bell tolls. (It's no accident, I think, that the run-up to the meaningful ting tinging and dong donging of 'Dipsychus' is a lovely bit of comic rhyming – a tribute to Venice-lover Byron's own love of daft comic rhymes – showing how pithy and pointful even the most trivial and desperate must-make-up-the-line seeming rhymes can be: 'What now? The Lido shall it be? / That none may say we didn't see / The ground which Byron used to ride on, / And do I don't know what beside on'.) But then so it is all over the Victorian place. The meaning, a certain fullness of meaning, however ironic, or etiolated, is, precisely, in the rhyming. 'These rhymes will furnish the reason', is how Hood put it in 'Miss Kilmansseg and Her Precious Leg' (line 2167). Which is not as extreme as AW Schlegel's famously strong claim about what poems do with words, that 'There is nothing ornamental about the style of a real poet: everything is a necessary hieroglyph'. Surely there can be, and are, you might think, verbal redundancies in poems, items which however hard you squeeze them won't yield any meaningful juice, even of the most deeply encrypted kind (a hieroglyph is an ancient Egyptian cryptic sign). But Hood's line points powerfully in Schlegel's demanding direction. In support of his own verse, naturally, but also, one might claim, of Victorian poetry at large. Hood's line should certainly make us think of his very moving poem 'The Bridge of Sighs' (in *Hood's Magazine* (May 1844) and then in his *Poems* of 1846), about a sad woman of the streets who has jumped to her death in the Thames (it joins Hood's 'The Song of the Shirt', about needle-working women out-workers, as one of the period's most potent social-protest poems).

'The Bridge of Sighs' allows its rhymes to build in nonce-fashion, especially adverbs in *-ly*; it even accepts the near-silly surprise of some of its collocations, but it makes even those very surprising rhymes carry large accusations against a heedless family, city, man-kind, and humankind.

Still, for all slips of hers
One of Eve's family –
Wipe those poor lips of hers
Oozing so clammily.

(27–30)

*

Who was her father?
Who was her mother?
Had she a sister?
Had she a brother?
Or was there a dearer one
Still, and a nearer one
Yet, than all other?

Alas! for the rarity
Of Christian charity
Under the sun!
Oh! it was pitiful!
Near a whole city full
Home had she none.

(36–48)

*

In she plunged boldly
No matter how coldly
The rough river ran, –
Over the brink of it,
Picture it – think of it,
Dissolute Man!
Lave in it, drink of it,
Then, if you can!

(72–9)

Always the Thames water is made horribly present: here turned, startlingly, into the medium of the heedless male punter's possible new thoughtfulness. And always the poem's revisioning challenges are done, like that, by rhyme. The woman is 'Rash and undutiful', but also 'Only the beautiful' (23, 26). And by half-rhyme. 'Perishing gloomily, / Spurred by contumely' (95–96) – where the noun in –*ly contumely* is brought in as a chance, but potent, rhyming ally of the adverb *gloomily*, to register the time's glooming contumely for prostitutes (a half-rhyme's pointed work not unakin to the echo of *rarity* and *Christian charity* (43–44), which pronounces a period's limit on its charitable feelings). The poem would have this corpse treated like a Christian penitent or saint. 'Cross her hands humbly, / As if praying dumbly, / Over her breast!' (100–103). Hers is a silence in death, an unheard prayer, conveyed wonderfully in the way *humbly* only partly chimes with *dumbly* – the still *b* of the latter answering to the now stillness of the woman. And so on, and on – in a poem unable to refrain from compassionate refraining. The loving second stanza:

> Take her up tenderly,
> Lift her with care;
> Fashion'd so slenderly,
> Young and so fair!

reappears later precisely as a refrain (80–84). And all this in a poem whose very subtitle, ' "Drown'd! drown'd!" *Hamlet*', makes for a multiple doubling: the repeated words of the Queen in *Hamlet* IV.vii.183, upon hearing of Ophelia's death by water, repeated now over a poem about another young woman's drowning, in a compelling intertextual move feminizing the melancholy of the Victorian period's favourite melancholic man.

Returning as Loss – And (A)gain

The largest cultural and literary echoes and returns are made to echo, to return, in yet one more Victorian poem that works through massive verbal returnings. Verbal returnings dramatically present – and naturally so, it's hard not to think – in what is perhaps the period's most potent poetic celebration of a return, namely Tennyson's 'The Charge of the Light Brigade'.

> I
> Half a league, half a league,
> Half a league onward,
> All in the valley of Death
> Rode the six hundred.
> II
> 'Forward, the Light Brigade!'
> Was there a man dismay'd?
> Not tho' the soldier knew
> Some one had blunder'd:
> Their's not to make reply,
> Their's not to reason why,
> Their's but to do and die:
> Into the valley of Death
> Rode the six hundred.
> III
> Cannon to right of them,
> Cannon to left of them,
> Cannon in front of them

Volly'd and thunder'd;
Storm'd at with shot and shell,
Boldly they rode and well,
Into the jaws of Death,
Into the mouth of Hell
Rode the six hundred.

IV

Flash'd all their sabres bare,
Flash'd as they turn'd in air
Sabring the gunners there,
Charging an army, while
All the world wondered:
Plunged in the battery-smoke
Right thro' the line they broke;
Cossack and Russian
Reel'd from the sabre-stroke
Shatter'd and sunder'd.
Then they rode back, but not
Not the six hundred.

V

Cannon to right of them,
Cannon to left of them,
Cannon behind them
Volley'd and thunder'd;
Storm'd at with shot and shell,
While horse and hero fell,
They that had fought so well
Came thro' the jaws of Death,
Back from the mouth of Hell,
All that was left of them,
Left of six hundred.

VI

When can their glory fade?
O the wild charge they made!
All the world wonder'd.
Honour the charge they made!
Honour the Light Brigade,
Noble six hundred!

Tennyson was stirred by reports in the *Times* newspaper of a disastrous charge upon mistaken orders, 25 October 1854, by the British cavalrymen of the Light Brigade against the Russian guns at Balaclava in the Crimean War. 'The British soldier will do his duty, even to certain death, and is not paralysed by feeling that he is the victim of some hideous blunder' (*Times* editorial, 13 November 1854). Tennyson wrote furiously for weeks, working hard on everything, but not least the rhymes, the repetitions. The poem was published 9 December in the *Examiner*. But still Tennyson couldn't let the poem go – revising it heavily for *Maud, and Other Poems* (1855), reworking it again for the New Edition of *Maud, and Other Poems* (1856). He claimed he wrote it 'in a few minutes', but there are some twenty 'states' of the poem extant.[29] They're all of them built on the accusatory rhyme word *blundered*, adapted from the Times's *blunder*: 'Some one had blundered'. Tennyson also claimed, mistakenly, that he'd found the phrase 'some one had blundered' in the *Times* and that 'this was the original of the metre of the poem'. But this 'original' line was all his own invention.[30] The much repeated 'six hundred' follows from it. The *Times* report of 14 November told of '607 sabres', which Tennyson rounded down to the rhythmically tighter 'six hundred'. He apparently toyed with 'seven hundred', but, as he wrote to *Examiner* editor Forster, 'six hundred is much better than seven hundred (as I think) metrically so keep it.' *Hundred* was allegedly pronounced *hunderd* in Lincolnshire, making a close rhyme with *blundered*, and also with *thunder'd* and *sunder'd* and the accusatory *wonder'd*. 'Volley'd and thunder'd' and 'All the world wonder'd' come twice. As do 'jaws of Death', 'jaws of Death', and 'mouth of Hell', 'mouth of Hell'. Much else comes more than twice. 'Half a league, half a league, / Half a league onward'; 'Cannon to right of them, / Cannon to left of them, / Cannon in front of them'; 'Cannon to right of them, / Cannon to left of them, / Cannon behind them'. Echoing, echoing; unrefrained refraining.

'Rode the six hundred' makes a refrain for the first three stanzas; its precursor line slightly modified each time: 'All in the valley of Death'; 'Into the valley of Death'; 'Into the jaws of Death, / Into the mouth of Hell'. In stanzas V and VI the refrain reappears rather drastically changed – a greatly altered refrain to register the greatly altered, that is depleted, Brigade. Tennyson knew that only 195 men came back.

> Then they rode back, but not
> Not the six hundred.
>
> *
>
> All that was left of them,
> Left of six hundred.

---

[29] Tennyson's extensive creative work is revealed and (hermeneutically excitingly) analysed by Edgar Shannon and Christopher Ricks, ' "The Charge of the Light Brigade": The Creation of a Poem', *Studies in Bibliography*, 38 (1985), 1–44.

[30] In his 1855 version Tennyson omitted lines 5–12, including the foundational 'Some one had blundered' – prevailed on by 'Some friends of excellent critical judgement': Hallam Tennyson, *Memoir*, I. fn, p411. Friends of better judgement helped persuade him otherwise. John Ruskin wrote, 12 Nov 1855, to say how 'sorry' he was that 'you put the "Some one had blundered" out of the "Light Brigade". It was precisely the most tragical line in the poem. It is as true to its history as essential to its tragedy'. His letter is reproduced in the *Memoir*, I,411.

And modified returning – the poignant mark of the Brigade's heroism which is the poem's main point – is an insistent feature of the poem's rhymings:

> Their's not to make reply,
> Their's not to reason why,
> Their's but to do and die.

The third line in that run makes a para-rhyming shift from the preceding negatives of silent military obedience to a positive uncomplaining action, a positive plunging of the cavalrymen into the final silencing negative of death in battle. It's an emphatic positive involving, of course, that rhyming soldierly finality of 'do *and* die'. The story is told that Mrs Tennyson, copying out the poem for publication, miscopied that phrase as 'do *or* die', which Tennyson, observing it, immediately corrected. He wanted that rhyming consequentiality: this sort of *doing* inevitably led to a *dying*. (Compare the end of Auden's poem 'September 1, 1939', 'We must love one another or die', which Auden came to think better about, correcting the line to 'love one another and die'.[31])

In this battle, and so in this poem, there's to be no mere unaltered returning. Like all battles – and poems about battles – this battle and this poem are all about positioning, placing, action in a place and places. So prepositions and adverbs of place naturally accumulate. They're one of the poem's most repeated parts of speech: *onward, in, into, thro', from, back*, and so on. Tellingly, they dominate the recurrence of stanza III as it morphs into stanza V. The Brigade rode *into* 'the jaws of Death' and 'the mouth' of Hell, and came *thro'*, came *back from* that mouth. They went *there* (29) and returned; an active *thereness* and *hereness*, a terrible journey of going and returning made utterly vivid by the verb-adverb repetitions – *storm'd at, storm'd at, plunged in, Reel'd from, rode back, came thro'* and the repeated double adverb phrases: *Right thro', Back from*. A returning which is, however, horrible because of its pronounced lack of absolute sameness. This returning is a repetition that won't be simply repeated. Words, phrases, are repeatable – that's poetry's proud prerogative, its essence – but are inevitably, at least in these circumstances, returns with a terrible alteration.

What was left of the Brigade is Tennyson's grave concern: 'All that was left of them / Left of six hundred'. 'All that was left of them' uncannily repeats the line about the cannons' deadly position: 'Cannon to left of them' (this is a very Ricksian observation in the Shannon/Ricks article named in

---

[31] A shift discussed compellingly in Julian Barnes's essayistic novel *A History of the World in 10½ Chapters* (1989).

my note 29). Because of the cannon that was 'to left of them' there's not much now 'left of them'. The way the rhyming line returns not quite intact – 'Cannon to left of them': 'All that was left of them' – announces the losses perhaps inevitable in poetry's favoured activity of 'incremental repetition'. Increments that are also decrements. The inevitable losses of returns, as of echoes in nature (and in poems like Christina G Rossetti's 'Echo' which stage echoes). Losses which are also, though, matters of some paradoxical gain. 'All the world wonder'd': twice. Here's a repeated, continuing marvelling. A matter for continuing honour. 'Honour' them, the poet exhorts, repeatedly. So here's honour, repeated honour, and not for the decremented Brigade, but for a 'Noble six hundred!' in the poem's last line: the Brigade still intact, all of them, after all, at least in the memory of the poem and its readers. A final, defiant, paradoxical plenitude witnessed to, one might observe, by the way stanza V puts on poetic weight: the stanza that repeats stanza III as a story of depletion, of not much being left behind, has acquired in the repetition two extra lines. Something is being said, once again, for the fullness of rhymes, in the face of rhyme's losses.

Doubling/Coupling in Rhyme

'The repetitions', said Tennyson's acquaintance the American poet Frederick Goddard Tuckerman of 'The Charge of the Light Brigade', 'are wonderfully effective'. And so they are, bearing as they do the burden of the poem's thoughts about returns as both loss and gain. Thoughts inevitably central, of course, to love poems which are, naturally, all about the positives and negatives of the repeated human act of coupling, of doubling, two people rhyming, or trying to rhyme, physically together. Love poems often make their point about the vicissitudes of bodily, sexual, personal rhyming, by making extensive and exemplary play with their rhymes. As in, it might be, Dante Gabriel Rossetti's eerily repetitive 'Troy Town' (written 1869–1870; *Poems* (1870)), a rather crude rewrite of the ancient story about the ruinous effects of the 'heart's desire' – desire multiplied across the ancient world, involving gods and humans, Aphrodite, Helen, Paris, and whose effects are repeated in every one of the poem's fourteen stanzas. This repetitive desirousness of all the poem's hearts involves an intricate doubling up of female breasts and the apples they resemble. The two lovely breasts of Helen of Troy are, the poem says, like a pair of lovely, edible apples, apples tempting Paris through the power of Aphrodite, who is fond of Paris because he once awarded her a golden apple in a lovelies' competition, and who now agrees to lead him astray, making him desire Helen of the twin breasts, who attains this favour from Aphrodite by giving her a lovely cup 'moulded' like her breast, which she bares enticingly to the goddess. The end result of which is the Trojan War and the destruction of Troy. It is certainly rough and ready, a lumpen voyeuristic mélange of mutual pimpings with far too many breast-like apples and apple-like breasts: ancient tragedy coarsely redone as modern street – or Pre-Raphaelite studio – theatre. But still, it is a tale of doublings and twinning made palpably awful in their outcome, as announced in the shock of every stanza's repeated, and internally rhyming, parentheses: '(O Troy's down, / Tall Troy's on fire!)'. The terrible results of desire's doublings and redoublings rammed home in a rather too unrefrained refraining.

Less global in its terrors, but still deeply concerned about body doublings, is the finely complex, and agreeably less hectic, and not at all vulgarizing, 'Two in the Campagna' by Robert Browning (in his second, *Men and Women* volume of 1855):

I

I wonder do you feel today
As I have felt since, hand in hand,
We sat down on the grass, to stray
In spirit better through the land
This morn of Rome and May?

II

For me, I touched a thought, I know,
Has tantalized me many times,
(Like turns of thread the spiders throw
Mocking across our path) for rhymes
To catch at and let go.

III

Help me to hold it! First it left
The yellowing fennel, run to seed
There, branching from the brickwork's cleft,
Some old tomb's ruin: yonder weed
Took up the floating weft,

IV

Where one small orange cup amassed
Five beetles, – blind and green they grope
Among the honey-meal: and last
Everywhere on the grassy slope
I traced it. Hold it fast!

V

The champaign with its endless fleece
Of feathery grasses everywhere!
Silence and passion, joy and peace,
An everlasting wash of air –
Rome's ghost since her decease.

VI
Such life there, through such lengths of hours,
Such miracles performed in play,
Such primal naked forms of flowers,
Such letting nature have her way
While heaven looks from its towers!

VII
How say you? Let us, O my dove,
Let us be unashamed of soul,
As earth lies bare to heaven above!
How is it under our control
To love or not to love?

VIII
I would that you were all to me,
You that are just so much, no more.
Nor yours, nor mine, – nor slave nor free!
Where does the fault lie? What the core
O' the wound, since wound must be?

IX
I would I could adopt your will,
See with your eyes, and set my heart
Beating by yours, and drink my fill
At your soul's springs, – your part my part
In life, for good and ill.

X
No. I yearn upward, touch you close,
Then stand away. I kiss your cheek,
Catch your soul's warmth, – I pluck the rose
And love it more than tongue can speak –
Then the good minute goes.

XI
Already how am I so far
Out of that minute? Must I go
Still like the thistle-ball, no bar,
Onward, whenever light winds blow,
Fixed by no friendly star?

XII
Just when I seemed about to learn!
Where is the thread now? Off again!
The old trick! Only I discern –
Infinite passion, and the pain
Of fine hearts that yearn.

Browning is lovingly addressing his wife after what she described as 'some exquisite hours on the Campagna' outside Rome in May-time 1854. The poem is about touching, contacts, tactility and their prospects: about the holding of hands and thoughts, the contact of souls and bodies, the meeting of faces in a kiss. A touching, a meeting, a pairing of two people, a two-ness, a doubling to make a one-ness, a bodily rhyming registered in the clearly never casual verbal rhymings: 'hand in hand'; 'your part my part'; 'I yearn ... touch ... kiss... catch ... pluck ... love'; 'I ... touch you close, I kiss your cheek, I pluck the rose'; 'kiss your cheek, Catch your soul's warmth.' For this story of bodily touching is also a story of verbal touching: the two kinds of rhyming are made to rhyme, to go together, to repeat, echo, each other in the poem. And very explicitly: on this outing the lyrical-I touches the woman 'close', 'catch[es]' the warmth of her soul (stanza X), and also, in parallel, 'touched a thought', an old thought that has 'tantalized' him 'many times' before and which he's tried 'To catch at' in 'rhymes' (stanza II). As he tries to catch that thought now – in these rhyming lines about rhyming, about the catching at a woman and at a thought about loving a woman.

This poet, with his anxieties about woman and rhymes about man-woman doubling, has been here before 'many times', and so, not surprisingly, have other poets: as Browning's intertextual trading (that particular brand of high literary rhyming) indicates. His opening query, 'I wonder do you feel today / As I have felt' – the troubling question of whether her feelings really chime with his, as the words 'you feel ... I have felt' rhyme, or at least part-rhyme – echoes the opening of John Donne's 'The good-morrow': 'I wonder, by my troth, what thou, and I / Did, till we lov'd' – that wonderful old example of the poetic rhyming of bodily and personal rhymings (Donne's 'My face in thine eye, thine in mine appears': a line whose pronominal doublings punningly net the *eyes* in which these *I*'s are reflected). The repeated summons in stanza VII, 'Let us ... / Let us be unashamed of soul / As earth lies bare to heaven', recalls Tennyson's recollection in *The Princess* (1847), VII.167, of the seduction of Danaë by Zeus in a shower of gold, 'Now lies the Earth all Danaë to the stars'. And, for that matter, apostrophizing the beloved as 'my dove' is to adopt the imploring voice of the Bible's lover in the *Canticles*, or *Song of Solomon*, 'O my dove' (*Canticles* 2.14). That's a long trail of love's rhymings for Browning's rhymes to *catch at* and *hold fast*. But also – and here's the poem's catch – to *let go*. For the moment of touching is evanescent – as fragile as the spiders' threads on the fennel sprouting from the broken brickwork of 'Some old tomb's ruin' (stanza III). This is 'Love', as another of Browning's pained Italian love poems has it, 'Among the Ruins', love threatened by ruination, lovers turning into more of the Roman ghosts that haunt the Campagna. Thread (II) and weft (III): they're old metaphors for literary text-makings (text: textile); here, troublingly, they represent a poetic work that's light as air, as wind-blown thistledown (XI). 'Where is the thread now? Off again! / The Old trick!' (XII). The thread that's so easily broken; the touching and holding, the body-rhymings, that are not to last. Twoness as one-ness, the old trick, the project of rhyme; but only for a moment. It's a peril the Donne poem was familiar with – lengthily announcing the two lovers as indubitably one, and yet having doubts after all about the repeated affirmation ('*If* our two loves be one ...'). A doubt, then, about the persistence of body-rhyming, lovers' doublings, announced, not least, in the negative rhymings of stanza VIII which culminate so painfully in that double 'wound'. 'To love or not to love?' (VII): loving so readily turns into the negative with which it so nearly rhymes, like Hamlet's question 'to be or not to be?' A nearly rhyming which is, after all the temporary rhymings which have gone on, all that the poem has to leave us with:

> ... Only I discern –
> Infinite passion, and the pain
> Of finite hearts that yearn.

An infinity of love discerned; but a finity of pain realized. A separation, a break, an end for lovers' body-rhyming actualized in a pronounced half- or broken-rhyme, *infinite-finite*.

Rhyming Apocalypse

It's a disjunctiveness, the actuality of non-rhyming, or of not-whole-rhyming that animates, as we've seen, so many of these virtuoso Victorian rhyme-workings. An anxiety that animates Gerard Hopkins very greatly. The most virtuosic rhymester of them all, he is in 'Spelt from Sibyl's Leaves' in such an evident panic about what rhyming as he would like to believe in it might mean and really achieve that he rather overdoes it (on the orator's notorious principle of raising your voice when you're in doubt about your point). This is a truly extraordinary sonnet – extraordinary by any standard in the intensity of its rhymings, and rather special in the extremity, even by Hopkins's extreme standards, of its verbal tight-bindings.

> Earnest, earthless, equal, attuneable, vaulty, 'voluminous, ... stupendous
> Evening strains to be tíme's vást, 'womb-of-all, home-of all, hearse-of-all night.
> Her fond yellow hornlight wound to the west, 'her wild hollow hoarlight hung to the height
> Waste; her earliest stars, earl-stars, 'stárs principal, overbend us,
> 5 Fíre-féaturing heaven. For earth 'her being has unbound, her dapple is at an end, as-

tray or aswarm, all throughther, in throngs; 'self ín self steepèd and páshed –
quíte
Disremembering, dísmémbering 'áll now. Heart, you round me right
With: Óur évening is over us; óur night 'whélms, whélms, ánd will end us.
Only the beak-leaved boughs dragonish 'damask the tool-smooth bleak
light; black,
10   Ever so black on it. Óur tale, O óur oracle! 'Lét life, wáned, ah lét life wind
Off hér once skéined stained véined varíety 'upon, áll on twó spools; párt,
pen, páck
Now her áll in twó flocks, twó folds – black, white; 'right, wrong; reckon
but, reck but, mind
But thése two; wáre of a wórld where bút these 'twó tell, each off the óther;
of a rack
Where, selfwrung, selfstrung, sheathe- and shelterless, 'thóughts agaínst
thoughts ín groans grínd.

Written in 1884–1885, it was not published till way after Hopkins's death
when his friend Robert Bridges brought out the poems in 1918. It's a sonnet,
one of the several 'terrible sonnets' Hopkins wrote at this most melancholy
time of his life, though unusual in the group for its outstandingly long lines
('the longest sonnet ever made' Hopkins called it: he can't have seen Maurice
Carpenter's 'Beautiful is the figure of the lusty full-grown groom' which
came out in *Towards Democracy* in 1883). Hopkins's lines are peculiarly
lengthened because each one is essentially two, split into a paired set, a mirrored couple or double. Hopkins marked where the dividing point (or caesura) comes. On either side of it the words are bound together ever so tightly
in a plethora of rhyming varieties – rhymed and half-rhymed words, rhyming phrases, medial rhymes, end-rhymes, front-rhymes. Especially front-
rhymes – in alliterating clusters – in tribute to the Anglo-Saxon verse
Hopkins so admired, verse built like this poem on line after line made up of
alliterating half-lines. The poem's invented pseudo-Anglo-Saxon compound
nouns – *hornlight*, *hoarlight*, *earlstars*, and so forth – continue this tribute
to the old Germanic mode. And of course the ends of this sonnet's whole
lines rhyme too – abba abba cdcdcd – end-rhyming in the anglo-francoph-
one manner, so that rhyme-wise we have here a palimpsest of older Germanic
and later Anglo-French systems – as well as echoes of the ancient alliterative
Welsh *cynghanned* – 'consonant-chime' as Hopkins glossed it in a letter to
Bridges – and the anaphoric Hebrew Psalms.

The *Sibyl's Leaves* of the title refer to the leaves with predictive messages
on them blown about by the winds inspiring the ancient prophetic Sibyl
(as featured in Virgil's *Aeneid*), but also to the *Dies Irae*, the Day of Divine
Wrath, celebrated in the Roman Catholic mass, the 'Day of Wrath, that day
when the world is consumed in ash as David [the Psalmist David] and the

Sibyl testify'. The poem is about the Last Day of all time, the end point of all existence, earth's *end* (5) that 'will end us (8), the end of the human journey from womb to coffin and on into time's Miltonic 'vast', the 'womb-of-all, home-of-all, hearse-of-all night' (2), when God, in the apocalyptic vision of the Bible, judges all persons. 'It is appointed unto men once to die', as the Bible has it, the Bible the one-time Protestant evangelical Hopkins was even more familiar with than his convert's Roman Catholic liturgy, 'but and after this the judgement' (Hebrews 9.27). This judgement day is a day of rift, of splitting, most appropriate for consideration in a poem whose every line is split and so a marker of splitting. It is to divide humanity into two, the godly from the ungodly, the sheep from the goats (in the metaphor from the Biblical Book of Apocalypse, the Revelation of St John, which line 12 draws on : 'two flocks, two folds – black, white; right, wrong'. Two groups only ('mind / But these two'): the sheep for eternal heaven, the goats for eternal damnation. Biblical, middle-eastern sheep are pretty indistinguishable from goats; they look alike, flock together; they appear, as it were, to rhyme. But God can tell them apart, knows that their rhyme, their apparent one-ness, is illusory, and He will divide them; will prove the falsity of the apparent chime. If rhyming is *remembering* (anaphora) and thus a *membering* (uniting separate verbal body-parts, making them 'members one of another', one body, as St Paul put it of the Christian church-body, Romans 12.5) – and it is – then this process of splitting, of breaking apart the apparent rhymesters, the apparently rhyming couples, is a *disremembering* and a *dismembering*, as line 7 indeed has it.

Disremembering: *dismembering* – this emblematic pair does what is commonly done in the poem, namely sounding, and looking, very like a full rhyme, but comprising only a broken rhyme. The second item of the pair returns, claiming rhyming partnership, but returns with a loss, with a bit broken off, amputated, *dismembered* in fact.[32] Like *hornlight*: *hoarlight*; *earliest stars*: *earlstars*; *reckon but*: *reck but*, and (less dramatically) *waned*: *wind*; *bleak*: *black*, these bitten-off part-rhymes register God's refusal of the fake rhymesters he's damning. On judgement day, in this poem, would-be orderly rhyming turns out to be disordered – *skeined* (11: tangled); *all throughther* (6: a dialect version of *through-other*, disorderly); a disjunctive *dapple* (5) and *damask* (9: the wavy pattern on beaten metal); a *veined*-ness (11). 'Glory be to God

---

[32]   Geoffrey Hill, the poet who is probably Hopkins's greatest successor, dwells powerfully on the force of *disremembering* as 'dismembering the memory', in his greatly Hopkins-centred review of the great Second Edition of the *Oxford English Dictionary* (published in 1989, centenary year of Hopkins's death): 'Common Weal, Common Woe', *TLS* (21 April 1989), in Hill, *Style and Faith* (Counterpoint, NY, 2003), 1–20; Geoffrey Hill, *Collected Critical Writings*, ed Kenneth Haynes (Oxford University Press, Oxford, 2008), 265–279. He tasks the OED with not feeling the full force of this and other important Hopkins words.

for dappled things', wrote Hopkins in his earlier poem 'Pied Beauty', happy with the gorgeous rhyming spots, the freckles, the 'couple-colour' of God's lovely natural creatures, cows, trout, finches' wings. Now all that is at an end, split up, divided, condemned. The godly and the ungodly are the only *two* that *tell* (13: i.e. count, matter, as well as speak), and now their apparent sameness doesn't count. Now, on judgement day, they 'tell, each off the other': their meaning, their selfhood, is in their difference from each other, their lack of rhyme (and *tell off* has the force, too, of rebuking, giving a 'telling off'). Judgement day is bad, in other words for guilty people: who will feel the force of God's violence as they are *pashed* (6: crushed, beaten); *whelmed* (8: overwhelmed, drowned – twice); *wrung* and *strung* (14) on God's rack (13). So no uniting on that Last Day, in the poem's last line, only a disuniting, a great separation of persons, a disjunction of selves (*selfwrung, selfstrung*) and of idea-systems (*thoughts against thoughts*), a *grind* of opposite categories up against each other, amid *groans* ('and there shall be weeping and gnashing of teeth', Matthew 8.28).[33]

A stress, then, on the stress of judgement day to come. It will continue the divine stress Hopkins feels right now – as in another of his 'terrible sonnets', '(Carrion Comfort)', the sonnet that is probably the one Hopkins described as 'written in blood' in May 1885, in which the poet feels like grain, threshed, or thrashed, by the divine rod and fan, or flail; feels trodden down by the divine foot, like the grapes in the Biblical winepress of the wrath of God (Revelation 19.15); and wonders, too, about who is fighting with whom ('O which one? is it each one?').[34] The priest and his God, like Old Testament Jacob wrestling with the antagonist Angel: not at one, but at odds, a disjunctively rhyming pair: a failure of union registered in the

---

[33] In his *New Bearings in English Poetry* FR Leavis celebrates 'Spelt from Sibyl's Leaves' at length 'as one of the finest things he [Hopkins] did; 'it exhibits and magnificently justifies most of the peculiarities of his technique'. 'In comparison with such a poem of Hopkins's as this, any other poetry of the nineteenth century is seen to be using only a very small part of the resources of the English language. His words seem to have substance, and to be made of a great variety of stuffs.' The poem is to be thought of as exemplifying Leavis's great tribute, in this momentous early critique of Hopkins, to the work of verbal repetitions in Hopkins: 'the pattern of and progression of verbal echo, alliteration, rime and assonance'. 'That need not be (indeed, is not) a mere musical trick, any more than conventional end-rime need be. Such devices may be used, as good poets use end-rime, to increase the expectancy involved in rhythm and change its direction, to control movement, to give words new associations and bring diverse ideas and emotions together, to intensify the sense of inevitability – in short to get new, precise and complex responses out of words'. *New Bearings*, New Edition (Chatto & Windus, 1950), 174, 182–186.

[34] Paul S Fiddes discusses the Christology of the crushed grain and grapes, especially in relation to the pertinent poem 'Barnfloor and Winepress' (taken as a genuine Hopkins poem, even though the MS is in another hand than his), and indicates Hopkins's indebtedness in the matter to George Herbert: 'GM Hopkins', Ch 40, *The Blackwell Companion to the Bible in English Literature*, eds Rebecca Lemon, Emma Mason, Jonathan Roberts and Christopher Rowland (Wiley-Blackwell, 2009), 565.

blasphematory broken-rhyme at the end of this sonnet, which so ironically recollects and pronounces this spiritual non-rhyming – 'That night, that year / Of now done darkness I wretch lay wrestling with (my God!) my God'. Polite Victorian Christians did not lightly disobey the third of the Ten Commandments, 'Thou shalt not take the name of the Lord thy God in vain' (Exodus 20), and especially clergymen did not. Swearing, even in parenthesis, '(my God!)', evidences the great stress Hopkins was under. The stress Geoffrey Hill wonderfully reflects on as a case of what Hopkins called in his sonnet 'Henry Purcell' the *abrupt self* : 'the rehearsal / Of own, of abrupt self' (*abrupt*: broken, broken off, breaking away, interrupted, truncated); the self torn between the rhyming contradiction of apostrophizing prayer (*my God*) and blasphemy (*my God!*). The self-revelation (in Hill's words) of 'man ... in his intense selfhood and in his most frightful splintering'. 'The abrupted experiences once more commune with each other: the expletive of a potentially filthy bare forked animal ('I wretch', 'carrion') and the bare word of faith'). These are contradictory 'movements of disjunction and junction', signalled by Hopkins's brackets: the brackets which, as ever in a poem, deliberately break a poet's 'syntactical stride', according to Christopher Ricks's brilliant reading of how brackets work in poems – and which Hill's own poetry repeatedly indulges in, as Ricks shows, on the model of what Hill admires in Hopkins as that abruption which, as Hill put it in an interview with Hallam Tennyson, is both 'a very technical thing' and also 'a very spiritual or psychological thing'.[35]

The rhyming abruption involves, of course, a transgression for which Hopkins will have to answer on judgement day: a prospect (to return to 'Sibyl's Leaves') distressing for all people, but not least for this most downcast of priests, anguished about his mortality and sinfulness (including guilt about his homosexuality which haunts his poems, and about his onanism: the night-time wrestle of '(Carrion Comfort)' suggests anxiety about masturbation to many readers). And more, judgement day looms as a dire prospect for poetry – that matter, as Hopkins' poetics has it, of getting the stresses in the right place. Every day is a judgement day for the poet for whom placing the stresses matters absolutely. How much more distressing the final judgement day when the stressed and stressing maker meets his stressing Maker. (Notable about 'Sibyl's Leaves' is the unusual number of stresses Hopkins has marked in.) As for the way of the rhymester, this arch-contriver

---

[35] Geoffrey Hill, 'Redeeming the Time', the best deep delve into Hopkins's poetic language ever (1972–1973), collected in Hill, *The Lords of Limit* (Deutsch, London and Oxford University Press, NY, 1984), and in Geoffrey Hill, *Collected Critical Writings*, ed Kenneth Haynes (Oxford University Press, 2008), 88–108. Christopher Ricks, *Geoffrey Hill and 'The Tongue's Atrocities'* (University College of Swansea, Swansea, 1978). Ricks quotes the 1977 BBC radio Hill/Hallam Tennyson interview, (1978), 27, & fn 35 p36.

of rhymes, the Last Day offers unremitting distress, for, as presented here, on That Day rhymes will be collapsing, breaking-up, getting dismembered, and where they survive, will be contriving and pronouncing a groaning and a grinding. If you're wise as a poet, as well as a mere Christian, you can only be wary (*ware*: 13) of the time when 'thoughts against thoughts in groans grind'. When the God of Hopkins the Jesuit will finally *disremember* and *dismember*, finally break up the rhymesters and the rhymes of earth – just as Hopkins's Jesuit Superiors have meanwhile vetoed his devoted rhyme-work: much more verbal goat than sheep-like Christian, in their view.

Part II

Contents and Discontents of The Forms

5

Down-Sizing

If the Victorian era is the Age of the Big Book – the Fat Novel and the Great Poem, those vast formal enclosures endeavouring to Get A Great Deal (if not quite Everything) In – and this is so – it is also the age of the small poem, the poem eschewing symphonic or epic stature, the text content to be rather midget, happy with the small size and the small subject. Alongside the bumper texts flourishes a counter aesthetic of the small time.

Sonnettomania

Small poems come, of course, in lots of shapes and indeed sizes. We can, though, take the sonnet, that compact little fourteen-line poem, as the obvious sign and flagship of the Victorian small-is-beautiful movement. And sonnets exist in almost daunting abundance. They're one of the period's obvious staples. Joseph Phelan's (good) study, *The Nineteenth-Century Sonnet*, talks of the 'sonnettomania' of the years around 1880.[1] But sonneteering flourishes throughout the period. Pointedly, *sonnettomania* and *sonnettomaniacs* got into the language in 1821, according to the Oxford English Dictionary.

A very large number of Victorian poets are sonnettomaniacs. The example of the grand old sonneteer Wordsworth, pouring out sonnets into his old age (he died in 1850 aged 80), was widely felt. John Clare's numerous sonnets on natural and erotic themes, tumbling out in the Northampton Asylum in the 1840s, are an evident homage to Wordsworth. Sonnets would be the

---

[1] Joseph Phelan, *The Nineteenth-Century Sonnet* (Palgrave Macmillan, Basingstoke, 2005), 134.

Victorian Poetry Now: Poets, Poems, Poetics, First Edition. Valentine Cunningham.
© 2011 Valentine Cunningham. Published 2011 by Blackwell Publishing Ltd.

period's most natural of homes for short bursts of succinct expressions of love, anger and devotion; for tidy feelings about nature, things, others, God; for the 'lyrical I' to be, well, briefly lyrical. Taking up the mantle of the feeling woman poet from sonneteering Felicia Hemans, Elizabeth Barrett Barrett of course fills her *Poems* (1844) with sonnets. Jotting down her compact private courtship thoughts about Robert Browning in verse, she naturally does it in a sonnet sequence, *Sonnets from the Portuguese* – published at Robert's insistence in 1850 (she wanted them to be called *Sonnets from the Bosnian*). Loving crisply in verse is what sonnets were for.

Charles (Tennyson) Turner, the Laureate's lesser known elder brother, wrote almost nothing but sonnets, beginning in 1830 with his *Sonnets and Fugitive Pieces*, bursting out again, after years of being deterred from publication because of brother Alfred's 'perfect work', with his *Sonnets* (1864), his *Small Tableaux* (1868), and his *Sonnets, Lyrics and Translations* (1873). Hallam Tennyson brought out his late uncle's *Collected Sonnets Old and New* in 1880: a very grand total of 342 of them![2] George Meredith's long sour 'sonnet' sequence (his have sixteen lines apiece) about unhappy marriage, *Modern Love*, appeared in 1862. Writing sonnets about beloved women and beloved paintings preoccupied Dante Gabriel Rossetti for most of his writing life. His ekphrastic 'forties sonnets about paintings started to appear in the Pre-Raphaelites' *Germ* magazine in 1850. He never stopped writing these little ekphrastic poems; they comprise the weighty 'Sonnets for Pictures' section of his 1870 *Poems* – expanded for his 1881 *Ballads and Sonnets* volume. Rossetti's even greater preoccupation, his great erotic 'House of Life' sequence of sonnets (those fleshly poems causing Buchanan such anxiety) massively fill the 1870 volume, stretching to a grand total of 102 in the 1881 collection (there would have been 103 had the notorious 'Nuptial Sleep' not been discreetly dropped). Never one for long poems – with the occasional narrative exception like 'Goblin Market' and 'The Prince's Progress' – Christina G really went to town on the sonnet in her sonnet-packed 1881 volume *A Pageant & Other Poems*. (It's easy to think she was rivalrously egged on by her brother's sonneteering example.) Her volume includes 'Monna Innominata: A Sonnet of Sonnets', a fourteen-sonnet sequence of melancholic lost-love poems (apparently about her unfulfilled love for the poet Charles Cayley), with a Preface invoking Elizabeth Barrett Browning, 'The Great Poetess of our own day and nation', and saying her 'Portuguese Sonnets' might have been like *this* had she 'only been unhappy instead of happy'. It also contains her twenty-four-strong religiously melancholic 'Later Life: A Double Sonnet of Sonnets'. Her brother's sequence opened in 1881 with a 'Sonnet on the Sonnet', extolling the

[2]   They're all gathered in *The Collected Sonnets of Charles (Tennyson) Turner*, eds FB Pinion and M Pinion (Macmillan, Basingstoke, 1988).

form as 'a moment's monument', an 'arduous fulness' (an earlier version had 'intricate fulness'), and his sister duly opened her volume with a self-referential sonnet about 'this my tome' with its 'many sonnets', and about what sonnets do. They are 'full of love'; 'so here now shall be / One sonnet more, a love sonnet', from 'me', 'To my first love, my Mother'. (Sonnets on sonnets and sonneteering rather abound in the period: as RE Egerton-Warburton's 'Il Sonnetto', in his *Poems, Epigrams and Sonnets* (1877) giving formal advice about quatrains and triplets and doing the rhymes; or Eugene Lee-Hamilton's 'What the Sonnet Is', in his 1894 *Sonnets of the Wingless Hours* (Dante's, Petrarch's, Shakespeare's and Dante Gabriel Rossetti's tears and loves); or Tennyson Turner's numerous faux-dismissals about the poem's tininess.)

One Sonnet More

'One sonnet more', said Christina G: it's a motto for Victorian poetic production. Wherever you look there's one sonnet more, and one more poet producing one. Especially about love's affairs and love affairs. JA Symonds's with men, it might be, in his own sonnets, or by proxy in his Michelangelo translations (all treated in Chapter 6, 'Selving'). Or Gerard Hopkins's relationships with male persons – at a hands-off distance, of course, with the farrier-parishioner 'Felix Randal', and 'Harry Ploughman' ('Hard as hurdle arms, with a broth of goldish flue / Breathed round'), and soldiers ('Yes. Whý do we áll, seeing of a soldier, bless him?'), and dangerously 'lovely lads' ('To what serves mortal beauty – dangerous'); and, much closer up, with the stressing and distressing deity of the so-called 'Terrible Sonnets' of the later 1880s. Or Tennyson, struggling with the recalcitrant heroine of *Maud*, patching together that long poem of distressed passion out of a lot of small poems, just occasionally with sonnet-like fourteen-line poems ('Cold and clear-cut face, why come you so cruelly meek' (I.iii.88–101); 'What, has he found my jewel out?' (I.x.2, 352–365); 'I trust that I did not talk' (I.xix.3, 695–708); 'My life has crept so long on a broken wing', and 'And it was but a dream, yet it yielded a dear delight' in the poem's final part, III.vi.1 and 2, 1–14 and 15–28), though more often with not-quite sonnets, little poems of eleven, twelve, thirteen, fifteen and sixteen lines ('Let it go or stay, so I wake to the higher aims', fourth poem of the poem's last part is a sixteen-liner): would-be sonnets, formal bosh-shots underlining, perhaps, that narrator's failures in love, the lover who can't quite get the lover's usual exercise in sonneteering quite right. Perhaps Meredith took a cue for his sixteen-line 'sonnets' from Tennyson. (It would be pleasing to think TS Eliot thought of Tennyson, as well as of JA Symonds and Michelangelo, when he made two half-hidden sonnets part of J Alfred Prufrock's 'Love Song': 'Let us go then, you and I' and 'Indeed there will be time', each ending with the couplet 'In the room the women come and go / Talking of Michelangelo'.)

An era, then, of sonneteering, of sonnet sequences. (*Sonnet Sequence*: a phrase first recorded in 1881 in Dante Gabriel Rossetti's *Ballads and Sonnets*, where 'The House of Life' got its sub-title, 'a sonnet sequence'.) Indeed the whole period is a kind of sonnet sequence, or a small-poem sequence, with sonnets as the style-leader of this mode. A time of dinky poems, in a period of intense imaginative and cultural shrinkage or dinkification. The small Victorian poem flourishes as a tiny house – a doll's house, no less – fit for the period's small subjects to live in. Indeed poems become as toys, dolls even: formal correspondents of their frequently small subject matter, the little people and little things Victorian writing provided in such abundance for the small, or small-minded, reader. This is the time when 'children's literature' takes off – when little people, juveniles, are so often the implied reader, the target audience of so much art, so many books. Imaginative works – paintings, novels, songs, poems – fill up with the small subject, in every sense. *Little Women*, as Louisa May Alcott's classic (American) novel of 1868 about a family of girls labels its young female subjects, are greatly in evidence. Little girls and little boys and their doings abound. The subject goes dramatically Peter Pan-ish. (*Peter Pan*, colossally popular 1904 play about the boy 'who wouldn't grow up', by children's writer and childless adopter of boys JM Barrie, is the quintessence of this obsession.[3]) For every Little Nell, say, or little Alice, or little Maggie Tulliver of the prose fiction (Little Nell, small heroine of child-obsessed Charles Dickens's *The Old Curiosity Shop* (1840–1841), she whose premature death cast a whole nation into mourning; Alice, whose instantly popular shrunken *Adventures in Wonderland* were brought out in 1865 to cash in on the kiddy-market success of Charles Kingsley's 1863 hit about a boy chimney-sweep, *The Water Babies*; Maggie Tulliver whose little girl adventures thrill the first parts of George Eliot's *The Mill on the Floss*, 1860), for every one of these there was a little poetic Laura and little poetic Lizzie (Christina G Rossetti's 'Goblin Market'), and a little Tennysonian Maud, and yet another little poetic sister (as in George Eliot's eleven-sonnet 'Brother and Sister' sequence of 1869).

Suffer The Little Children

Victorian writers and artists didn't invent the child and childhood – eighteenth-century sentimentalists and the Romantics, as convention has it, did that – but they dramatically cashed in on this newish imaginative field. They turned

---

[3]   See Andrew Birkin, *JM Barrie and the Lost Boys: the Love Story that Gave Birth to Peter Pan* (Constable, London, 1979).

enthusiastically to the child, adopting the perspective of the child, the notorious Child's Eye View. The child became a chief focus of the imagination, a focal point, a main focalizer. And poetry was in the vanguard of this Childish Turn. Children are right in the forefront of so many Victorian poets' thoughts and visions and dreams. Whose hair does Lewis Carroll first invoke in his poem 'Only a Woman's Hair', about 'woman's hair, the theme of poet's song / In every time and place'? Why, a little girl's: 'A child's bright tresses, by the breezes kissed / To sweet disorder as she flies'. In a period of intense literary emotionality, it's feelings for the young that pour out in abundance. It's a fulsome emotionality. Not least in the community of male-gay poems, yearning with Gerard Hopkins over the lovely and untouchable bugler boy in 'The Bugler's First Communion'; or with AE Housman, perennially saddened by the loss of the 'lads' of 'The Shropshire Lad' sequence – the 'Athlete Dying Young', the suicidal soldier youth who killed himself in guilt over some homosexual affair ('Oh lad, you died as fits a man'), the boy who turned (it seems) into an old tramp now lying dead out in a rough and rainy terrain ('Goodnight, my lad'), and Oscar Wilde, turned by Housman into a 'young sinner' punished 'for the colour of his hair' ('Oh who is that young sinner with the hand cuffs on his wrist?'[4]); or with Wilde himself in his many poems thinking of boys and lads, including *The Ballad of Reading Gaol* which turns its wife-murdering soldier into a juvenile figure in a boyish cricket-cap (in a poem dense with menacingly little things – 'the little tent of blue / Which prisoners call the sky'; the coarse Doctor's watch 'whose little ticks / Are like horrible hammer blows'; the chaplain's 'little tract'; the hangman's 'gardener's gloves'; the killing shed with its 'little roof of glass'; the 'little heap of burning lime' which destroys the dead boy-man's body). A strong emotionalism which gets even stronger in the many mothering poems – the poem as mother, cherishing her baby, especially one bereft of a father.

> Sweet and low, sweet and low,
> Wind of the western sea,
> Low, low, breathe and blow,
> Wind of the western sea!
> Over the rolling waters go,
> Come from the dying moon, and blow,
> Blow him again to me;
> While my little one, while my pretty one, sleeps.

[4]   One likes to think Housman knew Wilde's 'Wasted Days' sonnet about the 'fair slim boy not made for this world's pain, / With hair of gold clustering round his ears', which is featured in the 'Hair Pieces' section of Ch 7, 'Fleshly Feelings', below. It's unimaginable that Housman was unfamiliar with golden-haired Dorian Gray. What colour the hair of Housman's 'young sinner' might be is discussed in 'Hair Pieces'. Housman, *Poems*, ed. Archie Burnett (Clarendon Press, Oxford, 1997).

> Sleep and rest, sleep and rest,
> Father will come to thee soon;
> Rest, rest, on mother's breast,
> Father will come to thee soon;
> Father will come to his babe in the nest
> Silver sails all out of the west
> Under the silver moon:
> Sleep, my little one, sleep, my pretty one, sleep.

That's one of the interpolated poems in Tennyson's *The Princess*: at the end of section II. Tennyson made many drafts; his wife chose this version of the lullaby from the two Tennyson sent her, 'because it seemed to her more song-like'.[5] With *my pretty one ... my pretty one* it tugs poignantly on that most grievous moment in *Macbeth* when Macduff hears of the murder of his children – 'All my pretty ones? Did you say all?' (Act 4, scene iii, 215–216).

The grievingly endangered child is a recurrent poetic motif – as in the coalminer poet Joseph Skipsey's 'Mother Wept', about a 'lad' foolishly excited about going down the pit ('Father hid his face and sighed, / Mother turned and wept')[6]; or in Elizabeth Barrett Barrett's 'The Cry of the Children' (1843), inspired (like Benjamin Disraeli's 1845 novel *Sybil*) by the nation-outraging 1842 Children's Employment Commission report into child-labour in factories and coal-mines (one of whose commissioners was Barrett's friend the radical poet Richard Hengist Horne). 'Do ye hear the children weeping, O my brothers, / Ere the sorrow comes with years?' Children unschooled; so ignorant they don't know what the Lord's Prayer ('Our Father which art in heaven') means – a Christian country's spiritual orphans; children deprived of rest and play; dragging heavy waggons along in 'the coal-dark, underground'; driving the factory 'wheels of iron', 'round and round'; dying 'before [their] time'. ' "Little Alice died last year – the grave is shapen / Like a snowball, in the rime".'

Such poems of protest on behalf of the ill-treated young are, of course, highly Christianized, like Elizabeth Barrett's 'Cry': founded in a vision of Jesus as 'the friend of little children', who said 'Suffer the little children to come unto me, and forbid them not: for of such is the kingdom of heaven' (Mark 10.14), and that nothing was worse than offending against them (Mark 9.42). The poets share Dickens's anger that a so-called Christian country should fail its church's founder's wishes by plainly not heeding the plight of the working-class and under-class child. Not dissimilarly, Roman Catholic Coventry Patmore, guilty about striking his small motherless son

---

[5]   Hallam Tennyson, *Memoir*, I.255
[6]   In Skipsey's *A Book of Lyrics, Including Songs, Ballads and Chants* (new edn, revised, David Bogue, 1881).

in his poem 'The Toys', puts himself feelingly into the toy-sized child-world as a penitent who needs forgiveness from the child-loving Heavenly Father:

> And I, with moan,
> Kissing away his tears, left others of my own;
> For, on a table drawn beside his head,
> He had put, within his reach,
> A box of counters and a red-vein'd stone,
> A piece of glass abraded by the beach
> And six or seven shells,
> A bottle with bluebells
> And two French copper coins, ranged there with careful art,
> To comfort his sad heart.
> So when that night I pray'd
> To God, I wept, and said:
> Ah, when at last we lie with tranced breath,
> Not vexing Thee in death,
> And Thou rememberest of what toys
> We made our joys,
> How weakly understood,
> The great commanded good,
> Then, fatherly not less
> Than I whom Thou hast moulded from the clay,
> Thou'lt leave Thy wrath, and say,
> 'I will be sorry for their childishness.'
> (This is part of *The Unknown Eros* sequence
> of Patmore's *The Angel in the House.*)

Sick and dying children provoke poets as much as they do novelists. Death ran rampant among the young of the large Victorian families; burying a child was a terribly normal experience for poets as for everyone else.[7] WE Henley's daughter Margaret died at the age of five, to become the little lost London girl 'Reddy' in JM Barrie's novel *Sentimental Tommy: The Story of His Boyhood* (1896) and, it's been suggested, the Wendy of *Peter Pan*. The children whom hospitalized WE Henley 'play[s] a father to' in the 'Children: Private Ward' section (XVIII) of his (1875–1888) *In Hospital* sequence play ominously at being surgeons (one lad 'Saws, lectures, takes the artery up, and ties') while waiting innocently for death ('Willie's but six, and seems to like the place, / A cheerful little collier to the last'). Robert Bridges, who practised medicine in London hospitals in the 1870s, was acquainted at first hand with young death, not just on the wards but also in the family. His younger brother died in 1866; his cousin (and fag at Eton) the camp boy-poet

---

[7] See Pat Jalland, *Death in the Victorian Family* (Oxford University Press, Oxford, 1996), especially Ch 6, '"That Little Company of Angels": The Tragedies of Children's Deaths'.

Digby Mackworth Dolben died in 1867 aged nineteen: griefs which evidently animate Bridges's many elegiac poems. Such as 'I never shall love the snow again / Since Maurice died' (in Bridges's *Poems: Third Series*, 1880), about a boy (he sounds like an undergraduate) who comes home two days late for Christmas, a corpse: 'Wrapped in white, in solemn state / A flower in his hand, all still and straight / Our Maurice lay':

> And two days ere the year outgave
> We laid him low.
> The best of us truly were not brave,
> When we laid Maurice down in his grave
> Under the snow.

(This Christmas-tide grief is strongly echoic of *In Memoriam*, and the snow reminds us of Bridges's expertly observant way with snow in perhaps his finest poem, 'London Snow'.) And, of course, there's Bridges's 'On a Dead Child' (also in the 1880 volume), aweingly compelling voice of a father, not unreminiscent of King Lear with his dead daughter Cordelia, apostrophizing and touching a just dead child:

> Perfect little body, without fault or stain on thee,
> With promise of strength and manhood full and fair!
> Though cold and stark and bare,
> The bloom and the charm of life doth awhile remain on thee.
>
> Thy mother's treasure wert thou; – alas! no longer
> To visit her heart with wondrous joy; to be
> Thy father's pride; ah, he
> Must gather his faith together, and his strength make stronger.
>
> To me, as I move thee now in the last duty,
> Dost thou with a turn or gesture anon respond;
> Startling my fancy fond
> With a chance attitude of the head, a freak of beauty.
>
> Thy hand clasps, as 'twas wont, my finger, and holds it:
> But the grasp is the clasp of Death, heart breaking and stiff;
> Yet feels to my hand as if
> 'Twas still thy will, thy pleasure and trust that enfolds it.
>
> So I lay thee there, thy sunken eyelids closing, –
> Go lie thou there in thy coffin, thy last little bed! –
> Propping thy wise, sad head,
> Thy firm, pale hands across thy chest disposing.
>
> So quiet! doth the change content thee? – Death, whither hath he taken thee?
> To a world, do I think, that rights the disaster of this?

The vision of which I miss,
Who weep for the body, and wish but to warm thee and awaken thee?

Ah! little at best can all our hopes avail us
To lift this sorrow, or cheer us, when in the dark,
Unwilling, alone we embark,
And the things we have seen and have known and have heard of, fail us.

'Death, whither hath he taken thee?' echoes the fearful question of Mary Magdalene about the empty tomb of Jesus in John's Gospel, 'they have taken away the Lord ... and we know not where they have laid him'. And the note of challenge to Christian faith amidst such loss of the young – this father 'Must gather his faith together'; 'hopes', presumably Christian ones of union with the lost one after death, little 'avail us' and 'fail us' – the key-note challenge of *In Memoriam*, as of the peasant poet James R Withers' extremely touching poem 'On the Death of My Child' about his dead little girl (' "Thy will be done", Lord, I still wish to say, / Though a task very hard for frail flesh and blood')[8], and as Pat Jalland illustrates of so much Victorian reaction to the death of children (*loc cit*) – is at the core of the poem's seriousness.

A prevailing *religious* seriousness – as in Cosmo Monkhouse's (longish, eighty-six-line) poem 'Dead'. 'My son, my darling, all my joy is dead'. The boy is also 'my shame', and as the narrating father's poetic short story unfolds we learn why: the boy was some sort of Prodigal Son. He 'chose the wrong'; followed 'the fiend', albeit 'with hated steps and aching heart, /Yielding his body only with averted soul, / And died'. And the father is 'glad' ('Did I say glad? God help me'). It's a Victorian melodrama, of course, the stuff of evangelical tracts for the young – like the *Child's Guide* that the Revd Mr Brocklehurst hands to little *Jane Eyre*, with its 'account of the awfully sudden death of Martha G–, a naughty child addicted to falsehood and deceit': *Jane Eyre* (1847), Chapter 4. A narrative tradition whose melodramas not only registered its seriousness but laid it wide open to mockery, as at the hands of child-abuse protesting Charlotte Brontë, and of one of the key players in the children's-lit industry, the Catholic Christian Hilaire Belloc, whose *Cautionary Tales for Children* (1907) lampoons the bad-end-of-the-naughty-child syndrome it so gloriously plagiarizes. In, for example, 'Henry King, Who Chewed Bits of String, and Was Early Cut off in Dreadful Agonies': 'His Parents stood about his Bed / Lamenting his Untimely Death', as 'the Wretched Child expires' in midsentence, warning other kiddies off 'chewing little bits of String' between meals. Or in 'Matilda Who Told Lies, and Was Burned to Death': the

---

[8] In *Poems upon Various Subjects* (CW Naylor, Cambridge; Wertheim & Macintosh, London, 1854).

'little Liar' cried 'Fire' falsely once too often. Or 'Rebecca, Who Slammed Doors for Fun and Perished Miserably':

> Her funeral Sermon (which was long
> And followed by a Sacred Song)
> Mentioned her Virtues, it is true,
> But dwelt upon her Vices too,
> And showed the Dreadful End of one
> Who goes and slams the door for Fun.

What Belloc was poking fun at was poetry's going so often to Sunday School – seeking to teach children how to follow Gentle Jesus and be good little Christians, in the well-intended but keenly hortatory vein of Ulsterwoman Mrs CF Alexander. The verses of this Protestant evangelical clergy wife (her husband became Bishop of Derry and Rafoe and eventually Archbishop of Armagh and Primate of All Ireland) kept up the tradition going back to the Evangelical Movement of the eighteenth century which popularized hymn-singing in church and whose hymn-writing stars Charles Wesley and Isaac Watts made children a special target, as in Watts's *Divine Songs Attempted in Easy Language for the Use of Children* (1735), and Wesley's *Hymns for Children* (1763). In her *Hymns for Little Children* (1848), *Moral Songs* (1849) and *Hymns, Descriptive and Devotional for the Use of Schools* (1858) Mrs Alexander aimed to keep Irish Catholics and all the poor, but above all children, in their place. 'All things Bright and Beautiful', with its notorious verse about God ordering the difference between 'The rich man in his castle' and 'The poor man at his gate', is one of hers, from *Hymns for Little Children*. But even stronger in their theologized subordinating work are the messages for children in the lines in the same volume written to illustrate the Creed from the Anglican Church's *Book of Common Prayer*. Jesus dies 'to make us good' in (the quickly standard Easter hymn) 'There is a Green Hill Far Away'; 'He is our childhood's Pattern' in (the quickly standard Christmas Carol) 'Once in Royal David's City':

> And through all His wondrous childhood
> He would honour and obey,
> Love and watch the lowly maiden
> In whose gentle arms He lay.
> Christian children all must be
> Mild, obedient, good as He.

Francis Thompson, the child-adoring Roman Catholic (author of the desperately God-haunted 'The Hound of Heaven', keen addresser of Monica and Madeleine and Viola, the small daughters of Wilfred and Alice Meynell who took him off the street, a sad down-and-out opium addicted alcoholic who remained stuck in his own childhood and left nothing when he died in a hospice in 1907 except some papers and pipes and a toy-theatre he'd had since boyhood), clearly found the hard evangelistic driving of Mrs Alexander's kind hard to take. His extremely twee 'Little Jesus', in the voice of a little child addressing a 'little Jesus', wondering whether He too was kissed and tucked up at night by His mother, and so forth, gets close to mocking the affinities it claims:

> And did Thy Mother let Thee spoil
> Thy robes, with playing on *our* soil?
> How nice to have them always new
> In Heaven, because 'twas quite clean blue!
>
> ....
>
> Didst Thou kneel at night to pray
> And didst Thou join Thy hands, this way?
> And did they tire sometimes, being young,
> And make the prayer seem very long?[9]

Lewis Carroll's impatience with the kiddy-hymn writers is even clearer in his verses 'How doth the little crocodile / Improve his shining tail', about a diabolical crocodile cheerfully welcoming the little fishes of the Nile into his 'gently smiling' jaws. This is a put-down of Isaac Watts's Song 20, 'Against Idleness and Mischief', which offered little bees as models of puritanical good works and good conscience – 'How doth the little busy bee improve each shining hour':

> In works of labour, or of skill,
> I would be busy too;
> For Satan finds some mischief still
> For idle hands to do.
>
> In books, or work, or healthful play
> Let my first years be past;
> That I may give for ev'ry day
> Some good account at last.

The Sunday School instructors were easy meat for the child-protectionist mockers (Dickens's novels can hardly stop jeering at them). Obviously more compelling – and quite plainly harder to submit to the put-down treatment, for nobody at the time seems to try doing so – were poems whose instructional

---

[9] The 'Poems on Children' section of Thompson's *Poems* (1893) contains 'Daisy', 'The Poppy; to Monica', 'To Monica Thought Dying', and 'The Making of Viola'. This section is placed first in Volume I of Thompson's (posthumous) 3-volume *Works*, ed Wilfred Meynell, with 'Olivia' and 'Little Jesus' added. Thompson's *Sister Songs* (1895) makes up the second section of Vol I.

intentions for young behaviour came as narratives of youthful courage, endurance and daring: the Grace Darling-like stuff of that other kind of Sunday School literature, the *Adventure Book for Boys, and Girls*, often of an imperialist or foreign-missions stripe. I mean poems like Felicia Hemans' notorious 'Casabianca' about a thirteen-year-old lad who alone stuck to his guns as his ship went down ('The boy stood on the burning deck / Whence all but he had fled'), or Henry Newbolt's (wonderfully compelling; let no hard-hearted or post-colonially correct critic say otherwise) 'Vitaï Lampada' in which 'the voice of a schoolboy' is heard rousing the British soldiery hard-pressed in some desert campaign with the words of his old school's cricket captain (a lot of cricket and its implied codes for British and Empire boys knocks about in these verses for schoolboys):

> There's a breathless hush in the Close to-night –
> Ten to make and the match to win –
> A bumping pitch and a blinding light,
> An hour to play and the last man in.
> And it's not for the sake of a ribboned coat,
> Or the selfish hope of a season's fame,
> But his Captain's hand on his shoulder smote
> 'Play up! play up! and play the game!'
>
> The sand of the desert is sodden red, –
> Red with the wreck of a square that broke; –
> The Gatling's jammed and the Colonel dead,
> And the regiment blind with dust and smoke.
> The river of death has brimmed his banks,
> And England's far, and Honour a name,
> But the voice of a schoolboy rallies the ranks:
> 'Play up! play up! and play the game!'[10]

Dollanity

And one way or another quite grown-up poets kept playing childhood games. Childhood recall, the experience of the child, even nursery conscious-ness, were all the rage. It's only typical that between *The Prince's Progress and Other Poems* (1866) and her 1875 volume *Goblin Market, The Prince's Progress and Other Poems*, Christina G Rossetti should bring out her entirely baby-talk *Sing-Song: A Nursery Rhyme Book* (1872). Plainly,

[10] 'Vitaï Lampada', from Lucretius, *De rerum naturae*, II.79: 'Et quasi cursores vitae lampada tradunt', 'And like runners they hand on the torch of life'. Poem in Newbolt's *Admirals All* (Elkin Mathews, 1897); reprinted in the volume celebrating Newbolt's old school, Clifton School, Bristol, *Clifton Chapel and Other School Poems* (John Murray, London, 1908).

playing and replaying the world of the child, retreating into Nursery Rhyme, into *The Child's Garden of Verses* (as Robert Louis Stevenson's 1885 volume had it) was to re-enter, in the first place at any rate, an enticing lost world of remembered bliss, a glamorous imaginary wonderland of prelapsarian innocence, a happy enclosure of fairies and toys and other little things for little people. Characteristically, in Stevenson's *A Child's Garden* poem 'Block City', about a small boy's imaginative toy-city made out of his nursery building-blocks, the now grown-up poet contemplates that midget urbs again: 'And as long as I live, and where'er I may be, / I'll always remember my town by the sea'. Rather like the childhood-preoccupied James R Withers in his 'Little Rill'. 'I know a rill, a little rill'; it plays bo-peep as it rushes down the hill; 'Never still, never still, / Childhood is a little rill'. Childhood is where Withers's poetry wants to be. 'And I sigh for the pleasures when I was a boy', he says in the poem 'When I Was a Boy' – one more would-be Peter Pan.[11] Why this is childhood you might say, nor are they out of it. The poet and the poem have embraced *dollanity* as aesthetic home.[12]

Dollanity: that so canny label of Louisa May Alcott for these imaginative proceedings. It occurs in her *Little Women* (1868–1869), Chapter 4, to describe the doll-obsession of the novel's girls. Young Beth hoards dolls; she has six at least; she keeps a hospital for sick dolls, childish variant on Civil War infirmaries (Alcott nursed in one), where 'all were fed and clothed, nursed and caressed, with an affection which never failed'. One of these small parody infirm creatures had belonged to Jo: 'One forlorn fragment of dollanity'. It's utterly characteristic of this small-time time, that the dollanity taste and craving are shared by just about the biggest and bluffest and most amplitudinous of poets, namely Tennyson himself. His eye for the telling small subject, small person, small thing is wonderfully acute (result, it's suggested, of the close-up peering his shortsightedness necessitated). Here he is, apostrophizing a small flower, taken from a tiny fissure or cranny in a wall of crannies, to put in a tiny poem, itself occupying a mere poetic cranny alongside such flourishing poetic life-forms as 'The Coming of Arthur', 'The Holy Grail', 'Pelleas and Ettare' and 'The Passing of Arthur' in the 1869 ('1870') volume in which it first appeared, *The Holy Grail and Other Poems*:

> Flower in the crannied wall,
> I pluck you out of the crannies,
> I hold you here, root and all, in my hand,
> Little flower ...

[11]   Both poems in Withers's *Poems Upon Various Subjects* (1854).
[12]   Ann C Colley celebrates Stevenson's unabashed childhood nostalgias in ' "Writing Towards Home": The Landscape of A Child's Garden of Verses', *Victorian Poetry* 35, iii (Fall 1997), 303–318.

Line 3 originally began with just 'Hold', the 'I' being assumed. Tennyson added the 'I' by hand in his own copy of his *Works* (1881); he really wanted to bring home *his* holding the little flower in his hand – as he had done for real, apparently, when he plucked it at 'Waggoners Wells' near Haslemere. His poems would pause, deictically like this – *here* – as he did in life, over the tiniest natural thing. 'I have often known him stop short in a sentence to listen to a blackbird's song, to watch the sunlight glint on a butterfly's wing, or to examine a field flower at his feet'.[13] His son Hallam's *Memoir* is full of such moments. And so are Tennyson's poems. And it's no accident that, for instance, the lovely love-poem, 'Now sleeps the crimson petal, now the white', which oriental Ida reads aloud in 'The Princess', figuring the night-time desires of a lover in terms of the night-time behaviour of small natural creatures and things – 'Now folds the lily all her sweetness up, / And slips into the bosom of the lake: / So fold thyself, my dearest, thou, and slip / Into my bosom and be lost in me'– should be a sonnet. That it's declared to be from 'A volume of the Poets of her land' has prompted critics to suggest its form and images make it a Persian 'ghazal' – despite Tennyson saying he knew no Persian. But whatever the truth of this, it's a sonnet first and foremost, and one whose repeated end- and self-rhyming *me* (as emphatically personalizing as the *I*'s of 'Flower in the crannied wall') doesn't need any reference to the ghazal's repetitions of a 'single final word' to endorse or explain it.[14]

The poet and the lovely little thing. Hear Tennyson, attending the wedding of John Simeon's daughter, along with the poet Frederick Locker, and noticing a five-year-old bridesmaid: 'And as she knelt before us in sweet unconscious reverence, she displayed the soles of her little white shoes. These, and her little face and her general adornment were altogether very engaging, and Tennyson whispered to me: "She and her shoes remind me of one of your poems".'[15] Doubtless the poem 'My Mistress's Boots', by Locker (later known as Locker-Lampson):

> They nearly strike me dumb, –
> I tremble when they come
> Pit-a-pat:
> This palpitation means
> These Boots are Geraldine's –
> Think of that!

[13]   Mrs Richard Ward, daughter of Tennyson's great friend John Simon, quoted in Hallam Tennyson, *Memoir*, II.11

[14]   For the ghazal discussion see John Killham, *Tennyson and 'The Princess': Reflections of an Age* (University of London Athlone Press, London, 1958), 219–220, and for Tennyson's disclaimer see Christopher Ricks, 'Tennyson and Persian', *English Language Notes*, IV (September 1966), 46–47.

[15]   Hallam Tennyson, *Memoir*, II.78.

O, where did hunter win
So delicate a skin
For her feet?
You lucky little kid,
You perish'd, so you did,
For my sweet.

The faery stitching gleams
On the toes, and in the seams,
And reveals
That the Pixies were the wags
Who tipt these funny tags,
And these heels.

What soles to charm an elf! –
Had Crusoe, sick of self,
Chanced to view
One printed near the tide,
O, how hard he would have tried
For the two!

For Gerry's debonair,
And innocent, and fair
As a rose:
She's an angel in a frock, –
What a fascinating cock
To her hose!

Those simpletons who squeeze
Their pretty toes to please
Mandarins,
Would positively flinch
From venturing to pinch
Geraldine's!

Cinderella's *lefts and rights*
To Geraldine's were frights:
And, in truth,
The damsel, deftly shod,
Has dutifully trod
From her youth.

Come, Gerry, since it suits
Such a busy puss in boots
To be gone,
Set your dainty hand awhile
On my shoulder, dear, and I'll
Put them on.[16]

---

[16] Locker, *Poems* (private edition) (John Wilson, 1868). *London Lyrics*, '5th edn' (1872) claims the poem was first published in 1865.

In the 1876 edition of Locker's *London Lyrics* the poem acquired a fitting epigraph: 'She has dancing eyes and ruby lips / Delightful boots and away she skips'. The frontispiece of the first, private, presentation edition of Locker's *Poems* (later *London Lyrics*) is an illustration by Locker's friend (and Dickens's illustrator) George Cruikshank showing pixies making Geraldine's tiny footwear. (Cruikshank had established himself as an illustrator of fairies and fairyland when he did the pictures for the instantly popular *German Popular Stories* (first series 1823, second series 1826), first English translation of the Grimm Brothers' *Kinder und Haus-Märchen,* including 'The Elves and the Shoemaker' in the 1823 volume.) The 1881 edition of *London Lyrics* has an end-piece by Kate Greenaway, the by-then very well-known children's-book illustrator, entitled 'Little Dinky'.

Little Dinky: Little Kinky

If fetishism – always religiously and economically (Marx's 'commodity fetishism') as well as erotically charged – involves desirous substitution, synecdoche, the taking of a small thing for a larger one, then this is rampant fetishizing: small female as synecdochic substitute for grown-up woman, her shoes (shoes, those almost universal fetish objects) classically synecdochic of a forever out-of-reach desired female. And Locker's texts represent a wholesale Victorian fetishism of the a small female, a voyeuristic cult of the little girl as a doll or toy in a miniaturized nursery world of toys and dolls – where the female subject is reduced to a small effigy of herself in texts (and contexts) simply obsessed with dinky effigies and representations of the large world.[17] This is the Lilliputian world of children's writer William Brighty Rands. He's the author of *Lilliput Levée* (1864: illustrated by John Everett Millais), *Lilliput Revels* (1871), *Lilliput Lectures* (1871) and *Lilliput Legends* (1872): a career spent fantasizing over little girls, culminating in the posthumous collection issued by the glossy decadent publishers John Lane the Bodley Head. The cuteness of Rands's 'Doll Poems' doesn't at all assuage your worries over his paedophiliac patrolling of the underclothes of the doll 'Dolladine':

[17]   Giorgio Agamben's account of fetishism as a synecdochic literary/poetic phenomenon powerfully inspects dolls and toys as regular fetishistic objects, with reference to Baudelaire's 'enchantment' with things, and Rilke, as well to Baudelaire-obsessive Walter Benjamin and, of course, foundationally, Freud's 'Fetishism'. Giorgo Agamben, *Stanzas: Word and Phantasm in Western Culture*, trans Ronald L Martinez (*Theory and History of Literature*, 69; University of Minnesota Press, Minneapolis & London, 1993), especially Ch 10, 'Mme Panckoncke; or, The Toy Fairy', 59–60; but also Ch 6, 'Freud; or, the Absent Object', 31–36; Ch 7, 'Marx; or, The Universal Exposition', 36–40; and Ch 8, 'Baudelaire; or, The Absolute Commodity', 41–46.

> First, you observe her little chemise
> As white as milk, with ruches of silk;
> And the little drawers that cover her knees,
> As she sits or stands, with golden bands,
> And lace in beautiful filagrees.

That's from Rands's 'Doll Poems', III. 'Dressing Her' (in *Lilliput Lyrics*), but the dressing of this tiny effigy of a little Lolita reads more like an undressing. The repeated warnings of the poem's chorus against *crumpling* and *messing* it/her actually sound like a kind of gloating about what the sanctioned *pressing* might come to:

> Bless the Doll, you may press the Doll,
> But do not crumple or mess the Doll!
> This is the way we dress the Doll.

Just how far, you wonder, will the Lilliput Lyricist let himself go with his pressing? To its moral credit Francis Thompson's sonnet 'Olivia' tries to warn off little Olivia Meynell, ostensibly because love always leads to 'loss'.

> White flake of childhood, clinging so
> To my soiled raiment, thy shy snow
> At tenderest touch will shrink and go.
> Love me not delightful child.

Though, meanwhile, the poem rather delights in recording the clinging of this 'harmless-small' female creature to his 'soiled raiment' – *raiment*, Biblical, even Christological, garments, *soiled* literally by the filth of the streets where Thompson dossed down, and morally by his brothel contaminations. The poet will cling on to her clinging, relishing the great physical and moral contrast between this couple of ill-sorted 'lovers' which he affects to deplore. But even this contaminated degree of self-conscious self-cautioning is generally far from the thoughts of the small-tableaux merchants.

Small Tableaux: that's the very apt 1868 title of the period's mass-producer of sonnets, the Revd Charles (Tennyson) Turner. Neurotically productive, he's militantly defensive about the mode (his repeated defences make him the period's most sustained sonnet theorist). And smallness of scope is his major theoretical concern. The epigraph of his *Sonnets and Fugitive Pieces* (1830) is Wordsworth's line about 'The sonnet's humble plot of ground'. *Small Tableaux* is a translation of that volume's Latin epigraph, 'Hasce breves, oro pictor, ne sperne tabellas': 'I beg you, you painter, not to despise these small tableaux'. The volume's opening sonnet (CXLVIII in the Pinions' *Collected Sonnets*), 'My First and Last Strophe: On Being Asked to Write An Ode by a Friend', disclaims any power to do Odes. Tennyson

Turner's 'poor muse' cannot soar. The sonnet is 'Gossamer-Light' (Pinion CCLXXII); it's a stay-at-home mode, moving 'in modest round / Among my neighbours' (LI); it's always 'this little page' only (CXCVI). The best 'my sonnet-muse' can manage is 'her little best' (CXLIX). The sonnet works 'in one flash' only of illumination. And so it is too 'quick-spent' to cope even with such a tiny object as a 'sea-shell' ('The Sonneteer to the Sea-Shell', CCCXII). But sea-shells and their like are of necessity the mode's main subject in Turner's hands. His poems simply fetishize the small subject. They alight one after another on some tiny thing: coins, insects (especially bees and flies), birds (robin, wren, lark, corn-crake, bitterns, starling, nightingale, rooks, and so on and on), and especially on children – an occasional boy-child, but mainly a huge crowd of little girls: Kate, Lizzie, Minnie, Maud, Marie, Dora, Phoebe, Sophy, Agnes, Edith, Emeline, Alice, Ellen, Letty, Millie. Tennyson Turner was an unstoppable collector of little girls for his poems, not least at the seaside. He rivalled the Revd Charles Lutwidge Dodgson (Lewis Carroll) in his greed for young female company. He was Lincolnshire's own Lewis Carroll – Skegness's own poetic paedophile. The poet with the roving eye of the sonnet 'Little Sophy by the Seaside' (Pinion CCXXXIV: in his 1873 volume *Sonnets, Lyrics, and Translations*, which was dedicated to his niece Agness Grace Weld), watching little Sophy as a little Digger claiming 'her right of common in the land' armed only with a 'wooden spade', her 'little edgeless tools', a golden-haired mite in 'her pink sash', heading for the beach, 'childhood's ancient field of play', with 'a step of joy' (far removed from Browning's Duchess's 'spot of joy'). Or of 'Millie Macgill' (CCCXXXVII: in the posthumously published *Collected Sonnets, Old and New*), a memory of a beach encounter in July 1873, in Ardrossan, Scotland, with 'the little darling of the past'.

> I watch'd thy merry gambols on the sand,
> And ask'd thy name beside the morning sea;
> Sweet came thine answer, with thy little hand
> Upon the spade, and thy blue eyes on me,
> Millie Macgill.

Is she still alive, the poet wonders? He hopes she's not married; that nothing separates 'the silver sounds', 'Thy seaside names of Millie and Macgill'. It's important to the little-girl fetishizer that his objects of desire stay small – as the poem would preserve them, stuck in the aspic of memory. These poems cannot bear the negating of that temporary loveliness, the disappearance of the once accessible small girl. As in 'The Seaside: In and Out of Season' (CCXXXIX) – another act of little girl devotion from the 1873 volume, an elegy for the little girls of summer past with their very desirable, unknotted, loosened hair (based, Turner's editors suggest, on a holiday at Barmouth in North Wales in 1868):

In summer-time it was a paradise
Of mountain, frith, and bay, and shining sand;
Our outward rowers sang towards the land,
Follow'd by waving hands and happy cries:
By the full flood the groups no longer roam;
And when, at ebb, the glistening beach grows wide,
No barefoot children race into the foam,
But passive jellies wait the turn of tide.
Like some forsaken lover, lingering there,
The boatman stands; the maidens trip no more
With loosen'd locks; far from the billows' roar
The Mauds and Maries knot their tresses fair,
Where not a foam-flake from th'enamour'd shore
Comes down the sea-wind on the golden hair.

Those negatives – *no longer roam, No barefoot children, maidens trip no more, not a foam-flake … on the golden hair* – bear down heavily: the presence of a terrible absence; the enclosing bay, the beach, like the little enclosing space of the short poem, now a desolate scene of paradise lost.

Metonymic Eloquence

Many forces are at work in this pervasive poetic desire for the small thing, the small person, especially this repeated male fetishizing of the small female. What's very clear, though, is the lure of the possible sheer beauty of the small – small people, small things. Edmund Burke, great inspirer of the Romantics, had in his *Philosophical Enquiry into the Origin of our Ideas of the Sublime and the Beautiful* (1757) nicely and influentially put his finger on the contrastive aesthetic force of size: big natural things (mountains, for example) were *sublime*, but the *beautiful* was to be found in small things.[18] And the beautiful in the Burkean sense was what powered our poets' zest for the tininesses they packed their poems with: the snowflakes, raindrops, little flowers, leaves, petals, fruits and nuts, little birds and tiny creatures of Clare and Tennyson, of Hopkins and Hardy and Thompson and the rest; nature's lovely miniatures; God's fairy creations.

See what a lovely shell,
Small and pure as a pearl
Lying close to my foot,
Frail, but a work divine,
Made so fairly well,
With delicate spire and whorl,
How exquisitely minute,
A miracle of design!

[18]   See Valentine Cunningham, 'Charles (Tennyson) Turner and the Power of the Small Poetic Thing', *Victorian Poetry* 48, iv (Winter 2010), 1–13.

That's the runaway hero of Tennyson's *Maud*, consoled by the perfection of a seashell on a Brittany beach (*Maud*, Part II, ii, 1, 49–56).

> What heart could have thought you? –
> Past our devisal
> (O filigree petal!)
> Fashioned so purely,
> Fragilely, surely,
> From what Paradisal
> Imagineless metal,
> Too costly for cost?
> Who hammered you, wrought you,
> From argentine vapour? –
> 'God was my shaper.
> Passing surmisal,
> He hammered, He wrought me
> From curled silver vapour,
> To lust of His mind: –
> Thou could'st not have thought me!
> So purely, so palely,
> Tinily, surely,
> Mightily, frailly,
> Insculped and embossed,
> With His hammer of wind,
> And His graver of frost.'

That's Francis Thompson's 'To a Snow-Flake' (from his *New Poems*, 1897), the maker trying to enter the mind of *The Maker* (Dorothy Sayers's name for the Christian deity[19]) of this astoundingly made little object (and in *Goblin Market* rhymes, too). It's no surprise that when John Everett Millais, devotee of small children (think his painting *Bubbles*), as also of the tiny detailed foliage which packs Pre-Raphaelite paintings, sought to capture the loveliness of his little grand-daughter Phyllis he should have painted her enraptured by one of the two sprigs of speedwell she holds – a plant with tiny blue flowers, lifted from Tennyson's *In Memoriam* (LXXXIII), where the poet urges that flowers be brought to make funeral decorations: 'Bring orchis, bring the foxglove spire, / The little speedwell's darling blue'. '"*The Little Speedwell's Darling Blue.*" "*In Memoriam*"' is Millais's title (1891–1892) – an acknowledgement not just of the poet he loved, but a memorializing of Tennyson's potent way with miniature natural loveliness.

And what Millais was tapping into was not just Tennyson's mere relish for such tiny beauties, but his exploiting of the representational force of the tiny aestheticized thing or person, the way the poems keep making them

---

[19]   Dorothy Sayers, *The Mind of the Maker* (Methuen, London, 1941).

stand for more than just themselves. These little poetic items are offered as packed with meaning; as having allegorical, metaphoric, metonymic power; the synecdochic power of the fetish. What Jennifer Ann Wagner is getting at when she hails the expansionist force of what she calls the 'visionary sonnet': 'in which one poetic moment becomes an apocalyptic moment, containing all moments, in which the smallness of the form opens out through largeness of conception'.[20] That Breton seashell of Tennyson's 'is a miracle of design'; it's an argument for a designer God. Thompson's snowflake likewise talks theology. Apostrophizing the little flower he's grasped from the crannied wall, Tennyson thinks

> ... *if* I could understand
> What you are, root and all, and all in all,
> I should know what God and man is.

The sense of larger intimations, *there*, implicit, for the grasping, is a common feeling at such aesthetic moments. It powers Ruskin's approval of Pre-Raphaelite particularism, and his insistence that poetry must start with 'a little flower apprehended in the very plain and leafy fact of it' (in his attack on the Pathetic Fallacy of poetry – discussed in my next chapter, Chapter 6, 'Selving'). Browning's way, as ever, is to put the feeling under question, and in quotation marks, in his *Men and Women* poem 'An Epistle containing the Strange Medical Experience of Karshish, the Arab Physician'. Karshish has met the Biblical Lazarus, allegedly raised from the dead by Jesus, which raises huge questions about divinity and Incarnation and miracle. Should Karshish write about little things, when such big issues are pressing? 'Why write of trivial matters, things of price / Calling at every moment for remark?' (278–279). But straightaway he reports noticing a flowering herb.

> I noticed on the margin of a pool
> Blue-flowering borage, the Aleppo sort
> Aboundeth, very nitrous. It is strange!
> (280–283)

So what *is* the more arresting for the writer? Religious matters or tiny flowers? The run of Karshish's lines makes it unclear which is trivial, which pricey. But even as we reflect that Browning can't really think that little flowers are more pressing subjects than big religious issues, the question of which is the more important has sunk in, and we are indeed left noticing the little blue flower, left holding the suggestion that its meanings might actually be the more

---

[20] Jennifer Ann Wagner, *A Moment's Monument: Revisionary Poetics and the Nineteenth-Century English Sonnet* (Associated University Presses, Cranbury, NJ; London; Mississauga, Ontario, 1996), Ch 4, ' "Sonnettomania" and the Ideology of Form', 125.

momentous. Which takes us close to the contents of Tennyson's crannied wall: something like the aweing thought of George Eliot, rhapsodizing in her review of RW Mackay's *The Progress of the Intellect* (1850) about geology and the way geologists can deduce the earth's history from a single pebble.[21] 'To see', as Blake put it in his 'Auguries of Innocence', 'a World in a Grain of Sand, / And a Heaven in a Wild Flower, / Hold Infinity in the palm of your hand, / And Eternity in an hour'.[22] The metonymic eloquence of the small bit. Synecdochic truth. The transcendent glimpsed in the small empirical tot (the miniaturism that Gaston Bachelard lauds in *The Poetics of Space* as 'one of the refuges of greatness').[23] Which is what the poetry of the small thing and person desires and claims and, often, offers. A Victorian poeticity taking its place, then, alongside those two great Victorian inventions whose practice and meaning are also built on this assumption and manifestation of the revelatory meaning and truth contained in the small thing and small text – namely, the postage stamp and the photograph. Two meaning-packed Victorian textualities which are key examples of the new modes of aesthetic reproduction by mechanical means famously celebrated by Walter Benjamin as 'the Work of Art in an Age of Mechanical Reproduction'.[24] As machine-made pictorial miniaturizers of the real, the postage stamp and the photograph are akin to the factory-made, mass-produced Victorian metal toy, those dinky reproductions of the real, especially things, soldiers, animals, made of tin or lead – not to mention the dinky triumph of the age, the toy train.[25]

The Stamp of The Photographic Era

Here was a dramatic convergence of the aesthetic and the mechanistic, of – in that convenient and potent German concept rhyme – the *Aesthetik* and the *Technik*, which was witnessed with extreme picturesque force in the

---

[21]   *Westminster Review* (January 1851), 353–368. Jessica R Feldman is illuminating about Ruskin's (and George Eliot's) attachment to the meaning of the small detail in nature and art and architecture: *Victorian Modernism: Pragmatism and the Varieties of Aesthetic Experience* (Cambridge University Press, Cambridge, 2002), 16, 17, 23.

[22]   Written in 1803 or so; published first in Alexander Gilchrist's (posthumous) *Life of Blake* (1863).

[23]   Gaston Bachelard, *The Poetics of Space*, trans Maria Jolas (Beacon Press, Boston MA, 1969), 163.

[24]   In e.g. Walter Benjamin, *Illuminations*, ed. Hannah Arendt, trans Harry Zohn (Fontana, 1973). Originally in *Zeitschrift für Sozialforschung*, V.i (1936).

[25]   Lindsay Smith tries, with some success, to work the meaning and power of the new medium of the photograph into her discussion of the conflict between large meanings and the tiny detailism of Ruskin's polemics, Pre-Raphaelite practice and, in particular Morris's 'Defence of Guenevere': *Victorian Photography, Painting and Poetry: The Enigma of Visibility in Ruskin, Morris, and the PreRaphaelites* (Cambridge University Press, Cambridge, 1995).

career of Lewis Carroll. Carroll the author of the most famous of Victorian kiddy texts (including poems), namely the *Alice* books about a magically miniaturized world down a rabbit-hole; obsessed with fairy tininess of every sort; collector of little children, but particularly little girls and young actresses, for company and for photographing and writing about; badgering parents to let him get his hands on their young, but mainly their daughters; perpetually attentive to these little ones, writing poems and acrostic verses for Minnie, Ella and Emmie Drury, for Mary, Ina, and Harriet Watson, for Ruth Dymes, Marion Terry, Edith Denham, Florence Beaton, Mary Farshall, Rachel Daniel, and the rest, pursuing them by letter, holding their attention with his stories (which is how the *Alice* books began); a toy and gadget fetishist (he lectured Sunday Schools with a mechanized Humpty Dumpty); postal obsessive (inventor of 'The Wonderland Postage Stamp-Case', a pocket card-case for keeping postage stamps in, issued in 1890 with his pamphlet *Eight or Nine Wise Words About Letter Writing* – about beginning, going on with, ending, registering your letters, and above all using the one-and-only Wonderland Postage-Stamp Case); hoarder of the pictures of little girls and such, which he called his 'micro' photographs; his hands so scarily blackened with photographic chemicals that he wore gloves to conceal his own mechanical-era version of what Shakespeare called the stained 'dyer's hand' of the artist and not frighten off his little female friends.[26]

And as with Tennyson's little flower – he couldn't actually hold all meaning, all mankind, all divinity in his hand, but the little flower he could grasp might contain in its tiny self all of those things – so with toys, and toy-like poems, many of them about toy-size things and creatures. Cities and their inhabitants, for instance, belong to the big world outside the nursery, but in toy form they can be built at home, metonyms of grand buildings fit for the small citizen Robert Louis Stevenson, and now the grown-up Stevenson, to inhabit imaginatively. The boy with all the lead soldiers in his toy-box in Stevenson's poem 'My Treasures', the 'dolly sailor' of the toy-boat in the poem 'My Ship and I', lives on into his author's childhood-reeking adulthood. 'What are you able to build with your blocks?', asks Stevenson in his 'Block City', and the answer is, the whole caboodle: 'Castles and palaces, temples and docks'. A whole city in a lucky small child's small hands. A whole world, no less, if you're one of Tennyson Turner's luckiest little girls.

> When Letty had scarce pass'd her third glad year,
> And her young, artless words began to flow,
> One day we gave the child a colour'd sphere
> Of the wide earth, that she might mark and know,

---

[26] 'My nature is subdu'd / To what it works in, like the dyer's hand; Pity me, then ...': Shakespeare's Sonnet 111, 'Oh, for my sake do you with Fortune chide'.

> By tint and outline, all its sea and land.
> She patted all the world; old empires peep'd
> Between her baby fingers; her soft hand
> Was welcome at all frontiers. How she leap'd,
> And laugh'd, and prattled in her world-wide bliss.

That's little Letty holding a tin globe in Tennyson Turner's (much anthologized) sonnet 'Letty's Globe' (Pinion, CCCVI). He liked imagining the vast potential of the small toy-like object in a baby's hands. Or the kid holding, as it were, all the exploits of Alexander the Great between finger and thumb in the sonnet 'On Seeing A Little Child Spin a Coin of Alexander the Great' (Pinion, CCC):

> This is the face of him, whose quick resource
> Of eye and hand subdued Bucephalus,
> And made the shadow of a startled horse
> A foreground for his glory. It is thus
> They hand him down; this coin of Philip's son
>
> ...
>
> A coin his only presence: he is gone:
> And all but this half mythic image fled –
> A simple child may do him shame and slight;
> 'Twixt thumb and finger take the golden head,
> And spin the horns of Ammon out of sight.

(Both of these Turner poems are in his *Collected Sonnets*.) Lead soldiers, boats for dollies, tin globes, coins, and stamps and photographs: small objects packed metonymically with the largest meanings. As Walter Benjamin, keen childhood collector of toys and postage stamps, and great celebrator of Berlin's toyshops and stamp-shops, put it, marvellously, of postage-stamps:

> The child looks towards far-off Liberia through an inverted opera-glass: there it lies with its little strip of sea with its palms, just as stamps show it. With Vasco d Gama he sails around a triangle as isoscelean as hope and whose colours change with weather. A travel brochure for the Cape of Good Hope. ...
>   Stamps are the visiting cards that the great states leave in a child's room.
>   Like Gulliver the child travels among the lands and peoples of his postage stamps. The geography and history of the Lilliputians, the whole science of the little nation, is instilled in him in sleep ... . [27]

---

[27]   Walter Benjamin, 'Stamp Shop' section of *One-Way Street* (English version of *Einbahnstrasse*, written 1925–1926): *One-Way Street, and Other Writings*, trans Edmund Jephcott and Kingsley Shorter (NLB, London, 1979), 94.

The Victorians quickly realized something of the sort about photographs.[28] As Tennyson Turner has it in his sonnet 'A Photograph on the Red Gold: Jersey, 1867' (in *Small Tableaux*; Pinion, CCXXIX) about the image on the reflective back of his gold watch – a picture made of light, literally a *photo-graph*:

> About the knoll the airs blew fresh and brisk,
> And, musing as I sat, I held my watch
> Upon my open palm; its smooth bright disk
> Was uppermost, and so it came to catch,
> And dwarf, the figure of a waving tree,
> Backed by the West. A tiny sunshine peeped
> About a tiny elm, – and both were steeped
> In royal metal, flaming ruddily:
> How lovely was that vision to behold!
> How passing sweet that fairy miniature,
> That streamed and flickered o'er the burning gold!
> God of small things and great! do Thou ensure
> Thy gift of sight, till all my days are told,
> Bless all its bliss, and keep its pleasures pure!

A dwarfed tree, a tiny sunshine, a tiny elm: 'How passing sweet that fairy miniature'. The great world made very small; the small picture, though, telling amply of the world it reduces. A feature shared by the photograph-like portrait in Turner's sonnet 'Little Nora, or the Portrait' (in the 1873 volume; Pinion, CCXLII), where the poet is shown a portrait of a dead daughter by a grieving father, in which by this power of the small image, the dead girl still lives:

> Then came her portrait forth, which I had seen,
> And he had shown with pride, when last we met;
> The same bright smile – the rose-o'er laden arms,
> And all her pretty sum of infant-charms;
> But lo! a fair memorial tress was set,
> Facing the porcelain picture, where his child
> Still nursed her pile of summer-wreaths and smiled.

And as the photograph, the small picture, so the sonnet, the small poem, and not least ekphrastic ones like Tennyson Turner's dwelling, as Victorian sonnets rather tend to, self-referentially, on the small made thing and image. Dare the sonnet do its miniaturizing job on a grand creature such as an

---

[28]   Like childhood-conscious Graham Greene whose stamp-hoarding character Helen Rolt in *The Heart of the Matter* (1948) loves stamps because 'They are like snapshots'. *The Heart of the Matter*, Book II, Part I, Ch 3, section 1.

eagle, Turner wonders in 'The Eagle and the Sonnet' (CCLXXIV)? The Theban poet Pindar described in the first of his Odes a drowsy royal eagle perched on Zeus's sceptre, but what about an eagle in flight?

> If Pindar drew him best with drooping wings,
> And on a quiet perch his likeness took,
> How shall the sonnet, least of rhythmic things,
> Presume to take him flying? Will he brook
> To wheel and hover, while I hunt for rhymes?
> Returning at the Muse's fitful times,
> For yet another study? And, if so,
> Will he not yearn at last to strike one blow
> At his own miniature, and swoop from high
> To clutch my climax with an angry cry?

But the sonnet does so presume, confident in the force of its miniature takings – confident in the containing-expanding power of the small text, the one that likes to think it's presided over by the 'God of small things and great'. The poem, in other words, like Stevenson's childhood box full of metonymic lead soldiers; or the poetic 'drawer' of AE Housman in which, according to WH Auden's 1937 sonnet on him, he 'Kept tears like dirty postcards'; or, of course, Lewis Carroll's verbal *portmanteaux.*

Poetic Portmanteaux

It's no accident that Carroll, perhaps the greatest of the kiddy's rhymesters, should celebrate the expansive meanings of his art's apparently simple infant-speak in terms of travellers' clothes-bags into which much can be packed: hold-alls, *portmanteaux*. These verbal hold-alls get explained at yet one more jokily serious point in *Alice's Adventures in Wonderland* (1865) where Humpty Dumpty is being quizzed by Alice about 'whether you *can* make words mean so many different things' – in Dumpty's words, make 'one word do a lot of work'. Since Dumpty seems 'very clever at explaining words', Alice gets him to 'tell…the meaning of the poem called "Jabberwocky"':

> Twas brillig, and the slithy toves
> Did gyre and gimble in the wabe:
> All mimsy were the borogoves
> And the mome raths outgrabe.

It's apparent nonsense for the nursery, mere noise, full of weird nonce words; but, as Dumpty has it, it's actually full of meaning potential. ' "*Slithy*" means "lithe and slimy". "Lithe" is the same as "active". You see it's like a port-manteau – there are two meanings packed up into one word" '. And ' "*mimsy*" is "flimsy and miserable" (there's another portmanteau for you)'. (A port-manteau was originally a leather clothes bag hinged at the back and opening out into two equal halves; hence Dumpty's two meanings packed up into one.) Verbs, says Dumpty, are difficult to get to work overtime like this, whereas 'adjectives you can do anything with'. Carroll might have been thinking of his great Nonsense rival Edward Lear, the power of whose limer-icks draws almost entirely on the greatly unlimited outreach of the single adjective in their last lines: *umbrageous* old person of Spain, *illusive* old per-son of Woking, *abruptious* old man of Thames Ditton, *afficting* old man at a Station (an adjectival career beginning in Lear's *A Book of Nonsense*, 1846). Dumpty claims he 'can explain all the poems that ever were invented – and a good many that haven't been invented yet'. The portmanteau point and the stretchable-adjective claim certainly look forward as well as back-wards: fast-forwarding to Joyce's *Finnegans Wake*, that great lumbering machine of pun-full portmanteau words, as well as to WH Auden whose strong and tricky way with odd and uncontainable adjectives shows how much he'd learned from his admired Edward Lear. But even more than their prophetic potential, Dumpty's thoughts about words meaning more do indeed apply to 'all the poems ever invented'. Expansion, meaning more, speaking bigger than at first sight would appear, are what the poetic word aims for *per se*. The single word; the single image, single line, single poem; the small poetic item – a growth-power exemplarily registered in these mini-aturizing poets' obsession with the small things and person. The power memorably ascribed, in another of Stevenson's poems in *A Child's Garden of Verses*, 'Picture Books in Winter', to 'picture story books' read whilst 'Sitting safe in nursery nooks': 'We may see how all things are / Seas and cities near and far, / And the flying fairies' looks, / In the picture story-books'. An expandability of meaning manifested more troublingly, of course, in the way it becomes hard to distinguish childish subject matter from adult in these texts. 'Nonsense' limericks ostensibly for children segued into the flourishing Victorian underground industry of pornographic limericks for adults. Certain texts apparently for children are quickly indistinguishable from texts for adults, or are eminently readable, at least, as if child-adult portmanteaux.

Black Hands

Who, you wonder, are the *Alice* books really for? Linguists, chess players, and philosophers, not to mention mathematicians, have long supposed these are texts for them. Rather like the stories assembled by the Brothers Grimm – all at once notorious Nursery Story materials, but also full of adult-seeming nightmares, gothicisms, eroticisms, pathologies; a field, and field-day, of Freudian horror. All those lovely little doll-like female innocents of the poems (and the photographs) are also actors in a paedophile drama of a quite troubling adult fetishism. It's only characteristic that Carroll's Alice narrative of shrinkage, and the entry into 'gardens of delight' down the rabbit-hole, and then through the curtain and the little door and the passage smaller than a rat-hole, should sound so like a story of proxy sexual penetration of the female. Tenniel's illustration for that curtained orifice features a vagina-like shape complete with pubic-style hairy shading. Here's a kind of somatic nightmare of the virginal male author who can in real life only abide hairless pre-pubescent girls. In which real world, Carroll's chemically blackened fingers are all over the little white frocks of lovely little Alice Liddell that he carefully loosened for one of his ragamuffin photographs: a close, but only just not-too-close touching. No wonder Mrs Liddell started keeping her daughters clear of this eager poetic photographer. Some of the girls photographed by Carroll – and painted by Millais – stare back at the viewer with a very disturbing knowingness. Innocence often appears lost at the hands of the earnest collector of little seaside girls and little actresses to pose for his 'micro' photographs.[29] Max Müller's influential idea that baby noise, nursery talk, are fundamental to language and that nursery rhyming is basic to poetry, powerfully undergirds the going Victorian faith in the large reach of small talk, talk of the small, investment in words for and about the small things and the small person; but this linguist's notion that adult speak is inherently rooted in the infant also undergirds the very concerning way the juvenile aestheticizing keeps overlapping onto what seems a very grown-up kind of corruption.

It's a dark side of the repeated small-subject matter which the literature never quite represses. Making small in fictions is of course an act of domination, control, overpowering. It's the subjugating oppressiveness evident in all satirical writing – which makes a habit of reducing its targets to helpless and hapless miniature versions of themselves. Like Carroll's photographs of little girls with the carefully disarrayed clothing, the poetry of the small subject inevitably witnesses to some large, and thus powerful person's using, manipulating, subjugating others, and the Other, in a drama of unequal selves. The poet collects his small subjects, as the photographer collects photographs and the stamp-collector stamps: small effigies hoarded, row upon row, in albums, photo albums, stamp albums (albums of 'first-day covers' and postcards too) – books whose layouts oddly resemble many a volume of small poems. A concatenation of dubious collecting and collating ambitions. Post-cards and their collectors rightly haunt Jacques Derrida in *La Carte*

[29]   Sex, sexiness, and the child are the subjects of James R Kincaid's rightly serious and concerned *Child-Loving: The Erotic Child and Victorian Culture* (Routledge, London, 1992).

Postale / The Post-Card (1980/1987), a meditation on postage-systems that's greatly mindful of the oppressive role of the police mug-shot (*la bobine*, in French), the photograph on the Wanted Poster. Arrays of mug-shots on a multi Wanted Poster, which looks so like a page from a photo album or one torn from a stamp album, begin life, naturally, in those sheets of photographs arrayed by nineteenth-century criminologists like Lombroso and Francis Galton to define criminal types, degenerates, lesser breeds, racial inferiors. Arrangements of accusatory facial evidence that end up, of course, in the racially discriminating, pseudo-anthropological charts and posters of Nazi Germany. And the atmosphere in any poem's demonstration of aesthetic power over the Other can indeed be as discomfiting as it is in these practical manifestations of authority and power in the work of psychologizing, anthropologizing, policing, colonizing. What's more, the link between such powerful moves of defining, and subjugating, and perverse desire has long been clear; and the poets are not in the clear hereabouts. 'Girt with a boyish garb for boyish task, / Eager she wields her spade: yet loves as well / Rest on a friendly knee, intent to ask / The tale he loves to tell'. That's how Carroll's dedicatory verses to his poem *The Hunting of the Snark* begin: 'Inscribed To a Dear Child: In Memory of Golden Summer Hours and Whispers of a Summer Sun'. She's the little object of the narrator-poet's stories, held on his knee, a pre-pubescent androgyne creature, a beloved actor in, and occasion of, a paedophiliac-pederastic drama. (Carroll would fit his little friends out in the costumes he hoarded 'in a cupboard, to dress up children in when they came to be photographed. Some of the dresses had been used in pantomimes at Drury Lane: some were rags, to dress up beggar-children in': a sinister theatricality reminiscent of paedophiliac child-oppressor Fagin's merry little drama of pick-pocketing to initiate and ensnare innocent little Oliver Twist into a life of crime.[30])

Power on display. Modelling, playing the reduction game, is inevitably infected with the oppressive desires of subjugators. HG Wells's Little Wars game of 1913, in a way the apotheosis of the Victorian writers' obsession with tinification, makes an awful prelude to the Great War about to break out for real and for big. Doing 'Tin murder' with his little lead soldiers and tin guns, Wells was author as Kriegspieler, as war-gamer, doing what nineteenth-century generals were well practised at, namely modelling battle with metonymic soldiery as rehearsal for the real thing. Wells thought that waging Little War might substitute the Great War that was in the offing ('Here is a homoeopathic remedy for the imaginative strategist'), but he was wrong about an inevitable segue, the push from pleasant toy to painful real. He

---

[30]   The theatrical cupboard comes from Carroll's 1888 story 'Isa's Visit to Oxford' (1888): *The Works of Lewis Carroll*, ed & intro Roger Lancelyn Green, illustrated John Tenniel (Hamlyn, Feltham, 1965), 718–723.

recalled, as he should, his war-gaming predecessors, Sterne's old soldiers, kindly Uncle Toby and Corporal Trim in *Tristram Shandy*, 'playing Little Wars on a scale and with an elaboration exceeding even the richness and beauty of the contemporary game', but he overlooked the way their war games on the bowling green devastated the body and life of Toby's small nephew Tristram – greatly damaged when the sash-window, robbed of its lead weights and pulleys for making toy military hardware, crashed down on his penis as he was held by his nursemaid to pee out of it.[31] Authors who make small are perilously close to war-gaming generals proleptically expressing their domination desires over the powerless human material thus miniaturized.

'Letty's Globe' is in many lights fetchingly lovely with its picture of a little golden-haired child delighting in her grasp of a tin globe. But what's emphasized is that she is a little English girl, who contains 'old empires' in her little hand in the name of the now greatest of empires, the British one. Her powerful little hand reaches out to join the scarily oppressive hand of Carroll's Alice, a little girl's hand terrifyingly large in its way with shrunken others – snatching at the white rabbit in *Alice in Wonderland*, causing it to crash painfully into a splintering cucumber-frame; traumatizing the White King in *Through the Looking-Glass* as its laughing owner holds him between finger and thumb to dust ashes off him (' "The horror of that moment", the King went on, "I shall never never forget" ').[32] Letty occludes all Europe with her wonderful hair. She's a lovely and lucky little imperialist, but only in the gloating, condoning eyes of an infatuated poet who is at one with the child on the winning, oppressive side:

> But when we turned her sweet unlearned eye
> On our own isle, she raised a joyous cry.
> 'Oh! yes, I see it, Letty's home is there!'
> And, while she hid all England with a kiss,
> Bright over Europe fell her golden hair.

---

[31]   HG Wells, *A Game for Boys from Twelve Years to One Hundred and Fifty and for the More Intelligent Sort of Girls Who Like Boys' Games and Books*, With an Appendix on Kriegspiel (Frank Palmer, London, 1913), 8,97. Hillel Schwartz, who links Wells with modern military war-gamers, reproduces a photograph from *Little Wars: A Game ...* of 'giant' Wells in his garden manoeuvring his mini-troops: *The Culture of the Copy: Striking Likenesses, Unreasonable Facsimiles* (Zone Books, NY, 1966), 258. Discussion: 259ff.

[32]   UC Knoepflmacher compares and contrasts Tenniel's illustrations of these two Alice-hand moments in terms of different 'kinds of superiority': the 'retaliatory aggression of a giantess as childish as any of her underground foils and the solicitude shown by the would-be adult', who treats the White King as if he were a child. But what Tenniel's drawings rather bring out is the way every kind of superior grabbing and gripping bullies and hurts, however kindly intended. *Ventures into Childland*, edn cit (1998), Ch 6, 'Shrinking Alice: From Wonderland to Looking-Glass Land', 210–211.

Out of the mouths of 'babes and sucklings', you might say, come imperialist acknowledgements: imperialist brightness falling from a little Briton's hair. Tennyson Turner's sonnets elsewhere celebrate the bright light shed by England's 'fame in fight' and 'Her shining honour and her moral might' ('The South-Foreland Electric Light': XCVI), and the way Britain leads Europe in technology, science, invention, communication, intellectual power ('letters') as corollaries of her fighting force ('Greatness of England': XCVII). Discouraged, rather than encouraged, by what England's fighting men do, and have done to them around the world, Wilde's fine glooming about imperialist warfare in his 'Ave Imperatrix' sounds as if it remembers and is rebuking 'Letty's Globe': The earth, a brittle globe of glass, / Lies in the hollow of thy hand', its crystal heart darkened by 'The spears of crimson-suited war'. And, master of the rueful eloquence of the small thing, Wilde sees the little remainders and reminders of loved-ones killed in battle as 'toys' which give no joy: 'Pale women who have lost their lord / Will kiss the relics of the slain – / Some tarnished epaulette – some sword – / Poor toys to soothe such anguished pain'.

What Browning's wonderful 'My Last Duchess' dramatizes is precisely the distressing way ownership of a portrait – that reductive metonym of a person – inevitably involves an excess of authority over the person thus represented. The Duke had his wife painted and in a connected action had her killed because of the complicity between her and the painter which he believes the painting to portray. His command over the female subject of the painting was total, even unto death – 'I gave commands; / Then all smiles stopped together' – and now he's in interpretative command of the picture. The Duchess was his; the portrait is his; and now the portrait's meanings are his. He only can answer inquiries about 'that pictured countenance', 'since none puts by / The curtain I have drawn for you, but I'. He's a deranged policeman, detective, criminologist, who's got the evidential mug-shot he needs, the painting as Wanted Poster. And, I would say, this appalling ducal power plays on to all such picturing and photographing, all the period's dominating representations of the small human subject, all of its zest for metonymic manipulation of the subject in the text of the reduced scale.

It is, of course, only apt that in Browning's drama of male power over the human, and female, subject, metonymy should be so rampant. The Duke focusses for evidence of his wife's unfaithfulness on a sequence of metonymic bits of her body – cheek, wrist, throat, smile, blush, half-flush – 'that spot of joy' in her cheek, 'that spot of joy'. *That spot of joy*: terrible accusing repetition: the smallest of aestheticized parts, a mere *spot*; but (in the manner of all the poems using and focussing the small thing, and sponsoring the real as metonymn) one granted awfully large meanings, a whole story and history of alleged marital betrayal. What's terrifyingly at stake, then, for Browning – as a poet well used, of course, to misuse at the hands of strong readers and mis-readers; as a Nonconformist Christian accustomed to disablement by social and religious powers-that-be for the mere colour (as Housman might put it) of his religious hair – is the way that the loveliest of small aestheticized things, the tiniest of blushes on a lovely woman's cheek, the very stuff (and exemplar) of the Victorian poet's recurrent investment and faith in metonymn, in the telling power of the miniature, the dinky, can be made to tell thus against the ethical as well as the aesthetic worth of an artist and of his subject.

Small is beautiful; small can also be dubious. A dubiousness forcefully invading many such metonymized scenes; especially in the poetry of the revelatory body-part which the 'Fleshly Scholars' go in for – as, terrifyingly, in Browning's 'Porphyria's Lover', in which the jealous male lover's desire to possess his mistress for himself has him strangling her with her yellow hair – that favourite Victorian metonym of the desirable woman. The strangling is the apotheosis of the play of, and with, metonym going wrong, turning sour, awful culmination of a synecdochic catalogue of the bits of clothing the woman sheds and the body parts he touches in sadistic lust: dripping cloak and shawl, soiled gloves, hat; her waist, her smooth white bare shoulder, her eyelids, blushing cheek, little throat, little head. Here is a conjunction of body parts – hands, cheeks, shoulders, eyes, and so forth, that is quite usual for love poems, but this time these touchings are all foreplay to a murder. A bodily transaction in which the lover fantasizes – as rapists and other sex oppressors often do – that the woman wants to be possessed like this, is happy in fact to be the sex doll or puppet he turns her dead body into:

> I propped her head up as before,
> Only, this time my shoulder bore
> Her head, which droops upon it still:
> The smiling rosy little head,
> So glad it has its utmost will.

'[A]nd all her hair / In one long yellow string I wound / Three time her little throat around, / And strangled her'. Here's a trading in the small thing as an evil transaction – a transgressivity brought massively home by what passes for normalcy of being and acting, in fact, in the very pervasive Victorian dwarf-world of Fairy.

Shop of Little Body Horrors

Victorian Fairyology is everywhere (fairyology was a Victorian coinage).[33] And the Fairyologists' small creations are invariably menacing. Fairies are up to no good. Goblins mean you harm. Dolls – Victorian dolls at least – are

---

[33]   *Fairyology* was first used by Michael Aislabie Denham, *A Few Fragments of Fairyology, Shewing its Connexion with Natural History* (William Duncan and Son, Durham, 1854). The booklet provides Nicola Bown, *Fairies in Nineteenth-Century Art and Literature*, (Cambridge University Press, Cambridge, 2001) with the title and main subject of her Ch 3, 98–162,

scary, smiling menacingly with staring seeing-unseeing eyes, like the doll-like faces of the fairies in the paintings of John Anster Fitzgerald, *Ariel* (circa 1858), *The Fairies' Banquet* (1859), *The Fairies' Barque* (1860), *Fairy Lovers in a Bird's Nest Watching a White Mouse* (circa 1860). (Fitzgerald was the son of the minor Irish poet William Thomas Fitzgerald.[34]) They're as it were citizens of the frightening world of Fairy-master George MacDonald's influential novel *The Princess and the Goblin* (1872) – the bees' knees of the mode according to MacDonald's admiring successors, CS Lewis and JRR Tolkien – with its goblin miners, ugly and evil, surreal horrors out of Hieronymous Bosch, nightmarish as anything in the goblinesque line in Dickens's *The Old Curiosity Shop* (1840–1841), with its wheedling dwarf Quilp and its scary reduction of human beings to waxwork effigies in Jarley's travelling exhibition. For their part, the troops of 'little men' in William Allingham's famous 'The Fairies: A Nursery Song' – 'Up the airy mountain / Down the rushy glen' – look attractive in their green jackets and red caps with the cocks' feathers, but they steal and imprison little girls who then die of sorrow, and they put thorns in the beds of people who upset them, so though these 'wee folk' are called 'good folk' (in the Irish-folk way)

> We daren't go a hunting
> For fear of little men.

(The poem got a nicely eery illustration by the Pre-Raphaelite Arthur Hughes in Allingham's volume *The Music Master: A Love Story and Two Series and Day and Night Songs* (1855), for which Dante Gabriel Rossetti and John Everett Millais also provided illustrations; Allingham liked Hughes's best.) The Irish poet Dora Sigerson also sounds warning notes about the little prowlers of the Irish night-time:

> Go not to the hills of Erin
> When the night winds are about,
> Put up your bar and shutter,
> And so keep the danger out.
>
> For the good-folk whirl within it,
> And they pull you by the hand,
> And they push you on the shoulder,
> Till you move to their command.
> ('The Wind on the Hills', *Poems
> and Ballads*, 1899)

---

[34]   AS Byatt makes the doll-like menace point about Fitzgerald in her fine review-essay on the Dulwich Art Gallery Exhibition, 'The Age of Enchantment: Beardsley, Dulac and their Contemporaries 1890–1930': 'The Wild Ones', *The Guardian Review*, 24 November 2007.

The goblins of Christina G Rossetti's *Goblin Market* are likewise little monsters, sexual predators, luring sweet-toothed Laura into a kind of perdition with their pressing offers of sweet foodstuffs: she becomes *cankered*, a ruined person, fading away, in a damnation from which she's only saved by sister Lizzie putting herself through the malign violences of the little world. The tiny men – demonic, animalistic – *hug* and *squeeze* Lizzie; they *grunt*, *snarl*, *tread*, *hustle*, *elbow*, *jostle*, *claw*, *bark*, *mew*, *hiss*, *mock*, *tear* her gown, *soil* her stocking, *twitch her hair out by the roots*, *stamp on her tender feet*. This is assault by helter-skelter rhyming and repeating; they

> ... cuffed and caught her,
> Coaxed and fought her,
> Bullied and besought her,
> Scratched her, pinched her black as ink,
> Kicked and knocked her,
> Mauled and mocked her.

They try their hardest to *cram* the sweetly poisonous fruit-juices into her mouth, smearing them all over her face and chin and neck (so she's *syrupped*), but they fail because she keeps her mouth shut. She *uttered not a word*, like Jesus before His accusers in the Gospels. Rossetti wants an analogy between Lizzie and the Christ who died to save humanity from sin and the devil. Of course there's a pretty loud admission in all this of the heady mix of sexual, bodily fears and anxieties and desires which modern critics want to ascribe to Christina G – fear of what sucking and sucking and sucking Laura-like on the sweets of bodily pleasure might entail, combined with a desire for such bodily pleasures, even for the extreme feel of those dangerous syrups running down Lizzie's face, *lodging in dimples of her chin*, *streaking her neck*. But the poem should be read even more, I think, as a strong critique of the dollanities in which the male poets involve females, in the relishing, fetishizing, miniaturizing scene so much Victorian art contrives. *Goblin Market* is a poem of protest against the aesthetic and practice of dollifying.

It might almost be a comment in particular on Robert Browning's curiously relishing 1844 poem, 'Sibrandus Schafnaburgensis', about little creatures making sadistically merry ruin of an old book which Browning's 'I' couldn't stand and chucked into the watery hollow trunk of a plum-tree.

> VII
> How did he like it when the live creatures
> Tickled and toused and browsed him all over,
> And worm, slug, eft, with serious features,
> Came in, each one, for his right of trover?
> – When the water-beetle with great blind deaf face

Made of her eggs the stately deposit,
And the newt borrowed just so much of the preface
As tiled in the top of his black wife's closet?

VIII
All that life and fun and romping,
All that frisking and twisting and coupling,
While slowly our poor friend's leaves were swamping
And clasps were cracking and covers suppling!

The rhymings of the playfully violent attack verbs – *tickled, toused, browsed* – and the sinisterly sexual gerunds – *romping, frisking, twisting, coupling, swamping, cracking, suppling* – are so proleptically reminiscent of Rossetti's appalled rhetoric of rhymed assault. (Intriguingly for his poetry's smallness interests, Browning found Sibrandus of Aschafenburg, like so many other historical oddities such as the 'The Pied Piper of Hamelin', in the encyclopaedia of fact-fiction *curiosa* in his father's library which clearly entranced him mightily, Nicholas Wanley's *The Wonders of the Little World: or, A General History of Man. In Six Books* (1678). *The Little World*.)[35] For sure, 'Goblin Market' is a protest against the perversities of the miniaturizing branch of male aesthetics. Against what's going on, symptomatically, in the period's great cult of Shakespeare's *A Midsummer Night's Dream*, on stage and page, and in painting.

The painters – Richard Dadd, Robert Huskisson, Joseph Noël Patton, John Simmons – were magnetized by the as it were licensed marital violence and confusion, the perverse sexualities, of the play's fairy dream-land: the quarrel between the Fairy Queen and King, Titania and Oberon, over a changeling 'Indian' boy; the erotically wrecking work of their mischievous fairy servant Puck; tiny Titania's falling in love with big proley weaver Bottom metamorphosed into a beast-man in an ass's head; drugged human lovers falling for the wrong partners. And so were the poets. In 1856 Charles Kean's production ran for 250 nights with Puck played, to the delight of the male little-girl fetishizers, by the eight-year-old Ellen Terry. Lewis Carroll, great befriender of child actresses, devotee of little Ellen Terry, is reputed to have seen this production several times. Carroll was just as dotty about the little girls who played in the stage version of *Alice*. 'Dainty is the only epithet that seems to me exactly to suit' little Dorothy d'Alcourt, who played the Dormouse, he told readers of *The Theatre* magazine in April 1887, a piece recalling the origin of the Alice Story, the Liddell daughters' 'eager

---

[35] Nicola Bown is quite right, op. cit., 143–144, to offer this poem as an example of Browning's fairyological 'grotesquerie'; but her thinking of it as being about natural history misses the large point that it's about the sadism of wee creatures. A sadistically consuming pleasure which destroys books of course. (And oddly anticipatory of the fate of Rossetti's volume of poetry when it was exhumed from Lizzie Siddal's grave all wet and worm-eaten. For which see the end of 'Mourning and Melancholia', Ch 8, below.)

faces, hungry for news of fairy-land', and ' "Alice" the child of my dreams'. The little Dorothy was ripe now, he thought, to play Puck. In painting, Shakespeare's fairy-land allowed a plethora of naked flesh and naked people engaged in erotic activities undreamed of in any other Victorian aesthetic works, at least on such a large miniature scale – most notably, of course, in the quite bacchanalian scene in tininess-obsessive Noël Patton's *The Quarrel of Oberon and Titania* (1849). (Patton was very keen on literary miniaturism: he illustrated Kingsley's *The Water Babies*.) *The Quarrel* is an orgiastic sexual Eden of desirous naked little people, male, female and androgyne, enticing each other, embracing, dancing, writhing, in a scene of mass foreplay well-peopled with little Bosch-like monsters, all presided over by the lecherous nature-god Pan.[36] In 1857, Lewis Carroll, a great fan of Patton, stared and stared at the painting in the Scottish National Gallery in Edinburgh, eventually counting '165 fairies'. Admittedly he was number crazy, unable to leave numbers alone (like his little Isa in the story 'Isa's Visit to Oxford', who tried to count the raindrops of a shower, 'but when she had counted four millions, three hundred and seventy-eight thousand two hundred and forty-seven, she got tired and left off'). But what, you think, was he thinking as he did that? What, for that matter, was he thinking in his long career of cosying up, in his imagination, his art, his daily life, to little girls? 'Fairyland is nothing but the sunny country of common sense', thought GK Chesterton in 'The Ethics of England' chapter of his book *Orthodoxy* (1908). How wrong could a critic get? Fairyland is perverse as well as violent; indulging in it is a sign, in practitioners like Patton and Carroll, of profound self-estrangement, of an unhappy sexuality going terribly wonky, of a fetishism shading over in neurosis.

Carroll's writing about young females is haunted (as is Tennyson Turner's and, for the matter of that, Charles Dickens's) by the dementing prospect of their developing into unmanipulable grown-up women. 'Birdie', remembered as 'a small child who went to wade in the sea at Sandown', shocked Carroll with 'the astonishing photograph of the same microcosm suddenly expanded into a tall young person, whom I should be too shy to look at, even with the telescope which would no doubt be necessary to get any distinct idea of her smile, or at any rate to satisfy oneself whether she had eyebrows or not!' Neither little girls, nor photographs, were made for this. It was like, Carroll said, finding your small pet terrier turned into a hippopotamus overnight.[37] The grown-up poet has not, alas, in the photographed presence of the now adult object of onetime desire, an adult sexuality to

---

[36]　Well described by Adrian Poole in his excellent guide to Victorian ways with Shakespeare, *Shakespeare and the Victorians* (Arden Critical Commentaries, Thomson Learning, London, 2004), 56–57.

[37]　Letter of 10 February 1882, *Works*, ed Roger Lancelyn Green (1965), 716.

assume. The old fairy-dreaming has become a nightmare of distraught desire. The realm of Nonsense is a making of nonsense of anything approaching grown-up sexuality – the plight dramatically signalled in Edward Lear's distress over his nose (referred to in 'Fleshly Feelings', Chapter 7).

Noisome Noses

Lear was the 'dirty landscape-painter who hated his nose', as Auden's sonnet about him puts it, who 'wept to himself in the night': self-dramatized for the kiddy-audience of his child-centred Nonsense programme, as 'The Dong With a Luminous Nose'. The nose a great strap-on thing, 'Of vast proportions and painted red', with a bulbous end in which a luminous lamp' hangs, 'And with holes all round to send out the light, / In gleaming rays on the dismal'. The Dong is searching in vain for his lost Jumbly Girl, a lovely kind of fairy-monster, with 'sky-blue hands' and 'sea-green hair'. The light from the nose shines in vain. Noses are, traditionally, surrogate penises (think *Tristram Shandy*), and so is the Dong's. A surrogacy doubled by the noses's being a sort of vast dildo. A phallic thing quite scary in its carnivalesque grotesquerie. Enough to quite scare off any sensitive Jumbly Girl.

Nightmare is the standard proclivity of even would-be playful toy noses, as Dickens indicates in his *Household Words* article 'A Christmas Tree' (21 December 1850), a recollection of gadgets and tin toys and other Christmas dollanities in a catalogue of scary toys which gave him childhood nightmares, where he singles out the 'sinister expression' in the nose of the cardboard man who was hung against the wall and animated by a string. And Lear's Dong nose – overwrought sign of sexual distress and dementedness – is not playful at all. It registers not least the madness that thrives in Victorian fairyland. Richard Doyle, for example, one of the elite group of Victorian fairy painters, an artist with strong literary connections – he illustrated *The Fairy Ring* (1846), latest English translation of the Grimms' stories; his watercolour *The Enchanted Fairy Tree* (1846; exhibited 1868) is subtitled *A Fantasy Based on The Tempest by William Shakespeare*; his masterwork, *In Fairyland, or Pictures from the Elf World* (1870) is a set of thirty-six plates, 'The Fairy Queen Takes an Airy Drive', and so on, for which William Allingham provided poems – went mad. As did Richard Dadd. Dadd's tiny, obsessive masterpieces of Shakespearian miniaturization, *Contradiction: Oberon and Titania* and *The Fairy Feller's Master-Stroke* (accompanied by his brooding explanatory verses entitled 'Elimination of a Picture and its Subject', in which the Feller unlocks 'the secret cells of dark abyss' and releases a spell that 'Swindles soul, body, goods and purse'), were both painted in Bethlem Hospital, the notorious Bedlam lunatic asylum, to which this admired depicter of fairy, and especially of Titania, was committed in

1843 for murdering his father (Dadd died in the Broadmoor prison-hospital for the criminally insane, to which he'd been transferred in 1864).[38] Elizabeth Barrett thought that modernity and mechanization had unfitted the world for fairy writing. She'd heard in 1846 that Tennyson was writing a 'university' poem 'in blank verse and a fairy tale' (a mistaken rumour about 'The Princess'). 'Now isn't the world too old and fond of steam', she wrote Robert Browning, 'for blank verse poems, in ever so many books, to be written on the fairies?'[39] She was wrong to think that fairy art could not flourish in the age of steam. But she was right to wonder at the refusal of maturity implied in the poets' escape into fairyland; an immaturity, I would add, inevitably scathed by neurosis and madness.

---

[38]   All the details about fairy paintings and illustrations come from Jeremy Maas, Pamela White Irimpe, Charlotte Geer, and Others, *Victorian Fairy Painting*, ed Jane Martineau (Royal Academy of Arts, London; University of Iowa Museum of Art, Iowa; Art Gallery of Ontario, Canada; in association with Mervell Holberton, London, 1998). Afforced by Nicola Bown's *Fairies in Nineteenth-Century Art and Literature* (2001): particularly informative on Richard Dadd's madness, including reprinting key lines of 'Elimination of a Picture and its Subject', 160. Nicola Bown worked on the Royal Academy Exhibition, *Victorian Fairy Painting*.
[39]   *Letters of RB & EBB*, I, 444 (31 January 1846).

6

Selving

Who is *I*? Who speaks when the text says *I*? Whose *I* is it? Who are we meeting and hearing when we hear, or overhear, the 'lyrical I' speaking? What, in fact, is an *I*, a *self*? What is it to *be*; to be self-conscious; to imagine being, and one's own being; to try and see oneself, one's selfhood, in the mirror of a poem; to try out, to assume, selves in a poetic text? The old Hamletian, Protestant-era I-problematics on which the Novel was founded, and which got such vigorous renewing in the poems of the Romantic period, get continued with refurbished vigour, and renewed anxiety, in the writings of the Victorian period – before being passed on into early modernist, and modernist, times, as *the* question.

Selving, self-fashioning, striving with self-issues, are what Victorian poetry does. Poetic selving is at the solipsistic core of the vast Victorian enterprise of self-imagining, self-making in writing in the great array of contemporary self-discourses.[1] *Selving*, being *selved*, being *selved-up*: Hopkins, the great occluded, hidden-away voice of the Victorian imagination, as it were the great poetic unconscious of his age, invented these active parts of the verb to *selve*, which capture his and his period's preoccupation with making and trying to define selves and selfhood. This is in his private 1880 Retreat meditations on what was an absolutely main question for him and his poetry: 'my being-myself', 'my own being', how he *is*, how he makes and knows himself in his 'individuality', his 'selfbeing'. The issue is peculiarly human,

---

[1] For consideration of the theory and practice of self-writing in the mass of Victorian autobiographies and memoirs, novels and short stories, particularly good is Regenia Gagnier, *Subjectivities: A History of Self-Representation in Britain, 1832–1920* (Oxford University Press, New York and Oxford, 1991).

Victorian Poetry Now: Poets, Poems, Poetics, First Edition. Valentine Cunningham.
© 2011 Valentine Cunningham. Published 2011 by Blackwell Publishing Ltd.

he writes, since human nature is 'more highly pitched, selved, and distinctive than anything in the world'. Consideration of 'my selfbeing, my consciousness and feeling of myself' is a matter of sharp taste, 'that taste of myself, of *I* and *me*', the strongest taste there is, 'more distinctive than the taste of ale or alum, more distinctive than the smell of walnutleaf or camphor'. 'Nothing else in nature comes near this unspeakable stress of pitch, distinctiveness, and selving, this selfbeing of my own'. *Pitch* and *stress*: those key personal and poetic forces for Hopkins. He's compelled to ask these difficult questions of identity, to gulp them down however hard, 'to taste *self* but at one tankard'. The source of 'all that taste of self, that selfbeing' can be due, he argues, 'to chance', or 'to myself, as selfexistent', or 'to some extrinsic power'. Being a good as well as thoughtful Christian he argues that it's owed to an extrinsic power, ie God. The power he wrestles with unstoppably in his poems.[2]

Reflecting on selfhood, self-reflection: it's the perpetual way of the poet and the poem. Typically, for Browning's earliest published character, the narrator of *Pauline: A Fragment of a Confession* (1833), to be, to live intensely, means being self-conscious. For him, being *is* self-consciousness. He's the individual defined, in the momentous phrase of Hegel in his Berlin lectures on *Aesthetics* (1818 onwards), as 'self-reflective': *in sich selbst reflektiert*: a self reflected in, and reflecting on, itself.[3]

> I am made up of an intensest life,
> Of a most clear idea of consciousness
> Of self.
>
>   (268–270)

In this he's a modern Hamlet, reliving the plight of the character who, of all the persons from past literature who obsessed the Victorians, perhaps preoccupied them the most (and he looks forward, of course, to TS Eliot and Virginia Woolf and the insistences of modernist literature). The Browning notion is one Victorian poetry and poetics thoroughly endorse: being, life, the being of the poet, the being of the poet's characters, the being of the poem, consist of self-consciousness.

---

[2] 'First Principle and Foundation', *The Sermons and Devotional Writings of Gerard Manley Hopkins*, ed Christopher Devlin (Oxford University Press, London, NY, Toronto, 1959), 122–128.

[3] GWF Hegel, *Vorlesungen über die Aesthetik*, 2 vols (Berlin, 1842–1843), trans by TM Knox as *Aesthetics: Lectures on Fine Art*, 2 vols (Clarendon Press, Oxford, 1975), II. 1123. E Warwick Slinn's *The Discourse of the Self in Victorian Poetry* (Macmillan, Basingstoke, 1991) builds his most useful account of the central Victorian poetic business of writing the self on Hegelian assumptions and how they play in Tennyson, Clough, and Browning, especially Browning. It follows on from Slinn's also useful *Browning and the Fictions of Identity* (Macmillan, Basingstoke, 1982).

'Enough of me!' says the Browning voice after telling us at some length how he found on a Florence junk stall the 'old yellow Book' on which *The Ring and the Book* is based (I.773). It's time, he says, to move on from *me*, to 'The Book!'. But the Book – the old Italian book, and now Browning's book – are about nothing but *me*; and a whole shoal of *me*'s. Narratives about *me* are Browning's stock-in-trade: narratives in which an *I* keeps reporting about *me*, *me* the poet, *me*, *me*, *me* the poem's characters. Browning was flattered to find that John Stuart Mill had written on his copy of *Pauline* that 'this writer seems to me possessed with a more intense and morbid self-consciousness than I ever knew in any sane human being.' This accurately described him and his poetry, Browning told Elizabeth Barrett Barrett early in their correspondence, quoting Mill, albeit a bit loosely: 'the writer possesses a deeper self-consciousness than ever I knew in a sane human being.' 'Of course you are *self-conscious*', she assured him: 'How could you be a poet otherwise?'.[4] And no Victorian poet would demur at that. 'Face this *me*' shouts Browning's Aristophanes in his 'Apology' (line 1652). And the command keeps coming at you from all sides, like the cannon fire in 'The Charge of the Light Brigade', as you head into the pages not only of Browning, but of all the rest. The Victorian poem comes, like the Victorian novel, crowded with I-personae. It scarcely ever stops speaking in the first person – in the 'lyrical I' of the poet, in the 'I' of the poetry's vast array of fictional characters. Poets and characters keep coming before us as a great multiplicity of selves, owners of selves, self-asserters, self-knowers, persons and personae all owning up, one way or another, in the first person.

'*Whát I dó is me, for that I came*'. That's Hopkins in 'As kingfishers catch fire'. 'I am I'. That's Robert Browning in 'Life in a Love'. 'Just as I am ...': thus the evangelical hymn-writer Charlotte Elliott, presenting herself in verse after verse to God, and to the reader, in one of the period's most popular hymns, circulating in thousands of copies, 'Just as I am without one plea'. 'And I, because I am a woman – I ...'. That's Elizabeth Barrett Browning, of her life in Florence in her *Casa Guidi Windows* (II.95). 'I am black – I am black'. Thus Barrett Browning's escaped woman slave, repeatedly, in 'The Runaway Slave at Pilgrim's Point'. 'I, Marion Erle, myself, alone, undone': that's Barrett Browning's raped woman in *Aurora Leigh* (VI.1270). 'I am a verse-maker by trade'; 'I am the pink of courtesy as I smoke my cigar': this is James Henry, the Irish Virgilian in his *Poems Chiefly Philosophical* (1856) and *Poematia* (1866). 'I write' (Aurora Leigh in *Aurora Leigh*, I.29). 'I am not what I have or what I do; / But what I was I am, I am even I': that's Christina G Rossetti in 'The Thread of Life' (stanza 2), imitating the Biblical selfhood of God, 'I AM THAT I AM' – 'man's inherent feeling of personality

---

[4] Robert Browning to Elizabeth Barrett Barrett, posted 26 Feb 1845; EBB to RB, 27 Feb 1845: *Letters of Robert Browning & Elizabeth Barrett Barrett*, I.29 and 33.

seems in some sort to attest and correspond to this revelation: I who am myself cannot but be myself ... Who I was I am, who I am I am, who I am I must be for ever and ever' (as Rossetti puts it in her commentary on the Book of Revelation, *The Face of the Deep*).[5] 'I Sappho': thus Swinburne's Sappho in his 'Anactoria'. 'I cannot rest from travel; I will drink / Life to the lees ... / I am become a name / ... I am a part of all that I have met'. That's Tennyson's Ulysses. 'I am poor brother Lippo, by your leave!'. That's Browning's Fra Lippo Lippi: 'Yes, I'm the painter'. 'I will be patient and proud': thus Browning's Abt Vogler (line 90 of his poem). And so on and on.

They know who and what they are, it would seem. Or do they? In fact shakiness often attends the apparent confidence of all this self-assertion. Who they are, actually perplexes them greatly. 'Did I speak once angrily, all the drear days / You lived, you woman I loved so well', asks the narrator of Robert Browning's 'Too Late'. 'Who am I?' wonders his Lippo Lippi. 'Why I am I?' wonders the lyrical *I*, anxiously poking fun at the riddle of things in Tennyson's early poem 'The "How" and the "Why"'.' 'Who is this?' Christina G asks of herself, self-imagined as the Bride of Christ (in 'Who is this that cometh up not alone': entry for 30 October in *Time Flies: A Reading Diary* (1885)). 'Being – who?' demands Robert Browning's Asolando in the Epilogue to 'Asolando: Fancies and Facts'. Here in fact is a thicket, or maze, of severe self-troubling

> But I who saw such things as I have said
> Was overdone with utter weariness;
> And walked in care, as one whom fears oppress
> Because above his head
> Death hangs, or damage, or the dearth of bread.
>
> Each sore defeat of my defeated life
> Faced and outfaced me in that bitter hour;
> And turned to yearning palsy all my power,
> And all my peace to strife,
> Self stabbing self with keen lack-pity knife.

That's Christina G in 'An Old-World Thicket', feeling the self-inflicted pain of self-consciousness, 'Self stabbing self'. And the aesthetic, the resort of all

---

[5]   Christina G Rossetti, *The Face of the Deep: A Devotional Commentary on The Apocalypse*, 2nd edn (Society for Promoting Christian Knowledge, London, 1893), 47. An admittedly 'extraordinary' pure subjectivity not acceptable to Andrew and Catherine Belsey in their 'Christina Rossetti: sister to the Brotherhood', *Textual Practice* 2 (1988), 30–50, because this 'sovereign subject', resistant to her brother's impositions, knuckled under to its 'true Sovereign', the ultimate Patriarchalist deplored by the the the Belseys, namely God. Another example of deconstructionist critics' problems with the religious subject.

this turning of the self-problem into poetry, is no help. 'Sweetness of beauty moved me to despair': 'Brimmed full my cup, and stripped me empty and bare' (36–50). All this poetic fullness of self-awareness is actually an empty-ing, a vastation of the self – the feeling that there's nothing there self-wise, for all this self-inspection. 'We only hope', said Leigh Hunt, reviewing Tennyson's 1830 volume, that the 'piece of perplexity called *The "How" and the "Why"* is not sick writing'. But it was.[6]

Prosopopoeia

In this maze, Don Juan, the I-narrator of Robert Browning's *Fifine at the Fair*, pursues the clues to his own selfhood like a chemist unravelling the common thread of 'all diverse life'

> ... Just so I glut
> My hunger both to be and know the thing I am,
> By contrast with the thing I am not ....
> (1814–1816)

'The thing I am' harks back to Shakespeare's Parolles: 'simply the thing I am / Shall make me live' (*All's Well that Ends Well*, IV.iii.306). Hungering to be and to know that thing is self-evidently momentous, but is Don Juan, we are made to wonder, only playing at self-knowing – and playing dubi-ously, consciously engaging in a kind of fraud? He is at the Venice Carnival. It's a scene of masking, of people putting on masks, as actors do, assuming a false face – what was known in Greek as a *prosopon*, in Latin as a *persona* – a character, self, personality, not one's own: in the act of self-making known in ancient rhetoric as *prosopopoeia*; what we know as *personification*.

Juan will know himself, he hopes, know what it is to be a person, but in the only way possible, through this 'sham' of masking, through the putting on of *prosopa/personae*, through *prosopopoeia/personification*:

> ... so, through sham
> And outside, I arrive at inmost real, probe
> And prove how the nude form obtained the chequered robe.
> (1816–1818)

The self known thus is, he knows, only a surface thing, an outside, a *persona* rather than a person; it won't be stable, fixed; it's only temporary, and

---

[6]   Leigh Hunt, quoted in Ricks's headnote, *Poems* in 3 volumes, I,204.

subject to change. But he urges himself to be satisfied with this shallow being, this transitory self-knowing:

> ... we must nor fret
> Nor fume, on altitudes of self-sufficiency,
> But bid a frank farewell to what – we think – should be,
> And, with as good a grace, welcome what is – we find.
> (1881–1885)

As ever, Browning is talking about his own poetic explorations of selfhood – Don Juan is perhaps the strongest case of a Browning persona representing the poet himself. Through him Browning is evidently defending the method, the ethicity, and the results of the Dramatic Monologue – Browning's great machine for examinations of self, the acme of the Victorian obsession with self (no one does a Dramatic Monologue better than Browning; no one does as many of them as he), and the epitome of the Victorian preoccupation with fraught self-consciousness.[7] In particular Browning is resisting current accusations against the mode's inadequacy and dubiety. Accusations levelled, not least, against a poetry, and a poet, said to be fruitlessly stuck in morbid self-inspection.

The narrator of *Pauline: a Fragment of a Confession* is certainly confused about his selfhood – a confusion cognate with the poem's French epigraph (from a poem 'De lui-même', 'About himself', wrongly attributed to Clément Marot): 'Plus ne suis ce que j'ai été, / Et ne le sçaurois jamais être': 'I am no longer what I was / And nor would I ever know how to be that again'. This narrator is distressed over the self he's stuck with, over what he is: 'This is "myself", not what I think should be' (820). 'I am concentrated', he says (808); but this concentration in and on himself only confirms him in an unhappy earthly existence. Like Hamlet – and in words

---

[7] On the dramatic monologue, see: (foundational) Robert Langbaum, *The Poetry of Experience: the Dramatic Monologue in Modern Literary Tradition* (Chatto & Windus, London, 1957); (best handbook guide) Elisabeth A Howe, *The Dramatic Monologue* (Twayne, NY; Prentice-Hall, London, 1966); (most powerful) W David Shaw, *Origins of the Monologue: The Hidden God* (University of Toronto Press, Toronto, Buffalo, London, 1999); also: Park Honan, *Browning's Characters* (Yale University Press, New Haven, 1961); Roma A King Jr, *The Focussing Artifice* (Ohio University Press, Athens, Ohio, 1968); Donald S Hair, *Browning's Experiments With Genre* (University of Toronto Press, Toronto, 1972); A Dwight Culler, 'Monodrama and the Dramatic Monologue', *PMLA*, 90:1 (May 1975), 366–385; Frances Carleton, *The Dramatic Monologue: Vox Humana* (Salzburg University Press, Salzburg, 1977); E Warwick Slinn, *Browning and the Fictions of Identity*, edn cit (1982); Ekbert Faas, *Retreat into the Mind: Victorian Poetry and the Rise of Psychiatry* (Princeton University Press, Princeton NJ, 1988) and Herbert F Tucker, 'Dramatic Monologue and the Overbearing of Lyric', in *Lyric Poetry: Beyond New Criticism,* eds, Chaviva Hošek and Patricia Parker (Cornell University Press, Ithaca and London, 1985), 226–243 (focussed on Browning).

from *Hamlet* – he feels trapped in life because of uncertainty about what might lie beyond death:

> What would I have? What is this 'sleep' which seems
> To bound all? can there be a 'waking' point
> Of crowning life?
>
> (812–814)

He's consternated by the erratic tendency of his thoughts, his chaotic infixity of mind, and so of being. 'O God, where do they tend – these struggling aims?' (811). And at this point Browning supplies a truly remarkable footnote, a commentary, in French, allegedly by Pauline, on her interlocutor ('ma pauvre ami') and his confession. The poem, she says, is 'cet étrange fragment'; all 'songe et confusion', a dream and a confusion, not to be tidied up without damage to what's very revealing about it, namely its jumpiness:

> Ce début sans prétention, ce remuement des passions qui va d'abord en accroissant et puis s'apaise par degrés, ces élans de l'âme, ce retour soudain sur soi-même, at par-dessous tout, la tournure de l'esprit tout particulièrement de mon ami, rendent les changements presques impossibles.

'This unpretentious début, this stirring-up of the passions which proceeds first of all by great expansion then abates by degrees these bursts of soul, this sudden turning back on itself, and underneath it all, my friend's very special cast of mind, make changes all but impossible'. *Ce retour soudain sur soi-même*: this jumpy turning back on itself: nervy self-preoccupation, self-inspection, self-consciousness – it is, of course, as Browning is recognizing in this footnote, a founding characteristic of Browning's own poetry. It would be a main feature of his verse – if not always quite so disconcertingly as in *Pauline*. It resembles 'that return of the mind upon itself', which Arthur Hallam in 1831, in his run-up to his lauding of his friend Tennyson's 1830 *Poems*, thought a bad characteristic of 'the spirit of modern poetry'. This was a result, Hallam thought, of an imbalance between the interests of self and community productive of poetic 'idiosyncrasies' and 'melancholy'[8]. It was the erratic self-obsession that John Stuart Mill deplored as the 'selfishness' and 'morbid state' of *Pauline*'s narrator and which led him to write on his review copy that though 'this writer' (anonymous, of course) had 'considerable poetic powers' he seemed 'possessed with a more intense and

---

[8] Arthur Henry Hallam, unsigned review of *Poems, Chiefly Lyrical* (1830), *Englishman's Magazine* (August 1831), i.616–628; reprinted in *Tennyson, The Critical Heritage*, ed John D Jump (Routledge & Kegan Paul, London, 1967), 34–65.

morbid self-consciousness than ever I knew in any sane human being'. With which, as we've seen, Browning was not displeased.[9]

And, of course, for some readers, this 'morbid self-consciousness' was the welcome face of a new poetic. Dante Gabriel Rossetti sat in the British Museum Library in 1847 and copied out the whole of *Pauline*, greatly impressed (and suspecting the anonymous author to be Robert Browning). For his part Matthew Arnold, able reader of the poetic signs of the time, was as appalled as Mill or Hallam. In the Preface to his *Poems* (1853) he recognizes Browning's and Tennyson's kind of troubled self-consciousness as the very note of modernity. A modernity with a long back-story, stretching back through Goethe and Shakespeare to Empedocles, in whose work, Arnold claimed, 'the calm, the cheerfulness, the disinterested objectivity' of 'early Greek genius ... have disappeared: the dialogue of the mind with itself has commenced; modern problems have presented themselves; we hear already the doubts, we witness the discouragements, of Hamlet and of Faust'. And that morbidity – *monotonous*, *painful*, too *prolonged*, 'unrelieved by incident, hope or resistance', would not do for poetry, which should be 'dedicated to Joy', as Schiller thought. Which is why Arnold has dropped his poem 'Empedocles on Etna' from his collection, and is in effect ruling out Tennyson and Browning.

Literary modernity, then, as a doomy 'dialogue of the mind with itself': an unhappy self-dividedness, not to be got rid of just by erasing a poem. A reflexive subjectivity sad because the self knows itself as other, as double, *double-minded* as the Bible's Epistle of James has it in the Authorised Version, translating the Greek *dipsuchos*, two-souled man. The formula seized on by Arnold's one-time intimate AC Clough for his set of messy self-debating poems *Dipsychus*, in which a character Dipsychus, a 'double self' (*Dipsychus*, sc X, line 63) debates with a Doppelgänger, a combative personal Other, called Spirit.[10] And Clough was as unhappy as Arnold about this self-doubling; the Spirit, about whose identity there is much debate in the *Dipsychus* texts and their Epilogue, might be 'merely 'the hypothesis or subjective imagination', Clough said ('Epilogue'), but could be the Devil, Mephistopheles out of Goethe's *Faust* and Marlowe's *Dr Faustus*.[11] And this

---

[9]   See WS Peterson and FL Standley, 'The JS Mill Marginalia in Robert Browning's Pauline: A History and Transcription', *Papers of the Bibliographical Society of America*, LXVI (1972), 135–170.

[10]   The text was first published in the *Letters and Remains of Arthur Hugh Clough* (1865) with a note by Mrs Clough that she had earlier thought it 'too unfinished to be published among his poems'.

[11]   Daniel Karlin talks briefly about *Dipsychus*, and relates its doubleness to the nineteenth-century Doppelgänger tradition and Protestant self-scrutiny of which that movement is an offspring, in 'At home in the swell: AH Clough, hexameters and the triumphs of the flesh', *TLS*, 13 Jan 2006, 3–4.

unhappiness was widely shared; Arnold was right to suspect it was germane to all modern poets and their poetry, all of them the discouraged descendants of Hamlet the founding discouraged self-dialogist of western culture; all donning their fictional *prosopa/personae* for the purposes of self-dramatization, and thus endorsing the old Hamletian melancholy about the self. *Prosopopoeia/personification* – the inevitable post-Hamletian strain of the contemporary; and a poetic activity whose history granted it an inevitably bad name.

Pathetic Fallacy

Personification: it's the activity for which John Ruskin brilliantly invented the pejorative label, which has gone down in literary historicity for pointfulness, namely 'the pathetic fallacy'. Admittedly, what was most on Ruskin's mind in the 'Of the Pathetic Fallacy' section of his *Modern Painters* in 1856 (Vol III, Part 4, Chapter XII) as a deplorable tendency of modern poems was the way they granted an impossible selfhood to non-human nature. It was simply fallacious to suppose, as the Romantics and their successors did, that trees, and flowers, and hills have emotions. The foam of the sea is not 'cruel', nor does it 'crawl', as Charles Kingsley says it is and does in his poem 'The Sands of Dee' (1849).[12] Tennyson's *Maud* supplies 'exquisite' examples: the passionflower shedding a tear, the red rose crying, the white rose weeping, the larkspur listening, the lily whispering (*Maud*, Part I, section XXII, stanza x). This kind of personification is everywhere in poems, Ruskin observes. He might have been repeating Dante's observation, in Section 24 of the *Vita Nuova*, of the ubiquity of personification, though he shows no signs of doing so (and Dante Gabriel Rossetti's translation of the *Vita Nuova* didn't appear until 1861). Readers like personifications: 'if we think over our favourite poetry, we shall find it full of this kind of fallacy, and that we like it all the more for being so'. And where Dante is just a little perturbed at the unreality, Ruskin is enraged. Personification is an untruth; a refusal to accept reality; 'a falseness in all our impressions of external things.' It's the product of 'wilful fancy'; of 'an excited state of the feelings, making us, for the time, more or less irrational'; of a kind of madness, 'the reason unhinged by grief'. It's 'the sign of a morbid state of mind, and comparatively of a weak one.' For the sane, calm, unmorbid poet, 'the primrose is for ever nothing else than itself – a little flower, apprehended in the very plain and leafy fact of it, whatever and how many soever the associations may be, that crowd around it.'

[12]   The poem first appeared in Kingsley's social-problem novel *Alton Locke: Tailor and Poet: An Autobiography*, 2 vols (Chapman & Hall, 1850), vol II., Ch 5 (Ch 26 later), ascribed to Alton Locke, 'The Triumphant Author'. It was slightly altered in Kingsley's *Poems* (1872).

Ruskin rants. A rant that shows him sunk in an empiricist factualism, resistant to metaphoric working, to the power of metaphor – how it can actually grant roses emotions and turn them into people. And a rant that is evidently going much further than its immediate concern with its local branch of prosopopoeia, the personification of natural things. What appears to be more widely at stake is selfhood itself, the selfhood of the poet, self-hood in a poem – 'the thoughts of the poet himself ... the thoughts of the characters imagined by him'. Ruskin is appalled by the idea of the poet as a self, a person, who can be 'thrown off balance', whose emotions can quite overthrow him, can disrupt his perceptions, can generate language that's 'broken, obscure, and wild in metaphor'. Fallacious results, all this wrong-headed prosopopoeia, come from the poet's sorry susceptibility to such wrong feelings. It's the play of poetic selfhood as such which is discombobu-lating Ruskin – the allegedly morbid, weak, maddened selfhood of the poet which powers an excess of the personal in the poem, and an overly morbid, weak, disturbed set of *prosopa*, of *personae*, at that.

Ranting, yes; but still there is something – much, in fact – that's patently up with the contemporary sense of the self and the literary self-making that the Victorians go in for on such a grand scale.

> Like smoke I vanish, though I burn like flame;
> I flicker in the gusts of wrong and right,
> A shining frailty in the guise of might
> Before, a nothing – and behind a name.

That's WH Mallock, in his 'Human Life', in his *Verses* (1893), taking up Walter Pater's notorious manifesto about the necessary instability of the modern self in the Conclusion to *The Renaissance: Studies in Art and Poetry* (1873; 1888), and squeezing it, though not a lot. In a world we can know only by impressions – 'unstable, flickering, inconsistent, which burn and are extinguished with our consciousness of them' – Pater finds the self losing definition in a 'continual vanishing away, that strange, perpetual, weaving and unweaving of ourselves'. But still you can live successfully, Pater thinks, by accepting the heat, the ecstasy of the world's plethora of beautiful impres-sions (faces, hands, landscapes, seascapes), by burning 'always with this hard gem-like flame' induced by aesthetic joy in persons and things. For his part, Mallock accepts the *flickering* of things and self, of life as a totality of impressions (*flicker, impressions*: the tropes amply taken up by the early modernists Conrad and TS Eliot and Virginia Woolf). But he can't help real-izing that fires which give off flames also give off smoke – not only evanes-cent, but dark and murky, and (in Victorian cities) nasty, noxious, and smelly. So not for him, nor for most of his contemporaries, anything like Carlyle's bracingly confident Lutheran self-assertiveness – the upside of the

Protestant Reformation's promotion of the individual's uniqueness as a Bible-reading subject on its own before a beneficent God: impressive and appealing, and very lone-wolf. Carlyle translated Luther's notable Protestant hymn, 'Eine feste Burg ist unser Gott' into English – 'A safe stronghold our God is still': the translation that became standard in English hymnbooks and for English-language Christianity – as a sort of manifesto for a strong, centred selfhood rooted in Reformation individuality. In the rugged tones of Luther's poem, wrote Carlyle, introducing it and his translation in *Fraser's Magazine* in 1831, you could recognize the accent of the man who defied the powers of the day, German Emperor, Roman Pope, 'principalities and powers', the devil himself, and 'spoke these final and forever memorable words: "It is neither safe nor prudent to do aught against conscience. Here stand I, I cannot otherwise. God assist me. Amen!".' 'Hier stehe ich, ich kann nicht anders. Gott helfe mir. Amen!'.[13] But such indissoluble firmness of the self was rare to come by. Protestant Browning – Luther admirer, Carlyle admirer – tried to be a Luther. And he could match the rugged tones; but not the self-confidence. His *I* shatters and scatters into scores of fragments. He desires monologue, but he the single monologuist gets lost, his voice subsumed in the voices of his characters; his own face, his *prosopon*, hidden by the faces, the masks, the *prosopa* he puts on. Every dramatic monologue makes its author into some sort of actor, a ventriloquist, even (though Browning would hate the analogy) a medium. And this is as true for Tennyson and Swinburne, Augusta Webster and Amy Levy, as it is for Browning – though none of these invested in dramatic monologues to Browning's huge extent.[14]

Browning is especially troubled about the relationship. TS Eliot's confidence that 'when we read a dramatic monologue by Browning, we cannot suppose that we are listening to any other voice than that of Browning himself', because in a dramatic monologue it is 'surely' the second of the three voices of poetry, 'the voice of the poet talking to other people, that is dominant',[15] is over-strong. Now Browning's personae are him; now they're not; now they might be; now he can't tell whether they are or not. In his 1833 notes responding to Mill's annotations of *Pauline*, he talks of the poem

13 Thomas Carlyle, 'Luther's Psalm', *Fraser's Magazine*, no. 12 (1831); in vol III of Carlyle's *Essays, Critical and Miscellaneous* (Chapman & Hall, London, 1872), 61–64.

14 The monologues and soliloquies of Augusta Webster's *Dramatic Studies* (1866) and *Portraits* (1870,1893) – whose status as dramatic monologues proper is hotly debated – are now conveniently available in *Portraits and other Poems*, ed Christine Sutphin (Broadview Literary Texts, Letchworth, 2000), which usefully includes certain Webster essays, and some reviews of her poetry books. (Characteristically, Ekbert Faas puts Webster into his Appendix of 'Practitioners of the Dramatic Monologue Among Minor Poets', loc cit, 214–215. Amy Levy doesn't even make this list.)

15 TS Eliot, 'The Three Voices of Poetry' (1953), *On Poetry and Poets* (Faber & Faber, London, 1957), 96.

as part of a 'foolish plan' to 'assume and realize I know not how many characters', each of whom would be 'one and the same individual', that is himself. But only more or less. For *Pauline*'s narrator 'would have been more legitimately myself than most of the others'. So was he, or not? In the epilogue poem to the *Men and Women* volume, 'One Word More', dedicated to Elizabeth Barrett Browning (1855), Browning claims to speak with the mouth of his 'fifty men and women':

> Love, you saw me gather men and women,
> Live or dead or fashioned by my fancy,
> Enter each and all, use their service,
> Speak from every mouth, – the speech, a poem.
> (129–132)

Which seems plain enough: the mouth of the *persona*, considered simply as a hole through which the poet speaks (*persona*, from Latin *personare*, to speak through, as in the medieval (Chaucerian) parish *persoun*, modern *parson*, the figure through whom the Bishop spoke). Except that Browning goes on to wish to speak to her 'this once in my true person / Not as Lippo, Roland or Andrea' (137–138) – making a distinction between his own voice and the voices coming through the character masks, which he had just said were his own. A claim, what's worse, following the truly obfuscating four lines that followed the first statement:

> Hardly shall I tell my joys and sorrows
> Hopes and fears, belief and disbelieving:
> I am mine and yours – the rest be all men's,
> Karshish, Cleon, Norbert and the fifty.
> (133–136)

Does he mean that telling his own 'joys and sorrows', and so forth, through his *personae* was done *hardly*, ie with difficulty; or scarcely (*hardly*) at all? And what does 'I am mine and yours – the rest be all men's' mean? *I am* the things so expressed: they're *mine*? But if they're *mine*, they can't be *yours*. And what then are the *rest*? Perhaps 'I am mine and yours' is a declaration of loving allegiance: I am all myself, my own, I belong to me but am also *all yours* (along the lines of the possessives of the Biblical *Canticles*' female lover: 'My beloved is mine and I am his'). But that still leaves the problem of *the rest*: can Browning be all at once his own man, belong all to himself, and also to Elizabeth, and also to the *rest*, that is all the characters of his volume? (It doesn't help that for many years *Karshish* appeared in line 136 as *Karshook*, hero of Browning's 'Ben Karshook's Wisdom', a poem not in *Men and Women* – unlike 'An Epistle Concerning the Strange Medical Experience of Karshish the Arab Physician', and 'Cleon', and 'In a Balcony' whose hero is Norbert; nor, indeed, that 'Karshish, Cleon, Norbert and the fifty' make a total of fifty-three poems, three too many for the volume.)

All as confused and confusing as could be. No wonder Browning was irked by Ruskin's charge (as discussed in Chapter 1) that the *Men and Women* volume confirmed Browning's tendency to let himself be, and speak, through his people. Ruskin 'may be right', Browning conceded, but he was 'unwitting of the fact'; if he is in 'Pippa and other men and maids', he's sorry and repents of the sin (*peccavi*): 'I don't see myself in them, at all events'. But sometimes, and not least in 'One Word More' in the volume in question, he acknowledges that he did so see himself. So here, plainly, are muddy waters; and obscurities Browning could not stop himself muddying some more. In the 1867 Preface to his *Poems* he returned to *Pauline* – 'my earliest attempt' at '"poetry always dramatic in principle, and so many utterances of so many imaginary persons, not mine"'. *Pauline*'s narrator was not, after all, to be him; but then, again, the poet and his persona are quite close. *Pauline* was a 'crude preliminary sketch' that 'on reviewal, appears not altogether wide of some hint of the characteristic features of that particular *dramatis persona* it would fain have reproduced'.

There's something arrestingly fishy about Browning's kept-up switch-back owning and disowning of his people. Others might be able to pretend there was no problem, or not much of one, but he could not, and his indecisive blurring is the more impressive for it. Swinburne blustered as he tried to simply swat away the problem, defending his (publicly reviled) volume *Poems and Ballads* (1866) by breezily distinguishing himself from his people: 'the book is dramatic, many-faced, multifarious; and no enjoyment or despair, belief or unbelief, can properly be assumed as the assertion of its author's personal feeling or faith'; if he had wanted to attack 'sacred' things in his own person, as Byron and Shelley did, he would have done so 'to the best of my power'; but he did not so choose.[16] Augusta Webster (in her 'Poets and Personal Pronouns' essay) wouldn't allow 'the popular theory of poetry being, as it were, confessional'. On occasion, she had to admit, a poet might be 'distinctly' expressing 'emotions which belong to him in his actual life', but this was rare. The 'consoling evidence that, as a rule, I does not mean I' was clear: if poets had the 'mental state' of many of their I-characters they would not be 'able to correct their proofs and get their books through press'. Poets could easily tell the difference between themselves and their speakers, and a simple new printing code would clarify things: 'The use of a little i instead of a big I might have some effect as a sort of modest disclaimer of the writer's personality in the matter; but the printers would never stand

---

[16] In Swinburne's *Notes on Poems and Reviews* (JC Hotten, London, 1866): reprinted as Appendix I in *Poems and Ballads & Atalanta in Calydon*, ed Kenneth Haynes (Penguin, Harmondsworth, 2000), 403–416.

that'.[17] And, course, neither Swinburne's outright bravado nor Webster's rather wet psychologizings convince as attempted brushings-aside of the problem that Browning is obviously very alarmed about. They help make Browning's paltering, his inability to face up to the inherent *prosopon* or face problem – the question of the degree to which prosopopoeia is a self-facing, or self-defacing, or self-effacing truth to the self – look like the veriest honesty, the serious poet's grasp of the aweing difficulties hereabouts.

The Message of The Medium

It's inviting to read Browning's 'Mr Sludge, "The Medium"' as a reflection of the poet's anguished mixed feelings over the Dramatic Monologue, for a spiritualist medium is patently a type of the dramatic monologuist in alleging that others, the dead, communicate through him or her. 'Mr Sludge, "The Medium"' (first published in Browning's *Dramatis Personae* volume, 28 May 1864), one of Browning's angriest poems, is directed against the popular American medium Daniel Dunglas Home. To Browning's great annoyance, his wife had become infatuated with Home, convinced that he really was a conduit for dead people's thoughts, voices, and writings, that he produced their presence, their very touch. Browning thought him 'an unmitigated scoundrel', a beast, a piece of shit (a 'dung-ball'). He wanted to kick him, even though that would 'soil my shoe'. This was because of the 'vomit of lies' Home had uttered in a review of 'Mr Sludge', describing how in a séance at Ealing the 'spirits' had crowned Elizabeth Barrett Browning with a wreath of clematis, and alleging that this made Browning jealous, which prompted his gross poetic attack.[18] But for Browning the review's lies were only the latest in Home's mendacities – all the deceptions Sludge won't admit to ('Don't expose me! Just this once! / This was the first and only time, I'll swear').

Sludge's angry addressee has caught the medium out in a farrago of vulgar literary and historical nonsense, putting into the mouth of his dead 'sainted mother' some verses Lady Jane Grey, uncrowned Tudor Queen of England, allegedly 'composed / About the rosy bower in the seventh heaven / Where she and Queen Elizabeth keep house' (1470–1476). This is a classic

[17]   Augusta Webster, 'Poets and Personal Pronouns', *Examiner*, 2 March 1878, 268–270; collected with other of her *Examiner* articles in *A Housewife's Opinions* (Macmillan & Co, London, 1879), 150–156; reprinted in *Portraits and Other Poems*, ed Christine Sutphin (Broadview Press Ltd, Peterborough, Ontario, 2000), 366–372.

[18]   See Robert Browning's letter to Mrs WB Kinney, Jan 1871, *New Letters of Robert Browning*, eds WC DeVane and KL Knickerbocker (John Murray, London, 1951), 198–200; and 'Sludgehood', Chapter 3 of Daniel Karlin, *Browning's Hatreds* (Clarendon Press, Oxford, 1993), 47–67.

piece of dramatic monologuing, and blatantly crooked. And the dramatically monologuizing crook's long self-exculpatory plea in mitigation turns
into a defence of what a dramatic monologuist is about. At first Sludge
admits that the selves he impersonates in voice and writing and table-
rappings are all fake, a pretend reality, a pack of lies. All the mediums Sludge
knows are conscious pretenders. Browning supports that: 'medium' only
ever occurs in the poem, as in its title, in inverted commas. At one point
(167–169) there's a very apt little flurry over the word person. Learning
Greek, says Sludge, will make the interlocutor's son 'a Person ... / proficient
in the art of lies'. The listening father is thanked for correcting *Person* to
Porson, the eighteenth-century Greek scholar intended by Sludge. (He was
a nineteenth-century byword for drunkenness as well as minute scholarship:
Charles Reade called him an *oinomaniac*, mad for wine, in a lovely list of
lunatics in his novel *Hard Cash* (1863).) Person: Porson: Sludge's stutter
(repeated, interestingly, by the twentieth-century poet Stevie Smith in her
poem 'Thoughts about the Person from Porlock', the one who interrupted
Coleridge: he has to be Porson), the stutter nicely underscores the medium's
slipperiness over personation. He can't even get the word person right. And,
of course, to associate becoming a person with proficiency in lies, as his slip
of the tongue does, really brings home the link between mediumistic personation and untruth. Untruths which, having admitted to, Sludge immediately starts to defend. Very quickly, his skill as a tricksy rhetor, a canny but
dodgy argufier, kicks in – in the wonderful way with dubious argument
common to Browning's wicked personae. The deceptions, he says, are not
his fault. The public wishes to be deceived. His activities do good. The
faked-up spiritual phenomena encourage belief in the afterlife, the spiritual
world, and so confuse atheists, those liars who deny God and non-earthly
reality. So his lies are 'timely helpful' ones, 'laudable' deceptions, like chalk-
eggs placed under hens to help them lay real eggs (1306, 1308). His particular fictions are in good company, he declares; they're just what's provided
by novelists, dramatists and poets, even prose-writers, historians, biographers, and such:

> It's fancying, fable-making, nonsense-work –
> What never meant to be so very bad –
> The knack of story-telling, brightening up
> Each dull old bit of fact that drops its shine.
> (190–193)

All writing, says Sludge, is 'helpful lies' (1445) and more or less 'fancy'
(1464). Sludge speaks for – and as – 'the penman'(1463): ' "We writers paint
out of our heads, you see!" '(1467). So Sludge is, as Browning, or any such
poet, does. He's feeling Browning's collar. To ram home their affinity,

Browning has Sludge burst into the occasional pair of end-rhyming lines (1182–1183; 1283–1284). 'Bless us, I'm turning poet!' (1184). 'There's verse again, but I'm inspired somehow' (1285). Moreover, Sludge suggests, taking up the commonest critical thought about fiction, his feignings are actually truths:

> I'm ready to believe my very self –
> That every cheat's inspired, and every lie
> Quick with a germ of truth.
> (1323–1325)

'My self', this mobile theatre of lies, is a *veritable* thing too. Sludge really becomes, he really is, the persons of his brain's fancy – 'now the President, now Jenny Lind [the singer] / Now Emerson [the thinker], now the Benicia Boy [famous boxer]' [1268–1269]. 'All was not cheating'. At least, on some occasions he professes uncertainty about who's lifting the table, doing automatic writing, playing piano-accordion, and speaking. If the ventriloquialism is all pretence, how can it be 'I speak so much more than I intend, / Describe so many things I never saw'? (1311–1319).

> ... and pens, good Lord,
> Who knows if you drive them or they drive you?
> (196–197)

Automatic writing: pretence, or the real thing? The personations: fake or real? Prosopopoeia, self-making, self-existence: authentic or not? Sludge could not be closer to Browning's havering ownings and disownings of the selves in the selvings of his 'mediumistic' dramatic monologues. At issue in the ducking and diving of Sludge is nothing less than the truth of Browning, the truth of this whole genre of the dramatic monologue, which Browning so commands. Pens, good Lord, who does drive them? And who would want Mr Sludge as his or her counsel for the defence?

Human Sludge

'Mr Sludge' is, then, a poem of decidedly mixed feelings; its sympathies turning in quite opposite directions. We're convinced of Sludge's absolute wickedness and yet also made to be attracted to him. The poem won't allow us to think he's all bad. At least, his wickedness has a certain glamour. It's this mixture that obviously keeps Browning investing in this kind of persona. But of course, in the first place, there must be no doubt about the wickedness, the immorality.

Sludge is well-named: he's moral filth; in the moral sludge. To lie on his pattern is to inhabit the moral gutter, where the sludge of the city is. He 'gorges', he admits, 'On offal in the gutter' (263–264). Offal, *Abfall*, trash. *Cockered*, *cossetted* and *coddled* by his admirers, he has yearned to get away from them, like a child moithered by female relatives, kept from 'Good fun and wholesome mud', who longs to join 'The ragged sons o' the gutter at their game, / Fain would be down with them i' the thick o' the filth, / Making dirt-pies' (387–399). It's where Browning thinks Sludge, and his kind, belong.

Sludge excuses the *smuts* that have landed on him: it's the filth that alights on anybody's nose (500–504). He's no more filthy, he says, than 'your literary man', the realist writer, who makes a living out of reporting on human shit, 'the man for muck', painting as it were in excrement:

> Shovel it forth, full-splash, he'll smooth your brown
> Into artistic richness, never fear!

Such a writer would like to discover the whole world to 'roll' in 'the slime o' the slough, 'so he might touch the tip / Of his brush with what I call the best of browns.' (Painting in brown is, of course, a matter of browning.) The literary man's excrementitious browning work is 'ghost-tales, spirit-stories': just as filthy, because just as false, as Sludge's stories from the alleged spirit world. Except that writers get public credit, good repute, for their narratives and novels, as well as cash – which is all that Sludge gets (746–772). And this wide broadcasting of the moral sludge does indeed carry weight. Sludge is rather convincing about not being alone in the moral gutter. It's not at all the excuse for his degeneracy that he supposes, but what it does is confirm the feeling of the period's I-narration poems, and not just Browning's, that how Sludge is, so, one way or another, the contemporary self is.

Browning's talking heroes stack up pointedly as slick mongers of dodgy stories, dubious readings, questionable half-truths and outright lies on Sludge-lines. Like Sludge they're malefactors practised in slithy self-exculpation. Browning's wily Duke in 'My Last Duchess: Ferrara' claims to know the unique meaning of 'that spot of joy' in his wife's face, her *prosopon*, in her portrait. It's the sign, albeit a silent one, of adultery with Fra Pandolf the painter of the picture: the blush of unfaithful affections. But since the Duke is the owner of the painting and the controller of interpretative occasions – 'none puts by / The curtain I have drawn for you, but I' – and his is the only voice, the only reading, we hear, there's no gainsaying. And his array of claiming and disclaiming, his pseudo-hesitant parade of personal credits which instantly become her deficits – 'She had / A heart – how shall I say? – too soon made glad, / Too easily impressed; she liked whate'er / She looked on, and her looks went everywhere'; 'She thanked men – good!; but thanked / Somehow – I know not how – as if she ranked / My gift of a nine-hundred-years-old-name / With anybody's gift'; 'Oh Sir, she smiled, no doubt, / Whene'r I passed her; but who passed without / Much the same smile?' – turn that stubborn silence of hers into eloquent grounds for her death. This is self-serving falsifying eloquence; in which Browning's interest never flags, even after you might have thought it had peaked in the massive collection of dramatic monologues, 'my great venture, the murder-poem', *The Ring and the Book*. He is, of course, especially interested in the deviantly powerful – a duke, a bishop ('Bishop Blougram's Apology'), a Pope (Book X of *The Ring and the Book*, the sadistic ruler over millions ('Instans Tyrannus') – but by no means exclusively. And what unites these self-explaining, self-voicers, whether socially great or not-so-great, is their sheer untrustworthiness, their twisted take on, their perversion of, the straight, Lutheran, Protestant *I*. '[H]ere I stand', says murderous (and Papist) Count Guido (*The Ring and the Book*, V.247), in a contradiction of self-terms according to Browning (a paradox and untruth instantly proven by the fact he cannot actually stand, because of the pain in his *omoplot* (i.e. omoplate), his shoulder-blade: crooked plotter, crooked body, crooked self).

Browning's people tend to be in some way or other on edge, on the fringe – in scholarship, music, art, religion, and marriage. He's immensely drawn to failures, dropouts, flouters of convention of every sort, errant thinkers and poets and artists, the failed painter ('So die my pictures': 'Pictor Ignotus'), the out-of-fashion musician ('A Toccata of Galuppi's'), the scholar whose lifetime's work is misplaced and wasted, 'Dead from the waist down' ('A Grammarian's Funeral, Shortly After the Revival of Learning in Europe'), and so on. But it's the more clearly morally transgressive person he goes for most – unbelieving bishops, villains, con-men, cheats, heretics, wayward church functionaries, naughty monks, wife-killers, girlfriend stranglers: sinners all; people of the moral margin; in the gutter with Sludge. Or with Fra Lippo Lippi, the painting monk, a wonderful complex of low stuff, of waste matters and marginalities: the boy from the social margin, a street urchin, raised on *Abfall*, the thrown-out edges of food – 'On fig-skins, melon-parings, rinds and shucks, / Refuse and rubbish' (84–85); schooled in character, in 'the look of things', as *Abfall*, by 'Watching folk's faces to know who will fling / The bit of half-stripped grape-bunch he desires', which priest will let him catch sacramental candle-wax to sell, which dog will drop 'His bone from the heap of offal in the street' (114–125); drawing faces and bodies in the margins of music and reading books, on walls, benches, doors (129–135); grown up to be greatly transgressive as both artist and man. These people are Calibans: 'in the pit's much mire', where we find Browning's spokesman at the beginning of 'Caliban Upon Setebos'. They're distressing people in all sorts of distress – even mad; in the madhouse; in the poem as mental asylum.

Madhouse Cells

Johannes Agricola, founder of the Christian 'sect' of Antinomians, smuggest of hyper-Calvinists, confident his sins don't count against him because he's predestined to salvation, while the prayers and goodness of all Roman Catholics are religiously worthless because they are predestined to hell, was offered to readers as a madman. So was the man who calmly tells us how he strangled his beloved Porphyria with her hair, so that she could be his and no-one else's ('mine, mine'). 'Johannes Agricola in Meditation' and 'Porphyria's Lover' were originally a pair of poems, appearing in Browning's 1842 volume *Dramatic Lyrics* as simply 'Madhouse Cells', I and II. Even after they acquired their present titles in the *Dramatic Romances and Lyrics* volume of 1849, they were still subtitled 'I – Madhouse Cell', and 'II – Madhouse Cell' – subtitles only dropped when the poems were separated for Browning's three-volume *Poetical Works* of 1863. 'I believe I do unduly like the study of morbid cases of the soul', Browning confessed to Julia Wedgwood.[19] '[T]here can come no good of keeping this wild company', he wrote to Elizabeth Barrett, 26 February 1845, but he went on keeping it, never able to finally leave the mad-house behind.

Like, in effect, Tennyson, who knew, as did his brothers, what madhouses were like from the inside. Edward Tennyson went mad in October 1832. Alfred was in and out of mental homes and resorts for the hydropathic treatment of depressives. He and Septimus were both patients at Dr Matthew Allen's institutions for the mentally ill, High Beech, Epping Forest, Essex. When Alfred's brother Charles, the sonneteering clergyman Charles Tennyson Turner, died at Cheltenham, 25 April 1879, he was being treated for mental illness. And the Tennyson family's 'black blood', their tendency to bouts of despondency and melancholy amounting to insanity, ran rife in Alfred's poems as in his life.[20] From early to late in his career the self of his poems is prone to sadness and despair. Tennyson was morbid and suicidal even before the death of his beloved Arthur Hallam in September 1833 cast him into more or less permanent mourning. ' "I am half sick of shadows", said / The Lady of Shalott', quitting her loom, to be cursed unto death; ' "The curse is come upon me", cried / The Lady of Shalott'. 'Let us alone', 'Let us alone', 'Let us alone', cry The Lotos Eaters, so miserable they want to die. One of his two inner voices tempts the *I* of Tennyson's 'The Two

---

[19] Quoted by Daniel Karlin, *Browning's Hatreds*, 219.

[20] Ann C Colley amply charts the insanity in Tennyson's extended family and among his friends and colleagues, his friendships with 'mad doctors', his wide reading in the 'mentalist' literature, his 'clinical' interest in mad people in his poems, and 'madness as metaphor', especially in *Idylls of the King: Tennyson and Madness* (University of Georgia Press, Athens GA, 1983).

Voices' to kill himself, he being 'so full of misery'. A version of 'The Two Voices' was circulating among Tennyson's friends months before Hallam's death, under the title 'Thoughts of a Suicide'.[21] It reminded Tennyson's friend Carlyle of the Bible's Book of Job. It's certainly redolent of melancholic Hamlet's preoccupation with suicide. The selfhood of immortal Tithonus in the dramatic monologue 'Tithonus', another of the Hallam-death poems, is burned-out – 'And all I was, in ashes'. His beloved Aurora granted him endless life but not eternal youth. 'Me only cruel immortality / Consumes: I wither slowly in thine arms'. Empson said some of this poem's lovely lines were like 'mouldy wedding-cake', but the opening lines about the naturalness of death are unbearably fresh:

> The woods decay, the woods decay and fall,
> The vapours weep their burthen to the ground,
> Man comes and tills the field and lies beneath,
> And after many a summer dies the swan.
>
> (1–4)

(Small wonder Aldous Huxley wanted that last line for his 1939 satire on modern immortality-fantasies.[22])

> I loathe the squares and streets,
> And the faces that one meets,
> Hearts with no love for me;
> Always I long to creep
> To some still cavern deep,
> And to weep, and weep and weep
> My whole soul out to thee.
>
> (58–64)

That's the lover of 'Oh! that 'twere possible', demented by the loss of an alleged female beloved, but plainly grieving by proxy over the absent Hallam. The speaker is a tragically bereft *I* whose miseries keep overtaking the many moods of Tennyson's great 1850 poem, 'In Memoriam AHH, Obiit MDCCCXXXIII', the memorial poem for Hallam that Tennyson struggled for seventeen years to write, miseries especially challenging the poem's tries for consolation and religious hope in a desolate world, its brave whistlings

---

[21]   Christopher Ricks lists twenty-six Tennyson poems in which suicide appears as subject or event, even apart from the poems about martyrs and soldiers and the 'suicide-risk' poems, 'Geraint and Enid', 'Semele', 'The Ring' and 'The Sailor Boy': *Tennyson* (Macmillan, London and Basingstoke, 1972), fn pp 103–104.

[22]   *After Many A Summer* (Chatto & Windus, 1939). The American reprint of 1952 was titled *After Many A Summer Died the Swan*, because it was thought the American audience, unlike the British, would not have remembered how the whole Tennyson line went on.

in the glooms of a darkened universe. Miseries dramatically seeping and segueing into the even greater poem, Tennyson's very best poem in fact, 'Maud' (1855).

The germ of 'Maud' was 'Oh! that 'twere possible', and it is recycled in the longer poem. The I-narrator's dementing griefs are now ascribed to the suicide of his father, ground down in despair and madness over money speculations gone wrong through the manipulations of the men in the family of the beloved Maud – the new subject of 'Oh! that 'twere possible', estranged by the interfamily quarrels and, of course, the vengeful murder of her brother by her one-time lover, our narrator. The poem's original title was 'Maud, or the Madness'. Its narrator inhabits 'cells of madness' (III.vi.1). Tennyson called it 'the history of a morbid, poetic soul, under the blighting influence of a recklessly speculative age', which fits. He also thought the narrator was 'the heir of madness'.[23] Madness running in the narrator's family. Madness running, too, in Tennyson's family, emergent in Tennyson's own version of it. The poem's truly mad episodes, when the narrator thinks he's dead, 'And my heart is a handful of dust, / And the wheels go over my head', and so on (V.i), were thought by Tennyson's family to be based on observations of lunatics at High Beech.[24] They sound more like the dementias that drove Tennyson into High Beech, the mental upsets that were so massively egged on by Hallam's death. Madnesses inspired, too, of course, by Tennyson's closeness to the tradition of literary melancholy-madness. He thought of his poem as 'a little Hamlet'. Yet once more: the Victorian Hamlet and Hamletism.

Some contemporaries were reminded of the so-called Spasmodic School of Philip James Bailey, Alexander Smith and Sydney Dobell, and their long narrations of wild emotionality and frenzied gabblings, *Festus* (1839), *A Life Drama* (1853) and *Balder* (1854). (Tennyson thought *Balder* had good bits – like *Aurora Leigh*.[25]) A favourite charge against Browning was that he was a Spasmodic (leader of the 'Festus school' according to Bagehot in his review of *The Ring and the Book* in1869; if a poet at all (which he *isn't*) he's a poet of the *Festus* order, said Alfred Austin in his notorious jeering Browning overview in 'The Poetry of the Period', also in1869).[26] And it was

---

[23] He wondered why readers didn't 'find out that all along the man was intended to have an hereditary vein of insanity, and that he falls foul on the swindling, on the times, because he feels that his father has been killed by the work of the lie, and that all through he fears the coming madness'. Letter to Archer Thompson Gurney, 6 December 1855, *Letters of Alfred Lord Tennyson*, eds Cecil Y Lang and Edgar F Shannon Jr, 1851–1870 (Clarendon Press, Oxford, 1987), 137–138.

[24] Sir Charles Tennyson, *Alfred Tennyson* (Macmillan, London, 1949), 286.

[25] *Memoir*, II.506.

[26] Walter Bagehot, *Tinsley's Magazine* (Jan 1869), III, 665–674; Alfred Austin, *Temple Bar* (June 1869), XXVI, 316–333: both in Litzinger and Smalley's Browning *Critical Heritage* volume, 300–306; 339–356.

usual, too, for readers of 'Maud' to be reminded of Browning and the upset heroes of his dramatic monologues. Tennyson's psychologist friend Dr Robert James Mann dubbed the poem a 'mono-drama' in his defensive pamphlet of 1856, *Tennyson's 'Maud' Vindicated* (p72) (referred to earlier in the 'Stillicide' section of 'Making Noise / Noising Truths, Chapter 3).[27] He was doubtless thinking of Browning the Madhouse Cells specialist (he goes on and on about Tennyson's narrator as a *morbid*, mentally *rambling madman*, a maniac in 'the mad-house'; 'The grave where men are interred, but find no peace, is the madman's cell'; the 'blabbing' physician in there is 'perhaps ... the mad-doctor himself in the same boat with his mad-patients').[28] Tennyson, who liked his friend's booklet very much, readily adopted the Mann soubriquet as his sub-title in the 1859 edition, and 'Maud: A Monodrama' it has been ever since. Its monologues are not strictly 'dramatic monologues' as that label (invented by George W Thornbury for his *Songs of the Cavaliers and Roundheads, Jacobite Ballads, &c* (1857)) is applied to Browning and Swinburne, because there is no implied (silent) interlocutor in the poem (the narrator's apostrophizings of Maud, his own anger, a 'happy day', the stars and a prophet, don't count as that); but the selfhood on display in 'Maud' is *echt* Browning material.

As is Tennyson's poem 'Despair' of 1881, originally subtitled 'A Dramatic Monologue' – the complaint of a demented man who had with his wife attempted suicide in the sea out of post-Christian despair over a pointless universe, for which the monologuist blames their former Dissenting pastor, who 'bawled' on about God's anger for sinners, the 'dark side' of a Calvinist creed. It's oddly akin in subject to Browning's own dramatic monologue 'Ned Bratts' (*Dramatic Idyls*, 1879), confession of a wonderfully uncouth, vulgar-tongued and utterly crazy Bedford publican converted, with his wife, to Calvinist Christianity through reading *The Pilgrim's Progress* by Bedford's own John Bunyan. They repent of their crimes and petition at Bedford Assizes to be hanged before Satan can lure them from grace. No surprise that this poem was widely lampooned by critics for spasmodic grotesquery ('We wonder that his own fingers were not pulled from the joints as he wrote those dislocated and dislocating pages').[29]

---

[27] '[W]here can this unprofessional psychologist have acquired his accurate insight in the phenomena of insanity?', p10.
[28] The 'Blabbing' physician was taken by some as a poke at Dr Allen's taste for publicity, Tennyson having fallen out with him after losing much money in Allen's failed mechanical furniture production scheme.
[29] G Allen, *Fortnightly Review* (July 1879), XXXII, 149–153 ; and Anon, 'Three Small Books: By Great Writers', *Fraser's Magazine* (July 1879) NS XX, 103–124. Both in the Browning *Critical Heritage* volume, 458–460; 461–464.

'Maud' does, then, make a monodramatic presentation of self which is Browningesque in its kind, but a self proliferating, breaking up, in a way that never happens in a Browning poem. Each one of Browning's speakers is single; the narrator of 'Maud' is a split man. *I, I, I, I* he keeps pronouncing, but the mood, the emotionality, the implied kind or branch of selfhood varies with the occasion of the utterance, the point the narrative has reached, the state of his relationship with self and other. 'I hate'; I remember'; 'I think'; 'I have neither hope nor trust'; 'am I raging alone as my father raged in his mood?'; 'I am sick … I am sick'; 'My dreams are bad'; 'I will bury myself in myself'; 'Long have I sighed for a calm'; 'And most of all would I flee from the cruel madness of love'; 'I well would weep for a time so sordid and mean'; 'myself from myself I guard'; 'am I not, am I not, here alone?'; 'I hear the dead at midday moan'; 'I fear'; 'Did I dream?'; 'Sick, am I sick?'; 'At war with myself and a wretched race / Sick, sick to the heart of life am I'; 'And ah … / That the man I am might cease to be'; 'What matter if I go mad'; 'Scorned by one that I scorn'; 'I fancy her sweetness'; 'I thought as I stood'; 'I thought she was kind'; 'I … / Felt a horror'; 'I shuddered and thought like a fool of the sleep of death'. 'So dark a mind within me dwells'; '… if *I* be dear to someone else / Then I should be to myself more dear; … If I be dear / If I be dear to someone else'; 'what am I / That I dare to look her way?'; 'Shall I love her as well if she / Can break her word were it even for me? / I trust it is not so'; 'I must tell her, or die'; 'I … who am no more so all forlorn'; 'I … do accept my madness, and would die'; 'Dear heart, I feel with thee…;' 'do I dream of bliss?'; 'If ever I *should* forget, / May God make me more wretched /Than ever I have been yet!'; 'now I have sworn to bury / All this dead body of hate, / I feel so free and clear'; 'Strange, that I felt so gay'; 'I am … delighted'; 'till I die, till I die'; 'thinking of all I have lost'; 'So long / Shall I nurse in my dark heart … a spark of will'; 'Am I guilty of blood?'; 'I steal, a wasted frame'; 'I loathe the squares and streets'; 'Always I long to creep / Into some still cavern deep, / There to weep, and weep, and weep'; 'And my heart is a handful of dust'; 'I thought the dead had peace, but it is not so'; 'I know where a garden grows'; 'Maybe still I am but half-dead'; 'I thought that a war would arise in defence of the right'; 'I cleaved to a cause that I felt to be pure and true'; 'So dark a mind within me dwells'; 'I wake to the higher aims'; 'I have felt with my native land, I am one with my kind, / I embrace the purpose of God, and the doom assigned'.

It's a quite extraordinary trajectory or journey of the person, mapped as a forever shifting kaleidoscope of fluctuating emotion, thought, being. I-narration as a roller-coaster, a dizzying switch-back of self actualities and possibilities. The speaker wants, as he keeps saying, to be 'let … be', but what that being is to be never stays still: he's continually hindered in his being anything for long (there's a *let*, in other words, in the old sense that survives in tennis, as a hindrance) to the letting-be he craves.[30] Tennyson thought (according to his son Hallam) that 'The peculiarity of this poem is that different phases of passion in one person take the place of different characters'.[31] What he could, or should, rather have said, was that the great power of the poem is its gift of a self whose phases of passion constitute a variegation of character – identity in constant motion, the individual person as, essentially, a play, or field, of *personae*. A person unfixed, de-ranged, unhinged, decentred as we now say. Multiphrenic even. Not as actually multiphrenic as John Clare, but close enough for discomfort.[32]

When John Clare died in May 1864 he'd been for over twenty-two years in Northampton County Lunatic Asylum, a certified lunatic, delusively prone to thinking he was Byron, Shakespeare, Horatio Nelson, the Duke of Wellington with his head shot off, or a famous boxer of the day being fattened up for a big fight. From 1837 to July 1841 (when he ran away) he was also one of Dr Allen's High Beech patients, overlapping there with Alfred Tennyson. There is, alas, no record of these two poetic experts of the unsettled self ever meeting as they haunted the High Beech grounds, no whisper of an exchange of notes between the mad gent and the mad peasant on their shared condition and its aesthetic expression: the condition of so many of the period's many I-narratives, its obsessive poetic self-inspectings, its heaps of mono-dramatizations; the constant presenting of the self, and selves, as continually dislocated, relocating, forever on edge, in-between; the condition Browning elaborates through the mouth of Bishop Blougram.

---

[30] As Eric Griffiths sharply recognizes in his reflections on 'let it / him / me be' in 'Maud', there's avoidance as well as permission in 'let ... be'. *The Printed Voice of Victorian Poetry*, 120–121; and fn 70, p121, where Griffiths recalls Christina G Rossetti's 'Autumn': 'O love-songs, gurgling from a hundred throats / O love-pangs let me be'. Perhaps the canniest contextualizing *trouvaille* by David G Riede in his *Allegories of One's Own mind: Melancholy in Victorian Poetry* is to link the mental restlessness indicated by Browning's switch-back multitude of characters with the suicidally melancholy anomic *mentalité* described by Émile Durkheim in his *L'Éducation Morale* (1938)/*Moral Education: A Study in Moral Education: The Theory and Application of the Sociology of Education* (trans Everett K Wilson and Hermann Schnurrer, Free Press, New York, 1961): melancholy filling the gap left by desire, 'nervous agitation', the 'mind endlessly moving, a veritable kaleidoscope that changes from one moment to the next'. This 'anomic' condition of course closely fits the narrator of 'Maud'. David G Riede, op cit, 141, 179; quoting Christopher Herbert, *Culture and Anomie: Ethnographic Imagination in the Nineteenth Century* (University of Chicago Press, Chicago, 1991), 72–73.
[31] *Memoir*, I.396.
[32] The good of David Goslee's *Tennyson's Characters: 'Strange Faces, Other Minds'* (University of Iowa Press, Iowa City, 1989) is its narrative of Tennyson's poetic career as fraught lifelong struggle at self-presentation through his astonishing variety of fictional others, each related but each complexly different from 'himself'. Something similar applies, of course, mutatis mutandis, to the poetic career of Browning.

Endangered Edgings

Truth, says Blougram, has no 'simple self'. Truth's investigators inevitably 'confuse themselves'. There is no simple self. Blougram, like TS Eliot's Prufrock a trier-on of selves – no, he is not a Napoleon, a Shakespeare, a Luther – embraces a necessary incertitude as a principle both for his own being, and also, implicitly, for his author, as well as, by extension, for poetry as such:

> You see lads walk the street
> Sixty the minute; what's to note in that?
> You see one lad o'erstride a chimney-stack;
> Him you must watch – he's sure to fall, yet stands!
> Our interest's on the dangerous edge of things.
> The honest thief, the tender murderer,
> The superstitious atheist, demirep
> That loves and saves her soul in new French books –
> We watch while these in equilibrium keep
> The giddy line midway: one step aside,
> They're classed and done with. I, then, keep the line.
> ('Bishop Blougram's Apology', 392–401)

Holding the line between opposites – selves held in a kind of moral aporia between faith and doubt, good and evil – the character (and through him the poet) refusing to resolve contradictions and paradoxes of selfhood, to fix people and classify them and thus be done with interest and analysis: it's presented as a difficulty for the analysand and the analyst, the 'dangerous edge' of unresolved betweenness both for the persona and the poet. 'Our interest's on the dangerous edge of things' was Graham Greene's favourite line of Browning, appropriated by the sceptical and transgressive Roman Catholic novelist for his characters, stuck like him between Christian belief and unbelief, faithfulness and sin, and felt as apt not just for himself and his people but perhaps for western modernity. The positioning of interest and self is clearly not just Browning's, but shared by many Victorian poets and their characters. The poet of oxymoron: the good crook, the sane lunatic, the sinful priest, the outcast insider, the sceptic compelled by the supernatural, speaks representatively.

The attractions of the dramatic monologue – this mode of undercover self-othering, of confession without the price of overtness, of self-exploration and self-experiment within the privacy of a fiction of the self – were obvious for doubters of all kinds, for the many and various in-betweens of mind and of faith, gender, class and (even) race. It's no surprise that a poet like Amy Levy, divided on so many fronts – poet among leftwing politicals;

female in a man's world of London radicals; Jewish in a Christian university (first Jewish student at Newnham College, Cambridge); blurry about her sexuality (a troubled lesbian?); increasingly isolated by her deafness; sad and suicidal (she killed herself in 1889 at the age of twenty-seven by inhaling charcoal fumes in what was rumoured to have been a suicide-pact with the novelist Olive Schreiner which only Levy kept to) – should have been drawn to Browning and the Browningesque dramatic monologue for her writing in the person of Xantippe, Socrates's unhappy wife (in the title poem of *Xantippe, and Other Verse*, 1881), or a dying Magdalen (in her 'Magdalen' in *A Minor Poet, and Other Poems* (1884), or a suicidal failing poet (in 'A Minor Poet'). Levy's 'Last Words', a dying person's dramatic monologue (in her last volume, *A London Plane-Tree, and Other Verse* (1889), whose proofs she corrected just before killing herself), addressed to an other, not certainly a friend or foe (and not certainly a male or a female), comes with an epigraph, 'Dead! all's done with!', from Browning's 'Too Late', the poem addressed to a woman, now dead, who married another man than the speaker. Morbid, divided *I*; in a morbid poem publicly announcing the Browningesque heritage of its divided subjectivity, the fraught poeticity of the inbetween self.

Inbetweenness of all kinds, and all over the place. How black, for instance, was Elizabeth Barrett Browning? She seems to have been perennially anxious about inheriting the 'blood' of black slaves through generations of miscegenation on the Moulton Barrett family estates in Jamaica – the practice of white colonialists taking slave women for casual sex or even long-lived relationships, which produced lots of children. Elizabeth Barrett had relations who were wholly black, as did John Kenyon, Elizabeth's cousin and financial benefactor, and, apparently, Robert Browning, who was, like Alice Meynell, yet one more of Victorian literature's colonial offspring – Meynell's father was a Jamaican sugar-planter creole. Elizabeth Barrett's complexion, like Robert Browning's, was notably dark (both attracted speculations about what was popularly known in the era of British colonialism as a *lick*, or *touch*, or *dash*, of 'the tar-brush'). 'I am "little and black"', Elizabeth Barrett would announce.[33] And where better, we might say, to inhabit the troubling possibility of a black woman's self than in a dramatic monologue, namely 'The Runaway Slave at Pilgrim's Point', which she wrote for an American anti-slavery volume *The Liberty Bell* (1849)? 'I am black – I am black!' The voice of the black woman slave, whose black slave lover is beaten to death, mother of a white child with the face of her master (dramatic sign of ingrained inbetweenness, of the longstanding

---

[33]   For the blackness of the Brownings, and their plantation families, see Julia Markus's (controversial, but convincing) *The Marriage of Elizabeth Barrett and Robert Browning* (Bloomsbury, London, 1995).

colonial creolizing), which she kills to halt its future misery, blends into the voice of the little black sister of the Bible's *Canticles*: 'I am black, but comely'. It's an appeal to the oppressive white Christian slave-owners, and perhaps also to the prejudiced of colonialist England. An appeal which gets no sympathy for the poem's victim of colonialist boundary-crossing, of racial transgressivity.

Who or what is *I*? White? Black? Woman good, woman bad? Sexual transgressor or approvable lover? Is the runaway sane or insane to kill her child? 'I am not mad: I am black!' There's extreme edginess here. Racial on-edgedness factored into mental and moral and, of course, genderized edge questions.

On The Beach

Edginess right across the poetic park, then, but nowhere more pronounced than where edge-metaphor and edge-actuality converge: on the beach. Poet after poet, poem after poem, *I* after *I*, stand edgily at the most obviously dramatic literalization of inbetweenness that England and Englishness can offer, namely the coastline of this island, these islands. Being on the beach – the interzone that is for Robert Browning the quintessential dangerous edge, 'mere razor-edge 'twixt earth and sea' (*Red Cotton Night-Cap Country*, line 182); where boundedness becomes boundlessness, and knowableness and security and fixity of all kinds come to an end, and are challenged by the unknown and otherness and strangeness, are threatened by dissolution, and actually get dissolved – is a most common placing and condition for Victorian writing. More so even for poetry, than for the novel. '[W]e are still in our Aqueous Ages', declares Clough's character Claude in the (extremely watery) *Amours de Voyage* (Canto III, line 59) – a thought about the watery uncertainty of all life brought on by contemplating 'the waste of the rushing incurious billows' on the ship taking him from Marseille to Italy. The Victorian age of poetry is especially aqueous; and nowhere more so than when watery, dissolving, thoughts strike the poet at the border place where the water strikes the land.

This is where Tennyson's Ulysses find himself – between action and inaction, life and death, in a poem stuck between the sounding of the sea's furrows and the sounding of the old man's complaining voice. ('Ulysses' is a sort of replay of Tennyson's early sonnet, 'Conrad! why call thy life monotonous?' upbraiding one 'Conrad' for not pushing Life's boat out onto the 'living eddies' and for perpetually hanging about 'by one beach'.) Here stands the narrator of 'Maud', a refugee from the consequences of his mad murder of Maud's brother, on 'the dark sea-line' of the Brittany coast, where Briton, we're told, dissolves into Breton. When they land on 'Breton sands' (in Tennyson's 'Merlin and Vivien') is when Merlin's troubles with snaky Vivien really begin. It's on the shoreline at Dover in Arnold's 'Dover Beach' that the poem's *I*, and we his readers, hear his faith and the faith of the Christian ages being sucked away like shingle at the mercy of a receding tide. Arnold's little clutch of forlorn 1849 'Marguerite poems', about the absence and loss of the French girl with whom he fell in love in Switzerland – a watery love from the start: developed on 'the strand' of the Lake of Thun – repeatedly lament the separation enforced by the English Channel, the sea that now 'rolls between us'. Arnold stands as it were on Dover Beach not just as forlorn Christian, but as forlorn lover: 'In the void air, / towards thee, / My stretched arms are cast; / But a sea rolls between us –' ('Parting', 62–64). And the frustrated longings of this lover beached beside 'The unplumbed, salt, estranging sea' ('To Marguerite – Continued', 24), at once enforce and emblematize the despairs of the one-time Christian believer:

> Yes! in the sea of life enisled,
> With echoing straits between us thrown,
> Dotting the shoeless watery wild,
> We mortal millions live *alone*.
> ('To Marguerite – Continued', 1–4)

(Joseph Bristow's suggestion that 'Dover Beach' is addressed to Arnold's old school and Oxford chum Clough rather than as usually thought to Arnold's wife, and that the aqueous doubtings of the poem have to do with uncertainties about sexual orientation and worries by a pair of as it were boyfriends about the prospect of upcoming marriage, doesn't hold water. Arnold's Dover Beach is a perplexed, but heterosexual scene.[34])

The narrator of Swinburne's dramatic monologue 'Félise' (rhymes with 'seas') is yet one more beached lover, holdings out his hands to a beloved across a strait of water, 'Grey sea between', in an unending unfulfilled yearning. The narrator of yet one more dramatic monologue of Swinburne's, 'By the sea-side', likewise contemplates his beloved's departure on the morrow, when 'long miles will sweep between us'.[35] For Dante Gabriel

---

[34]   See Joseph Bristow, ' "Love, let us be true to one another": Matthew Arnold, Arthur Hugh Clough, and "Our Aqueous Ages" ', *Literature and History*, series 3, vol 4, no. 1 (Spring 1995), 27–49. 'I am not trying to concoct a previously unknown homoeroticism between Arnold and Clough' Bristow says; but that is what he is trying. In her otherwise rather sharp 'The poetry of Victorian masculinities', in *The Cambridge Companion to Victorian Poetry* (2000), 203–227, Thaïs E Morgan suggests agreement with Joseph Bristow's case about 'Dover Beach' (p223); but then he is the editor of the *Companion*.

[35]   One of the 'Three unpublished poems by Algernon Charles Swinburne', in *The Whole Music of Passion: New Essays on Swinburne*, eds Rikky Rooksby and Nicholas Shrimpton (Scholar Press, Aldershot, 1993), Appendix, 175–180.

Rossetti the beach is where at some unknown time life will encounter death, on 'the strand / Of the pale wave which knows thee what thou art' (*The House of Life,* Sonnet XCIX, first of the pair 'Newborn Death'). This is the death-reminiscent border where the mirror-image of the fraught *I* of Sonnet XCVII, 'A Superscription' – 'my name is Might-have-been; / I am also called No-more, Too-late, Farewell' – has 'the dead-sea shell' held up to his ear which was 'Cast up thy Life's foam-fretted feet between'. Paddling in the sea you don't just get your feet wetted, you get them fretted with life anxieties. *The House of Life's* parting note is provided by Song XI, 'The Sea-Limits', which orders the reader to 'Consider the sea's listless chime':

> Time's self it is, made audible, –
> The murmur of the earth's own shell.

The sea's noise is the voice of 'the lapse of time', and of pain, death, loneliness. We are to 'Listen alone beside the sea' to this voice. It's the twin of the noise you hear in lonely woods – 'Hark where the murmurs of thronged men / Surge and sink back and surge again, – / Still the one voice of wave and tree' – but especially audible at the sea's edge where we're to 'Gather a shell from the strown beach / And listen at its lips' and hear the melancholy 'desire and mystery, of 'Earth, Sea, Man'. (This 1849 poem was composed on the French coast and at first entitled 'At Boulogne. Upon the Cliffs. Noon'.)

Almost to a man, and woman, Victorian poets get serious at the beach. It takes a CS Calverley, one of the period's most devoted mockers, to eschew the regular troubledness of the watery border: in his 'On the Beach', the comic 'lucubrations' of a 'Private Tutor' who has no girl-friend but has bought himself a cheap locket to moon over on the beach in the contemporary glooming fashion (a poem whose merriment is greatly enhanced by its absurdist rhymes, not least the eleven nicely silly ones – *screech, leech, peach, bleach,* and so on – for *beach*).[36] The frivolity is rare; the majority note is of habitual certainties dissolving at the watery border. Hopkins is just one of the period's many seaside observers struck by the sea's emblematic unreadability. He'd like to 'unpack' the 'huddling and gnarls' of the sea-water, to 'law out the shapes and sequences of the running'; but cannot (*Journal*, p.223). George Meredith's troubled sonnet-sequence *Modern Love* (1862), about unhappy marriage and the dismaying unfaithfulness of a wife, ends with a reflection on how 'in this

---

[36]   *The English Poems of Charles Stuart Calverley*, ed Hilda D Spear (Leicester University Press, 1974), 91–92.

our life' the soul only gets 'a dusty answer' when 'hot for certainties' – doubts affirmed on a midnight beach:

> In tragic hints here see what ever more
> Moves dark as yonder midnight ocean's force,
> Thundering like ramping hosts of warrior horse,
> To throw that faint thin line upon the shore.
>
> (Sonnet 50)

In his *Fifine at the Fair*, Browning doesn't just celebrate his new-found love of swimming, of going 'Amphibian' as the poem's 'Prologue: Amphibian' has it, but figures the seaside encounter between earth-bound body and the watery medium as one more emblem of difficult epistemic betweenness – 'my spirit's life / 'Twixt false, whence it would break, and true, where it would bide' (1040–1041). The sea in *Fifine* is a *disassociating* medium, where selfhood (and truth) find themselves shattering. The poem has, of course, utterly absorbed the contemporary spirit of seaside doubting. But, more, in a cunningly inset sonnet (1428–1441) it draws on the Third Ode of Roman Horace, the one praying for a safe voyage to Greece for the poet Virgil. Horace called the sea *dissociabilis*, estranging, disuniting, and so does Browning as *Fifine*'s narrating Don Juan joins Horace in thinking that embarking on that 'disassociating sea', the 'turgid main' – the 'sea-tracklessness' – is a risky business. Ships are '*impious* vessels', says Browning, closely following Virgil. Browning patently knows Clough's 1847 version of the Horace (he uses some of Clough's phrasing), but, notably, he refuses to take up Clough's translation of *dissociabilis* as the *uncompanionable* deep. Browning doesn't find the sea merely unfriendly: for him it's the medium of a severe breakup of the self.

And this is not the only divergence from Clough. Where Clough translates Horace's *impius* as *godless*, Browning follows Horace closely with *impious*. Neither Horace nor Browning imagines impiety to be godlessness; Browning can see through godless Clough's illicitly slipping some uncovenanted atheism into Horace's poem. The water's edge is for Browning where *doubt* is in play, not the positives of either faith or unbelief. Doubt, the watery irresolution of self (and other) that commands Arnold's 'Marguerite' series, whose tone and theme are continued so forcefully in 'Dover Beach' and, of course, in Arnold's 'Self-Dependence' – where the *I*, embarking in a state of self-weariness and confusion of being ('Weary of myself, and sick of asking / What I am, and what I ought to be') appeals to the sea for its former calming effects (' "Ye who from my childhood up have calmed me, / Calm me, ah, compose me to the end!" '), but hears only an exhortation to be and to find himself in stoic individualism ('"Resolve to be thyself; and know that he, / Who finds himself, loses his misery!"'). This is good old advice, but no more than that; it's not the calming that was requested. The sea offers discomforts, not comforts. Browning's Don Juan thinks Virgil 'Much reassured by this so comfortable ode' of Horace (*Fifine*, 1441); but that's not how any of these seaside poems reads – including Horace's. At this particular razor's edge you obtain small consolation, if any at all.

The (Self)destructive Element

You might manage to stay afloat – with Swinburne, fearless sea-swimmer: in the tempestuous North Sea above all, but also anywhere he could (for instance in the English Channel where in 1866 he would have drowned in strong currents off the coast of Normandy, had he not been rescued by French fishermen). The successful sea-swimmer is one who defies what Joseph Conrad came famously, in his novel *Lord Jim* (1900), to denote as 'the destructive element' which modernity demands we immerse ourselves in. Swinburne celebrates his meeting of that challenge again and again in his water poems. 'My heart swims blind in a sea / That stuns me': that's Swinburne in his 'Satia Te Sanguine' (in *Poems and Ballads*), speaking as an unhappy lover, surviving in metaphor over a sea blown hard 'to windward and lee' with 'Lamentation, and mourning, and woe' (The poem's title, translating as 'Satiate thyself with blood', is the fabled words of Queen Tomyris as she drops the head of Persian king Cyrus, severed because he killed her son, into a bowl of blood: the adversities represented by the sea join up with an even more horrible liquidity.) In 'The Lake of Gaube' Swinburne relishes a survivor's suicidal-erotic plunge into the depths of the French Pyrenees lake (in a locals-astounding dive and swim of his in 1862) – deadly dark, silent and unfathomable as the sea and colder even than the North Sea in winter.

> Far down through the fathomless night of the water, the gladness of silence and gloom.
> Death-dark and delicious as death in the dream of a lover and dreamer may be,
> It clasps and encompasses body and soul with delight to be living and free:
> Free utterly now, though the freedom endure but the space of a perilous breath,
> And living, though girdled about with the darkness and coldness and strangeness of death:
> Each limb and each pulse of the body rejoicing, each nerve of the spirit at rest,
> All sense of the soul's life rapture, a passionate peace in its blindness blest.
> So plunges the downward swimmer, embraced of the water unfathomed of man,

The darkness unplummeted, icier than seas in midwinter, for blessing or ban;
And swiftly and sweetly, when strength and breath fall short, and the dive is done,
Shoots up as a shaft from the dark depth shot, sped straight into sight of the sun;
And sheer through the snow-soft water, more dark than the roof of the pines above,
Strikes forth, and is glad as a bird whose flight is impelled and sustained of love.
As a sea-mew's love of the sea-wind breasted and ridden for rapture's sake
Is the love of his body and soul for the darkling delight of the soundless lake:
As the silent speed of a dream too living to live for a thought's space more
Is the flight of his limbs through the still strong chill of the darkness from shore to shore.
Might life be as this is and death be as life that casts off time as a robe,
The likenesss of infinite heaven were a symbol revealed of the lake of Gaube.

Published in *A Channel Passage and Other Poems* (1899) 'In Memory of William Morris and Edward Burne-Jones', Swinburne's dark excitements sound like a blacked-up version of the homoerotic rhapsodizing about young men swimming in Clough's swimming and swimming-hole obsessed 'The Bothie of Tober-Na Vuolich' (1848):

>   here the boiling, pent-up water
> Frees itself by a final descent, attaining a bason,
> Ten feet wide and eighteen long, with whiteness and fury
> Occupied partly, but mostly pellucid, pure, a mirror;
> Beautiful there for the colour derived from green rocks under;
> Beautiful, most of all, where beads of foam uprising
> Mingle their clouds of white with the delicate hue of the stillness.
> Cliff over cliff for its sides, with rowan and pendent birch boughs,
> Here it lies, unthought of above at the bridge and pathway,
> Still more enclosed from below by wood and rocky projection.
> You are shut in, left alone with yourself and perfection of water,
> Hid on all sides, left alone with yourself and the goddess of bathing.
> Here, the pride of the plunger, you stride the fall and clear it;
> Here, the delight of the bather, you roll in beaded sparklings,
> Here into pure green depth drop down from lofty ledges.
>
> Hither, a month agone, they had come, and discovered it …
>
>   ….
>
> Rounded a craggy point, and saw on a sudden before them
> Slabs of rock, and a tiny beach, and perfection of water,
> Picture-like beauty, seclusion sublime, and the goddess of bathing.
> There they bathed, of course, and Arthur, the Glory of headers,
> Leapt from the ledges with Hope, he twenty feet, he thirty;

There, overbold, great Hobbes from a ten-foot height descended,
Prone, as a quadruped, prone with hands and feet protending;
There in the sparkling champagne, ecstatic, they shrieked and shouted.

....

Lo, on the rocky ledge, regardant, the Glory of headers,

....

And they looked, and wondered, incredulous, looking yet once more,
Yes, it was he, on the ledge, bare-limbed, an Apollo, down-gazing,
Eyeing one moment the beauty, the life, ere he flung himself in it,
Eyeing through eddying green waters the green-tinting floor underneath them,
Eyeing the bead on the surface, the bead, like a cloud, rising to it,
Drinking-in, deep in his soul, the beautiful hue and the clearness,
Arthur, the shapely, the brave, the unboasting, the Glory of headers ...

(III. 34–81)

What's missing in the Swinburne is Clough's lightness – the daylight, but also the perennial tendency of Clough to undercut his intensities by sending them up.

'"Hobbes's gutter" the Piper entitles the spot, profanely' (III.63). Which can't fail to remind you of the anti-climactic mickey-taking in *Dipsychus* (sc V. 200ff), where Dipsychus, excited by the waters around Venice ('to the sea!'), urging himself and his double to plunge Byronically in ('Quick, quick! in, in!'), has his enthusiasm undermined by the Spirit, his bare feet stung by thistles, worried about what will happen to the watches and purses they'll leave behind on the bank, and how they'll get dry once they get out:

> Well; but it's not so pleasant for the feet;
> We should have brought some towels and a sheet.

Swinburne's moodily serious homoerotic intensity is aloof from Clough's comic practicalities. His tight rhyming (and long line) and the dourness of his homoerotic fervour make you think rather of Edward Carpenter. Swinburne sounds as if he's learned quite a lot from Carpenter's 'Beautiful is the figure of the lusty full-grown groom on his superb horse' which came out in the 1883 edition of *Towards Democracy*, with its 'Wild songs in sight of the sea, wild dances along the sands', and 'the sight of the naked bodies of the bathers, bathing by the hot sea-banks'.

Browning's delight in surviving in the dangerous medium against all odds in 'Prologue: Amphibian' – his relief at getting back on dry land – is patent ('Land the solid and safe – / To welcome again (confess!)' (69–70). In her commentary on Revelation 21.1 where John the Revelator sees 'a new heaven and a new earth' in which 'there was no more sea' Christina G Rossetti, a Londoner clearly inclined to take a seaside-visitor's holiday view of the sea, takes a bit of persuading about this absence in the heavenly future that she so greatly hankers after ('How shall we be consoled for our lost sea with its familiar fascination, its delights, its lifelong endearedness?'). (She returned to this text again and again.) But she quickly brings herself round to recognizing that 'the long-drawn wail of our bitter sea' won't do in heaven, and caps her reflections in *The Face of the Deep: A Devotional Commentary on the Apocalypse* (home of so many of her poems) with the verses later entitled, in some words from Habbakuk 3.8, ' "Was Thy Wrath against the Sea?" ' The poem begins 'The sea laments with unappeasable / Hankering wail of loss' – which is made to rhyme pointedly with 'clamorous waves which toss.' Rossetti's Jesus is the one who said 'Peace, peace, thou sea!', as the poem puts it.[37] Arriving in heaven will be a thankful stepping onto dry land: the feeling common to Victorian poetry's returning swimmers and sailors, whether religious or not. 'Home is the sailor home from the sea': it's the relieved note of 'Requiem' by Robert Louis Stevenson, the much-travelled descendant of Scottish lighthouse builders who, in text after text (like his 'Christmas at Sea'), shows he knew all about the sea's dangers; and a homecoming celebration repeated by AE Housman, a poet as familiar as anybody with the great tradition of endangered sea writing, in his lovely elegy for Stevenson, 'RLS' – 'Home is the sailor…'. An islanded, sea-girt people, so many of them immigrants, or children of immigrants from across the sea, with fishermen and sailors and travellers across the Empire galore in the family, was the ripest possible audience for these reflections. And for the heroizing of sea-people. Such as Grace Darling, young daughter of the Northumbrian Longstone Lighthouse keeper, who became a national legend in 1838 for (with her father) rowing some shipwrecked travellers to safety in foul seas. The poets could not refrain from hymning her praises – old Wordsworth ('Grace Darling', 1842), Thomas Hood (in 'Address'), Henry Francis Lyte (author of the famous hymn 'Abide With Me', in 'Grace Darling's Death-bed'), and Swinburne ('Grace Darling', in his *Astrophel And Other Poems*, 1894).

The rowing girl's fellow-Northumbrian, the North Sea swimmer himself, regrets being 'too young to have seen thee', but – inveterate toucher – Swinburne has 'touched thy father's hallowed hand' (line 106). His roaring, banging, sea-noisy tribute dwells on 'the madness of the storming surf' (61), which he well knows regularly defeats the would-be swimmer. Deep is

[37] *The Face of the Deep: A Devotional Commentary on the Apocalypse* (London, SPCK, 1892), 478–79. The poem was reprinted in Rossetti's 1893 volume *Verses. Reprinted from 'Called to be Saints', 'Time Flies', 'The Face of the Deep'* (London, SPCK, 1893) alongside ' "And there was no more Sea" ', which also started life in *The Face of the Deep*. Good publication detail, as ever, in Betty S Flowers' notes to RW Crump's Penguin *Complete Poems* of CGR (2001).

calling unto deep here, in every sense. 'Deep calleth unto deep': they're the words of Psalm 42.7, which go on, 'all thy waves and thy billows are gone over me'. It was one of the period's favourite expressions of misery, the watery 'deep' of the metaphor calling loudly to the deeps of the poets. 'O God, O God!', cries Clough's split man Dipsychus, 'The great floods of the fiend / Flow over me! I come into deep waters / Where no ground is!' (scene XI, 105–107). In Swinburne's 'A Leave-Taking' – a poem addressed to his 'songs', urging them to 'go seaward' – the beloved 'will not care':

> Though all those waves went over us, and drove
> Deep down the stifling lips and drowning hair,
> She would not care.
>
> (33–35)

Drowning is the repeated result of Swinburne's poems 'going seaward' – as they repeatedly do. Not much is salvageable for person or poetry from venturing on to the beach and out into the straits:

> It is not much that a man can save
> On the sands of life, in the straits of time
> Who swims in sight of the great third wave
> That never a swimmer shall cross or climb.
> Some waif washed up with the strays and spars
> That ebb-tide shows to the shore and the stars;
> Weed from the water, grass from a grave
> A broken blossom, a ruined rhyme.

That's from 'The Triumph of Time' (81–88), which, like so much Swinburne, takes masochistic pleasure in the sea's adversarial whip-hand over the sea-farer and the swimmer. In this poem, characteristically, the sea is 'the great sweet mother' whose 'fugitive pain' is of course painful, but also 'sweet'. The pains of revolutionary action are necessary, says Swinburne, and to be endured like terrible storms at sea ('A Song in Time of Revolution. 1860'). Resisters of despots (in 'A Song in Time of Order. 1852') have to 'Push hard across the sand'; feel 'The quiver and beat of the sea!'; go 'Forth, with the rain in our hair / And the salt sweet foam in our lips; / In the teeth of the hard glad weather'. Salt in your teeth, in the teeth of bad weather at sea: here's a perverse pleasure in an ironic sweetness, paradoxical as the 'hard glad weather' at sea.

   A good deal of the lure of Sappho and Sapphics for Swinburne seems to be the attractions of death by salty water, a masochistic salt-water erotics, the enjoyment of 'broken kisses salt as brine'. That's how 'Anactoria' puts it, Sappho's jealous dramatic monologue, a sado-masochistic threnody from the lover who desires death by water, a merging of 'Lotus and Lethe' in

'Thick darkness and the insuperable sea' (in one story Sappho did kill herself by leaping into the sea). Swinburnean Sapphics are inseparable from the sado-masochistic 'quiver' of the sea, the seaside mix of love, pain, fear, and pleasure – as in the Sappho monologue 'On the Cliffs' in (naturally) the very watery collection *Songs of the Springtide* (1905). Bloody, red-handed Dolores, masochistic Swinburne's favourite sadistic saint, 'Our Lady of Pain', is also Our Lady of the Sea, the 'Thalassian', 'Foam-white, from the foam', the one who drowns mariners, 'by foam of the waves overtaken' ('Dolores', 223–224, 235).

Only a Swinburne, one might feel, would think Dolores's painful attentions a sweetness. In general, drowning appals the period's poets. They fear death by water. Shelley's death by drowning stains the collective poetic memory, gets felt as proleptic of the poet's worst fate. The death of Arthur Henry Hallam, not strictly a death at sea, becomes so in Tennyson's grief by virtue of the long sea-voyage home undertaken by his corpse. The early parts of *In Memoriam* prayerfully ask for a safe voyage – lest 'the roaring wells / Should gulf him fathom-deep in brine; / And hands so often clasped in mine, / Should toss with tangle and with shells' (X) – much as if Hallam were a living person. (*Tangle* is 'oar-weed', according to Tennyson.) There's a curious echo here of the mysterious words of Tennyson's Ulysses in the poem written just after Tennyson heard of Hallam's death: 'It may be that the gulfs will wash us down', where the gulf washing down could be benign, a gulf-stream, say, driving Ulysses's vessel towards the Happy Isles, or could be a more sinister inundation. Whatever the truth of that, the prayers of *In Memoriam* IX and X do not, as the poem's Section VI has it, protect the sailor. Even as the mother is praying for her sailor son, 'His heavy shotted hammock-shroud / Drops in his vast and wandering grave'. God's providence is no defence against the 'roaring wells'. It did not save Hallam. (Isobel Armstrong thinks this Section is directed with bitterness at the Revd Robert Montgomery's popular evangelical poem about God's providence, including His special protection for real Christians, *The Omnipresence of the Deity* (1828), which had a long passage about a shipwrecked mariner saved from drowning through the prayers of the girlfriend he left grieving on 'the yellow beach' (*Omnipresence*, II, 124–191). The suggestion holds water.[38]) Nor did Providence intervene to save Elizabeth Barrett Barrett's favourite brother Bro from drowning in the sea at Torquay in 1840, or to save Robert Bridges's cousin the extremely pious young Anglo-Catholic poet Digby Mackworth Dolben from drowning in a swimming-hole in 1867, or to save the pious Oxford Classicist George Augustus Simcox from falling to his death in the sea off the cliffs at Ballycastle in Northern Ireland in 1905. Nor, for that matter, to save the five Franciscan nuns drowned in the mouth of the Thames

[38]   Isobel Armstrong, *Victorian Poetry: Poetry, Poetics and Politics* (1993), 74–76.

on the night of 7 December 1875, who are the troubling victims of Hopkins's 'The Wreck of the Deutschland'. Nor indeed to halt the great inundation of the coast of Lincolnshire which is the occasion of Jean Ingelow's 'The High Tide on the Coast of Lincolnshire (1571)'.

Drowning, death by water, is certainly bad for its victims. It was unarguably good, though, for Victorian poetry, which thrives on the imagining and writing of watery depredations and deaths. *In Memoriam* has a sure claim to be among Victorian England's greatest poems. Hallam's so to say honorary death by water is fundamental to one of the two greatest poetic careers of the reign, namely Alfred Tennyson's : it was the restart of the career, beginning with 'Ulysses', of the poet already drawn to the force of death by water and the power of the swansong in 'The Lady of Shalott' (1832). 'The Idylls of the King', Tennyson's great medieval epic, begins with King Arthur's death and swansong – the fictional death of King Arthur sponsored by the fantasized death of Arthur Hallam – the poetic of, and from, the 'dusky barge / Dark as a funeral scarf from stem to stern': 'And slowly answered Arthur from the barge'. The poem is the answer to Arthur's death; Tennyson's whole career is in that answering. 'Morte d'Arthur', founding text of the *Idylls*, was written 1833–1834 under the immediate shock of the news of Hallam's death: the shock that sustains Tennyson's imaginings right to the end. Afforced, with awful irony, by the death of his sick son Lionel, who died and was buried at sea on the way home from India in 1886, lamented in the very late poem 'To the Marquis of Dufferin and Ava'. This poem is in the *In Memoriam* stanza, repeats the old *In Memoriam* questions and hopes: why should the young die, a son before his father – who hopes to meet him soon in heaven – soon because the poet is nearing his own end-time. An ending that Tennyson inevitably imagines, and writes, as a watery one in 'Crossing the Bar'.

'And may there be no moaning of the bar' – the barrier between earth and heaven, modelled on the notorious sand-bar in Southampton Water on the way to Tennyson's home in the Isle of Wight – at the hour of his crossing, but rather a gentle tide, 'Too full for sound and foam'. Tennyson's last words – 'Mind you put my *Crossing the Bar* at the end of all editions of my poems' – will be like his earliest ones: sea-conscious, and sea-anxious. From first to last, what's done at and on and by the sea, was the prompter of Tennyson's verses. Especially the sea's adverse doings.

> Break, break, break
> On thy cold gray stones, O Sea!
>
> ....
>
> Break, break, break,
> At the foot of thy crags, O Sea!
> But the tender grace of a day that is dead
> Will never come back to me.

Waves break on the shore; they come in as breakers, in every sense; they break things and people – cliffs, hearts. The broken-hearted Tennyson, in this emotionally raw little poem provoked by Hallam's death, all at once acknowledges the sea's unstoppably heart-breaking work ('Break, break, break' as address of ironic acceptance: 'you do, you will, break cliffs and people and hearts'), and wearily commands it to carry on ('Break, break, break': 'go on, you always have, you might as well carry on your grieving work; my beloved is never going to come back to me'). And breaking seas come to emblematize all of the underminings of Tennyson's hopes and faiths which followed that death as it were by water. Our ears are bashed as a full tide bashes the cliffs with all of Tennyson's onomatopoeic strength: it

> Rose with ground-swell, which, on the foremost rocks
> Touching, upjetted in spirts of wild sea-smoke,
> And scaled in sheets of wasteful foam, and fell
> In vast sea-cataracts – ever and anon
> Dead claps of thunder from within the cliffs
> Heard through the living roar.

Swelling into a great ridge, a 'thunderous fulness', the sea smashes into other, well eroded cliffs, bringing down a cliff-top cathedral, making great 'gaps and chasms of ruin', sweeping away people and effigies – 'The men of flesh and blood, and men of stone' – 'To the wasted deeps together'. And these violent, ruining waters from Tennyson's 'Sea Dreams' (published in 1860) – one a description of natural events; the other a bad dream – are in effect allegories of the adversities and economic ruin endured by the poem's city-clerk and his wife (orphan of an 'unknown artist') through investing in a fraudulent Peruvian mining scheme got up by an unctuous religious crook (a version of the Revd Dr Matthew Allen, the lunatic-asylum keeper, who lost a lot of the Tennysons' money in a disastrous mechanical wood-carving business).

The linkage between distress and the sea's work is normative for Tennyson. He apparently got the idea of eroded cliffs and churches fallen into the sea from a memorable passage in Charles Lyell's best-selling *Principles of Geology* (first version 1830–1833) illustrating the protracted, changing work of time: the book that prompted much of the anxieties about Biblical, Christian assumptions about creation and geological time and a human-centric world which so animate *In Memoriam*: the message of the 'scarpèd cliff' in the notorious 'Nature, red in tooth and claw' section of that poem (LVI). *Scarped*: cut away, torn up, eroded, by the sea. When Tennyson's poems are occasions of, and occasioned by, pain, as they so often are, the sea is not far to seek as in some way the promoter of the distress, and so of the poem. It's simply typical of Tennyson's seaside forebodings that Merlin, in 'Merlin and Vivien', should foresee his own doom as victim of Lilith-like

Vivien's desires in 'the curled white of the coming wave' watched by someone lying on the shore – the danger-filled beach. It's a by no means 'pleasurable' vision. 'You seemed that wave about to break upon me / And sweep
me from my hold upon the world, / My use and name and fame' (300–302).
And so Vivien proves.

And Tennyson's poems are not unique in this. Bad water is incitingly good
for many poets. Think of those impressive poems about suicides in the
Thames, discussed earlier, Theo Marzials' 'A Tragedy: DEATH!' (in Chapter
3) and Thomas Hood's 'The Bridge of Sighs' (in Chapter 4). The death-
dealing Thames prompts a small genre of impressive suicide-verse. In
Clough's London-based fragment, 'Dipsychus Continued', Dipsychus, now
the eminent Lord Chief Justice, is visited by a destitute woman, his former
mistress, and it turns out, a sometime prostitute, whose story he refuses to
take time to attend to ('the court, the nation waits'), and who then departs
to throw herself into the Thames.

> ... I searched
> Newspaper columns through to find a trace
> Of some poor corpse discovered in the Thames,
> Weltering in filth or stranded on the shoals.

(Dipsychus is haunted by her parting words, 'You called me Pleasure – my
name now is – Guilt'.) The Edinburgh poet Henry Bellyse Baildon's plaintive
'Alone in London' is yet one more poem about a sad woman who jumps to
her death in the indifferent river: 'Sheer down the black abyss she falls; – /
The river washes by its walls' (published in *Morning Clouds: Being Divers
Poems* (1877)). One of the most telling sections of James Thomson's threnody about melancholic London, *The City of Dreadful Night*, is Part XIX
about the Thames, 'the River of the Suicides':

> The mighty river flowing dark and deep,
> With ebb and flood from the remote sea-tides
> Vague-sounding through the City's sleepless sleep,
> Is named the River of the Suicides;
> For night by night some lorn wretch overweary,
> And shuddering from the future yet more dreary,
> Within its cold secure oblivion hides.
>
> One plunges from a bridge's parapet,
> As by some blind and sudden frenzy hurled;
> Another wades in slow with purpose set
> Until the waters are above him furled;
> Another in a boat with dreamlike motion
> Glides drifting down into the desert ocean,
> To starve or sink from out the desert world.
>
> (1–14)

The two best poems of Jean Ingelow, a generally mediocre poet (for all of Christina G Rossetti's 'envy' of her, and the admiration of Edward FitzGerald) are, not accidentally, bad-watery ones: her 'Divided', narrated by a woman separated from her beloved by an ever-widening stretch of water, a 'beck' that gradually becomes a grand estuary of the sea; and the very moving 'The High Tide on the Coast of Lincolnshire (1571)' about the death of a milk-maid overtaken by the rising floodwater: ' "Cusha! cusha! Cusha!" calling'; no longer. (Ingelow's *Poems* (1863) with these two poems in it, sold hugely: 200,000 copies it is said.)

For his part, Hopkins is a very great example of these bad-water inspirations.

> They fought with God's cold –
> And they could not and fell to the deck
> (Crushed them) or water (and drowned them) or rolled
> With the sea-romp over the wreck.
> Night roared, with the heart-break hearing a heart-broke rabble,
> The woman's wailing, the crying of child without check –
> Till a lioness arose breasting the babble,
> A prophetess towered in the tumult, a virginal tongue told.
>
>   * * * *
>
> Sister, a sister calling
> A master, her master and mine! –
> And the inboard seas run swirling and hawling
> The rash smart sloggering brine
> Blinds her; but she that weather sees one thing, one;
> Has one fetch in her; she rears herself to divine
> Ears, and the call of the tall nun
> To the men in the tops and the tackle rode over the storm's brawling.

Those are stanzas 17 and 19 of 'The Wreck of the Deutschland'. A disaster at sea has provoked Hopkins into being Hopkinsian. This is the first of the recognizably 'Hopkinsian' poems, with its defiantly broken beat, its 'sprung' rhythms; its broken syntax; intense multi-rhyming, punning loops (*heart-break, heart-broke*); its wonderfully forceful noisy consonantalisms (*sloggering brine; swirling, hawling*, brawling (and what's *hawling? – hauling? howling?–* here's the fuzziness of the gerundive at its most audible). Hopkins's poetic innovativeness, wonderfully hard and violent on the ear and in the mouth, not least in the matter of what he wanted to call 'sprung rhythm', begins in the breaking sea breaking up a ship and its passengers.

He was out of practice, he told his new correspondent RW Dixon in the 'Ding Dong Bell' letter of October 5 1878 – 'my hand was out': he'd written almost nothing since becoming a Jesuit, when he'd 'burn't' his poems as unbefitting his 'profession' as priest – when his Rector suggested someone ought to write a poem about the nuns whose drowning had so 'affected' him. But he went ahead nonetheless, returning to poetry writing with a dramatic difference. 'I had long had haunting my ear the echo of a new rhythm which I now realized on paper ... I do not say the idea is altogether new ... but no one has professedly used it and made it the principle throughout, that I know of.' In narrative terms the poem is one more conventionally weepy Victorian tale of the unfortunate watery demise of females – and one wrapped in very conventional Roman Catholic biases about nuns: inevitably heroic in their lion-like faith; and about Protestants (they're refugee German nuns, religious kin of St Gertrude of Wittenberg, not of Wittenberg's Martin Luther, that 'beast of the waste wood', a murderous Cain to these innocent Catholic Abels (stanza 20)). But formally, linguistically, it is radically new. So new that Hopkins 'had to mark the stresses in blue chalk'. And this, and the dense anaphoric work ('rhymes carried on from one line into another and certain chimes suggested by the Welsh poetry I had been reading (what they call *cynghanedd*)'), plus 'a great many more oddnesses', 'could not but dismay an editor's eye'. And so it was rejected by the Jesuit magazine *The Month*, which at first accepted it, then, on second thoughts, 'withdrew and dared not print it'. So Hopkins went private as a poet, not publishing his revolutionary new work, showing it only to close friends, Robert Bridges and Co. All in all a poetry of stress: the distress of the saddened poet, the distress of the drowned nuns smashed to death by the 'sloggering brine', the stress on faith that such tragedies provoke (God's 'mystery must be instressed, stressed': stanza 5). A new poetic of the verbal stress: this new, heavy combination of verbal stresses, the massive combined beating of the poem's sheer noise, the clanging, dinging of its sound, its rhythm. All initiated by the stress of the wronging sea. The great agent and medium of human dissolution. Good for the poem which it is stressing into being, but bad for people, the poem's subjects, the poet, for selfhood in general and particular. The nuns drown, their bodies to be dissolved under water. And Hopkins' would-be public career is dissolved, under Jesuit orders.

Dissolving/Disselving

Self-dissolution: what happens, or what's initiated, at the land's edge, where in Virginia Woolf's words at the opening of her *Mrs Dalloway* (1925) you might 'plunge' into the killing medium of water, where the solidity of solids is challenged by the dissoluteness, the liquefaction of liquid, is what the poets widely announce as their plight. The knowable, fixable self ending in a dissolving: death of the self in, indeed as, water.[39] As Pater put it at the end of the

---

[39] Varieties of self-dissolution – vanishing, fading, diminishing, dimming – are the good, though critically rather too mild and narrow, subject of James Richardson, *Vanishing Lives: Style and Self in Tennyson, DG Rossetti, Swinburne, and Yeats* (University Press of Virginia,

first version of the passage from his notorious 'Conclusion' to *The Renaissance* about the 'dissolution' of our impressions which dismays 'analysis' – 'that strange, perpetual, weaving and unweaving of ourselves': 'Such thoughts seem desolate at first; at times all the bitterness of life seems concentrated in them. They being the image of one washed out beyond the bar in a sea at ebb, losing even his personality, as the elements of which he is composed pass into new combinations. Struggling, as he must, to save himself, it is himself that he loses at every moment'.[40] Such thoughts of personality loss, self-dissolution, seem to animate several poems (and paintings) involving reflections on and reflections of persona, of selves, especially in water: the troubled self caught in the act of self-reflection, of knowing itself as double, doubled, seeings its Doppelgänger in the mirror, especially a watery one.

'I look into my glass', as Hardy's poem of that title has it (in his *Wessex Poems* (1898)), and what 'I' see in 'my wasting skin' is a disconcertingly doubled abiding: here's an old man utterly changed by time, but also the same as ever: still painfully full of the old emotions, the 'throbbings of noontide'. 'When I look forth at dawning' ('Nature's Questioning' in the same volume), 'Field, flock, and lonely tree' and pool 'gaze at me' – reflect my gaze – wondering in school-child-like 'lippings' 'Why we find us here!'. And 'I' have no reply ('No answerer I ...'): self and its reflection in nature, in that pool, are 'still the same', stuck with each other as doubles, are 'neighbours nigh', like 'Life and Death'.

It occasions no surprise that when Swinburne – wateriest of water-gazers – writes an ekphrastic poem – that is a poem looking at itself metatextually, in the mirror of a painting – he should be drawn to Whistler's painting of a woman before her mirror, *Symphony in White no 2: The Little White Girl*, and that his poem about the painting, 'Before the Mirror', should end by fantasizing that the girl is being dissolved in her mirrored self-image, her doubled self:

> Face fallen and white throat lifted,
> With sleepless eye
> She sees old loves that drifted,
> She knew not why,
> Old loves and faded fears

Charlottesville, 1988), in which the best chapter is IV, 'The Tennysonian Flow', 58–81, on flowing and ebbing in Tennyson.

[40]   The 'Conclusion' began life as the ending of a review of a clutch of William Morris's poetic volumes, *Westminster Review*, ns XXXIV (October 1868), 300–312. Some passages, like this one, did not make the transition to *Studies in History of the Renaissance* (1873), nor to the 'third edition', *The Renaissance: Studies in Art and Poetry* (1888). The whole 'Conclusion' was omitted from the 'second edition', because Pater 'conceived it might possibly mislead some of those young men into whose hands it might fall'.

Float down a stream that hears
The flowing of all men's tears beneath the sky.

John Hollander is rightly reminded, and suggests Swinburne was mindful, of Tennyson's Lady of Shalott whose life and work, all her being, are shattered with the cracking of her mirror – when, induced by the river-song of Sir Lancelot, she exchanges mirrored reflections of Camelot river for the real water and 'With a glassy countenance' floats to her death.[41] (There's more about this momentous ekphrastic encounter in the ekphrastic discussion in my final Chapter 'Victorian Modernismus'.)

And it is, I'd say, no accident that Gerard Hopkins's sonnet 'As kingfishers catch fire', which is about the infixity and multiplicity of the self – of the self as person and poet, Christian and priest – should do its usual great repetitive rhyming, its verbal ringing, on this not just with reference to what bells do when they give tongue, but by calling on the noise stones make when they're 'tumbled' over the edge, or 'rim' of a well, that is when solids are lost in water:

As kingfishers catch fire, dragonflies dráw fláme;
As tumbled over rim in roundy wells
Stones ring; like tucked string tells, each hung bell's
Bow swung finds tongue to fling out broad its name;
Each mortal thing does one thing and the same:
Deals out that being indoors each one dwells;
Selves – goes itself; *myself* it speaks and spells,
Crying *Whát I dó is me: for that I came.*

Í say móre: the just man justices;
Kéeps gráce: thát keeps all his goings graces;
Acts in God's eye what in God's eye he is –
Chríst. For Chríst plays in ten thousand places,
Lovely in limbs, and lovely in eyes not his
To the father through the features of men's faces.

It's a tortured poem about and by a tortured self; its tortured language reflects this priest-poet's difficulties with knowing and writing *I*. Every mortal thing (including people) speaks itself, has an identity to utter (like those stones and bells and the tucked/plucked strings of musical instruments). This speaking is a selving, self-identifying, self-making, an assertion of the self's purpose, its teleology ('Selves – goes itself; *myself* it speaks and spells, / Crying *Whát I dó is me: for that I came*'). But there's more to the *I*, and thus more to say: *I* (have to) *say more*. The *just man* is not *just* one thing,

[41] John Hollander, *The Gazer's Spirit: Poems Speaking to Silent Works of Art* (University of Chicago Press, Chicago and London 1995), 191ff.

not just a man in a single sense. For Hopkins the reason for this is that (in the theological orthodoxy which Christina G Rossetti and the other Christians were also clear about) he *is*, he has his being, as the Bible puts it, 'in Christ'; he 'dwells', in another Biblical metaphor, in Christ, and Christ dwells in him. He lives, then, and acts 'in God's eye'. In a not-so-clever pun, God's *eye*, which is God's *I*, gives his *I* its meaning: he 'Acts in God's eye what in God's eye he is'. And if he is, in God's eye, in Christ, he is all over the place. '[F]or Christ plays in ten thousand places': Christ is simultaneously everywhere, in his people and in the bread and wine of the eucharist wherever it is celebrated, as all Christians hold, and, as Roman Catholics believe, in the 'reserved' sacramental wafers kept in the holy boxes called 'tabernacles' in Roman Catholic churches. And while this multiple being of Christ might be a consoling thought for a Christology and for Christian sacramentalism, it would seem less consoling when it's applied to the individual self, to a Hopkins as human being. To be all over the place is, presumably, to not know exactly where you are, is to be greatly unsettled.

The poem's unsettling thought about unsettledness is, though, granted some late appeal in the turn to the attractions of the body of Christ as manifest in His male followers. Christ's loveliness (the subject of much Hopkins meditating) is expressed in the limbs, the eyes, the faces – the *prosopa*, no less – of the men whom Christ indwells. They're eyes and *I*'s, at once Christ's and Christ's male surrogates, the *prosopa* through whom He presents himself: selves – and of course bodies – magnetizing the fascinated gaze – the eye, the *I* – of the poet. And thus the question of the self's instability turns out to be very much a gender matter, coloured and textured by anxieties about the gender of the speaking subject.

The Deep Blue Gender Sea

This is true, variously, of Tennyson and Swinburne, of Pater and John Addington Symonds, as well as of Hopkins (though not, I'm sure, for all Joseph Bristow's hints in his 'Aqueous Ages' article,[42] that it's true of Arnold and Clough). Bereft by Hallam's death Tennyson's grieving self resolves itself into womanhood. He is Hallam's widow. For his part, Hopkins, perennially troubled male-watcher (and not accidentally Pater's tutee at Oxford), shrinks from a married man's heterosexual destiny, but also from the pederastic joy with boys that was fashionable in his time at Oxford. This double averting and flinching is what's going on, I take it, in Hopkins's arrestingly fragmented attempt at a poem known as 'Epithalamion'.

---

[42]   The one cited above, p216: *Literature and History* (Spring 1995), 27–49.

'Epithalamion' (traditional title for a wedding poem) was to have been an Ode for his brother Everard's wedding in April 1888; and Hopkins simply cannot get it done. He cannot think, cannot write, about a male person finding himself in the body of a woman, in wedlock. An *I* speaks. 'Hark, hearer, hear what I do'. He (we assume he) asks us, the 'hearer', to 'make believe' that 'we' are together in a cleft (a 'Southern dean or Lancashire clough or Devon cleave') of the landscape's 'loins', a 'between' place where water dances down, 'boisterously beautiful'. It's a sexualized landscape, in which 'we' come across some 'boys from the town', bathing: young proletarian males. The *I* clearly wants to look on, at the loveliness of their 'bellbright bodies', even to join them in the water. But he represses this desire for himself transferring it to a third person, 'a listless stranger', who 'unseen' by the boys, 'Sees the bevy of them'. A desirous, but frustrated, voyeur. Who hurries in a state of high excitement to 'a pool neighbouring', gets undressed, plunges into the water. He's so excited he can hardly undo his bootlaces ('frowning, lips crisp / Over finger-teasing task'). Indeed, he sheds his trousers and underwear ('down he dings / His bleachèd both and woolwoven wear') before taking off his boots, which is a curious way around. Nonetheless, at last, 'walk the world he can with bare his feet' (the condition for Hopkins of ultimate earth-relating purity: human boots are anathema[43]), and, hesitating a bit, as a naked person well might when faced with cold water ('Here he will then, here he will the fleet / Flinty kindcold element let break across his limbs'), he dives in: 'Where we leave him, froliclavish, while he looks about him, laughs, swims'.

But this is all a diversion from the 'sacred matter' of marriage, the starting subject of the poem, which the poet cannot bring himself to go on with. To be sure, as this abandoned fragment tells us later on, the 'delightful dean' is 'Wedlock' and the water is 'Spousal love'. But these are not in prospect for the *I* of the poem, nor for his third-person surrogate: the *he* who can think only of naked boys, whose frolics he can only (and no doubt for the usual look-but-you-may-not-touch reasons of Hopkins the priest) join in with by proxy, in an adjacent pool.[44] Certainly for this poet there's to be no contact either in actuality or imagination with a female's private parts. These are

---

[43] See the important discussion of feet and boots and sandals in Joseph Bristow, ' "Churlsgrace": Gerard Manley Hopkins and the Working-Class Male Body', JELH, 59:3 (1992), 694–711, and my discussion, Valentine Cunningham, 'Fact and Tact', *Essays in Criticism*, 51:1 (Jan 2001), 119–138.

[44] Queer Theory critics, such as Joseph Bristow, want to emphasize the hands-on aspects of Hopkins' gay desirings, and avoid the plain fact of Hopkins's hands-off warnings to himself about touching boys such as the boy soldier in 'The Bugler's First Communion'. Joseph Bristow. ' "Churlsgrace"…', loc cit. Compare Gregory Woods, *A History of Gay Literature: The Male Tradition* (Yale University Press, Hew Haven and London, 1998), 171–173. For counter arguments see Valentine Cunningham, 'Fact and Tact' (2001).

kept at an absolutely safe distance, mirrored, metaphoricized, in the land-scape's 'delightful' dean/clough/cleave, or Hopkins' favourite *quain* (a wedge-like angularity) or *quaining*. Here the rocks 'chancequarrièd, self-quainèd' make the damming wall that creates the stranger's swimming hole. *Quain*, like its neighbour *quoin*, is cognate with Latin *cuneus*, wedge, at whose shoulder always hovers the unspoken *quaint* – or *cunt:* for Hopkins the utterly unspeakable word and thing, the signifier and centre of hetero-sexual desire. Which the boys, and words about the boys, interrupt, not just at one remove, but at two. There's to be no leaping into wedlock joys, not even, in this stunted stuttering poem, for Hopkins's brother; no joining in either with the swimming lads. Hopkins is a poet who cannot refrain, as his Journal shows, from paddling, getting his feet wet, jumping into pools, when he's on his own, or when they're the healing waters of a virginal female saint, as at the well of St Winefred (subject of Hopkins's unfinished Tragedy about her murder and her miraculous well, 'St Winefred's Well' (1879)), but who is utterly thrown by the waters of wedlock, and also by a pool full of naked boys.[45] He'll never plunge in sexually, not even as a boy-watcher, not even through his poem's surrogate boy-admirer. Here, truly, is a male self stuck on the the watery selfhood edge as genderized problematic. 'Epithalamion' is a key indicator of how, for Hopkins, the self challenged at, by, and as, a wateriness is a truly harsh gender business. (His letter to Robert Bridges about his failure to complete 'Epithalamion' is not only astoundingly off-hand about the married couple – 'The honeymoon was in Paris; they wrote thence in ecstasy; but had not been home long when the bride's mother died' – but strangely reminiscent of one of his touch-only-as-a-priest male poems, 'Felix Randal' – 'O is he dead then?' – and its cagey take on endearment. 'This seeing the sick endears them to us, us too it endears' (the poem); 'But perhaps an affliction endears husband and wife' (the letter). About endearment he was always shaky, this old master.).

Gender perturbation at the water's edge is not, of course, unique to Hopkins. His 'Epithalamion' makes you think he must have Swinburne's 'Lake of Gaube' half in mind, and Clough's 'Bothie' wholly so. (He doesn't mention either poem in his letters – though he was marvellously rude about the 'long waterlogged lines' of the third series of Swinburne's *Poems and Ballads* (1889) – thinking perhaps of the Spanish Catholic disaster-at-sea poem 'The Armada'.[46]) Clough, double-minded in almost the Hopkinsian

---

[45]   *Journals and Papers*, eds Humphrey House and Graham Storey (OUP London, 1959), 224, 235, 261.

[46]   Letter to Bridges, 29 April 1889, *Letters* to Bridges, edn cit, 304. Another letter, 1 Jan 1885, describes a Swinburne attempt at describing a sunset over water, perhaps the breathily impressionistic 140-line 'Evening on the Broads' in *Studies in Song* (1880), as 'overlaid with

way about swimming – it's all at once what lovely naked youths do, to the pleasure of a not all that reluctant homoerotic gaze, but also the troubling activity of heterosexual couples. It seems rather apt to this troubledness that Clough's original title was 'The Bothie of Toper-Na-Fuosich', until the *National Gazette* pointed out his mistake: 'Fuosich' in Scots Gaelic meaning 'bearded well' – waving a titular flag as a sort of subconscious metaphor for the worrying private parts of females which the poem's frequently visited bathing-hole rather plainly also represents. The undergraduate Piper, swimming refusenik and cynical commentator on the ephebic swimmers, dubs the swimming-hole a *wash-hand-stand basin* (II.230): the standard primitive ablution facility in Victorian Oxford's undergraduate bedrooms, nostalgic metaphor for the familiar stuff of male single-sex existence and eroticism and also an insulting gibe at the plunge into heterosexual marriage with the peasant girl Elspie that his radical undergraduate friend Philip is heading for. Rudely diminishing the threatening torrents of nightmarish heterosexual implication. In one of the poem's most powerfully erotic passages Elspie dreams of heterosexual union as like the salt sea forcing its way up an inland waterway. Just narrating her nightmare requires self-steeling effort.

> You are too strong, you see, Mr Philip! just like the sea there,
> Which *will* come, through the straits and all between the mountains,
> Forcing its great strong tide into every nook and inlet,
> Getting far in, up the quiet stream of sweet inland water,
> Sucking it up, and stopping it, turning it, driving it backward,
> Quite preventing its own quiet running: and then, soon after,
> Back it goes off, leaving weeds on the shore, and wrack and uncleanness:
> And the poor burn in the glen tries again its peaceful running,
> But it is brackish and tainted, and all its banks in disorder.
> That was what I dreamt all last night. I was the burnie,
> Trying to get along through the tyrannous brine, and could not;
> I was confined and squeezed in the coils of the great salt tide, that
> Would mix-in itself with me, and change me; I felt myself changing;
> And I struggled, and screamed, I believe, in my dream. It was dreadful.
> You are too strong, Mr Philip! I am but a poor slender burnie,
> Used to the glens and the rocks, the rowan and birch of the woodies,
> Quite unused to the great salt sea; quite afraid and unwilling.
>   (VII.120–136)

At the end of Book VI the narrator tells the Muses and Graces and Loves that he will be 'Indirect and evasive no longer, a cowardly bather, / Clinging to bough and to rock, and sidling along by the edges', but will plunge into

---

such phantasmata, secondary images, and what not of delirium-tremendous imagination that the result is a kind of bloody broth'. *Letters*, 202.

the story of the courtship of Elspie and Philip from their perspective. 'I will confront the great peril, and speak with the mouth of the lovers' as they sit at the water's edge. But try as he may Clough's boy-minded imagination is still prone to cowardice, evidently flinching, not unlike Hopkins, at taking the heterosexual narrative plunge, dithering at the edge of the dualistically gendered water. Clough rebuked poets elsewhere, in one of his radical short poems, for trembling at the water's edge of political commitment. 'Come, Poet, come! / A thousand labourers ply their task, / And what it tends to scarcely ask, / And trembling thinkers on the brink / Shiver, and know not how to think'.[47] But dither at this gendered water's edge Clough does.

For his part John Addington Symonds responds to the perturbing call of the genderized sea, specifically the waters at Venice, with a kind of resigned joy. 'The Sea Calls' is the title of one of his Venetian sonnet sequences (in his volume *Vagabunduli Libellus* (1884)): a summons to give himself entirely to sex with Venetian boatmen – 'comradeship' he calls it – about which he nonetheless never stops feeling guilty.

Symonds knows himself only as 'Twy-natured', a self in two, as sonnet LIV in his 'Stella Maris' sequence puts it.[48] (*Stella Maris*, one of the Virgin Mary's titles, is appropriated challengingly for Venice, home for Symonds of droves of desirable men, and specifically his particular friend, the gondolier Angelo Fusato, inspiree of most of the 'Sea Calls' and 'Stella Maris' sonnets.) Symonds is a variegated 'personality'; so variegated, as his pair of sonnets entitled 'Personality' (in his *Animi Figura* (1882)) has it, that 'I know not what I am' – a confusion that spreads to others: 'Each self, from its own self concealed, is caught / Thus in a cage of sense'. Which gets in the way of 'comradeship', because 'His own self no man sees, and none hath seen / His brother's self'. And he's a striated, confused self, precisely at Venice, sexually attractive, sexually confusing Venice. Venice of the dramatic land-water borderlines, where sea and land blend and clash theatrically: the *terraqueous* city – Symonds' own word for this place whose mix of land and water mirrors as it signifies his gendered self-confusion, 'my more terraqueous mould', as he puts it in sonnet LIV.

It's a confusedness that runs deep and wide across Symonds' writing. On the one hand there are homosexual rhapsodies, rhapsodies in blue so to say, Symonds' Blues, as a post-jazz-age might label them, about the blues – the blues of the Venetian lagoon, and the blues of Venetian working-men's blouses. Of twenty-three years old Angelo Fusato: picked up in Venice in 1881, with his lilac shirt and his opalesque eyes (*opal*: anything from blue-green to almost black), 'as though the quintessential colour of the Venetian

---

[47] 'Come, Poet, come!', *Putnam's Magazine*, II (July 1853), 74.

[48] Did gay Australian novelist Patrick White, one wonders, have Symonds in mind in naming the eponymous gender-switching hero of *The Twyborn Affair* (1979) as he did?

waters were vitalized in them and fed from inner founts of passion. This marvellous being …':

> Wide lucid eyes in cavernous orbits set
> Aflame like living opals or the sea,
> Vibrant with floods of electricity,
> The soul projected in each fiery jet:
> This thy fierce fascination haunts me yet;
> And I have dreamed all Venice into thee.

That's Symonds' 'A Portrait', one of the many Fusato tributes in *Vagabunduli Libellus*. It's a celebration of desire for the terraqueous male focussed in Symonds' most remarkable essay, 'In the Key of Blue'. (*In the Key of Blue: And Other Essays* (1892), 1–16; a characteristic Nineties volume in design, from the 'decadent' publishers Elkin Matthews and John Lane, At the Sign of the Bodley Head in Vigo Street, London, with title page and binding by Nineties design darling CS Ricketts.) The essay is about the difficulties literature has in describing colours, the inadequacies of its colour vocabulary, which falls well short of nature's variegations. 'These thoughts were in my mind at Venice, where the problem of colour gradations under their most subtle aspect presents itself on all sides to the artist.' Some painters have lately done justice to the blue of Venetian women's clothing, but no one has tried 'reproducing the costumes of men in single figures or in masses'.

> Yet it is just among the working people – fishermen, stevedores, porters, boatmen, artizans, *facchini* – that the best opportunities are offered for attempting symphonies and harmonies of blue. Whole classes of the male population attire themselves in blouses, sashes, and trousers of this colour. According to the fancy of the individual, or the limitations of his wardrobe, the arrangements of tints are infinitely varied in the same costume. Stuffs faded by washing and exposure blend with the new crude dyes. Dirt and stains of labour, patchings of harder upon softer tones, add picturesqueness. And whether the flesh-tints of the man be pale or sun-burned, his complexion dark or fair, blue is equally in sympathy with the model. Some men show remarkable taste in the choice and arrangement of the tints combined. It is clear that they give no little thought to the matter. Modulations from the main chord of three decided blues are made by tones of lavender or mauve in the blouse, the sash, or the stockings. Under strong sunlight, against the greenish water of the canals, the colour effect of such chromatic deviations are piquant and agreeable.
>
> (pp3–4)

Symonds will make up the lack, assiduously celebrating this attractively mixed, deviant, washed-out Venetian blueness – mirror of his own gender blur – in a set of poems which he calls 'blues and blouses', a sequence of

'Studies' mainly featuring the nineteen-years old Augusto Zanon, a *facchino* (or porter) 'with whom I have been long acquainted', 'posed' 'in a variety of hues in combination' (p 4). Symonds calls these gay love poems 'symphonies' – symphonies of 'Blues and white', 'blues and brown', 'pink and blue', 'blues and gold', 'blues and green', and so forth. They're Symphonies after Whistler, cult painter of the decadent Nineties (Charles Ricketts who did the cover for this volume lodged with Whistler). They celebrate the joys of the 'confused' self, happy in devouring the sexually inviting look, the clothes, body, *prosopon* of the young male Venetian – and, in fact, bisexual – other. As in 'A symphony of black and blue':

> *A symphony of black and blue –*
> *Venice asleep, vast night, and you.*
> *The skies were blurred with vapours dank:*
> *The long canal stretched inky-blank,*
> *With lights on heaving water shed*
> *From lamps that trembled overhead.*
> *Pitch-dark! You were the one thing blue;*
> *Four tints of pure celestial hue:*
> *The larkspur blouse by tones degraded*
> *Through silken sash of sapphire faded,*
> *The faintly floating violet tie,*
> *The hose of lapis lazuli.*
> *How blue you were amid that black,*
> *Lighting the wave, the ebon wrack!*
> *The ivory pallor of your face*
> *Gleaned from those glowing azures back*
> *Against the golden gaslight; grapes*
> *Of dusky curls your brows embrace,*
> *And round you all the vast night gapes.*
>
> (pp5–6)

In this mood Symonds can gaze desirously in his own person on and on, can hold the gaze that Hopkins had to keep averting from his attractive lads, especially naked bathing ones. He haunted London's Thames Embankment for the purpose. (There's a poem, 'The Song of a Swimmer', about watching a proley lad going for a London swim, 'His firm and vital flesh, white, rounded, radiant', pasted in the manuscript of Symonds's Memoirs.[49]) Julia Saville associates the loving paintings of naked bathing boys by Henry Scott Tuke with Symonds' rhapsodies in blue, especially Tuke's famous painting *August Blue* (1893–1894). Tuke took his title from Swinburne's poem 'The

---

[49] Reported by Matt Cook, *London and the Culture of Homosexuality, 1885–1914* (Cambridge University Press, Cambridge, 2003, 132–133 (in 'The Hellenic City', Ch 5, which strongly features Symonds).

Sundew', about the weedy little marsh-plant of that name, 'renascent' in sea-water, emblem for Swinburne of mysterious betweenness: 'how it grows, / If with its colour it have breath, / If life taste sweet to it, if death / Pain its soft petal, no man knows'.[50] There is a syndrome here of rapturous acceptance of sexual boundary-crossing. *Erethism*, Symonds liked to call it, a nineteenth-century medical term for extraordinary bodily arousal, agitation, mental and emotional restlessness: 'The pulses beat, the nerves thrill and tingle. To escape the tyranny of the impossible vision which keeps the mind upon a rack, "libidinous joys" present themselves under seductive colours, and the would-be hierophant of artistic beauty is hurried away upon the wings of an obscene Chimaera'.[51] The evidence of this state, said Symonds, was in his Fusato sonnets. It's also in his symphonies in male-Venetian blue; in his *Memoirs*' fantasies of gazing at bathing boys, touching up compliant males in lectures, kissing desired men's faces; in its lists of desired and obtained male companions and temporary partners; in his long poem 'Phallus Impudicus' (also in his *Memoirs*), relishing 'The crimson glory of the lustrous gland' and 'Masculine draughts of rapture epicoene', watching a questing man pick up a lovely Venetian youth, 'Rank stuff of sex'; in his protracted meditations on Greek boy-love, pederasty, 'Dorianism', especially in *A Problem in Greek Ethics: Being An Inquiry into the Phenomenon of Sexual Inversion Addressed to Medical Psychologists and Jurists* (1901); in his crusading autobiographical admissions as Case XVII in his and Havelock Ellis's *Sexual Inversion* (1897) – where, as Case XVII, 'He likes sound and vigorous young men of a lower rank from the age of 20 to 25'; has 'no moral sense of doing wrong'; his lungs and neuroses became better when he abandoned his wife for 'indulgence' in his 'inborn homosexual instincts'; he gets instantly healthy when he 'indulges in moderate homosexual pleasure'.[52] And, of course, in his enthusiasm for Michelangelo's sonnets to Tommaso Cavalieri, which he translated, and for Walt Whitman's celebrations of the 'intense, throbbing, sensitive, expectant love of man for man'.[53]

[50] Julia F Saville, 'The Romance of Boys Bathing: Poetic Precedents and Respondents to the Paintings of Henry Scott Tuke', *Victorian Sexual Dissidence*, ed Richard Dellamora (University of Chicago Press, Chicago and London, 1999), 253–277.

[51] Phyllis Grosskurth, ed, *The Memoirs of John Addington Symonds* (Hutchinson, London, 1984), 239–40.

[52] Havelock Ellis and JA Symonds, *Studies in the Psychology of Sex*, I, *Sexual Inversion* (Wilson & Macmillan, London, 1897), 283ff.

[53] *The Sonnets of Michael Angelo Buonarroti & Tommaso Cappanella, Now For the First Time Translated in Rhymed English* (Smith, Elder, & Co., 1878); *Renaissance in Italy*, Vol 3, *The Fine Arts* (Smith, Elder, & Co., 1877), Ch 8, 'Life of Michael Angelo', especially 432–435, and Appendix II, 512–528, 'Michael Angelo's Sonnets'; *Walt Whitman: A Study* (George Routledge & Sons, London; EP Dutton, NY, 1893), 97–98; *The Life of Michelangelo*, 2 vols, 2nd edn (John C Nimmo, London, 1893).

On the one hand, as I say, there are these polemical raptures; but, on the other, there are the massive despondencies, an invasive sense of sin, and bouts of melancholy approaching madness, which frame these joys. The *erethistic I* of Symonds' writings has a very downcast Doppelgänger. The second sonnet of the 'Personality' pair talks of the self and his desired comrade carrying

> ... with them to the void
> Without, the void more terrible within,
> Tormented haply by the smart of sin
> And cursing what their wilful sense enjoyed.

The *Animi Figura* volume, in which the 'Personality' sonnets appear, contains a 'Self-Condemnation' sequence. 'Thine am I, thine, thou irresistible!' declares the *I* of 'Stella Maris' XXV, but this is 'Damnation palpable'. The beloved offers love and calm 'of all convention free' in 'Renunciation, II', in *Vagabunduli*, but these are 'Calm as the salt dead lake; easy as sin; / Sweet as love-apples hiding dust within'. (Symonds described this poem as being about Fusato and also an Oxford Cathedral choirboy called Alfred Brooke.) In his review of *Vagabunduli* in the *Academy* (19 November 1884), Hall Caine could see no way out for the author of the 'Stella Maris' sonnets except madness. 'Alas! he did not know perhaps that he had given voice to my soul's darkest apprehensions', Symonds confided to his Memoir (Grosskurth, p 240).

Hall Caine was no doubt mindful of the palpable gothicities attendant on Symonds' immersion in the 'Stella Maris' blue. 'I dreamed we were together on blue waves'; a sixteen-year-old Love is at the helm; but on the boat's red sail is depicted a horse bearing 'A dead man oe'r blue waves for evermore' (XXVIII). Here was a deadliness for the self, for the poet and for poeticity; the widely felt dangers of wateriness breaking over the poet, even in wonderfully blue Venice, with its lovely boys in blue. Venice was utterly enticing, but also dementing. As the poet and critic Arthur Symons inevitably found. The missionary voice of the decadent Nineties and their inspirations the French Symbolist *poètes maudits* (in his greatly influential *The Symbolist Movement in Literature* (1899, extended 1919), who was naturally roped in by Symonds to endorse the 'Key of Blue' defence ('see how beautiful' is 'the young man in a blouse', whom the world calls 'immoral'), Symons went melancholy mad in Venice, his 'subtle terror growing up out of' the 'insidious coiling of the waters – waters with two madhouses in them, echoing with the sounds of the insane'. The mental plight of Symons' character Henry Luxulyan, in the 'Extracts from the Journal of Henry Luxulyan', echoes his author's. Luxulyan was, Symons told Symonds, 'a pathological and psychological study of one who was intensely morbid and restless, a study of nerves and disillusions, and there is a great deal of self-analysis in it'. Death in Venice; madness in Venice. The utter fearfulness for self and for writing of invasive wateriness.[54] It should make you think, perhaps, of the book of Dante Gabriel Rossetti's manuscript poems disinterred in 1869 from Lizzie Siddal's grave and coffin after seven mouldering years: 'soaked through and through', they 'had to be still further saturated with disinfectants' before being dried out very slowly, 'leaf by leaf'. Much was lost, erased by water – 'a sad wreck'. Embarrassed, Rossetti tried to limit knowledge of the events to friends like marsh-minded Swinburne; 'but I suppose the truth must ooze out in time'. Oozing poems; oozing truths. Wateriness palpably bad in every way for these poems, especially physically; bad for the physicality, too, of the poet.[55]

In Symonds' sonnet 'O, Si! O, Si!', about the Fusato relationship (in *Animi Figura*), the poet addresses a persona, himself presumably, who has turned away from the holiness of marriage, to be besmirched by the lust of the gendered in-between, with his 'incurable malady' of the self:

> The good thou cravest might have once been thine,
> Hadst thou not made thy will the instrument
> Of forceful folly, on vain rapture bent.
> Thou from the boughs didst rend that fruit malign,
> Which, slowly ripening 'neath the touch divine
> Of hours and days and season, should have leant
> At last to bless thee with the full content
> Of wedded lives in love's most holy shrine.
> Now with intemperate fingers having torn,
> Thou findest beauty but a poisonous lure
> Unto thy soul's destruction, joy a thorn,
> Love's orient wings smirched with the mire impure
> Of frustrate lust, friendship no sooner born
> Then tettered with disease what skill can cure?

Tetter is a skin disease. This persona, this self, bears the marks of his incurability, the foreverness of his unease, his dis-ease, on his body: *smirched*, *mired*, *tettered*. He's a divided self with his perturbations pronouncedly marked on his body.[56]

[54] AJA Symons to JA Symonds in Arthur Symons, *Collected Works* (Martin Secker, London, 1924), II,691. 'Extracts from the Journal of Henry Luxulyan', *Collected Works*, V,200. Karl E Beckson, *Arthur Symons: A Life* (Clarendon Press, Oxford, 1987), 254. Symons, 'Fragment of an Autobiography', *Horizon* 8 (1943), 139.
[55] Rossetti to William Michael Rossetti, 13 and 15 October 1869, and to Ford Madox Ford, 14 October and later October 1869, *Letters of Dante Gabriel Rossetti*, eds Oswald Doughty and John Robert Wahl, II, *1861–1870* (Clarendon Press, Oxford, 1965), 751–754.
[56] Joseph Bristow is good in his *Effeminate England: Homoerotic Writing after 1885* (Open University Press, Buckingham, 1995) on later Victorian gay male distresses of self-definition

Contralto Parts

The divisions of selfhood as manifested in the body are what Swinburne is magnetized by in his 1863 'Hermaphroditus' sequence of four sonnets (published in the notorious *Poems and Ballads* volume of 1866). They are, as Barry Bullen has ably shown, at the centre of the Victorian, aestheticist, Paterian, fantasy of the androgynous self: the lovely boys indistinguishable from girls, and young females indistinguishable from boys, especially in their faces, their *prosopa*, dotingly painted by Dante Gabriel Rossetti and Simeon Solomon and Ted Burne-Jones.[57] Swinburne's sonnets are ekphrastic, addressed to the marble statue of the Greek Hermaphroditus in the Louvre Museum. Hermaphroditus was the son of Aphrodite, that is Venus, goddess of love, and of Hermes, the god of tricksters and interpreters; a beautiful boy who used to bathe in a fountain near Halicarnassus (birthplace of Dionysus). He's the original naked boy of the swimming-hole. Salmacis, nymph of the fountain, fell in love with him, embraced him, prayed to the gods to make them one body, and she had her wish. The result was a lovely boy with female breasts, a perfect androgyne. (Hermaphrodites get their name from Hermaphroditus.) The statue in the Louvre intensely captured the nineteenth-century European imagination. Walter Pater, greatly drawn to Greek ideals of androgynous loveliness, praised in his *The Renaissance* the 'Hermaphrodite of the Louvre' as a 'perfect blending' of male and female beauty. The poem 'Contralto' by Théophile Gautier, haunter of the Louvre Museum (he wrote a guide to its art), star of Symons's (expanded) *Symbolist Movement in Literature* for his aestheticist anti-Christian Greekism ('I am as much a pagan as Alcibiades or Phidias. I have never plucked on Golgotha the flowers of the Passion, and the deep stream that flows from the side of the Crucified and sets a crimson girdle about the world, has never washed me in its flood'), is a rapt meditation on the statue's ambivalences as a model for the singer Ernesta Grisi's androgynous voice. The poem appeared in Gautier's *Émaux et camées* (1852) and evidently helped affirm Swinburne's attention to the carving. Fragoletta, cross-dressing lesbian heroine of the French novel by Henri de Latouche, *Fragoletta* (1829), was also inspired by the Louvre statue. Swinburne took her name for the hermaphrodite subject of his poem 'Fragoletta' (also in *Poems and Ballads*). Swinburne's 'Hermaphroditus', addressing the Louvre's figure as 'sweet', imagines the confusion of blind Cupid, god of love, at the blend of male and female attractions in this person who was physically and sexually

---

and self-writing, and especially good on Symonds' sexological writing plights; but is not animated by the water-sea-lake metaphoricity and metonymicity.

[57]   JB Bullen, *The Pre-Raphaelite Body: Fear and Desire in Painting, Poetry, and Criticism* (Clarendon Press, Oxford, 1998), especially 182–194.

disordered in a watery encounter gone evidently wrong (freshwater counterpart of the destructive salt-water encounters discussed earlier in this chapter).

> 'Yea, sweet, I know; I saw in what swift wise
> Beneath the woman's and the water's kiss
> Thy moist limbs melted into Salmacis,
> And the large light turned tender in thine eyes,
> And all the boy's breath softened into sighs;
> But Love being blind, how should he know of this?'
>
> (sonnet IV)

The keynote for Swinburne is frustration for both the would-be lover and the beloved, confusion of self and body for both gazer and gazed-upon, in transgressive desire present and transgressive sexuality in prospect. Sweet Hermaphroditus should

> Choose of two loves and cleave unto the best;
> Two loves at either blossom of they breast
> Strive until one be under and one above.
>
> (sonnet I)

But he/she is doomed never to be able to choose – stuck in absolute aporetic doubleness and dividedness, in an irresoluble body/gender plight. Nothing

> Shall make thee man and ease a woman's sighs
> Or make thee woman for a man's delight.
>
> (sonnet III)

'Sex to sweet sex with lips and limbs is wed'. But for the desirous outsider this means the (usual) 'fruitful feud of hers and his' will turn 'To the waste wedlock of a sterile kiss' (sonnet II). Hermaphroditus is 'a thing of barren hours' for ever. Perpetually chiasmic, as it were, lost in the stasis of perpetually each-way crossing-over body-parts – a chiasmic nightmare registered, as critics have nicely observed, in the sonnets' rhetorical habit of chiasmus: 'A strong desire ... great despair ..., / A great despair. strong desire' (I); 'not love but fear ... not fear but love' (IV); and so on.[58]

The desirous nymph Salmacis gets the blame for all this, of course (it's always the females in Swinburne who give, Dolores-like, the pain), and in 'Fragoletta' Swinburne takes up the lure of the hermaphroditic as lesbian,

---

[58] JB Bullen (1998), op. cit., acknowledges the discussion of the poem's chiasmic riches in Catherine Maxwell's Oxford DPhil thesis – which is now incorporated into her *The Female Sublime from Milton to Swinburne: Bearing Blindness* (Manchester University Press, Manchester and NY, 2001), 204–205.

with the female body-parts foremost. But still, as before, the bosom is 'barren'. Worse, Fragoletta's kisses would be bloody and 'sting'. Fragoletta has turned into Dolores. So here's a prospect of pain, and, for desirous Cupid, a matter of incest – Fragoletta-Hermaphroditus is, like Cupid, the child of Venus. 'Say, Venus hath no girl, / No front of female curl, / Among her Loves'; but she does, because Hermaphroditus became one; and Cupid's having sex with her/him would be the ultimate transgression:

> How should he greet thee? What new name,
> Fit to move all men's hearts, could move
> Thee, deaf to love or shame
> Love's sister, by the same
> Mother as Love?

It's a shame-full loving which evidently appeals to Swinburne but also appals him, imbued as the love and desire are with (in the chiasmic terms of 'Hermaphroditus') fear and despair. Love: fear; desire: despair – delights frightfully backed by horrors; as they are in the chain of paradoxical attractions and repulsions in the Gautier poem 'Contralto', whose entranced and repelled celebration of the hermaphroditism of his mistress the opera singer Ernesta Grisi's voice is, as it were, the backing track for Swinburne. Contralto – name for the lowest female singing voice, and (once) the highest male voice: ambivalent tone, voice as doubled self:

> Que tu me plais, ô timbre étrange!
> Son double, homme et femme à la fois,
> Contralto, bizarre mélange,
> Hermaphrodite de la voix!

Bizarre mélange: a pleasing creature, beautiful, charming, graceful – the tributes pile up – but simultaneously disquieting, accursed, monstrous, strange, doubtful: *inquiétante beauté*; *beauté maudite*; *sexe douteux*; *Monstre charmant*; *timbre étrange*. Gautier speaks very loudly the anxiously paradoxical attraction-revulsion you can hear as tone and undertone in 'Hermaphroditus' and 'Fragoletta'. Or, indeed, in Oscar Wilde's Swinburne-tribute poem 'The Burden of Itys' (*burden* once again: act of poetic repetition, and also heavy load, plight even).

In the standard version of his story, standardized by Ovid's *Metamorphoses* (the one recycled by TS Eliot in *The Waste Land*, Part II, 'A Game of Chess'), Itys was the son of Procne, the mother who stabbed him to death and cooked him as a meat-dish for husband Tereus in revenge for his rape and silencing tongue-excision of her sister Philomela, who had nonetheless told her story in a weaving. To save their lives Philomela was metamorphosed into a nightingale and Procne into a swallow. In Homer, it's Procne who becomes the nightingale and Philomela the swallow. In Swinburne's 'Itylus' (using Homer's name for Itys, but following Ovid's version), the nightingale Philomela chides her swallow sister Procne for forgetting the death of her first-born.[59] For his part, Wilde sings as Itys, cruising the countryside, especially around Oxford – much as Matthew Arnold did in his 'Thyrsis'. Itys hopes to bump into 'the ancient Gods of Grecian poetry', the doomed male lovelies of the ancient world, Hyacinth, Endymion, Narcissus, Adonis, even Antinous (beloved of emperor Hadrian, the youth who drowned mysteriously in the Nile), and always failing to do so. Modern Oxfordshire is no revived ancient pastoral scene. It's ghosted, alright, by literary presences, as Arnold's 'Thyrsis' landscape was ghosted by his dead friend Clough, but these are only ghosts, figments of the imagination. There are, to be sure, some real-life lovely lads about, modern gay sex-objects – the 'roving comrades' who can meet up in the 'mossy dells', the 'troop of laughing boys' who cheer on a college 'racing eight' from the Thames tow-path: this is Arnold's Oxfordshire overtly gayed up. But the longed-for Greek and Roman boys never materialize. 'It was a dream, the glade is tenantless, / No soft Ionian laughter moves the air, / The Thames creeps on in sullen leadenness' ('The Burden of Itys', 295–297). And the poem is utterly fraught, burdened no less, with frustrated desire. 'A moment more, the startled leaves had stirred, / Endymion would have passed across the mead / Moonstruck with love' (265–268). And it's not just the boys who fail to appear. 'A moment more ... lonely Salmacis, // Had bared his barren beauty to the moon (280). Barren: Swinburne's word. Salmacis, who is one of the Wilde/ Itys 'diviner memories', earlier in the poem: 'memories of Salmacis / Who is not boy or girl and yet is both, / Fed by two fires and unsatisfied / Through their excess, each passion being loth / For love's own sake to leave the other's side / Yet killing love by staying' (120–126). The unsatisfying doubleness of the hermaphroditic, the torn duality of the bi-genderedness that effectively kills love. And here is grievous anxiety about the stability, coherence, knowability and hence the clear speakability of the self, especially about gender identity, which helps motor, I think, one of the most obvious problems in reading Victorian poetry, namely the constant difficulty of actually identifying the gender of the speaking, the 'lyrical' *I*.

---

[59] Matthew Arnold's 'Philomela' (?1852–1853) hesitates messily between versions. It celebrates the nightingale for her song of 'Eternal passion! / Eternal pain!'. In his first draft this is Procne ('Dost thou still reach / Thy husband, weak avenger, through thyself?). He dropped the lines when, according to his editor Kenneth Allott, 'he realized how firmly established was the identification of Philomela with the nightingale'. But his published version nevertheless asks of Philomela 'Dost thou again peruse / With hot cheeks and seared eyes / The too clear web, and thy dumb sister's shame', as if it wasn't her tongue that was torn out, but Procne's. *Poems of Matthew Arnold*, ed Kenneth Allott (Longmans, 1965), 347–349.

Garbling Identity

Trying to obscure your identity as a writer is very common among Victorian poets, and for all sorts of reasons, some of them only guessable; but gender issues never seem far away from the widespread self-shroudings. Who knows what drove Robert Browning to call himself 'Z' as the author of 'Porphyria' and 'Johannes Agricola', the Madhouse Cells poems, when they appeared in the *Monthly Repository* (1836)? Not the first-night nerves, as it were, which had *Pauline* published anonymously in 1833, for *Paracelsus* had already appeared in 1835 in the name of 'Robert Browning'. Was it wishing 'Robert Browning' not to come out starkly as a radical Unitarian like the founder of the *Monthly Repository*, WJ Fox? Impossible to tell. But what is striking is the gender-story implicit in Oscar Wilde's claim in the title of 'The Ballad of Reading Gaol' that it is 'By C.3.3', the number on Wilde's cell-door in Reading Gaol, his convict identity. This is not, I think, an attempt to dodge the scandal loaded onto the name of 'Oscar Wilde', disgraced writer, fallen Satan-like from the hubristic heights of his one-time public fame, after his conviction for homosexual activity, but rather an act of defiance, from a man victimized for his sexuality. 'Here I stand, C.3.3, convict under a bad law.' The poem's sub-title – 'In Memoriam CTW, Sometime Trooper of the Royal Horse Guard, Obiit HM Prison, Reading, Berkshire, July 17th 1896' – not only memorialized a criminal soldier, Charles Thomas Woolridge who murdered his wife, the very sort of man Wilde was in jail for having sex with, but loudly echoed the title of Tennyson's poem about a dead male, 'In Memorian AHH, Obiit DCXXXIII'. With the strong implication, I think, of a heavily ironic complaint that while Tennyson became the most celebrated poet in England for writing about his bereavement as another man's 'Widow', Wilde went to prison for his way of preferring men.

Mary Coleridge (friend of the imperial poet Henry Newbolt and of Robert Bridges and RW Dixon – she did an Introduction to Bridges's 1905 edition of Dixon's last poems) published as 'Anodos', 'for fear', she said 'of tarnishing the name which an ancestor [her great-great uncle Samuel Taylor Coleridge] has made illustrious in English poetry'. Belated woman disclaims the patriarch's precedent force: *anodos*, a-nodos (not knotty), anodyne; female poet waives any desire to muscle in on the male patch, and does so under a gender-unspecific name. Women poets are especially exercised about their trade names. Elizabeth Barrett Barrett hides behind the gender-anonymous EBB. The Brontë sisters publish their poems as by Currer, Ellis, and Acton Bell, not-quite male names, close to androgynous ones. Augusta Davies writes at first (two volumes of verse and a novel) as Cecil Home – Cecil, one of the handful of genuinely androgynous names in English culture. Mathilde Blind's first collection (1867) appeared as by Claude Lake – Claude, another of the small English androgynous group, borrowed perhaps from Clough's protagonist in *Amours de Voyage* (surname, though, if Arnold's biographer Park Honan is to be believed, of the female beloved of Arnold's Marguerite Poems, Mary Claude), attached to the distinctly watery Lake.[60] Young Alice Thompson's first poetic outing, *Preludes* (1871) is by the gender non-specifying AC Thomson. The anarchist Louisa Sarah Bevington's first pamphlet of poems, *Keynotes* (1876) is by Arbor Leigh – an arrestng m/f *mélange*: Leigh adopted from Elizabeth Barrett Browning's heroine Aurora Leigh, but Arbor patently masculine (*arbor*, Latin for tree: hard, phallic). Katherine Harris Bradley, likewise Barret Browning inclined, wrote at first as Arron Leigh (*The New Minnesinger*, 1875), then joined up with her niece Edith Emma Cooper as Arron Leigh and Isla (*Bellerophôn and Other Poems*, 1881), after which this lesbian couple decided to appear as Michael Field. And the genderized complexity of what was going on in all this was evident at the time. The two sonnets 'To George Sand', by Elizabeth Barrett Barrett (*Poems*, 1844), for instance, are arrested by the contradictions of a woman 'Self-called George Sand': the acquired double self, the 'large-brained woman and large-hearted man', but also the female writer who was unwilling to hide her 'woman's nature' in 'manly scorn', thus 'Disproving thy man's name'.

The commonly alleged pragmatic reason, that assuming a male name or a gender-blurring one made it easier for females to get published, does not really hold water. It was not at all difficult for Victorian women to find publishers, whether single or married. Elizabeth Barrett Barrett might still travel after her marriage under her old title of EBB, the B for married Browning silently replacing the B for spinster Barrett – but being a married woman was even less of a bar to getting published than it was before. Publishers had no qualms about women, single or married, as such. When Alice Thompson and Augusta Davies marry they publish happily as Alice Meynell and Augusta Webster. What seems to have been at stake in adopting gender-blurring or outright male pseudonyms is a wide desire by women, especially when starting out, not to be read, and thus dismissed, as just female, especially as just young and female, as 'girly' in modern terms. That seems to be what's inciting Augusta Webster, Alice Meynell, Mathilde Blind

---

[60] Park Honan, *Matthew Arnold* (Weidenfeld & Nicolson, New York and London, 1981), 149ff. Marie Claude was a German-born French Protestant writer for children and of hymns, a northern acquaintance of Arnold, only with difficulty to be identified as the (unidentified) Swiss girl of the Margeurite poems, as Miriam Allott rather easily shows in 'Arnold and "Margeurite – Continued", *Victorian Poetry*, 23 (1985), 125–143.

and Louisa Bevington, as neophyte poets. (Louisa Sarah Bevington never appeared as such, nor even as Mrs Guggenheim her married name; her *Poems, Lyrics, and Sonnets* (1882) are by LS Bevington, 'Author of *Keynotes*, Etc': *Keynotes*, the Arbor Leigh volume, the *Etc.* being her anarchist pamphlets.) The Brontës' self-rechristenings seem, symptomatically, to be precisely laying claim to be taken seriously as poets, not type-cast as young women ones. They were, of course, in direct competition with their adored, but pushy, brother Branwell. What they're after is recognition of their own poetic talent, which means shedding a female identity. The avoidance of female identity is more complex in the case of Katherine Harris Bradley and her niece Edith Emma Cooper – androgynous Arron Leigh and her niece 'Isla' sheltering behind Michael Field. What the shared male identity was concealing wasn't a simple femaleness, but their rather peculiar personal tie, the lesbian relationship between an aunt and a niece sixteen years her junior. Not because lesbian relationships were illegal – they never have been in Britain – but, one guesses, because of the age difference (was there a whiff of paedophilia here?), and because of the echo of a relationship forbidden by canon law, namely the one between an aunt and a nephew. (What won't do is Yoppie Prins's notion in her protracted prowling around the problematic identity of 'Michael Field' that in assuming it Bradley and Cooper 'perform a self-doubling signature that unsettles conventional definitions of lyric as the solitary utterance of a single speaker'. Even if such 'conventional definitions' exist, that feels very wide of any motive they might have had.[61])

For their part, male gay, or bisexual male poets were driven by more pressing concerns. There was strong traditional prejudice against effeminate men, perennially thought of as potential catamites, plainly up to no good. 'Masculine' women have always attracted sneery notice – Dante Gabriel Rossetti finds it easy, for example, to jeer at the 'falsetto muscularity' of his sister and Elizabeth Barrett Barrett – but nothing like the kept-up mocking

---

[61]   Yoppie Prins, *Victorian Sappho*, edn cit, 16. Celebrators of the life and poems of 'Michael Field' do tend to either not feel there is much of a problem here, as e.g. Chris White, ' "Poets and Lovers evermore": the poetry and journals of Michael Field', in *Sexual Sameness: Textual Differences in Lesbian and Gay Writings*, ed Joseph Bristow (Routledge, London and NY, 1992); or, like Yoppie Prins, they rather bark up the wrong tree. Prins's thoughts on Michael Field first appeared as 'A Metaphorical Field: Kathleen Bradley and Edith Cooper', *Victorian Poetry* 333, 1 (Spring 1995), 129—148 in the *Victorian Poetry* 'Women Poets' Special Number, which contained Dorothy Mermin's rather valuable piece on Victorian poetic writing and reading 'as a woman': ' "The fruitful feud of hers and his": Sameness, Difference and Gender in Victorian Poetry', (*Victorian Poetry* 'Women Poets' Special Number, 149—165 (miles better than Mermin's much-reproduced 'The Damsel, the Knight, and the Victorian Woman Poet', *Critical Inquiry* 13 (1986), 64–80, which is full of sweepingly dubious allegations about Victorian gender conventions and the possibilities for Victorian women and women poets.

of *mollies* (a term from the early 18ᵗʰ century), *sissies* and *nancies* (the later, Victorian terms). Buggery had been outlawed in England since 1533. It was notoriously difficult to prove in court; the evidence required was much reduced in 1828; but it remained a capital crime until 1861. No other form of gay male sexual activity was criminalized until 1895, when Henri Labouchère, Liberal MP for the staunchly Nonconformist seat of Northampton, got 'gross indecency' of all sorts by men added to the Criminal Law Amendments Act, which was actually brought in to outlaw child sex and to curtail prostitution. But long before 1895 public prejudice and legal force kept gay males cautious. And no gay male writer or artist was unmindful of what happened to the painter Simeon Solomon, arrested in a public lavatory in London, 11 February 1873, for 'attempting to commit sodomy'. He was fined the huge sum of £100, and sentenced, 24 March 1873, to eighteen months' prison with 'light', as opposed to 'hard', labour – commuted to police supervision only through the intervention of his cousin Meyer Solomon (the Solomons were big in London's Jewish business community, rich and influential). The other man, George Roberts, got eighteen months hard labour, and had no powerful friends to help get him off.

Solomon was a renowned Pre-Raphaelite, his paintings of androgynous boy-girls/ girl-boys recognizably close to those of Dante Gabriel Rossetti. His paintings were, as it were, the public face of his friend Walter Pater's Platonism. Swinburne idolized him for the androgyny of his pictures. Swinburne's poem 'Erotion', an ekphrastic interpretative commentary on Solomon's painting *Damon and Aglae* (in *Poems and Ballads*), relishes the hermaphroditism of Damon – his lover Aglae talking of girls' fingers 'nestling through' his 'beautiful boy's curls / As mine did', and their lips meeting 'those curled lithe lips of thine', as hers did. In the painting, Damon's hair is more loosely abundant than hers, because not tied back; his lips are far more luscious. What's striking is how the androgyny of the male makes the poem and the painting move in the direction of sapphic lesbian love that's more explicit elsewhere in Swinburne (in 'Anactoria' for instance), but is still not sapphic. It was the edgy implicit bisexuality of the painting which Swinburne especially liked. The first eight lines of his poem were printed in the 1866 Royal Academy Exhibition catalogue's entry for *Damon and Aglae*. Swinburne's prose celebration of the painting and his discussion of 'Erotion' as a 'comment' on it, appeared in his July 1871 survey of Solomon's work, 'Simeon Solomon: Notes on his "Vision of Love" and other Studies' in the journal *The Dark Blue* (shades of JA Symonds!). This essay is very keen on Solomon's sadism, and especially aroused by the cruel face of the Rossetti-esque woman giving the thumbs down to a defeated gladiator in Solomon's painting *Habet!*: 'delicious thirst and subtle ravin of sensual hunger for blood visibly enkindled in every line of the sweet fierce features'; 'ravenous relish for fleshly torture'; 'cunning and cruel sensibility which catches fire from the stroke it deals, and drinks as its wine of life the blood of its sentient sacrifice'.[62]

A few months earlier, in April 1871, *The Dark Blue* published Swinburne's 'The End of a Month', yet one more of his watery poems about lovers parting 'At the sand's edge'. It was illustrated by 'S. Salaman', that is Solomon, featuring a pair of androgynous lovers whose only distinguishing feature is the longer, floating, hair of one of them.[63] The Solomon-Swinburne association was a meeting of proclivities, minds, desires, selves; but when the law caught up with Solomon Swinburne immediately dropped him. As did Dante Gabriel Rossetti. The galleries shunned him. The public ratting was like St Peter denying Christ ('I never knew him'). It anticipated the flight of London gay men heading for the Channel ports and France when Wilde was convicted. Some of Solomon's gay admirers, like Pater and Wilde, hung on to his pictures (Wilde's were sold at his bankruptcy sale, 1895). Lionel Johnson would paper his flat with Solomon reproductions. But public friends had he few; and poor, ill – hospitalized in 1880, 'not only ragged but actually without shoes', Dante Gabriel Rossetti reported to Janey Morris – drunk, his talent struggling, desperately flogging photographic reproductions of his work to make ends meet, he ended up in the St Giles workhouse where he died in 1905.

What panicked Solomon's public associates was, precisely, the publicity. Same-sex desires, having an illegal sexuality, being gender-doubtful, were most safely expressed by implication, in code, in coy metaphors, in distractingly lavish paintedness, through high-minded scholarly talk of Greek practices, behind a mask of Greek allusion and Sappho revivalism and the concealments of translation, in the diary and the unpublished memoir, and in privately printed texts. How noticeably the period's polemics in favour of pederasty, 'Greek' friendship between older men and youthful ones, tended to etherealize it, stressing this same-sex attraction's high aesthetic appeal, distancing it from low bodily vulgarity and the lure of illegalized buggery. Symonds could not in all honesty deny his well-known interest in sodomy – after all he was known, in Swinburne's words, as 'Mr Soddington Symonds'.[64] And he frankly admits that 'Greek love was tainted with a vice obnoxious to modern notions'. But, though 'strange and incomprehensible as this must always seem there were two brief moments, once at Athens, and once at Florence, when amorous enthusiasms of an abnormal type presented

[62]   *The Dark Blue*, I (July 1871), 568–577.

[63]   *The Dark Blue*, I (April 1871), 217–220. The poem was retitled 'At A Month's End' in the *Collected Works* but was otherwise almost unchanged. Details of Simeon's life and works, with many illustrations, are in Colin Cruse, *Love Revealed: Simeon Solomon and the Pre-Raphaelites* (Birmingham Museums and Art Gallery; Merrell, London and NY, 2005).

[64]   Letter to Theodore Watts, 1 September 1894, *Letters*, ed Cecil Y Lang (Yale University Press, New Haven and London, 1959–1962), Vol 6, *1890–1909*, 74.

themselves to natures of the noblest stamp as indispensable conditions of the progress of the soul upon the pathway toward perfection'. (That's in his essay on 'The Dantesque and Platonic Ideals of Love', defining 'Dorian comradeship', in *In the Key of Blue*, 81.) Pederasty on the Symonds plan would not be too physically scary, and would be very pleasant despite the illegality. A tone of aesthetic high-mindedness, of 'Platonic' relationships transcending the mere flesh, characterizes everything that Pater and the Paterians, Symonds, Wilde, wrote about admiration for lovely young male bodies – culminating in Wilde's very pained passage in his prison letter to Bosie *De Profundis* (1905) complaining of how his letter expressing the most beautiful of elevated Greek love for the youth got into the hands of blackmailers and was travestied and vulgarized in court.[65] Most of Michelangelo's sonnets are 'devoted to love and beauty', said Symonds, discussing his translations of them in *The Contemporary Review*:

> In relation to both he was a Platonist of the purest and most exalted type. As an artist, he admired the human form for the intellectual splendour it displayed. As a lover, he discoursed upon the soul of his beloved, and praised the body only as the prison-house of a divine idea. ... The elevation of Michael Angelo's conception of love is so unmistakeable in his poems that we do not need the emphatic testimony of both Condivi [Michelangelo's biographer] and Vasari [the art historian] to the fact that neither in word or deed was he ever known to have departed from the strictest purity.[66]

In Pater's persistent campaign for a revolutionary revival of a non-puritan Greekist and Renaissance aesthetic of the male body and of gay male admiration, affection and desire, the wish for a missionary clarity runs up repeatedly against an opaqueness, caginess, hintfulness obviously invested in for fear of public – and Oxford University – opinion, as well as, ultimately, fear

---

[65] 'I compare you to Hylas, or Hyacinth, Jonquil or Narcisse, or someone whom the great god of Poetry favoured and honoured with his love. The letter is like a passage from one of Shakespeare's sonnets .... It can only be understood by those who have read the Symposium of Plato, or caught the spirit of a certain grave mood made beautiful for us in Greek marbles. Look at the history of that letter ... into the hands of a loathsome companion ... to a gang of blackmailers ... forms the basis of your father's worst attack ... denounced by your father's Counsel as a revolting and insidious attempt to corrupt Innocence ... forms part of a criminal charge .... The judge sums up on it with little learning and much morality: I go to prison for it at last'. *De Profundis* (1905; 1949): *Complete Works of Oscar Wilde*, Intro Vyvyan Holland (New Edition, Collins, London, 1966), 889–990. The letter features in Ch 7 in my discussion of gay/androgynous writing's interest in Hyacinthus. For the jeering, leering use of the letter in the Wilde trial, see the transcripts in *Irish Peacock & Scarlet Marquess, The Real Trial of Oscar Wilde*, ed Merlin Holland (Fourth Estate, London and NY, 2003).

[66] JA Symonds, 'Twenty-Three Sonnets for Michael Angelo', *The Contemporary Review*, XX (September 1872), 509.

of the law.[67] This is especially true of Pater's major pieces gathered into *The Renaissance: Studies in Art and Poetry*. His dealings with Michelangelo's sonnets to Tommaso Cavalieri characteristically mix plainness and fluffiness. 'The Poetry of Michelangelo' chapter (originally in *The Fortnightly Review* (November 1871) under Pater's name) hints at the unconventional homosexual passions of so many of Michelangelo's poems:

> Beneath the Platonic calm of the sonnets there is latent a deep delight in carnal form and colour. There, and still more in the madrigals, he often falls into the language of less tranquil affections; while some of them have the colour of penitence, as from a wanderer returning home. He who spoke so decisively of the supremacy in the imaginative world of the unveiled human form had not been always, we may think, a mere Platonic lover. Vague and wayward his loves may have been; but they partook of the strength of his nature ....

Pater plays down the role of the woman Vittoria Colonna in Michelangelo's life and literature. Michelangelo's editors, his great-nephew in 1623, and Cesare Guasti in 1863, had tried to make her the main, characteristic, and of course female object of Michelangelo's verses. But Pater presents her and the aged Michelangelo, nearly seventy, spending time discussing art and the Pauline epistles, 'already following the ways and tasting the sunless pleasures of weary people'. That was not the main direction of Michelangelo's desire. In the first (1873) volume version of the essay Pater adds a footnote, noting that *The Contemporary Review* of September 1872 had published translations of 'Twenty-three Sonnets from Michelangelo, 'executed with great taste and skill' from Guasti's text. He copies out three of them, giving them his own titles, one 'To Night', one 'To Vittoria Colonna', and also one 'To Tommaso Cavalieri':

> Why should I seek to ease intense desire
> With still more tears and windy words of grief,
> When heaven, or late or soon, sends no relief
> To souls whom love hath robed around with fire?
> Why needs my aching heart to death aspire,
> When all must die? Nay death beyond belief
> Unto those eyes would be both sweet and brief,
> Since in my sum of woes all joys expire!
> Therefore because I cannot shun the blow
> I rather seek, say who must rule my breast,
> Gliding between her gladness and her woe?

---

[67]   The story of English gay Greekism in its especially Oxonian dimensions is well told by Linda C Dowling, *Hellenism and Homosexuality in Victorian Oxford* (Cornell University Press, Ithaca and London, 1994).

If only chains and bonds can make me blest,
No marvel if alone and bare I go
An armèd knight's captive and slave confessed.[68]

Which is plain enough; but only up to a point. Hedging slightly, Pater omits the name of the translator, already the more openly same-sex crusader, JA Symonds ('To Tommaso Cavalieri' is Sonnet XXXI in Symonds' 1878 volume of Michelangelo and Campanella translations). Symonds had (a bit embarrassingly for Pater?) offered his *Contemporary Review* translations as a 'supplement' to Pater's *Fortnightly Review* essay that, he'd said, 'reveals the purest and most delicate sympathy with the poet's mind'. Pater can't be accused, though, of hedging over the last line of the 'To Cavalieri' sonnet, with its lower-case *knight*. In the book of Michelangelo translations Symonds underlines the pun on Cavaliero's name and so the maleness of Michelangelo's subject by capitalizing *Knight*. The word should have 'a large K', Symonds pointed out to his friend Horatio Brown, 'since Michael Angelo designed a pun upon the young man's name'. But in the *Contemporary Review* version Pater is quoting from there's only a lower-case *k*.

But still Cavalieri had been named and, of course, Pater concluded his 1873 volume with those ecstatic paragraphs from his (anonymous) 1868 William Morris piece in the *Westminster Review* linking aesthetic uplift with excitement over lovely young male friends: 'some form ... perfect in hand or face ... burn with this hard gem-like flame ... ecstasy ... all melts ... exquisite passion ... spirit free for a moment ...stirrings of the senses ... curious odours ... the face of one's friend'. So it was for him frighteningly bad luck that *The Renaissance* came out, 15 February 1873, only four days after the Solomon arrest. Willy-nilly he'd got himself caught up in the quickly mounting reaction against Solomon and aestheticized gay sexuality. The irrepressible Solomon was arrested in a public lavatory in Paris, 3 March 1874, and jailed for three months in France. In 1874 love letters between Solomon and WH Hardinge, the 'Balliol Bugger', were passed to Benjamin Jowett, the Platonizing Master of Balliol; Hardinge was rusticated (i.e. sent away from Oxford for a time); Pater was called in to answer for the bad influence of his writings and friendships. (Wilde read *The Renaissance*, already a cult book, in his first term at Oxford, autumn 1874: 'that book which has had such a strange influence over my life', he says, ruefully, in *De Profundis*.) In 1875, in the same wave of reaction, Oscar Browning – Pater's friend and Solomon's one-time lover – was dismissed from Eton for going too far with the boys in his charge. Pater, his hopes of high public office at Oxford – Proctor,

---

[68]   Quoted in the Textual Notes to Walter Pater, *The Renaissance: Studies in Art and Poetry. The 1893 Text*, ed Donald L Hill (University of California Press, Berkeley, LA, London, 1980), 225–226.

Professor of Poetry – dashed, needed some damage limitation and sought it in the savage amendments to the second edition of *The Renaissance* (May 1877): the dropping of the hard gem-like 'Conclusion' and the Michelangelo sonnets. The sonnets never returned; their residue is a mere footnote in the 1888 third edition (after the Solomon fuss had died down) informing that they'd been 'translated in English, with much skill, and poetic taste by Mr J.A. Symonds'. The Conclusion reappeared in the third edition with the half-apologetic explanation that it had been earlier omitted 'as I conceived it might possibly mislead some of those young men into whose hands it might fall' and with an advertisement for his novel *Marius the Epicurean* (1885), in which 'I have dealt more fully' with 'the thoughts suggested by' the Conclusion.[69] *Marius* is a plangent, soft fiction about high-minded male-Greek friendship existing in a welter of pre-Christian aestheticized stoicism. Dreamy Victorian Platonism at its soggy worst.

Pater's coynesses, panics, self-qualifyings were symptomatic, and probably well-advised.[70] This was indeed a time for caution, of writing for initiates, chums, those in the know, who could read between the lines. The textual equivalent of going abroad for gay sex. Like the poems of William Johnson, Eton Classics master, drooler over beautiful pupils such as Digby Mackworth Dolben, whose *Ionica* volumes (1868–1897), with their yearning Greekist pastoral lines about the likings of and for 'Dorian' shepherds, became cult-books carried lovingly around the Empire by Old Etonians and other pederastically inclined subalterns. (Sacked in 1872 for overstepping even Eton's loose sexual bounds Johnson changed his name to Cory and retreated abroad; got married; ended up as a private Classics tutor to ladies in Hampstead.) Johnson changed his name; more common was changing, or otherwise blurring, the pronouns.

[69]   Walter Pater, *The Renaissance: Studies in Art and Poetry, The 1893 Text*, ed Donald L Hill (University of California Press, Berkeley, Los Angeles and London, 1980) – with full textual history and variants. JA Symonds, 'Twenty-Three Sonnets from Michael Angelo', *The Contemporary Review*, XX (September 1872), 505–515. JA Symonds, *The Sonnets of Michael Angelo and Tommaso Campanella, Now For The First Time Translated into Rhymed English* (Smith, Elder, & Co., London, 1878). Horatio F Brown, ed, *Letters and Papers of John Addington Symonds* (John Murray, London, 1923) 53 (JAS to Horatio Brown, 3 March 1873).

[70]   At his trial Wilde admitted he had, on the advice of Pater, omitted from the book version of *Dorian Gray* a passage 'liable to misconstruction' – in all likelihood the discussion between Basil Hallward and Dorian suggestive of gay male sex that was read out by the prosecuting counsel. This was in the first *Lippincott's Monthly Magazine* version (July 1890) which caused huge public outcry, prompting WH Smith's to withdraw the 'filthy' magazine from its bookstalls. For his part, Pater would not review the unpurged *Lippincott's* version, as being 'too dangerous', but was happy to review the slightly revised (Wilde refused to accept 'purged' in court) 1890 book version in the *Bookman* (November 1891). See *Irish Peacock & Scarlett Marquess: The Real Trial of Oscar Wilde* (2003), passim.

Blurring The Pronouns

It was simply perverse of Swinburne in his *Dark Blue* piece to complain about the incoherences of Solomon's rhapsodic prose narrative *A Vision of Love Revealed in Sleep* (1871: privately printed, but distributed by Dante Gabriel Rossetti's publisher SF Ellis) – sometimes referred to as his 'prose poem' – and about what you come to realize, with the aid of its frontispiece's depiction of two males gazing absorbedly at each other, is a vision of beatific same-sex sex. For Swinburne well knew that the 'atmosphere of such work' had to be 'Dim and vague'. That was the convention, Swinburne's own convention, the evasive gender-blurring convention of all the dippers in the deep blue of unconventional and illegal desire. Swinburne presumably recognized, in Solomon's kept-up refusal of specificity about the *I* meditating on lovely male forms, his own obscuration techniques.

> Should love disown or disesteem you
> For loving one man more or less?

But who is *you*? A man? A woman? And who is the poem's *I*? Male? Female?

> Across, aslant, a scudding sea-mew
> Swam, dipped, and dropped and grazed the sea:
> And one with me I could not dream you;
> And one with you I could not be.

We're in Swinburne's 'The End of a Month', in *The Dark Blue*, the pronouns, for personal and legal safety's sake, tantalizing us with the androgyne possibilities of Solomon's illustration, but refusing even to affirm that. And so it goes across a whole swathe of such writing. Who, for example, are 'We' in 'We Two', one of the many poems of love and loss, by George Cecil Ives, in his volumes *Eros's Throne* (1890) and (the anonymous) *Book of Chains* (1896)? Hard to tell, except by his gay friends, Edward Carpenter, Wilde, and Symonds. Although he was a public crusader for the legalizing of homosexuality, he was not going to let on by indulging in genderizing pronouns.[71] Who speaks as *I* in Michael Field's poems? The femaleness that you'd assume from knowing the gender of their authors is inevitably occluded in the claim that the poems are by one 'Michael Field'. Even the couple's apparently sapphic poems, with epigraphs addressed from Sappho

---

[71]   This advocate of night-time public-parks retreats for male sexual encounters, *spoonitaria* as he called them, was not at all keen to go Wilde's punished way – the anonymity of the *Book of Chains* has no doubt something to do with the Wilde trials. Ives is rather a star in Matt Cook's *London and the Culture of Homosexuality* (2003).

herself to women, have their pronouncements blockaded by the alleged male presence of M Field. 'I love to see thee in thy grace, / Dark, virulent, divine': the addressee of 'Come Gorgo, put the rug in place' (in the Bradley/Cooper volume *Long Ago*, 1889) is explicitly the 'foolish woman' of the poems' untranslated Greek epigraph from Sappho, but even within this frame that *I* is gender-opaque.

Such poems rely on the *intrinsic* tendency of pronouns to referential obscurity. As Hopkins does in his sonnet 'I wake and feel the fell of dark', where the night-time cries of an agonized *I* ('I am gall, I am heartburn') are 'like dead letters sent / To dearest him that lives alas! away', and it's impossible to decide whether *him* refers to God or to some absent male object of desire filling Hopkins's masturbatory ('sweating') thoughts ('I see / The lost are like this, and their scourge to be / As I am mine, their sweating selves; but worse').[72] Symonds assiduously cultivated this handy pronominal opacity in his double sonnet 'A Dream':

> I yearn for you, my dearest; for you came
> In visions of the night and stood by me:
> I took your hand, and set you on my knee,
> And stroked your hair, and drank the sunny flame
> Of your large eyes: I kissed your cool moist lips,
> And laid your cheek to mine, and asked you why
> You stayed so long away; for lovers die
> In one short week of waiting, tears eclipse
> The moonlight of their eyes, where hope hath lit
> Radiance reflected from the brows they love:
> And then you laughed, and playful seemed to prove
> Whether or no I loved you, frowned and knit
> Brows all unused to anger, smiled again,
> And nestled to my side and breathed away my pain.
>
> *(New and Old*, 1880)

Occasionally in Symonds's *oeuvre* the poem is openly about a *him*, as in the double sonnet 'Vintage', where

> I found him lying neath the vines that ran
> Grape-laden o'er grey frames of oak and beech;
> A fair and jocund Faun, whose beard began,
> Like dewy down on quince or blushing peach,
> To soften chin and cheek. He bade me reach
> My hand to his, and drew me through the screen
> Of clusters intertwined with glistening green.
> Sunrise athwart us fell – a living fire,

---

[72]   I'm grateful to my colleague Helen Moore for pointing out that *fell* meant *gall*.

That touching turned our tendrilled roof to red;
Network of shade from many a flickering spire
And solid orb upon the youth was shed;
With purple grapes and white his comely head
Was crowned, and in his a hand a bunch he pressed
Against the golden glory of his breast.

(New and Old, 1880)

But the homoerotic frankness here relies on the conventional reader assuming that the adored 'Faun' is indeed an ancient Greek pastoral deity and not a metaphor for a lovely adolescent with embryonic downy beard just appearing on a cheek that's like a quince or peach. Otherwise Symonds relies on letting the conventional assumption reign that the *you* of a love poem by a male poet or one with a male name or written in the person of a male character will be female. To keep the conventional, the puritan, the prurient, and maybe also the legalists guessing about him and his objects of desire, Symonds will even sprinkle some female pronouns around – as in the sonnets 'Renunciation' I and II (in *Vagabunduli Libellus*):

I woke; the present seemed more sad than hell;
On daily tasks my sullen soul I cast;
But, as I waked, a deeper sorrow fell
Like thunder on my spirit; for she past
Before the house with wondering wide blue eye
That said, 'I wait! why will you not reply?'

In the diary version of the poem (and the event it describes) *she* is *he*: he being the choirboy Alfred Brooke (Grosskurth, *Memoirs*, p124). The published poem is lying.

In a large sense, of course, the gender opacity of the pronouns in poems by Swinburne and Hopkins, Michael Field and Symonds, does not matter. Desire, whether homosexual, heterosexual, or bisexual – and for that matter desire constrained and shaped by the forces of class and economics and race and the historical moment – is desire; love is love; a lover a lover; a beloved a beloved; a love poem a love poem. (The literary evidence from around the world and across history indicates something like the 'unchanging human heart' so jeered at by some critics, for all the obvious *differentiae* affected by varieties of language and ideology and assumptions about what's natural and unnatural.) The similarities of the emotions and the rhetorics in play are too close for fundamental differentiation. And poems refusing gender specificity may well be making such a point – firing a polemical shot in the longstanding quarrel about the orthodoxy and legitimacy of same-sex desire (the polemical point of Jeanette Winterson's pronoun-blurring novel *Written on the Body*, (1992), and the point, I take it, of Wayne Koestenbaum's suggestion about the lyrical 'field' of Michael Field, that this poet, in his/her/their evasions of gender specificity, 'frees the love lyric, long a genre of possession, into an ownerless, borderless "field" '[73]). But in another important sense this form of identity obscuration does matter – because covertness, however induced, by whatever understandable pressures, political, social, ideological or merely privately personal, is bad for literature. It allows the untrue, the unreal, to pass as the true and the real. Nothing is more hostile than truth-evasion to poetry's conduct of the autobiography, confession, testimony. witness-bearing and – even – historiography that poems are good at going in for; and going in for which helps make poems good. Covertness, euphemism, half-truth cut poetry off at the root, ream out its core, betray its purposes. As JA Symonds himself recognizes when he berates Michelangelo's great-nephew for amending the masculine pronouns (and otherwise obscuring the male target) of the sonnets addressed to Tommaso Cavalieri in his 1623 edition, and challenges Cesare Guasti, editor of the first modern edition (1863), to take the sonnets literally as 'an expression of the artist's homage for the worth and beauty of an excellent young man'. The poems were 'mutilated' in 1623 in a 'garbling process' that renders them 'unintelligible'. Michelangelo is dishonoured by these obscurantist tricks. And Symonds is right; garbling is never good for poetry, for any writing, whether the garblers are readers, critics, editors, or writers themselves.[74]

[73] Wayne Koestenbaum, *Double Talk: The Erotics of Male Literary Collaboration* (Routledge,London, 1989), 174. Quoted by Yoppie Prins, *Victorian Sappho*, 95, as the lead-in to her wrestle with the claims of specific lesbian identity in Michael Field's Sapphic writing and rewriting, a struggle involving conflict with Angela Leighton's and Margaret Reynolds's sympathy for a specific lesbian voice and poetry, not least of 'Michael Field'. Prins, op cit, Ch2, 'Sappho Doubled: Michael Feld', 74–111, versus Angela Leighton in *Victorian Women Poets: Writing Against the Heart* (Blackwell, Oxford, 1995) and Margaret Reynolds, ' "I lived for Art, I lived for Love": The Woman Poet Sings Sappho's Last Song', in Angela Leighton, ed, *Victorian Women Poets: An Anthology* (Blackwell, Oxford, 1996), 277–306.

[74] JA Symonds, *Renaissance in Italy*, Vol 3, *The Fine Arts* (Smith, Elder, & Co.,1877), Appendix II, 'Michael Angelo's Sonnets', 517–522. Symonds' 1872 *Contemporary Review* translations and comments, and his 1878 edition of Michelangelo's sonnets set the textual record straight. See also Symonds, *The Life of Michelangelo Buonarroti, Based on Studies in the Archives of the Buonarroti Family at Florence*, 2 vols (2nd edn, John C Nimmo, 1893), II, 147–179, for his account of Michelangelo's relations with men and the poems about them. The story of Michelangelo's Victorian reception is quite carefully set out in Lene Ostermark-Johansen, *Sweetness and Strength: The Reception of Michelangelo in Victorian England* (Ashgate, Aldershot, 1998).

7

Fleshly Feelings

The story of the poetic self in the last chapter turned inevitably into a story of the poetic body. And how could it not? Self and body: it's the large conjunction which helps make bodies, the flesh, so central a Victorian subject. Bodies are ubiquitous in Victorian poems. 'The fleshly feeling is everywhere', declared 'Thomas Maitland', aka Robert William Buchanan, minor poet and devoted Browning imitator, of Dante Gabriel Rossetti's poems in his intemperate 1871 attack on what he called 'The Fleshly School of Poetry'.[1] And he was right. He was aiming in the first place at Swinburne as well as at Rossetti, but he intended the charge to stick more widely, and it does.

The attack got him into very bad odour – 'Foetid Buchanan', Ezra Pound called him in his poem 'Hugh Selwyn Mauberley'. Swinburne was extremely rude about him, again and again, especially after the Maitland mask was torn off. Buchanan was well-known to both Rossetti and Swinburne as an enemy. Nothing, wrote Swinburne, cursing Rabelaisianly, could 'adequately prepare the human nose' for the stink coming from the shit-house where such 'turdilousifartishitical buggeraminous ballockwaggers' as Buchanan prepared their attacks.[2] Rossetti let off one of his rude limericks:

---

[1] 'Thomas Maitland', 'The Fleshly School of Poetry: Mr DG Rossetti', *The Contemporary Review*, XVIII (October 1871), 334–350, reviewing Rossetti's *Poems*, 5th edn. Reissued as a pamphlet.

[2] In response to Buchanan's review of William Michael Rossetti's edition of Shelley, in the *Athenaeum* (Jan 29 1870): letter of Swinburne to Dante Gabriel Rossetti, Feb 12 1870, *Letters of Algernon Charles Swinburne*, ed CY Lang, II (Yale University Press, New Haven, and Oxford University Press, London, 1959), 89. Earlier Rossetti had referred to 'the obscene organ' of Buchanan's speech, i.e. his anus, 'when it is hitched up for an utterance': *Letters of DGR*, eds Doughty and Wahl, II (Clarendon Press, Oxford, 1965), 793.

Victorian Poetry Now: Poets, Poems, Poetics, First Edition. Valentine Cunningham.
© 2011 Valentine Cunningham. Published 2011 by Blackwell Publishing Ltd.

As a critic, the Poet Buchanan
Thinks Pseudo much safer than Anon.
Into Maitland he shrunk,
But the smell of the skunk
Guides the shuddering nose to Buchanan.[3]

An outspoken riposte by Swinburne in the *Examiner* (28 December 1871), 'The Devil's Due', cost him £5 in libel damages. Buchanan later recanted. 'Mr Rossetti, I freely admit now, never was a fleshly poet at all; never, at any rate, fed upon the poisonous honey of French art;' 'how false a judgement ... how conventional, and Pharisaic a criticism, which chose to dub as "fleshly" the works of this most ethereal and dreamy – in many respects this least carnal and most religious – of modern poets'.[4] Buchanan certainly overdid the abuse and the jeering; was wrong to dismiss Rossetti (and Swinburne) as the period's utterly second-rate ones, mere 'walking gentlemen' of the stage, Rosencrantz and Guildenstern to Tennyson and Browning, the stars who play Hamlet 'on alternate nights'; and he was indeed being pharisaical, or puritanical, in his dislike of these poets' body interests. But he had been correct about the prevalent fleshliness of the poetry (and of the painting of the Pre-Raphaelite school to which Rossetti – and Simeon Solomon, named twice in the attack – belonged); correct, too, about fleshliness as a prevailing Victorian phenomenon. It's only apt that Tennyson, Browning, and Morris should make pointed appearances in the wings of Buchanan's assaulting main stage.

At every turn of his piece Buchanan illustrates the most telling analysis of the Victorian discourse of the body, namely Part One of the first volume of Michel Foucault's *History of Sexuality* (1978: English version of *La volonté de savoir*, 1976), 'We "Other Victorians"'. Foucault was revising Steven Marcus's influential picture. Marcus called his classic 1969 study of Victorian sexuality and pornography *The Other Victorians*, to denote the marginality of Victorian sex writing: an unofficial, fringe affair, not central to the being, selfhood, imagination, and writings of the repressed, prudish, puritanical majority – familial, schoolmasterly, preacherly – which averted its gaze, its interests and its pens. Foucault turned the (once conventional) Marcus model upside down. By contrast, he argued, the Victorians were as preoccupied with sex as 'we' are. 'We' are all 'other Victorians', and so were the Victorians. The Foucauldian argument is that sex, and the sexualized body, were simply ubiquitous in Victorian times, especially in art and literature.

---

[3]   In the 'Juvenilia and Grotesques' section of *The Works*, edited by William M Rossetti (revised edn 1911), 275; in the 'Uncollected Writings' section of DGR, *Collected Poetry and Prose*, ed Jerome McGann (Yale University Press, New Haven and London, 2003), 375.
[4]   Letter to the *Academy* (1 July 1882) ; 'A Note on Dante Rossetti', in *A Look Around Literature* (1887).

Sex was busily transformed into 'discourse', that is texts of all kinds, analytical, documentary, narrative, fictional, pictorial, poetic. Sex became (in a wonderfully apt Victorian metaphor) a kind of *railway junction* of Victorian discourses: medical, sociological, psychiatric, economic, and of course moral and aesthetic. Foucault highlighted four effects, or discursive characterizations, of Victorian sexuality: the hysterical woman (the female body, 'saturated with (pathological) sexuality'); the masturbating child (focus of the institutionalized war, at home, at school, against the perpetual lure of unnatural and perverse onanism); the Malthusian couple (male-female couples, or married partners, seen as a battleground of Malthusian anxiety about family size – whether to procreate, hugely, minimally, or not at all, in the name of social preservation); the perverse adult (grown-up sexuality defined by the rising schools of psychiatry as key to the normalization or pathologization, of the individual, the self). Foucault's categorizings are rather French-polished – dominated by his knowledge of modern psychiatry's roots in the work on 'hysteria' and with 'hysterical' females at the hands of the great French neurologist Jean-Martin Charcot (Freud's inspirer) at the Salpêtrière hospital in Paris. And it's hard to believe that Malthusian arguments about the dangers of over-population were a main preoccupation of Victorian married couples. But Foucault's large allegation holds good, namely that Victorian growing up, being, identity, action, social function were all considered in contemporary discussion as matters of bodiliness, of the sexualized body, and strong body perturbation at that. Women, children, married couples, or adults seeking self-definition: all perceived, and textualized, in their sexual, that is bodily, dimensions, and all construed, at least potentially, as in some way somatically transgressive – dubious, sinful, pathological, perverse, both individually and socially. And defined thus, loudly, publicly. With the discourse of sexuality, of bodiliness, as a universal one, and, of course – perhaps Foucault's canniest observation – shared even, or especially, by repressive, censoring, policing persons, discussions, efforts.

It was indeed easy for Buchanan to hit on the flesh – and troubled, troubling fleshliness – in contemporary poetry and its pictorial cognates, for there was so much of it. He singles out Tennyson's 'Vivien' (as the 'Merlin and Vivien' section of *The Idylls of the King* was titled when it first appeared in 1859). In it, Tennyson 'has concentrated all the epicene force which, wearisomely expanded, constitutes the characteristic' of Dante Gabriel Rossetti and Swinburne. 'The fleshliness of "Vivien" may indeed be described as the distinct quality which becomes unwholesome when there is no moral or intellectual quality to temper or control it.' Buchanan doesn't say whether he thinks Tennyson escapes the unwholesomeness of his successors; and it would be hard indeed to greatly differentiate Vivien's enticing Merlin-undoing sexiness – lissom limbed, writhing and sliding on Merlin's lap, clinging to him, hugging him ('hugged him close ... hugged him close' (943, 946)), a Victorian lapdancer in a body-revealing frock: 'a robe / Of samite without price, that more exprest / Than hid her clung about her lissome limbs' (219–221) – from any of Rossetti's satanically lovely females, his Liliths and Prosperpines, or even from Swinburne's demonic female lovers, his ladies of pain.

What's going on in what is for Buchanan a most provocative reduction of human relationships to their merely bodily aspects is a worrying dualism of the self, which divides the person into body and soul and prefers the body. '[T]he fleshly gentlemen have bound themselves by solemn league and covenant to extol fleshliness as the distinct and supreme end of poetic and pictorial art; to aver ... by inference that the body is greater than the soul ... and that the poet, properly to develop his poetic faculty, must be an intellectual hermaphrodite ... .' Buchanan is not clear what particular distinction '*intellectual* hermaphrodite' is making, but he'd managed to work in the word hermaphrodite, in a calculated swipe at the body-perplexed, hermaphrodite-obsessed Swinburne.

Swinburne's particular fleshliness gets very condescendingly dismissed as juvenile, and so *Poems and Ballads* falls short of Rossetti's brand for 'thorough nastiness':

> Mr Swinburne was wilder [than Rossetti], more outrageous, more blasphemous, and his subjects more atrocious in themselves; yet the hysterical tone slew the animalism, the furiousness of epithet lowered the sensation; and the first feeling of disgust at such themes as 'Laus Veneris' and 'Anactoria', faded away into comic amazement. It was only a little mad boy letting off squibs; not a great strong man, who might be really dangerous to society. 'I will be naughty!' screamed the little boy; but after all, what did it matter?

Grown-up Rossetti, though, a man actually experienced in adult sex, is a different matter when he shamelessly 'chronicles his amorous sensations'. And there are lots of these for Buchanan to identify. He picks out the sensationally sexy lines from 'A Last Confession', Rossetti's ostentatiously Browning-tribute dramatic monologue, confession to a priest by an Italian Nationalist of how he stabbed his onetime mistress to death when she spurned him with a laugh which reminded him of a prostitute he heard laughing three hours earlier (512–519):

> A woman laughed above me. I looked up
> And saw where a brown-shouldered harlot leaned
> Half through a tavern window thick with vine.
> Some man had come behind her in the room
> And caught her by her arms, and she had turned
> With that coarse empty laugh on him, as now
> *He munched her neck with kisses, while the vine*
> *Crawled in her back.*

Sexual frankness; naked prostitute, her body alluringly half-revealed, explicitly *brown*-shouldered; woman as edible flesh, her neck *munched* with kisses by her customer, with the troilistic participation of the vine's tendrils (tendrils affirmed by Rossetti's favourite Milton in *Paradise Lost* Book IV as a sexy analogue of a woman's, i.e. Eve's, 'wanton ringlets'). The vine *crawled* over the woman's naked back: so nature is made complicit in transgressive sex, an analogue of human lustfulness, as the oldest of rhetorical tricks, prosopopoeia, or the pathetic fallacy, works the new Pre-Raphaelite ticket. Rossetti is endorsing transgressive sex as natural, and making the poem's celebration of it sound natural too. Which upsets Buchanan so much that he italicizes the two munching lines: for him, men munching prostitutes' necks won't do, and neither will poems that have men behaving according to fallen nature and crawling all over women's bodies.

Other offending bits of Rossetti get their italics too. The last line of Sonnet XLIX, 'Willow wood I', for instance, from Rossetti's life's-work sonnet sequence *The House of Life* (first edition 1870), in which Cupid's lips, reflected in water in a well, turn into the narrator's beloved's lips and, rippling, meet his as he stoops to sip them: they 'Bubbled with brimming kisses at my mouth'. And sexually avaricious Lilith's prayer ('Eden Bower', 187–188) to the 'God-snake of Eden!' to embrace and tongue her body: '*Grip* and *lip* my limbs as I tell thee!' Buchanan also quotes a couple of lines from 'Jenny', Rossetti's dramatic monologue addressed by a rather shame-faced customer to the lovely disarrayed body of the sleeping whore he uses for the usual blood-money, in which the john reflects on how knowing children have observed her in the Haymarket, the notorious London street for soliciting, on a Saturday night, 'market-night': 'Have seen your lifted silken skirt / Advertise dainties through the dirt' (146-7). *Dainties*: that wonderful Keats word for a beloved's kissable breasts, 'Those dainties made to still an infant's cries', in his 'Bright Star' sonnet, which Rossetti seems to be thinking of as his narrator gazes at Jenny's body in her unlaced silk clothing in some of the poem's most extraordinarily loving, tender lines: 'And warm sweets open to the waist / All golden to the lamplight's gleam' (49–50). This time there were no Buchanan italics: as if the awfulness, for him, of a poetic display of desirable female ankles – even if in aid of a moral-satirical advertisement of the fleshly truth about Christian England, bourgeois Christian men's hypocritical purchasing of sex from downtrodden women in the fleshpots of London's Haymarket – goes without saying. Not so, though, the sonnet 'Nuptial Sleep', main attraction in this hostile display of Rossetti's erotic bodiliness: it's quoted in full with all of its first part, the octet, italicized:

> *At length their long kiss severed, with sweet smart:*
> *And as the last slow sudden drops are shed*
> *From sparkling eaves when all the storm has fled,*

> *So singly flagged the pulses of each heart.*
> *Their bosoms sundered, with the opening start*
> *Of married flowers to either side outspread*
> *From the knit stem; yet still their mouths, burnt red,*
> *Fawned on each other where they lay apart.*

> Sleep sank them lower than the tide of dreams,
> And their dreams watched them sink, and slid away.
> Slowly their souls swam up again, through gleams
> Of watered light and dull drowned waifs of day;
> Till from some wonder of new woods and streams
> He woke, and wondered more: for there she lay.

Here is a full-grown man, presumably intelligent and cultivated, putting on record for other full-grown men to read, the most secret mysteries of sexual connection, and that with so sickening a desire to reproduce the sensual mood, so careful a choice of epithet to convey mere animal sensations, that we merely shudder at the shameless nakedness. We are no purists in such matters. We hold the sensual part of our nature to be as holy as the spiritual or intellectual part, and we believe that such things must find their equivalent in all; but it is neither poetic, nor manly, nor even human, to obtrude such things as the themes of whole poems. It is simply nasty.

Buchanan was right to guess *careful* work on the poem's words – and canny indeed at spotting Rossetti's most considered work: 'A Last Confession', 'Eden Bower', 'Jenny', the sonnets of *The House of Life*, were high among the poems Rossetti 'would wish to be known by'. Buchanan would have been, perhaps, shocked at the extent of the work that went into arriving at the sonnet's final result (as reported in my Chapter 1, 'Words, Words, Words and More Words'), the rich range of bodily possibilities at Rossetti's erotically versatile disposal – *chirped at, kissed at, moaned to* – before 'Fawned on each other' was arrived at. He would also have been surprised, I guess, to learn (as also reported in Chapter 1) that the sonnet's original title 'Placatâ Venere', implying any sort of sexual relation, had been replaced by 'Nuptial Sleep' with its more respectable and less offending suggestion of married lovers, and that Dante Gabriel and his brother William had worried about whether the poem was too intimate to appear in public print at all. (And, in fact, Rossetti took Buchanan's point about public unfitness by dropping 'Nuptial Sleep' from the 1881 reprint of *The House of Life*.)

Very revealing is Buchanan's vexed concession that there are two opposed Victorian publics, two audiences, two readerships, two 'kinds' of English Society, one tastefully averse to seeing, smelling, touching, knowing the body, the other, 'the coarse public', before which Mr Rossetti satisfyingly 'parades his private sensations'. This latter is the section of society that 'goes into ecstasy over Mr Solomon's pictures' (two years this, before Simeon Solomon's trial for soliciting for gay sex in London lavatories) – 'pretty pieces of morality, such as "Love dying by the breath of Lust" '. (That's a lost picture by Solomon, known only in a photographic print of a lost drawing by Frederick Hollyer based on the Solomon – showing AMOR, a naked, swooning, pubescent youth being ardently embraced by a classically androgynous-faced, flowing robe, flowing hair, Rossetti-Burne-Jones-Solomon type, LIBIDO.[5]) Even more revelatory is Buchanan's own manifest zest for what, speaking in the name of the body-averse readership, he deplores. His appalled glossings – *sexual connection, sensual mood, animal sensations, shameless nakedness* – denote enthusiasm rather than deprecation. The bubbling heat of his shocked catalogues of the bodily ways of the poets and the women of their poems matches – outdoes even – anything in his deplored texts for sweaty hecticness. Passages like the ones from 'A Last Confession' and the rest inspire 'wonder', Buchanan says,

> at the kind of women whom it seems the unhappy lot of these gentlemen to encounter. We have lived as long in the world as they have, but never yet came across persons of the other sex who conduct themselves in the manner described. Females who bite, scratch, scream, bubble, munch, sweat, writhe, twist, wriggle, foam, and in a general way slaver over their lovers, must surely possess some extraordinary qualities to counteract their otherwise most offensive mode of conducting themselves. It appears, however, on examination, that their poet-lovers conduct themselves in a similar manner. They, too, bite, scratch, scream, bubble, munch, sweat, writhe, twist, wriggle, foam and slaver in a style frightful to hear of.

But if the poets' style is frightful, Buchanan's repeating lists co-opt that frightfulness. 'We get very weary', he says, 'of this protracted hankering after a person of the other sex; it seems meat, drink, thought, sinew, religion for the fleshly school. There is no limit to the fleshliness ...'. But the hankering and unlimitedness are Buchanan's too. They illustrate very well Foucault's point about censoring voices sharing in and greatly supplementing the large Victorian discourse of sexuality; and amply imply the greatly shared interests of both of the 'kinds' of readership Buchanan adduces. Neither kind, it would seem, is not utterly fascinated by the period's fleshliness without end.

---

[5] No 98 in *Love Revealed: Simeon Solomon and the Pre-Raphaelites* (Birmingham Museums and Art Gallery, & Merrell, London and NY, 2005), 144 – with the misinforming note that Robert Buchanan suggested the picture was exhibited at the Dulwich Gallery. He did not. Though, obviously, Buchanan must have seen the painting somewhere.

Bodily Sign Language

The body magnetizes writing because, as the sociologist Anthony Beavis would so magnificently put it in Chapter XI of Aldous Huxley's ultra-body-conscious novel *Eyeless in Gaza* (1936), it is 'indubitably there'. It has, as we would say now, material presence, the presence of materiality.[6] Beavis is at that point meditating on the consequences of modern metaphysical doubt, the disappearance of the old Christian faith that sustained 'knowledge' of God and of the human soul and spirit. Only by faith can these be known, because they can't actually be seen, smelled, touched, let alone presented on stage, displayed for an audience, a reader. So in modern sceptical times – the sceptical era arriving with force for Victorians – their physical non-presence pronounces them unknowable and in effect denotes their non-existence. They go missing, beyond human grasp and grip; but they leave the body behind – undeniably visible, smellable, touchable – as a sure ground of knowledge about the human. The only ground for science, old and new, as far as the sceptic is concerned; and a main ground even for Christians trying to hang on to the old metaphysical confidences. So for Victorians the body settles in, unsettlingly of course, as the ultimate sign – ultimate signifier, ultimate signified – displacing spirit and soul as reliable referents, and of course displacing God as the ultimate referent. The body in being indisputably real, becomes the essence of the real. Once Jesus and his Way, his metaphysic, were Truth; now the body was.

The irrefutable thereness of the body – ground of what was thought the irrefutable truth-telling of the body: this was a faith widely shared by philosophy, medicine, criminology, the new psychology. The body is thought to tell the true story of the person. It's a most legible text, a knowable sign-system, a semiotic fullness, a source of narrative, an iconography even. Jean-Martin Charcot's influential work was publicized from 1862 on in his journal titled the *Nouvelle iconographie de la salpêtrière*, and celebrated in the *Iconographie photographique de la salpêtrière, service de M Charcot*, edited by the neurologists Desiré-Magloire Bourneville and Paul Regnard, 1877–1880. In her book *Ventriloquized Bodies: Narratives of Hysteria in Nineteenth-Century France* (1994), Janet Beizer rightly stresses the body-textualizing abounding

---

[6] Selfhood in its material dimensions: of course a dominant of modern critical realization. For a characteristic (though especially good) look at the self-material conjunction in Victorian thinking see 'Subjectivity, the Body and Material Culture', Ch 2 of Regenia Gagnier, *A History of Self-Representation in Britain, 1832–1920* (Oxford University Press, New York and Oxford, 1991).

in and around Charcot's work: the 'narrative staging', the theatrical
'performance' of female hysteria Charcot induced in his lecture-theatre;
the turning of women's bodies into 'lithographs', their 'welts' interpreted
by doctors as meaningful texts; the hospital's published photographs
as records of body eloquence; the 'ventriloquism' of the silent hysterical
females' bodies, their meanings 'dubbed' by a male narrator. Athena
Vrettos, in her *Somatic Fictions: Imagining Illness in Victorian Culture*
(1995), nicely thinks of the speaking (and ventriloquized) bodies in
Harriet Beecher Stowe's anti-slavery novel *Uncle Tom's Cabin* (1852) and
in Louisa May Alcott's American Civil War *Hospital Sketches* (1863) as
participants in an 'affective hermeneutics'. (Vrettos aptly cites the pioneering British doctor William Osler describing sick bodies as an 'endless
narrative source' – 'a sort of Arabian Nights' entertainment', which
nurses must discreetly refuse to indulge in.) Phrenology – the art of reading the character from the bumps and declivities of the skull – flourished
in this faith in the body as the true-story-teller of the self. So did what
was called physiognomy – reading the character from facial details (every
man is now 'a great physiognomist', we're told in George Eliot's *Adam
Bede* Chapter 15, reading the 'language of nature' in the lovely face, the
cheek, lips, chin, eyelids, lashes, eyes, of Hetty Sorrel). Henry Frith's popular 1891 guide to physiognomy, *How to Read Character in Features,
Forms, & Faces. A Guide to the General Outlines of Physiognomy* lumps
physiognomy together with phrenology, palmistry, chiromancy (hand
work) and pathognomy (gait and gestures) as revelatory of character,
morals, race, class. Every body part and bit of body attire from hair to
boots tells – forehead, eyes, teeth, chin, handshake, tread, angle of hat,
tightness of glove, the lot. Victorian body-scientist Francis Galton discovered the fingerprint as unique to the individual, the never-failing sign and
signature of the person, and launched his career of grouping human types
by characteristic facial features and measurements of the skull – visual
evidence of goodness and immorality ('degeneracy' a speciality) afforced,
of course, by photographs, the new medium of truth-registering ('the
camera never lies'). Phrenology and physiognomy were, like the fingerprint, essential to the new criminology. Cesare Lombroso, renowned contemporary criminologist, was able to read the signs of criminality from the
mere shape of a person's jaw, his cheekbones, the size of his ears. So could
the Paris police chief: assembling his systematic sets of criminal ears, noses,
mouths, foreheads, and so on, in *Tableau Synoptique des Traits
Physiognomiques* (1901–1916). In *The Criminal* (1890) Havelock Ellis, the
sexologist friend of JA Symonds, tells how the photos of prison inmates are
utterly revelatory of, for example, homosexuality. Charles Darwin felt he
could read off the emotions of people (and animals) from the 'expression'
on their faces (see his rather astounding *The Expression of The Emotions in*

Man and Animals, 1872). And so on.[7] And this widely held faith in the readable, ventriloquizable truths of the body was inevitably embraced not just
by novelists (Henry Frith keeps citing Dickens) but by the poets.

The body is the fullest, most reliable sign that poetic deixis keeps pointing
to. Robert Browning expounds the faith at length through his Fra Lippo
Lippi (*Men and Women*, 1855). Lippi is a realist painter, a materialist, an
artist of the flesh. As he admits to the night-watchmen who've accosted him
out on the razzle, he's been a body realist ever since he was a homeless gut-
tersnipe, surviving only by knowing the 'look of things', learning to read
faces, to know who would discard a 'half-stripped grape-bunch', who curse
and kick him, which priest would wink and let him collect wax-candle droppings, which would call the cops in. He inhabits a completely materialist,
bodily world, an affair of food and drink (he's plainly drunk) and sex.
A Rabelaisian monk, he haunts loose women, plays 'hot cockles' with other
men's wives (*hot cockles*: a game, sparky sex – *cockles*: *cock* – and food).
'[Z]ooks, sir, flesh and blood, / That's all I'm made of' (60–61). And his art
is all flesh and blood. He's an expert at faces – 'eyes and nose and chin' –
and the faces in his frescoes of Bible stories, apostles, saints, are all recognizable as local individuals. 'That's the very man!' people say; 'it's the life!'.
The *very man*; the *life*: person, being, life; the reality, truth of persons as,
and in, their face. Person indeed as mere *prosopon*, as his or her face. By
their bodies shall ye know them: 'Faces, arms, legs and bodies like the true /
As much as pea and pea!' (177–178). Which upsets the Prior and the theologically 'learned', the church authorities who commission Lippi's work.
For these Pauline Christian Platonists the soul is the real, the truthful essence;
the body's an interfering shell, the flesh a distraction from spirit, a zone of
sin, of sinful sex.

> Your business is not to catch men with show,
> With homage to the perishable clay,
> But lift them over it, ignore it all,
> Make them forget there's such a thing as flesh.
> Your business is to paint the souls of men –
> (179–183)

---

[7]   Much of the historical detail is handily collected in *Spectacular Bodies: The Art and Science
of the Human Body from Leonardo to Now*, catalogue of a Hayward Gallery body-herme-
neutics exhibition, eds Martin Kemp and Marian Wallace (Hayward Gallery/University of
California Press, 2000). The 'Reading the Signs' section, 94–123, is especially pertinent. Lucy
Hartley, *Physiognomy and the Meaning of Expression in Nineteenth-Century Culture*
(Cambridge University Press, Cambridge, 2001) usefully takes the history of physiognomy
back to Johann Lavater and Charles Bell, and is good on Darwin, in particular on Darwin and
blushing, but has almost nothing to say about literature, and gets quite bogged down on the
Pre-Raphaelites and the subject of the expressibility of 'ordinariness'.

The Prior cannot actually define what and where the soul is

> ... it's a fire, smoke ... no, it's not ...
> It's vapour done up like a new-born babe –
> (In that shape when you die it leaves your mouth)
> It's ... well, what matters talking, it's the soul!
> Give us no more of body than shows soul!
>
> (184–188)

The soul's thereness is, precisely, debatable; it is, *per se*, unspeakable. Unlike the body – and the Prior is caught out acknowledging this, recognizing his mistress (passed off by everybody as his niece) in the picture of Salomé whose dance pleased Herod and who, at her mother Herodias's suggestion, got John the Baptist's head cut off as a reward: 'Oh! that white smallish female with the breasts, / She's just my niece (195–196). (By mistake he calls Salomé Herodias – a mistake that was in Browning's source for the Lippi story, Vasari's *Lives of the Painters*, and that Browning enjoys recycling.) The body holds guilty secrets. So 'Paint the soul, never mind the legs and arms!' is the advice. But if for Lippi-Browning 'soul', the evanescent, untouchable, inner realities of the person, are to be accessed, this will only be through rendering the body. The 'life's flash' of the mistress (213) will only be made manifest through painting her body, her face. *Flash*, so close to *flesh*; the flash of life manifest in the living flesh. It's a rhyming relationship Brown would later exploit in *Fifine at the Fair* (1872), rescuing fallen Fifine with the 'lavish limbs' and eloquent 'haunch' from the disregard of the good Elvira: claiming through narrator Don Juan that the divine 'flash' appears through the 'coarsest' female's 'couverture'. Here's 'the inward grace, sacramentally manifest through 'the outward sign' even of this immodest, debauched, black, whorish performer's body – a piece of human 'filth', whose 'brand' – a prostitute's punishment burn-mark – she freely displays, urging you to 'pry', 'Your finger on the place', in a replay of St Thomas being urged to touch the wounded side of Jesus (*Fifine at the Fair*, 253, 278–283, 287, 330–338, 339–355, 376–391).

The lovely face and body of the Prior's niece painted by Lippi are also outward sacramental signs. So far from being a distraction for 'soul', they're the only access to it:

> Take the prettiest face,
> The Prior's niece ... patron-saint – is it so pretty
> You can't discover if it means hope, fear,
> Sorrow or joy?
>
> (208–211)

Lippi will not allow that there's bodily beauty without soul. But even if, for the sake of argument, there were, you would 'get about the best thing God invents', and beholding it you would 'find' in your self, 'the soul' that was missing, because you'd be compelled to 'return' God 'thanks' (215–220). 'Rub all out'; 'Have it all out!' the Prior keeps commanding: erase the breasts, the bodiliness, in aid of picturing the soul. But that wouldn't only annihilate Lippi the painter (' "Rub all out!" Well, well, there's my life, in short'), it would do away with any chance of revealing the soul of the pictured one. To absent the body is to keep the soul absent; only by the body's continued presence might the soul be rescued for presence. Which is a critical line Elizabeth Barrett Browning has her character the painter Vincent Carrington endorse in a Lippi-tribute at the end of the First Book of *Aurora Leigh* (1856):

> The rising painter, Vincent Carrington,
> Whom men judge hardly as bee-bonnetted,
> Because he holds that, paint a body well,
> You paint a soul by implication, like
> The grand first Master ....
>
> (I. 1095–1099)

Body first. Elizabeth Barrett Browning is following the sequence of the Bible's creation story. Creating the human person in the Garden of Eden, God ('grand first Master') first made a body out of clay and then 'breathed into his nostrils the breath of life; and man became a living soul' (Genesis 2:7).

What's being offered here are the potent body fictions of real presence. 'That's my last Duchess painted on the wall / Looking as if she were alive', declares Browning's Duke in 'My last Duchess: Ferrara'. Only *as if*, of course, for she is mere paint, a piece of art, a fiction. But whatever life, truth, reality, presence she has, it is by dint of her pictured body, the somatic access route to knowledge about her. Real presence manifested through the accredited legibility of the body. A difficult legibility, naturally, because paint is silent, like the body, a wholly silent sign, awaiting words, hermeneutic, on and about it. But the more provokingly inviting for being silent – like blushes, that most recurrent case of Victorian body-speak. How enticing bodily redness keeps trapping the body-ventriloquizing, interpreting poet's gaze (in acts of what Peter Brooks nicely calls *scopophilia* and *epistemophilia*, the desirous eroticizing and narrativizing gaze of the writer[8]). The exciting red

---

[8]   Peter Brooks, *Body Work: Objects of Desire in Modern Narrative* (Harvard University Press, Cambridge MA and London, 1993). Brooks' interest in 'modern' writers' scopic desire (what M Jay has called 'The Scopic Regime of Modernity') is greatly inspired, as are most recent discussions of the body, by Michel Foucault's insistence on the gaze as key to modern discourses of power – educational, penological, medical. M Jay is quoted from *Vision and Visuality*, ed Hal Foster (Bay Press Seattle, 1988), 3–23, by Carlo Ginzburg, *Wooden Eyes: Nine Reflections on Distance*, trans Martin Ryle and Kate Soper (Verso, London and NY, 2002), 149.

buttocks of Swinburne's S-M *Whippingham Papers*; the 'burnt red' mouths of the lovers in Rossetti's 'Nuptial Sleep', the great red lips of the lovely demonic women in his paintings; the 'signature' of 'the conscious glow' rising up the body of a woman claimed, dubiously, as *promising* in the Charles Tennyson Turner sonnet that was eventually titled 'A Blush at Farewell'; 'the crimson-throbbing Glow' of the body of Coventry Patmore's now dead wife in remembered sexual congress (in 'To the Body', in *The Unknown Eros* volume of the *Angel in the House* sequence, Book II, Part VII (1879)); Alfred Tennyson's obsessive roster of poems for and about his failed beloved Rosa Baring, 'Early Verses of Compliment to Miss Rosa Baring', 'The Rosebud', 'The Roses on the Terrace' – aka 'The Rose' – peaking in the poem 'Go not, happy day' inserted into 'Maud': each one eloquent about disappointingly eloquent roseate glowing and blushing rosiness ('Rosy is the West / Rosy is the South, / Roses are her cheeks, / And a rose is her mouth'); and so on and on. (How apt, you think, for these blush-obsessed times that Tennyson should have an elusive object of desire named Rosa; or, for that matter, that Elizabeth Barrett's beloved but vulnerable dog – the one held to ransom by London dog-thieves – should be called Flush.) And it's necessary to note that these rednesses are to be thought of in the first place not as allegorical but as tokens of *realia* – actual red buttocks and lips and glowing bodies. They have, of course, metaphorical propensity, as all that Tennysonian rosiness, not least, indicates – but what 'Maud' brings fiercely home is the actuality of the shed blood that begins the poem, flows through it, taking in the murder of Maud's brother, and climaxes in the bloody redness of the Crimean War. All of it real, like that opening 'red-ribbed hollow' as it's later called (Part II,I,i, 25), 'its lips ... dabbled with blood-red heath / The red-ribbed ledges' that 'drip with a silent horror of blood' (Part I,I,i, 2–3), with absolutely no thought of the crude allegorizing that knocks around busily in the criticism (the blood is menstrual blood; those metaphorical lips are read in a gothic act of über-metaphoricizing as a vagina; and so forth). The horrors of the bloodied real. And there is, to be sure, something up like this with the period's aestheticized rednesses, especially the blushing and the blushers. Blush-readers do keep, we feel pretty sure, getting things wrong: like the murdering lover in Browning's 'Porphyria's Lover' who deludedly takes her dying blush ('her cheek once more / Blushed beneath my burning kiss'), as a sign of her satisfaction in the *Liebestod* he contrives for her; or Browning's Duke who confidently reads the painted Duchess's (half) flushes and blushes, the *spots of joy* in her face, as signs of a transgressive love-affair with her painter, and is, we suspect, misreading them. But the manifest potential for mistaking the body's signs, the body as sign, is not taken by Browning as a reason for rejecting the potential of the body for truth-telling and for ditching faith in its legibility. Browning by no means spurns the Duke's faith in the body's legibility, only suspects his analysis, his conclusions. Which is why Lippo Lippi (and Browning) will 'Fag on at flesh' ('Fra Lippo Lippi', 237).

In the end what makes Browning happy with Lippi's bodiliness is its root-edness in traditional Christian incarnational (and sacramental) theology, the idea of God present, presenced, in the human form of Jesus. This is Browning's, and Lippi's, theology of sanctified flesh – the belief of Browning's Paracelsus in spiritual truth as body truth, divine knowledge felt in the body:

> I knew, I felt, (perception unexpressed,
> Uncomprehended by our narrow thought,
> But somehow felt and known in every shift
> And change in the spirit, – nay in every pore
> Of the body, even,) – what God is, what we are.
> What life is – how God tastes an infinite joy
> In infinite ways – one everlasting bliss
> From whom all being emanates, all power
> Proceeds; in whom is life for evermore,
> Yet whom existence in its lowest form
> Includes; where dwells enjoyment there is he.
>   (*Paracelsus*, Part V, 638–648)

Spiritual body-truth in downright bodiliness ('in every pore / Of the body, even'). What angers Browning about Sludge-Home spiritualism is its fake bodiliness, its lying materialization of spiritual presences – the table rap-pings and liftings, the deceiving touch of the medium's hand pretending to be a dead child's. 'The tiny hand made feel for yours once more' ('Mr Sludge, "The Medium" ', 474). Touching, the mark of the true, granting access to the truth of persons and of God in a person, was not for religious-theatrical exploitation. Browning, compulsive toucher – always getting people to feel how low his pulse was ('Do me the honour to feel my pulse'): this 'low-pulsed forthright craftsman's hand of mine' – felt contaminated when Home tried his touching tricks on him, fiddling with his leg under the table, at a séance.[9] The sacredness of body, this somatic location of sacred-ness, was not for playing or tinkering with. For the divine treasure was indeed concealed in 'the earthen vessel', as the end of 'Christmas-Eve' put it, in words from Scripture (first part of *Christmas- Eve and Easter- Day* (1850), 1313). And the divine was especially present in the least attractive vessels: in 'The hot smell and the human noises' of the Mount Zion Dissenting Chapel of 'Christmas-Eve', in its poor, unlovely, unwashed, bedraggled, fat, wizened, coughing, sickly Christians ('The man with the handkerchief untied it, / Showed us a horrible wen inside it': 'Christmas-Eve', 177–178). God extremely incarnate in human bodies which the

---

[9]   Pulse-taking reported by Lady Burne-Jones at Ruskin's house, 12 December 1862: David J DeLaura, 'Ruskin and the Brownings: Twenty-Five Unpublished Letters', *Bulletin of the John Rylands Library*, 54 (1971–1972), 345.

lyrical-I has to learn to discern and tolerate. Roman Catholic Christians worship the same incarnated Christ in the poem's Rome; but there His particular incarnation lacks the force of the principle: the place and its version of divine worship betray the professed theology in their costly theatricalism – 'buffoonery', 'posturings and petticoatings' (1324–1325), 'the raree-show of Peter's successor' (1242) – modern detractors of 'brave weather-battered Peter' of the work-hardened hands (942–945). What Browning is advocating is a low-Protestant religion of the ordinary person, which means a sacramentalism of the ordinary body, wens and all – a religion sustaining, and sustained by, brutal somatic realism. What Walter Bagehot – a Unitarian, rather close to the demythologyzing Göttingen professor Browning debunks in 'Christmas-Eve' – precisely disliked in Browning: 'the realism, the grotesque realism of orthodox Christianity' ('a suspicion of beauty, and a taste for ugly reality, have led Mr Browning to exaggerate the functions, and to caricature the nature of grotesque art'; like a soldier with 'an appetite for slaughter, a tendency to gloat on carnage, to love blood, at least for the moment, with a deep eager love').[10] Browning's was not Unitarian-inclined Dickens's kind of Christianity, or Christian art, either. Dickens's notorious attack on the Pre-Raphaelites and in particular on John Everett Millais's painting 'Christ in the Carpenter's Shop (Christ in the House of His Parents)', not only anticipates Bagehot's hostile line on Browning's body-realisms; it also sounds startlingly like a gloss on Browning's Zion Chapel Christians, who had appeared in public only two months earlier in April 1850. Here was a most unlovely Holy Family, a badly-bodied lot:

> ... prepare your selves ... for the lowest depths of what is mean, odious, repulsive, and revolting.
>
> ... In the foreground of that carpenter's shop is a hideous, wry-necked, blubbering, red-headed boy, in a bed-gown; who appears to have received a poke in the hand, from the stick of another boy playing in an adjacent gutter, and to be holding it up for the contemplation of a kneeling woman, so horrible in her ugliness, that (supposing it were possible for any human creature to exist for a moment with that dislocated throat) she would stand out from the rest of the company as a Monster, in the vilest cabaret in France, or the lowest gin-shop in England. Two almost naked carpenters, master and journeyman, worthy companions of this agreeable female, are working at their trade ... Wherever it is possible to express ugliness of feature, limb, or attitude, you have it expressed. Such men as the carpenters might be undressed in any hospital

---

[10] 'Wordsworth, Tennyson, and Browning; or Pure, Ornate, and Grotesque Art in English Poetry', *The National Review*, XIX (Nov 1864), 27–67. Parts of the Browning discussion, in Litzinger & Smalley, *The Critical Heritage*, edn cit, 274–276.

where dirty drunkards, in a high state of varicose veins, are received. Their toes have walked out of Saint Giles.[11]

The boy with the (proleptic) wound in the hand is Jesus, and the monstrously ugly woman is his mother. This Holy Family is oddly akin to Browning's chapel people, who if they didn't walk in from London's notorious, crime-ridden St Giles's slum, lived somewhere very like it, in a Sodom and Gomorrah, beyond 'the safeguard border' of the street lamps, in 'certain squalid knots of alleys, / Where the town's bad blood once slept corruptly' ('Christmas-Eve', 29–47).

'What's filth?', the Corinthian woman Lais is reported as asking, towards the end of Browning's *Aristophanes's Apology* (15 April, 1875) – quoting Euripides (his lost play *Aeolus*, as reported in Athenaeus's *Deipnosophists*: the moment is deep down in the cocoon of Browning's complex intertextuality!). She continues the question with the old answer: 'unless who does it, thinks it so?' (line 5336). Which is Browning's thought: there's nothing objectively filthy, and thus excludable as too disquieting, about bodiliness in art. *Aristophanes Apology*, this very long poem, is patently Browning's highly wrought, and fraught, response to the Buchanan piece of three and a half years earlier. Browning invents a sculptor called Lachares to stand for all portrayers of the naked body who resist the charge of 'Outrageous sin' from the shuddering, offended 'elders'. ' "Sinned he or sinned he not?" ' No he didn't: Pallas Athene is the 'more beautiful' for being unclothed. 'And there the statue stands / Entraps the eye severer art repels' (5087–5093). (Browning's son Pen was one of the many Victorian sculptors who wanted to present the utterly naked human form.) *There* the statue is, because *there* the human being's body is: Browning's insistently deictic truthfulness will have no other. ' "I paint men as they are – so runs my boast – / Not as they should be" ', says Aristophanes in the tones of Lippo Lippi (2129–2130). The true poet wants 'the real', the physical real, 'not falsehood'. The truth of bodies – however ugly – will serve for aesthetic *beauty*: it has it own beauty (2166–2169).

> 'I stand up for the common coarse-as-clay
> Existence, – stamp and ramp with heel and hoof
> On solid vulgar life, you fools disown.'
>   (2683–2685)

The poet must never 'Despise what is – the good and graspable'. And Aristophanes promptly grasps some examples of what should be grasped by

[11]   Charles Dickens, 'Old Lamps for New Ones', *Household Words*, I, no. 12 (15 June 1850), 265–267.

poets – physical things to be preferred to 'the out of sight', the spiritual and mental subject:

> '... village joy, the well-side violet patch,
> The jolly club feast when our field's in soak,
> Roast thrushes, hare-soup, pea-soup, deep washed down
> With Peparethian; the prompt paying off
> That black-eyed brown-skinned country-flavoured wench
> We caught among our brushwood foraging'.
>
> (1956–1961)

(Peparethian is an Aristophanic wine.) The edible woman – 'country-flavoured' flesh among all the other rural comestibles – is, of course, Browning's defiant revival of the 'brown-shouldered harlot' whose neck is 'munched' with kisses in Rossetti's 'A Last Confession', whom Buchanan so took against. The 'well-side violet patch' draws our attention to another of Buchanan's main dislikes, the well of Rossetti's 'Willow wood' in which reflected kisses bubbled up. The younger Fleshly School-mate finds thus a well-defended home in Browning's own very physical and most fleshly lines. Lines in which a nipple might pop up at any time as simply allowed fact and force of the natural – like the sexy (blush-coloured) mushrooms the poet comes across in his imagined morning stroll through the feminized bodily Italian landscape with Elizabeth Barrett, in 'By the Fire-Side' (*Men and Women*, 1855):

> ... the rose-flesh mushrooms, undivulged
> Last evening – nay, in today's first dew
> Yon sudden coral nipple bulged,
> Where a freaked fawn-coloured flaky crew
> Of toadstools peep indulged.
>
> (stanza XIII, 61–5)

The bulging coral nipple. No wonder the Pre-Raphaelites looked to Browning as a kind of bodily leader. '[T]en lines of Browning whack / The whole of the zodiac', wrote Dante Gabriel Rossetti to John Lucas Tupper around the time *Christmas-Eve and Easter-Day* came out (and it was a volume Rossetti and his chums competed to be the first to read).[12]

And Robert Browning's stoutly defended bodily practice indeed leads the way for a whole period's traders in body truths, body realities. Traders *en masse*, dealing in bodies of every sort – bodies all along the spectrum from lovely ones to vile ones, above all bodies giving off troublingly mixed messages.

---

[12] Letter of April 1850. *Letters of Dante Gabriel Rossetti*, eds Doughty and Wahl, I, *1835–1860* (Clarendon Press, Oxford, 1965), 89.

All Sorts and Conditions of Bodies

Desirable and desired bodies stack up, of course, in huge numbers. The desirable body of the beloved is the traditional focus of the love poem, and Victorian love poems abounding so much, so do bodily eroticizings. Victorian poets simply cannot abate their fascination with the desirable body of the beloved other. They're scopophiliacs to a man, and woman. RH Hutton dismissed the soured erotics of George Meredith's *Modern Love* sequence of pumped-up, sixteen-line sonnets as 'Modern Lust'. But lusting after the body of a beloved has always been the love-poem's main prerogative, and Victorian poets do not eschew the mode's traditional opportunities. Especially the sonneteers, the likes of heterosexual Dante Gabriel Rossetti, Elizabeth Barrett Browning, George Meredith, and for that matter, the Revd Charles Tennyson Turner, Alfred Tennyson's sonneteering elder brother and devoted fetishist of lovely little girls (who featured so heavily above in 'Down-Sizing', Chapter 5), and bisexual Swinburne, and the gay-body celebrators Edward Carpenter and John Addington Symonds, all of them keen investors in the most erotic of western erotic modes. Buchanan was quite right to remark the large welcome afforded the eroticized body by Rossetti and Co. He was wrong only in finding this deplorable and in implying it was a merely hole-in-corner obsession limited to a junior branch of the poetic business conducted at an ill-attended Fleshly School. Of course Rossetti and Swinburne and later Decadents like JA Symonds stand out for the warm detail of what eventuates when desirous human bodies meet and touch and hold and penetrate each other, but their difference from their so many other eroticizing contemporaries is only in the detail and tone of their erotic Gestalt, and not in the fact and presence of pleasurable fleshly encountering.

Of course the so overwhelmingly present bodies of Victorian poetry are not all of them lovely and conventionally desirable. Victorian body-poems are full of repellently diseased, sick, wounded, decaying, broken, ruined, dying and dead bodies. Victorian poets are frequently morbid (the subject of my next chapter, 'Mourning and Melancholia'), and their body encounters are often grim in the extreme. Poets and poems frequent hospital wards, death-beds, morgues. Poems commonly pathologize the body. Bad-body consciousness keeps driving poet and poem to some sick person's bed-side, into hospital, down to the morgue. Tormented poetic spirits engender poem after poem about tormented bodies. The poetic atmosphere is intensely psychosomatic. Stories of body illnesses as mirrors of mental ones, abound. Tellingly, even before the death of Hallam put the morbidity and mortality of the body at the centre of his consciousness Tennyson's poems were thriving on the body in distress. So awful was what the extremely agonized confessional poem from around 1832 which begins 'Pierced through with knotted thorns of barren pain' was registering that Tennyson could not manage to finish it. The poem's *I*, 'Deep in forethought of dark calamities' and 'Sick of the coming time and coming woe', lies on his bed at night feeling like someone walking across a volcanic plain afraid his body is about to be consumed in spouts and showers of 'scorching fire':

> and I lay with sobbing breath,
> Walled round, shut up, imbarred, moaning for light,
> A carcase in the coffin of this flesh,
> Pierced through with loathly worms of utter death.
>
> (15–18)

His body's a coffin containing a putrefying carcase. He's in a 'spiritual charnel house', in 'an unutterable tomb', a place and plight too terrible to continue writing about. Broken body; broken poem. A distracted body lament written out of extreme mental and spiritual distress that was followed a year later (and still before news of Hallam's death reached Tennyson) by 'St Simeon Stylites', monologue of an early Christian hermit pillar-dweller with a spectacularly rotting body. The poem is commonly taken as a satire on the claims of Christian asceticism (and aimed in particular at the influential contemporary Cambridge evangelical vicar the Revd Charles Simeon). Fitzgerald claimed that Tennyson would later on read it 'with grotesque Grimness', 'laughing aloud at times'. Tennyson might have managed a grim laugh later, but the poem's gruesome somatic detail doesn't sound as if he found anything funny at the time of writing. '[H]alf deaf', 'almost blind', toothless Stylites suffers 'superhuman pangs', 'coughs, aches, stitches, ulcerous throes and cramps'. 'From scalp to sole' he's 'one slough and crust of sin'. So he's a modern Job, a version of the Old Testament character tormented by Satan with God's permission, covered in boils whose excretions he scrapes off with a broken bit of pot, a 'potsherd'. Of course Stylites' body ills are a self-induced penance; he's punishing his flesh because it's 'this home / Of sin'. He's chosen to live outside in all weathers just as, when a young monk, he wore rough rope tied 'about my limbs', 'Twisted as tight as I could knot the noose' – so tight that ulcers formed, 'eating through my skin'. He's a Catholic masochist for Christ; which Protestant Tennyson no doubt deplores. But Stylites' profound spiritual burdenedness, his sharp sense of sin in the flesh, which have provoked this life of body torture, make for a psychosomatic compound that Tennyson evidently feels terribly close to.

And these early sufferers of Tennyson's simply mature in their psychosomatic distress along with their never really undistressed creator. Tennyson's early miserabilist whose body feels entombed in a charnel house of the spirit horribly anticipates the melancholy mad narrator of 'Maud' interred under the London street in that poem's 'Dead long dead' passage. Anticipates, too – for these body plights are to be found all across the period – the extraordinarily gothic/surrealist poem 'In the Room' (1867–1868) by the vastly pessimistic Tennyson-watcher James Thomson, author of the great and notorious melancholy vision of London, 'The City of Dreadful Night', the poet so glooming he was known as the 'Laureate of Pessimism'. In Thomson's 'In the Room' the furniture and fittings of a lodging-house bed-sit talk about its late inhabitant, a failed writer who has just killed himself by swallowing poison. His corpse lies on the bed; which describes him/it:

> XX
> The bed went on, This man who lies
> Upon me now is stark and cold;
> He will not any more arise,
> And do the things he did of old.
>
> XXI
> But we shall soon have short peace or rest;
> For soon up here will come a rout
> And nail him in a queer long chest,
> And carry him like luggage out.
> They will be muffled all in black,
> And whisper much, and sigh and weep:
> But he will never more come back
> And someone else in me must sleep.

Swinburne is peculiar, of course, not for being so obsessed with bad bodies, but for liking them. His *algolagnia* (as Bonamy Dobrée dubbed it, using a twentieth-century technical term from psychiatry[13]), his pathological pleasure in body pains and the pained body – the beaten-in joys of the Eton flogging-block, the delights of the brothel for flagellants in St John's Wood and what the Ladies of Pain could do for his flesh in reality as well as in imagination, the kept-up Sadeian cult of getting the 'sob of pleasure' from the 'pulse of pain' (as Swinburne's poem 'Rococo' puts it) – finds its dire corollary, apotheosis even, in his truly terrible poem 'The Leper' (*Poems and Ballads*, 1866). A lover confesses his continuing love for a beloved who contracted leprosy, physical expressions of which love he keeps up for six months after her death. God cursed her with this plague. Everybody but the lover cursed her too and 'cast her forth for a base thing'. But he secreted her in a 'wretched wattled house', which became an abode and retreat of love (oddly proleptic, in its building materials at least, of Yeats's cabin hideaway on 'The Lake Isle of Innisfree' – 'of clay and wattles made'). Feeding and watering the diseased

---

[13] Bonamy Dobrée, Introduction to his *Swinburne* selection (Penguin, Harmondsworth, 1961), 11.

woman, the lover-narrator keeps her alive for 'forbidden' sex (line 80), done in a Swinburnean menu of sado-masochistic, pleasure-pain terms – straining, staining, sobbing, breaking, sharp, bites, stings – a rhetoric so usual with Swinburne he can produce it almost as casually as if it were simply normal, nothing to make a great fuss about. It's a dark erotics that's continued, thrillingly, burningly, after death as the narrator holds her dead feet and kisses her 'half ruined' hair (so that the poem draws arrestingly close to 'Porphyria's Lover', the Browning dramatic monologue Swinburne greatly admired, in which Porphyria, strangled with her own hair, is used in necrophiliac erotic play by her killer, who kisses her dead cheek, and props her head against his shoulder, caressingly, 'as before'). Swinburne's lover concedes that his necrophiliac doings 'may be' a love gone wrong, a 'Spoilt music', a wonky, 'blurred' writing (129–132), but he quickly brushes the concession aside. 'Nothing is better, I well think', he declares at the poem's start, 'Than love', and he means his own sado-masochistic, necrophiliac loving, desire for, and sex with, a very un-well beloved. The word *well* occurs a defiant three times in the poem's opening stanza. The poem carefully challenges notions of what's sexually, bodily *well*; challenges the reader to not think that the narrator and his woman and the poet are un-well, are doing something that's not well done. We're being invited not to think less than well of these lovers, this poet, this poem. The lover gives his woman *well-water* to drink (73). Well-water, pure water, something well from the well – from deep down in the earth, hidden water, brought blessingly into the light. And 'hidden-well-water / Is not so delicate to drink' as this love the poet is celebrating: 'This was well seen of me and her'.

A delicate love, then. *Delicate*: a wonderfully complex word, as William Empson gleefully shows in one of the best of his lovely riffs on poetic vocabulary in *The Structure of Complex Words* (1951). It means *fastidious, fine, refined, innocent, pure, natural*, as well as *pleasurable, delightful*; with the sense of *fastidious* growing close to *sickly*, and the *pleasurable* acquiring senses of excess of pleasure, *voluptuousness*, even *effeminacy*. Victorian readers would also (though Empson doesn't say this) hear the word *cate* in *delicate*: *cate*, as in *cates*, pleasing food (it belongs to the *catering* set of words), delicious eating stuffs, *dainties*, body-pleasing comestibles you put in your delighted mouth (what's provided by the 'catering hand' of the lover Porphyro in Keats's 'The Eve of St Agnes (1820)). Empson thinks Swinburne is directing 'The Leper' at 'drawing-room' ideas of love, lovers, and love poems, which is probably right. He also thinks Swinburne is subversively getting at that view of the 'refined' – aesthetically fastidious, tasteful, art-loving – Victorian female which equates refinement with sickliness of body, physical weakness, wasting away, by suggesting there's self-sadism (and so masochism) in such delicacy of taste and body (Empson mentions the posh Victorian female fashion of body-punishing corsetry, 'tight-lacing').

Which is as may be. He thinks the poem 'very fine'. It confirms his early and lasting liking for Swinburne. Having no time for God, Empson no doubt approved strongly of the poem's blaming God for the woman's leprosy. Above all he thinks the poem's sadism justified: 'the sadism is adequately absorbed or dramatised into a story where both characters are humane, and indeed behave better than they think; Swinburne nowhere else (that I have read him) succeeds in imagining two people'.[14] But what kind of humanity? The narrator's goodness in succouring a plague victim (leprosy was in Swinburne's time thought highly contagious) is undoubted. But his humanity comes with a very inhumane price tag: this lover is looking after her, keeping her to himself, because, sadistically and masochistically, he likes sex with a diseased woman. And sadism – let alone necrophilia – doesn't become morally agreeable merely by being 'adequately absorbed or dramatised' in a story. And, of course, ironically, in granting respect to this sado-masochistic necrophiliac's deviances Empson is thwarting the poem's keen challenge to normalcy, depleting Swinburne's pronounced pleasure in disconcerting minority sexuality, spoiling the fun Swinburne gets from assuming the bad-boy parts. Who's 'The Leper' of the title? The leprous woman, of course; but also the lover himself; and in moral as well as medical senses. As the alleged medieval original story that Swinburne appended to his poem in cod Old French made clear: this 'wicked man' and 'damned cleric' 'took pleasure in kissing the dead body lots on her foul and leprous mouth and embracing her gently with amorous hands', thus catching her disease – her 'abominable malady' – and dying of it. The hero is a moral leper as well as a physical one. Which is presumably what Swinburne wants to be thought, and wants us, horrified but attracted, to take him as: the sick erotic connoisseur of (and with) deviant, transgressive, awesomely bad-body tendencies.

Swinburne's sick and sad pleasures are indeed difficult to think well of (and they weren't: the *Spectator* of 22 September 1866 rightly described 'Anactoria' and 'Phaedra' as 'foul stuff' and 'The Leper' as 'worst of all').[15] For their part, Tennyson and Thomson might be craving our sympathy for the bad-body plights of their poems, but they take no pleasure in them and do not expect us to do so either. The painter-poet and 'Nonsense'-monger Edward Lear tries hard, one supposes, to make light of the nose he deplores, but his horror at his own face keeps intruding into his would-be light verses as a dementing pathology. 'How pleasant to know Mr Lear'; but 'His nose

---

[14]   William Empson, *The Structure of Complex Words* (Chatto & Windus, London, 1951; Hogarth Press, London, 1985), 76–79.
[15]   And as Yoppie Prins enjoys reporting, 'Swine-born' Swinburne as he was dubbed, the sado-masochist connoisseur of the abused body, took rather happily to the critical abuse, the whippings of the critics. Prins, *Victorian Sapphics*, 158ff.

is remarkably big; / His visage is more or less hideous'; and 'He weeps by the side of the ocean, / He weeps on the top of the hill'. This non-pleasure taking poem of 1879 was published as 'By Way of Preface' to Lear's *Nonsense Songs and Stories*, and came to be titled 'Self-Portrait of the Laureate of Nonsense', but its nose horrors are not at all nonsensical. Not dissimilarly, the Dong in 'The Dong with a Luminous Nose' who is unhappily in love with a Jumbly girl, searches the world for her in vain by the light of a lantern in the monstrous nose he's made out of Twangum Tree bark. Persona – mask – as well-lit monstrosity:

> And he wove him a wondrous Nose, –
> A Nose as strange as a Nose could be!
> Of vast proportions and painted red,
> And tied with cords to the back of his head.
> – In a hollow rounded space it ended
> With a luminous lamp within suspended
> All fenced about
> With bandage stout
> To prevent the wind from blowing it out; –
> And with holes all round to send the light,
> In gleaming rays on the dismal night.

This poem appeared in Lear's *Laughable Lyrics* (1876), but its bodily apprehensions are not at all laughable. Lear's nose-upsets merit him a place alongside Nikolai Gogol, the Russian laureate of nose-neurotic writers. They're as un-amusing as the Crimean War sonnets with which Sidney Dobell, the wine-merchant poet, made some claim to be taken seriously as a poet rather than being known only as the author of the wildly, crazily gothic 'spasmodic' dramatic poem about a poet's life and work, *Balder* (1854).

> 'Thou canst not wish to live', the surgeon said.
> He clutched him, as a soul thrust forth from bliss
> Clings to the ledge of heaven! 'Wouldst thou keep this
> Poor branchless trunk?' 'But she would lean my head
> Upon her breast; oh, let me live!' 'Be wise'.
> 'I could be very happy; both these eyes
> Are left me; I should see her; she would kiss
> My forehead: only let me live'. – He dies
> Even in the passionate prayer ... /

That's from 'The Wounded' in *Sonnets on the War* (1855), by Dobell and by Alexander Smith, the Scottish Spasmodic whom Dobell met in the years he spent in Edinburgh in search of medical treatment for his wife. The physical horrors of *Sonnets on the War* almost merit it a place alongside another Russian's writing, namely Leo Tolstoy's accounts of war-wounded and dead on the other side, his extraordinary reports from the Russian field-surgery tents at Sebastopol in the Crimean (English version: *Sebastopol Sketches* (Penguin, 1986)). Dobell was never at the Crimea but his sonnets' vivid body-horrors combine images from the traditional apocalyptic repertoire (he was obsessed by the Book of Revelation and thought the Crimean War was a fulfilment of Biblical prophecy, 'Sebastopol' being, he reckoned, etymologically related to 'Armageddon'), and by what he'd seen in Edinburgh hospitals.

It was his own later experience in Edinburgh hospitals which inspired WE Henley's unique and outstanding hospital sequence. This crippled Gloucester poet had a leg amputated when a boy (some sort of tubercular illness) and spent two years, 1873–1875, in Edinburgh Infirmary in a (successful) effort to save his other leg. His long graphic sequence of poems, *In Hospital* (many of them sonnets) about being a patient, hospital routine, nurses, doctors, medical students, visitors, other patients, was published finally in 1888. Written by a man with a mutilated body, fighting against further mutilation, Henley's sequence comprises a society of pain in miniature, a village of somatic distress, eloquent with stumps of limbs, splints, plasters, bodies in ruin through accident and surgery – ghastly body truths which are also heart-breaking personal and social narratives:

> As with varnish red and glistening
> Dripped his hair; his feet looked rigid;
> Raised, he settled stiffly sideways:
> You could see his hurts were spinal.
>
> He had fallen from an engine,
> And been dragged along the metals.
> It was hopeless and they knew it;
> So they covered him and left him.
>
> As he lay, by fits half sentient,
> Inarticulately moaning,
> With his stockinged soles protruded
> Stark and awkward from the blankets,
>
> To his bed there came a woman,
> Stood and looked and sighed a little,
> And departed without speaking,
> As himself a few hours later.
>
> I was told it was his sweetheart.
> They were on the eve of marriage.
> She was quiet as a statue,
> But her lip was gray and writhen.

That's poem XIII, 'Casualty'.

> You are carried in a basket,
> Like a carcase from the shambles,
> To the theatre, a cockpit
> Where they stretch you on a table.

That's the narrator in poem V, 'Operation', not *like* a patient etherized upon a table as in TS Eliot's 'The Love Song of J Alfred Prufrock', but actually a patient etherized upon a table (Henley had gone to Edinburgh to be treated by Joseph Lister the pioneer of anaesthetics).[16] Oscar Wilde was scornful about *In Hospital*. He was very upset by Henley's hostile review of 'The Ballad of Reading Gaol' (1898). Wilde had been diverted by harsh legal circumstances from celebrating the bodies of beautiful young men to anguish over his fellow-prisoner, the young soldier hanged in the Gaol for the crime of wife-murder, his dead body burned by quick-lime in an unmarked grave (the fate of murderers in England). 'In Reading gaol by Reading town / There is a pit of shame, / And in it lies a wretched man / Eaten by teeth of flame, / In a burning winding-sheet he lies, / And his grave has got no name'. It was as if the nightmare of *Dorian Gray* – male beauty overtaken by age, ugliness, decay – had really come home to Wilde's art. And he clearly expected sympathy for a poem whose body-horrors make it a kind of parallel to *In Hospital*. Not getting it he turned on Henley: 'so proud of having written *vers libres* on his scrofula that he is quite jealous if a poet writes a lyric on his prison'. There is, of course, nothing free about the verse of *In Hospital* – always regular rhythmically, with regular line lengths, and comprising numerous sonnets – and it's not about scrofula. But Wilde was right about the revoltingness of Henley's bodies and body-experiences. Only a Swinburne, perhaps, would find them desirable.

And what is, of course, striking is how so many Victorian poems find something up with even the most desirable body, how often some cause for body-revulsion is let in to disrupt a poem's scopophilia, to contaminate the love-making, to trespass on a poem's bedroom, or bedroom-like, scene of desire. The body of the young woman in Hood's 'The Bridge of Sighs' is beautiful – 'Fashion'd so slenderly, / Young, and so fair!' – but it's just been fished from the Thames ooze, a muddied suicide. Rossetti's Jenny is 'full of grace' (like the Virgin Mary in the Roman Catholic 'Hail Mary'), her lovely

---

[16]   A sharp encapsulation of Henley's life, doings and works is James Campbell's review of *The Selected Letters of WE Henley*, ed Damian Atkinson (Ashgate, Aldershot, 2000), *TLS* (11 Aug 2000), 3–4, cruelly entitled 'Legless to the Last' in token of one-legged Henley's ending up as a drunkard.

Keatsian breast 'All golden in the lamplight's gleam', but she's a sleeping prostitute, tired out from her transgressive erotic labours. Before long she'll have turned into one more of those sad women of Margaret Woods' appalled Nineties poem about prostitutes, 'Under the Lamp': 'Like a crushed worm in the mire of the city', 'A shop-soiled, meagre, / Night-wandering woman', her used-up body sadly illuminated as she stands soliciting on 'The obscene pavement's horrible slime, / Spittle of smokers, foulness of feet'. Edward Carpenter's rhapsodic extended sonnet on the beautiful 'figure of the lusty full-grown groom on his superb horse', ecstatic about friends cleaving 'flesh ... to flesh' and naked human animals bathing in the sea, their muscular bodies inviting 'kisses all over', is overtaken by thoughts of these lovely male bodies being wounded and killed in battle (Whitman-inspired, one guesses: Whitman the lover and celebrator of boys and men wounded and killed in the American Civil War). Carpenter tries to make these bodies in pain a tribute to 'glorious War'. And some of these wounded men are lucky to have 'quick-healing glossy skin'. But this attempt to turn battle-fields into places where bodily love-affairs are consummated – 'O swift eager delight of battle, fierce passion of love destroying and destroying the body!' – is utterly unconvincing. No such whistling in the dark can mollify the thought of warfare's somatic ruinations.

For his part, it's priestly and theological propriety which intervenes between Father Hopkins and the wonderfully touchable body of the soldier-boy dressed in his 'regimental red' in 'The Bugler's First Communion'. The boy 'Yields' to Hopkins's teaching, 'tender as a pushed peach'. The homosexual priest clearly imagines touching, kissing, even eating this peachy boy from the Cowley barracks.[17] The 'Breathing bloom' of his 'mansex fine' has excited him into verse. But Hopkins has to turn his lips away, turn down the invitation of the soldier-boy's edible body, devote his lips rather to 'pleas', that is to prayers. He can put 'Christ's royal ration', the sacramental wafer, in the boy's 'sweet' mouth, but that's all. The priest is only allowed priestly contact, priestly touching, whatever his body might desire otherwise. Other bodily communions would be unholy.

As in that other great eucharistic poem of Hopkins, the sonnet 'Felix Randal', about touching a male parishioner and being touched by him, but only (despite everything Q-theory inspired readings might suggest)

---

[17]   'I cannot stop to defend the rhymes in the Bugler. The words "came down to us after a boon he on My late being there begged of me" mean "came into Oxford to our Church in quest of (or to get) a blessing which, on a late occasion of my being up at Cowley barracks, he had requested of me": there is no difficulty here, I think'. Hopkins to Robert Bridges, 22 Oct–Nov 1879, *The Letters of Gerard Manley Hopkins to Robert Bridges*, ed Claude Colleer Abbott, 2nd (revised) impression (Oxford University Press, London, 1955), 97.

sacramentally.[18] 'My tongue had taught thee comfort, touch had quenched thy tears, / Thy tears that touched my heart, child, Felix, poor Felix Randal'. Hopkins does tongues, as we say, but only doctrinally. 'To what serves mortal beauty?', Hopkins asks in the sonnet that's known by that opening line. And the answer is that it's 'dangerous' because it's erotically exciting: it sets the blood 'dancing', which won't do in a priest. 'I think ... noone can admire beauty of the body more than I do, and it is of course a comfort to find beauty in a friend or a friend in beauty. But this kind of beauty is dangerous'. That is Hopkins to Robert Bridges on the subject of the 'beauty' of Bridges's poems in a letter so anxious about the danger that it rambles and quite stutters in its effort to sort out the allowed kinds of beauty from the disallowed. Beauty 'of the mind' and of the soul is obviously 'greater than beauty of the body', and not dangerous. But, then, isn't it good 'Aristotelian' Catholicism to believe that 'bodily beauty' emanates from the soul? The 'soul may have no other beauty, so to speak, than that which it expresses in the symmetry of the body'. Though, of course, there are always going to be 'blurs in the cast' of the body not 'found in the die or mould' of the soul.[19] Hopkins really is troubled; even when trying to as it were defuse the dangers of (male) bodily attraction, to calm the 'dancing' of his blood, by reminding himself that it's basically soul-beauty that's at issue. The 'mortal beauty' sonnet seeks similar reassurance by recalling Pope Gregory's attraction towards the fetching English slaves he saw in the Forum at Rome, 'lovely lads': 'Non Angli, sed angeli' – 'Not Angles, but angels'. The sight of these lovely boys inspired Gregory to send Augustine on a missionary journey to Britain. And that, Hopkins is reminding himself, is the priestly way: to seek the good of the soul of beautiful boys – the persona inside, the grace of God in them that transcends the undoubted physical lure which marks their bodily person:

> World's loveliest – men's selves. Self flashes off frame and face.
> What to do then? how meet beauty? Merely meet it; own,
> Home at heart, heaven's sweet gift; then leave, let that alone.
> Yea, wish that though, wish all, God's better beauty, grace.

What Hopkins is doing is, as Foucault would put it, earnestly policing his desires with constant theological and sacerdotal cautions and reminders.

---

[18]   See Joseph Bristow, ' "Churlsgrace": Gerard Manley Hopkins and the Working-Class Male Body', *Journal of English Literary History*, 59:3 (1992), 694–711, and Gregory Woods, *A History of Gay Literature: The Male Tradition* (Yale University Press, New Haven and London, 1998), 171–173, and my opposition to their readings of 'Felix Randal' in 'Fact and Tact', *Essays in Criticism* 51:1 (Jan 2001), 119–138.

[19]   Hopkins to Bridges, 22 October–November 1879, *Letters to Robert Bridges*, edn cit, 95.

So too is Coventry Patmore. The poems of *The Angel in the House*, Patmore's impeccably chaste meditation on married love, with his wife's enrapturing moral and physical superiority constantly jostling her theologically endorsed subordination – it appeared in two sequences, *The Betrothal* (anonymously, 1854), and *The Espousals* (1856) – are, as every Victorianist knows, thoroughly policed. They're a by-word of restraint about what might happen in the Christianized conjugal bedroom. They weren't Patmore's last word on the subject of Christian marriage, though. He couldn't stop writing about it – and much more freely after his devoutly Protestant first wife (daughter of a Congregationalist minister) died. But always there's policing. Hopkins thought that much of Catholic-convert Patmore's material was too frank for publication. On Christmas day 1887 Patmore burnt his large collection called *Sponsa Dei*, 'Bride of God', which was about love, physical and spiritual, blaming the repressive Hopkins, who had suggested it might lead astray 'the general reading public'. Patmore did, though, follow up *The Angel in the House* with *The Unknown Eros*; and the public must have found it in many aspects surprisingly open about the wifely beloved's body. As in 'To the Body' (referred to earlier for its arousal by blushing): a hymn to the 'pleasures' the poet found in the body of a now dead wife. What, Patmore wonders, are heaven's delights going to be like, if the bodily bliss he found 'in thee' – that 'crimson-throbbing glow' – are their mere 'first-fruits'? The poem fights off the wish of 'shameless men' to 'cry "Shame!"', to declare shameful the riches of the beloved's body – a 'little, sequester'd pleasure-house' – 'Every least part' of it:

> Elaborately, yea, past conceiving, fair,
> ... from the graced decorum of the hair,
> Ev'n to the tingling, sweet
> Soles of the simple, earth-consoling feet,
> And from the inmost heart
> Outward unto the thin
> Silk curtains of the skin,
> Every least part ... .

But even here the (lovely) celebration is monitored, and constrained, by harsh theological considerations. The beloved's hair and feet and skin are not fair 'past conceiving' in themselves, but because they hear and reply to the music of 'the spheres', and as such are in tune with heaven. But, of course, being a Protestant, the beloved wife died 'unshriven', and so she cannot go, yet, or ever, to the paradise which in Patmore's belief dead Roman Catholics can enjoy straightaway. She lies 'in the grave's arms, foul and unshriven', stuck in her 'sin', her outsiderliness, like the Jebusites of the Old Testament who, as Patmore puts it, lived in the Holy City of Jerusalem, allowed by God, 'by formal truce and as of right', but in a 'false fealty', never finally part of the Chosen People. And the poem ends with the poet anticipating heaven's joys for himself while the body of the admired partner of his blissful earthly bodiliness is rotting in the grave. Sex with a lovely Protestant wife, however beloved, has to be placed as wonderful, alright, but, in effect, sinful, doomed and damned.

Here was a body-transgressivity not to be relished unless you're truly decadent, like the paid-up masochist Swinburne and his poetic heirs, the late-century Decadents, or those merely leaning that way, like Rossetti. And, of course, whatever the pleasure bodily paining confers it remains painful, which is the aspect of masochism perplexing to everybody except masochists. The masochism which, according to Freud, is intrinsic to certain kinds of high aesthetic activity, and which make masochists of us all. Freud's 'Beyond the Pleasure Principle' dwells on the puzzling attraction of tragedy: why do we keep returning, repeatedly, to take pleasure in the theatrical playing, and playing out, of the most awful, painful events? *Why Does Tragedy Give Pleasure?* wonders AD Nuttall as the title of his 1996 book about this puzzle puts it. Why indeed? The critical tradition has long wondered. And the body-work which enamours so-called decadent love poems is as emotionally confused as anything offered by Aeschylus or Shakespeare. Even hardened masochistic Swinburne flinches on occasion: 'I dare not always touch her, lest the kiss / Leave my lips charred' ('Laus Veneris', 169–170). The craved touching of lovers in Rossetti's 'Penumbra', one of the Songs (not sonnets) in *The House of Life*, is to be shunned as too hot to handle:

> Because it should not prove a flake
> Burnt in my palm to boil and ache.

A lover's palm should not be a flake of fire to make your palm 'boil and ache', but this kind of lover's does. In Rossetti's 1870 painting 'La Donna dell Fiamma', the Woman of the Flame, a gorgeously sultry woman (actually Janey Morris) holds a small winged figure of Love in the form of a flame, seemingly aloof to its heat for herself and the pain it would give a poet-painter-lover who might grasp it. Press this hot woman's cheek in a kiss, be cherished by those hands, and you get burnt. 'Pity and love shall burn / In her pressed cheek and cherishing hands' ('The Stream's Secret', stanza 19). The poetic notion of woman as hot stuff is very old and endorsed by Dante's vision of Beatrice in the *Vita Nuova*, translated by Rossetti in 1848. But traditional or not, having the hots for, and being burnt in, the heats of the desirable other's body is still a burning. Love, according to *The House of Life* sonnet 'Love's Fatality', is sweet but deadly. 'Desire of Love' is 'most dread', a *thwarting* of life. What should be a loving touching, 'hand to hand', is a form of bondage, of slavery. Rossetti's lovers are as if shackled together, bound at hand and foot, 'Linked in gyves' (ankle fetters). Which is to be in the shared shackles of misery and frustration – 'Love shackled with Vain-longing'. The lips of the man, made for pleasurable kissing are instead 'two writhen flakes of flame'; that is, they're wrenched, twisted in pain, for their own part, and hot providers of pain to any beloved. Those lips *moan* in pain and complaint to Love about the chaining involved in being a 'self' in love and talking about love, naming it. It's 'Life's iron heart, even Love's Fatality'.

Those Troubling Synecdoches

These male poets are haunted by lovely women whose most fetching body parts, the absolute sources of sexual pleasure, the intensest focusses of desire – their mouths, the hair, those recurrent, eloquent, legible, and perennially visible, manifest Victorian synecdoches of the body – are in practice occasions, locales, instruments, of horror and pain, even of death.

The fabulous desirable women in Rossetti's paintings and their accompanying poems have what Swinburne celebrated in 'Laus Veneris' as 'marvellous' mouths. But those huge, intensely kissable, lips belong to killing females, demonic mistresses, from Hell – Pandora, Astarte, Lilith, Fazio's mistress, Helen of Troy, the Venus of 'Venus Verticordia' ['turner of hearts'], Prosperpina. They're lusciously lipped, flame-haired women, temptresses, doing worrying things with their hands, holding out tempting foodstuffs, enticing eats for the lover's mouth – versions of the Bible's Eve offering the apple of temptation and damnation to Adam. The woman of *Venus Verticordia* holds an apple and a little spear: '"Alas! the apple for his lips, – the dart / That follows its brief sweetness to his heart"', as Rossetti's accompanying sonnet ('Venus Verticordia (For a Picture)' has it. ('She's fraught with peril', thought the *Athenaeum*, 21 October 1865, with reason.) Proserpina, bride of Pluto, Empress of Hell, in Rossetti's *Prosperpina* painting of 1873–1877 holds a pomegranate. Because she's bitten it, partaking of the fruits of Hell, she'll never return to earth. The red of the bitten portion is like an open mouth with the seeds looking like teeth. It presents itself as a version of the teeth undoubtedly concealed by Proserpina's large, pursed lips (the lips, in fact, of Janey Morris). It is, of course, the classic *vagina dentata* of ancient male nightmare. Be seduced by this mouth – the painting loudly pronounces – kiss these lips, and you too will be bitten, be engulfed for ever in the hell that awaits those suckered by such loveliness. Here, as the English version of Rossetti's accompanying sonnet, 'Prosperpina (For a Picture)' has it (there was an Italian version too) is 'cold cheer' – 'this drear / Dire fruit, which, tasted once, must thrall me here'. Thralling: thrilling and enslaving, the enthralling lips and mouth, enthralling sweets for the mouth that will thrall their consumer hellishly.

Rossetti's *House of Life* sonnet 'The Kiss' plays the same note of a love lost to Hell: 'my lady's lips' are said in kissing to play 'With these my lips' a 'consonant' tune such as the one Orpheus played to rescue his Eurydice from Hell – a music that worked only up to a point, because Orpheus lost her irrevocably soon after. And an aesthetic of hellish mouth work captivating everyone in Rossetti's vicinity. Negatively on the part of his (pious and virginal) sister Christina, whose 'Goblin Market', written in April 1859 and published in 1862, reads like an extended moral rebuke to her brother's bad-mouth/bad eating fascinations. Sweet-toothed Laura crams damnation into her mouth in the form of the irresistibly sweet fruits of the goblin men – biting and sucking, on and on, more and more. ' "You cannot think what figs / My teeth have met in, / What melons icy-cold" '. 'She never tasted such before'. 'She sucked and sucked and sucked the more'. She's only saved from the death that comes from these bad-mouth engagements because of sister Lizzie's resisting this tempting mouth work, not opening her lips as the goblins 'squeezed their fruits / Against her mouth to make her eat': 'Would not open lip from lip / Lest they should cram a mouthful in: / But laughed in heart to feel the drip / Of juice that syruped all her face, / And lodged in dimples of her chin, / And streaked her neck which quaked like curd'. The mouth-dominated poems and paintings that came after *Goblin Market* show Dante Gabriel doing more of his same, laughing as it were in the face of his sister's rebuking poem (despite his help with her poem, providing its title, and the 'suggestive wit and revising hand' she later said she was indebted to). And Rossetti's images of damnable mouths and their temptations were ones that Swinburne, for his part, couldn't get enough off.

When Swinburne saw Dante Gabriel's 1859 painting of the full-lipped Fanny Cornforth, *Bocca Baciata* ('Kissed Mouth': title taken from a Boccaccio sonnet inscribed in Italian on the back of the panel: 'The mouth that has been kissed loses not its freshness...'), he thought it 'more stunning than can be decently expressed'. These 'stunners' (as the Pre-Raphaelite Brotherhood came to call the ruinous attractions of the large proley red-lipped, red-haired young women they couldn't stop painting) quite stunned the small masochist, and indecently. He relished the pain they suggested – swooning, for example, over Rossetti's 1863 *Helen of Troy*: the burning red mouth, 'a keen red flower-bud of fire, framed in broad gold of wide-spread locks, the sweet sharp smile of power set fast on her clear curved lips', with the burning city of Troy behind her reddening the heavens with the light of pain and destruction. In Swinburne's own 'Laus Veneris' it's the mouth of Helen of Troy that's held to be particularly 'marvellous'. Just so, in that poem, the 'large pale lips of strong Semiramis' – mythic Assyrian Empress and strong woman, associated in some readings with warlike Astarte, or Ashtaroth, downmarket Hebrew demon of lust, Egyptian version of Aphrodite, assigned by Dante to the second circle of the Inferno, the place of the lustful – curl back like a tiger's, a beast ready to devour its prey, lips red with the blood of 'the last kiss' that 'made them bleed'. There's blood because these kissings are also bitings. As in Swinburne's sonnet 'A Cameo' (also in *Poems and Ballads*), once more an arranged meeting been Pain and Pleasure, in which 'lips and teeth bite in their sharp indenture'. *Indenture*: a contract, so named because ancient written contracts were two pieces of a signed document cut in two in a wavy, tooth-like, indented pattern. 'And lips love's indentures make', as Philip Sidney's Elizabethan sonnet put it – the lovers' lips and teeth meeting in a kiss that punningly makes a contract between them, not at all anticipating Swinburne's sharpening of the teeth to emphasize the biting. *Sharp indenture*. These are 'strange loves' indeed, as 'A Cameo' has it. Or as another *Poems and Ballads* sonnet, 'Love and Sleep', fantasizes the erotic encounter: 'my love' leans over 'my sad bed', with 'hotter hands than fire', her lips open and speaking of 'Delight', her face 'honey to my mouth', 'pasture' for the eyes, though not for the eyes alone but also for the teeth: 'with bare throat made to bite'. This poet-lover is not just parasitic; he's vampiric. Like Arthur Symons's late-Victorian lover who scoops up Swinburne's toothy, toothsome desires and filters them through Bram Stoker's *Dracula* (1897), to turn a deft tribute to the European motor of poetic decadence, Charles Baudelaire himself, in 'Hallucination: I':

> One petal of a blood-red tulip pressed
> Between the pages of a Baudelaire:
> No more; and I was suddenly aware
> Of the white fragrant apple of a breast
> On which my lips were pastured; and I knew
> That dreaming I remembered an old dream.
> Sweeter than any fruit that fruit did seem,
> Which, as my hungry teeth devoured it, grew
> Ever again, and tantalised my taste.
> So, vainly hungering, I seemed to see
> Eve and the serpent and the apple-tree,
> And Adam in the garden, and God laying waste
> Innocent Eden, because man's desire,
> Godlike before, now for a woman's sake
> Descended through the woman to the snake.
> Then as my mouth grew parched, stung as with fire
> By that white fragrant apple, once so fair,
> That seemed to shrink and spire into a flame.
> I cried, and wakened, crying on your name:
> One blood-red petal stained the Baudelaire.[20]

---

[20]   In Symons, *Poems* (2 vols, William Heinemann, 1902), Vol I, 'London Nights' section.

Hair Pieces

And if Victorian erotic poems are mouthpieces for the troubling desirability of the synecdochic female mouth, how much more are they troubled hair pieces. The Victorians are terribly preoccupied by hair. It's no accident that hair fetishism – the stimulation of sexual desire through this particular part of the human body – was first defined in Victorian times (Havelock Ellis, the Victorian poet and sexologist who features rather a lot in these pages, is credited by the Oxford English Dictionary with the first talk of it in English in his *Studies in the Psychology of Sex* of 1897). Hair on the head, on the face, was of course so visible, so present, as an obvious manifestation of the persona, the person, the face it adorned. It was felt to be significantly metonymic, synecdochic of the person, to be utterly eloquent of the self. It contained depths of meaning. It was *deep* hair. (Aphrodite has 'deep hair' in Tennyson's 'Oenone' in the 1842 *Poems* version, line 173: much more deeply meaningful than the merely *dark* hair of 1832.) Here was a very speakable metonym of the person, and the publicly available, socially acceptable, outward sign of the sexual person. The fetishized synecdoche that was allowed open expression, it was the speakable synecdoche of the other, less respectable, body hair: the public face, so to say, of the unpublishable pubic. (In the completest study of hair in Victorian literature and culture, Galia Ofek – incited by Giorgio Agamben's thoughts on fethisism ('If fetishism was the nineteenth-century model perversion, surely hair was the flagship fetish') – as fetishized hair working very hard as synechdochic of the female genitalia, as well as the whole social body in sexual perspective.[21])

Hair was felt to speak clearly about character. Face-curtained Elizabeth Barrett Browning, carrot-topped Swinburne, filthily hirsute Tennyson were, of course, known by their hair. Early in his correspondence with the much-haired Elizabeth Barrett, Robert Browning is naturally egged on by thoughts of big hair – 'the heap of hair' in a Titian painting, an image for Robert of the muchness of Elizabeth's locks. He is 'pulled', he writes, 'by the head and hair, into letter-writing' (*Letters of Robert Browning and Elizabeth Barrett Barrett*, I. 5–6). Tennyson's shaggy locks and beard made the most obvious emblem of his being and his verse. As he knew – endowing the magician Merlin with his own hairiness, 'The vast and shaggy mantle of his beard', which Vivien draws 'Across her neck and bosom to her knee' (*Merlin and Vivien*, 244–245). Arthur Arundel, 'The Poet' of the alternative draft songs for *The Princess* – 'rough his hair but fine to feel' – was thought a portrait of Tennyson (*Collected Poems*, ed Ricks, p1768). Oscar Wilde's new curly

---

[21]   Galia Ofek, *Representations of Hair in Victorian Literature and Culture* (Ashgate, Farnham, Surrey and Burlington VT, 2009), 7, 20, 21.

hair-cut, modelled on busts of Nero in the Louvre, which he went specially to Paris to obtain in December 1882, was held the outward sign of his deviance and degeneracy.[22] Hair was widely thought to embody a person's force, his or her very essence. The Biblical story of Samson, whose strength was in his hair, haunted the popular imagination. People sought hair as mementoes of the notable, the special, the heroic. Grace Darling, famous as the lighthouse-keeper's daughter with the windswept hair rowing shipwrecked people to safety, complied with so many requests for locks of hair that she was in danger, says the *Dictionary of National Biography*, of baldness. Leigh Hunt was seeking to endow Browning with a great predecessor's force when he gave him a lock of Milton's hair. When courting couples exchanged locks of hair, it was as a foretaste of bodily contacts and exchanges to come. Lovers wore the other person's hair in lockets and rings, portable, handleable, present synecdoches of the beloved's desirable body. Sonnet XVIII of Elizabeth Barrett Browning's *Sonnets from the Portuguese* celebrates that special anticipatory synecdochic giving to Robert Browning:

> I never gave a lock of hair away
> To a man, dearest, except to thee,
> Which now upon my fingers thoughtfully
> I ring out to the full brown length and say
> 'Take it'....

'I ring out': the hair is wrapped around her fingers like a ring, proleptic of the ring the hair might well be destined for; and as it were making a noise, ringing out like (wedding?) bells, in a declaration of the speaker's love, which the ring is. Every commentator on Victorian hair is entranced by courting Robert Browning's begging of some of her hair ('give me so much of you .. as may be given in a lock of your hair'), by Barrett's stuttering reluctance (too 'prude', she said, to give away hair except to 'nearest relatives' and a few of her 'female friends'), her coy hints that she'd trade some of hers for some of his, the exchange of hair-containing rings, her talk of tying thus silken knots, his of living and dying comforted and blessed by 'your beautiful ring, your beloved hair'.[23] In the poem Barrett was offering her whole self in this bit of her self – self as woman, and also as poet, the hair of the poet and the poem about it being one. Hair as poem; poems as hair. A conception hair-obsessed Yeats readily shared. 'He Gives His Beloved Certain Rhymes', as the 1895 poem beginning 'Fasten your hair with a

---

22   Norman Vance, *The Victorians and Ancient Rome* (Blackwell, Oxford, 1997), 259.
23   Letters 2110–2112, 2115, 2119–2120, 2124 (23 Nov–2 Dec 1845), *The Brownings' Correspondence*, eds Philip Kelley and Scott Lewis, Vol 11, July 1845–Jan1846 (Wedgestone Press, Winfield Kansas), 194–203. Ofek, op. cit., 25–27; Elisabeth G Gitter, 'The Power of Women's Hair in the Victorian Imagination, *PMLA*, 99(i), Jan 1984, 943.

golden pin, / And bind up every wandering tress', was eventually titled. The gift of the rhymes, the poem, is a celebration of the beloved's hair. And the fastening and binding of her hair are made one with the 'building' of the rhymes which the poem also celebrates. (The poem appeared first in the story 'The Binding of the Hair' in the *Savoy* magazine, 1896.)

The force, the *mana*, of hair was deeply connected with the way hair out-lives its owner. Hair doesn't die. The melancholy narrator of Robert Browning's 'A Toccata of Galuppi's' (in the *Men and Women* volume) – he who wonders 'What of soul was left … when the kissing had to stop?' – hardly has the heart, he says, to rebut Galuppi's answer: 'Dust and ashes!', and thinks of dead women and their lovely hair as evidence for that gloom:

> Dear dead women, with such hair, too – what's become of the gold
> Used to hang and brush their bosoms?

(*Such hair*, and so wonderful that brushing: the much brushed hair of women that also invitingly brushed their breasts.) But, of course, what has become of that hair is that it has survived its wearer, is not in fact dust and ashes. This survivability of hair is what fired the rumour that Lizzie Siddal's hair was found to have grown to fill the coffin when Rossetti had it dug up to retrieve his poems.

Keeping a dead person's hair was a way of keeping her or him alive in effect as well as in memory, in an act of approved piety and bereft love. In 'Only a Curl' Elizabeth Barrett Browning comforts some friends whose child has died leaving them with only 'a single gold curl in the hand': the hair defies mortal-ity; it links them encouragingly with their little angel now in heaven – ' 'Tis easy for you / To be drawn by a single gold hair / Of that curl, from earth's storm and despair, / To the safe place above us'. Out of despair, via some hair. Just so, Dante Gabriel Rossetti celebrates a 'tress' of his dead wife's hair in 'Life-in-Love' (Sonnet XXXV of *The House of Life*), as the living remnant of the old 'heart-beats' and 'fire-heats': 'all that golden hair undimmed in death'. Little Nora in Charles Tennyson Turner's 1873 sonnet 'Little Nora, or The Portrait' has died but lives on in the portrait her father preserves and also in the 'memorial tress' that is 'set / Facing the porcelain picture, where his child / Still nursed her pile of summer-wreaths and smiled'. Though *still*, stilled in her tomb, and still unmoving (a 'still life') in her portrait, she is still (yet) present: in that pictorial representation, but also in the metonymic 'tress'.[24] The narrator of *Maud* is most upset, demented even, by the thought that Maud's brother, whom he has killed, wore his mother's hair in a ring:

---

[24]   Sonnet CCXLII, in *The Collected Sonnets of Charles (Tennyson) Turner*, eds FB and M Pinion (Macmillan Press, 1988).

> And now I remember, I,
> When he lay dying there,
> I noticed one of his many rings
> (For he had many, poor worm), and thought
> It is his mother's hair.
> > (Part II, section II, stanza viii, 114–117)

The piety indicated by that ring of hair outweighs all the nasty rich-boy ostentation betokened by the other rings. Here was the absolute moral value-added of mother-remembrance embodied in hair. The added value that's part of the meaning-load of Elizabeth Barrett's gift to Browning:

> I thought the funeral shears
> Would take this first; ... but Love is justified –
> Take it, thou, ... finding pure, from all those years,
> The kiss my mother left here when she died.

Here the female hair comes laden with doubled female meaning – the woman lover's and her dead mother's. And though men's hair is thought of as telling, especially in gay men's poems, it's women's hair that, the period finds, tells so much more. And Victorian women know it. The poets' women *are* their hair. They are hair solipsists. 'The Way of a Maid', according to Francis Thompson's cynical poem of that title (*New Poems*, 1897) is to belittle her high-minded lover by thinking only of her hair:

> And, while she feels the heavens lie bare,
> She only talks about her hair.

She knows her hair is her 'glory' – even the Bible has said so – and the male poets are almost helpless before that knowledge. The first noticeable feature of an attractive woman in Browning's 'A Pretty Woman' (in *Men and Women*) is her hair: 'That fawn-skin-dappled hair of hers'. Hair rhymes – in this brilliantly self-rhyming poem – with 'that infantine fresh air of hers'. Hair of hers; fresh air of hers. A pretty woman's *air* – her aspect, demeanour, being, as well as her tune, her poeticity; even the rather slight tune, as seems to be the case in this poem, of what we would call an *air-head* – is her *hair*. The one repeats and is repeated by the other. *Such hair*, indeed, as Browning liked saying – and from the start: about Andromeda in *Pauline*, her 'hair / Lifted and spread by the salt-sweeping breeze ... such hair' (659–662). '[F]awn-skin-dappled' is lovely: hair dappled like the skin of a young deer, inviting you to imagine touching and stroking even as you look. The colour's a carefully observed variant of the usual clichéd gold or red. Not, though, that any poet, or painter, of the time ever tires of golden hair.

There are, of course, some non-red-heads around. The creolized Elizabeth Barrett has dark hair. It's celebrated in Robert Browning's 'By the Fireside' as 'That hair so dark and dear'. The pair exchange curls of hair as 'purply black' as the 'purpureal tresses' the Roman poet Pindar imagined adorning the white brows of the Nine Muses, according to Elizabeth's Sonnet XIX 'From the Portuguese'. (She imagines Browning's lock is 'so black' because of the shadow on it of the poet's traditional crown of laurel-wreath; she'll preserve the warmth of the brow the hair came from by keeping it 'on my heart' until her brow 'grows cold in death': lovers' hair always has this *memento mori* air.) For her part, Matthew Arnold's French lover has brown hair – 'soft brown hair' in Arnold's poem 'Calais Sands'; 'lovely brown hair' in his 'Separation'. The 'lily girl' of Wilde's enigmatic 'Madonna Mia' sonnet (is she the Virgin Mary or just any girl?) has 'brown, soft hair braided by her ears'. The two Spanish girls in Browning's 'Soliloquy of a Spanish cloister', 'brown Dolores' and her friend Sanchicha, have 'Blue-black, lustrous' hair, 'thick like horsehairs' (as Spanish females tend to). The girl murdered in Rossetti's 'A Last Confession' has 'thick/Dark hair' (as females from Lombardy, again, tend to). The cheek of the speaker in Ernest Dowson's 'Terre Promise' (*Verses*, 1896) is 'brushed' by 'the fragrant darkness' of a woman's hair. Swinburne's Faustine has hair that's 'black imperious' as well as 'Red gold' (59–60); the 'lights' in it 'Shift from dead-blue to burnt-up black' (155). The woman tempting the monk in Hopkins's friend the Revd RW Dixon's 'A Monk's Story' (in his *Christ's Company and Other Poems*, 1861) has 'a gloss of purple hair' (70). The female addressee of Swinburne's 'Before Parting' had hair 'full of purple colour' as well as of 'hid spice' (31–32). Queen Ahinoam's hair, in Swinburne's 'The Masque of Queen Bersabe' (also in *Poems and Ballads*), is 'pure purple'. (The hair in 'Before Parting' inspires a nice learned note on purple and purple hair in literature at large from Kenneth Haynes in the Penguin Classics edition of *Poems and Ballads*.[25]) The boy Antinous in Wilde's 'The Burden of Itys' has 'black and clustering hair' (line 283); Wilde's 'Endymion' refers to Endymion's brown hair twice: 'And brown and curly is his hair'; 'the lad's brown hair'. The wicked witch in William Morris's 'Rapunzel' has black hair. And there's sometimes something of the Western film's sign-system hereabouts: bad cowboy in black hat: dubious female in black hair. But this code is by no means absolute; and by the same token, not all of the poetry's golden-haired women, Victorian poetry's equivalent of the Western hero in the white hat, are as good for their lovers as they might be.

---

[25] *Poems and Ballads & Atalanta in Calydon*, ed Kenneth Haynes (Penguin, Harmondsworth, 2000), 361.

But still, some shade of gold is the norm, and the normative sign of the most desirable other, especially the female other.[26] The red-gold hair of women spreads in huge mats, webs, nets across Rossetti's paintings, and so across his poems about them. The poets can't get enough of golden locks. Mary, the drowned milkmaid in Charles Kingsley's (1849) 'The Sands of Dee' has 'golden hair'. Tennyson's Maud has 'sunny hair'. Barrett Browning's *Aurora Leigh* opens with Aurora remembering how her beloved father 'Stroke out my childish curls across his knee' and the maid Assunta's 'daily jest' about 'how many golden scudi [Italian gold coins] went / To make such ringlets'.[27] The 'back-hair' of the widow in Browning's *Red Cotton Night-Cap Country* is 'a block of solid gold' (900). The girl with 'eager eyes 'who awaits the narrator in Browning's 'Love Among the Ruins' has golden hair. The hair of Dante Gabriel Rossetti's 'Blessed Damozel', 'lying down her back, / Was yellow like ripe corn' (a 'lying' he wanted his brother to help him get as vividly right as possible – as discussed in Chapter 1). Charles Tennyson Turner's fetishistic collection of little girls is usually golden-haired, like his little Nora, and his 'Little Sophie by the Seaside', and his famous three-year old Letty of the much anthologized 'Letty's Globe'. The hair of Rapunzel/Guendolen in what must be the most spectacular hair-fantasy of the period, William Morris's 'Rapunzel' is, you guessed it, inevitably golden. And so on and on. Golden hair, female gold: it denotes, boldly and crudely, the value, the sexual value of girls and women sited in their hair.

A valuation not at all limited to straight-sex transactions. Victorian androgyne fantasies commonly feature hair – think the hair in Simeon Solomon's male-fetish paintings (and Swinburne's poem 'Erotion' about Solomon's androgynous *Damon and Aglae* painting: discussed in 'Selving', Chapter 6), and the hair of Aubrey Beardsley's numerous bi-gendered figures and in Rossetti's androgynous paintings, and the way some boys were aestheticized.[28] And the androgynous boy-object of male desire is, characteristically, golden-haired. Oscar Wilde's Dorian Gray has 'gilt' hair ('Dorian',

---

[26]   So much so that Elisabeth G Gitter's (pioneering) study, 'The Power of Women's Hair in the Victorian Imagination' loc. cit., knows *only* golden hair.

[27]   In the manuscript drafts an uncle 'fresh from Spain' asks how many (Portuguese) moidores were 'melted down' to 'make those glittering curls'. Textual note to *Aurora Leigh* I, 20–25, in Margaret Reynolds, ed, *Aurora Leigh* (Norton, NY and London, 1996), 316.

[28]   I'm thinking of the much-discussed photograph of Lewis Carroll lounging with George MacDonald's androgynous children, three much-haired Alice-like daughters and a long-locked little boy (reproduced and discussed in UC Knoepflmacher, *Ventures into Childland: Victorians, Fairy Tales and Femininity* (University of Chicago Press, Chicago and London, 1998), 160ff), as well as of the ringleted 'Pen' Browning, his hair kept long and girlie (a sort of double of his mother's locks) until he was twelve and his mother died (ringlets snipped off by father on the day after her funeral in 1861).

name for ancient Greeks, is curiously close to French *doré*, golden or gilt). It was modelled on Wilde's beloved Bosie's blond locks (by awful contrast Wilde's wife had brown hair).[29] The boy in Wilde's 'Wasted Days' sonnet, made for a love which is as yet painfully (to his admiring poet) unfulfilled, is a Bosie-like blond.

> A fair slim boy not made for this world's pain,
> With hair of gold thick clustering round his ears,
> And longing eyes half veil'd by foolish tears
> Like bluest water seen through mists of rain;
> Pale cheeks whereon no kiss hath left its stain,
> Red under-lip drawn in for fear of Love,
> And white throat whiter than the breast of dove –
> Alas! alas! if all should be in vain.
>
> Corn-fields behind, and reapers all a-row
> In weariest labour toiling wearily,
> To no sweet sound of laughter, or of lute;
> And careless of the crimson sunset-glow
> The boy still dreams: nor knows that night is nigh:
> And in the night-time no man gathers fruit.

(The androgynous tug of the poem is well revealed in the way Wilde could recycle most of the first seven lines of 'Wasted Days' in 'Madonna Mia' – which interestingly denies that female the boy's feminized golden hair.[30]) One of the incriminating nubs of the letter addressed to Bosie, and labelled a 'sonnet', that was produced in court to prove Wilde's 'unnatural' affections (referred to earlier, in 'Selving'), was its infatuated insistence on Bosie's goldenness: 'Your slim gilt soul walks between passion and poetry'; 'I know Hyacinthus, whom Apollo loved so madly was you in Greek days'.[31] Hyacinthus: persisting type of the adorable fragile male; from whose blood in Greek mythology the hyacinth flower was said to have sprung – hyacinths

---

[29]   Wilde wanted his *Salome* (1893) bound in 'Tyrian purple' to go with Bosie's 'gilt hair': Richard Ellmann, *Oscar Wilde* (Hamish Hamilton, 1987; Penguin, Harmondsworth, 1988), 353. *Salome*, a drama much concerned, of course, with hair, not least on the head of its beheaded John the Baptist figure: hanging down frightfully like a Medusan nest of snakes as Salome holds it in the Aubrey Beardsley illustration for the 1894 John Lane/Bodley Head English edition. Wilde had been attracted to Beardsley as illustrator by his drawing of Salomé holding the Baptist's head in the *Studio*, April 1893: Ellmann, 355.

[30]   Both poems, of course, are in the Oxford World's Classics *Complete Poetry* of Wilde, ed Isobel Murray (1997), with minimal, but useful, noting in the matter.

[31]   For the extended role of the letter in the Wilde trial, see the transcripts in *Irish Peacock & Scarlet Marquess: The Real Trial of Oscar Wilde*, ed Merlin Holland (Fourth Estate, London and NY, 2003).

of various colours, but taken as yellow when applied to poetic hair, from Homer on (*Odyssey* VI, 231), because the epithet *hyacinthine* there ('looks like the hyacinthine flower') was understood to mean golden since the hair is immediately compared to gold. And, in the tradition, there were concerning hints of femaleness, or androgyny, about such hair. So that Milton goes out of his way in *Paradise Lost* Book IV to insist that Adam's 'hyacinthine' locks 'manly hung': he doesn't want them confused with Eve's 'golden tresses', though that's easily done. Ovid's *Metamorphoses* X, 211 immortalized the idea that the hyacinth's petals were inscribed *Ai, Ai* to register the grief of Hyacinthus. That's the legendary inscription which William Allingham thinks of in suggesting in his little elegy for Keats entitled 'Hyacinth' that the flower mourns for the dead poet: 'Were but thine old inscription legible / 'Twould suit our modern loss too sadly well'.[32] What plainly concerned Milton (known, not incidentally, as 'the lady of Christ's' when he was a boy at Cambridge for the girlishness of his long hair) was that *hyacinthine* might be too plainly legible as unmanly. Which is, maybe why the major nineteenth-century male poets, all except Byron – and Wilde – eschew hyacinthine for hair. Are they worried by what Wilde plainly celebrates in addressing Bosie as Hyacinthus, and in dwelling on the beloved blond boy's ephebic blondness, the hinting at the effeminacy Milton so carefully rebuts?[33] In Housman's very movingly glum, horrified poem 'O who is that young sinner with the handcuffs on his wrists?', about Wilde's imprisonment, 'the colour of his hair' is code for Wilde's innate homosexuality. 'Oh they're taking him to prison', and 'hailing him to justice', and 'He can curse the god that made him', all 'for the colour of his hair'. (He's tried, in vain, 'To hide his poll or dye it of a mentionable shade'.) This is, in the first place, not a poem about the mentionability of hair-colour, but about the speakability of same-sex desire. Which Housman felt it wiser to write about only in code, and in fact to keep altogether quiet about in his lifetime: he never published the poem, which only came out, so to say, posthumously in 1937 in his brother Laurence Housman's *AEH: Some Poems, Some Letters and a Personal Memoir*. The poem 'says something', Laurence said, 'which AEH very much wished to say, but perhaps preferred not to say in his own lifetime'. And, of course, what AEH preferred not to say does, emphatically, repeatedly, involve the colour of that young sinner's hair. No doubt, one guesses, it was the tell-tale *hyacinthine*, allusion to which got Wilde into

---

[32]   In Allingham's *Flower Pieces and Other Poems* (1888).

[33]   It's more than interesting about the ambivalent sexual tradings in the Hyacinth Garden of Part One of *The Waste Land* that we are never actually told the gender of TS Eliot's 'hyacinth girl' – referred to again, like the hyacinth's melancholic inscription, in my final chapter, 'Victorian Modernismus'.

legal trouble. The hair-colour that dare not speak its name, even in a poem destined to be kept in the closet.[34]

Swinburne asks 'To what strange end ... some strange god' has hidden 'love in all the folds of all' the hair of bi-gendered Hermaphroditus. Every poet – hetero, of course, but gay as well – knew the 'end' for which 'love', that is sexuality, had been disposed 'in all the folds' of all the hair of the desired other. Hair is projected as the constant locale of sexual invitation and desire; it's the place, literally, of sexual intercourse in Victorian poems. The hetero poets are as uniformly fetishistic about female hair as the gay ones about androgynous locks. Hair turns poets on; it turns their characters on. Hair in all kinds and fashions. Wet hair, it might be, the hair of, say, Guinevere or Jehane in William Morris's 'The Defence of Guinevere' and 'The Haystack in the Floods'.[35] But especially loose, untied, flowing hair: the kind of hair that fills that volume of Morris's (dedicated 'To My Friend, Dante Gabriel Rossetti, Painter'– Rossetti the women's-hair specialist), the hair-besotted book that's natural home of 'Rapunzel', story of the greatest amount of hair known to story and literature, the floating, unloosed, undone hair of Rapunzel/Guendolen – 'fathoms' of it (a fathom is 6 feet or 1.8288 metres) which she lets down from up in her tower-prison to make a stair-way (*stair-way*: *hair-way*) up which Prince Sebald can climb to rescue her. Women's loosened hair is indeed, as Isobel Armstrong rightly puts it in her discussion of Morris in her chapter on 'The Grotesque as Cultural Critique', 'a Victorian code for released sexual feeling'.[36] 'Rapunzel, Rapunzel / Let down your hair', chants the wicked witch in that poem. Rapunzel/Guendolen yearns for the sexual consummation that will come when she can 'free' her golden hair and let it down for Sebald to employ as the stair-way to her body. The witches have plaited it, that is bound it, so they can swing on it in the likeness of 'Devil's bats'.[37] Freed, it floats down, to help fulfil Sebald's dream of access to her body. A dream registering Rossetti's vision of entry to the desired female, both body and soul, via the hair. Hair that's the absolute essence of the female 'Body's Beauty' in Rossetti's sonnet LXXVIII of *The House of Life*. And what's notable about the attraction of the woman's soul in the parallel sonnet LXXVII, 'Soul's Beauty' is how bodily and hairy

---

[34] I'm full of admiration for Christopher Ricks's argument that ultimately the poem is about deadly prejudices, of which anti-semitism is the model, so that the un-named hair-colour would the red of traditional anti-semitic labelling and libelling. But that leap is too far-fetched. Ricks, 'AE Housman and "the colour of his hair"', *Essays in Criticism*, 47 (1997); in *Allusion to the Poets* (Oxford University Press, Oxford, 2002), 282–294.

[35] In *The Defence of Guenevere and Other Poems* (1858).

[36] Isobel Armstrong, *Victorian Poetry: Poetry, Poetics and Politics* (1993), Part II, Ch 9, p 242.

[37] Galia Ofek is at her historical-critical best in weighing the Victorian attraction-repulsion of 'the Medusa-Rapunzel Dichotomous Paradigm', *Representations of Hair in Victorian Literature and Culture* (2009), 74–77.

it is – a matter of 'her gaze' which strikes 'awe', of her enslaving eyes, but also of her 'flying hair'. The woman's 'flying hair' is paralleled with her 'fluttering hem'. This female is 'known' – 'long known' – by her 'flying hair and fluttering hem'. And the hem of the fluttering dress is indeed enticing, directing the desirous male gaze to the woman's ankles, but not as enticing as the unloosed hair, because its revealings are also a coy concealing. The key erogenous operator, the sign and means of open sexual invitation, is the wholly visible, flying hair. Woman – 'Lady Beauty' in Sonnet LXXVII – seduces most by her loose hair. Such hair is what makes the poet's 'voice and hand shake still' – causes the 'beat' of his 'heart and feet' as he pursues her 'daily'.

Hair invites to thoughts of sex, and to sex. Poets – and painters – fantasize constantly about that invitation. They want to climb Rapunzel's hair-stair, and be pleasurably enclosed in it: the hair pathway and gateway as triumphant enshrining, as bedroom. The lyrical-I of Rossetti's 'The Blessed Damozel' imagines his sainted beloved leaning out from the 'gold bar' of Heaven, her yellow hair hanging down in an invitation precursive of Morris's Rapunzel, so that 'now, in this place / Surely she leaned o'er me – her hair / Fell about my face ....' This is only a stuttering dream, registered in the strange staccato of that fourth stanza. 'Nothing' actually happened, except 'the autumn-fall of leaves', which perhaps provoked the dream; but it's a potent and continuing one. (Rossetti's painting *The Blessed Damozel* not only features the lengthily red-haired Janey Morris with a halo of stars, but features a background superabundance of embracing couples each of whose women has red-hair also trailing lengthily down her back.) In 'The Love-Letter' (sonnet XI of *The House of Life*), the poet puts himself as it were in the position of the love-letter he's received, which was 'Warmed by her hand and shadowed by her hair' and was 'closelier press'd' to her 'bosom' as she wrote, 'at some fond thought'. The text of love, the paper gift, comes heavily charged with bodily presence and especially the erotic charge of the hair: the warming bodily touch of love and the lover's hair-shadowing, enjoyed by proxy. It's a dream Browning's men enjoyed right from the start of his career, as in Browning's very first published words in *Pauline* (1833), his poetry's genesis moment:

> Pauline, mine own, bend o'er me – thy soft breast
> Shall pant to mine – bend o'er me – thy sweet eyes,
> And loosened hair and breathing lips, and arms
> Drawing me to thee – these build up a screen
> To shut me in with thee, and from all fear;
> So that I might unlock the sleepless brood
> Of fancies from my soul, their lurking-place[.]
>
> (1–7)

In the screen of the beloved's hair: a place of love, and also of poetry; where memory, and the characters of the poetic monodrama, are released. The echo here in this genetic unlocking of the brood of fancies, of Milton up in his high lonely midnight tower in 'Il Penseroso' seeking to 'unsphere' the spirit of Plato and 'unfold' 'vast regions' for the imagination, the 'immortal mind', is deliberately hubristic of this young poet. But the difference at this career-beginning moment from puritanical Milton – the hair-obsessed poet who associates the let-down hair of women with the pagan spirits who are banished by the young Christ in 'On the Morning of Christ's Nativity', and the troubling attractions of lovely long-haired Eve, mother of all the sinful and fallen, in *Paradise Lost* – is abundantly clear. This new poet's inspirations will come from accepting, rather than spurning, the creative erotic charge of sexy female hair.

And yet, before very long, guilty Miltonic thoughts about the fatal attractions of women's hair were striking Browning hard. It's difficult to find a description of sex and post-coital satisfaction anywhere in Victorian literature that's more enticing and attractive than the affair of adulterous wife Ottima and her German lover Sebald in Browning's 'Pippa Passes' – the woman recalling herself on top in sex, that superior position so much craved by male poets for their women, covering the man with her unloosed hair:

> While I stretched myself upon you, hands
> To hands, my mouth to your hot mouth, and shook
> All my locks loose, and covered you with them –
> You, Sebald ... .
>
> (Part I, 198–201)

Sebald: who wants Ottima to slow her narrative orgasmically down, in echoes of Catullus's famous 'lente, lente', 'slowly, slowly', as she half recalls Keats's 'Now more than ever seems it rich to die' (' "Let death come now! 'Tis right to die! " ... Who said that?') and remembers her hair in his mouth: ' "such bliss" '. Blissful memories contrived by the blissfully hair-greedy mouth of the poet:

> I felt you
> Taper into a point the ruffled ends
> Of my loose locks 'twixt both your humid lips.
>
> (I.211–13)

But immediately the moral force of *loose* intrudes. Ottima declares herself a *loose*, a *fallen* woman. 'My hair is fallen now: knot it again', she says, urging Sebald to bind her hair thrice about her brow and to repeat after her that she's his queen, his 'spirit's arbitress, / Magnificent in sin'. Which he tries to

do; but is stymied at the word 'Magnificent'. He can't declare their sin magnificent: he's cut off by the song of the passing innocent peasant Pippa about
how 'God's in his heaven' and 'All's right with the world'. These words
about divine rightness instantly put him off his lover. 'Go, get your clothes
on – dress those shoulders!' 'Wipe off that paint! I hate you'. Ottima's
undressed body and painted face have lost their appeal. And 'the very hair, /
That seemed to have a sort of life in it, / Drops, a dead web!' (237–247). It's
no accident that Guido Franceschini in *The Ring and the Book* fantasizes
that his impotence (his body's *ice*) would be solved by a loose woman with
unloosed hair and unloosed clothes who would 'tumble[] flat and frank on
me / Bareheaded and barefooted, with loose hair / And garments all at large',
crying ' "Take me thus!" ' (V.686–688).

Hair, the loveliest, most desirable bodily part that Victorian poetry allows
itself to dwell on, turns out to be deadly stuff, the site and sign of transgression, of guilt about the body, metonym of the deadly attractions of sexuality
itself. (It's not hard, hereabouts, and not at all by the way, to recall Ruskin's
disturbed 1848 wedding night when the sight of Effie's pubic hair altogether
unmanned him: the tragedy of the keenest advocate-to-be of the hair-
dominated Pre-Raphaelite painters and poets, disabled not so much (common story) by the shock of a woman having the pubic hair that the marble
statues he was used to did not, as by his not having grasped the synecdochic
force of all that aestheticized Victorian hair already filling the poems if not
yet actually the paintings, the public face of the privately pubic.) All that
lovely hair is indeed, one way or another, perturbed and perturbing, the
occasion of so much disturbed imagining. Think of Aphrodite, Goddess of
Love, whose lovely hair entrances Victorian poets of all kinds and qualities,
letting it down in grief for the dead Adonis she adores in Elizabeth Barrett
Browning's translation of first-century BC Bion of Phlossa's poem, 'A Lament
for Adonis':

> And the poor Aphrodite with tresses unbound
> All dishevelled, unsandaled, shrieks mournful and shrill
> Through the dusk of the groves.

Just, or nearly, so, the floating, unbound hair of Calypso in 'Calypso
Watching the Ocean' by LEL (Letitia Landon), is the mark of a lover abandoned (by Odysseus), 'type', as the poem has it, of everyone, 'mortal or
celestial', who submits to the 'passion and power' of the heart:

> Downwards floateth her bright hair,
> Fair – how exquisitely fair!
> But it is unbound.
> Never since that parting hour

Golden band or rosy flower
In it has been wound;
There it droopeth sadly bright,
In the morning's sunny light,
On the lone and lovely island
In the far-off southern seas.[38]

Distressed air, distressed hair. Hair as a sign of a great deal that's felt to be up with gender, the body, sexual desire, sexual relations. In Elizabeth Barrett's strange tribute sonnet 'To George Sand: A Recognition' (in her *Poems* of 1844), the sexually radical French woman writer 'George Sand' is represented as having tried to deny her 'woman's nature'; breaking 'away the gauds and armlets worn / By weaker women in captivity': the adornments of women slaves, that is married women; cutting off her hair, to look like a man, to go with her 'man's name'. George Sand shore off what St Paul said was a woman's, a wife's, *glory*, her hair; making a heretical glory of what St Paul thought the 'shame' of short hair (it was 'a shame for a woman to be shorn or shaven', I Corinthians 11.6). But Sand can't, Barrett is glad to think, after all, deny her true womanliness – the womanliness of submission to men: the father Barrett was obedient to even as she wrote, the husband she was still looking forward to in 1844:

Thy woman's hair, my sister, all unshorn
Floats back dishevelled strength in agony,
Disproving thy man's name.

The 'woman-heart' of the French poet beats in her poems, despite herself. She should give up her 'unsexing' pretence (and Barrett's use of that verb from Lady Macbeth's invoking the murderous spirits to 'unsex' her, to remove any womanly compunction against murdering King Duncan, is full of horror). Sand should leave all unsexing to God and the after-life – the 'pure' unsexing of 'the spirit-shore', or heaven, where, as Jesus said in Mark 12, there is no marrying nor giving in marriage (no women there are 'given in marriage' by a senior family male to another male, as the Anglican Prayer Book Wedding Service has it), because 'in Christ' there is neither male nor female (St Paul again: Galatians 3.28). Sand should accept the womanly submissiveness signified by orthodox Christian women's hair – Barrett's own, it might be, that grim curtain of 'black ringlets'; even if it's an 'agony', it's an orthodox one, and thus a 'strength'. But what, one wonders, about that 'dishevelled strength'? Dishevelled hair is always a sign in Victorian art of

---

[38] 'Subjects for Pictures', *The New Monthly Magazine and Literary Journal*, 47, Part III (1836), 20–21.

sexual willingness. Is the virginal Barrett thinking fearfully of the reputed initial agony of sexual intercourse for women, the necessary painful bodily submission of the good Christian wife? Whichever way the poem turns there's some sort of trouble for woman – all turning on the way hair is worn.

The shifts of Lawrence Kramer's way with this poem are most suggestive as he scoops it into his very insightful discussion of the 'mandated' sexual violence of men against women in western culture, *After the Lovedeath: Sexual Violence and the Making of Culture* (1997):

> The dangling gauds and clutching armlets unmask the normal condition of Western womanhood as one with that of a Turkish odalisque or, perhaps, of an Israelite slave girl in Egypt. The pleasure such women give, by both their ornamentation (hence their sexuality) and their servitude, is further identified with the agony proper to woman as subject. That agony, in turn, takes material form as the woman's crowning glory, her unbound hair, an object of much fetishistic desire in the nineteenth century.
>
> Barrett Browning [though she was, in fact, only Barrett Barrett when she wrote the poem] is not only in on a secret that femininity is, and is meant to be what hurts. She also knows that part of her willingly embraces the duty to dishevel her strength in agony. We might be tempted to dismiss this as a moral failure ... as the poet meekly kisses the rod. But Barrett Browning thinks that the moral failure is Sand's, not her own; it is just too easy to play a manly part. What is hard, what is heroic, is to wear one's feminine hurt as a badge of defiance. Wear the gauds, the armlets, and the hair at a certain angle, and the slave girl become a tyrant: Dalila, Turandot, Salome.[39]

Turandot, Dalila and Salome: notorious *femmes fatales*; Dalila and Salome: sexual victims who turn masterful in Biblical story. And in terms of hair. Philistine Dalila cuts off her Jewish lover Samson's hair and so emasculates him; Salome overwhelms King Herod with the erotic force of her dancing and gets the hairy head of John the Baptist on a platter as a reward. Salome goes into throes of memorably morbid ecstasy over the prophet Jokanaan's head in Wilde's characteristically relishing version of the popular story in his *Salome* (French version 1893, English version 1894). Aubrey Beardsley's notorious illustration of the scene, known as 'The Climax', has the snake-haired head of Iokanaan as the mirror image of Salome's richly flowing and curling black locks, a monstrous coupling of a be-haired hermaphroditic pair. The lethality of these entrancing women is greatly bound up with what they do to hair. Because their threat to men is embodied in the dangerous challenge embodied in eroticized hair as such. It's the Lamia-effect – after Keats's poem 'Lamia', in which the witch-woman Lamia has a serpent's

---

[39] Lawrence Kramer, 'Odd Couples', *After the Lovedeath: Sexual Violence and the Making of Culture* (University of California Press, Berkeley, Los Angeles and London, 1997; pbk 2000), 235.

head ('ah, bitter-sweet'); a Medusa-tribute, of course, in which women's fetching locks appear as deadly snakes. A disturbed vision no less (much drawn by Simeon Solomon): close to what the Austrian psychiatrists Josef Breuer and Sigmund Freud thought of as hysterical symptoms in the case (foundational for modern psychoanalysis) of Anna O, who hallucinated her hair as black snakes.[40] And so it is with Dante Gabriel Rossetti's Lilith obsession. In his dramatic 'Body's Beauty', for example, where the beauty with the fetching hair is indeed Lilith, legendary demonic lover of Adam, deadly predecessor of the fatal Eve. Eve was the lovely temptress seduced by Satan in the form of a snake; Lilith is the snaky seductress whose hair is as deadly as any snake bite.

> Of Adam's first wife, Lilith, it is told
> (The witch he loved before the gift of Eve,)
> That, ere the snake's, her sweet tongue could deceive,
> And her enchanted hair was the first gold.
> And still she sits, young while the earth is old,
> And, subtly of herself contemplative,
> Draws men to watch the bright web she can weave,
> Till heat and body and life are in its hold.
>
> The rose and poppy are her flowers; for where
> Is he not found, O Lilith, whom shed scent
> And soft-shed kisses and soft sleep shall snare?
> Lo! as that youth's eyes burned at thine, so went
> Thy spell through him, and left his straight neck bent
> And round his heart one strangling gold hair.

Here's death as a very peculiar *Liebestod*, strangulation by desirable hair. The very agent of pleasure as weapon of man's destruction. It's a suicidalism zanily paralleled by the deadly love-making in Robert Browning's most awful love poem, his most terrible hair-piece, the dramatic monologue 'Porphyria's Lover', in which Porphyria, an adulterous golden-haired wife, 'Too weak' (according to her lover) to leave her husband, invites death by her own hair:

> She put my arm about her waist
> And made her smooth white shoulder bare,
> And all her yellow hair displaced,
> And, stooping, made my cheek lie there,
> And spread, o'er all, her yellow hair,
> Murmuring how she loved me ...

[40]   Full account in Breuer and Freud, *Studien über Hysterie* (Leipzig and Vienna, 1895): *Studies in Hysteria*, trans and ed James & Alix Strachey (Hogarth Press, London, 1956).

In that perennially desirable shrine of hair, in which 'she was mine, mine, fair, / Perfectly pure and good', the lover-narrator 'debated what to do'. And

>   I found
>   A thing to do, and all her hair
>   In one long yellow string I wound
>   Three times her little throat around,
>   And strangled her.

His tone is uncannily akin to Rossetti's woman killer's in that Browning-tribute poem 'A Last Confession': 'And then I found her laid against my feet / And knew that I had stabbed her' (538–539): a woman whose hair is a main attraction and, eternally wet with her blood, haunts his guilty dreams as she keeps wringing it out with a hissing noise. 'Porphyrias's Lover' is a Lilith story in gender-reversal, but still the inevitable *Liebestod* which lies in store whenever Victorian lovers tangle with Lilithian hair. Here was an older Romantic strain being given momentous push into the Victorian present:

>   Hold thou thy heart against her shining hair,
>   If, by thy fate, she spread it once for thee;
>   For, when she nets a young man in the snare,
>   So twines she him he never may be free.

That's Rossetti's 'Lilith. From Goethe', written in 1866 – a version of the lines in Goethe's *Faust*, where Mephistopheles introduces Faust to the witch Lilith in the Witches' Sabbath on Walpurgisnacht up on the Brocken Mountain. Rossetti knew well the pedigree of his erotically hairy night-mares. It was a tradition of ancient evil – temptation to sin and fall – whose immorality his devout sister easily recognized and, on the face of it, readily repudiated. The good Prince in her poem 'The Prince's Progress' (in *The Prince's Progress and Other Poems*, 1866), falls from grace, distracted from the grail pursuit of true love, when – like Bunyan's Christian in *The Pilgrim's Progress* wandering into Bypath Meadow – he falls for the charms of the 'wave-haired' but evil milkmaid

>   Who twisted her hair in a cunning braid
>   And writhed it in shining serpent-coils
>   And held him a day and night fast laid
>   In her subtle toils.

Sonnet No. 8 of Christina G Rossetti's 14-sonnet sequence *Monna Innominata: A Sonnet of Sonnets* (in *A Pageant and Other Poems*, 1881), one of the most astonishing of her so many astonishing love poems, has a much more complex take on the wiles of snake-haired women. In her self-deprecating role as one the Unnamed Women of the sonnet, the love-poem tradition, as one of history's anonymous beloveds – not Dante's Beatrice, not Petrarch's Laura, not the heroine that 'the Great Poetess of our own day and nation', author of *The Portuguese Sonnets*, that is Elizabeth Barrett Browning, might have written about had she been 'unhappy instead of happy' – Christina G thinks of the Bible's Queen Esther, who saved the exiled Jews, her Jewish kindred, from destruction by appealing to her infatuated husband King Ahasuerus: using her attractive body to get her way with a man. Rossetti had long been attracted to Esther's bold self-assertiveness. 'If I perish, I perish', Esther had said, putting herself forward (*Esther* 4.16). Rossetti repeated the phrase three times in her 1851 poem 'A Royal Princess' in which an Esther-like princess defies her oppressive, revolution-crushing, imperialist father and risks her neck to take bread to famished workers clamouring violently at the palace gates: 'I, if I perish, perish; in the name of God I go'.[41] Now, in Sonnet No. 8, meditating ruefully on her missed opportunities with one of her repudiated suitors, the poet and translator Charles Bagot Cayley – these are indeed unhappy love poems – she thinks of how she might have done an Esther on Cayley, might have used her body, and especially her hair, to secure him; and had not done so:

> 'I, if I perish, perish' – Esther spake:
> And bride of life or death she made her fair
> In all the lustre of her perfumed hair
> And smiles that kindle longing but to slake.
> She put on pomp of loveliness, to take
> Her husband thro' his eyes at unaware;
> She spread abroad her beauty for a snare,
> Harmless as doves and subtle as a snake.
> She trapped him with one mesh of silken hair,
> She vanquished him by wisdom of her wit,
> And built her people's house that it should stand:–
> If I might take my life so in my hand,
> And for my love to love put up my prayer,
> And for love's sake by Love be granted it!

The last three lines mark a melancholy, even regretful, 'If only': if only she could be like an Esther, luring and entrapping her man with perfumed hair. But she will not, because she cannot. That's Lilith's way, the way her brother's

[41] The poems was first published in 1863 as Christina G's contribution to the fund-raising effort on behalf of Lancashire mill-workers laid off when the American Civil War interrupted cotton supplies, in the collection *Poems: An Offering to Lancashire. Printed and Published for the Art Exhibition for the Relief of Distress in the Cotton Districts.*

hair-infatuated poems and paintings approve (her 'one mesh of silken hair' obviously comes from his 'one strangling golden hair'). Off her own bat Christina G has turned Esther into Lilith (the Bible tells how Esther was perfumed a lot to make her attractive to Ahasuerus, but makes no mention of hair, and not even the perfume is alluded to as Esther approaches her husband on the climactic 'If I perish, I perish' occasion). And Lilith's way is not for a good Christian woman, a would-be bride of Christ, even if snakiness gets a sort of endorsement from the advice of Jesus to his followers to be 'wise as serpents, and harmless as doves', which is seemingly followed by Esther in line 8, 'Harmless as doves and subtle as a snake', and even if the cause – Christian marriage – is as good as Esther's. This sonnet's epigraph from Dante (each one of the series has an epigraph from Dante and Petrarch) reads (in William Michael Rossetti's translation), 'As if he were to say to God, "I care for nought else"'. That's not an 'As if' for Christina G: she'd never tell God she cared for nothing else than a human love. But still the tone of regretful 'if only' pushes hard against the rhetoric of the deplorable – *lustre, pomp, bride of life* (so close to *pride of life*) – denoting the strategies and ends – *trapped, mesh* – the moral woman will not stoop to. The most highly moral women in Christina G's Anglo-Catholic Christian book are nuns, who cut off their golden hair when they become Brides of Christ, as in the case of the three nuns in the three (unpublished) poems of the 'Three Nuns' group.

> When my yellow hair was curled
> Though men saw and called me fair,
> I was weary in the world
> Full of vanity and care.
> Gold was left behind, curls shorn
> When I came here; that same morn
> Made a bride no gems adorn.

Thus the first nun, embracing financial poverty, and physical unattractiveness, for Christ, signified and performed in the loss of golden hair ('for this white veil / I gave my golden hair' says the third nun). Her chosen lot is uglification and earthly impoverishment, swapped, she tells herself, for the 'treasure' of an undying love in heaven – 'where / Nought perisheth'. But the theological rectitude here – the divine husband of these brides is above the low hair-attractions earthly lovers are magnetized by – quite fails to assuage the sequence's much regret at the loss of earthly suitors who cared for such vanities. 'I sacrificed, he never bought'. The second nun looks forward to dying and receiving her heavenly 'crown of glory' from her heavenly husband – the reward whose very name jars really unconsolingly with St Paul's claim that a woman's hair is her 'glory' – that golden stuff she can't help wishing she'd 'bought' an earthly love with. These poems are heavy with apparent (and terrible) autobiographical regret and angst over the poet's chosen life as unmarried and virginal, as the one refusing the sexual allure of hair. The deplored attractiveness of hair refuses to be outweighed by the moral considerations.

It's a conflict going on rather widely in the period. Men find the artfully contrived Lilithian allure of woman's hair overwhelmingly attractive, even though this is a torturing loveliness. Especially when, as in the case of the spouse in George Meredith's extremely bitter sequence of anti-love sonnets *Married Love* (1862), the woman is using her hair to attract other men. (The anger of *Modern Love* is directly related to the betrayals of Meredith's wife, the writer Mary Ellen Nicolls, who ran off with the Pre-Raphaelite painter Henry Wallis. And not, perhaps, all that by the way, Meredith was lodging with his great friends the hair-cultists Dante Gabriel Rossetti and Swinburne even as he wrote the sequence.) Meredith blames disgustingly over-coiffeured male hairdressers for complicity in the creation of modern Liliths. All the golden-haired lovelies have serpent potential; 'that oil'd barber', 'That long-shank'd dapper Cupid with frisk'd curls', brings it to life:

> The gold-eyed serpent dwelling in rich hair
> Awakes beneath his magic whisks and twirls.

For his part the Aesthetic Nineties poet John Gray (alleged inspirer of Oscar Wilde's *Dorian Gray*) dreams in his lushly Beardsleyesque poem 'The Barber' of being such a hairdresser and being led on into the body intimacies that time spent in the beauty parlour is, apparently, all about. One kind of touch leads inevitably to others:

> I
> I dreamed I was a barber: and there went
> Beneath my hand, oh! manes extravagant.
> Beneath my trembling fingers, many a mask
> Of many a pleasant girl. It was my task
> To gild their hair, carefully, strand by strand;
> To paint their eyebrows with a timid hand:
> To draw a bodkin, from a vase of kohl,
> Through the closed lashes; pencils from a bowl
> Of sepia to paint them underneath;
> To blow upon their eyes with a soft breath.
> They lay them back and watched the leaping bands.
>
> II
> The dream grew vague. I moulded with my hands
> The mobile breasts, the valley; and the waist
> I touched; and pigments reverently placed
> Upon their thighs in sapient spots and stains,

Beryls and crysolites and diaphanes,
And gems whose hot harsh names are never said.
I was a masseur; and my fingers bled
With wonder as I touched their awful limbs.

From the public head-hair reaching down the body to the pubic hair, down to the publicly unspeakable treasures of the female body – 'gems whose hot harsh names are never said', except when they're used as synonyms for female private parts, as *diaphanes*, or crystal, apparently was (the louche French symbolist poet Jules Laforgue hails the *géraniums diaphanes* of women in a poem offered for admiration by TS Eliot in his essay 'The Metaphysical Poets'). *Valley*, slangy word for the zone between female breasts, was also a synonym, borrowed from French, for vagina. And as the touch of the barber turns into an erotic masseur's probe, gothicity sets grotesquely in. The massaging fingers bleed 'with wonder'; these limbs are 'awful'. And the beauty parlour turns into a plague hospital: the sweet desired body of the woman metamorphosing into a dementing sick monstrosity:

III
Suddenly, in the marble trough, there seems
O, last of my pale mistresses, Sweetness!
A twylipped scarlet pansie. My caress
Tinges thy steelgray eyes to violet.
Adown thy body skips the pit-a-pat
Of treatment once heard in a hospital
For plagues that fascinate, but half appal.

IV
So, at the sound, the blood of me stood cold.
Thy chaste hair ripened into sullen gold.
The throat, the shoulders, swelled and were uncouth.
The breasts rose up and offered each a mouth.
And on the belly pallid blushes crept,
That maddened me, until I laughed and wept.

The two 'lips' of the 'twylipped' vagina of the white-bodied woman (her 'marble trough') heat up, flowering into a 'scarlet pansie', under the barber-poet's warming, whole-body blush inducing, caress: a nightmare of uncouth swelling, and breasts turning surrealistically into mouths. The poem appeared in Gray's *Silverpoints* volume, published by Elkin Matthews and John Lane in 1893 – *the* decadent *fin de siècle* publishers: it was John Lane who published the English version of Wilde's *Salome* in 1894, whose Beardsley illustrations include 'The Toilette of Salome', with a masked pierrot primping a Sade-reading female seated in a very phallic arm-chair, in a scene curiously reminiscent of Gray's barbering dream.[42] Beardsley's own spryly nightmarish barber poem, 'The Ballad of a Barber', features an asexual/bisexual fop ('nobody had seen him show / A preference for either sex') who breaks down while doing a little Princess's long golden hair (it 'fell down to her feet / And hung about her pretty eyes'), fails to get the curling right, scorches her frock with his curling irons, stumbles in her copious 'train', and stabs her fatally with the broken neck of a Cologne bottle.[43]

The hair in Gray's body metamorphosings endorses the barbering nightmare. It 'ripened into sullen gold': the token of value tarnished; the currency of female loveliness devalued. '[C]an hair be false?' asks the narrator of *Red Cotton Night-Cap Country* about the widow's hair that's 'a block of solid gold' – 'Hair / So young and yellow crowning sanctity'. And of course it can: it belies her real age. Lilith's hair in Rossetti's 'Body's Beauty' is 'the first gold' alright, token of primal value, but sin and death are what are purchased with it. Here's the betrayal of the body's face-value that's repeatedly signalled by dubious bodily transactions, bad-body commerce, around golden hair. As in 'Goblin Market', mightily concerned with the moral and physical price to be paid for sexual pleasure, with the false value of merely bodily satisfactions. Foolish Laura, girl with the 'gold upon [her] head' (123), pays for the sweet fruits the sinister goblin men offer on their 'golden dish'. Her cash is her golden hair. 'Buy from us with a golden curl', they urge, and she does (125): an event gloatingly illustrated by Dante Gabriel with a Madonna-like Laura cutting off a lock of her hair with a pair of (naturally) phallic scissors while the demonic salesmen smooch and leer and slaver.[44] Pleasured, satiated, but cankered and sick, her hair gone grey, Laura lies dying with thoughts of her friend Jeanie, who fell sick and died of the 'joys brides hope to have' (314). Laura's saved only by her golden-haired sister Lizzie running the gauntlet of the violent sweetness-traders who won't take her coins. She holds out as they try to 'cram' fruit into her mouth, smearing her shut lips with the dangerous juices. 'Like a rock of blue-veined stone / Lashed by tides obstreperously, – / Like a beacon left alone / In a hoary

---

[42] 'The Toilette of Salome' is reproduced, along with Beardsley's 'The Climax' and one of Solomon's many Medusas, in *The Age of Rossetti, Burne-Jones, and Watts: Symbolism in Britain, 1860–1910*, eds Andrew Wilson and Robert Upstone (Tate Gallery Publishing, London 1997), 221, 226, 237. On *Silverpoints*, see Linda C Dowling, 'Nature and Decadence: John Gray's *Silverpoints*', *Victorian Poetry*, 15:2 (Summer 1977), 159–169.

[43] In *The Savoy*, no. 3 (July 1896), 91–93, accompanied by Beardsley's illustration of a much be-curled and raddled old roué of a barber.

[44] The illustration was the frontispiece to Christina G's *Poems*, New and Enlarged Edition (Macmillan, London and New York, 1895). See Maurice McInnis, 'Allegorising on their Own Hooks: The Book Illustrations of Dante Gabriel Rossetti & Arthur Hughes', in Susan P Casteras, *Pocket Cathedrals: Pre-Raphaelite Book Illustrations* (Yale Centre for British Art, New Haven, 1991), 67–77.

roaring sea, / Sending up a golden fire, – / ... / Like a royal virgin town / Topped with gilded dome and spire / Close beleaguered by a fleet / Mad to tug her standard down' (410–421). It's a triumph of heaven's moral gold-standard asserted by Lizzie's Christ-like substitutionary atoning suffering, her bearing of Laura's bodily sin in her own abused body. And of course the redeemed Laura's hair regains its golden colour; her renewed moral currency overtly signalled in that golden hair is restored to her. Unlike the heroine of Browning's 'Gold Hair', or Andrea del Sarto's Lucrezia, or Dante Gabriel's Jenny – all of them unremittingly contaminated by the cash nexus of their golden hair.

The 'beautiful girl' of 'Gold Hair: A Story of Pornic' (in Browning's *Dramatis Personae*) has masses of hair that outshines gold ('Hair, such a wonder of flix and floss, / Freshness and fragrance – floods of it, too! / Gold, did I say? Nay, gold's mere dross'). She insists it be left uncut at her death; it fills her coffin spectacularly, 'not flowing free' but crowning her, framing her face, spreading down across her breast till it 'reached her gown'. Her dead face is 'like a silver wedge' surrounded by her 'yellow wealth'. She becomes legendary as a saintly soul, an angel 'meant for heaven', one whose only 'crime' was 'she knew her gold hair's worth'. Until in later times her coffin is unearthed to reveal a skull wedged in a heap of the gold coins she kept hidden in her hair. She'd ostensibly looked forward to 'Gold in heaven' but put her real faith in earthly coinage, 'gold, the true sort', as she thought (stanza XXV). But it's the wrong sort – a sign of her moral corruption, of original sin, says the poem's narrator, taking her 'As the text of a sermon' (stanza XXVIII), as someone laying up treasure on earth rather than in heaven. She's an exemplum of the deceptiveness of the shiny stuff – women's golden hair, the debased values it stands for, and confirms them in.

In 'Andrea del Sarto', a poem preoccupied with questions of value – how much is a painter, a painting worth? – cash-strapped, gold-obsessed del Sarto might still paint his golden-haired wife Lucrezia as the Virgin Mary ('Let my hands frame your face in your hair's gold / You beautiful Lucrezia that are mine!'), but meanwhile she goes off with her 'Cousin', to acquire some money for her 'smiles', a golden-haired lovely getting gold for betraying her husband. '[L]et smiles buy me', he pleads (223); but her preferred cash-transactions are extra-marital ones. The promise and loveliness of her golden hair are utterly contaminated by the bad money dealings it attracts. Not unlike Rossetti's Jenny, the sadness of whose plight – lovely young woman driven into prostitution – is affirmed by the 'golden coins' her punter leaves in 'her golden hair' as she sleeps. He departs too casually, classically educated gent that he is, imaging her as Danaë: 'I think I see you when you wake, / And rub your eyes for me, and shake / My gold, in rising, from your hair, / A Danaë for a moment there.' But what woman would want to be a Danaë – supposing she knew who Danaë was, as poor Jenny no doubt does not – victim of a rape by Jove in the shape of a shower of gold coins? 'Jenny, my love rang true!', the john says; but no it's only the gold coin that rings true: a money truth that gives the lie to any claims of 'love' in their transactions. The 'love' that needs the 'tinkling' of coins to make it 'audible', as the client goes on cynically to admit, is worth nothing. (That 'tinkling' gives the game away: as all Rossetti's readers would know, this was St Paul's metaphor in 1 Corinthians 13 to signify the moral hollowness of the love-less: if I 'have not charity, I am become as a sounding brass, or a tinkling cymbal.')

Moral guilt, sin, satanism even, are all over these tradings. In Rossetti's 'Eden Bower' (written in 1869 for the 1870 volume of his poems) snake-woman Lilith is actually the lover of Satan, the Snake himself. They're both beautifully golden-haired. Just 'come' from sex with Adam, Lilith urges the Snake to have sex with her ('What more prize than love to impel thee? / Grip and lip my limbs as I tell thee'), and to permit her to go in snake-shape to tempt Eve to eat the forbidden fruit. Golden hair, one snaky strand of which is enough to strangle the 'youth' in 'Body's Beauty', is the tie that binds Lilith and her 'God-Snake of Eden' in this poem:

> Wreathe thy neck with my hair's bright tether
> And wear my gold and thy gold together!

'With my body I thee worship', declares the bridegroom in the traditional wedding service of the Church of England. Here, by contrast, was a satanic parody of that orthodox body worship: worship at the altar of Lilith's body, where her hair dominated, was to do satanic sex, to be in a demonic marriage. Which is indeed just how Swinburne seems to like it. Confronted by Rossetti's painting of 'Lady Lilith' whose story the 'Body's Beauty' sonnet narrates – yet one more of Rossetti's big-hair productions, with the woman's copper-coloured hair spreading massively across the canvas, held out and up by her combing as she narcissistically contemplates her face (those big red lips) and hair in a hand-mirror – Swinburne went into raptures. Lilith, he drooled, 'draws out through a comb the heavy mass of hair like thick spun gold to fullest length: her head leans back sleepily, superb and satiate with its own beauty ... The sleepy splendour of the picture is a fit raiment for the idea incarnate of faultless fleshly beauty and peril of pleasure unavoidable'. Only a masochist, you think, would enjoy that perilous combination and relish it as *unavoidable*.[45]

---

[45] Swinburne, 'Notes on Some Pictures of 1868', in his *Essays and Studies* (1875); discussed by Andrew Wilton, 'Symbolism in Britain', in *The Age of Rossetti, Burne-Jones and Watts: Symbolism in Britain 1860–1910* (1997), 11–33. 'The Lilith and Her Daughters' section of this catalogue of a Tate Gallery exhibition of 1997–1998, pp 94–107, is particularly illuminating on the period's Lilith preoccupation.

As Swinburne reads Lilith, she becomes the Faustine of his much deplored poem 'Faustine', his own Satanic woman with the notably seductive hair:

> Lean back, and get some minutes' peace;
> Let your head lean
> Back to the shoulder with its fleece
> Of locks, Faustine.

Faustine's particular 'fleshly beauty', as Swinburne puts it in his defensive commentary on his poem, is 'doomed ... from the first to all evil and no good'. It's this idea, he said, that gives his lines 'such lift as they have'.[46] And that's true. The poem's energy consists in the repeated announcement of Faustine's 'no good' aspects. The poem rings unforgettably with her name; every stanza ends with her name rhyming with her attributes – rhymes that ring out her terrible character, and the poet's terrible delight in it, rendered with all Swinburne's rhyming ingenuity: *unclean, epicene, obscene, mean,* and so forth. She's a bi-gendered *love-machine*; she worships the *Lampascene* (the God Priapus with the huge phallus); she's from *Mitylene* (like lesbian Sappho). The poem's Latin epigraph – *Ave Faustina Imperatrix, morituri te salutant,* version of the address of gladiators in the Roman arena to the presider over their violent sport: 'Hail Empress Faustina, those about to die salute you' – makes Faustine a judge of men's life or death. Simeon Solomon's notorious painting *Habet!* ('Let Him Have It!') depicting noble Roman women, fascinated and horrified onlookers at the gladiatorial combat, with the presiding woman, a gorgeous red-haired Pre-Raphaelite icon, cruel, gloating, eager for a death, giving the thumbs-down to a loser, is an evident tribute to Swinburne's poem and its relish for female cruelty.[47] Its pictorial richness evidences its utter seriousness, the seriousness of the poem. These men are nothing if not earnest in their sado-masochism, and, actually, compelled by a very grown-up brand of sadness at their disturbed condition. Buchanan was quite wrong to suggest Swinburne was just a naughty little boy trying hard to shock the grown-ups with big bad show-off words. What's impressive and rather moving about 'Faustine' and other such Swinburne poems is a sort of caring wonderment about the wicked woman and what she might do. The poem's opening lines urging her to lean back and get some rest are kindly ones. Real love is in the

---

[46] *Notes on Poems and Reviews* (1861); reprinted as Appendix I of the Penguin Swinburne's *Poems and Ballads & Atalanta in Calydon,* ed Kenneth Haynes (2000), 403–416.

[47] Painting reproduced in e.g. *Love Revealed: Simeon Solomon and the Pre-Raphaelites,* ed Colin Cruise (Birmingham Museums and Art Gallery, and Merrell, London and NY, 2005), 121.

air. The narrator raises the possibility of actually loving this classically hostile Pre-Raphaelite danger woman. And is she really, despite that catalogue of accusing rhyme words, capable of doing a Lilith on him?

> If one should love you with real love
> (Such things have been,
> Things your fair face knows nothing of,
> It seems, Faustine);
>
> That clear hair heavily bound back,
> The lights wherein
> Shift from dead-blue to burnt-up black;
> Your throat, Faustine,
>
> Strong, heavy, throwing out the face
> And hard bright chin
> And shameful scornful lips that grace
> Their shame, Faustine,
>
> Curled lips, long since half kissed away
> Still sweet and keen;
> You'd give him – poison shall we say?
> Or what, Faustine.

Terrible things are occurring in the give and take of these Swinburne relationships – pain, violence, bondage, death – but still they're impressively founded not just in a human need for sexual fulfilment and delight, come what might, but in a very touching regard for the desired other, even if so many of the pleasuring touches going on are repellent and wronging, endangering, neurotic, pathological even. And this patently applies, I'd say, to very many of even the most rebarbative of the Victorian hair-poems, even to 'Porphyria's Lover' and its extreme kind.

> Kissing her hair I sat against her feet,
> Wove and unwove it, wound and found it sweet;
> Made fast therewith her hands, drew down her eyes,
> Deep as deep flowers and dreamy like dim skies;
> With her own tresses bound and found her fair,
> Kissing her hair.
>
> Sleep were not sweeter than her face to me,
> Sleep of cold sea-bloom under the cold sea;
> What pain could get between my face and hers?
> What new sweet thing would love not relish worse?
> Unless, perhaps, white death had kissed me there,
> Kissing her hair.

'Kissing her hair' (this is Swinburne's 'Rondel'): nothing can substantially undermine or detract from the wondrous tenderness of the act, and the loveliness of its desired object, whatever else the lover and his woman get up to. Just as the cynical, brutal even, posture in Swinburne's 'Before Parting' of being bored and tired of the mere repetition of loveless kissing – the 'Cold sweet recurrence of accepted rhyme' (line 3) – and of not knowing, and frankly not really caring, how the other's hair has lost its old look and fragrance ('Less full of purple colour and hid spice'[32]), cannot erase the poet's recall of the good times when 'your soft hair lay / All blurred and heavy in some perfumed wise / Over my face and eyes' (10–12). And so, albeit filtered through the mesh of troubling perverse imaginings, the poet and his poems, these poets and their poems, have this way of ending up in the erotically unspecialized zone occupied by, say, the actress Fannie Kemble's unneurotic, though compellingly sad 'Song' (it's in her *Poems*, 1883), about the fading of love and so also of the once fresh body of the beloved: her peachy, rosy cheek; her sunny eyes; her golden hair:

> Pass thy hand through my hair, love;
> One little year ago,
> In a curtain bright and rare, love,
> It fell golden o'er my brow.
> But the gold has paled away, love,
> And the drooping curls are thin,
> And cold threads of wintry gray, love,
> Glitter their folds within:
> How should this be, in one short year?
> It is not age – can it be care?

The trope of once beloved woman's hair letting you down is familiar. Though Lilith she is not. And that the Lilith-type could be redeemed, her transgressions forgiven, her *Unheimlichkeit* domesticated, at the same time as her fallen, diabolical, wicked-witch charms went on being kept fully in play and in the picture, is obviously the essence of the period's huge fascination with the figure of 'Mary Magdalene'.

All The Magdalenes

'Mary Magdalene'– her name the ancient generic label for prostitutes, 'Magdalens' all in Victorian times (Christina G Rossetti helped at the characteristically named St Mary Magdalene 'house of charity' for former prostitutes in London's Highgate, 1859–1870) – was a traditional and popular conflation of several Mary stories in the Gospels. There's the 'Mary Magdalene', a demoniac out of whom Jesus casts seven devils (Mark 16.9; Luke 8.2), who goes to Jesus's tomb to anoint his dead body with 'sweet spices' (Mark 16.10) and who weeps when she finds the tomb empty (John 20.11). And there's the anonymous fallen woman – prostitute, adulteress, the text doesn't specify – who comes weeping to the house of 'Simon the Pharisee' (Luke 7.37ff), washes Jesus's feet with her tears, wipes them with 'the hairs of her head', kisses the feet, anoints them with very expensive ointment from an 'alabaster box', has her many sins forgiven her because her 'faith' has saved her, and whose 'love' for Jesus is said to be 'much' because of the muchness of her forgiven sins (the pious Pharisee meanwhile thinking orthodoxly that Jesus should not have let a sinful, unclean woman touch him). There's the unnamed woman in Matthew 26 and Mark 14 at the house of 'Simon the Leper' at Bethany, who pours an alabaster-box-full of 'very precious' ointment onto Jesus's head, against the protests of the disciples (Matthew) or onlookers (Mark) at the waste of what could have been sold to help the poor, and is excused because, as Jesus says, while they have the poor always with them Jesus will soon be leaving, and the woman is anointing his body, he says, in anticipation of his death and burial. And there's also Mary, the sister of Martha and of Lazarus, whom Jesus raised from the dead, a female favourite of Jesus, who at the family house at Bethany took 'a pound of ointment of spikenard, very costly, and anointed the feet of Jesus, and wiped his feet with her hair: and the house was filled with the odour of the ointment' (John 12.3) – against the protests of Judas Iscariot, the disciples' treasurer, about waste and the poor, which elicit the justification about Mary's anointing Jesus 'against the day of my burying', for which Jesus says she's 'kept' the ointment (John 12.4ff).

Out of all of which traditionally overlapping narrative materials comes the Victorian poets' Magdalene composite: lovely woman, highly desirable, with wonderful temptress hair, a gorgeous figure, well-off on the proceeds of paid-for sex (that alabaster box of lovely unguent did indeed cost a lot), but now penitent, weeping for her sins, a lover of Jesus and loved by him in return; a so bodily female whose tender attentions to Jesus's body, his hair, his feet, with her unguents, her tears, her kisses, her hair, body touching body, an interaction especially of hair, are also a religious occasion, redemptive, happy for her (and for Jesus), but also melancholy because this intercourse is signed with mortality in its anticipation of Jesus's bodily demise and anticipated decay (what the anointing and spices were designed to cover up, but were unable to prevent).

The gorgeousness of the woman with the big hair on the threshold of Simon the Pharisee's house, straining away from her lover and other roisterers, magnetized by a stern-looking Jesus across the way, is wonderfully rendered in Rossetti's 1850s painting 'Mary Magdalene at the Door of Simon the Pharisee', albeit at the expense of a lot of sexing-up.[48] Charles Ricketts – promoter of Pre-Raphaelite artists, friend and publisher of John Gray and Oscar Wilde, painter of Salomé, designer of the first production of Wilde's *Salome* (1906) – reproduced Rossetti's painting as the frontispiece for his volume *The Pageant* (1896) after he'd discovered it in a shop on London's Brompton Road. The Magdalene's attraction for the fleshly brigade of Decadents and Ur-Decadents is clear. Frederick Sandys' painting 'Mary Magdalene' does her in a frailer, but still gorgeous version, with long vari-tinted copper-coloured hair, holding a small jar apparently of ointment, approaching an off-stage Jesus with parted lips and half-closed eyes (patently a model posing as a penitent with no great conviction). Rossetti thought Sandys had ripped off his watercolour 'Mary Magdalene leaving the House of Feasting'.[49] In RW Dixon's poem 'St Mary Magdalene',[50] the Magdalene is absorbed into a scene of heavily eroticized English Anglo-Catholic devotedness, as a woman kneeling in a religious trance before an altar, holding her 'casket rare' of alabaster, remembering her past lives, quitting a mad 'rout of mirth' (as in Rossetti's painting), tormented by her seven swinish devils, visiting Christ's empty tomb. She hears many voices, a 'sobbing' flow, murmuring 'About things happened long ago / Of utter woe'. A Simeon 'was there and looked at her', the male focalizer, surrogate for the desirous male gaze of the poet and his readers, taking her in with a Pre-Raphaelite painter's eye, noting the line of her body and clothes and the hair which won't be controlled, a rebellious, still erotic, sign of the quondam transgressor:

> Kneeling before the altar step
> Her white face stretched above her hands;
> In one great line her body thin
> Rose-robed right upwards to her chin;
> Her hair rebelled in golden bands
> And filled her hands.

Her hair is a handful (*she's* a handful, as South London Browning would say) – a hand-full that's discrepant, one might think, with the alabaster

---

[48] Galia Ofek (2009), 66ff, takes Rossetti's Magdalene as based entirely on Luke 7.37ff, which is I'm sure wrong, and seems to assume Luke's is the Bible's only Magdalen story and so, again mistakenly, the essence of 'Magdalen'. She seems unaware of the tradition's, and so the poets' composite, bricolage Magdalen.

[49] Details in *The Pre-Raphaelites* (Tate Gallery/Penguin Books, London, 1984), 284; and *The Age of Rossetti, Burne-Jones and Watts: Symbolism in Britain 1860–1910* (1997), 104–105 ('Lilith and Her Daughters' section).

[50] In Dixon's *Christ's Company and Other Poems* (1861).

casket she's 'likewise' holding in the next stanza. But then this is fantasy not realism. Her body sways in time with the hymn she can also hear 'from within': 'Discordant, but with weighty rhymes'. She's rhyming with Rossetti's heavy-breathing vision, especially with its excessive gorgeousness – a discordancy, not least, with the note of penitential austerity, repentance, and graveyard melancholy so prominent in the Gospel stories. And a discordancy that Swinburne – of course – would extend. His Faustine might rhyme in crucial ways with the Bible's Magdalene as a demonic sexual temptress with 'imperious hair', and Swinburne is alert to a rhyming of names; but always Faustine's a demon-lover Swinburne is celebrating as beyond repentance and exorcism:

> Even he who cast seven devils out
> Of Magdalene
> Could hardly do as much, I doubt,
> For you, Faustine.
>
> (49–52)

There's more than a touch, I'd say, of Swinburne's refusenik Magdalene in Ernest Dowson's blasphemous unpicking of the orthodox Magdalen components in his 'Impenitentia Ultima', in which a defiantly impenitent sinner's last request before death and an end in Hell is for an hour's 'grace' with a woman whose hair will 'stream down and blind me' and whose feet he will 'bathe' with his tears.[51] And there's a good deal of Swinburne's parody Magdalen in Tennyson's Lilithian Vivien, the slithy demon-lover in 'Merlin and Vivien', an obvious case of Magdalene-*manquée*, kissing Merlin's feet 'As if in deepest reverence and in love' (217–218). Vivien's a sexually ardent female at a large remove from the Mary of *In Memoriam*, who weeps at the grave of her dead brother Lazarus and is an analogue in her grief of Tennyson's own sister, left bereft at the death of her fiancé Arthur Hallam: a most pious Mary who loves Jesus so much for restoring her brother to life that she washes and anoints his feet:

> Her eyes are homes of silent prayer,
> Nor other thought her mind admits
> But, he was dead, and there he sits,
> And he that brought him back is there.
>
> Then one deep love doth supersede
> All other, when her ardent gaze
> Roves from the living brother's face,
> And rests upon the Life indeed.

---

[51] In *The Savoy*, no. 1 (Jan 1896), 131.

> All subtle thought, all curious fears,
> Borne down by gladness so complete,
> She bows, she bathes the Saviour's feet
> With costly spikenard and with tears.

Not for Emily Tennyson any such gratitude to the Lord: her beloved was not raised from the dead so she has to content herself with a life of mourning prayerfulness and spiritual devotion to Jesus:

> Thrice-blest whose lives are faithful prayers,
> Whose loves in higher love endure;
> What souls possess themselves so pure,
> Or is there blessedness like theirs?
>   (Section XXXII)

By sticking to the Mary-sister-of-Lazarus segment of the Gospels' Mary-composite, Tennyson has turned down the sexual temperature, thinned the erotic content of his sister's frustration as bereaved fiancée and of the love she has for Jesus. And the Mary stories are indeed ripe for selective application, not least in the direction of piety. There's no distracting foot-drying hair in the *In Memoriam* version, as there are no tears at all, let alone feet and hair, in Isa Craig's 'The Box' (in her *Songs of Consolation*, 1874), subtitled 'Mark xiv.3'. Craig follows Mark's tear-less, feet-less, hair-less story as text for a little sermon about the need for Christian generosity to 'enrich' the poor. Which is all very well, but a de-sexualized effort that's less than concordant with the obvious erotic core of the gathered Mary stories, even at their most pious – an insistent eroticism that invades the Victorian Magdalene encounters even at *their* most pious. As for example in Laurence Housman's extremely devout 'Spikenard', envoi poem to his Christ-adoring 1898 volume *Spikenard: A Book of Devotional Love-Poems*, in which the poet turns himself into the Magdalene, offering 'This broken spikenard of my speech!' at the 'awful Feet' of Jesus, 'from a body full of blame / And tongue too deeply versed in shame.' Metaphoric cross-dressing in which the poet arms himself, rather startlingly, with the Magdalene's precious box. And you don't need to have read Freud on the meanings of his famous analysand Dora's handbag – womb-like container, emblem of female sexual potency and fear - to feel the gender oddity of that as well as the erotic force of all of the Victorian appropriations of the broken box of pricey ointments dedicated to a male body from a woman with the sexually broken, intruded-on body. The erotic implications of that highly charged (and discharged) box won't ever go away, even in Isa Craig's hair-less 'The Box'. They resonate, however obliquely, in the gay male grievings of Wilde's *The Ballad of Reading Gaol*, where the broken hearts of the prisoners at the execution of their fellow are likened to the Magdalene's broken box whose scent filled the house of the unclean Leper redeemingly:

> And every human heart that breaks,
> In prison-cell or yard,
> Is as that broken box that gave
> Its treasure to the Lord,
> And filled the unclean leper's house
> With scent of costliest nard.
>   (607–612)

This poem's catena of brokennesses – Magdalene's box, body of executed murderer, prisoners' hearts – makes redeemable Magdalenes of them all ('How else but through a broken heart / May Lord Christ enter in?' [617–618]): the murderer, and all the Gaol's broken-hearted criminals, including the gay male transgressor and male-prostitute user, the fraught gay griever over the ruined body of an attractively ruined male, Oscar Wilde himself.

The broken box's presence – often literally, but always anyway implicitly, as analogue of the female (and in Wilde's case feminized) body as attractively disturbed and disturbing erotic container – mightily afforces the sexual stresses of the period's Magdalene encounters of whatever kind. Whether in the gorgeous overdoings of the pictorial Magdalenes; or the aweing sadnesses of perhaps the period's best Magdalene poem, Rossetti's 'Jenny' (where potent rearrangings of Magdalene components occur as Jenny sleeps with the punter's coins in her hair, and it's *her* hair that's perfumed with 'fine fumes' and delicate 'musk', and the 'magic purse' of *her* body acquires 'New magic' as the john takes money from *his* purse); or in the grieving mournfulness of Amy Levy's 'Magdalen', her dramatic monologue in which an abandoned female, dying now in some hospice for fallen women, gently berates her once 'tender' seducer (in *A Minor Poet And Other Verse*, 1884); or in Lewis Carroll's 'Only a Woman's Hair' (17 February 1862), one of his very best poems, which reflects on the various 'dreamy' incitements of female hair – 'the theme of poet's song / In every time and place' – prompted by the discovery of a packet among Jonathan Swift's papers containing a single lock of hair dismissively labelled 'Only a woman's hair' – a dream about hair from a container that takes the poet back to Bethany and a weeping woman bathing 'the sacred feet with tears' and 'wip[ing] them with her hair', scorned by Pharisees but not by Jesus and thus a story rebutting 'scorn' for that Swiftian lock: 'the eyes that loved it once no longer wake: / So lay it by with reverent care – / Touching it tenderly for sorrow's sake – / It is a woman's hair'; and, of course, in Richard Le Gallienne's extremely moving, highly personal and arrestingly innovative take on the Mary stories, his 'An Inscription', elegiac sonnet for a dead beloved with once 'sunlit hair', whose coffin containing the precious remains reminds the poet of Mary's box of precious ointment in a meditation yearning for the resurrection that Lazarus's sister witnessed:

> Precious the box that Mary brake
> Of spikenard for her Master's sake,
> But ah! it held nought half so dear
> As the sweet dust that whitens here.
> The greater wonder who shall say:
> To make so white a soul of clay,
> From clay to win a face so fair,
> Those strange great eyes, that sunlit hair
> A-ripple o'er her witty brain, –
> Or turn all back to dust again.
>
> Who knows – but, in some happy hour,
> The God whose strange alchemic power
> Wrought her of dust, again may turn
> To woman this immortal urn.
> (In *Robert Louis Stevenson,
> An Elegy*, 1895)

Who knows indeed? God *may*, of course, perform a Lazarus miracle. As these Christian poets believe, he *could* do that. But we know that he did not do so for Tennyson's sister; nor for Richard Le Gallienne. The sunlit hair stayed stuck fast in its dark urn.

8

Mourning And Melancholia

Melancholy reigns over Victorian poetry. James Thomson, the cyclical depressive known as the Laureate of Pessimism (binge-drinking down-and-out, a stinky derelict haunter of the British Museum Reading Room, wandering the streets in carpet-slippers, jailed for setting fire to his lodgings, collapsing and dying of a stomach haemorrhage in June 1882 in the rooms of the blind poet Philip Bourke Marston), has the hellish London of his poem 'The City of Dreadful Night' (1870–1873, first published in 1874) presided over by a statue of 'Melencolia'.[1] A colossal winged woman in bronze, she's described as a version of the large downcast woman who represents *Melencolia* in Albrecht Dürer's famous 1514 engraving. Dürer's effigy of a person stymied, aporetic, in her work – surrounded by instruments and tools of architecture, carpentry, and other building work, which are lying idle; sitting next to a ladder pointing heavenward, which she displays no interest in; her gaze averted too from a shining sun and rainbow

---

[1]   Written 16 Jan 1870–29 October 1873. Published in the *National Reformer*, 22 March–17 May 1874. Collected in *The City of Dreadful Night and Other Poems* (1880). Referring to the absence of High Victorian melancholia from Juliana Schiesser's historical chart in *The Gendering of Melancholia: Feminism, Psychoanalysis, and the Symbolics of Loss in Renaissance Literature* (Cornell University Press, Ithaca and London, 1992), 2–3 – nothing between Romantics and 1890s Decadents and Freud – David G Riede in his sometimes acute book *Allegories of One's Own Mind: Melancholy in Victorian Poetry* (Ohio State University Press, Columbus OH, 2005), 4, surprisingly evinces little surprise, because he thinks the Victorians 'seem to have produced no literary monument to melancholia' comparable to Burton's *Anatomy of Melancholy*, *Hamlet*, Milton's 'Il Penseroso' or Keats's 'Ode to Melancholy' – 'if only because' of 'insufficient recognition of James Thomson's *The City of Dreadful Night*'. Aside from the weird confusion there between production and recognition, this is absurd. 'The City of Dreadful Night' is such a monument; so is 'Maud' (which Riede devotes proper length to).

Victorian Poetry Now: Poets, Poems, Poetics, First Edition. Valentine Cunningham.
© 2011 Valentine Cunningham. Published 2011 by Blackwell Publishing Ltd.

(traditional signs of hope) rather blocked off by a flying rat-like goblin bearing a banner inscribed 'Melencolia I' – came to seem a symbol of the aporetic selfhood, the burdened lonely self-consciousness of the Protestant Reformation, and the western European selfhood it generated. Dürer's Melencolia is the mother, so to say, of Hamlet, and the grandmother of Hamlet's consciousness-burdened offspring.[2] Prominent among whom are the Victorian poets.

Thomson's bronze version, described in section XXI of his poem, sums up for him the spirit of stoical, indomitable, but terribly downcast modernity: 'sick of soul' herself, the 'City's sombre Patroness and Queen' presides 'Over her Capital of teen and threne' (*teen*: woe; *threne*: lamentation, dirge). She's filled with

> The sense that every struggle brings defeat
> Because Fate holds no prize to crown success
>   ...
> That all is vanity and nothingness.
> (XXI. 64–65, 70)

Her subjects often gaze up at her

> The strong to drink new strength of iron endurance,
> The weak new terrors; all, renewed assurance
> And confirmation of the old despair.
> (XXI. 82–84)

So Queen Melancholy confirms both the enduring strong and the terrified weak equally in their 'old despair'. And Victorian poets are among her loyalest citizens. In a fan-letter to George Eliot, Thomson compared her, admiringly, to 'that grand and awful *Melencolia* of Albrecht Dürer which dominates the City of my poem'. He might have sent a circular-note to something like this effect around the whole British literary world.

Downcastly

For Victorian poems are multiplied scenes, extended cries, of desolation. Characteristically of his own and the period's greatly agonized writing, Lewis Carroll's *The Hunting of the Snark* (1876) is subtitled 'An Agony in Eight Fits' (with *fit*, old word for a section of a poem or song, doubling up

[2]   See eg Walter Benjamin, *Ursprung des Deutschen Trauerspiel* (1928)/*The Origin of German Tragic Drama*, Trans J Osborne (NLB, 1977), and Julia Kristeva, *Soleil noir: dépression et mélancholie* (1987)/*Black sun: Depression and Melancholia*, trans. LS Rondiez (Columbia, NY, 1989).

as meaning also an emotional bout, as of melancholy). 'A sadness ever sings': as in Sydney Dobell's 'Desolate' – bleak landscape poem, in Dobell's greatly saddened Crimean War-time volume *England in Time of War* (1856) (referred in Chapter 3, 'Making Noise/Noising Truths'), in which raindrops beat out an onomatopoetic rhythm of a wet-day's gloom: 'From the sad eaves the drip-drop of the rain!'; 'And alas, alas, the drip-drop of the rain!'. The poets come downcast, or *downcastly*, in William Renton's wonderful coinage (not recorded in the Oxford English Dictionary) in his little poem 'Dull December' (in *Oils and Watercolours*, 1876), about horses getting tired ploughing a wintry field and finding the return, up a ridge, harder than going down it: 'More downcastly they come'. Ever downcastly, the Victorian poets keep finding just cause for weeping. They imitate the Bible's Jeremiah, the 'weeping prophet', ascribed author of the Bible's *Book of Lamentations*. Hopkins's sonnet of complaint to God, 'Thou art indeed just Lord, if I contend / With thee' of course repeats the weeping prophet's complaint from the Authorized Version text of Jeremiah 12.1 – calqued on the Latin of the Vulgate Version which provides the poem's epigraph. Chapter 2 of *Alice's Adventures in Wonderland* (1865) is entitled 'The Pool of Tears'. They're Alice's tears; she swims in them. Victorian poetry swims with tears. The poets shed tears all the time. Tennyson labelled his tears as *idle*, but there's nothing *idle* about the tears shed in that inset poem in 'The Princess', 'Tears, idle tears': they're prompted, quite un-idly, by every stanza's recall of 'the days that are no more'. Tennyson has gone down in literary memory as the tear-shedder. Wilfred Scawen Blunt's memorial sonnet 'Alfred Tennyson' remembers him as the weeper who compelled other poets to tears: 'Tears, idle tears! Ah who shall bid us weep, / Now that thy lyre, O prophet is unstrung?'; 'We know not how to weep without thy aid, / Since all that tears would tell thyself has said' (in Blunt's *Poetical Works*, 1914). Francis Thompson blamed Tennyson's endless smoking, the 'tobacco, tobacco, tobacco' for 'manufacturing' the Laureate's 'blood into a saturated solution of melancholy' (a shallow accusation: tobacco was more a symptom than a cause of Tennyson's melancholies).[3] Robert Browning admitted to Julia Wedgwood, 'I believe I do unduly like the study of morbid cases of the soul'.[4] Tennyson was mightily drawn to such cases; and was one himself. 'Close weary eyes, breathe out my weary breath,/ One only thought I have, and that is death', is how Tennyson's (unpublished) 1830–1832 sonnet, 'Alas! how weary are my human eyes', puts his morbid inclinations. '[M]y hopeless melancholy gloometh': the line rhymes doomily with this 1831 sonnet's opening: 'Me my own Fate to lasting sorrow gloometh'. Like others of these gloomy sonnets – poems bearing heavily the weight of the exem-

---

[3]   Francis Thompson, 'The Life of Tennyson', *New Review*, no. 102 (Nov 1897), 542.

[4]   Quoted by Danny Karlin, *Browning's Hatreds* (Clarendon Press, Oxford, 1993), 219.

plary poem 'Il Penseroso', the melancholy musings of Milton's Melancholy Man – this one is addressed to his friend Arthur Henry Hallam: the confidant of Tennyson's confessed morbidities, the contextualizer of them in his review of *Poems* (1830), and whose unexpected death would soon make him the cause of more of them. Tennyson's 1830 persona Mariana would rather be dead than alive. 'She said, "I am aweary, aweary, / I would that I were dead"': the refrain chimes harshly all through her eponymous poem 'Mariana'. Her feeling was evidently Tennyson's own in the early 1830s. '[S]peak low, and give up wholly / Thy spirit to mild-minded Melancholy', Tennyson exhorts himself in his 1831 sonnet 'Check every outflash, every ruder sally'; and, receptive to the proclivity, he didn't have to put much effort into the urging. And the gloomy feeling never abated; rather it picked up velocity and volume with the resounding devastation of Hallam's death, and remained more or less Tennyson's lifelong note. You keep hearing that wish for death in his lines. A huge, unstoppable sadness:

> Immeasurable sadness!
> And I know it as a poet,
> And I greet it, and I meet it,
> Immeasurable sadness!
> And the voice that apes a nation –
> Let it cry an affectation,
> Or a fancy or a madness, –
> But I know it as a poet,
> And I meet it and I greet it,
> And I say it, and repeat it,
> Immeasurable sadness!

These lines appear as 'Sadness' in Hallam Tennyson's *Memoir*, II.17, assigned to the year 1864. The persisting sadness makes Tennyson perhaps the period's most melancholy man. But this was a time of melancholy men – and women. Mariana is in a deep sense the spokesperson for the times. 'I am like Mariana in the moated grange' Elizabeth Barrett confessed to Robert Browning (June 7 1845, *Letters of EBB & RB*, I.91). Melancholy pervades the poems of Christina G Rossetti and Matthew Arnold, of AE Housman and Thomas Hardy, to name no others. James Thomson is certainly a candidate for 'Laureate of Pessimism', but he's more properly to be thought of a Laureate of the Pessimists. His contemporaries are all, by and large, pessimists. They groan an awful lot in their verse. Not for nothing did Christina G Rossetti's family know her poems as her 'groans'. Arnold's poems are only typical of the period's output in rarely escaping from the cramps of despondency.

The thoughts that rain their steady glow
Like stars on life's cold sea,
Which others know, or say they know –
They never shone for me.

Thought lights, like gleams, my spirit's sky,
But they will not remain.
They light me once, they hurry by;
And never come again.

That's Arnold's little poem 'Despondency' – in *Empedocles on Etna, and Other Poems* (1852), that immensely dispirited volume. Despondent in his 'Despondency', Arnold, in Switzerland, hears for himself the *sobs* of *human agony* audible in the lone mountain torrents and the 'brooding' of the 'mountain-bee', which he says brought on the glooms of the French writer Étienne de Senancour and 'the melancholy eloquence' of *Obermann*, Senancour's collection of epistles from Switzerland. In his 'Stanzas in Memory of the Author of "Obermann": November, 1849' Arnold asks:

Is it for this, because the sound
Is fraught too deep with pain,
That Obermann! the world around
So little loves thy strain?

The 'moody' Greek philosopher Empedocles, eponymous hero of Arnold's soon-to-be deplored 'Empedocles on Etna: A Dramatic Poem', commits suicide by throwing himself into the crater of the volcano on Mount Etna, unable to carry on living: 'dead to life and joy' (321) in 'this meadow of calamity, / This uncongenial place, this human life (365–366)'. All is irredeemably melancholy in the 'deep-buried' self of Empedocles (371) – a favourite deep preoccupation of Arnold's. 'I feel a nameless sadness o'er me roll' is how Arnold feels in 'The Buried Life', yet one more of his unhappy 1852 poems:

Light flows our war of mocking words, and yet,
Behold, with tears mine eyes are wet!

He has 'A longing to inquire / Into the mystery of this heart which beats / So wild, so deep in us'. *The mystery of this heart which beats in us*: he's recalling Hamlet's challenge to Rosencrantz and Guildenstern – 'you would pluck out the heart of my mystery' (*Hamlet*, III. iii. 356). But 'this heart' is not all that mysterious to Arnold: he knows that deep down – and all through – he is, like Hamlet, melancholic. 'How weary, stale, flat, and unprofitable, / Seem to me all the uses of this world!', thinks Hamlet (I.ii.133–134), feelings shared by the ageing man and woman in Arnold's

'The Youth of Man' (also in the 1852 volume) – 'they see, for a moment, / Stretching out, like the desert / In its weary, unprofitable length, / Their faded ignoble lives'. 'Well I know what they feel!' exclaims their narrator. According to the famous downcast Preface to his *Poems* of 1853, from which 'Empedocles on Etna' was dropped, Arnold offered Empedocles as a melancholic precursor of Hamlet. In the surviving fragments of Empedocles' work, 'calm' and 'cheerfulness' and 'disinterested objectivity have disappeared' as 'the dialogue of the mind with itself has commenced' and 'modern problems have presented themselves' and the *doubts* and *discouragement* of Hamlet and of Faust (Goethe's Faust: offspring of Shakespeare's Hamlet) have set in. In his notes to 'Empedocles on Etna' Arnold says that the philosopher's 'spring and elasticity are gone: he is clouded, oppressed, dispirited, without hope and energy'.[5] Are we not all 'travellers in a hurry to arrive, / To whom their destination when 'tis reached / Soon seems as tedious as each tedious stage / They posted through to reach it?', according to one of the fragments for Arnold's aborted tragedy on Lucretius, some of whose bits he recycled in his 'Empedocles'.[6] *Tedious, tedious*: it's the modern condition, as Arnold goes on painting it in his 1857 essay 'On the Modern Element in Literature': 'a state of feeling unknown to less enlightened but perhaps healthier epochs – the feeling of depression, the feeling of *ennui*'.[7] The *ennui* and *discouragement* of Senancour are not, though, to be blamed wholly on the times: their *root* is in Senancour himself (according to Arnold's 'Obermann' essay of 1869).[8]

And ennui and discouragement are rooted, seemingly ineradicably, in so many Victorian poets. In his hugely influential First World War-time paper 'Mourning and Melancholia' (1915; published 1917), Sigmund Freud helpfully distinguished *mourning*, grief over the death of a beloved, a very normal reaction, from *melancholia*, an illness, a neurosis, brought about by protracted mourning which the patient is failing to recover from.[9] On that reckoning Tennyson's lifelong stretch of mourning for his dead friend Arthur Hallam, beginning with the seventeen years it took him to complete his 'In Memoriam AHH: Obiit MDCCCXXXIII', would certainly make him a melancholic. A melancholic like Tennyson's Queen, Victoria herself, who never stopped mourning for her dead consort Albert, and whose favourite book,

---

[5]   Quoted in the (standard) *Poems of Matthew Arnold*, ed Kenneth Allott (Longmans, 1965), 148.

[6]   Allott ibid. 587.

[7]   Allot ibid. 148.

[8]   Allot ibid. 155.

[9]   'Mourning and Melancholia', in Sigmund Freud, *Standard Edition of the Complete Psychological Works*, ed and trans James Strachey et al (24 vols, Hogarth Press/Institute of Psycho-Analysis, London, 1953–1966), XIV, 243–258.

it was said, after the Bible, was her Poet Laureate's 'In Memoriam'. And the poets mourn royally. Mourning is so ubiquitous in Victorian verses that elegy, the poetry of mourning, is simply the period's most omnipresent genre. (For a long time Tennyson's title for 'In Memoriam' was simply 'the "Elegies" '.) And this poetic grieving is so unassuagable, the tears poems shed over the dead so unstoppable, that you could say that the period and its poetry are, in Freudian terms, all under the melancholic cosh. Elegy, *the* melancholic mode, persists unstoppably.

Trading in Death

Personal ending, ending-up, worry over endedness: they've animated so much of the world's writing, but never more so than in Victorian times. 'Marley was dead to begin with': the opening words of Dickens's story 'A Christmas Carol' might be a motto for so much Victorian composition, a signal for the prevailing way Victorian aesthetic production owes its genesis, its origin, its life, to somebody's death. All writing has been, in the words of TS Eliot's poem 'Intimations of Immortality' about the Jacobean playwright John Webster, 'much possessed by death'. Death is indeed, as the American poet Wallace Stevens's 'Sunday Morning' has it, 'the mother of invention'.[10] As so much of Dickens's writing arises, as it were, from his repeated visits to morgues, in Paris, in London, so does Victorian poetry, and not just allegorically but literally. As in the case of Robert Browning's 'Apparent Failure' (in *Dramatis Personae*), about stalking (his word) one time into the Paris morgue on a visit to that city and taking in the 'sermon's text' (about death) proposed by the three latest bodies of suicides fished out of the Seine. Or of Dante Gabriel Rossetti's 'From Paris to Brussels (11pm 15 *October to half-past* 1pm 16) Proem at the Paris Station', a close-up vignette of a murdered man fished from Seine after days in the water, seen 'In passing by the Morgue' ('The face was black, / And, like a negro's, swollen; all the flesh / Had furred, and broken into a green mould'). Angela Leighton is right to take Dorothy Mermin to task for her misguided suggestion that 'a woman poet who identified herself with such a stock figure of intense and isolated art' as Tennyson's Mariana, as Elizabeth Barrett did, 'would hardly be able to write at all'. To object that that was 'not quite true' is putting the criticism mildly. Mermin was mistaking not just the grounds of Barrett's creativity, but a whole epoch's. Out of the living coffin of Barrett's melancholically shut-in existence came abundant writing, 'a multitude', as she said when comparing herself with Mariana, and so, *mutatis mutandis*, it was for

---

[10]   Quoted by Karen E Smythe, *Figuring Grief: Gallant, Munro, and the Poetics of Elegy* (McGill-Queen's University Press, Montreal and Kingston, Ontario, 1992), 8.

her time.[11] Hélène Cixous was correct in her *Three Steps on the Ladder of Writing* lectures (1993) to suggest that all reading begins with a death, in the sense that a death – an absence – is needed before we can begin reading (not least, the absence of the author), and that all reading goes on in a place of absence, of death. But how dramatically true this is of the reading of Victorian poetry. Its favourite imagined habitation is the scene of death – deathbed, funeral, graveside, churchyard, charnel-house, cemetery, morgue. Like a pathologist, as described by the writer-pathologist F. Gonzalez-Crussi, poetry makes a living out of the dying; but Victorian poetry does so especially.[12] Death is its business. It trades in death. 'Trading in Death': it's what Dickens deplored about sellers of Duke of Wellington memorabilia, relics, letters, locks of hair, window-seats overlooking his State Funeral route, and so forth, in his *Household Words* piece of that title (27 November 1852). Much of whatever aesthetic force Victorian poetry achieves is, like Dickens's fiction, purchased at the expense of the most melancholic event or experience humans know: our mortality, the fact of dying and death, our inevitable human ending-up. The beauty of this aesthetic is, as the poet DJ Enright once nicely put it, the beauty of requiems. It's not the devil who has all the best tunes: 'Literally, it's requiems that have the loveliest tunes – Fauré, Berlioz, Verdi, Mozart'.[13]

Victorian poetry certainly had cause enough for grief. For death was everywhere, at home and abroad. Christopher Herbert points suggestively towards two great areas of national morbidity: the suicidalism of the age, ascribed particularly by Émile Durkheim, the great student of suicide, to contemporary *anomie*, the melancholy generated when rules and frames of meaning and value are suspended, and rampageous desire is frustrated; and the great national depression prompted by what the 'Indian Mutiny' and its horrifically violent suppression revealed about the failures of the great imperialist project and the 'unspeakable horror' of the violence at the heart of 'our civilisation and our Christianity'.[14] The ordinary daily uniform of Victorian bourgeois men was funereal black. 'Dickens, Ruskin, Baudelaire

---

[11]   EBB to RB, Feb 3 1845, *EBB & RB Letters*, I.91. Angela Leighton, 'Stirring "A Dust of Figures": Elizabeth Barrett Browning and Love', *Browning Society Notes*, 17, 1–3 (1987–1988), 11–13 ; reprinted, *Critical Essays on Elizabeth Barrett Browning*, ed Sandra Donaldson (GK Hall & Co, New York, 1999), 218–232. Versus Dorothy Mermin, 'The Damsel, the Knight and the Victorian Woman Poet', *Critical Inquiry*, 13 (1986), 64–80.

[12]   F. Gonzalez-Crussi, 'The Dead as A Living', *Notes of An Anatomist* (Pan Books, London, 1986), 62–71.

[13]   In a conversation with me for a BBC radio Proms interval programme on literary and musical Endings.

[14]   Christopher Herbert, *Culture and Anomie: Ethnographic Imagination in the Nineteenth Century* (University of Chicago Press, Chicago, 1991); and *War of No Pity: the Indian Mutiny and Victorian Trauma* (Princeton University Press, Princeton and Oxford, 2008).

all asked why it was, in this age of supreme wealth and power, that men wanted to dress as if going to a funeral'.[15] It was because they *were* going to a funeral, either for real or in fantasy. Certainly, as WE Henley put it in 1877 in 'To WR', 'Death goes dogging everywhere'. This was not long after his nearly two years stay in Edinburgh Royal Infirmary, being dogged daily by death. Death is 'the ruffian on the stair' in this Henley poem, the pimp of 'Madame Life', lurking to put the squeeze on her customers. She's a lovely 'piece in bloom', and a source of 'fun', of pleasure. 'But he'll trap you in the end, / And he'll stick you for her price.' Death is ineluctable; it's all 'around us', as James Withers has it in his poem 'Insensibility to Death Around Us', about the endless 'sad procession' of dead neighbours which he will one day join. A Procession the world is callously 'insensible' to:

> Thus it has been for ages past
> And so 'twill be when I am gone;
> The world will hurry on as fast,
> Like water o'er the sunken stone.
> When I return to parent earth,
> And mingle with forgotten clay,
> It will not check a moment's mirth,
> Nor scarce be known a mile away.
> (*Poems Upon Various Subjects*,
> II, 1856)

These are understandably harsh accusations from the 'Hedge-Side' poet, a barely subsistence labourer, always desperately poor, his family in and out of the workhouse: of course the world does not care for him and his kind. But Withers and his poem are by no means insensible. And Withers' sensibility unites him with the mass of Victorian poets, who are perpetually, in the words of the down-and-out Irish poet James Clarence Mangan (poor, starving, sick, an Irish James Thomson), 'gazing gravewards'. (That's in 'The Night is Falling', which appeared in the *Irish Monthly Magazine* in 1845, a 'weary', grieving, night-time, 'chill December' lament about the 'death-valse' of this life.) Living, surviving, *sur-vivre*, living-on, according to Charlotte Brontë, means *per se* to be in mourning. 'He that lives must mourn', is her feeling in her extremely grieving '24 December', and she professes herself happy that her sister Emily, who died five days earlier 19 December 1848, is no longer alive to share that unrelieved pain of the living.

The pain of the lonely heart. Victorian poetry is a school of surviving lonely hearts.

---

[15] The paperback cover declaration of John Harvey's wide-ranging investigation of black clothing in the nineteenth (and twentieth) century: *Men in Black* (Reaktion, London (1995), 1997).

Show not, O Moon! with pure and liquid beam,
That mournful spot, where Memory fears to tread;
Glance on the grove, or quiver in the stream,
Or tip the hills – but shine not on the dead:
It wounds the lonely hearts that still survive,
And after buried friends are doomed to live.

That's 'On the Moon-Light Shining Upon a Friend's Grave', published in the Tennyson brothers' collaborative volume of 1827, attributed to Charles Tennyson, but surviving in manuscript in Alfred's hand. Alfred already, then, in the role of relict, the widowed one, six or seven years before Hallam's death. Victorian poets and poems are commonly widowed, literally and metaphorically. Tennyson keeps casting himself as Hallam's widow in 'In Memoriam'. It's the most regular of Victorian poetic postures. Poet and poem keep finding themselves as coming 'After' – as Philip Bourke Marston's poem 'After' has it (in his *All in All: Poems and Sonnets*, 1875). And it's an afterwards of grieving. 'Afterwards' – Hardy's poem (in his *Moments of Vision*, 1917) about what people will think and say after his death – 'When the Present has latched its postern behind my tremulous stay, / ... will the neighbours say ...?' – is where Victorian poets and poems keep imagining themselves, because it's where they keep finding themselves: post mortem; ghosted, ghostly; left behind; one of Hardy's 'fellow – wight[s] who yet abide'. The woman Marston's lyrical-I in 'After' kissed and clung to for just 'A little time' (repeated six times), just 'A little while' (three times), has died, leaving him 'like a ghost alone', with 'long, long years to weep in, / And comprehend the whole'. Poet and poem are often left behind like this, with a prospect of years ahead trying to make sense of the preceding death. They're belated; too late for happiness. 'Too late, too late' is their refrain – with WH Mallock in his poem 'Too Late' (*Poems*, 1880). It's the authentic note of the saddest American mode, the Blues. Mallock's repetition anticipates the particular Blues which so attracted the modern apostle of belatedness, melancholy Philip Larkin: 'Too late, too late, too late, too late, too late'.[16] Bluesy Mallock expresses himself surprised, taken aback, by an unacceptable death. 'What, dead – quite dead?' (Terrible reversing echo of Othello's awful cry in the presence of the Desdemona he's just murdered, 'Not dead? Not yet quite dead?' (*Othello*, V.ii.85); compare Hopkins' 'Felix Randal the farrier, O is he dead then?') Death, however anticipated, tends to come, like this, as a surprise, a shock, as the unacceptable fact of life. Being left bereft – bereaved: dispossessed, robbed, *berauben*, of a loved one – is no less painful for being utterly normal.

---

[16]   It's perpetually 'too late', or about to be so, in Larkin's poems: 'Latest Face', 'Annus Mirabilis', 'Fiction and the Reading Public', 'Lock the door, Lariston, lock it, I say to you', and 'Now'.

Without Her – And Him, And Them

> What of her glass without her? The blank grey
> There where the pool is blind of the moon's face.
> Her dress without her? The tossed empty space
> Of cloud-rack whence the moon has passed away.
> Her paths without her? Day's appointed sway
> Usurped by desolate night. Her pillowed place
> Without her? Tears, ah me! for love's good grace,
> And cold forgetfulness of night or day.
>
> What of the heart without her? Nay, poor heart,
> Of thee what word remains ere speech be still?
> A wayfarer by barren ways and chill,
> Steep ways and weary, without her thou art,
> Where the long cloud, the long wood's counterpart,
> Sheds doubled darkness up the labouring hill.

That's Dante Gabriel Rossetti in 'Without Her', Sonnet LIII of *The House of Life*, remembering, it would appear, his wife Lizzie Siddal, who has departed this world, her place, his place, as in life she departed his heart (displaced and replaced by Janey Morris). This is an elegy, then, for a double death, the death of a wife, and the death of a heart. A double loss, 'a doubled darkness', in fact, as in the poem's final line, marked and re-marked in the places and things she once inhabited and touched – her mirror, dress, pillow, her paths, his heart. They are all now utterly empty of her. Her mirror reflected her once – doubled her – as the poem's pool of water once reflected, doubled, the moon, and she was doubled in her lover's heart; but there's no doubling now. At least not in the mirror which is, like the dress and all else, presently without her. *Without her*, five times: one of the most touching repetitions in Victorian poetry (repeated in Rossetti's 'Life-in-Love', Sonnet XXXVI, another poem about the absent Siddal: 'Look on thyself without her'). They're all as blank and gloomy as a now dark, once moonlit, pond or sky, as grim as the night itself, where once day shone. But the glass, dress, pillow, paths are still, by language's curious enablings, *hers* still – they're *her* glass, *her* dress, and so forth. Her *pillowed place* – intimate recall of Keats's 'Bright Star' sonnet ('Pillow'd upon my fair love's ripening breast') – is, linguistically at any rate, pillowed still. The pillow, like the mirror, dress, paths, lacks her, is *without* her, and yet memory – elegiac recall – grants it her presence still: her old *place* bears her imprint, her trace, like a pillow indented by a head no longer there – *pillowed* still. Only the poet's heart is emphatically dispossessed – it's *the* heart, not *her* heart – and how could it be *hers*; it's his; it always was, now it's his *without her*; without her in every sense, including 'outside of her'. However heart-felt Rossetti's grief, his sense of loss, his being moved about Siddal's death, she is gone, and he is without her, lacking her, on the outside of her one-time presence. Siddal is, in Ophelia's words in her song about her dead father Polonius, 'dead and gone', and for ever (*Hamlet*, IV.iv.29–30). She's present in memory, present in the poem, reflected in the elegiac poem's reflective, reflecting words about reflection, its doublings, albeit negative ones; but she's also physically absent – caught in an arresting aporia of absence-presence, presence-absence, an aporia whose pressing negativity outweighs the poetic optimism it just about wears.

Being bereft, the being of the bereft; words about absence, words without, from the place of the departed, from the surviving one now emphatically without the absent one, mourning her or him as quite 'lost': this is the sadness of the elegiac condition, the unavoidable tragedy of this survivalist mode, the voice of the survivor. Here surviving, survival, are paradoxically, if naturally enough, grounds not for rejoicing or satisfaction, but for their very opposite: survivor unhappiness, shading into anger (King Lear's anger over the death of his daughter Cordelia: 'Why should a dog, a horse, a rat, have life, and thou no breath at all?'), but not, I think, into that modern clichéed emotion, 'survivor guilt'. And this grim affect infects most of the many kinds of Victorian elegy.[17]

Elegiac Notes

Elegy: death rhymes. Elegiac notes echoing from the poetry's multiplied scenes of death. As the line at the opening death scene of *Maud* has it: 'And Echo there, whatever is asked her, answers "Death!".' Ubiquitous elegy. **Elegies for family dead, for wives and children, siblings and cousins.** As in Richard Le Gallienne's many verses about his dead wife Mildred, including 'An Inscription' and (perhaps) 'Jenny Dead'; Dante Gabriel Rossetti's 'Without Her'; Leigh Hunt's Sonnet 'On the Death of His Son Vincent'; Robert Bridges' 'On a Dead Child', and 'I never shall love the snow again / Since Maurice died'; James Withers' 'On the Death of My Child''; Charlotte Brontë's '24 September', mourning sister Emily, and '21 June 1849', grieving for Anne; Thomas Ashe's 'Cousin Carrie'; Coventry Patmore's (guilty) recollections of his dead wife seeded across *The Unknown Eros* volume;

---

[17]   For the best recent discussions of English elegy, see Peter M Sacks, *The English Elegy: Studies in the Genre from Spenser to Yeats* (Johns Hopkins University Press, Baltimore, 1985); Jahan Ramazani, *The Poetry of Mourning: the Modern Elegy from Hardy to Heaney* (University of Chicago Press, Chicago, 1994); Eric Smith, *By Mourning Tongues: Studies in English Elegy* (Boydell Press, Ipswich, 1997); also Angela Leighton, in *On Form: Poetry, Aestheticism, and the Legacy of the Word* (Oxford University Press, Oxford, 2007).

William Barnes's utterly compelling memories of his late spouse in dialect poems like 'Since I no mwore do zee your feäce'; Matthew Arnold's heroizing tribute to his late father, headmaster of Rugby School in 'Rugby Chapel, November, 1857' (elegy as a sort of Official Biography); Arnold's more moved lines for his younger brother William, organizer for the East India Company of Education in the Punjab, who died at Gibraltar on the way home from India, 9 April 1859 ('Stanzas from Carnac' and 'A Southern Night'); Tennyson's 'To the Marquis of Dufferin & Ava', on the death in the Red Sea in 1886 of his 32-year old son Lionel returning home sick from his post in India:

> And sacred is the latest word;
> And now the Was, the Might-have-been,
> And those lone rites I have not seen,
> And one drear sound I have not heard,
>
> Are dreams that scarce will let me be,
> Not there to bid my boy farewell,
> When That within the coffin fell,
> Fell – and flashed into the Red Sea.

(Tennyson's use of the *In Memoriam* stanza make this poignant declaration of parental loss all the more touching: would the loss of a loved one in a foreign place, Hallam's kind of death, never cease? It can't be a coincidence that the multi-elegiac 'Locksley Hall Sixty Years After', an old man's dramatic monologue grieving for dead kindred, including a 'sailor son ... Leonard early lost at sea', was written in the few months following Lionel's death.)

And **elegies for friends and lovers:** as Thomas Hardy's 'Friends Beyond' ('Gone, I call them, gone for good, that group of local hearts and heads': strikingly echoing the litany of the 'Gone' in Tennyson's 'Locksley Hall Sixty Years After'); Augusta Webster's 'Dead Amy'; Matthew Arnold's 'Thyrsis: A Monody, to Commemorate the Author's Friend, Arthur Hugh Clough, Who Died at Florence, 1861'; Tennyson's 'In the Valley of Cauteretz', written in August 1861 in a valley of the Pyrenees that he had visited with Arthur Hallam, 'one I loved two and thirty years ago', and hearing again the 'living voice' of his dead friend; and his 'In the Garden at Swainston' (1870) written on the occasion of the funeral of his friend and neighbour Sir John Simeon, 'weeping' for 'three dead men' the poet has loved with an everlasting love, Simeon, Henry Lushington and Arthur Hallam; and his sonnet 'To the Rev WH Brookfield' (1874), his old Cambridge friend 'Brooks', a sort of 'humorous-melancholy' Jacques out of Shakespeare's *As You Like It*, and whose death (constant note of these friend rememberings) reminds Tennyson of the death of their mutual friend Hallam, 'the lost light of those dawn-golden times, / Who loved you well!'; and Tennyson's lovely little 'In Memoriam WG Ward' (1889) for his Isle of Wight friend the Roman Catholic theologian; and of course the elegy which overshadows all of the Victorian elegiac enterprise, Tennyson's massive 'In Memoriam' for his friend, and beloved, Arthur Henry Hallam; and AE Housman's 'AJJ', upon the death in India of his friend Adalbert J Jackson.

And **elegies provoked by deaths in the news, in the newspaper, sensational deaths, accidental deaths, deaths as symptoms of social evil and the ways of a wicked, or just sad, world:** such as J Stanyan Bigg's 'Hartley Pit Catastrophe'; LEL's 'A Suttee'; Gerard Hopkins's 'The Wreck of the Deutschland'; Sidney Dobell's 'Song of a Mad Girl, Whose Lover Died at Sea'; Dobell's Crimean War poems in *Sonnets on the War* (1855) and *England in Time of War* (1856); Elizabeth Barrett Barrett's 'The Cry of the Children' and (as Barrett Browning) 'The Runaway Slave at Pilgrim's Point'; the cluster of sad poems about women jumping to their death in the River Thames – Hood's 'The Bridge of Sighs', Henry Bellyse Baildon's 'Alone in London', Theo Marzials' 'A Tragedy', George Cecil Ives's 'Ellen Marian Smith. "No control over the other servants". Found in the Thames, April 18, 1896' (in Ives's anonymous volume, *Book of Chains*, 1897); Tennyson's 'In the Children's Hospital: Emmie' (1880), a nurse's Jesus-minded narrative about the death of a little girl in a charity hospital, a story Tennyson heard from Mary Gladstone but also read about in the papers; Oscar Wilde's capital-punishment protesting 'The Ballad of Reading Gaol'; Housman's 'Shot? so quick, so clean an ending?' ('Oh that was right, lad, that was brave'), Poem XLIV of *A Shropshire Lad*, about a soldier-boy's suicide over some homosexual misdemeanour (reported in a newspaper cutting which Housman preserved in his copy of *A Shropshire Lad*).[18]

And **elegies for dead poets, fellow-members of the household of writing, that is elegy as a dead poets' society:** as Elizabeth Barrett at and on 'Cowper's Grave'; Matthew Arnold, the non-stop elegist, at 'Heine's Grave' in Paris's Montmartre Cemetery and in 'Haworth Churchyard' (in his imagination only, the poem mistakenly thinking 'the grass blows' from grave to grave of the 'sisterly band' of Brontës, when in fact Anne was buried in Scarborough, and Charlotte, Emily, and Branwell were buried in a vault inside the church); Arnold in 'Stanzas In Memory of Edward Quilligan' in whose house he met Charlotte Brontë and Harriet Martineau; Arnold in 'Thyrsis' in memory of Clough; Arnold's 'Stanzas In Memory of

---

[18]   The next poem on *A Shropshire Lad*, XLV, even more bitterly ironic about being homosexual, recommends suicide in Biblical words to the same lad, for being sexually 'sick' of 'soul': 'If it chance your eye offend you, / Pluck it out, lad, and be sound'; 'And if your hand or foot offend you, / Cut it off, lad, and be whole; / But play the man, stand up and end you, / When your sickness is your soul'.

the Author of "Obermann"'; Eliza Cook's '"Poor Hood" (Written at Kensal-Green Cemetery)'; 'An Epitaph for Keats', by Dante Gabriel Rossetti ('Here lieth one', stabbed to death by a forgotten *Quarterly* reviewer, but who will live as long as Time flows flows on, 'His great name writ in water': which sounds a lot too soluble for the permanence Rossetti is positing – elegy deconstructing itself); and elegy-freak Swinburne's 'Ave Atque Vale: In Memory of Charles Baudelaire', and his 'In Memory of Walter Savage Landor'; William Allingham's 'Three Sisters', remembering the Brontë women (in his *Evil May-Day*, 1883); and Amy Levy's (1889) 'London Poets (*In Memoriam*)'; Victor Plarr's 'On a Reading of Matthew Arnold' (in *In the Dorian Mood*, 1896: 'Arnold is dead'); and all the women establishing tight poetic sisterhoods in the gloom of a connected chain of elegiac contemplations and offerings – LEL's 'Felicia Hemans'; Elizabeth Barrett's 'Felicia Hemans', dedicated 'To LEL, Referring to her Monody on that poetess'; Dora Greenwell's 'To Elizabeth Barrett Browning in 1861' (*Poems*, 1867); and, of course, massively, dominatingly, Tennyson's *In Memoriam*, grandest of elegies to a dead poet as well as a dead friend. (The prevailing death-bed, graveside, tomb-confronting sadness in these mourning tributes of course marks them off from the so to say mere tributes to bygone poets, of which there are also many – for instance, Tennyson's 'Milton: Alcaics', his 'To Virgil: Written at the Request of the Mantuans for the Nineteenth Centenary of Virgil's Death' (1882), his 'To Dante', and Anne Brontë's 'To Cowper'.)

And also those two rather distinct categories of elegy, much employed by Victorian poets, which eschew grieving on what may be thought elegy's traditional plan, namely **elegies for pets and other creatures, and elegies for heroes. Elegies for animals and birds** are full of the patent affection the English commonly feel for their dumb friends, rooted in impossible anthropomorphism and a kindly but irrational pathetic fallacy. These poems memorialize earnestly, like the rows of little tombstones for dogs and horses to be found at every stately home. Their pet-owning authors are evidently in earnest, but their best efforts at a kind of seriousness – as, say, in Matthew Arnold's elegies for his dead dogs Kaiser and Geist ('Geist's Grave' and 'Kaiser Dead: April 6, 1887'), and his pet canary, 'Poor Matthias' (a poem also rehearsing the demise of a whole kennels-full of canines, Rover, Atossa, Geist, Max, Kaiser) – never manage to sound much more than parodic of the genre, just as those animal tombstones look and read like the pastiches of human tombstones which, of course, they are.

> Poor Matthias! – Found him lying
> Fall'n beneath his perch and dying?
> Found him stiff, you say, though warm –
> All convulsed his little form?

The Monty Pythons' Dead Parrot sketch is not far away. The would-be kindliness of this kind of animal-caring verse – as in Christina G Rossetti's poem about the unheeding ploughshare that chopped up a mole and earthworm ('A handy Mole who plied no shovel') and the one about the careless Frog which got run down and mangled by a 'broadwheeled waggon' ('Contemptuous of his home beyond / The village and the village pond') – is, of course, morally commendable. 'Pity the sorrows of a poor old Dog / ... Despise not even the sorrows of a Frog' urges the Mole's and the Frog's neighbouring poem 'A Word for the Dumb' in Rossetti's *Time Flies: A Reading Diary* volume: a poem sold to help the Anti-Vivisection Movement she ardently supported. But the tone is never far from the merely twee ('Spare Bunny once so frisky and so free': 'A Word for the Dumb'). At their best such verses work the mock-heroic ticket, which is a way of tarting up the ridiculous in the tonally suspect armour of the sublime – in a long tradition, alright, going back to Catullus's sparrow, via Thomas Gray's 'Ode on the Death of a Favourite Cat' (1747), and deranged Christopher Smart's lovely considerings of his cat Jeoffroy (in the huge fragmentary eighteenth-century poem 'Jubilate Agno'), and Renaissance (helter-skelter) John Skelton's 'Speke Parrot' – but they're none the more finally rateable for all that.

> What, Kaiser dead? The heavy news
> Post-haste to Cobham calls the Muse,
> From where in Farringford she brews
> The ode sublime,
> Or with Pen-bryn's bold bard pursues
> A rival rhyme.

Thus Arnold's 'Kaiser Dead, April 6, 1887', his very last poem, on the death of his favourite mongrel dachshund. The muse brewing Odes sublime at Farringford on the Isle of Wight is the one inspiring Tennyson – into sublime Odes including the altogether serious one on the Death of the Duke of Wellington. The bold bard at Pen-bryn is the bad but best-selling Welsh poet and educationalist Lewis Marris, whose reputation is said to have been second only to Tennyson's, and who only missed the Laureateship after Tennyson's death when Queen Victoria learned of his common-law 'marriage' to his American housekeeper. 'O for the croon pathetic, sweet, / Of Robin's reed', sings Arnold in his role as temporary pasticheur of the elegiac Ode, in lines 11–12 of 'Kaiser Dead', referring to Robert Burns's 'Poor Mailie's Elegy', that threnody for a dead sheep, the same creature featured in Burns's 'The Death and Dying Words of Poor Mailie, the Author's only pet yowe: an Unco Mournfu' Tale':

O a' ye bard on bonie Doon!
An wha' on Ayr your canters tune!
Come, join the melancholious croon
O' robin's reed!

Thus 'Poor Mailie's Elegy'. Arnold's 'Kaiser Dead' has pinched Burns's
stanza form, and his summons to the bardic Tennyson and Lewis to croon
along in elegiac chorus is as mocking as Burns's own invocation. Arnold
may not be sniggering as evidently as, say, WH Mallock's jaunty 'Lines on
the Death of a Pet Dog, Belonging to Lady Dorothy Nevill (June 1878)' –
rhyming 'You who but yesterday sprang to us' bathetically with 'One little
grace and a pang to us' – but he's getting very close. Poetic pangs for humans
don't spring like that.[19]

Soldiering On

By great contrast, **elegiac Odes for human beings, especially heroic ones,** are
precisely not light and springy. Of course what marks the great public elegies like Tennyson's 'Ode on the Death of the Duke of Wellington' – acme
of his publicly dutiful, Laureate elegies (of which there are indeed quite a lot,
for example the 1892 elegy for Queen Victoria's grandson who died prema-
turely at the age of 28, 'The Death of the Duke of Clarence and Avondale:
To the Mourners': subject, as it happens, of Christina G Rossetti's 'A Death
of a First-born: January 14th, 1892') – is the way that, in the fashion of their
mode, they control grief, holding it at bay, and we have to allow that this is
out of a regard for due decorum, for a public styling of remembrance, not
from any fear of showing private emotion. Tennyson's great Wellington
'Ode' is, of course, about real bereavement, the bereavement of a nation.
A nation mourns; at least a nation is exhorted to mourn. 'Let us bury the
Great Duke / To the noise of the mourning of a mighty nation' (3–4). 'Let
the long procession go, / And let the sorrowing crowd about it grow, / And
let the mournful martial music blow; / The last great English man is low'
(15–19). 'Mourn ... Mourn ... Mourn...' (19, 24, 27). 'Let the bell be tolled':
the commanding wish tolls three times (47, 53, 58). The poet himself joins
this mourning crowd: 'Let *us* bury ...'; 'Mourn, for to *us* he seems the last'
(19). Wellington is the man 'whom *we* deplore' (twice: 8, 40; *deplore*:
lament). It is, though, always a matter of *we* and *us* and *ours* – our island

[19]   Seamus Perry's rather astute chapter 'Elegy' in *A Companion to Victorian Poetry*, eds
Richard Cronin, Alison Chapman, and Anthony Harrison (Blackwell Publishers Ltd, Oxford,
2002), 113–133, grants animal elegy an all too rare critical sympathy.

guarded by such 'great men' as Wellington (154ff), 'our noble England' (161); 'our rough island story' (201), 'our fair island-story' – never *I* and *me* and *mine* from the poet (the *my* of 'my rest' in 83 belongs, apparently, to the late Lord Horatio Nelson, enquiring about Wellington). The voice of the poet is subsumed into the voice of the people (four times, 142, 144, 146, 151), which is to *echo* down through the centuries in honour of Wellington (*honour*, five times, 149–150). The muse Tennyson invokes isn't a private one, it's the 'civic muse' (75). Tennyson's private grief, however great it might be for the soldier-politician whose reactionary hostility to the extension of the franchise, and all that, was close to the mature Tennyson's own political inclinations, is not in question. This is 'Duteous mourning' as Dante Gabriel Rossetti's 'Wellington's Funeral: 18th November 1852' has it. Tennyson speaks as the Laureate speaking for the nation; egging on a public lamenting. Which is why elegy turns into eulogy: praise of the national Lord of 'hosts' (171: the poem getting close to blasphemy, offering Wellington as the Biblical God), its 'rugged' truth-teller, and all that. Public elegies of this kind have this way of turning into public praise poems – anciently the work of bards for hire, court poets, poets laureate, publicly performing emotions not necessarily their own.

Which is, more or less, the case with all of Tennyson's imperialist poems and epitaphs for soldiers and such, his elegies for the historically and publicly heroic: as in 'Havelock' (hero of what the British knew, and know, as the Indian Mutiny; Indians as the Great Sepoy Rebellion); 'Epitaph on General Gordon' (stubborn evangelical colonialist, killed in the Sudanese rebellion against British rule, one of the butts of Lytton Strachey's demythologizing *The Great Victorians*); 'The Defence of Lucknow' (bloody episode in the Indian Mutiny, engraved in the collective English national psyche as one more colonialist episode where 'we' were rescued scathed but last-minute victorious over ungrateful uprisers with 'dark faces' by British soldiers with the 'wholesome white faces'); 'The Revenge: A Ballad of the Fleet' (English naval heroics of Sir Richard Grenville and crew in the Elizabethan Spanish Wars); even in the angry 'The Charge of the Light Brigade'. It comes as no surprise to find Laureate Tennyson in his 'Battle of Brunanburgh' modernizing the Old English poem about Athelstan and Atheling slaughtering their Norse enemies – a piece of revived bardic praising, traditionally cool and laconic about death in war. Such was the way of Victorian soldierly heroizing – with grieving banished in talk of honour and glory, of national pride and national character, a poetry of the stiff English upper-lip, of British soldiers whose bravery is modelled on fantasies of ancient Roman stoicism in battle, drummed-in to schoolboys as part of their lessons in the Classics. (An aesthetic ideology fiercely derided and debunked by Wilfred Owen and Siegfried Sassoon and Co. in the First World War, and now, of course the object of much – overmuch? – automatic 'post-colonialist' critical disgust.)

It's the ethic and aesthetic of TB Macaulay's 'How Horatius Kept the Bridge'; or AE Housman's '1887', written for the fiftieth anniversary of Queen Victoria's enthronement, a tribute to the 'Lads' of Shropshire's 'Fifty-third' regiment who've fought and died as national 'saviours' in overseas campaigns ('It dawns in Asia, tombstones show / And Shropshire names are read; / And the Nile spills his overflow / Beside the Severn's dead'); or in the extremely memorable and influential chain of imperialist verses by the graduate of Clifton School, Bristol, and of Classics-promoting Corpus Christi College, Oxford, Henry Newbolt, in his 'Vitaï Lampada', and its ilk. 'Vitaï Lampada': the torch of life, handed on, according to the Roman poet Lucretius, from runner to runner in life's race – or flung by 'the falling' in battle to the host of young men coming behind them, closing up the ranks of the heroic dead in Newbolt's poem, whose young hero rallies a depleted band of British soldiery, about to die on some far-flung imperialist battlefield, by repeating the message his Old School cricket-captain gave him as he went in to bat as Last Man at the desperate end of a school cricket match:

> The sand of the desert is sodden red, –
> Red with the wreck of a square that broke; –
> The Gatling's jammed and the Colonel dead,
> And the regiment blind with dust and smoke.
> The river of death has brimmed his banks,
> And England's far, and Honour a name,
> But the voice of a schoolboy rallies the ranks:
> 'Play up! play up! and play the game!'
> (*Admirals All* (1897); reprinted in
> *Clifton Chapel and Other School
> Poems* (1908))

'Where are you, Poets', asks Sidney Dobell in 1875, 'that a Hero dies / Unsung?' He was lamenting the poetic silence over the death in the Ashantee Wars in South Africa of Eardly Wilmot, leading his men though wounded, 'till killed by a second wound'. Heroically dead, 'He looks a Poem', a 'model' for a poem 'thrown ... down' by 'the Bardic Heavens'. But Dobell is not weeping, and nor would the Duty-praising poems that he calls for weep. That wouldn't be playing the heroic-eulogy game, wouldn't be cricket. It's a lesson Tennyson's poetic wives have absorbed. In 'Home they brought her warrior dead', inset in 'The Princess', the grieving wife of a soldier killed in battle (one of those fighters, as Tennyson likes to think, emboldened by memories of wife and children at home), represses any expression of sorrow – 'nor swooned, nor uttered cry', not even when looking at her husband's dead face. Tears are allowed at last, but only when 'his child' is placed on her knee: "Sweet my child, I live for thee". In the alternative version of this poem, 'Home they brought him slain with spears', there's natural sorrow, but no tears at all, not even when the child plays with his father's lance and shield, only a desire for a respectful silence from the little survivor: ' "O hush, my joy, my sorrow" '. The repression is shocking enough, though not as shocking as Tennyson in 'Little bosom not yet cold', turning his stillborn first child of 1851 into one of his dead warriors for whom weeping is held inappropriate. The boy died, 'bold and resolute', his little fists clenched: 'He had done battle to be born, / But some brute force of Nature had prevailed / And the little warrior failed'. Tellingly, there are no first-personal pronouns in this poem; and you feel that the Romanesque fantasy of a soldierly death is provoking a terrible denial. It's usual for critics to suggest a close parallel with the stillborn baby in 'The Grandmother' (1859), and to suggest that Tennyson was thinking there of his own baby: 'There lay the sweet little body that never had drawn a breath. / ... I wept like a child that day, for the babe had fought for his life. / ... I wept like a child for the child that was dead before he was born'. But the difference between the two poems is mightily telling. In 'The Grandmother' the mother's tears are unrestrained and the metaphor of the baby's fight for life is not allowed to transform him into one of those heroic warriors for whom tears are *infra dig*. The dead baby is allowed its proper place in the ranks of the everyday dead for whom elegy's customary sorrowing is allowed in what one is compelled to feel is a most appropriate outlet. Here is the unrepressed mourning of 'In Memoriam' – Tennyson's vast compelling model of an elegy which subsequent poems regularly declared affinities with.

The title of Oscar Wilde's 'The Ballad of Reading Gaol by C.3.3., In Memoriam CTW Sometime Trooper of the Royal Horse Guards, Obiit HM Prison, Reading, Berkshire, July 7th, 1896' starkly recalls Tennyson's *In Memoriam AHH Obiit MDCCCXXXIII*. Of course the title is alerting us to the poem's offered challenge in the matter of gender and ethics. It's a hit from behind bars (C.3.3 was Wilde's cell-number) at the gender prejudices which let Tennyson the lover of a man stay free while men-loving Oscar Wilde is locked away; a calculated strike, too, against the public turning of a blind eye to the patent homoerotic grieving of *In Memoriam*. A protest which AE Housman had made earlier, albeit in private, in the poem of 1892 kept out of *A Shropshire Lad*, about his dead friend Adalbert J Jackson, which he pointedly titled 'AJJ'. These memorials of AJJ and CTW are, of course, engagements in a gender warfare with *In Memoriam*; but even more, they're declaring the potency and authenticity of the *In Memoriam* model. 'AJJ' is, like most of *A Shropshire Lad*'s poems, built out of the *In Memoriam* stanza. In it the greatly Roman-minded Latinist Professor Housman dwells on silence, on the unsaid, on how, sadly, the mourning *I* will never speak again to the dead man. Here's an instance, if you like, of the old stoic silence. But in the meantime the poet is not silent; he speaks to us readers in the position of the dead man. 'I mourn you', he says, 'and you heed not how'. But *we* heed. 'Unsaid the word must stay'; but the mourner nonetheless says it, to us. The poem breaks the silence it bewails, the silence of the tomb. Which is elegy's usual paradox. The dead man of Wilde's poem is a soldier. Not for him, though, any heroizing silence. He's a most unheroic soldier, dead because of unheroic violence, the killing of his wife. As a subject he's a sharp rebuke to the assumption that all Victorian soldiers are heroes and ripe for dry-eyed elegy. This soldier, at least, is demoted to the ranks of ordinary weeping elegy, where grief reigns, and the weight of death, of memory of the dead, is unrelieved. As in Thomas Ashe's 'Pall-Bearing' (in Ashe's *Poems, A New Edition*, 1871, revised for the *Complete Edition* of the *Poems*, 1886, as 'Corpse-Bearing'), story of a man asked to help carry his dead friend's coffin to his grave, and who feels the weight of it ever after:

> But, what a weight, O God!
> Was that one coffin to bear!
> Like a coffin of lead!
> And I carry it everywhere [.]

He's vowed 'Never to carry a corpse / Again, to my dying day'; but the remedy comes too late, for there's no alleviating the burden of the memory he bears. Which is all an allegory, as well as an instance, of elegy's plight: the poetry which cannot shed the weight, cannot lighten the burden of being *in memoriam*.

Like memories of the dead, writing in and about melancholy is very hard, if not impossible, to let go of. In poem LXII of 'A Shropshire Lad' the perennially elegiac Housman rebukes himself for being so 'Moping melancholy mad' in his verses: '"Terence, this is stupid stuff"'. (Terence Hearsay was one of Housman's soubriquets; *The Poems of Terence Hearsay* was the original title for the *Shropshire Lad* sequence – melancholy man naming himself ironically after the comic Roman playwright Terence.) Terence should, instead, 'pipe a tune to dance to, lad'. But as for that, Terence replies that beer is even better than poetry. 'Ale, man, ale's the stuff to drink / For fellows whom it hurts to think'. He knows because he's drunk himself into oblivion at Ludlow Fair, and was happy lying intoxicated in the gutter: 'And down in lovely muck I've lain'. But the world had not changed for the better when he woke up. 'I was I, my things were wet'. There was nothing for it but to carry on handing out stuff whose 'smack', its taste, is sour, growth of 'a weary land', words fit for 'an embittered hour' in a 'dark and cloudy day.' And this Terence ends with a little parable of King Mithridates IV, who lived a long life, resisting his enemies' repeated poisoning attempts by dosing himself regularly on a sort of homeopathic diet of poisons growing from 'the many-venomed earth'. As it were, a steady intake of melancholic stuff as the only prophylactic against being utterly overwhelmed by morbidity and mortality.

When I Am Dead

And this prophylaxis of melancholy – melancholy as a medicinal condom – is pretty universal. It's what drives, as well as sanctions, the steady production of elegy, especially in poems for dead poets, dead people naturally close to the nerve of poets' feelings. It has so many poets brooding on their own end, imagining themselves, or someone like them, dying and being dead: Thomas Hardy, for example, wondering in 'When the present has latched its postern' what the neighbours will say of him when he has passed on; or Pessimism Laureate Thomson in his 'In the room' getting the wretched furniture, curtain, cupboard, mirror, bed, to discuss the writer lying there on his Grub Street bed after a misery-ending drink of poison; or the *I* of George Eliot's ' "O May I join the Choir Invisible" ' imagining herself among the heavenly singers 'whose music is the gladness of the world' (the poem, in Eliot's *The Legend of Jubal & Other Poems*, 1867, has a Latin epigraph from Cicero which translates as 'That long time, when I shall not exist, moves me more than this short time'); or Charlotte Brontë in 'The Missionary' writing as St John Rivers, the missionary to India out of *Jane Eyre*, anticipating a martyr's death; or Tennyson wanting to die and feeling dead after his failure with Rosa Baring, advising, proleptically in 1851–1852, against any mourning over his grave in 'Come not, when I am dead' ('Come not, when I am dead, / To drop thy foolish tears upon my grave .../ But thou, go by') and then, in the poem's second stanza, actually getting into the grave and speaking from there: 'Pass on, weak heart, and leave me where I lie: / Go by, go by.' And these imaginings were not confined to 1851–1852; Tennyson dwelt on dying, and his own dying in particular, more or less all his creative life.

'Dead, long dead, / Long dead!', that cry from the 'shallow grave' of the melancholy mad narrator of *Maud* – *Maud or the Madness*, Tennyson's 'little Hamlet' – said it all in 1855. But Tennyson had long been dead, or dying, in his fraught imaginings. He's 'A carcase in the coffin of this flesh, / Pierced through with loathly worms of utter Death' in the 'charnel damp', the 'unutterable tomb', in 'Perdidi Diem' – one of his undergraduate poems. He recycled those wormy lines in 'Pierced through with knotted thorns of barren pain', an unfinished – and by the horror it – unfinishable poem of 1832, which has him 'Walled round, shut up, imbarred, moaning for light' in what the poem's earlier version called "darkness visible" (quoting Milton's *Paradise Lost* on Hell), in a 'spiritual charnel low and damp'. 'My life is full of weary days', admits the lyrical-I of that poem in *Poems* (1832) addressing (it seems) Hallam – shaking hands with him 'across the brink / Of that deep grave to which I go'. The speaker says he doesn't want any 'dusky cypress tree' planted over his grave, nor is his friend to wear 'doleful crape' in his hat.

He should wear none of what the Victorians knew as 'weeds', that is the black mourning clothing of a widow, 'widow's weeds'. Rather, natural weeds ('darnel') should be allowed to grow over the grave, and Hallam should come on 'still' days and 'whisper low, / And tell me if the woodbines blow'. Such 'cheerful tones' will be 'welcome to my crumbling bones': 'If any sense in me remains'. These sentiments were among the many leapt on so mercilessly by JW Croker in his savaging review of the 1832 volume. 'We take upon ourselves to reassure Mr Tennyson, that, even after he shall be dead and buried, as much *"sense"* will remain as he has now the good fortune to possess' (*Quarterly Review*, April 1833). Which sarcasm utterly missed the serious point about Tennyson's fears as to what sensibilities, if any, the dead might have – not least the ongoing anxiety about being buried alive that would emerge so terribly in *Maud* – as well as obscuring the force of that aweing 'welcome to my bones'. How greatly unhappy with himself a person must be, one feels, to tell a friend about to be bereaved that he's welcome to have his mortal bones. Upset by Croker, Tennyson dropped the poem. When it was let back into the public domain in 1865 it was shorn of the verses about Hallam's visits and Tennyson's *sense*, which were only restored in 1872 among the 'Juvenilia'. Juvenile they might be, but such feelings from a premature grave were utterly foundational for Tennyson. Even before Hallam's own death, Hallam was clearly an actor in Tennyson's extensive morbid fantasies. Hallam's dying of course increased Tennyson's morbidity – the wrong man died, so to say. The would-be dead man was now the *survivant* – left behind to revivify with renewed death consciousness a morbid poetic career almost killed off by Croker's unsympathetic jeers.

The death of Hallam inspired not only *In Memoriam*, but affected everything that followed that decease. From then on Tennyson cultivated his death plots with renewed vigour. From the death of Arthur Hallam springs, of course, the death of King Arthur that's the culmination of the great epic plot of the *Idylls of the King* with which Tennyson's career culminates. Arthur, whose end is in his epic's beginning. ' "My end draws nigh" ', ' "Place me in the barge" ', Arthur's farewell words from his floating coffin about the old order changing; his swan-song from the barge which 'Moved from the brink' (of the land, but also the brink of death) like a dying swan, 'some full-breasted swan / ... fluting a wild carol ere her death': all this, the finale of the *Idylls* and Tennyson's career, is written down first in 'Morte d'Arthur' in 1833–1834, in the immediate aftermath of the other Arthur's demise. The career of the *Idylls* models Tennyson's own; it too begins with deaths, with endings up. 'Dead, long dead', indeed. It's a very long career in mortality-broodings, only outdone for protracted death-thoughts by Christina G Rossetti.

Christina G rarely lets up on her dying concerns. A devoted Anglo-Catholic Christian she might be thought the laureate of the four last things which the Christian Church traditionally insisted Christians should meditate on: Death, Final Judgement, Heaven and Hell. She spent much effort commenting on the Bible's last book, the Apocalypse, or Revelation, of St John, that treasure trove of last things and End-times events, in her volume *The Face of the Deep: A Devotional Commentary* (1892; it went into several editions). Scores of her late poems arise in its pages out of her reflections on the Last Book's eschatological, apocalyptic verses. But such had been her preoccupation from the start – very much to do with Heaven, but even more with Death. Her poems gorge themselves on death throughout her career, and on her own death above all. 'I must die': it's the sad, five times refrain of 'Wife to Husband'. *Die* rhymes every time matter-of-factly with 'Goodbye'. The matter-of-factness keeps at bay any pinch of over-sentimentalism, let alone the perverse hysteria Germaine Greer rants about in her sloppy, un-understanding attack on Rossetti in her *Slip-Slop Sibyls*.[20] That death is the sad, depriving *hap*, the inevitable chance of life, what always happens, and which might bring its own kind of *happiness*, consciousness and memory in some afterlife, or might, *haply*, not do that, is the burden of Christina G's sad 'Song', one of the saddest among so many sad ones, telling a relict beloved not to sing any sad songs for her (that repeated Tennysonian note):

> When I am dead, my dearest,
> Sing no sad songs for me;
> Plant thou no roses at my head,
> Nor shady cypress tree:
> Be the green grass above me
> With showers and dewdrops wet;
> And if thou wilt, remember,
> And if thou wilt, forget.
>
> I shall not see the shadows,
> I shall not feel the rain;
> I shall not hear the nightingale
> Sing on, as if in pain:
> And dreaming through the twilight
> That doth not rise nor set,
> Haply I may remember,
> And haply may forget.

Rossetti is constantly, like this, as it were 'Dead Before Death' (as the sonnet that comes next in *Goblin Market and Other Poems*, 1862, has it). In 'Rest', a couple of poems after that, Rossetti invites *Earth* to 'lie heavily' on the

---

[20]   Germaine Greer, 'The Perversity of Christina Rossetti', in *Slip-Slop Sibyls: Recognition, Rejection and the Woman Poet* (Viking, 1995), 359–389.

'eyes' of a dead female as she lies 'Hushed' and 'curtained' in her coffin awaiting 'the morning of Eternity' (*Earth* rhyming with absent *mirth*, and 'a
blessèd dearth / Of all that irked her from the hour of birth'). Hamlet was
appalled at the thought of crossing 'the bourne', the boundary, between life
and death, from which 'no traveller returns' (*Hamlet* III.i.79–80); Christina
G's poems cross it again and again, and not least in 'The Bourne' (in *The
Prince's Progress & Other Poems*, 1866), about the grave in which 'we'
won't be counting the hours and their passing shadows. Dark thoughts
about becoming physically corrupt, in the dark of the grave, are what she
likes thinking, as in 'By the Waters of Babylon. BC 570', written in the voice
of an Israelite exiled from God's presence: 'And we, as unclean bodies in
the grave / Inheriting corruption and the dark / Are outcast from His presence which we crave' (this is one of the poems in the first Rossetti collected
edition of 1875). 'Life is not sweet', says this most sweet-toothed of poets in
'Life and Death' (in *The Prince's Progress*), but 'One day it will be sweet /
To shut our eyes and die'. Life *is* sweet, but death is sweeter, she thinks elsewhere, in the *Goblin Market* volume's 'Sweet Death', while 'crossing the
green churchyard thoughtfully'. The grass withers; 'And youth and beauty
die'; but the 'glad company' of heaven are 'Better than beauty and than
youth'. And, as ever, when Rossetti thinks of dying, she thinks of eating and
food-stuffs. Heaven is 'our full harvest'; why, then, be satisfied with the
mere *gleanings* of earth, the bits of corn traditionally left around for the
landless poor to collect? Why – in one of her wonderfully layered Biblical
metaphors – 'Prefer to glean with Ruth?' The Bible's Ruth: widow, relict,
poor, gleaning in the fields of her kinsman Boaz, who fancies her as she toils
in his field and has his labourers leave lots of gleanings for her, and who gets
her, gleaning the gleaner, as his wife. Heaven is much better than being left
behind, a relict, one of the posthumous bereaved ('I suppose a few posthumous groans may be found among my remains', she said to her brother
Dante Gabriel); better, of course, than being a man-less woman, like the
widowed Ruth; better even than being a woman who gets her Boaz – what
virginal Christina G only ever dreamed of. Unsatisfied now, she will be satisfied in heaven, where the harvest is, in the Bible's words, plenteous.

The prospect of being satiated after death does, though, get extremely
gothic, as Rossetti thinks, along with the Bible's Job, of what worms do
to buried bodies. Andrew Marvell, the seventeenth-century 'Metaphysical'
poet, notoriously thought that reminding his 'coy mistress' of how worms
will one day 'try', test, taste, feed on, her 'long preserved virginity' in the
grave would be enough to scare her into his eager embrace while the going
was still good ('To His Coy Mistress'). Disconcertingly, virginal Christina
G seems happy to think of those worms satisfying their sweetness-cravings
on dead bodies like the one she keeps imagining herself as. 'The worm
feeds sweetly on the dead': a sweetness that's a nourishing meal, for 'The

ı is fattened with our dead' (all this in 'A Testimony', in *Goblin* *ket* – one more of her many *Vanitas Vanitorum*, The Vanity of Earthly Vanities, poems).

Among The Ruins

That welcoming of physical corruption, embracing the wormy realities, of the grave, if only prophylactically, is part and parcel of a wide Victorian poetic apprehension of decay, fall, ruin. All the personal dying of the poems is taking place in a large context of poetically imagined ruin. The period's mood music is a heavy consciousness of ruin – bodily ruin (looked at in 'Fleshly Feelings', Chapter 7, above), the fall of cities and civilizations, the fall of trees (death and decay in nature), the death of God (doubt's ruinous encroachments on faith). The poets see through the eyes of Walter Benjamin's Angel of History (a version of Dürer's winged Melencolia), his face turned toward the past as he's propelled backwards into the future, with the events of the past a mounting catastrophic pile of debris in front of him, 'wreckage upon wreckage'.[21]

Victorian poets inherit and grow the fetishistic Romantic cult of ruined buildings and sites. (Giorgio Agamben is right to link the Düreresque Melencolia-effect with the Romantic and post-Romantic taste for the meaning of ruins, the potent scene of broken fragments, torsoes, under the aegis of fetishism's absolutizing of the synecdochic bit.[22]) Tennyson thought the line 'Whose dwelling is the light of setting suns', in Wordsworth's ruin-celebrating (and celebrated) poem 'Tintern Abbey', was 'almost the grandest in the English language'. 'Tears, idle tears' 'came to' Tennyson, he said, 'on the yellowing autumn-tide at Tintern Abbey' – that momentous ruin, made all the more poignant because Hallam was buried nearby. Tennyson haunted this doubly sanctified ruin – haunted by Hallam as well as Wordsworth. Section XIX of *In Memoriam*, about the rivers Severn and Wye and the hills around, and about Tennyson being 'hushed' in grief for Hallam, was actually written at Tintern Abbey.[23] Tennyson's Mariana mopes in a very Romantically mouldering 'grange': its thatch 'weeded and worn' (the weeds sprouting in it

---

[21]   Walter Benjamin, 'Theses on the Philosophy of History', IX (first published, posthumously, 1950); in *Illuminations*, trans Harry Zohn, ed Hannah Arendt ((Cape, London, 1970) Collins/ Fontana, London and Glasgow, 1973), 259–260.

[22]   *Stanzas*, (1993), 33. Agamben's thoughts on fetishism are founded, aptly enough, on reflections on Melancholy and Dürer, pp11–18.

[23]   Stephen Gill's *Wordsworth and the Victorians* (Clarendon Press, Oxford, 1998), 188–204, fills out Tennyson's relationship with Wordsworth and his poems, including Tennyson's unease over Wordsworth's 'thick-ankled' tendency, and his slashing and cutting in his copy of 'Tintern Abbey' of what he thought its excessively repetitive parts.

reminding of widow's 'weeds': mourning garb), its garden sheds 'broken' and 'sad', the pear-tree espaliered against the gable-end falling away because its nails are all 'rusted'. The attractive rot of Romantic ruins survives strongly like this for the Victorians. Whoever the traveller is in Robert Browning's ' "Childe Roland to the Dark Tower Came" ', and whatever the meaning of his quest in that notoriously obscure poem, it's pretty clear that the Dark Tower is some kind of magnetic relic. Browning doesn't care greatly for this Romantic lure – the narrator of 'By the Fireside' feeding his memories of pursuing 'the ruined chapel ... / Half-way up in the Alpine gorge!' should perhaps get out of his compelling ruin-cravings; the woman at Asolo in the wonderfully dyspeptic late poem 'Inapprehensiveness', quite taken up with the nearby ruin towering over the valley and wishing she had her 'perspective glass' with her to check out 'a missing turret', and wondering whether Ruskin had '"noticed ... / That certain weed-growths on the ravaged wall / Seem" ... ' (or was it Ruskin?), is culpably 'inapprehensive' of what matters more, namely the unnoticed man at her side, who'd like to catch her gaze and have her spot his 'dormant passion'. But Browning has to acknowledge the prevalence of the ruin cult. The busy ruin promotions of John Ruskin, Victorian doyen of Italian ruin-connoisseurship and aestheticizing, praiser-up in text after text of the attractions of the melancholically decayed building and town, who has to be put in his place. But his influence can't be denied.

Christina G Rossetti's take on ruined cities is, like that of so many others in this so Bible-minded age, refracted colourfully through her keenness on Biblical eschatology and apocalypse. She's devoted to the idea of a New Jerusalem, the revived City of God in the Book of Revelation, as her hope for life after death, but also much taken by the Fall of Revelation's Babylon the Great, the great wicked city, Jerusalem's antonym, whose foundations are the Biblical Tower of Babel anciently put an end to by God. Biblical eschatology – religious ending talk – is built on the fall of the great city, the city punished for its transgressions. Rome is, clearly, intended by the Book of Revelation's writer. This ferocious end-times talk, devotedly endorsed by Christina G, is eager to write 'Ichabod', ancient Hebrew curse ('the glory has departed'), over the once great urban place. 'The Glory hath departed, Ichabod!' exclaims the narrator of Rossetti's 'By the Waters of Babylon. BC 570'. He (clearly a male self) is an exile from Jerusalem, God's city shattered by Babylonian enemies, his body wasted 'to skin and bone', feeling (as we just saw) as if he's dead and buried, a ruined man from a ruined city, both him and his place perishing in God's 'ire'. This is traditional Biblical judgement. City and citizen are 'As Sodom and Gomorrah scourged by fire, / As Jericho before God's trumpet-peal'. 'The curse is come upon me', he says, twice, repeating the words of Tennyson's Lady of Shalott when her mirror and her world shatter and she embarks on her death-voyage down to Camelot.

This note of post apocalyptic desolation and abandonment sounds widely. 'Wail! fallen Salem! Wail' urges Tennyson's 1827 poem 'The Fall of Jerusalem', twice – infected no doubt by one of Byron's multi-apocalyptic *Hebrew Melodies* (1815), 'On the Day of the Destruction of Jerusalem by Titus'. The city should mourn its fall – its lustre darkened by the shadow of the Roman eagle, its 'fane' now polluted by 'Mohammed's votaries'. The poet certainly mourns. 'Jerusalem! Jerusalem! / Thou art low!' The voice is that of Jesus in the Gospel, lamenting the coming desolation of the Holy City: 'O Jerusalem, Jerusalem ...'. 'Where is the Giant of the Sun, which stood / In the midnoon the glory of old Rhodes?' asks Tennyson's 'Fragment' of 1830, opening a catalogue of *Ubi sunt?* ('Where are they now?') enquiries about ruined cities and civilizations. Where are the obelisks of 'Mysterious Egypt', and the fabled statue of Memnon near Thebes which made music when the rays of the rising sun struck it, and the glorious Egyptian city of Memphis? 'Old Memphis hath gone down: / The pharaohs are no more'. The manuscript of the 'Fragment' goes on to recall the great Ephesian temple of Diana, burnt down by one Eratostratus in the night Alexander the Great was born.

At the end of Tennyson's (1828) Cambridge Prize Poem 'Timbuctoo', the spirit of the fabled African city looks forward gloomily to its inevitable demise and later discovery as didactic ruin:

> 'Oh City! oh latest Throne! where I was raised
> To be a mystery of loveliness
> Unto all eyes, the time is well-nigh come
> When I must render up this glorious home
> To keen *Discovery*: soon yon brilliant towers
> Shall darken with the waving of her wand;
> Darken, and shrink and shiver into huts,
> Black specks amid a waste of dreary sand,
> Low-built, mud-walled, Barbarian settlements.
> How changed from this fair City!' 236–245

The tones of Milton's *Paradise Lost*, apocalyptic poem moved by thoughts of Hell as Pandaemonium, a mighty Babylonian, and London-like, urbs, destined for doom, echo through 'Timbuctoo' – composed, with great aptness, out of huge sections of Tennyson's unfinished 'Armageddon'.

Timbuctoo was visited for the first time by a modern European in 1826, and the Victorians were kept conscious of such sites of now diminished glory, and their apocalyptic object lessons, by the formidable nineteenth-century exploration and archaeology enterprise, visiting, digging, unearthing, drawing (and eventually photographing) especially in places rich in associations of Biblical story and prophesied apocalyptic destruction. 'Howl, desolate

Babylon, lost one and lone!' urges Tennyson's 'Babylon' in the voice of the avenging Old Testament 'Lord' (in the 1827 volume *Poems by Two Brothers*), a poem replete with notes pointing to the Old Testament passages it's built out of. 'Babylon' picks up on the Biblical-apocalyptic revelations in the (first) *Memoir on the Ruins of Babylon* by the Baptist explorer and diplomat Claudius James Rich which appeared in 1815 – the ruinous subject of several of Byron's Biblical-apocalyptic poems, such as 'Vision of Belshazzar' (about the Book of Daniel's story of Belshazzar's Feast and the mysterious handwriting on the wall interpreted by Daniel as predicting the Fall of Babylon), 'By the Rivers of Babylon We Sat Down and Wept' and 'The Destruction of Sennacherib', in his *Hebrew Melodies*, which appeared in the same year. (Byron's Biblical drama *Cain, A Mystery* (1821) reveals more of his strong taste for catastrophe, drawing as it does on the geologist-palaeontologist Baron Cuvier's theorizing of the geological record as only explicable by a series of 'catastrophes' occurring before the 'creation of man' narrated in the Book of Genesis.) The apocalyptic painter John Martin (who became the Brontës' favourite painter) drew heavily on the Byronic market in Biblical apocalyptic in his *Fall of Nineveh* (finished in 1826: Nineveh being the sinful city whose destruction the Bible's prophet Jonah was sent to prophesy), and his *Belshazzar's Feast* (completed in 1830). The monstrous Assyrian epic *The Fall of Nineveh* by John Martin's friend the poet Edwin Atherstone (cited for its unmisgiving protractedness in Chapter 1) was started, on the back as it were of Martin's painting, in 1828–1830. Hot with Christian relish for such downfalls – 'So sank, to endless Night, that glorious Nineveh' – it was published in two huge volumes in 1847, as news of AH Layard's excavations in Mesopotamia, begun in 1845, was leaking out. Layard's reports from ruined Nineveh in his *Nineveh and its Remains* (1849) and *A Popular Account of Discoveries at Nineveh* (1854), were a sensation. WD Paden, invaluable archaeologist of Tennyson's interest in such ruins, thought that the gibe in 'Maud' against Maud's nasty brother as 'That oiled and curled Assyrian Bull' suggested just how much Tennyson had caught the excitement over Layard's sensational unearthing of the great Assyrian winged bulls.[24] Happening to come out of the British Museum in 1856 just as one of Layard's 'wingèd' beasts from Nineveh was being unloaded, Dante Gabriel Rossetti was moved to meditate on the passing and pastness of Greece, Egypt, and Rome, and the fall of Babylon, Thebes and Rome, as well as of Nineveh (in the poem whose composition is inspected in my opening chapter 'Words, Words, Words ...'). The bull is 'A dead disembowelled mystery: / The mummy of a buried faith / Stark from the charnel' – emblem of a dead culture, elegiac icon, a kind of 'zealous tract' preaching urban

[24] WD Paden, *Tennyson in Egypt, A Study of the Imagery in His Earlier Works* (1942; Octagon, NY, 1971), n.235, p.161.

doom. It foretells London's own inevitable ruin. 'The Burden of Nineveh' is the poem's title; its original subtitle was ' "Burden. Heavy calamity; the chorus of a song" – Dictionary'. In this way the poem announced the spiritual and cultural burden of its repeated poetic burden about the meanings of Nineveh as eloquent 'corpse': the repeated burden, in both senses, of Victorian poets. Of poets such as James Clarence Mangan doing the voice of an Arab mourner in his 'Gone in the Wind' (1842).

> Solomon! Where is thy throne? It is gone in the wind.
> Babylon! Where is thy might? It is gone in the wind.

Italian Jobs

'I am Rome, / Tadmor and Cairo' says the speaker of Tennyson's early (unpublished) 'The Idealist'. Cairo, mistakenly thought the same as ancient Memphis; Tadmor, 'a noble city of ancient Syria, now in ruins' according to the 1802 *English Encyclopedia*, which Tennyson's father owned, and which showed two engravings of the ruins.[25] And Rome, of course, the most aweing example for Rome-obsessed England of the Decline and Fall of empires, of the potential of great cities for ruin.[26]

Of all the nineteenth-century traveller's lures, ruinous Italy was the strongest. Painters, classicists, art-historians, Roman Catholic converts, and of course poets, just couldn't stay way. Walter Savage Landor, the Brownings, Frederick Tennyson, Isa Blagdon, Eugene Lee-Hamilton all resided in Florence. Swinburne – like so many others, Edith Wharton, Henry James, and so on – passed through. JA Symonds' paiderastic love-life flourished in Venice (Byron's favourite city). George Eliot and her new husband Johnny Cross went to Venice for their honeymoon. Venice was the centre of John Ruskin's aesthetic universe. George MacDonald spent half his time in the last twenty years of his life (1885–1905) at his place in Bordighera. Edward Lear's painting trips to Rome and other scenic Italian places went consciously

---

[25]   Information, as ever, from the invaluable Ricks edition(s) of the *Poems*.

[26]   Wide survey in Kenneth Churchill, *Italy and English Literature: 1764–1930* (Macmillan, London, 1980). The Romantic period is well covered in Sophie Thomas, *Romanticism and Visuality: Fragments, History, Spectacle* (Routledge, NY, 2008) and Jonathan Sacks, *Romantic Antiquity: Rome in the British Imagination 1789–1832* (Oxford University Press, NY, 2009). Anne Jarowitz, *England's Ruins: Poetic Purpose and the National Landscape* (Blackwell, Oxford, 1990) has a strong chapter 'Ruinists in Rome', ranging widely from Spenser to Byron, 21–53. And the analysis of the apprehension of the 'discourse' of European ruins in the wake of the French Revolution in the 'Ruins' chapter of Peter Fritzsche, *Stranded in the Present: Modern Time and the Melancholy of History* (Harvard University Press, Cambridge MA and London, 2004), 92–130, plays powerfully onto the Victorian situation.

in the footsteps of JMW Turner, and, for that matter, of Byron and his Childe
Harold, and Stendhal and Goethe. Clough wrote his touristic love poem
Amours de Voyage actually in Rome. Roman Catholic to-be, John Henry
Newman thought Rome the 'most wonderful place in the world' when he
visited with his friend JA Froude. John Gray studied for the Roman Catholic
priesthood there. But for all the sun and fun, the pleasures of art and (for
some) of the religion, Italy meant, above all, disaster, death, ruin; especially
ruins. AJA Symons had a terrible nervous breakdown in Venice; Johnny
Cross tried to kill himself by jumping into Venice's Grand Canal (not quite a
Death in Venice, but close). Savage Landor died poverty-stricken and sick in
Florence, where he'd been looked after by the Brownings. Elizabeth Barrett
Browning died, of course, at Florence, having been sick almost unto death
in Rome. She's buried in the Protestant Cemetery at Florence. So is Clough.
Eugene Lee-Hamilton died in Florence after a long depressive illness and is
buried in the New Protestant Cemetery. George MacDonald died and is bur-
ied at Bordighera. The Protestant Cemetery of Rome turned into a momentous shrine to the English Romantic poets, Shelley and Keats, buried there.
(Leigh Hunt, who was present with Byron at the burning of drowned Shelley's
dead body near La Spezia, wrote the epitaph for Shelley's Roman tomb.)
Mary Howitt and JA Symonds joined their Romantic predecessors in the
graveyard – Symonds' grave is very close to Keats's. (Almost the first thing
John Ruskin does in Rome in 1841 is look up Keats's surviving companion
the painter Joseph Severn and visit Keats' grave.) In January 1888 Edward
Lear died and was buried at San Remo where he'd lived for many years; his
tomb has words from Tennyson's tribute poem, 'all things fair / With such a
pencil, such a pen, /You shadowed forth to distant men, / I read and felt
and I was there'. The Italy of their imagination and writing and art was also
a kind of morgue for English poets. As it was, of course, for the Roman and
Italian art, the poetry and civilizations, which so obsessed the poets.

And Victorian poem after Victorian poem constructs some kind of elegy
for Italian culture. In his 'Old Pictures in Florence' (in the *Men and Women*
volume) Browning, for instance, walks us round a Florence of frescoes flak-
ing away, or 'rasped, / Blocked up, knocked o'er', 'crumbly tempera', Fra
Angelicos in scraps, the frescoes and paintings of Taddeo Gaddi and Lorenzo
Monaco in so bad a state that Browning can't decipher their subjects. The old
Yellow Book (source of *The Ring and the Book*) which Browning found on
a stall in Florence's Piazza di Lorenzo in June 1860, among the ordure, shards
and weeds', is in a state of *crumblement*; it's metaphorically one of Florence's
ruined buildings, an awful allegory of Italian ruination (*The Ring and the
Book*, I.670ff). According to 'Old Pictures in Florence', art 'departed' the city
when it lost its freedom to the Hapsburgs; the city's aesthetic life is 'incomplete', as incomplete as Giotto's campanile. Florence's dying paintings – their
'pulse-tick' getting fainter and fainter – weakening and waning 'till the latest

life in the painting stops' – are an object lesson in *sic transit!* It's a ghastly transitoriness, though, whose sites, Italy's archaeological sites, actual ruins, the poets and painters can't resist.

Pompeii and Herculaneum, buried in hot lava and ash from nearby Mount Vesuvius in AD 79 – those very vivid Italian cases of Apocalypse Then, and potent reminders of apocalyptic possibility Now – led the interest. *Pompeiana* (1817–1819), the first account in English of the disaster and the state of the ruins by their excavator William Gell (with John Gandy) created instant awed response from British artists, art and poetry. Pompeii became the hottest aesthetic property. Shelley visited the sites in 1819. The Oxford setters of the English Poem Competition chose 'Pompeii' in 1819. Macaulay won. Robert Stephen Hawker's Oxford Newdigate Prize poem on the same subject was mainly lifted, people said, from the Macaulay. John Hughes's *Pompeii: A Descriptive Ode* appeared in 1820. Atherstone brought out *The Last Days of Herculaneum & Abradates & Panthea: Poems* in 1821. The 'last Days' tag loudly invoked Biblical apocalypse: what happened at Pompeii and Herculaneum was a foretaste of what Biblical prophecy was read as foretelling for the Last Days of Time. John Martin's painting *The Destruction of Herculaneum & Pompeii* followed in 1822. (The father of the poet John Leicester Warren, Lord de Tabley, commissioned a half-size version of Martin's typically vast production.) Bulwer Lytton stayed with William Gell, and wrote most of his 1834 bestseller *The Last Days of Pompeii*, in Naples. The novel is dedicated to Gell. Macaulay followed in the footsteps, as it were, of Lytton's novel in 1838. His *Lays of Ancient Rome* followed in 1842. Its interest in Roman glories now past became the commonest of Victorian tropes.

Byron had, as ever, led the poetic way with his invocation of lost Italian glories of art, poetry, architecture and empires in Canto IV of *Childe Harold's Pilgrimage* – written in Venice in 1818, grieving over the 'ashes' of 'Rome imperial' and a Florence ungrateful to its entombed society of dead poets, Dante, Petrarch, Boccaccio, and over the physical wreck of Rome, the 'Ruins of years'. What a ruin the Colosseum is, Childe Harold exclaims (IV.cxlii) – inspired to utter some of the most memorable of lines in all English verse, the ones with the wounded gladiator, dying in the arena, remembering his family back home in Transylvania: '*There* were his young barbarians all at play / *There* was their Dacian mother – he, their sire / Butcher'd to make a Roman holiday' (IV.cxli). Everything was 'A ruin' now. Rome burned itself in the Victorian imagination because it had burned in Turner's apocalyptic sketch, *Rome Burning* (dating from about 1834). Rome was a wreck and a heap of wrecks: cultural heritage as depressed ruin. 'Drove up to the Capital – a fitting, melancholy-looking, rubbishy place; and down to the forum, which is certainly a very good subject; and then a little further on, among quantities of bricks and rubbish, till I was quite sick'. Thus John Ruskin's diary note, November 30ᵗʰ1840.[27] 'With disgust', he hastened to add in his *Praeterita* of 1885. 'There is a strange horror lying over the whole city ... it is a shadow of death, possessing and penetrating all things', he wrote home.[28] 'Rome disappoints me much', writes traveller Claude to his friend Eustace in Clough's big tourist poem, *Amours de Voyage* (1858). He keeps saying so in Canto I. This is because the city is so '*Rubbishy*': 'All the foolish destructions and all the sillier savings' (I.20–21).

> Would to Heaven the old Goths had made a cleaner sweep of it!
> Would to Heaven some new ones would come and destroy these churches!
>
> (I.24–25)

Rome 'is like its own Monte Testaceo, / Merely a marvellous mass of broken and castaway wine-pots. / Ye gods! what do I want with this rubbish of ages departed?' The traces of the distant past are rubbish – 'the Forum? An archway and two or three pillars' – and so are the remains of the less distant past, like the church of St Peter's, full of trashy Bernini sculpture. Emperor Augustus 'vaunted': ' "Brickwork I found thee, and marble I left thee!" '; ' "Marble I thought thee, and brickwork I find thee" the Tourist may answer' (II. 39–50).

The rubbishiness of Roman modernity was of course endorsed by what Protestants like Clough took for granted was a rubbished form of Christianity as practised and represented in the main Roman Catholic shrine of St Peter's. The Vatican was focus of Protestantism's standard equation between 'Babylon the Great' of the Biblical Book of Revelation, that apocalyptic city's presiding Scarlet Woman, and the Church of Rome. 'Babylon the Great is fallen' announced the Book of Revelation, proleptically; a fall proved, as every Protestant visitor agreed, by Roman ruins and the trash of Roman religion. '[N]o music worth hearing, a little mummery with Pope and dirty cardinals'; thus Ruskin's Protestant Evangelical inflected reaction in the Sistine Chapel on Advent Sunday, 29 November 1840: 'Outside and west façade of St Peter's certainly very fine: the inside would make a nice ball-room, but it is good for nothing else'.[29] In St Peter's on a Christmas-Eve, the narrator of Robert Browning's 'Christmas-Eve' section of *Christmas-Eve and Easter-Day* (1850) tries to make himself believe in the religious virtues of the Roman version of the Christian faith, but can't shrug off Browning's in-built Protestant nose for 'Rome's gross yoke', its obscuring 'errors and perversities' (614ff). The 'raree show of Peter's successor' (1242)

---

[27]   *Praeterita* (1885); Intro Tim Hilton (Everyman's Library, NY and London, 2005), 250.
[28]   Quoted by Tim Hilton, *John Ruskin, The Early Years, 1819–1859* (Yale University Press, New Haven and London, 1985), 58.
[29]   *Praeterita*, edn cit, 250.

won't do; it's a 'buffoonery, / Of posturings and petticoatings' (1324–1325). The uncouth, illiterate, proley London Dissenters he visited earlier offer a purer, less rubbished form of the faith. 'How very hard it is to be / A Christian!', the narrator goes on in 'Easter-Day' (1–2), but he finds it especially hard to stomach the Roman decadence. And, not surprisingly, this sequel goes on to dream of Judgement Day. The dreamer misses the usual catalogue of Second Adventist events predicted in the Bible (' "And where had place the great white throne? / The rising of the quick and dead? / Where stood they, small and great? Who read / The sentence from the opened book?" '), but still the Judge of the End times appears in a pall of smoke reminiscent of Sodom's destruction, and declares the end of all the preceding religious 'shows' – Dissenting, Roman, German Higher Critical, but in particular the Roman, I'd say, given the usual Protestant links between Roman religion and apocalyptic destruction. In play here are the associations George Eliot all at once appreciates and satirizes in the Protestant Evangelical perturbation of her Dorothea Brooke in Rome in *Middlemarch* (1871): the young English Calvinist, 'fed on meagre Protestant histories and on art chiefly of the hand-screen sort', mentally overthrown by Rome's 'stupendous fragmentariness', 'the gigantic broken revelations of the Imperial and Papal city', the double 'wreck' of the city and its religion:

> Ruins and basilicas, palaces and colossi, set in the midst of a sordid present, where all that was living and warm-blooded seemed sunk in the deep degeneracy of a superstition divorced from reverence ... and all this vast wreck ... degradation, ... jarred her as with an electric shock ....

She's left aching. And she never forgets; ever after she sees a mental 'magic-lantern' picture-show of Roman images: vast St Peters', its mosaic prophets and evangelists, 'and the red drapery which was being hung for Christmas spreading itself everywhere like a disease of the retina' (Chapter 20). Roman scarlet; Scarlet Woman; Protestant unease and dis-ease in the presence of the seemingly apocalyptic Roman wreckage. Which is what Clough and Robert Browning, Ruskin and George Eliot herself all felt. (The Holy Week celebrations at Rome in 1860 were 'a melancholy hollow business', 'wearisome' and 'empty'; trashy religion in a trashy city, George Eliot thought, storing her dismayed responses in her 'Recollections of Italy 1860' diary for use later in *Middlemarch*.)

To be sure, the responses of Clough's Claude are those of a shallow and irresponsible tourist, too easily softened when he falls briefly in love with the English traveller, Mary Trevelyan – 'Cupolas, crosses, and domes, the bushes and kitchen-gardens, / Which by the grace of the Tiber, proclaim themselves Rome of the Romans' (III.234-235) – and Clough is jeery about this dilettante who can worry about the amount of *latte* in his *caffé-latte* while Garibaldi's Republicans are fighting for control of the city (II.102).

But those first impressions of a rubbished city remain inerasable.[30] And not even the rosier tints of love's spectacles can make those bushes and kitchen gardens seem noble.

'Love among the Ruins', as Robert Browning celebrates it (in the *Men and Women* volume) may be 'best', certainly better than 'the whole centuries of folly, noise and sin' which caused the wars that demolished the city once 'great and gay', reducing the 'site' of one-time urban splendour to 'Miles and miles' of empty sheep pasture. But it won't restore the spires and towers and palace, the 'causeys [causeways], bridges, aqueducts', the marble 'wall / Bounding all', of which only 'a single little turret' survives to mark the spot of a once 'sublime' tower and 'burning' amphitheatre. The girl 'with eager eyes and yellow hair' waits there for her lover, most attractively, but their anticipated embrace's clash and annihilations – 'Ere we rush, ere we extinguish sight and speech / Each on each' – disconcertingly mimic the destructiveness that has left them only ruins to make love in. The solitary turret and miles of empty plain make the site sound like the Campagna outside Rome – the desolate scene, ghosted by a 'decease[d]' Rome, of Browning's 'Two in the Campagna', another *Men and Women* poem, about a pair of lovers whose love, 'This morn of Rome and May', is not quite in ruin but seems getting on that way. (The Campagna was much painted by ruin-bibbing English artists, like Edward Lear – *Campagna di Roma: via Prenestina* (1865) – and Turner, an engraving of whose *The Campagna*, was used to illustrate 'The Campagna of Rome' section of the best-selling 1830 edition of rich, radical, touristic art-collecting Samuel Rogers's *Italy : A Poem* (first published in 1822).[31]) Browning turns the setting of 'Love Among the Ruins' into a Biblicized apoc-

---

[30] A point nicely made by John Schad in his critically handy *Writers and their Work* volume, *Arthur Hugh Clough* (Northcote/British Council, London, 2006), 16.

[31] Old Rogers, generous in every way, especially financial, to other writers, used to read *Italy* to the young Tennyson and consult him about the notes for the poem. ' "He liked me", Tennyson said, "and thought that perhaps I might be the coming poet, and might help to hand his name down to future ages" '. Hallam Tennyson's *Memoir*, II.72. Actually Rogers was offered the Laureateship in 1850 in succession to Wordsworth but turned it down in favour of Tennyson. The 1830 edition of *Italy*, with engravings by Turner, Stothard, and Prout, sold 7,000 copies by 1832 – after poor early sales (*Italy* 'would have been dished', quipped Lady Blessington to Byron, 'were it not for the plates': quoted in the new Oxford DNB). The last edition was in 1834. It became a standard handbook for Victorian visitors to Italy. Macaulay was a fan. Ruskin claimed the first sight of Turner's plates affected the entire course of his life. If you'd become indifferent to Venice, said Ruskin, you were instantly cured by reading Rogers's 'Venice' section beginning 'There is a glorious City in the Sea'. Very informative Introduction in JR Hale, ed, *The Italian Journal of Samuel Rogers* (Faber & Faber, 1956) about British tourists, the French clean-up of Roman debris, and so forth. 'The Pantheon! What a walk from the Vatican to the Coliseum! So long a spectacle of ruin and of scorn', wrote Protestant Rogers, 25 November 1814, *Journal*, 207. For Lear and Turner see *Imagining Rome: British Artists and Rome in the Nineteenth Century*, eds Michael Liversedge and Catharine Edwards (Bristol City Museum and Art Gallery/Merrell Holbertson, London, 1996), 123–124.

alyptic Omni-ruin. It's certainly an 'abomination of desolation' in the redolent phrase from the Bible's apocalyptic Book of Daniel. The fallen tower and the 'brazen pillar high / As the sky' recall the Tower of Babel. The 'gourd' which has 'overscored' the plains sounds like the one God has a 'worm' destroy to teach Jonah a lesson about how He can destroy, or spare, Nineveh as He wishes. And every pair of lines in the poem wonderfully arranges a fall, as each set of rhyming words drops bathetically away. This is a poetry of absolute, repeated falling; it can't be voiced in any other way:

> Where the quiet-coloured end of evening smiles,
>   Miles and miles
> On the solitary pastures where our sheep
>   Half-asleep
> Tinkle homeward through the twilight, stray or stop
>   As they crop –
> Was the site once of a city great and gay
>   (So they say)
> Of our country's very capital, its prince
>   Ages since
> Held his court in, gathered councils, wielding far
>   Peace or war.

And here's devastation refusing to be read as picturesque in any kind of Romantically fantasizing way! The poem's rhymes arrange a line-by-line negating of any aesthetic delight in ruinousness as strong in poetic effect as the scepticism voiced in the lengthy debate about the picturesqueness of ruins, and the symbolism of 'ravage', in Browning's *Red Cotton Night-Cap Country*. What's 'picturesque'?, is this poem's ask. A 'travelled lady' is advised to ponder 'Some work of art gnawn hollow by Time's tooth, – / Hellenic temple, Roman theatre, / Gothic cathedral, Gallic Tuilieries / But ruined', and to question their so-called picturesqueness. Poets, painters want their 'crumblings' left untouched, even if they're a danger to children, for the sake of art. '"Disturb no ruins here!"', they say; but their 'picturesque' isn't a moral or aesthetic absolute because ruins do not stay still; they change, and thus so does any sense of 'picturesque'. And nobody having ruins fall on his 'pate' or tripping over debris thinks 'picturesque' the word to describe his feelings. Far better to be practical and clear up ruins, 'For conservation's sake / Clear the arena forthwith!' And certainly, if you don't, the tramp of touristic feet will turn everything to 'one blank / Mud-mixture, picturesque to nobody' (1031–1168). I paraphrase, and cut and paste, what seems to me a more than ordinarily obscure set of contending Browningesque voices. But the poem's main point is clear: ruins are disconcerting, if not dangerous, and nobody should be allowed to soften their grim reminders with bogus aestheticizing glosses or talk.

Autumn's Leavings

Something similar emerges from the massive amount of natural declining and falling – another *Überrest* of Romantic consciousness – that goes on in and around, and is an intimate part of, the prevailing ruin-consciousness. Autumn, Winter, snow and cold, falling leaves, falling and felled trees, strike loud negative notes of nature's challenge to its own more cheerful counter-factuals of Spring and Summer, renewal, return, growth and flourishing. Our melancholics revel in bad weather, in the natural woefulness of coming Autumn and Winter.

> On a bare hill a thin elm's spindle crest
> Was glorified by kisses of the sky,
> Where harvest sunshine made the shrill wind die
> Till evening, and the waning year had rest.
> Only about a blackened empty nest
> Some lonely rooks kept an unrestful cry;
> Below the babbling brook of reeds was dry
> In the green valley trending to the west,
> Green still; on either side the lands were ploughed,
> Whence carrying scanty sheaves of ill-saved grain
> On creaking wheels went by a broken wain,
> Whereon three harvest men who whistled loud;
> But in the shadow of a rising cloud
> Two scarlet leaves fell in a pool of rain.

That's the wonderful autumnal sonnet 'Falling Leaves' by the Oxford Latinist George Augustus Simcox (in his *Poems and Remains* volume of 1869). And you're reminded constantly in such poems as this of elegy's per-ennially anti-pastoral subject-matter and feeling, and that elegy is, as Classicists like Simcox and Housman (and for that matter, Arnold, Tennyson, Hopkins and Robert Bridges) well knew, the mode of winter, and, we might add, of autumn turning into winter, of the season of natural dying, the time of and for elegy.[32] Matthew Arnold's dead father comes to his mind in

---

[32] Curiously, elegy is scarcely mentioned in Northrop Frye's influential *Anatomy of Criticism* (1957), which sought very ambitiously to systematize (like a Puritan Systematic Theology) all literature by genre and archetypal 'mythos'. If elegy were really on Frye's radar it would surely have come under his 'Mythos of Autumn' and, more particularly, his 'Mythos of Winter'. As it is, his 'Mythos of Winter' oddly embraces only Irony and Satire, and Tragedy is what comes under his 'Mythos of Autumn'. Elegy gets put in a miniscule box in his 'Theory of Genres' discussion, coming right after panegyric, as 'panegyrical funeral ode', epitaph, and the 'poem of melancholy in its extreme form of accidia or ennui', as in Baudelaire, which latter is classed as a branch of 'tragic irony'. So touches of 'Winter' and 'Autumn' there; but only glancingly.

'Rugby Chapel, November, 1857') as 'The autumn-evening' descends 'Coldly, sadly' over Rugby School's playing 'field / Strewn with its dank yellow drifts / Of withered leaves': 'There thou dost lie, in the gloom / Of the autumn evening'. Arnold does, of course, try and cheer his poem up with thoughts of Dr Arnold's 'radiant vigour' as a leader of young men – it's not been long, after all, since son Matthew was banishing melancholy from his published pages and embracing Schiller-esque Joy as poetry's must-monger. 'But ah! that word, *gloom*, to my mind / Brings thee back, in the light / Of thy radiant vigour, again'. But gloom keeps invading (three times in lines 14–19).[33] In Bridges's 'The north wind came up yesternight', the northerly wind blows the New Year's new moon across 'The frost-bound country', a landscape unable to resist winter's killing power and 'wrath' ('There scarce was hanging in the wood / A shrivelled leaf to reave', i.e. steal). Thus Nature shows her 'Dim indications of the power / That doometh man to woe', that is the Fall and original sin. Thinking of these bare 'tree-skeletons', the poet passes the churchyard, and his 'spirit' enters a 'Grey, melancholy and vast' land where Memory, 'The widowed queen of Death', reigns,

> And ghosts of cities long decayed
> And ruined shrines of Fate
> Gather the paths, that Time hath made
> Foolish and desolate.
> (*The Shorter Poems of Robert
> Bridges*, Book V, 1894)

The graveyard of nature, of the seasons, is where all the ruins are.

'The woods decay, the woods decay and fall'; and Tennyson's Tithonus, cursed with immortality, would like to die as the woods do. It's only natural; and natural for melancholics and elegists, especially elegists of past civilizations, to think of such demises. 'On Wenlock Edge, the wood's in trouble; / His forest fleece the Wrekin leaves; / The gale, it plies the saplings double, / And thick on Severn snow the leaves'. Thus Housman in Poem XXXI of *A Shropshire Lad*. Falling leaves, like snow; autumn turning into winter; as they did in this very place when the Romans were in Britain. ''Twould blow like this through holt and hanger / When Uricon the city stood'. Uricon: Uriconium, Roman name for modern Shropshire's Wroxeter. And the falling leaves of the troubled wood are a portent of inevitable decline and fall to come for the (presently very alive) 'English yeoman'. They're reminders of

---

[33] 'Rugby Chapel November 1857' must make you recall TS Eliot's 'Preludes. I', which plainly recalls the Arnold, in which 'The winter evening settles down / With smell of steaks in passageways. / Six o'clock' – an apparently cheering and inviting smell for a winter evening, which can't, though, greatly alleviate the sadness of such 'burnt-out ends of smoky days', as 'a gusty shower wraps / The grimy scraps / Of withered leaves about your feet / And newspapers from vacant lots'. *Withered leaves* – of several sorts.

how 'To-day the Roman and his trouble / Are as ashes under Uricon'. Thomas Hardy titled his 1867 poem about fallen leaves as signifying reminders, 'Neutral Tones' (it's in his *Wessex Poems*, 1898). But it's the colours of the poem not its tones of voice that are neutral – the lack of bright colour in the 'white' sun of a winter's day in which 'gray' leaves from an ash tree fell 'on the starving sod', 'And a pond' was 'edged with grayish leaves', and a woman's smile was 'the deadest thing / Alive enough to have strength to die' – all of this making 'keen lessons' for memory in the deceits and wrongings of love. Like so many of these poems of autumnal and wintry falling the feelings are anything but neutral; rather, anguish reigns. 'I never shall love the snow again / Since Maurice died': Bridges's take on the deadliness of winter is to be forever marked by the accidental collusion in it of a private grief, the doubled wintriness of the wintry season (compare Auden's 1939 elegy 'In Memory of WB Yeats': 'He disappeared in the dead of winter'). But this seasonal lowering of spirit differs from the usual in degree rather than in kind.

Fallen Trees

These grievers over nature's fallings are angry. William Barnes's apparent stoical acceptingness in his poems about the chopping down of trees – 'Zoo the girt elem tree out in the little huome groun' / Wer a-stannen this marnen, an' now's a-cut down' ('Vellen the tree', in the 'Dorset Dialect' version of *Poems of Rural Life, in the Dorset Dialect*, 1844) – is not widely shared, and certainly not by Gerard Hopkins. Hopkins's consternation over the chopping down of poplar trees at Binsey, on the edge of Oxford, provoked him into one of his very best poems – one of the very best of Victorian poems, indeed of English poems of any period – 'Binsey Poplars: Felled 1879':

> My aspens dear, whose airy cages quelled,
> Quelled or quenched in leaves the leaping sun,
> All felled, felled, are all felled;
>   Of a fresh and following folded rank
>   Not spared, not one
>   That dandled a sandalled
>   Shadow that swam or sank
> On meadow and river and wind-wandering weed-winding bank.
>
> O if we but knew what we do
>   When we delve or hew –
>   Hack and rack the growing green!
>   Since country is so tender
>   To touch, her being só slender,
>   That, like this sleek and seeing ball
> But a prick will make no eye at all,

8

15

Where we, even where we mean
    To mend her we end her,
    When we hew or delve:
After-comers cannot guess the beauty been.
20   Ten or twelve, only ten or twelve
    Strokes of havoc únselve
        The sweet especial scene,
    Rural scene, a rural scene,
    Sweet especial rural scene.

It's an elegy for fallen trees. The poet mourns for the fallen. He's an 'After-comer', as all mourners, all elegists, are. Unlike the ignorant 'After-comers' Hopkins imagines in line 19, though, this one does know the beauty that has been and is now gone. This is the elegist's perennial tragedy. Hopkins has loved these trees. They're imagined as people he has loved. The pathetic fallacy is running rampant. The trees are 'My aspens dear'. They're womanly. They've been like a woman in his life; the only woman, in fact, that he, as a priest, has been allowed to touch. '[C]ountry is so tender / To touch'. These trees have been, what's more, a maternal presence. They 'dandled' their shadows in the river flowing about them. Dandling is what mothers do, bouncing children in their lap. And now this beloved woman has been raped, sexually assaulted, even unto death. An untender 'prick' has done its worst. 'Ball' (14) – like 'prick' (15) – is no accident. Hopkins's anger has driven him to use low slang, *ball*, and *prick*. The bad country-matters of the tree-felling have got him talking, like angry Hamlet (III.ii.112), 'country matters' (*country*: *cunt*). In his anger he's let his anxiety about the threat to his own body – his anguished eye-talk – provide the strong testicular meta-phoricity, *ball*, *prick*, for the threat to nature's body. The loss to his entranced vision of his beloved landscape – 'The sweet especial scene, / Rural scene, a rural scene, / Sweet especial rural scene' – has provoked his customary anxiety over the fragility of his eyesight; the 'seeing ball' which just 'a prick will make no eye at all'. No eye; no I: it's the old Hopkins double meaning (remember the discussion of 'As kingfishers catch fire' in 'Selving', Chapter 6). Not seeing is not being. The scene has been *unselved* (line 21), and so, unsighted now, is the poet. His own being has been *hacked* and *racked* and not *spared*, like the trees. There's a double loss going on here, the one to the country and the one to him. As ever, Shakespeare comes to Hopkins's mind, and, fittingly, terrible death-minded Shakespeare. As my Balliol colleague the poet and scholar Carl Schmidt has nicely pointed out, 'All felled, felled, are all felled' harks awfully back to Macduff lamenting the murder of his wife and children on Macbeth's order: 'Did you say all? ... All? / What, all my pretty chickens and their dam / At one fell swoop?' (*Macbeth*, IV iii.217–9). And 'Strokes of havoc únselve' (21) surely brings together

Anthony's expecting the ghost of murdered Caesar to 'Cry "Havoc!" and let slip the dogs of war' (*Julius Caesar*, III.i.274) with Lady Macbeth's 'unsex me here' as she works herself up for the murder of King Duncan (*Macbeth*, I.iv.38).[34] But even more, I'd say, it's the fall in the garden of Eden, that primal ruin of Arcadia, of pastoral bliss, which floods Hopkins's vision of these fallen trees. They have been *felled* (three times). They have been made to fall, like soldiers, who of course fall in battle when a leader cries havoc (pillage, devastation) and lets slip the dogs of war; but more, like Adam, the original delver, or digger ('When Adam delved...'), cursed by the Fall to a lifetime of hard labour, of delving and hewing. To *hew* (line 10) is to cut, to cut wood – to chop down trees especially. 'Hewers of wood' in the Bible are servants, labourers, mean fellows, outsiders, the cursed ones. The Binsey trees have been hewn down, subjected to a felling, a Fall, a Paradise Lost; and by fallen man, fallen Adam's descendants, the hewers and delvers. Among whom is, of course, Hopkins himself. He includes himself in the collective *we* of hewers and delvers. 'O if we knew what we do / When we delve or hew' (9–10). 'Father forgive them', prayed Jesus on the cross to God, 'for they know not what they do'. Priestly Hopkins knew that, orthodoxly, he needs such forgiveness. It's the human need. For 'When we hew or delve' (18) – sweet chiasmic inversion of line 10's 'When we delve or hew' – we always commit a sin against the country, 'the growing green' (11), God's pastoral. Even when we mean well: 'even / Where we mean / To mend her we end her.' Inevitably we are ending people: condemned to end, to die ourselves; and, however well meaning, we are the cause of ending in, and the ending of, others. Hopkins's frustrated *mend* has got *end* inscribed ineluctably in it. There is, for this Christian poet, no mending the human disposition to death and deadliness; at least no natural way of amending the inevitability of human endings. What's signalled by the mediating human word *men*, embedded in that *mend*. Mend, *men*, end. It's the men in there who are the problem. Men, man, humankind. The tragedy of ending is all human; all too human.

You'd expect a Jesuit to talk in this theological way. And Hopkins's post-Romantic taste for ruins is understandably churchy. He pokes, awed, poeticizing, admiring the decrepit beauties, round the remains of the Cistercian Abbey at Netley near Southampton ('every thing ... beautiful, the ruins, the ivy, the ashtrees ... dead ... dying ... one notable dead tree in the NW corner of the nave, the inscape markedly holding its most simple and beautiful oneness up from the ground through a graceful swerve ... The finest of all stands (I think) in the monks' day-room'); and around 'the little ruined chapel of Kirk Trinnian' on the Isle of Man ('growing ashes now and half

---

[34] Carl Schmidt in an admirable lunchtime lecture on 'Hopkins and the Natural World', St Giles Church, Oxford, 6 December 2008.

pulled down by them'); and the nearby ruin of Peel Castle, with its ruined Cathedral of St German and its ruined 'red chapel', and the castle's cliff base smashed against by 'great seas ... glass-green, as loose as a great windy sheet, blown up and plunging down and bursting upwards from the rocks in spews of foam'. He's certainly what Philip Larkin in his 1950s poem 'Church Going', about church visitors' taste for old religious buildings, called a 'ruin-bibber': a tippler of ruins, after the Biblical 'wine-bibber'. But the tippling is driven by a theological sense of flaw, damage, fall in nature. It's no accident that Hopkins's attraction towards those churchy ruins is infected by natural processes of ruination (those strong seas) and natural ruin, the falling and dying of ash trees (and how apt that they're *ash* trees, whose name is the word for burnt-out remainders). The impact of what Larkin also meant by church-going, namely the decline and end of Christianity is, for sure, a pros-pect hanging around these visits. It's held, though, as it were in abeyance, just as the crashing seas at Peel are not being consciously linked to anything like an Arnoldian sea of faith: Hopkins's Peel is some way distant from Dover Beach. What's getting the prominence here is the fallenness of the natural: nature's *fatiscere* factor as this theologian poet would have it. '[N]ature in all her parcels and faculties gaped and fell apart, *fatiscebat*, like a clod cleaving and holding only by strings of roots', he recorded in his jour-nal, of his weary trudge towards Clitheroe, Lancashire, and some dire Jesuit lodgings. Latin *fatiscebat*: nature was breaking up, giving way; was weary, downcast from exhaustion (*fatiscere* is related to Greek *chasma*, chasm, gulf). The melancholy of nature mirrored his own (at the time he was feeling in 'darkness and despair', 'quite downcast': a priest in distress reading his own and nature's distress inevitably through theology's lens).[35]

Recessionals

But the theologizing of elegy was by no means limited to paid-up theolo-gians and ministers of religion like Hopkins, nor even to unremittingly Christian poets, like Christina G Rossetti, and the hymn-writers – one should, of course, say 'Christian G and the *other* hymn-writers' for she was one too – whose main business was with the Christian story, and not least the narrative of personal and cosmic ending-up offered by the Bible and Christian theology. In one way or another, theologizing the subject of death, of ending-up, of reaction to death, is nearly universal for Victorian poets. It's hard to find any one of them, including – especially including – agnostics and atheists and other sceptics, doubters and renegers on faith, who was not so Christianized, so steeped in the Judaeo-Christian narrative, as to be

---

[35] Hopkins, 1873 Journal, *Journals and Papers*, edn cit, 236.

unable to escape thinking theology in some sort at deathbed or graveside. And dominantly, and for believers as well as unbelievers, elegy and the elegiac provoke – seem to demand, even – some questioning of faith's certainties, if not outright doubting.

Such is the assault on his orthodox faith in life after death which Bridges feels, inspecting the body of his little son in its coffin, in 'On a Dead Child':

> So quiet! doth the change content thee? – Death, whither hath he taken thee?
> To a world do I think, that rights the distaste of this?
> The vision of which I miss,
> Who weep for the body, and wish but to warm thee and awaken thee?

> Ah! little at best can all our hopes avail us
> To lift this sorrow, or cheer us, when in the dark,
> Unwilling, alone we embark,
> And the things we have seen and known and heard of, fail us.

> (*Poems: Third Series*, 1880)

The momentousness of Browning's 1864 poem 'A Death in the Desert' (in *Dramatis Personae*) consists not in its being simply a kind of elegy for the Bible's John, supposed author of John's Gospel, the Book of Revelation and the Epistles of John, imaginatively forceful though that is, but because of how it responds to contemporary writers of sceptical elegies for Christian history and orthodoxy. Dying John, lengthily defending the veracity of his memories of an historical Jesus and so of his Gospel's foundational record, against the forerunners of the so-called Higher Criticism of the Biblical texts, particularly the European underminers of Biblical, and so of ecclesiastical authority – the likes of Ernest Renan in his *La Vie de Jésus*, which Browning read in November 1863, soon after it appeared, and David Friedrich Strauss, whose *Das Leben Jesu* Browning had long been familiar with in George Eliot's 1846 translation, and whose new *Life* of Jesus of January 1864 Browning seems also to have read. The poem's John won't have either himself or his Gospel erased from history. ' "Was John at all, and did he say he saw?" ', he has John's detractors, early version of the Higher Critics, say (twice: 196, 345). Yes, John replies, he did exist and he did, and does, say he saw: 'Look at me who was present from the first! / Ye know what things I saw' (301–302); 'I saw the power' (221). And now, although Jesus is dead, and still has not yet returned in the promised Second Coming, 'I see the Love' (221). The critics are 'glozers' of John's texts and his history, commentators whose *glosses* are *glozes*, that is lies. John's self-defence is firm, even if a bit longwinded. Nonetheless, Browning can't entirely escape John's worries about the critics pulling down the shutters on Bible factuality. This end-preoccupied poem ends with the sceptics' question about Jesus's non-reappearance, ' "Where is the promise of his coming?" ' (177). The next-to-last voice in the poem, an affirmer of the dead John's credibility, says that the hundreds of believers who'll welcome the returning Christ in ten, or at most twelve, years' time are proof of Jesus Christ's divinity which John wrote about. If you don't believe this, you're 'lost'. The poem's very last words tell us that one of its main named critics, the man Cerinthus, is indeed lost. But, of course, the question of who and what exactly are lost remains. John is dead; Jesus is dead; and so are those believers whose faith at the Second Coming was to affirm Christ as God. So many ends; and still no promised end. (And, not at all by the way, it's a poem like this, struggling for faith on the cusp of engulfing doubt, that rather nullifies Thomas Hardy's remark about Browning's 'smug Christian optimism worthy of a dissenting grocer'.[36])

Ruin, dissolution of persons, cultures, cities, inevitably set the poets think-ing of the ruin and dissolution of church and churches, of belief, of Biblical certainties. Just typical is Dante Gabriel Rossetti's reaction to the arrival of that winged god from Nineveh. The effigy is an emphatic sign of the ruin of Nineveh's ancient religion and its supercession by newer Christianity. But what brushes over the poem's ending is the nightmarish apocalyptic thought that as that old religion disappeared so might London's Christian faith; future generations coming across this Nineveh relic might not know 'us' as a race 'That walked not in Christ's lowly ways'. This worried thought is a consider-able part of the burden of 'The Burden of Nineveh'. Just so, when a sense of 'Ichabod', the Glory is Departed, is appealed to, it comes inevitably laden with its original, Biblical, sense of the departure of divine glory. The period's extremely common feeling of belatedness, the sense of the good times being past, of good things and good persons passing away, of the fleetingness of what's pleasant, of the loss of pastorals – expressed so well in the pair of 'decadent' Ernest Dowson poems of the 1890s, their titles taken from two of Roman Horace's ancient songs of lament, 'Vitae Summa Brevis Spem Nos Vetat Incohare Longam' ('The brevity of life prohibits us from any far-reaching hope': Horace, *Carmina* I.iv.15) and 'Non Sum Qualis Eram Bonae Sub Regno' ('I am no longer the man I was when ruled over by [my beloved] Cynara': *Carmina*, IV.i. 3–4), with their wonderfully affecting and soon-to-be deservedly famous lines like 'They are not long, the days of wine and roses' and that far-reaching phrase 'gone with the wind' – keeps getting scooped into the feeling that Christianity, the viability of its faith and practice, are

---

[36] A criticism curiously endorsed by Donald Davie, 'Robert Browning, *Dissentient Voice: The Ward-Phillips Lectures for 1980 With Some Related Pieces* (University of Notre Dame Press, Notre Dame and London, 1982), 36. Davie's claim that Browning's faith 'comes with a great head of emotional steam behind it', but 'has virtually no intellectual substance whatever', Davie (1982), 37, is rubbish.

waning, or even over. The feeling and its Christianized shudder are vividly present in Rudyard Kipling's great challenge poem 'Recessional: 1897)' (in Kipling's *The Five Nations* volume, 1903), which warns England not to forget in its swaggering imperialist boastfulness the 'God of our father, known of old', whose desired 'sacrifice' is still 'An humble and a contrite heart.' England's 'pomp' has gone, and is going, the way of Nineveh and Tyre. The national and political rot is leading to ruin, because of the loss of the Christian morality which once guaranteed the gun-power (the morality and theology of *that* assumption are, of course, deeply dubious and disquieting, along with the poem's notorious reference to the 'lesser breeds without the Law', the lower orders of the foreign Others, who are Christian England's uncivilized adversaries). Kipling's title 'Recessional' refers, utterly aptly in this Christianizing atmosphere, to the traditional hymn sung by clergy retiring to the vestry at the end of a church service. 'The tumult and the shouting dies; / The Captains and the Kings depart'; and the bemoaned imperialist receding is modelled on the clerical. It's all up with all the old reverence and reverencers. 'Retrocessional' was a variant title for this poem; 'After' was another.

'Recessional' could well be the title of the period's most melancholy of elegies for the dying of faith, Matthew Arnold's classic poem of Victorian doubting, his 'Dover Beach' (published 1867). He stands at the very edge of England, the border as it were between England and France – metonymic and metaphoric location of the liminality, the between-ness, where old faith and modern doubt converge for the divagator of his 'Stanzas from the Grande Chartreuse': 'Wandering between two worlds, one dead, / The other powerless to be born' (85–86). As he listens to the tide tearing at the shingle as it pulls away down the beach, he hears the 'Sea of Faith' once at high tide ('at the full') ebbing loudly away:

> But now I only hear
> Its melancholy, long, withdrawing roar,
> Retreating, to the breath
> Of the night-wind, down the vast edges drear
> And naked shingles of the world.

It's the old melancholic note of time and tide which people perpetually hear on tidal beaches,

> Where the sea meets the moon-blanched land
> Listen! you hear the grating roar
> Of pebbles which the waves draw back, and fling
> At their return, up the high strand,
> Begin, and cease, and then again begin,
> With tremulous cadence slow, and bring
> The eternal note of sadness in.

And this ancient prompter of melancholic thoughts (Sophocles heard it 'long ago ... on the Aegaean') is now specially prompting melancholy over the waning of faith.

It's typical of Arnold to claim continuity of his seaside melancholy with his beloved Greeks. His poem blankly refuses to own up to more recent overhearings. Undoubtedly this beached melancholic has in his ear Letter iv of *Obermann* in which Senancour positions himself on a beach and hears the waves 'expiring' towards daybreak as the moon sheds 'l'ineffable mélancolie de ses dernières lueurs' (the unspeakable melancholy of its final glimmers) on the water; not to mention the seaside melancholics of Tennyson's many poems, and not just 'Ulysses', where the melancholic moan of the sea is aweingly audible.[37] But Arnold was never going to admit publicly to sharing the tropes of his great rival Tennyson. And the Greek claim is, of course, Arnoldian moonshine – Sophocles never heard any such thing because the Aegean is not a tidal sea. Too, Arnold overlooks the metaphoric force of his own noticing of how tidal waters perpetually flow back as well as perpetually ebb away. But these illogics do not, oddly, soften the force of the elegizings, and especially not the self-dramatizing of the poet and his female addressee as a version of Milton's Adam and Eve quitting Paradise (at the end of *Paradise Lost*) with 'wandering steps and slow' (a slowness Arnold has passed on to the tide) for a world of solitary exile – beguilingly lovely in appearance, as Arnold has it, but which 'Hath really neither joy, nor love, nor light, / Nor certitude, nor peace, nor help for pain'. A world that's without any of the old consolations and confidences traditionally offered to Christian believers, the old *certitude* in Arnold's most memorably haunting word (absence of doubt or hesitation, subjective certainty, assurance, according to the OED): the 'only unignorable use of the word in our literature' according to Christopher Ricks.[38] A world Arnold defines with a most memorable image from Thucydides's *History of the Peloponnesian* War, about the confusions of the Athenian soldiers in a night-time battle (a passage well-known at Rugby School in Dr Arnold's translation of Thucydides, and a standard reference for classically educated boys like Arnold: Rugbeian and Oxonian Clough refers to it his *Bothie of Tober-na-Vuolich*, IX. 51–54):

[37]   Robert Douglas-Fairhurst cannily remarks the many Tennyson places that link the sea with moaning – in 'Ulysses', of course, but also in *In Memoriam* and 'The Palace of Art', all pre-'Dover Beach', and all likely familiar to Arnold; as well as 'The Passing of Arthur' and 'Demeter and Persephone' (both coming after the Arnold, in 1869). *Victorian Afterlives* (2002), 2, 7–8.
[38]   In 'Yvor Winters: Allusion and Pseudo-Reference', rebutting Yvor Winters's sneers at 'Dover Beach', exposing Winters's heavy use of the Arnold in his poem 'The Slow Pacific Swell' – 'Half-drenched' in Arnold, in Winters's phrase ('Half-drenched in dissolution', no less) – and noting the telling recurrence of *certitude* in Winters's oeuvre: Ricks, *Allusion to the Poets* (Oxford University Press, Oxford, 2002), 295–318.

> And we are here as on a darkling plain
> Swept by confused alarms of struggle and flight,
> Where ignorant armies clash by night.

Darkling: in the dark; a favourite nineteenth-century poetic word. It would be surprising were Arnold not thinking of Keats listening, *darkling*, to the nightingale in his 'Ode to a Nightingale', or the lovers in Keats' 'The Eve of St Agnes' making their 'darkling way' down the stairs. Hardy might be thinking of Arnold when he calls the old thrush 'darkling', as it sings to the 'corpse' of the old century in the 'crypt' of a winter landscape on December 31 1900 ('The Darkling Thrush'). Hardy was certainly thinking of Arnold when he had the mourners in the funeral procession of God in 'God's Funeral' (1908–1910) confess to being *darkling*, as they grieve the death of this 'man-projected Figure' (the 'projection', a divinity made in human image as described by the Higher Critical 'Teachers', the ones Browning's John resists in 'A Death in the Desert'):

> 'So, toward our myth's oblivion
> Darkling and languid-lipped, we creep and grope
> Sadlier than those who wept in Babylon
> Whose Zion was a still abiding hope'.

The Death of God

The death of God, or at least the disappearance which mimics a death.[39] Noisily announced by the tidal shingle on Dover Beach, but an absence more usually denoted by silence, the silence of the grave and thoughts of the grave as a final silencer. The silence of the grave troubles poets mightily. Especially the silence of the poets they keep elegizing – so horribly reminding of the eventual fate they fear looming for their own voice, their own poems. And the terrible silence of death's absentings keeps nudging them into panic about what's happening in their time, the time of the alleged death or disappearance of God, to the voice, the *word*, the *logos*, of the God of the Bible, which is His defining foundational aspect ('And God said ...'. Genesis 1; 'In the beginning was the word', John's Gospel 1). Momentously for poetry. It's the way that Tennyson's *In Memoriam* looks into the heart of these divine absences, silences, darknesses, which helps grant this large piece

---

[39]   Death: disappearance: the terminological and conceptual issue (and what Nietzsche actually meant by the notorious 'death of God') which J Hillis Miller bats about at the beginning of *The Disappearance of God: Five Nineteenth-Century Writers* (1963), his foundational study of the absence-presence-absence of God in De Quincey, Robert Browning, Emily Brontë, Arnold and Hopkins. (It's the interplay replicated in the question of the death or disappearance of the author: 'death' (Roland Barthes), 'disappearance' (Michel Foucault).)

of poetic grieving (perhaps the largest ever piece of aesthetic elegizing, the largest ever verbal monument, or *Denkmal*, built to the memory of a dead loved one) helps grant it its momentousness, makes it the most momentous of Victorian elegies, perhaps the most momentous elegy of all time.

Hallam 'is gone', like the master of a house, mourned by his children and his servants: his 'vacant chair' (XX) is a daunting signifier of a lost presence (much like the creaking basket-chair in Virginia Woolf's novel *Jacob's Room*). Gone. Hallam is, in Ophelia's haunted words for her dead father, 'dead and gone'. He's gone, as all the dead do: 'They are all gone, and thou art gone as well!'; 'Yes thou art gone!' (Arnold's 'Thyrsis', 130–131). Such is the tragic finality of death – Polonius will 'not come again' (Ophelia); nor will Cordelia. In her grieving father King Lear's words, 'She's gone for ever': 'Thou'lt come no more, / Never, never, never, never, never'. Grieving in the night, unable to sleep (*In Memoriam* VII), Tennyson is drawn, bereft, to the London house where Hallam had lived, 67 Wimpole Street, where he'd once stood, heart beating, looking forward to the touch of his loved one's hand. The house is now 'Dark', the street unlovely, the weather bad, the breaking dawn grim. 'And ghastly through the drizzling rain / On the bald street breaks the blank day', because 'He is not here'. Tennyson has entered the long vastating history of elegy – the literature of suddenly *bald* and *blank* existence, and the sense of religious blanking-out that this experience of terrible baldness imposes on the Christian poet and the poetry of the believer. 'Grave doubts' Tennyson calls them in a compellingly terrible pun (XLVIII): serious doubts inspired at the graveside. 'He is not here': the words of the two men 'in shining garments' at the empty tomb of Jesus (Luke 24.6). For the moment, at any rate, Tennyson cannot appropriate the angelic continuation: 'He is not here, but is risen'. Standing by the dark, empty, silent house of Hallam, Tennyson feels no resurrection consoling, no sense of any life after death, of existence after life's end. The house's darkness and silence and emptiness insistently affirm the poem's nightmare: metaphysical negation, transcendental blankness, the terrifying presence of religious darkness (there's very little light …), the silence of God, the emptying out of the old and once present Christian meanings. All the 'grave doubts' which keep poking into the poem.

Hallam's death challenged Biblical origins and thus Biblical teleology and ontology; his ending deeply unsettled the Bible's asserted narrative of beginnings with and for God in Christ: 'In the beginning God', 'In the beginning was the word'. At the very least it was an ending that seemed to affirm all the unsettlings of the Grand Narrative of Genesis and of the Gospels already coming on strong from the Higher Criticism and, of course, contemporary science.[40] The falterings of Tennyson's faith in a not-very-old, God-created

---

[40]   See Daniel Brown, 'Victorian poetry and science', *The Cambridge Companion to Victorian Poetry*, ed Joseph Bristow (Cambridge University Press, Cambridge, 2000), 137–158.

anthropocentric world that had been induced by Charles Lyell's *Principles of Geology*, which Tennyson read in 1837 ('I falter where I firmly trod': LV), were made vivid by this most traumatic demise. Hallam is just one of Nature's anonymous victims: Nature, the evolutionary force at work during Lyell's long geological ages, 'red in tooth and claw', and which couldn't care less about humans as such, and so is at odds with the orthodox Christian's 'creed' in a creative God of love – 'love Creation's final law' (LVI; LV)). LVI ends despairingly: faith overwhelmed by feelings of futility brought on by the silence of God – whose silence is one with Hallam's ('thy voice', it would appear, is a blend of God's and Hallam's; they've been silenced in unison).

> O life as futile, then, as frail!
> O for thy voice to soothe and bless!
> What hope of answer, or redress?
> Behind the veil, behind the veil.

Hallam's presence has been obscured, is 'veiled', and so is God's. That last line has prompted much desperate critical debate, but its meaning is very clear in terms of orthodox Biblicism. The veiling of God's face is one of the New Testament's horrors for unbelievers, especially Jews, the ones who can't *see* (II Corinthians 3). In Judaic practice only the High Priest met God behind the curtained, or veiled, Holy of Holies of the Tabernacle and Temple. The Veil of the Temple was 'rent from top to bottom' at the crucifixion, signifying for Christian commentary, led by St Paul, the opening of access to God for all people. Hence the (unreferenced) passage from Hebrews 6.19 quoted by Christopher Ricks in his Notes at this point, about the Christian's 'hope' as 'sure and stedfast' because it 'entereth into that within the veil'. To doubt, as Tennyson is being made to, access to the Christian consolations from 'within the veil' is to be horribly stuck in a hopeless, meaningless dark, where, in Derridean terms (which draw greatly on the Biblical rhetoricity of the veil), there's only consternating confusion and aporia.[41]

Verbum In-Fans

Tennyson is, for the time being anyway, an outsider to the Christian faith, with the face, the revelation, of God, occluded for him. 'Our dearest faith' has become 'our ghastliest doubt'(CXXIV): extreme version of the doubt of the one shut out of Hallam's emptied house on that 'blank' and 'ghastly' day

---

[41] Derrida's engagement with *voiles*/veils, and similar textually aporetic textiles, especially in Biblical terms, is extensive. But see eg Jacques Derrida/Hélène Cixous, *Veils*, trans Geoffrey Bennington (Stanford University Press, Stanford, CA, 2001).

in VII; ghastliest version of a ghastly doubt in the Holy Ghost induced by Hallam's having become a ghost. Tennyson is ghosted by doubt; doubt brought on the ghosting of Hallam. Doubts haunting Tennyson terribly because they seem focussed not just on the genesis of the world, but on the origins of Christianity itself, the Gospel narratives of Jesus' birth. The insistent nagging of *In Memoriam* at its three Christmases makes it sound as if Tennyson has been reading George Eliot's translation of David Friedrich Strauss's *Life of Jesus* (1846) as well as Lyell.[42] It's a critical convention to note that the poem is structured around three Christmases (XXVIII, LXXVIII, CIV), but the strong reason for this dwelling on the celebration of the Advent of Christ in the teeth of Hallam's non-appearance, his non-advent ('Expecting still his advent home', VI), is usually missed by commentators.

If, as Strauss had argued, the Christmas story is merely fictional, Tennyson's faith is foundationless, and the challenge engineered by Hallam's absence and silence merely affirmed. So Christmas must be celebrated, to keep up some sort of faith in the Advent of Christ, the 'welcome guest' of tradition, as some sort of rebuttal of the aweing absences that Hallam's death signifies. 'How dare we keep our Christmas-Eve; // Which brings no more a welcome guest?' asks XXIX. The 'baptismal font' in the neighbouring church is *cold*, signifying cold comfort for any beginning-of-faith ritual; but still it is entwined with 'holly boughs', traditional emblems of the redemptive death Christ was born for. And while a 'wreath' will once again hang on 'the portals of the house', denoting death (its leaves 'will die'), 'we' did 'weave / The holly round the Christmas hearth'. 'With trembling fingers', granted, but still it's the festive holly (XXX). The poem's second Christmas (LXXVIII) is still possessed by awful silences and absences – 'silent snow possessed the earth''; 'The quiet sense of something lost'; dry eyes. But 'dance and song' denounce them. And again there's defiantly Christian holly ('Again at Christmas did we weave / The holly round the Christmas hearth'). The third Christmas (CV) is the most strained of all, the grave's silences and blankings getting affirmed in a spate of negatives – the single church-bells, 'not the bells I know', the laurel ungathered, the holly boughs uncut, no dancing, no 'bowl of wassail', no 'song, nor game, nor feast', and so forth. 'For who would keep an ancient form / Through which the spirit breathes no more?' Grave absences all – aporias for the faithful, a non-practice of Christmas because it lacks the creative, genetic, spirit which God (the Word) breathed into Adam; immediately overcome, though, by the noisiest section of the whole poem (CVI): 'Ring out, wild bells'. These New Year's bells are elegiac – they ring out the dying

---

[42] David Friedrich Strauss, *The Life of Jesus Critically Examined*, trans MA Evans, 3 vols (London, 1846). The only book George Eliot published in her own name of MA [Mary Ann or Marian] Evans.

year – but they're also prophetic of life after death; a new advent with the living Christ of the Advent. 'Ring in the Christ that is to be.' And it's no accident that the poem's next section (CVII) celebrates Hallam's own birthday (1 February 1811). A 'bitter day', with no 'flowers or leaves / To deck the banquet' because it's still winter; but for all that a 'festal' day, with music and toasts 'to him, whate'er he be'. Whatever he be. The poem's 'honest doubt' (XCVI) won't admit any more than that. But there is a birth to be celebrated; a presence to be claimed; as with the Jesus of history whom Tennyson finds himself affirming. Something to be wildly, even spasmodically, excited about. (It's been noticed how CVI resembles passages in PJ Bailey's *Festus*, the much jeered-at 'spasmodic' poem Tennyson rather admired.[43])

The silence of death of course offers a direct challenge to any poet. Tennyson's apprehension that Hallam's silencing adumbrated the silence of God and of Christ the Word and sustainer of word – an end for what Derrida has labelled Judaeo-Christian logocentrism – particularized and afforced a general apprehension. Thinking of the inevitable depredations of time – the old ruin melancholics given scientific spin by the likes of Lyell – Tennyson sees little hope for the survival of his own verse (*dumb* lays and *vain* songs, LXXVI). 'What hope is here for modern rhyme?' His elegy – 'These mortal lullabies of pain' – is bound to end up on some bookstall of old stuff, a record of ancient 'grief' for any casual passer-by to flick through, something 'Sung by a long-forgotten mind' (LXXVII). This section is an elegy for elegy – it's an elegy doubled. Time, like death, the emptier-out of faith, as it were infantilizes the poet, makes him an *in-fant*: *infans*, a person without speech. The poet dreams of divine purpose in the world:

> So runs my dream: but what am I?
> An infant crying in the night:
> An infant crying for the light:
> And with no language but a cry.
>
> (LIV)

But there is, after all, a chance for the poet's voice if the Christmas story be true – the story of the Word which became an infant (the '*Word* without a *word*; the *aeternall word* not hable able to speak a word', in the words of the 1618 Christmas Day sermon of Bishop Lancelot Andrewes, which so entranced TS Eliot on his way to Christian faith), in order to save word-users from silence.[44] It's a faith which Tennyson embraces even as he is impelled by the bad news of Hallam's death to doubt it. The gloom in

---

[43] Details of that enthusiasm – Tennyson's marked copy of *Festus*; his evangelizing FitzGerald with the goodness of *Festus*; etc – are in Ricks's Note to CVI, *Selected Edition*, 453.
[44] Lancelot Andrewes, *Sermons*, ed GM Storey (Clarendon Press, Oxford, 1967), 85.

LXXVII over the hopelessness of modern rhyme immediately precedes LXXVIII, the second of the poem's Christmases. The Christmases whose meanings might well negate the going negations. 'But what of that?', Tennyson demands, rounding on his post-Lyell ruin thoughts:

> My darkened ways
> Shall ring with music all the same;
> To breathe my loss is more than fame,
> To utter love more than sweet praise.

'Ring out, wild bells' indeed. Celebratory noise driving out depressed silence; words putting up a fight against in-fantilization. In other words, poem – form, the created literary object – rising out of the linguistic confusions and ruins wrought, or threatened at least, by the linguistic erasures and blanks of post-Christian doubt.

Tessellation

Much has, of course, been written about the formal disruptedness of *In Memoriam*, its patchy construction over so many years, a formal fragmentariness mirrored in the poem's disrupted syntax which is, in turn, a mirror of its jerky, intermingled, intermittent play of faith and doubt: the 'contradiction of the tongue' (CXXV).[45] But the overall result is coherence, formal wholeness achieved by an accumulation of poetic bits – not unlike the great poem by the poet Tennyson's elegiacs keep reminding us of, namely TS Eliot's 'The Waste Land'. 'These fragments I have shored against my ruins', as Eliot's poem put its formal building programme. For which Robert Browning's word is *tessellation*: the making of new wholes out of broken fragments – as in tessellated pavements, or mosaics, made of little bits of stone, marble, glass, called *tessera* or *tesserae* (plural). The word occurs in that part of *Red Cotton Night-Cap Country* where the fate of ruins is debated. Keep them crumbling picturesquely? Renovate entirely? Preserve as 'partial-ruin'? But do remember the virtues of tessellation:

> ... experiment yourself
> On how conducive to a happy home
> Will be the circumstance your bed for base
> Boasts tessellated pavement ...
> (1071–1074)

---

[45]   Julian Wolfreys is especially good on the incoherences, formal and conceptual, of the poem, and records the history of these critical anxieties, in 'Tennyson's Faith', Ch 2 of *Victorian Hauntings: Spectrality, Gothic, the Uncanny and Literature* (Palgrave, 2002), especially 57–58, 65–67, 69–70, and fn 5, p159.

Tesserae, the little building blocks of tessellation: it is (importantly) one of Harold Bloom's famous 'ratios of influence' – one of the techniques he suggests poets deploy in re-using their predecessor's materials.[46] A model of the way the poets are after all variously busy making their poems out of their contemplation in, and confrontations of, ruination, especially aesthetic, textual ruin. Poetry among the ruins. New verse out of, as it is about, the old debris. Ancient ruins daunt you, as Sophie Thomas has it, by their 'incompletable' because 'passed away' fragmentariness.[47] But in and through and out of that incompletability come new textual completions. *Tessellation.* A model, not least, for the way elegies do *mnemotechnik*, building their epitaphic memorials, their poetic monuments, out of the ruins of memory and presence. Their *cenotaphs*, empty tombs ('He is not here'), thrown up in the effort to keep memory alive and the dear departed present. 'Methinks my friend is richly shrined' (LVII, stanza 2). Tennyson made it clear he was offering his poem as that shrine (*shrine*: memorial container or building preserving venerated relics of the dead). 'The poet', said Tennyson of this stanza, 'speaks of these poems. Methinks I have built a shrine to my friend'; but, he added, 'it will not last'. The stanza goes on in that vein: 'But I shall pass; my work will fail'. And stanza 3 turns from the enshrining poem to the poet himself, the living shrine; at least the memorializing will last as long as he lives.

> Yet in these ears, till hearing dies
> One set slow bell will seem to toll
> The passing of the sweetest soul
> That ever looked with human eyes.

A deleted stanza 3 insisted, unconsoled, on the poem's shortcomings as a time-resistant monument:

> So might it last and guard thy dust
> For ever! Would indeed for this
> My skill were greater than it is!
> But let it be. The years are just.

The poem of memory will not last. Even the most 'powerful' of memorial rhymes, the ones, as Shakespeare's Sonnet 55 has it, that can outlive 'marble' and 'the gilded monuments / Of princes', are doomed to fail as 'living record of your memory', despite Shakespeare's claim to the contrary. (Sonnet 55 hangs over *In Memoriam*'s memorial anxieties, as it does over all the

---

[46] Harold Bloom, *The Anxiety of Influence: A Theory of Poetry* (Oxford University Press, New York, 1973).
[47] Sophie Thomas, *Romanticism and Visuality*, edn cit., 42.

grand elegies of the English tradition, Milton's *Lycidas*, Shelley's *Adonais*, and so on.) And Tennyson could not bring himself to share Shakespeare's faith in the power of memorial verses. His friend James Spedding did not like the clarity of Tennyson's despondency about his poetic weakness in that original stanza 3, and got Tennyson to drop it.[48] But the worry still stands in the published work – 'my work will fail'. Time – and death – will finally defeat elegy's hubristic, hope-full, work of trying to make the absent present, keep the dead alive, in a memorializing text.

Living On?

But for all this in-built scepticism, Tennyson does hang on to a faith in the provocation of elegy – as a technique for survival, of *sur-vivre*, survival, living on.[49] The faith that elegy is a means of combating the erasures of death, of joining in the Biblical victory of Christ over death – the 'last enemy that shall be destroyed' according to the resurrectionist I Corinthians 15.

Hangs on, describes it, though. 'What will survive of us?' The profound question of Philip Larkin's poem 'Arundel Tomb' clearly frets Victorian writers immensely. The credibility of orthodox Christianity's allegation of life continuing after death, the promise of bodily resurrection and everlasting life and consciousness in heaven (or hell), was widely challenged. The very assertiveness of the ultra-orthodox Christian poets – Christina G Rossetti, it might be, or John Henry Newman – indicates the pervasiveness of faith's wobblings. What shows in Christina G's seemingly unstoppable fetishistic engagements with the end-times themes of the Book of Revelation and the prospects of a future life, after death, in heaven is neurotic anxiety rather than Christian confidence. '[M]y soul shall walk in white', she insists in one of her earlier heaven-minded poems, 'From House to Home' (in the *Goblin Market* volume, 1862). And she went on fantasizing about becoming one of John the Revelator's 'Multitudes – multitudes ... in bliss, / Made equal to the angels, glorious, fair; / With harps, palms, wedding-garments, kiss of peace, / And crowned and haloed hair', as her poem 'From House to Home' has it. Her poems keep reading like the orthodox obverse of Swinburne's blasphemous unbelievings. (She read Swinburne with aggression as well as horror: for instance, erasing line 1151, 'The supreme evil, God' in her copy of Swinburne's *Atalanta in Calydon*, 1865.) But still she never gets to sound wholly reassured. Such poems as 'From House to Home', said her brother William in his notes to it, were 'evidence of a spirit sorely

[48] See the notes in Ricks's *Selected Edition*, 401.
[49] See Jacques Derrida, 'Living On: Border Lines', in Harold Bloom et al, *Deconstruction and Criticism* (Seabury, New York, 1979), 75–175. (French version: 'Survivre'.)

wrung, and clinging for dear life to a hope not of this world'; and he was right.[50] (It's a terrible mistake of Jerome McGann to think she fell into the ancient Christian heresy, which tempted Milton and Donne, of believing in 'soul sleep' after death and before the 'general resurrection' at the end of time; she patently thinks, or hopes, that dead Christians go straight to be 'with God' in heaven, a fate which can't come soon enough for her – like the Second Advent of Christ, which would preclude her from dying, but which, she keeps lamenting, is horribly deferred.[51])

John Henry Newman's *The Dream of Gerontius* (1865) has the orthodox hope that death is not the absolute end persistently offered to a panicked old priest on his deathbed. Angels assure him of salvation from the 'horror' of 'that shapeless, scopeless, blank abyss, / That utter nothingness, of which I came' (lines 24–25). Mary and all the Saints are praying for him. God will 'spare' him. Purgatory (for this is a very Roman Catholic poem) certainly waits, in which he can prayerfully work his way up to heaven. Angels are ready to 'tend, and nurse, and lull' him on his deathbed (900). Good Catholics will say 'Masses' for him, which will 'aid' him 'at the Throne of the Most Highest' (901–902). Choirs of 'Angelicals' keep singing verses, some of which came to comprise one of English Christianity's most frequently sung hymns – 'Praise to the Holiest in the height, / And in the depth be praise: / In all His words most wonderful; / Most sure in all His ways!'. But the choirs are tinny; their repetitive verses not to be relieved by recall of Edward Elgar's lovely later settings. The comforts on offer are lukewarm. Mere liturgical and theology text-book iterations clonk heavily on the page. The poet writes as if the answer to theological questionings is to be found in the mere repetition of the liturgy and other church phrase-books. None of the poem's busy orthodox Catholic assurances manages to assure, and the old man's death-bed panics are not assuaged.

As for the outright sceptics, the essence of their negative faith is belief in death as the utter end of life, being and consciousness. Swinburne's blaspheming negations draw powerfully on this anti-creed. His 'Ilicet', that

---

[50] *The Poetical Works of Christina Georgina Rossetti, with Memoir and Notes by William Michael Rossetti* (1904), 461. Quoted by WR Crump, ed, *Christina Rossetti: The Complete Poems*, 910.

[51] For Jerome McGann's mistake, see 'The Religious Poetry of Christina Rossetti', *Critical Inquiry*, 10 (September 1983), 127–144. Reprinted in McGann, *The Beauty of Inflections: Literary Investigations in Historical Method and Theory* (Clarendon Press, Oxford, 1985). Awfully influential. Unhappily acclaimed by Joseph Bristow, in his sanctifying reprint of it, as 'the first serious re-evaluation of Rossetti's position as a writer employing a distinctive and unusual form of Anglican eschatology': *Victorian Women Poets: Contemporary Critical Essays* (Macmillan, Basingstoke, 1995), 184. Michael Wheeler, in that best book on death and the afterlife in Victorian literature, *Death and the Future Life in Victorian Literature and Theology* (Cambridge University Press, Cambridge, 1990), does not, of course, include Christina G in his examination of the Protestant Victorians' growing interest in an 'intermediate state', e.g. 78ff.

most carefully fashioned of ultimate poems – *end, end, end*, it keeps saying – professes characteristic certainty in its denials of afterlife, of resurrection, of John the Revelator's heaven. 'None that has lain down shall arise / The stones are sealed across their places' (27–28). Jesus didn't rise from the dead and nor shall anyone else. 'No soul shall tell nor lip shall number / The names and tribes of you that slumber' (37–28). The Book of Revelation talks of the number of people in heaven 'that no man can number'; but that's the numberless crowd of the dead 'in Christ'. Jesus, the New Testament, the Christian tradition, say you should stay awake, keep watching and praying, anticipating the Second Advent, the arrival of Christ 'the Bridegroom' who will take the Church off to heaven as his Bride. 'Nay', says Swinburne to all that; no point (123–124). All that talk, the theological Bible story, is over, quite dead. The poem's title 'Ilicet' is Latin for 'It's all over': a word anciently used at the end of an assembly or funeral party. Swinburne is speaking at Christianity's funeral. This death is final, as death, for Swinburne, always is: 'An end, an end, an end of all'.

> The grave's mouth laughs unto derision
> Desire and dread and dream and vision,
> Delight of heaven and sorrow of hell.
> (34–36)

The grave might laugh, but Swinburne is not smiling. His Latin title 'Ilicet' signposts a rather impressive ancient stoicism in the face of the death of the old Christian assurances: Roman impassiveness, Greek even. 'We are born with travail and strong crying, / And from the birth-day to the dying / The likeness of our life is thus' (106–108). The borrowed tones are from the Book of Job; they anticipate the post-Christian bleakness of the 'born astride of a grave' speech in Beckett's *Waiting for Godot* (in French 1952, in English 1956), that death-arrested text so saturated in Greek epicurean stoicism. It's the fortitude expectable enough, one might think, in the poems of AE Housman, Kennedy Professor of Latin at Cambridge, but the more powerful for coming from so close to the pre-Christian source. Repeating the inevitability and finality of death, whilst refusing every time to do other than take on the chin the shock of this human doom, to keep practising what the Greek epicureans advised as stoic *apathia, athambia* (imperturbability), and *galenismos* (the unperturbed calm of a stilled sea) in the face of human suffering, is what make Housman's *A Shropshire Lad* so moving and compelling.[52]

---

[52] The stoic attributes of the epicurean self are described in A-J Festugière's *Épicure et ses dieux* (Presses Universitaires de France, Paris, 1946 (*Epicurus and His Gods*, trans CW Chiltern, Blackwell, 1955)), a book Beckett undoubtedly read in French before writing *Godot* (*athambia* is one of the 'characteristics' of God in Lucky's great rambling speech).

When I watch the living meet
And the moving pageant file
Warm and breathing through the street
Where I lodge a little while,

If the heats of hate and lust
In the house of flesh are strong,
Let me mind the house of dust
Where my sojourn shall be long.

(XII)

Housman's mourning impresses in its never flinching from the fact of mortality – as a mourning over mortality, particular and general, which lives with the
realistic emotions of the sad heart. So, not a refusal to mourn, but a refusal to
make funerary acts do anything but suggest finality. To Housman's grave-sides
you bring only anti-wreaths – no evergreens, nothing that would suggest life
after death by flowering in spring (spring-time, Easter blossoms: those hung-
onto tropes of resurrection in *In Memoriam*), and not even any rosemary
(what Ophelia would strew on Polonius's grave: rosemary 'for remembrance')
because it's too encouragingly bright (with *rime* (and for *rhyme*?)). Only dead
bits of harvest leftovers will do – chaff (*awns*), a dead stalk (*haulm*), any old
dead vegetation that's around on this cold (and plainly anti-Tennysonian)
Christmas-tide, just so long as it'll never flower, resurrection-style, again.

Bring, in this timeless grave to throw,
No cypress, sombre on the snow;
Snap not from the bitter yew
His leaves that live December through;
Break no rosemary, bright with rime
And sparkling to the cruel clime;
Nor plod the winter land to look
For willows in the icy brook
To cast them leafless round him: bring
No spray that ever buds in spring.

But if the Christmas field has kept
Awns the last gleaner overstept
Or shrivelled flax, whose flower is blue
A single season, never two;
Or if one haulm whose year is o'er
Shivers on the upland frore,
– Oh, bring from hill and stream and plain
Whatever will not flower again
To give him comfort: he and those
Shall bide eternal bedfellows
Where low upon the couch he lies
Whence he never shall arise.

(XLVI)

Housman's refusal of resurrection is as emphatic and almost as impressive as 'Last Words' by Amy Levy – the suicidal urban depressive, a female version of James Thomson, whose Jewishness and socialism precluded her from anything like Christian after-life hopes:

> These blossoms that I bring
> This song that here I sing
> These tears that now I shed
> I give unto the dead.
>
> There is no more to be done,
> Nothing beneath the sun,
> All the long ages through
> Nothing – by me for you.

Art – 'These blossoms' – for and about the dead; a nothing-but death-consciousness, because death is all there is. 'Nothing beneath the sun': Levy picks up her *vanitas vanitorum* pessimism from its Biblical source in Ecclesiastes 1: 'Vanity of vanities saith the Preacher, vanity of vanities; all is vanity. What profit hath a man of all his labours which he taketh under the sun?' Her poem's subtitle, 'Dead! all's done with!', is from Robert Browning's 'Too Late', about its narrator's dead female beloved who went off with a rival poet – utterly silent, now, in the churchyard ('you cannot speak / From the churchyard'). On 10 September 1889, after correcting the proofs of the volume *A London Plane-Tree and Other Poems* in which 'Last Words' would appear a few weeks later, Levy killed herself by inhaling charcoal fumes.

Not for Levy any of that (rather grating) breeziness infecting Hopkins's priestly announcement of a parishioner's death: 'Felix Randal the farrier, O is he dead then?' But it is not incidental that she draws on Browning for her subtitle. For clearly even the Christian and more or less orthodox Browning could feel daunted by the apparent finality of the grave. His faith in an after-life is manifestly a fraught thing. The poem 'La Saisiaz', which the sudden death of his friend Annie Egerton Smith on their Swiss walking tour in September 1877 shocked him into, endorses that fragility. It doesn't go as far as his Cleon, the Greek poet, who thinks the Christians' idea of heaven and after-life insane ('Cleon', 353), but it is racked with end questioning. '"Was ending ending once and always, when you died?"' 'What of you remains ...?' was the question raised as he 'lifted' her 'form', 'as it lay' (172–175). They'd been discussing Frederic Harrison's articles in *The Nineteenth Century* magazine (June, July, 1877), 'On the Soul and Future Life' (164). Her death brought the contemporary debate and its doubtings dramatically home, with painful reminders of Elizabeth Barrett's own shattering death. Can Browning really believe Annie Egerton Smith is a living soul in heaven with Dante's Beatrice and his own Elizabeth?

... How much, how little, do I inwardly believe
True that controverted doctrine? Is it fact to which I cleave,
Is it fancy I but cherish, when I take upon my lips
Phrase the solemn Tuscan fashioned, and declare the soul's eclipse
Not the soul's extinction? take his 'I believe and I declare –
Certain am I – from this life I pass into a better, there
Where that lady lives of whom enamoured was my soul' – where this
Other lady, my companion dear and true, she also is?

(209–216)

The poem has to acknowledge that an after-life cannot be proved as fact. It ends with a debate between Fancy and Reason, which Fancy loses, and a refusing of any sort of resurrection except the memories this poem has lived through.

And all over the Victorian poetry scene there are signs like this that belief in personal survival is hard, even, or perhaps especially, for those who crave the belief. Section XLVII of *In Memoriam* would like something more explicit than just a vague faith in a person's surviving as part of some 'general Soul'. Tennyson wants to meet, to be with, to 'know' Hallam, in an eternal after-life, even as, according to the Bible, he himself will be eternally known. 'And I shall know him when we meet' ('then I shall know even as also I am known': I Corinthians 13.12). This is the only 'dream' that can satisfy the bereaved lover. But what Tennyson fears is that there will only be some temporary meeting after death (like those in Virgil's underworld in the *Aeneid*), before final dissolution in the 'general Soul':

Before the spirits fade away
Some landing-place, to clasp and say,
"Farewell! We lose ourselves in light".

Which would be pleasant ('If we are to be finally merged in the Universal Soul, Love asks to have at least one more parting before we lose ourselves', said Tennyson), but not 'sweet' enough, for this would only be a version of the pagan or atheist saying his final farewell at the graveside. To be in Roman Catullus's shoes in fact. As at the end of *In Memoriam* LVII (the 'my work will fail' section) where Tennyson hears Hallam's passing-bell:

I hear it now, and o'er and o'er,
Eternal greetings to the dead;
And 'Ave, Ave, Ave' said,
'Adieu, adieu' for evermore.

There Tennyson is recalling the 'terribly pathetic lines' of Catullus's Poem 101, an elegy for Catullus's dead brother: 'Accipe fraterno multum manantia fletu, / Atque in perpetuum, frater, ave atque vale' – 'Receive these, wet with a flood of brotherly tears, / And goodbye (hail and farewell) to you, my brother, for ever and ever'. No 'modern elegy', Tennyson wrote to Gladstone, can 'equal in pathos the desolation of that everlasting farewell', 'so long as men retain the least hope in the after-life of those whom they loved'. The utter pathos of the farewell is because Catullus has no resurrection hope; Christians are raised from that depth of despondency because of their hope, however faint. But to recall and imitate Catullus in his poem rather suggests that Tennyson shares that ancient gloom, and is saying a hopeless farewell to Hallam 'for evermore'. 'In those sad words I took farewell' (LVIII). Certainly the Catullan gloom stuck in Tennyson's mind, to be uttered again in some farewell verses to his own brother Charles (the sonneteer), ' "Frater Ave atque Vale" ' – actually written on a visit to Sirmio, the peninsula where Catullus lived:

> There beneath the Roman ruin where the purple flowers grow,
> Came that 'Ave atque Vale' of the Poet's hopeless woe,
> Tenderest of Roman poets nineteen-hundred years ago,
> 'Frater Ave atque Vale' – as we wandered to and fro
> Gazing at the Lydian laughter of the Garda Lake below
> Sweet Catullus's all-but-island, olive-silvery Sirmio![53]

In his fine attempt at laying the spectre – or 'spectral signs' – of 'Tennyson's Faith', Julian Wolfreys wants to play up the force of Tennyson's adding a Christian-era double 'Adieu, adieu' to the triple 'Ave, Ave, Ave' in LVII, and to do so by invoking Jacques Derrida's compelling 'Adieu' to Emmanuel Levinas (the Christianizing Jewish hermeneute), which in turn embraced Levinas's hope-full praise of elegy as the mode of non-final farewells. 'The greeting of *à-Dieu* does not signal the end. "The *à-Dieu* is not a finality", he says, thus challenging the "alternative between being and nothingness", which "is not ultimate" '. Such *adieux*, Wolfreys hopes, are where the ghost of Tennyson's shaky faith in an afterlife (of elegies as well as of persons) sidles into *In Memoriam*. But even when we arm them with the potent death-defyings of Derrida the master elegist, himself clad in the Judaeo-Christian memorializing faith of Levinas, those *adieux* of Tennyson don't put up a very strong fight against the old despondent Catullan farewellings.[54]

---

[53]   Tennyson's letter to Gladstone about the Catullan pathos was in reply to Gladstone comparing Tennyson's 'Prefatory Poem to My Brother's Sonnets' to the unsurpassable beauty of Catullus's 101. Letter in Hallam Tennyson's *Memoir* II.239. Details in Ricks's *Selected Poems* notes to *In Memoriam* LVII and ' "Frater Ave atque Vale" '.

[54]   Julian Wolfreys, *Victorian Hauntings* (2002), 72–73. Jacques Derrida, 'Adieu', in *Adieu to Emmanuel Levinas*, trans Pascale-Anne Brault and Michael Naas (Stanford University Press, Stanford, CA, 1999), 13; expanded version of 'Adieu' in Derrida, *The Work of Mourning*, trans ditto (University of Chicago Press, Chicago and London, 2001), 197–209.

Lazarus: Come Forth

What the *adieux* of elegy arrange and celebrate in the Derrida-Levinas conception is survival as memory, the living-on of the dead in some memorializing act and text – epitaph, tombstone, memorial object, elegiac verse. This is the most ancient of elegiac desires. Elegy is indeed a *mnemotechnik*, a technique for attempted remembering; aesthetic, textual remembering as an effort to keep a dead person alive. Tennyson knows the great 'shrine' of *In Memoriam* will eventually pass and fail; it's mortal like him (LVII), but still he keeps building his would-be memorial monument.

Like so many of his contemporaries, Tennyson would like to believe in a literal, physical life after death, in resurrection as such, in the resurrected Jesus, who raised Lazarus exemplarily from the dead in John's Gospel Chapter 11. Lazarus haunts Tennyson, as he haunts the period. But he's a difficult, even tormenting model. The non-arrival of Hallam at the first Christmas of *In Memoriam*, where a bereft brother and sister, Tennyson and his sister, Hallam's fiancée, try to rejoice in the advent of 'Hope' (XXX), segues into the tauntingly opposite scene at the house of Lazarus's sister Mary, to which her dead brother, raised from his 'charnel house', has returned alive. Jesus, the 'Life' ('I am the resurrection, and the life', John 11.25), has restored Lazarus to life, and to his loving sister: 'he was dead, and there he sits, / And he that brought him back is there'. And turning her 'deep love' for her brother onto his resurrector, 'She bows, she bathes the Saviour's feet / With costly spikenard and with tears' (XXXII). Clearly, implicit here, is the haunted question of why Tennyson and his sister have not been likewise blessed with a resurrection. The Gospel's Mary's 'eyes are homes of silent prayer', and so, it is suggested, are Emily Tennyson's. Emily (and Tennyson) love Hallam, as Mary loved Lazarus. They even, as Christians, 'love' Jesus, if not quite like Mary. But their Christ has failed them; their loved one stays dead – with hard implications for any faith in the Christ of the Gospel's resurrection. And, tellingly, Tennyson lets in some of the traditional doubts about the Lazarus story. Why, notoriously, the clamant silence of the Gospel's Lazarus, back from the dead?

> When Lazarus left his charnel-cave
> And home to Mary's house returned,
> Was this demanded – if he yearned
> To hear her weeping by his grave?
>
> 'Where wert thou, brother, those four days?'
> There lives no record of reply,
> Which telling what it is to die
> Had surely added praise to praise.

> From every house the neighbours met,
> The streets were filled with joyful sound,
> A solemn gladness even crowned
> The purple brows of Olivet.
>
> Behold a man raised up by Christ!
> The rest remaineth unrevealed;
> He told it not; or something sealed
> The lips of that Evangelist.
>
> (XXXI)

There's a hole in the Gospel story. 'And would it have been worth it, after all, / To say: "I am Lazarus come from the dead, / Come back to tell you all, I shall tell you all" ', wonders TS Eliot's J Alfred Prufrock. But Lazarus didn't tell, and so neither can Prufrock. Which silence and absence are, rightly, felt to shake faith in the Gospel, and resurrection, and Tennyson, greatly shaken by Hallam's death, endorses the shaking. Section XXXI was one of the very first parts of the poem to be written. So Tennyson's Lazarus yearnings and doubtings are clearly foundational to his elegiac work and concept. The absence for Tennyson and his sister of Mary's Lazarus joy is a clear sign of Tennyson's disquieted faith. Earlier, in 'To –' (1828–1830) ('Thou mayst remember what I said'), he'd rejoiced that a doubting friend had with Tennyson's help been resurrected like Lazarus from the 'charnel-place' of doubt into renewed 'spiritual life'. In that poem's third stanza the poet compared his joy at this recovery to Mary's at the raising of Lazarus:

> Not Mary felt such full delight
> When having heard her brother's name
> Joined with 'Come forth' and waiting mute
> Forth in the open sunshine came
> The languid corpse bound hand and foot
> Winking his eyelids at the light.

Hallam Tennyson dropped this stanza when he put the poem into his *Memoir* (I.60), perhaps because its presence would have brought home, by contrast, the negativity of the Lazarus story in *In Memoriam*, and shown up doubting Tennyson's not being able there to put himself in Mary's happy shoes.[55]

Hesitation about Lazarus's testimonial force is the subject of Robert Browning's pastiche New Testament Epistle, written by an Arab doctor to his Arab mentor, 'An Epistle Containing the Strange Medical Experience of Karshish, the Arab Physician' (in *Men and Women*, 1855, i.e. five years after *In Memoriam*). Karshish has met a Jewish madman called Lazarus, who is

---

[55] Full version of the poem from the Trinity College Tennyson Notebook 23 (embargoed earlier): first in Ricks's three volume edn of the *Poems*, I.307.

convinced he was dead and buried for three days, 'and then restored to life /
By a Nazarene physician of his tribe: / – 'Sayeth the same bade "Rise", and
he did rise' (99–101). This Lazarus, Karshish suggests, must have been in a
prolonged epileptic trance from which he recovered by 'some drug / Or
spell, exorcization, stroke of art' (82–83). Karshish wishes he knew the trick
behind this 'crazy tale' (224). His scepticism runs deep. There's no evidence
except Lazarus's own word. The Nazarene 'leech' died 'many years ago'.
But still, Lazarus's 'conviction', while not in itself proof, is impressively
'Ardent' (217). Often his face lights up, 'As if he saw again and heard again /
His sage that bade him "Rise" and he did rise' (192–193). As if. Agreeably,
Lazarus is no proselytizer, as religious madmen tend to be – though of course
(and you keep hearing again the characteristic Browningesque to and fro of
argument, the jostle of the negative and positives, of the claimings and waiv-
ings) mere personal conviction would be no 'real ground' for any preacher,
so perhaps that's the reason for his avoidance of evangelism.

   Still, Karshish has made Lazarus break the Gospel's silence. And he's
impressed, despite himself, by Lazarus's claim that his resurrector was, 'God
forgive me! who but God himself, / Creator and sustainer of the world, /
That came and dwelt in flesh on it awhile! / – 'Sayeth that such an one was
born and lived, / Taught, healed the sick, broke bread at his own house, /
Then died.' Suppose, Karshish writes, he were 'very God!', 'the All-Great',
and 'the All-Loving too', offering love and saying ' "thou must love me who
have died for thee!" '. Thus Lazarus told Karshish: 'The madman saith He
said so' (312). The (critically notorious) capitalized H is Karshish's. Clearly,
for Browning, as for Tennyson, the whole edifice of Christian theology and
belief – God incarnate in Jesus, redeeming death of Christ, God's offer and
demand of 'love' – hangs on this 'Nazarene physician' and what it is said he
did for Lazarus. And the whole affair is, as Karshish says twice, 'strange'
(282, 312). A strange story, and one strange to relate. Lazarus has spoken,
but actually not much. He's mainly 'apathetic' (226); disinclined to push his
'crazy tale' (224). And, crucially, Karshish's own narrative lapses twice into
silence, goes all elliptical, in the face of what he (and Browning) find
unrepeatable and indeed unsayable. Jesus

> ... died, with Lazarus by, for aught I know,
> And yet was ... what I said nor choose repeat,
> And must have so avouched himself, in fact,
> In hearing of this very Lazarus
> Who saith – but why all this of what he saith?
> (273–277)

And with this endorsement of the silence of the Gospel's Lazarus, Karshish
turns to what he calls less 'trivial matters' – some 'Blue-flowering borage' on

'the margin of a pool' (280–281). Thus the sceptic tries to trivialize Lazarus, his story and theology, and shrug off the *awe* Lazarus *touches* him with (289). But Lazarus is not to be trivialized like this. So much hangs on him, as shown by Browning's 'prolix' poem (285), and the widespread literary worry Lazarus attracts. We've already heard (end of Chapter 6) Richard Le Gallienne's doubting 'Who knows' in his poem 'An Inscription' about God's 'strange alchemic power' really to raise his beloved from her funeral 'urn'. Elizabeth Barrett Browning's engagements with Lazarus are symptomatically edgy. His brief appearance in *Aurora Leigh* at that cryptic moment when Aurora's widowed father is said to have suddenly 'through love' 'Thrown off the old conventions, broken loose / From chin-bands of the soul, like Lazarus' (I.176–178), is enticingly enigmatic. What conventions? What loosening? Barrett Browning's comment on Robert Browning's 'An Epistle' – 'The way in which Lazarus is described as living his life after his acquaintance with the life beyond death, strikes me as entirely sublime' – comes in a letter to her sister Henrietta defending the poem against her charges of lack of reverence and even blasphemy. It's 'a view *from without* of the raising from the dead, &c – and shows how this must have impressed the thinkers of the day, who came upon it with wondering, unbelieving eyes, for the first time'.[56] Elizabeth plainly counted herself among the believers. But feeling Lazarus's life after death as the sublime part is curious, for it indicates enthusiasm precisely for the withdrawn, 'apathetic', silences of Robert's Lazarus, the man with the resurrection story he can't ever prove. And what about Elizabeth's failure to do a Lazarus poem? 'Lazarus would make a fine poem, wouldn't he?', she wrote to her friend HS Boyd, 8 July 1840, from Torquay. Lazarus is among her 'great many schemes'.[57] Three days later her beloved brother Edward drowned in the sea off Torquay. And she went into utter decline, nearly dying of grief, gave up writing for months, and her Lazarus project was never resurrected. She did, though, take up spiritualism in a big way, the nineteenth century's sub-Christian, DIY resurrectionism.

One way or another, Lazarus keeps letting the poets down as reassuring case and model of literal resurrection. He would, though, manifestly do as model for the next best thing so far at least as writers are concerned, namely the survival of the dead in and as text. 'Lazare, veni foras', Jesus's command to Lazarus in the Latin of the Vulgate Bible – 'Lazarus, come forth' in the

---

[56]   *Elizabeth Barrett Browning: Letters to her Sister, 1846–1859*, ed Leonard Huxley (John Murray, London, 1929), 235–236.
[57]   *Letters of Elizabeth Barrett Browning*, ed Frederic G Kenyon (2 vols, Smith Elder, 1897, I.82. Margaret Reynolds points to these Lazarus interests in her ever-useful edition of *Aurora Leigh* (Norton, NY, 1996), fn2, p11.

Authorised Version's English – is, according to the great French theorist of writing and reading Maurice Blanchot, what every reader in effect asks of a text. On this view, reading gives life to the dead, or otherwise absent, author, bringing him or her back from the dead, from the place of the missing, making the absent present.[58] Which is, of course, what elegy seeks to do, this quintessential mode of *prosopopoeia*, or personification, that basic rhetorical function of fiction, of characterization, of all imaginative writing, the making and granting of a *prosopon* (Greek: mask, face, self, character), or *persona* (Latin for the same), where they didn't exist before. Or, in the case of elegy, giving life to the person who has died and would otherwise stay dead. 'To paraphrase Hillis Miller, the dead continue to live on, to survive beyond life in the afterlife of what we call reading'.[59] The dead Lady of Shalott lives on, in effect, as a piece of writing, a text, being read by the people of Camelot – 'And round the prow they read her name, / *The Lady of Shalott*'. She's 'become a name', like Tennyson's 'Ulysses', a written character (character: a person, and also pieces of alphabetical stuff) in a piece of writing, whose reading is a device for her survival. Which Tennyson well recognizes in *In Memoriam* (XCV) where the grieving narrator reads a letter of Hallam's which vividly brings back the past, reanimates Hallam, speaks in Hallam's voice:

> A hunger seized my heart; I read
> Of that glad year which once had been,
> In those fallen leaves which kept their green,
> The noble letters of the dead:

[58]   Maurice Blanchot, 'Reading', in *The Space of Literature* [*L'Espace littéraire* (Gallimard, Paris, 1955)], trans and intro Ann Smock (University of Nebraska Press, Lincoln NE and London, 1982), 191–198. Favourite Blanchot model. Developed in e.g. his *L'Entretien infini* (Gallimard, Paris, 1969) – a place well discussed by John Gregg, *Maurice Blanchot and the Literature of Transgression* (Princeton University Press, Princeton, 1994), 58–59. One of the most telling parts of W David Shaw's *Origins of the Monologue: The Hidden God*, edn cit (1999), and fundamental to his fruitful notion that Victorian dramatic monologues stage the voice of a masked deity behind the mask of the poets, is his 'Ghostly Vocatives: The Genesis of the Monologue' section, 81ff, which names 'Lazarus, come forth' (along with Orpheus's summons to Eurydice) as 'the paradigmatic narrative of all ghostly conjuring', the 'fictive raising of the historical or legendary dead through the invocation and personification' occurring as part of the dramatic monologue's self-reflexive textuality – 'a mirror version of itself in a narrative about conjuring ghosts by means of deictics, apostrophes, or other words of power'. Gustave Doré's engraving *The Resurrection of Lazarus*, frontispiece of Shaw's book, is invoked as powerful illustration. But Blanchot's reflections, which would have helped enlarge and strengthen the Lazarus resurrection thought are not, alas, known to Shaw.

[59]   Julian Wolfreys, 'Afterword: Prosopopoeia, or, Witnessing', *Victorian Hauntings*, 141, referring to J Hillis Millers's *Topographies* (1995) from which he'd just quoted Hillis Miller's (correct) reflection on prosopopoeia as a 'a voice or a face of the absent, the inanimate, or the dead' (Miller, 140).

> And strangely on the silence broke
> The silent-speaking words, and strange
> Was love's dumb cry defying change
> To test his worth; and strangely spoke.
>   (21–28)

Leaves that fall from trees fade and die; leaves, pages, of writing 'keep their green', stay fresh, don't alter; and nor does the voice they convey, unlike the rotting body in its grave. The touch of that untouchable body is still tangible in the written page. 'So word by word and line by line, / The dead man touched me from the past' (XCV. 33–34). All *strangely*, as the poem says, twice. (*Strange* is Karshish's repeated word for the revenant Lazarus.) It's no accident that Hallam's old letter seems to be directed against 'doubts' (30), and that it induces a 'trance' (43) in which the 'soul' of the relict is united with the 'living soul' of Hallam as if with God ('And mine in this [or his] was wound, and whirled / About empyreal heights of thought' (37–38)). The dead man's survival in his letter is a religious affair: this is real resurrection for a sceptical age. (The resurrection-reading scene gets repeated in the additions to 'Mariana in the South' written at the same time as XCV (1841–1842), where Mariana's deserting lover reappears as she reads his 'old letters' – itself a replay of Goethe's *Wilhelm Meister* in which the dead Mariana speaks to her lover through her letters.[60]) Here, in his poem, Tennyson enacts, and self-reflexively, the Lazarus work of elegy – emphasizing the way Lazarus can as it were rise from the dead, can speak and touch; advertising elegy as a method for doing what even the most believing Christian finds it hard to believe is literally possible.[61] This literary resurrecting is still an oxymoronic, questioned activity – these words from the past are *silent-speaking*, a *dumb cry*. The raised Lazarus of the Gospels said nothing: a silence haunting the early Christian church: what Blanchot is getting at in his 'Reading' discussion when he ends up dwelling on the 'opening' of the tomb which then remains 'closed tighter', effecting a 'transparency' that 'belongs to the greatest opacity'[62]. But they do in their way constitute a material presence. Which is one reason why, I take it, elegy is so dominant

---

[60]   Noted by Paul Turner, *Tennyson* (Routledge & Kegan Paul, London, 1976), 122.

[61]   Angela Leighton is impressive on the touching touches of Tennyson's elegiac transactions, *On Form, Poetry, Aestheticism, and the Legacy of a Word* (Oxford University Press, Oxford, 2007), 61ff.

[62]   *The Space of Literature*, trans cit, 195. It's the oxymoron developed in 1969, when Blanchot was thinking, allegorizingly, of two Lazaruses, the one in his still clean white grave bandages, the other already decomposing under that agreeable whiteness: one returned (*rendu*), the other still lost (*perdu*). John Gregg, op. cit., 59.

a mode in growingly sceptical Victorian times; is why, for example, the Christian-resurrection eschewing Swinburne is such an elegy-mad poet.[63] Survival in memorializing poems doesn't beggar belief like Biblical resurrection does.

Hauntology

And there is indeed confidence of a sort to be had in the abidings of elegy. Arthur Munby's 'A Deathbed: July 1st 18 –' celebrates a wife who has gone, the poem declares, to meet her late husband in heaven; 'We too' might 'join her at the last'. 'Meanwhile, she still is with us; and abides, / A charming Presence, in the faithful hearts / Of many folk, and most of all in mine'. But actually the only hope of ensuring that presence, that abiding, is in elegiac texts like this one. And Munby produced oodles of obituary, epitaph poems, unstoppably arranging voices, presences, from beyond the grave (including the startling, comi-tragic, 'Post Mortem' whose narrator speaks from his tomb, where he has words with his loquacious dead wife in the next coffin along and records the dead weight of his suicidal son who is banged down on top of him). 'The dead abide with us! Though stark and cold / Earth seems to grip them, they are with us still'. That's Mathilde Blind in her son-net 'The Dead' (in her *Songs and Sonnets*, 1893). But this classic Victorian atheist (German-Jewish radical crusading New Woman, translator of Strauss's demythologizing *The Old Faith and the New* (1873–1874), admirer of Shelley and George Eliot and Swinburne, as well as Christina G Rossetti) is not thinking of anything like a Christian kind of survival or presence, but of memory living on, the 'heritage' of the dead's 'imperishable will' incorpo-rated in 'Our perishable bodies', that is the continuing life of tradition. In fact: the abiding of the dead in elegiac texts like hers; in the afterlife of words about dead people; in the person, prosopon, persona, of Lazarus as textual survivor and returner.

---

[63]   A religious sceptic's elegy-fetishizing reciprocated in Hardy's 1910 elegy for Swinburne, 'A Singer Asleep (ACS 1837–1909)', composed at Bonchurch, Isle of Wight, where Swinburne was buried, and 'I can still hear the brabble and the roar' that greeted Swinburne's Sapphically sado-masochistic verses, a roar now 'spent like spindrift on this shore', gone like Swinburne's drowned 'singing mistress' Sappho, while Swinburne's voice 'swells yet more and more'. Elegy on this beach denies the total annihilations of Arnold's 'Dover Beach'. The original initials 'ACS' of Hardy's title, spelled out in later versions of the poem, were, I hope, Hardy's gesture towards recuperating a sexual bad-boy with a defiant recall of Tennyson's 'In Memoriam AHH' along the lines of Housman's 'AJJ' and Wilde's 'CTW', discussed earlier in this chapter. Yopie Prins misses the elegiac point entirely: 'Having memorized the Sapphic cadence of Swinburne, how-ever, Hardy never fully remembers him; the elegy is also a way of forgetting Swinburne, a repeti-tion that leaves behind an empty form.' Precisely not! Prins, *Victorian Sappho* (1999), 121.

The Mellstock folk in Hardy's 'Friends Beyond' have all ' "Gone ... gone for good" '; they all 'lie in Mellstock churchyard now!'; but still 'They've a way of whispering to me – fellow-wight who yet abide'. They 'murmur mildly to me now'. The poet thinks he hears their voices from the grave, and writes them; and we hear them, as we read. Which is what elegy's for: for readers, as relicts, to encounter, and hear from, the dead. (Hardy's Swinburne elegy imagines the ghost of Swinburne coming down to the beach every night to meet Sappho's ghost rising from the waves, and being assured that 'orts' of her verses live now in her disciple's lines.) The dead, as Browning's Duke puts it of the portrait of his Duchess, there in the elegiac text's representation 'as if ... alive'. Enjoying, if that's the word, the life of a ghost. And Victorian poets are haunted men and women, their poems haunted houses: living witnesses to Harold Bloom's final model of poetic influence offered in *The Anxiety of Influence* – apophrades, the return of the dead to their old abodes. Apophrades: the activity that sustains an ontology which is (to borrow a lovely suggestive word from Julian Wolfreys) a *hauntology*.[64]

Victorian poetry comprises a great theatre of ghost stories – presided over, of course, by the ghostly presence of Dante, whose grieving poetry in his prose-poetry confessional *Vita Nuova* (1292–1295) weeps, self-reflexively, for the death of his adored Beatrice, basis of the vision that gave us the most sustained Christian ghost-story ever, his *Divine Comedy*, itself a greatly haunted text, full of ghosts, but especially ghosted by the *Aeneid*, classic pre-Christian story of a journey to the underworld, and by its author Virgil, who is Dante's chosen guide to the *Inferno*. The childhood of the young Rossettis was utterly haunted by the author who so preoccupied their father Gabriele, Professor of Italian at London University, Dante scholar and Dante crank (he read the *Divine Comedy* as a cryptogrammic work of anti-papal prophecy). It's only germane that when Christina G did a ghost story, as in her early *Goblin Market* poem 'The Hour and the Ghost', about a Bride dementedly haunted by a dead lover who would break up her marriage, it should be haunted by the story of Paolo and Francesca, the famous grieving lovers from Canto V of the *Inferno*. Dante Gabriel focussed himself as poet and painter and (proleptically) as career-griever over his dead beloved Lizzie ('Sid') Siddal by translating (and annotating) the *Vita Nuova* – actively modernizing and personalizing Dante's great poems of grief over Beatrice and regret over falling in love again so soon after her death (shades of Rossetti's later falling in love with Janey Morris). When he finished his main

---

[64] Julian Wolfreys, op cit, 2, on the 'hauntological disturbance' of modernity. The story of nineteenth-century literature as such, rather brilliantly displayed in Robert Douglas-Fairhurst's persistingly apophraditic *Victorian Afterlives*, edn cit (2002), is of writers irresistibly haunted by their predecessors and haunting their successors. So many poets (and novelists) a crossroads or (as Foucault might have put it) a railway junction of ghostings.

updating work in around 1850– 'a rite of passage that sets [him] on the path of a new existence centered in a devotional pursuit of art and beauty': Jerome McGann[65]), to be published in later 1861 in his *Early Italian Poets*, revised and rearranged in 1874 as *Dante and His Circle* – he changed his name from Gabriel Charles Dante Rossetti to Dante Gabriel Rossetti, signalling a new poetic progenitor, his new (ghostly) father. And, plainly haunted by the melancholy / guilty poeticity of the *Vita Nuova*, ventriloquizing it even, his *House of Life* is a truly haunted house, with Lizzie Siddal playing the (resurrected) role of Dante's Beatrice, an absentee recalled to life (she died in 1862) with, as it were, her dead baby in her arms (as in Sonnets XCIX and C, 'Newborn Death').

And so it goes in the poetic haunted house. In more or less everything Tennyson writes from 'Ulysses' on – its aged narrator's story a textually haunted replay, of course, of the ancient hero's narrative in Dante's *Inferno*, which Tennyson read in the standard nineteenth-century translation by the Revd HF Cary. For his part, Matthew Arnold's hauntings found their apotheosis in the death of Arthur Clough, the subject of his *Thyrsis* (1861). Arnold subtitled that poem 'A Monody', to recall Milton's 'Lycidas', a 'Monody' bewailing Milton's 'learned friend' Edward King. 'Thyrsis never more we swains shall see'; but the poet will not 'despair' (192) because Thyrsis-Clough survives as a ghost, companion of the ghost of the legendary Oxford poor scholar, the Scholar-Gipsy whose ghostly presence in the leafy slopes around Oxford was the subject of Arnold's 1853 poem 'The Scholar-Gipsy', an elegy for the passing of Arnold's and Clough's undergraduate years spent happily tramping that ghosted ground. A set of passings haunted by Tennyson's Hallam griefs in *In Memoriam* ('amongst us one, / Who most has suffered, takes dejectedly / His seat upon the intellectual throne; / And all his store of sad experience he / Lays bare of wretched days': 'The Scholar-Gipsy', 182–186). So, ghostings upon ghostings upon ghostings: all hallowed at the end of *Thyrsis* by the 'whisper' of Clough's ghostly assurings, as invoked by Arnold:

> *Why faintest thou? I wandered till I died.*
> *Roam on! The light we sought is shining still.*
> *Dost thou ask proof? Our tree yet crowns the hill,*
> *Our Scholar travels yet the loved hill-side.*
> (237–240)

The poets assiduously attended seances – grief-stricken Dante Gabriel and his brother William hoping to hear from Lizzie, imagining the table-rapping sessions at Cheyne Walk were her communications ('rubbish ... bogies ... simply

[65]   Dante Gabriel Rossetti, *Collected Poetry and Prose*, ed Jerome McGann, notes p. 401.

childish', thought their Pre-Raphaelite friend William Bell Scott)[66]; Elizabeth Barrett desirous of talking to her dead brother Bro (egged on by Harriet Beecher Stowe who claimed she'd contacted her dead son this way). But as places for hearing from and talking with the dead, elegiac poems were plainly a lot less dodgy, and a lot more consoling. Elizabeth Barrett was not the only one to draw comfort from the ancient Greek drama *Alcestis* by Euripides, with its story of Heracles rescuing Alcestis from death and restoring her to her grieving husband Admetos. In the haunting aftermath of his wife's death Robert Browning made this cult Euripidean resurrection fiction his own. (William Morris did a version of it in the first, 1868, volume of *The Earthly Paradise*; Frederick Leighton's painting *Hercules Wrestling With Death for the Body of Alcestis* was exhibited at the Royal Academy in 1871.) Browning's long (2,705 lines) *Balaustion's Adventure: Including a Transcript from Euripides* (1871) is mostly Browning's own version of *Alcestis*. The frame narration is by one Balaustion, a Euripides fan rather resembling Elizabeth Barrett – whose tribute to Euripides in her poem 'The Wine of Cyprus' ('Our Euripides, the human, / With his droppings of warm tears') – utterly haunts Robert's poem. Those two lines are part of *Balaustion*'s epigraph. The cut-down version of their second occurrence is ascribed to a poetess who is said to live on, like Euripides, in such poetic words:

> I know the poetess who graved in gold,
> Among her glories that shall never fade,
> This style and title for Euripides,
> *The Human with his droppings of warm tears.*
> (2668–2671)

She is, of course, the dead Elizabeth Barrett Browning, celebrated elsewhere in the poem in Admetos's 'passionate' address to the wife he's about to lose, 'Who wast to me as spirit is to flesh' (2561). Her haunting lines come from a haunted poem, and a haunted relationship. 'The Wine of Cyprus' (1844) is subtitled *Given to me by HS Boyd, Author of 'Select Passages from the Greek Fathers'*. Hugh Stuart Boyd was Elizabeth Barrett's blind Greekist confidant, who taught her Greek, and had her read to him the Greek authors her poem lauds. She wrote three sonnets in his memory after his death in 1848: 'Hugh Stuart Boyd: His Blindness', '... His death' and ' ... His Legacies' – which latter recalls Boyd's three dying gifts: a copy of Aeschylus and of Gregory Nazianzen and a chiming clock. The clock is to 'Chime in the day which ends these parting days!' (her death-day?); its chimes join the

---

[66]   See Appendix 7, 'Dante Gabriel Rossetti and Spiritualism', *The Correspondence of Dante Gabriel Rossetti, The Chelsea Years 1863–1872, Prelude to Crisis*, Vol V, *1871–1872*, ed William S Freadman (DS Brewer, Cambridge, 2005), 401–403.

'murmurous / Sad echoes of my young voice' reading Boyd Greek, which 'Return and choke my utterance'. The poet and poem speak, about the silence of death and the silence of a dead author's gifted books, and her own utterances of long ago, which are nonetheless heard again in the echoes of memory, the continuing chiming of the clock – returning utterances which are however choked, and chimes which anticipate the grieving poet's own end.[67] It's a complex play with echoes both heard and choked off, echoes of Elizabeth's dead youth, of her dead teacher, and old Euripides, all made to echo and re-echo in Robert's refracting his survivalistic story through faith in the survivor powers of elegizing Elizabeth Barrett. What an echo-chamber 'Balaustion' is! It ends (2672–2697) with Balaustion's ekphrastic praise of another death-defying text, namely Leighton's painting – the 'women-wailers' looking on 'in fear's rhythmic sympathy' as mighty Herakles fights the 'envenomed substance', the 'poisonous impalpability', of Death for the life of dead Alcestis. 'I pronounce that piece', says Balaustion, 'Worthy to set up in our Poikile', that is London's National Gallery. A fine tribute, you might well think, to the power of the Alcestis story, an endorsement of the art which would celebrate art's wrestle with death, of art like Leighton's which would join in that struggle. But those 'women-wailers' do wail on, caught in the horror of an as yet unresolved contest. Alcestis lies there, dead yet, for all the 'rhythmic sympathy' of the women mourners. And it is 'fear's rhythmic sympathy', evidently shared by Robert Browning – despite his own 'rhythmic sympathy', sympathy in verse, with the Alcestic (and Lazarus) stories. In the matter of how art might keep the dead alive, Balaustion's echo of the Duke's praise in 'My Last Duchess' of Fra Pandolf's portrait of the wife he's had killed – 'I call that piece a wonder now' – is decidedly unsettling.

Danny Karlin is right, in these connections, to invoke Browning's very late poem 'Dubiety' (in *Asolando: Fancies and Facts*, 1889), which is about remembering a dead woman, presumably Elizabeth Barrett, trying to kiss him – 'Of what came once when a woman leant / To feel for my brow where the kiss might fall'. 'What is it like that has happened before?', the poem asks. A question pertinent to every poem seeking to remember, to bring back past events and people. Is it a dream? 'No dream, more real by much'. Is it a vision? No, he's had many 'fanciful' visitations, and this is not one of those. This is more than 'mere musing'. So it's 'a memory, after all!' A truthful one – 'Truth ever, truth only the excellent!' But, still, 'but a memory, after all': only a memory; and no substitute for the real thing which it re-enacts. Elegy's claims for the value of presence are, then, all ersatz; they're a

---

[67] She makes Boyd audible again in the epigraph from his *Reflections on the Atoning Sacrifice of Jesus Christ* (1817) to her poem 'The Mediator' (1838). Their protracted correspondence, 1827–1847, appears in Barbara P McCarthy, ed, *Elizabeth Barrett to Mr Boyd: Unpublished Letters of Elizabeth Barrett Browning to Hugh Stuart Boyd* (John Murray, London, 1955).

'Dubiety'. And, most suggestively, Karlin recalls Milton's sonnet on his dead wife, 'Methought I saw my late Espoused Saint / Brought to me like Alcestis from the grave'. She's 'Such, as yet once more I trust to have / Full sight of her in heaven'. The return, though, is delusory: 'But O as to embrace me she enclin'd / I waked, she fled, and day brought back my night'. The tradition of Christian elegy will not sustain Browning in his Alcestis dreamings.[68]

The Far-Off Interest of Tears

Obviously a certain consolation is gained in these ghostly returnings which elegy keeps arranging – or elegists would stop arranging them. There's a certain gain in relived pain. Right at the beginning of *In Memoriam* Tennyson invokes the ample idea of *interest* as sustaining his persistent recall of Hallam, his kept-up Lazarus-raising attempts, his poetic hauntings and ghostings, his reaching a hand back 'through time to catch', to touch, and be touched by, the dead. Here is *interest*, activity that *interests*, engages the imagination and mind; and there is *interest* to be got in the sense of accumulated wealth, moral, and spiritual gain, as it were money growing in the poetic bank. But this is an *interest of tears*. (Christopher Ricks's notes to his *Selected* Edition pointfully suggest Tennyson is remembering Shakespeare's Sonnet 31 – 'How many a holy and obsequious tear / Hath dear religious love stolen from mine eye, / As interest of the dead' – and *Richard III* (IV.4.322–324), 'the liquid drops of tears that you have shed / Shall come again, transformed to orient pearl, / Advantaging their loan with interest'; as well as 'my sorrow's interest' of the *Rape of Lucrece*, line 1797.) What's gained in this poetic investment is not an assuaging of tears, but more of them. Tennyson said he was thinking of 'The good that grows for us out of grief'. But who would venture, Tennyson wonders, for a gain that might match loss but only in continued pain

> And find in loss a gain to match?
> Or reach a hand through time to catch
> The far-off interest of tears?
> (*In Memoriam*, I)

Notably, the *interest* is *far-off*. Elegy's interest is indeed in the *far-off*: in presently dead persons, but also, as this opening passage of *In Memoriam* makes clear, in far-off writings. Elegy's relationship with the dead is readerly and textual, to do with old books and texts and their writers, with, in other words, tradition, as much as with persons merely; with the 'dead selves' of writing as much as with the 'dead selves' of people. As, in their different

---

[68]   See Danny Karlin, *Browning's Hatreds*, 31,32.

ways, Tennyson and Browning both realize in their haunted regard for the story of the prophet Elisha bringing a dead boy back from the dead (2 Kings 4). Browning offers it in Book I of *The Ring and The Book* as a rather moving justification of his poem (based as it is on the old Roman murder-trial papers he picked up on a junk-stall in Florence), but also poetic creativity as such: acts of literary resuscitation, a matter of dead writings brought back to life. Only God can create *ex nihilo*; the human poet resuscitates rather: 'Makes new beginning, starts the dead alive' (I.733). The contemporary poet is a raiser of dead texts, like Old Testament Elisha:

> ... Was not Elisha once? –
> Who bade them lay his staff on a corpse-face.
> There was no voice, no hearing: he went in
> Therefore, and shut the door upon them twain,
> And prayed unto the Lord: and he went up
> And lay upon the corpse, dead on the couch,
> And put his mouth upon its mouth, his eyes
> Upon its eyes, his hands upon its hands,
> And stretched him on the flesh; the flesh waxed warm:
> And he returned, walked to and fro the house,
> And went up, stretched him on the flesh again,
> And the eyes opened. 'Tis a credible feat
> With the right man and way.
>
> (I.760–772)

Not just the prophetic, poetic kiss of life, but the whole-body – and of course erotically heated – touch of resuscitator and resuscitatee. And the triumphalist implication is that Browning is the 'right man' for this kind of job ('Enough of me!' he says, as he finishes recalling Elisha, 772). Which detracts rather from the aweing emotionality of the Biblical story of love and hope and desire triumphing over the pain of great loss. By huge contrast, it's the recorded pain of his failure to succeed straightforwardly in an Elisha attempt that makes Tennyson's appropriation of the exemplum the more compelling. This is in *In Memoriam* XVIII, where the poet would like to perform the resurrection work of elegy, 'the ritual of the dead', provoking violets (as it might the flowering of new life, the new life of elegiac literature), to spring from Hallam's 'ashes'. Tennyson was thinking, he said, of the burial scene in *Hamlet*, V.i.232–234, where Laertes asks that from his dead sister Ophelia's 'fair and unpolluted flesh / May violets Spring!'. Ricks's Note compellingly thinks that Tennyson was also mindful of Hallam's tribute to him in his piece in the *Gentleman's Magazine* of August 1832, taking words from Persius's *Satires* i about violets springing up from the fortunate ashes and burial mound of a dead poet. The dead Hallam is also a dead poet. So the 'violets' are his words, which 'may' be heard again in Tennyson's resurrection efforts. But Tennyson, the would-be Elisha, is driven by grief almost to extinction himself, so that he has almost no breath left himself, the breath of life that he might impart, the breath needed to utter as elegist:

> Ah yet, even yet, if this might be,
> I, falling on his faithful heart,
> Would breathing through his lips impart
> The life that almost dies in me.

But there is a kind of surviving. The 'life'

> ... dies not, but endures with pain,
> And slowly forms the firmer mind,
> Treasuring the look it cannot find,
> The words that are not heard again.

The poet finds he has breath still, if only just; not enough for a full Elisha event; but still there's something to treasure: the look, the words – present, audible; lost, inaudible. An odd kind of 'interest', small credit in the poetic bank, oxymoronic stuff, that is, of course, to do with the poet's wordy, breathed, engagement with a dead poet's words, his vocables, his breathings. They're what are at stake; intertextual relations.

Tennyson's interest is indeed intertextual. Revealingly, in *In Memoriam* I, his run-up to the 'far-off interest of tears' has him thinking of Goethe: 'I held it truth, with him who sings / To one clear harp in divers tones / That men may rise on stepping-stones / Of their dead selves to higher things'. 'I alluded to Goethe's creed', Tennyson said; 'Among his last words were ... "from changes to higher changes"'. (Lost words, apparently, but that only thickens and enriches the complexity of these Lazarus/Elisha attempts.) Elegy's investment in 'dead selves' is also, like this moment in Tennyson, an investment in old texts, or it resembles such. On this plan elegy will combine its intertextual modelling with actual intertextuality. It is, of course, not at all necessary that the elegiac subject should be a literary person – far from it – but it so happens that Tennyson's Hallam, like his Virgil and Dante, and Arnold's Clough and Heine, and Robert Browning's Dora Greenwell and Elizabeth Barrett, and Barrett Browning's George Sand, and Dante Gabriel Rossetti's Siddal, and LEL's Felicia Hemans, and Charlotte Brontë's sister Anne, and Victor Plarr's Arnold, and Eliza Cook's Thomas Hood, and so on and on, are dead writers. Elegy, this generic work that's so like the act of reading ('Lazarus Come Forth!'), particularly enjoys, as it were, trying to raise writers from the dead. This reading matter commonly concerns those whose reading matter mattered and matters. And by the same sort of apt confluence, it is most striking that not only is the *elegiac* subject commonly embraced in a frame of intertextual adherings and lineage markings – Tennyson thinking of Hallam at Wordsworth's Tintern Abbey, it might be, or Browning embracing his wife's ghost through revivals of Euripides, or Protestants galore reading the ruins of Rome though the Book of Revelation's story of the Fall of Babylon, Housman refracting his modern desolations through his widely garnered readings in Roman literature and culture, Arnold doing modern tedium as a replay of Etienne (*Obermann*) de Senancour, and all that – but also that the ordinary and usual Victorian intertextual tradings – the poets' vast habitual array of literary translations, versions, revisings, reworkings, remindings, revisitings, refractings – are with a past literature of a relentlessly melancholic, tearful, wintry, death-darkened, elegiac kind. That is the writing that moves writers, sticks in their imagination, and fires their own work. Fetchingly prominent in the list Hallam Tennyson gives us of those who, his father thought, 'enrich the blood of the world' (*Memoir*, II. 284ff) are profoundly melancholic notes from Keats, who 'would have been among the very greatest of us if he had lived' (tearful Ruth among the alien corn, and the faery lands forlorn, of 'Ode to a Nightingale'), and Wordsworth ('The line "Whose dwelling is the light of setting suns" is almost the grandest in the English Language'), and Shakespeare. Three lines from the Bard 'always bring tears to my eyes' – including Posthumus's words in *Cymbeline* when his resurrected wife Imogen embraces him, 'Hang there like fruit, my soul, / Till the tree die' (Act V. sc v.263–264), the passage that would feature strongly in the narrative of Tennyson's death-bed (described below). '*Hamlet* is the greatest creation in literature that I know of', Tennyson thought. He liked reading aloud Goethe's saddest lyrics: 'he had *les larmes dans la voix* when he read the second stanza' of 'Der Abschied' (The Farewell), 'Traurig wird in dieser Stunde ...' (This will be the hour of sadness ...). Tennyson was moved by the 'solemn pathos of that great but heart-saddening Elegy on Cornelia by Propertius'. Reading aloud Cowper's 'Lines on my Mother's Portrait' brought on the tears; so did Petrarch's 'etherially-beautiful lines on the death of Laura' in the 'Trionfo della Morte' ('The Triumph of Death').[69] And these are the intertextual notes Tennyson keeps striking in his verse – persistently replaying the melancholy of Hamlet, not least in *In Memoriam*; taking up his position as the latest in the long historical line of elegists; his frequent poetic tears repeating Virgil's[70]; recycling the Book of Job in his 'Saint Simeon Stylites'; reliving Lucretius's apprehensions of cosmic void ('atom

---

[69] Hallam Tennyson, *Memoir* II. 500–505.
[70] See the Virgil section of Norman Vance's *The Victorians and Ancient Rome* (Blackwell, Oxford, 1997), 149–153.

and void, atom and void': 'Lucretius', 257), and Dante's mournings (his Ulysses coming from the *Inferno* rather than from Homer).[71]

> And I too dreamed, until at last
> Across my fancy, brooding warm,
> The reflex of a legend past,
> And loosely settled into form.
>   ('The Day-Dream', 9–12)

And the legends-past settling into Tennyson's forms are commonly dire ones. Which is how it goes across the whole Victorian field: Browning embracing the subject of poeticity through the enigmatic words of pretend melancholy-mad Tom from *King Lear* which form the title and the last line of his 'Childe Roland to the Dark Tower Came'; Dante Gabriel Rossetti putting Dante's mournful 'Vita Nuova' into English; James Thomson certifying the London of his 'The City of Dreadful Night' as a modern version of Dante's Inferno, borrowing the signposting words at the entrance to Dante's Hell for his epigraph, 'Per me si va nella città dolente' ('This way for the sorrowful city') and his line (section I) 'They leave all hope behind who enter there' (Dante's 'Lasciate ogni speranza voi ch'entrate': 'Abandon all hope, you who enter here', the Inferno's most remembered line); William Morris repeatedly redoing grim old poetic stories, such as the *Aeneid* (his version, 1875) and *Beowulf* – in *The Story of Beowulf* (1895), a loose rhyming up of AJ Wyatt's prose translations of the Anglo-Saxon poem; and AE Housman continually reworking the for him familiar tropes and forms of classical sadness (epitomized in his only published translation of Latin verse (1897), the multi-elegiac 'Diffugere Nives', after Horace's Ode IV.7 – 'The snows are fled away' – the poem he read to his students one day in 1914, in Latin and in his own version, on the verge of tears, saying 'That I regard as the most beautiful poem in ancient literature'). And so on and on. A busy intertextual commerce which was emphatically an interest in, and a bid to poetically cash-in on, the accumulating interest of far-off literary tears. An activity suffused with the elegiac notes of the form which these intertextual interests make it resemble most.

---

[71] For Tennyson and Lucretian sadnesses, see Angela Leighton, *On Form*, 66ff. The period's Lucretianism is discussed at some length in 'Modernizing the Subject', Ch 9 below, and owes a lot to Norman Vance's *The Victorians and Ancient Rome*. For Tennyson's intertextualities of sadness at large Wilfred Mustard's old account, *Classical Echoes in Tennyson* (Columbia University Press, NY, 1904) is especially valuable. The 'Tragedy' chapter of Richard Jenkyns's *The Victorians and Ancient Greece* (Basil Blackwell, Oxford, 1980) is most informative. And how noticeably full of sadness, distress, awfulness are the wide-ranging examples of Victorian translation in the handy anthology *Daphne into Laurel: Translations of Classical Poetry from Chaucer to the Present*, ed Richard Stoneman (Duckworth, 1982).

Making a Good End

Survival in these circumstances is all literary; the resurrection that's allowed is textual – even if these emergers from the literary tomb are, like the Biblical Lazarus, wrapped in their grave-clothes, clothed in the marks of the mortality, the endedness and closures of death, the ending-up inevitability which elegiac stratagems are all about endeavouring to subvert. 'How dull it is to pause, to make an end', says Tennyson's old man Ulysses ('Ulysses', line 22). And while *dull* might be the word for an old traveller's slowing down period before death, being bored at the inactivity of as it were the retirement home – fear of which leads Ulysses to think of putting to sea again and doing 'something', 'some work of noble note', 'ere the end': stalling death's imposition of uselessness, staging the productive if marginal 'penultimateness' which William E Fredeman influentially observed as a desire and device of Tennyson for his characters, himself, and his poems – *dull* is far too mild for describing the poem's and in general the period's, utter panic about making an end.[72]

Death's finality ('Death closes all', as Ulysses puts it, line 51) is more than just a dullness. This doorway into what Ulysses, and his author (in this very early response to Hallam's death), fear is the 'eternal silence' (l.27), can't be shrugged off as merely boring. It is indeed to be fended off by any means, and by some work of note, if possible of noble note. Which includes trying to arrange a good death, and since that's never altogether within one's own powers, at the least trying to fix how you will be remembered, especially by writing your own epitaph, your own elegy, using your poems as what Michael Wheeler has called a 'Testamentary Act'.[73] Doing an elegy for someone else, memorializing others,

---

[72] 'Tennyson's poem explores the denouement of ... not the end, but as so often in Tennyson's dramatic monologues and lyrics, the penultimate moment before the end, which is unrevealed': William E Fredeman, ' "A Sign Betwixt the Meadow and the Cloud": The Ironic Apotheosis of Tennyson's "St Simeon Stylites" ', *UTQ*, 38 (1968), 72. Rightly advertised by Christopher Ricks as 'one of the most acute statements ever made about Tennyson' in his *Tennyson* (Macmillan, London and Basingstoke, 1872), 111. Acutely afforced by Martin Dodsworth: 'the characteristic Tennysonian conclusion ... superficially emphatic, actually inconclusive': 'Patterns of Morbidity: Repetition in Tennyson's Poetry', in *The Major Victorian Poets: Reconsiderations*, ed Isobel Armstrong (Routledge, 1969), 17. Standard doctrine now about Tennyson; generalized for the period by E Warwick Slinn's inspection of the refusal of meaningful closure at the end of Elizabeth Barrett Browning's *Aurora Leigh* and Robert Browning's 'Childe Roland': 'Experimental Form in Victorian Poetry', *The Cambridge Companion to Victorian Poetry*, ed Joseph Bristow (Cambridge University Press, 2000), 48–50. Seamus Perry's suggestion of *pending* as a synonym and substitute for penultimate (from Latin *pendere*: to be suspended, about to fall) diminishes the poems' sense of being finally aporetic, stuck, and stymied 'ere the end': *pending* suggests a mere delay for the nonce, something in the office pending-tray sure to be seen to shortly. Seamus Perry, *Alfred Tennyson* (2005), 20.
[73] Michael Wheeler, *Testamentary Acts: Browning, Tennyson, James, Hardy* (Clarendon Press, Oxford, 1992).

combating death that way, is clearly pretty noble; it's a kind of ennobling of someone else's memory. Writing your own epitaph, trying to guarantee your own survival in, and as, text of course, but still on your own terms – as it were a do-it-yourself resurrection work – is less morally noble because of its innate selfishness, but it does involve action, rather than just throwing in the towel, and as a death-defiant refusal to go quietly it is admirable enough in its way.

To 'make a good death' is an old ambition – to be peaceful and unafraid, and so forth, on your death-bed has long been thought of in the Christian tradition as a sign of being 'right with God' and 'ready to meet your Maker', as well as a good advertisement for the consolations of Christian faith. Victorian Christians, especially the majority Protestants, were greatly ani- mated by what Jeremy Taylor, the favourite author of George Eliot's *Adam Bede*, called *Holy Dying*.[74] The Christian poets and their loved ones were very keen on the putting up of a good show at the end. Not possible of course in many a case – think Christina G Rossetti, the poet of perennial hope in the ultimate joy of unity with her Saviour in heaven, perennially sustained by the orthodox thought that our rather painful existence was a mere matter of 'abiding' just a short time ('yet a little while' as her poem 'Yet a Little While' puts it) before the heavenly joys set in, but dying (December 29 1894) in extreme agony of spirit and body, anxious about her sins and her prospects in an after-life, her screams from the pain of her recurred breast cancer so awful that a neighbour of her Torrington Square flat sent in a complaining note. Not the kind of ending Robert Browning would have his friend John Forster remember Elizabeth Barrett by.

Browning writes to Foster at great length about his wife's last moments in July 1861: her persistent cheerfulness despite bad pains in her chest (the doctor talks of the 'serious' state of her lungs) and the need for morphine that's administered through her last night by her devoted husband; she knows Robert ('Know *you*!'); she feels 'Beautiful'; she says 'Our lives are held by God', 'And my hands too'; she takes two saucers of jelly, which she normally hates, because Robert insists; 'Then she bade, "God bless me" repeatedly till I laid her down to sleep again'; and she dies in Robert's arms, her head 'supported' by his: 'no struggle, no sigh even, only a dreadful sus- pense for a minute or two then a silence'. He thought she had fainted, her head on his arm, 'then there was one least contraction of the brow', and their servant Annunziata cried 'The blessed Soul has passed away!'. There

---

[74] Jeremy Taylor, *The Rule and Exercises of Holy Dying* (1651). Pat Jalland, *Death in the Victorian Family* (Oxford University Press, Oxford, 1996) is very good on the 'Good Death' in the period, especially in its Protestant Evangelical form, drawing on the excellent Michael Wheeler, *Death and the Future Life in Victorian Fiction and Theology* (Cambridge University Press, Cambridge, 1990) and Geoffrey Rowell, *Hell and the Victorians: a Study of the Nineteenth-Century Theological Controversies Concerning Eternal Punishment and the Future Life* (Clarendon Press, Oxford, 1974).

are words too private for Browning to repeat, things that 'I can't write', that 'must stay in my heart'. He's aware that he might be thought guilty of betraying too much private matter, but still the needs of the poet's published good-death portrait must be served: 'Why should I not have tried to tell you so much of this as will give you my own one comfort in some degree and not leave you to fancy there was pain, struggling, or the consciousness of departure and separation? – She went, like God's child, in his presence with no more apprehension or difficulty that *that*! ... there was no pain.' She was taken to the Protestant Cemetery in Florence, along mourning streets, to be buried in the presence of grown Italian men 'crying like children', of Italian Independence politicians and journalists there to honour her siding with their cause, and of 'all' the English and American expats. This was public mourning for a publishable end: Forster is commissioned to tell 'the sum' of the story 'to any friends that may have been apprehensive of worse news'. Forster passed on the letter itself to Thomas and Jane Carlyle.[75]

Robert Browning is writing for Elizabeth Barrett's posterity. Even more successful in this mission – in fact the best publicized, and best arranged literary death-bed of the period – are the last days in September and October 1892 of Laureate Tennyson, as narrated in Ch XXIII, 'The Last Chapter' of his son Hallam's *Memoir* (Vol II. 420–432). A plethora of lastnesses, the chapter opens with Tennyson's own epitaph poem, 'Crossing the Bar'. Some of the poet's 'last talks' are recorded – about death's nearness, life after death, God, and poets' views of God. 'So much to do, so little done'. 'The life after death, Lightfoot [Bishop of Durham, theologian and Bible commentator] and I agreed, is the cardinal point of Christianity'. Tennyson is still thinking of glossing *In Memoriam* XLIII, with its suggestion that if sleep followed death and was like a flower folding its petals at night then memories of the loved one would survive in the dead person like scent and colour in the flower ('silent traces of the past': XLIII, line 7): 'and in that case the memory of our love would last as true, and would live pure and whole within the spirit of my friend until after it was unfolded at the breaking of the morn, when the sleep was over'. Wordsworth is quoted a lot, especially lines from 'Yarrow Revisited' about changing with age but still being able to recover the old brightness of soul when visiting a loved valley. Alfred de Musset's poem 'Tristesse' is 'perfect'. Victor Hugo was a genius, but ridiculous when he said 'Napoleon irked God'. Some of Walt Whitman's writings 'are quite unreadable from nakedness of expression' (are too openly homoerotic?), but 'a fine spirit' breathes through them, and he has sent Tennyson a book about Giordano Bruno – whose 'view of God is in some ways mine ... believing in an infinite universe as the necessary effect of the

---

[75] July 1861. *New Letters of Robert Browning*, ed WC de Vane and KL Knickerbocker (John Murray, London, 1951), 137–140.

infinite divine Power'. The death of Bruno, burnt as a misunderstood here-
tic, might be a good subject for a poem. Spinoza was called an atheist, but
he was 'full of God ... "Gott betrunken".' Tennyson 'often now longed for
the quiet Hereafter when all would be made clear'. He reads in the Book of
Job and St Matthew and Anna Swanwick's *Poets the Interpreters of the Age*
(just published).

At 8 o'clock on the morning of Monday 3 October Tennyson sends
Hallam for his Shakespeare, and the son brings him George Steevens's edition of *Lear*, *Cymbeline* and *Troilus and Cressida*, plays 'which he loved
dearly'. He can only manage two or three lines himself, but Hallam reads
some more at his request. Tennyson thinks he's been walking in the garden
with Gladstone, showing him 'my trees'; talks to his physician about death,
and how 'men cling to what is after all but a small part of the great world's
life'. Hallam kisses the proofs of Tennyson's latest volume, *The Death of
Oenone, Akbar's Dream and Other Poems*, which will be published posthumously, 28 October. Tennyson keeps asking for his Shakespeare ('Where is
my Shakespeare? I must have my Shakespeare'), tries several times to read
it, lies 'with his hand resting on it open'. On the Wednesday his last words,
apart from 'a farewell blessing' to wife and son, are the enigmatic 'I have
opened it'. Hallam wonders if this refers to the page of *Cymbeline* which
Tennyson had opened at the words (mentioned earlier among those provoking Tennyson to tears) of Posthumus embraced by returned Imogen, 'Hang
there like fruit, my soul, / Till the tree die'; or whether Tennyson is thinking
of the reassuring lines spoken by God to a dying person who's afraid his
'tiny spark' will 'vanish' in God's vast cosmos – 'Rush of suns, and roll of
systems, and your fiery clash of meteorites ' – lines 'of which he was fond'
from the little poem 'God and the Universe' (in the *Oenone* volume):

> 'Fear not thou the hidden purpose of that Power which alone is great,
> Nor the myriad world, His shadow, nor the silent Opener of the Gate'.

'[H]is own lines of comfort from "In Memoriam" were strongly borne in
upon' his family gathered round. As he dies, at 1.35am Thursday October 6,
holding Hallam's wife's hand, Hallam 'spoke over him his own prayer, "God
accept him! Christ receive him!" because I knew that he would have wished
it'. These are, of course, the last words of Tennyson's great memorial poem
for yet one more of the Arthurs in his life, Arthur Wellesley, the 'Ode on the
Death of the Duke of Wellington'. The next day's medical bulletin continued
the heavily literatured and Arthurian note: 'On the bed a figure of breathing
marble, flooded and bathed in the light of the full moon streaming through
the oriel window; his hand clasping the Shakespeare which he had asked for
but recently, and which he had kept by him to the end; the moonlight, the
majestic figure as he lay there, "drawing thicker breath," irresistibly brought

to our minds his own "Passing of Arthur"'. '[D]rawing thicker breath' (line 316) is the dying King Arthur's plight as he nears his breath-less end ('breathing hard', 330; 'panted hard', 344) in 'The Passing of Arthur' – the final part of the *Idylls of the King* (only slightly recast from the earlier 'Morte d'Arthur') and makes his famous 'slow' speech about the old order changing, and more things being wrought by prayer than this world dreams of, and his having done what he's done, before heading off now to the healing, pastoral utopia of Avilion.[76] (The bulletin's picture of the supine Arthurian poet anticipates the grand scene of Arthur lying dead, surrounded by mourning royal and musical females, in the gigantic *Sleep of Arthur in Avalon* by Tennyson-obsessed Pre-Raphaelite survivor Edward Burne-Jones – 24 feet long; 16 year's work; until Ted Jones's own death at the age of 65 in 1898 left the vast painting still not quite finished.[77])

The local clergyman bids farewell with the words 'Lord Tennyson, God has taken you, who made you a prince of men!' *Cymbeline* is placed with the body, 'and a laurel wreath from Virgil's tomb', and 'some of his Alexandrian laurel, the poet's laurel'. The funeral service takes place in a crowded Westminster Abbey, the coffin covered in a Union Jack flag lent by the Brigade of Guards. The Abbey's nave is lined by soldiers of the Balaclava Light Brigade. 'Many' people are seen reading *In Memoriam*. The anthems include a setting of 'Crossing the Bar'. Hallam quotes the last sixteen lines of the Wellington Ode. Tennyson is interred next to Robert Browning, and in front of Chaucer's monument. The Chapter closes with a reproduction of a fair copy of the manuscript of 'Crossing the Bar'. Letters to Tennyson from Queen Victoria supplement this extended death-narrative – each one, though Hallam doesn't mention this, written on her black-bordered notepaper, arriving in black-trimmed envelopes, and sealed with the black wax customary since Prince Albert's death in 1861. The epistolary series ends with Victoria's letter of condolence to Hallam, thanking him for the copy of Tennyson's 'Silent Voices', 'which I conclude were the last he ever wrote' – the verses requesting the 'Silent voices of the dead' not to call him back in memory to the sunlit past, but to call him forward to the 'glimmering' heights ahead ('On, and always on!'). The Queen is touched by the beautiful story of his ' "passing away" with Shakespeare in his hand'; she encloses a copy of her journal entry about her meeting with 'the great poet Tennyson' in August 1883 at Osborne, on the Isle of Wight, Tennyson's home and hers,

---

[76]   CY Lang dwells carefully on the relations between the four Arthur-fixated poems, 'Morte d'Arthur', *In Memoriam*, *Idylls of the King*, and the Wellington 'Ode', in *Tennyson's Arthurian Psycho-Drama* (University of Nebraska Press, Lincoln, NE, 1983).

[77]   Very nice account of the painting: Fiona McCarthy, ' "Secure Me a Famous Wall" ', *Saturday Guardian*, 17.v.2008, 12–13, in aid of this painting's rare visit (a resurrection?) to London's Tate Britain Gallery from its usual exile home in the Museo de Arte of Ponce, Puerto Rico. Exhibition brochure: Alison Smith, *The Sleep of Arthur in Avalon* (Tate Publishing, London, 2008).

'in dearest Albert's room', when Tennyson 'talked of the many friends he had lost, and what it would be if he did not feel and know that there was another world, where there would be no partings', and 'I told him what a comfort "In Memoriam" had been to me, which pleased him'.

And so the death of the national poet Tennyson is artfully passed on to memory as a great literary event. Tennyson's poetic stature is affirmed in a lineage stretching from Virgil through Chaucer and Shakespeare, especially Shakespeare; his own funeral note an echo, a replay, of all the passings he's turned into great elegies, especially those poems of his for all the Arthurs. Tennyson's dying is textualized: it becomes a death on his own elegiac plan, a textualized ending-up scenario that the great Arthur elegies, *In Memoriam* above all, made him famous for. It's the effort to achieve this status of memorial, as textual *mnemotechnik*, that his poem 'Crossing the Bar, the key-note of the *Memoir*'s 'Last Chapter', Tennyson's own epitaph written in 1889 while crossing the Solent, the stretch of water between England and his, and Victoria's, Isle of Wight home, plainly manifests. And this poem's hesitancies reveal the worries that are endemic to the self-elegizing need. The anticipated crossing of the 'bar' between life and death, from 'our bourne of Time and Place' over to the Hamletian 'bourn' from which 'No traveller returns', will involve, like Hallam's and King Arthur's (and for that matter the Lady of Shalott's) a watery passage. Tennyson wants the journey to be silent – no 'sadness of farewell', just the 'evening bell'; no 'moaning'; and the silent moving of a sleepy tide, 'Too full for sound or foam'. He'll be going 'home'; but where that is is kept vague – 'the flood may bear me far'. And will he actually see his Pilot 'face to face' when he has crossed over? (The treacherous sand-bar in the Solent required Pilots to steer the ferry boats safely.) Tennyson hopes so: 'I hope to see my Pilot face to face / When I have crost the bar'. It's only a hope, though; Tennyson eschews St Paul's certainty in I Corinthians 13.12: 'For now we see through a glass, darkly; but then face to face'. The hesitancy of *In Memoriam* is still palpable, for all the uplifting revisions this poem underwent before publication. 'For though from out our bourne of Time and Place / The flood may bear me far, / I hope to see my Pilot face to face / When I have crost the bar', was originally 'Alone from out the bourne of Time and Place / Alone I sail and far, / But hope to see my Pilot ...'. That *But* was the third one in the early version to go; and Tennyson got rid of the emphatically melancholy and prominently self-rhyming *Alone ... Alone*. But even the final result finds Christian confidence about dying unforthcoming. The poem's opening 'call' ('Sunset and evening star, / And one clear call for me!') is indeed, as Christopher Ricks's note has it, 'ominous'. 'The pilot has been on board all the while, but in the dark I have not seen him', Tennyson explained. And the poem's words remain darkling ones. Thus the poet's very own end-text resists every effort to go out (and survive textually) with flags flying and guns blazing.

The habitual mockers, of course, found it easy to mock the good literary death. Swinburne's *Lesbia Brandon*, for instance, is a protracted parody of the pious death-bed ('And that was the last of Lesbia Brandon, poetess and pagan'), and comes replete with cynical poems about bad deaths ('Some die weeping, and some die sleeping, / And some die under the sea; / Some die ganging, and some die hanging'). For such cynics the manufacturing of reputation-targeted self-epitaphs was an easy target. As for Edward Lear, for instance, in his absurdist 'Incidents in the Life of my uncle Arly':

> On a little heap of Barley
> Died my agèd uncle Arly,
> And they buried him one night; –
> Close beside the leafy thicket; –
> There, – his hat and Railway-Ticket; –
> There, – his ever-faithful Cricket, –
> (But his shoes were far too tight).
>   (*Nonsense Songs and Stories*,
>   ed Sir Edward Strachey (1895))

Browning himself could be jeery too, as he is, at least initially, about his sixteenth-century Bishop whose dying concern (in 'The Bishop Orders His Tomb at Saint Praxed's Church') is securing a plum 'niche' (20) in that church at Rome, and so a prize niche in history, in memory, 'through centuries' (80), by means of a splendid monumental tombstone. His tomb must be best 'antique-black' marble. His epitaph must be carved 'aright' in 'Choice Latin, picked phrase' (76–77). His motives are utterly low – to outdo in splendour his old rival Gandolf's tomb. 'Vanity, saith the preacher, vanity!' is the poem's opening line. This was in the 1840s,[78] long before reputation-securing entered Browning's calculations on the death of his wife (who, interestingly, as the as yet unmarried Elizabeth Barrett Barrett made several suggestions to improve the poem). Browning's satire was directed, not least, at possible low motives behind the ancient memorial splendours of Roman and Roman Catholic Churches which his despised Oxford Movement Anglo-Catholics seemed to admire so much. (Browning can't stop himself having the Bishop wanting, incredibly, to lie where he can hear 'the blessed *mutter* of the mass'; 'see God *made and eaten* all day long', and 'taste / Good strong thick *stupefying* incense-smoke': 81–84, my italics). But for all his mocked-at ecclesiastical pridings, Browning's Bishop becomes steadily more sympathetic. His 'nephews', or sons (he's appealingly vague: 'ah God, I know not!') do indeed seem bent on squandering the worth of the 'villas' he's bequeathed them, and on building him some cheapo monument

---

[78]   The poem appeared in *Hood's Magazine* and then in Browning's *Dramatic Romances and Lyrics* in November 1845.

('Bricked o'er with beggar's mouldy travertine', 66), bearing a low Latin inscription (*Elucescebat*, 99), instead of the high Ciceronian *elucebat*, for 'he shone'). And we're made to feel the frustrations, anger and despair of (yet one more) dying man on the extreme border of life ('Do I live, am I dead?' he asks, twice: 13, 113), knowing that death is coming soon. All too soon, he feels – along with the Bible's Jacob ('Evil and brief hath been my pilgrimage', 101, after Genesis 47.9), and Job ('Swift as a weaver's shuttle fleet our years', 51, after Job 7.6). And then what? The Bishop shares the horror of so many of the period's anticipators of the end. 'Man goeth to the grave, and where is he?' (52). And his unconsoledness is Job's: 'he that goeth down to the grave shall come up no more' (Job 7.9); 'man giveth up the ghost, and where is he?' (Job 14.10). Death's touch is the great unwanted familiarity: nothing like the welcome ghostly touch of the dead man from the past, Tennyson's Hallam. Death's touch is what that other dodgy ecclesiastic of Browning's, Bishop Blougram, fears, with his story of the actor who played Death rather glitzily on stage ('pasteboard crown, sham orb, and tinselled dart') and then in his dressing-room afterwards 'Got touched upon the sleeve familiarly' – the awful reality behind the stories. This is the touch which really finds you out, like the touch of the judging God which Christian orthodoxy believed death led you towards. 'Thus God', says Blougram, 'might touch a Pope / At unawares, ask what his baubles mean, / And whose part he presumed to play just now' ('Bishop Blougram's Apology', 66–76). All of which is, Browning and his people agree, the greatly to be feared awesomeness of ending-up considerations: the so often unrelieved horror of last things; of what might happen, or not, at the last; of being a 'last' one, a person at his or her last moment – sunk in the morbid finalities of Lizzie Siddal's *At Last* poems – 'And, mother, when the big tears fall / (And fall, God knows they may), / Tell him I died of my great love' – rather than the fulfilled erotic satisfactions of Dante Gabriel Rossetti's (unpublished) sonnet 'At Last' where past and future meet in 'Love's deepest lair', 'In the warm darkness underneath thine hair'. It's the persistent worry about Last-ness patently animating Browning even whilst drumming up a hope in something good, prelapsarian even, awaiting him after death – at the end of his Paris morgue poem 'Apparent Failure': 'My own hope is, a sun will pierce / The thickest cloud earth ever stretched; / That, after Last, returns the First, / Though a wide compass round be fetched; / That what began best, can't end worst, / Nor what God blessed once, prove accurst'. Some hope of that, you might say in Browning's South London lingo, the poem's tone being set by its trio of emphatically dead men.[79]

---

[79]   Carol T Christ features 'Apparent Failure' in her (all too brief) discussion of Browning and Victorian poetry's interest in life after death and in doing funerary remembrance: 'Browning's Corpses', *Victorian Poetry* 33, iii–iv (Autumn–Winter 1995), 391–401.

Unto this Last

Victorian poets are mightily haunted by Jesus's parable of the labourers in a vineyard who all get the same 'penny' at the end of the day even if they started work very late, 'about the eleventh hour'. 'I will give unto this last', says the master, the same wage as 'unto' the first (Matthew 20.14). The parable was traditionally read as being about the uncertainites of eschatology and apocalypse, of the Last Day of Divine Judgement run by an arbitrary deity, of the unpredictable fate of last ones, at the last. The Authorised Version's catchy phrase, 'unto this last', caught on as a catch-all of ending-up fears. *Unto this Last*: it echoes premonitorily across the Victorian scene of writing. It's the title of Ruskin's anti-capitalist polemic of 1860; of Francis Thompson's 1897 poem about a man finding a late love; of Isa Knox's 1874 poem about how to live the Christian life in the light of the presently deferred end of the world. There's a strong touch in the Knox poem of Christina Rossetti's anxiety at Christ's deferred Second Coming ('the end may be ... some ages hence') – part of the poem's pressing end anxieties. 'The end! When will it be?'

'What know'st thou of the end?' It's the motoring doubt of so much Victorian verse. It drives the period's great investment in monument making, in poetic Lazarus work, especially the desire for a personal monument: the desire of Browning's Bishop for a Denkmal of lasting stone and the inscribing of fine and living words, something touchable and knowable to be set against the awful fear that there's no living after death except like this. If the ooze of the rotting corpse is all there is, at least a fine monument will hide it. Angeringly to their father, the Bishop's sons are wishing only crumbly gritstone on their forebear: 'clammy squares which sweat / As if the corpse they keep were oozing through' (116–117). The ooze of mortal corruption which some of our poets had awful first-hand experience of. Hardy, for example, in what should be thought of as one of the most important of his imagination-fuelling experiences, when as a young London architect he was pressed into service as a Resurrection Man, supervising the removal of hundreds of coffins and their human remains from the old St Pancras Church graveyard on a wintry night in 1866 by the light of ghastly flares, to make way for the new Midland Railway line into St Pancras. And, momentously, Dante Gabriel Rossetti, who in October 1869 had Lizzie Siddal's coffin in Highgate Cemetery dug up and opened (by night and by the light of a great infection-warding-off fire) to recover the manuscript book of his poems which he had lain with her dead body, in a frantic burst of guilty dedication, seven years before. Rossetti, timid Resurrection Man, who could not face actually being present at the Lazarus moment, was shocked at the book's rotting condition: 'soaked through and through', oozy with mortality. It had to be 'further saturated with disinfectants'. The truth about the disinterment 'must ooze out in time', he wrote to his brother.[80] The poems had already oozed out, marked by death's depredations: stinking and rotting. Worms had made 'a great hole right through all the leaves of *Jenny*'.[81] 'Oh Lizzie, Lizzie, come back to me', Rossetti had lamented over her dead body. But she was not to be resurrected. The poems, though, were. The Lazarus verses of the Resurrectionist poet could, did, and do, survive, vivid emblems of how poems, the words, can defeat their subject death, and the death of their subject. But never, however much they're saturated in the disinfectants of the poetic act, to be utterly free of the grave's stink. The worminess, the sticky ooze of the grave, will always stick to the literary Lazarus.[82]

[80]   DGR to William Michael Rossetti, 13 October 1869. *Letters*, ed Oswald Doughty and John Robert Wahl, II, *1861–7* (Clarendon Press, Oxford, 1965), 751–752. Details of Lizzie's death, interment and disinterment are in the best Rossetti life: Oswald Doughty, *A Victorian Romantic: Dante Gabriel Rossetti* (Oxford University Press, London, 1960). DGR's take on 'Unto this Last' is in 'The Husbandman', *The House of Life* LXXVI.

[81]   DGR to Ford Madox Brown, 14 October 1869, *Letters* (1965), II, 753.

[82]   Samantha Matthews' lively investigation of nineteenth-century poets' textualized deaths, burials, graves, bodily remains, is aptly framed by its opening bravura narrative of the resurrection of Rossetti's poems and its ending account, splendidly detailed and pictorially illustrated, of Tennyson's dying, funeral and interment: *Poetical Remains: Poets' Graves, Bodies, and Books in the Nineteenth Century* (Oxford University Press, Oxford, 2004).

9

Modernizing The Subject

Engaging with the modern subject, with 'modern problems', in that phrase of Matthew Arnold's from his Preface of 1853 – 'modern problems have presented themselves' – was, evidently, a major challenge for Victorian poets, however one construes 'modern'. In one large sense of it, the modern subject was what the best Victorian novelists, our great fictional realists – Dickens and George Eliot, Thackeray, Meredith, Disraeli, Mrs Gaskell, Charles Kingsley, Gissing, Hardy – and Dickens's guru, the great steaming and storming social prophet and critic, Thomas Carlyle, welcomed into their texts with such critical relish and satirical fervour, even anger. The city and the factory, poverty and money, power and crime, justice and injustice, war and class, the modern woman and wife, the contemporary labourer, the demented urbanite, the abandoned child, waifs and strays: these were topics which the Novel and non-fictional prose polemics – the pamphlet, the sermon, journalism, Parliamentary Blue Books – all realistic, documentary writing, made their own.

Genre Wars

There was a widely accepted opposition, even warfare, of genres: prose was for this outer, modern world; poetry was for other than such worldly measures. Oscar Wilde's dismissing WE Henley's hospital sequence of poems 'In Hospital' as 'the beautiful poetry of a prose-writer' endorses the opposition: Wilde thought hospitals were a subject fit only for prose. The nagging urban and suburban realist John Davidson's triumphalist acclaim in his great

Victorian Poetry Now: Poets, Poems, Poetics, First Edition. Valentine Cunningham.
© 2011 Valentine Cunningham. Published 2011 by Blackwell Publishing Ltd.

'Pre-Shakespearianism' essay (the *Speaker* XIX, 28 January 1899) for a poetry that sings 'the offal of the world' – Hood's 'The Song of the Shirt' about poor outworking women needle-workers and James Thomson's London threnody 'The City of Dreadful Night' – builds on the customariness of the opposition even as he's saying it is happily now, in 1899, being overthrown. The 'offal of the world' is the usual subject of 'statistics' and 'prose fiction'. Hood got 'The Song of the Shirt' 'out of the newspapers'. Poetry has usually 'passed by on the other side': as the Pharisee and the Priest did in Jesus's parable of the Good Samaritan. In Davidson's view, the Victorian Good Samaritan, modern version of the man who went to the aid of the traveller robbed and left injured by the roadside, has been the prose writer. Poetry has 'hid its head like the fabled ostrich in some sand-bed of Arthurian legend'.

That prose is actually the better medium for the modern subject was naturally axiomatic with the prose-writer par excellence, critical Thomas Carlyle, who constantly advised socially concerned poets to take up prose instead. Tennyson, he characteristically said, was 'a life-guardsman spoilt by making poetry'. When Thomas Cooper, the Chartist verse-maker sent Carlyle his radical prison epic *The Purgatory of Suicides: A Prison Rhyme* (a poem actually dedicated to the great crusader) he got sent in return Carlyle's *Past and Present*, that great volume of radical prose polemics against capitalist England, plus advice to do his work in prose ('Certainly the *music* that is very traceable here might serve to irradiate into harmony for profitabler things than what are commonly called "Poems"'). It comes as no surprise that Thomas Hardy, that wonderful poet of modern anxiety, should have nonetheless tried his hardest at confronting the devastating social problematics of modernity in prose fiction, novels such as *Tess of the D'Urbervilles* (1891) and *Jude the Obscure* (1896). No surprise either that when the socialist Arthurianizer William Morris wanted to really take on modern society he should do so in his dystopian prose romances *The Dream of John Bull* (1888) and *News from Nowhere* (1891). Nor that when Elizabeth Barrett Barrett wanted to write 'the poetry of the world', to compose a 'completely modern' poem, 'meeting face to face and without mask the Humanity of the age, and speaking the truth as I conceive it out plainly', she knew it had to be 'a sort of novel-poem'. Such was the only course for this admiring disciple of Carlyle. And the result was her great modern, *engagé*, and greatly novel-imitating, *Aurora Leigh* (1856).[1]

---

[1] Letters to Robert Browning, *Letters of Robert Browning and Elizabeth Barrett Barrett*, I.25 (17 February 1845) and I.29ff (27 February 1845). The sharpest account of *Aurora Leigh*'s modernity is Matthew Reynolds, 'The Scope of Narrative: *Aurora Leigh*', Ch 5 of his *The Realms of Verse: English Poetry in a Time of Nation-Building* (Oxford University Press, Oxford, 2001) – though for Reynolds the modernity which matters most is Barrett Browning's Italianism, reflecting her enthusiasm for Italian liberation.

There was, of course, a tradition of recent-ish British poets being public radical and democratic – namely Blake and Burns, Byron and Shelley, carry Wordsworth and Coleridge. The old ghost of radical, political Milton still haunted. But this heritage was in constant danger of being blanketed over by poetry following just as traditional escape routes from disturbing modernity into privateness, solitude, and meditation, into pastoralism, and nostalgia for past times and old modes, poems preferring the mountain, the lake, the garden as relief from and deliberate counter to the noise of the demos and the city, the jostle of the street, the voices of massness, the thrum of the factory, in other words the modern technological-industrial-urban complex and all its demands and problems. The Victorian escapists preferred coming after Keats and his kind of romanticism, rather than, say, Blake's. Not for nothing had 'sublimity' – label for the highest kind of emotion art could supply, and for the essence of the best kind of aesthetic vision – been defined by the great Romantic theorist Edmund Burke as what you experienced by being out in nature, high on some Lakeland crag, up a Swiss Alp, well above the 'bathos' of the earth's low places, down in the gutter, where the socially lowly were. The beauty of poetry on this view was the beauty of uplift: out of the reach of, say, Dickens's urban waif Jo in *Bleak House* who scrapes a living from the tips he gets sweeping a crossing for high-end pedestrians through the horse-shit laden London street. As William Hale White ('Mark Rutherford'), the late-Victorian Nonconformist from Bedford, lamented when he found himself alone and downhearted in London: Wordsworth's pastoral pantheism, the blessings of nature, hills and lakes and mountains, were simply not possible among the teeming bricks of the urban desolation.[2] For many poets the modern city meant aesthetic and aesthetico-spiritual death. Which is why there's so much flinching from the social modern in Victorian poetry (and painting), and so many retreats into pastoralism, medievalism, Arthurianism and classicizing, so much nostalgic harking back to pre-modernity, to pre-industrial times, imaginings, practices: Tennysonian medievalizing and classicizing, Oxonian Pre-Raphaelitism, Ruskinian Guild Socialism, Morrisian Arts and Crafts, and their kind, with all their associated pictures and poems.

---

[2] *Mark Rutherford's Deliverance: Being the Second Part of his Autobiography*, 'edited by his friend, Reuben Shapcott' (Trübner & Co, London, 1885), Ch 1: '... the literature of my own day ... has an evil side to it which none know except the millions of sensitive persons who are condemned to live in great towns .... The long poems which turn altogether upon scenery, perhaps in foreign lands, and the passionate devotion to which they breathe, may perhaps do good in keeping alive in the hearts of men a determination to preserve air, earth and water from pollution; but speaking from my experience as a Londoner, I can testify that they are most depressing, and I would counsel everybody whose position is what mine was to avoid these books.'

Class Warfare

In this contest of subject-matter, this struggle between presentness and past-ness, there's more than a whiff of class warfare, the clash of Gentlemen and Players, a split along the lines of Matthew Arnold's notorious demarcations, as in his 1867–1868 *Cornhill* Magazine essays, collected as *Culture and Anarchy* (1869), between the 'cultured' and the rest, between elitist, con-servative, orderly, Church of England, Oxford and Cambridge educated per-sons who have and are the 'tone of the centre', and the 'philistine' others, provincial, Liberal, democratic (and so disorderly), religiously Nonconformist persons excluded from the two ancient English Universities and thus deemed substantially uneducated. And how 'modern' in the politico-social sense Victorian poems are, is indeed greatly constrained by their authors' class and their (usually) related religious background and affiliations. It's poets of working-class and Dissenting-religious origin, poets of the Arnoldian edge, provincial, Liberal, incapable of speaking in the tones of 'the centre', men and women of the socio-religious margin (a fat margin: on Census Sunday in 1859, half the population attended non-Church of England places of wor-ship) who are more likely to be modern in the manner of the great realist novels. It comes as no surprise to find that the poets who celebrate the life of the slum, street, and factory, who speak up for the wage-slave and the slave, for the subjugated and downtrodden, the poets who are the voice of political and social and economic protest, tend not to be in that large group of poets from the gentry, the nobs and snobs, the sons and daughters of vicars and landowners and Masters of the Hunt. These poets have not sashayed smoothly from Rugby and Harrow Schools and Eton College to the Colleges of Oxford and Cambridge, are not persons of independent means, are cer-tainly not in that large category of male Victorian writers whose profes-sional status is registered in Censuses as 'Called to Bar but never practised', but are, rather, themselves factory boys and girls, down-at-heel, subject to terrible fluctuations of economic fortune, are products of Nonconformist Sunday Schools and Unitarian Academies, of Dissenting Colleges, and, of course, evening classes for working men – many of them self-taught students to whom entering the mainstream of the European literary tradition flowing from Greece and Rome and Italy was dauntingly hard.

I mean poets such as Ebenezer Elliot, the Yorkshire 'Corn-Law Rhymer', one of the eleven children of a radical Nonconformist and Calvinist iron-worker, a largely self-taught Chartist and iron-founder, who lectured on Burns and Milton to northern Mechanics' Institutes, whose *Corn-Law Rhymes* (1831) agitated against a government whose policies made 'Bread dear and labour cheap' ('a voice', Carlyle enthused in the *Edinburgh Review*, July 1832, 'coming from the deep Cyclopean forges, where labour, in real soot and sweat, beats with his thousand hammers "the red son of the furnace" '). And Thomas Cooper, autodidact shoemaker from Leicester (taught himself Latin, Greek, and Hebrew), a Methodist preacher turned Chartist agitator turned Christian Socialist, put in jail for 'seditious' speeches to strikers, where he wrote his prison epic *The Purgatory of Suicides: A Prison Rhyme* (1843), the volume dedicated to Carlyle; author of Chartist chants and songs ('Toil, brothers, toil, till the world is free – till Justice and Love hold Jubilee': 'Chartist Song'), and Chartist rhymes ('God of the earth, and sea, and sky, / To Thee Thy mournful children cry'). And Ebenezer Jones, son of London Calvinist parents, impoverished by the death of his father, made to slog for twelve hours a day as a tea-merchant's clerk, radicalizing himself on the writings of Shelley and Carlyle and the socialist Robert Owen, preaching democratic anger in his Chartist verses ('What'll we do with the workhouses? million, million, men! / Shall we all lie down, and madden, each in his lonely den?': 'A Coming Cry', in *Studies of Sensation and Event*, 1843). And Thomas Hood, born in the Poultry in the City of London, son of a bookseller, who was put in a counting-house at the age of thirteen, a long-time consumptive who was always close to the financial bottom, never making money in his attempts at radical journalism (*Hood's Magazine*, which published lots of early Browning), one of the period's finest crusaders for the poor – the suicidal woman of the streets ('The Bridge of Sighs'), the ill-rewarded woman home-worker ('The Song of the Shirt'). And Gerald Massey, son of illiterate Hertfordshire canal bargees, put to work in a silk-mill at the age of eight, falling in love with books by reading *Robinson Crusoe*, *The Pilgrim's Progress* and Methodist tracts, schooling himself in socialism by reading Tom Paine, turning Chartist propagandist and then Christian Socialist, and becoming perhaps the country's most famous libertarian poet: 'Fling out the red Banner! ... Tyrants are quaking!' ('Song of the Red Republican', first published in *The Red Republican*, no. 1, 1850); 'Good People! put no faith in Kings, nor in your Princes trust, / Who break your hearts for bread, and grind your faces in the dust' ('They are but giants while we kneel': first in *The Friend of the People*, March 1851). Massey naturally reminded his readers of the self-improving working-class hero of Charles Kingsley's novel *Alton Locke* (1850), and was rumoured to have contributed character aspects to his friend George Eliot's eponymous working-class hero of *Felix Holt, the Radical* (1866) – they'd both worked together on John Chapman's radical paper *The Westminster Review*.

And then there's Alexander Smith, Glaswegian poor-boy, apprenticed at age twelve to the lace-pattern business, beginning a long process of social self-betterment (he ended as Registrar of Glasgow University), getting his poems in the Glasgow *Evening Citizen*; dubiously famous as a wild 'Spasmodic, poet, but, with Sydney Dobell, a more than decent Crimean War sonneteer (in their collaborative *Sonnets on the Crimean War*, 1855), and, for his own part, a rather good celebrator of modern Glasgow in his *City Poems* volume (1857) – especially in the poem 'Glasgow' ('A sacredness of love and death / Dwells in thy noise and smoky breath'). And Joseph Skipsey, sometime Northumberland coal-miner, who went down the coal-pit at the age of seven, never attended school but taught himself to read and write, and poured out simple, moving celebrations of and lamentations about northern coal-mining life in volumes such as *The Collier Lad, and Other Lyrics* (1864), to the delight of Tennyson and Morris, Dante Gabriel Rossetti, and the Ruskinites (Oscar Wilde pointedly compared Skipsey's 1886 volume *Carols from the Coalfields* with Blake's *Songs*). And James Thomson, whose naval father was disabled and so unable to support his family, and whose mother died when he was eight, leaving him as a charity boy to be educated at the Royal Caledonian Asylum for sons of poor Scottish soldiers and sailors in Islington, a world-wanderer, whose grim experience as an alcoholic down-and-out in London (leaking shoes, rough lodging-houses, keeping warm in the British Museum Reading Room) fed the most sustained Victorian poetic portrait of London as Dantesque hell, 'The City of Dreadful Night' (1874). And WE Henley, Gloucester bookseller's son and grammar-schoolboy, a young cripple with an amputated foot, whose twenty-months in Edinburgh Infirmary to which he'd been consigned in an effort to save his other leg, resulted in perhaps the best-ever hospital poems in any language, the 'In Hospital' sequence (1873–1874) – a poet thoroughly at home in what readers like Oscar Wilde thought the most unpoetic of materials (who ever visualized town-life in the rain better than Henley did, in his sensationally good sonnet 'Rain'? – 'Black chimney-shadows streak the shiny slates'; 'And to the wall the dank umbrellas crowd': *A Book of Verses*, 1888). And there is also, of course, John Davidson, from Greenock, yet another Scottish poor-boy, brought up in the wake of the theological contentions that split the Calvinist Churches of Scotland in the 1840s, put to work aged thirteen in the chemical laboratory of Greenock's Walker's sugar factory, who never made money at writing (first in Glasgow, then in London), though he tried hard (reviewing, he said, brought in scarcely enough to keep him in tobacco), who became the laureate of bitterly harsh modern, especially urban, life – 'With shelves for rooms the houses crowd, / Like draughty cupboards in a row': 'A Northern Suburb' (1896). Davidson's eclogues were always of the ironic urban kind (as in *Fleet Street Eclogues*, 1893, and *A Second Series of Fleet Street Eclogues*, 1896). And he was, of course, author of the duly famous, sharp, colloquial and courageous critical complaint of a clerk trying to survive on 'Thirty Bob a Week':

> But I don't allow it's luck and all a toss;
> There's no such thing as being starred and crossed;
> It's just the power of some to be a boss,

And the bally power of others to be bossed:
I face the music, sir; you bet I ain't a cur;
Strike me lucky if I don't believe I'm lost![3]

And then, too, even more strikingly perhaps, there's the bustling group of rather eminent proletarian women poets, writing poems of close involvement with the modern social-economic condition against all odds. Women such as Janet Hamilton, the blind Scottish Calvinist spinner and weaver and mother of ten children, author of numerous forthright poems about oppression, slavery, 'The Horrors of War' in the Crimean, poverty, drunkenness, Sabbath-breaking, the role of ordinary mothers. And Eliza Cook, youngest of the eleven children of a Southwark 'brazier', entirely self-educated, who achieved exceeding popularity as poet and journalist (*Eliza Cook's Journal* outsold Dickens's *Household Words* at three half-pence per issue), chatty and homely, feminist-inclined, with a radical eye to the plight of shop-workers and other city artisans ('The Old Arm-Chair', May 1837, 'I love it, I love it; and who shall dare / To chide me for loving that old arm-chair', was a particular Victorian family favourite; her 1864 poem 'Poor Hood', celebrating Hood as 'the Poet fool / Who sung of Woman's woes and wrongs', led to the erection of Hood's monument in Kensal Green Cemetery). And Isa Knox, orphaned child of an Edinburgh hosier and glove-maker, largely self-taught (she left school at the age of nine), who was close to London's Langham Place group of feminist activists, published a book against slavery (1863) and many poems promoting Christian consolations especially of a womanist turn (like her Magdalene poem 'The Box', discussed in 'Fleshly Feelings', Chapter 7, above). And Ellen Johnston, 'The Factory Girl', put to work at the age of eleven in a Glasgow weaving mill, whose poems about the Crimean War, democratic struggles in Italy and Poland, Scottish workers and poor people, published in Glasgow newspapers, especially the *Penny Post*, got her national attention (though Queen Victoria's personal addition of £5 to Johnson's Royal Bounty Fund benefit of £50 didn't prevent her dying in penury and of malnutrition in a Glasgow workhouse).[4] And Elizabeth Duncan, Dundee ploughman's daughter, minimally schooled, sent away from home aged seven to work on a farm as an all-round hand, minding the cows, gathering gorse for fodder, growing up to do handloom weaving and domestic work, eventually marrying

[3] The poem first appeared in no.2 of the Nineties Decadents' house journal, *The Yellow Book*, July 1894. Davidson thought of himself, rightly, as contributing necessary 'blood and guts' to the Yeats-Symons Rhymers' Club. See *The Poems of John Davidson*, ed Andrew Turnbull, 2 vols (Scottish Academic Press, Edinburgh, 1973), and John Sloan, *John Davidson, First of the Moderns: A Literary Biography* (Clarendon Press, Oxford, 1995).
[4] Susan Zlotnik has much that's informative about Ellen Johnston in ' "A Thousand Times I'd be a Factory Girl": Dialect, Domesticity, and Working-class Women's Poetry in Victorian Britain', *Victorian Studies* 35, 1 (Autumn 1991), 7–72.

an Arbroath flax-dresser, bearing eight children, trying to supplement the family income (husband injured in an accident) with her booklets of devout, protesting poems about American slavery, prisoners, the arrogance of the powerful, and in particular worried mother's verses about the Crimean War to which her second son Willie went as an ordinary soldier – hero of the Sebastopol siege as well as of his mother's 'The Death of Willie, My Second Son' (he was killed aged thirty-five in 1866, mangled in an unfenced hair-teasing machine in an Aberdeen factory). And the dye-factory-worker from Chorley in Lancashire who published as 'Marie' poems celebrating manual labour in the radical pacifist *People's and Howitt's Journal*, and gently satirical pieces in *Eliza Cook's Journal* ('Posted Books', for instance, gibing at 'men of merchandise' for having no room in the 'ledgers' of their hearts for moral considerations). And Ruth Willis, the lame Congregationalist factory-worker from Thomas Cooper's Leicester whose poems, full of sympathy for workers and Chartism, for poor English *emigrés* 'self-exiled' to Australia in hopes of freedom from 'want, and despair', and for Polish revolutionaries, appeared in the Chartist-sympathetic *Leicester Mercury* and were collected in two series of *Lays of Lowly Life* (1861–1862, and 1868). And Fanny Forester, Salford-Irish dye-worker, author of eighty-plus narrative poems of northern urban proletarian life, work, and death – sob-stories, actually – which appeared in the 1870s and early 1880s in the popular *Journal* of *Ben Brierley*, Mancunian textile worker turned journalist, versifier and Lancashire-dialect story-teller. And Mary Smith from Cropredy in Oxfordshire, daughter of a Nonconformist (Independent or Congregationalist) cobbler, who attended Methodist Sunday-School and day-school, was a domestic servant in the Carlisle ménage of radical Baptist minister JJ Osborne, worked domestically for Quakers, moved gradually towards Quakerism, founded a primary school, ran free classes for poor females and spoke out loudly for women's education, suffrage, equality. Her 'great aim', she said in *The Autobiography of Mary Smith, Schoolmistress and Nonconformist. A Fragment of a Life* (posthumous, 1892), 'was to use simple, natural language, avoiding metaphors, as Wordsworth did'. Her poem ' "Women's Claims": Written on Reading of Viscountess Amberley's Lecture at Stroud' (Viscountess Amberley, Bertrand Russell's mother, was a women's suffrage campaigner), looks forward utopianly to the 'coming' future of ' "Equal Rights" ' in the rhythm of Tennyson's futuristic 'Locksley Hall'. It appeared in Smith's volume *Progress, and Other Poems; The Latter Including Poems on the Social Affections and Poems on Life and Labour* (1873). Her long dissenting (and Dissenting) poem 'Progress' about the loving spirit of England which ennobles especially the poor, includes a eulogy of the country's 'myriad' proletarian, 'humble poor' poets:

> The simple priests of nature, with her still,
> Poets unknown to fame, whose numbers pure,

Dear to the lowly, bless the hearts they thrill;
How have ye tuned your lyres unceasing, sweet,
While labour's stony ways have gall'd your feet.

She singles out Ebenezer Elliott as 'The People's Bard', who has notably caught the 'strain' of the 'Muse of the Poor' in his 'stormful song', against oppressors and for justice and true patriotism:

No college bred these men: they snatched their lore
From books incongruous, in their hours of rest;
Their chambers the free fields, where evermore
Thought made them welcome to her banquets blest.
Nor did they murmur that the impassive years
Sped on oblivious of their hopes and fears;
Theirs was the courage true, which works and waits,
Alike amid all seasons and all fates.

Smith's 'Progress' evidently owes much of its political sentiment to Thomas Cooper's *The Purgatory of Suicides*. Like Cooper's poem, Smith's *Progress* was dedicated (with permission) to Carlyle, 'one of the greatest writers, profoundest thinkers, and purest moralists that this or any age has produced'. (Smith's first volume, *Poems*, 'By M.S.', was dedicated 'To Mrs Carlyle, Wife of Thomas Carlyle, Esq.'.)[5]

Dissenting (Dis)abilities

So much outsiderliness, then, of one kind or another, of nonconformity in general but also of Nonconformity in particular. And it really is no accident that some kind of religious difference and dissidence, actual Dissent as well as general dissenting, unites so many of the radical poets whose family and financial circumstances and education might suggest something otherwise than strong affinity with the poor and needy and the lower class. Theirs were the animating politics proudly announced in that subtitle of *The Nonconformist* magazine, 'The Dissidence of Dissent and the Protestantism

[5]   All these proletarian women poets, except Isa Knox, feature in the excellent collection of verse and prose *Working-Class Women Poets in Victorian Britain: An Anthology*, edited by the doyenne of proletarian women poet studies, Florence S Boos (Broadview Press, Peterborough, Ontario, 2008). Working-class women of course feature strongly in Florence Boos's compendious chapter 'Working-Class Poetry' in the Blackwell *Companion to Victorian Poetry*, eds Richard Cronin, Alison Chapman, and Anthony H Harrison (Blackwell, Oxford, 2002), 204–228. Surprisingly few of these proletarians – only Eliza Cook and Ellen Johnston, in fact – are in the standard anthology *Victorian Women Poets*, eds Angela Leighton and Margaret Reynolds (Blackwell, Oxford, 1995).

of the Protestant Religion' which Arnold lampooned by jeering repetition in the opening chapter of *Culture and Anarchy* (1869). This was the mark of the middle-class beast, the national enemies of 'Sweetness and Light'.[6] These middle- and upper-middle-class Dissenters followed, as it were, in the religio-political footsteps of the great dissident Carlyle himself, who was brought up in a strict Calvinist faction of the Scottish Secession Kirk, close friend of Edward Irving the leader of the charismatic Irvingite Catholic Apostolic church, married to Jane Welsh a descendant of John Knox the founder of Scottish Calvinism, a classic Victorian post-Christian humanist whose ethic and aesthetic were utterly shaped by that beginning in dissident Christianity. Naturally enough Carlyle venerated Martin Luther, Europe's foundational radical Protestant, as prophet and world-changer, but also as poet. Carlyle translated Luther's defiant hymn 'Eine feste Burg ist unser Gott' in the version that became a battle-cry for worldwide anglophone Protestantism – 'A safe stronghold our God is still' (*Fraser's Magazine*, no.12, 1831).

This remarkable tribe of the un-needy Carlylean Dissenting radicals prominently includes the poets influenced by Unitarianism: the liberal satirical journalist and poet Leigh Hunt, friend of Shelley as well as of his London neighbour Carlyle, son of a Unitarian preacher; and James Henry, the Irish Virgil scholar and satirical pamphleteer, his politico-religious scepticism fuelled by Unitarian schoolmasters, author of the 1862 poem protesting against coal-owners who neglected their workers' safety, 'Two hundred men and eighteen killed / For want of a second door!'; and Sarah Flower Adams, the radical anti-Corn-Law League poet, daughter of the crusading Unitarian and libertarian Essex printer and journalist Benjamin Flower, adopted into the family of WJ Fox the renowned radical London Unitarian minister, founder and sometime editor of the libertarian *Monthly Repository*, in which her poems appeared, as did those of her great friend the Congregationalist poet Robert Browning;[7] and Sydney Dobell, the prosperous Gloucester wine-merchant, brought up in his parents' apocalyptic Unitarianism (his mother's father founded a Unitarian church in London at the end of the eighteenth century), who not only achieved notoriety as author of the slamming-banging Spasmodic poem about a poet's life *Balder: Part the First*, but wrote numbers of poems in favour of Spanish, Hungarian and Italian freedom (Mazzini loved Dobell's long pro-Italian democracy poem *The Roman*, 1850), and about Crimean War horrors, which he viewed in the light of his inherited Biblical apocalypticism (he thought – as mentioned

---

[6] 'Sweetness and Light', Ch 1 of *Culture and Anarchy: An Essay in Political and Social Criticism*, one volume edition (Smith Elder, London, 1869).

[7] The politicized aesthetics of Fox, Browning's first poetic patron, and of *The Monthly Repository* and Browning's elaborate dance with it, are major themes of Isobel Armstrong's *Victorian Poetry: Poetry, Poetics and Politics* (1993).

in the little discussion of Dobell in my 'Fleshly Feelings', Chapter 7 above –
that Sebastopol was etymologically related to 'Armageddon'). For her part,
Mary Howitt, author of many pleasant moralizing celebrations of ordinary
life (including 'The Barley-Mower's Song'), who through *Howitt's Journal*,
edited with her husband William, was at the forefront of progressive causes –
against enclosures of commons, slavery, factory abuses, vivisection, and in
favour of extending the suffrage (they published, for example, Eliza Cook) –
was for a time a Unitarian before becoming a heavy Spiritualist and death-
bed Roman Catholic, though her political aesthetics and aestheticized
politics were never not steeped in the values of the (well-off) Quakerism which
she and her husband were bred in. Likewise Mary Sewell, best-selling author
in her sixties of long sentimental ballads about the virtuous poor – end-
game of a Quaker's life of philanthropy and radical campaigning against
slavery and such (even though she converted to Anglicanism), supported by
her Quaker-banker husband. Not dissimilarly, Mary Kendall's 'The Sandblast
Girl and the Acid Man' (*Songs from Dreamland*, 1894), about frustrated
love in a stained-glass factory in 'Muggy Manchester', comes out of a life of
devoted polemic, in verse and prose, for liberal reformist causes and against
overseas oppression (Turkish massacres of Armenians, for example), owing
much to Nonconformist feeling and value (her father was a Methodist minister). Kendall worked for years without salary for the reformist Quaker
Rowntree family of York, researching and speech-writing for the pro-
worker campaigner B Seebohm Rowntree. Too, it's arguable that Rudyard
Kipling's wonderful feel for the demotic tones of his soldier subjects in his
Barrack-Room Ballads (1892), in poems like 'Tommy' and 'Mandalay' and
'Gentleman-Rankers' (poems first published, not at all by chance in WE
Henley's papers), is greatly indebted to the democratic traditions of the
Potteries Methodism Kipling's extended family was steeped in on both sides,
his father's Kiplings and his mother's Macdonalds – generations of Methodist
ministers going back to John Wesley's time. In his wonderful 1889 essay
'My Great and Only', Kipling pays tribute to the inspiration he got from the
songs of London Music Halls, the 'Songs of the People'. But there's more
than an air also of Methodists hymns, those religious songs of the people,
about Kipling's verse (try singing his 'Recessional', for example, 'God of our
father's known of old', to the tune of, say, Charles Wesley's 'Long my imprisoned spirit lay / Fast bound in sin and nature's night').

The radical drive of Unitarianism and Quakerism and much Methodism
was a Victorian by-word. So was the political disposition of those as it were
honorary Dissenters, namely Jews – a tradition shared by two notable Jewish
women poets, Mathilde Blind and Amy Levy. Mathilde Blind, German
Jewish banker's daughter, sister of an attempted assassin of Bismarck, a
feminist, atheistic New Woman, friend and colleague of every radical in
sight, Garibaldi, Mazzini, Eleanor Marx; editor of Byron and Shelley; first

biographer of George Eliot; close to Swinburne (in fact sexually keen on him); full of polemical verse, like her long poem *The Fire on the Heather* (1886) against the Scottish landowners who evicted their peasant tenants in the awful Highlands clearances; a sonneteer whose subject in *Songs and Sonnets* (1893) could indeed be the lovely-bleak 'A Winter Landscape' (a kind of Darwinian atheist riposte to Christina G Rossetti's widely-admired and Christian 'In the bleak mid-winter'), but who was still more at home in 'Manchester by Night', absorbing traditional leftist urban desolation, the *smoky*, *black crush* and *rush* of the hellish urbs, into the *hush* of a desolate universe from which a creator God is now absent. Mathilde Blind left her estate to Cambridge's Newnham College for women. Newnham's first Jewish student was Amy Levy, the satirical socialist novelist, author of feminist dramatic monologues in the manner of Robert Browning (like 'Xantippe', complaint of Socrates's unhappy wife, title poem of the volume *Xantippe and Other Poems* which appeared when Levy was still an undergraduate). Levy, at the core of 1880s London's Jewish radicalism (Eleanor Marx translated her 1888 novel *Reuben Sachs*, a satire on Jewish-materialism, into German), but also the melancholy drop-out from Newnham who killed herself at the age of twenty-seven having just corrected the proofs of *A London Plane-Tree and Other Verse* (1889) – a volume pervaded by desolated urban survivalism, as in 'In the Mile End Road', as well as pseudo-cheerfulness on a sad London omnibus ('Ballade of an Omnibus'). Her sonnet 'London Poets (*In Memoriam*)' makes Tennyson's tones of grief for Hallam stand for the whole tribe of sad London poets now dead, as she herself would be when the book appeared:

> They trod the streets and squares where now I tread,
> With weary hearts, a little while ago;
> When, thin and grey, the melancholy snow
> Clung to the leafless branches overhead;
> Or when the smoke-veiled sky grew stormy-red
> In autumn; with a re-arisen woe
> Wrestled, what time the passionate spring winds blow;
> And paced scorched stones in summer: – they are dead.
>
> The sorrow of their souls to them did seem
> As real as mine to me, as permanent.
> To-day, it is the shadow of a dream,
> The half-forgotten breath of breezes spent.
> So shall another soothe his woe supreme –
> 'No more he comes, who this way came and went'.

Her last words, these, about lonely belatedness in the modern city; her final volume's aweing finalities about the angst of the desolated urban modern. As announced in her poem 'Last Words', whose epigraph, as reported in the discussion of resurrection-refusing poems in 'Mourning and Melancholia', my preceding chapter to this one, is from Robert Browning's 'Too Late': 'Dead! all's done with'. 'All's done with' Levy's 'Last Words' keeps saying (the only resurrection she allows is the 're-arisen woe' of the London Poets); and what's important to perceive here, is that this is one outsider by religion repeating the words of another, namely of Robert Browning the Congregationalist.

Congregationalist Aesthetics

Congregationalists: old Dissenters, and nothing at all honorary about their Nonconforming status – an historical edged-out-ness which dramatically infects and inspires the work, as it did the lives, of Robert Browning and Elizabeth Barrett Barrett/Browning and their co-religionist George MacDonald. George MacDonald was a Scottish Congregationalist who pastored an English Congregationalist chapel for a while, drifted away into freelance preaching, but stayed true to his desire to bring an *engagé* Christianity to workers stuck in the industrial heart-lands. In Manchester he ran a kind of private socialist chapel for working men in a rented room. His poetic output was slight beside the prose he's best know for, his autobiographical novels of fraught searching after modern faith – especially his *Robert Falconer* (1863) – and his very influential fairy writing (CS Lewis said MacDonald's *Phantastes* (1858) baptized his imagination; GK Chesterton claimed that *The Princess and The Goblin* (1872) changed his life). But MacDonald was well capable of transposing the radical post-Christianity for urban people of his novels into the poems he did write. As in 'A Manchester Poem', this poet's daydream of a Manchester couple, man and woman, denizens of the 'chimneyed city', whose streets are mired in the 'black precipitate' falling from carbon-filled clouds, two shrunken wage-slaves in a shuddering prison-like factory of gigantic clashing machines, who escape on a Sunday and bring a snowdrop plant back to their slummy room. The poem is a classic of George Eliot-type humanist Feuerbachian re-casting of Christian symbols and meanings in ordinary existence: the pair's simple meal is 'their Eucharist'; the window-frame casts a shadow of a cross; the stones in the city's 'dull pavement' comprise a Bethesda (Bethesda: the pool in Jerusalem in the Gospels where sick people wait for an angelic cure, and a favourite name for Nonconformist chapels); the snowdrop in the house is like the Annunciation – the angel announcing Jesus's birth to Mary. Which is all very sentimentalizing. But still the poem never shrinks from detailing the industrialized Mancunian horrors for which it is busily offering this post-Christian redemption. (The poem appeared in MacDonald's *Works of Fancy and Imagination*, III (1871), and was heavily revised for his *Poetical Works* (1893).)

MacDonald was a close friend of Robert Browning, that rich-boy Congregationalist – well, fairly rich-boy, son of a Congregationalist banker who was by no means poor, even though he had turned down, on moral grounds, the lucrative management of his mother's St Kitts sugar plantations which he would have otherwise inherited. (He paid for most of Browning's first volumes of verse.) Symptomatic of the continuing anti-Establishment sympathies of Browning and MacDonald was their attendance at the Congregationalist Chapel of the Welsh preacher-poet Thomas Jones. Browning's usual hostility in his poems towards tyrannous oppressors, managers, doers-down (of all sorts, including religious ones) undoubtedly comes from his being steeped in the legal and political, social and cultural 'disabilities' of Dissent, and the anger that marginalizing engendered (he was one of the many intellectually able English Dissenters prevented by their religion from going to the Established Church's universities of Oxford and Cambridge). It's utterly pertinent that Browning was early in his career so mixed up with the Unitarian Flower sisters and published in the radical *Monthly Repository* founded by the notoriously radical Unitarian WJ Fox. Just so, Elizabeth Barrett's kept-up poetic siding with the poor and oppressed – children in factories, slaves, and (as Mrs Browning) Italians struggling for freedom from foreign occupation[8] – all rather unexpected from the likes of privileged, cosseted, rich Miss Barrett Moulton-Barrett (life at daddy's place Hope End in Gloucestershire, financed by West Indian slave plantations, was extremely *haute-bourgeois* existence) – is utterly explicable with reference to her native Congregationalism.

At a lovely warm moment in their early correspondence Elizabeth and Robert discovered their shared Dissenting roots and proclivities. 'Can it be you', Robert writes on a Sunday evening in August 1845, 'my own you past putting away, *you* are a schismatic and frequenter of Independent Dissenting chapels? And you confess this to *me* – whose father and mother went this morning to the very Independent Chapel where they took me, all those years back, to be baptised – and where they heard, this morning, a sermon preached by the very minister who officiated on that other occasion!' She had just told him of her Dissenting preferences. Dissenters have 'an arid, grey Puritanism in the clefts of their souls: but it seems to me clear that they know what the "liberty of Christ" *means*, far better than those do who call themselves "churchmen"; and stand altogether, as a body, on higher ground' (RB & EBB *Letters*, I. 145–146; 147–148). A year later Elizabeth repeated her position as the couple was plotting where to get married. She can 'pray anywhere and with all sorts of worshippers from the Sistine Chapel to

---

[8]   *Casa Guidi Windows: A Poem* (Chapman & Hall, London, 1851), celebration of Florence and Italy and the 'bella libertà' of the unification cause: rightly taken up by modern feminist critics as exemplary of Barrett Browning's strong feminized political radicalism and of poetic Victorian women's fighting strength. See, e.g., Sandra M Gilbert, 'From Patria to Matria: Elizabeth Barrett Browning's Risorgimento', *PMLA*, 99:2 (1984), 194–211, and Esther Schor, 'The Poetics of Politics: Barrett Browning's Casa Guidi Windows', *Tulsa Studies in Women's Literature*, 17:2 (1988), 305–324.

Mr Fox's', but 'I like beyond comparison best, the simplicity of the dissenters ... the unwritten prayer, ... the sacraments administered quietly and without charlatanism! and the principle of a church, as they hold it, *I* hold it too, ... quite apart from state necessities ... pure from the law'. She's not as theologically left-wing as the Unitarians (or Socinians) and so is not happy in chapels like Robert's friend 'Mr Fox's' ('The Unitarians seem to me to throw over what is most beautiful in the Christian Doctrine'), but it's utterly clear where she stands religiously, and thus politically, and so of course poetically. These letters of hers swing the way of Browning's 'Christmas-Eve and Easter-Day'; she and her husband-to-be are in rather complete religio-political-poetical tune.[9]

Barrett Browning's 'Poetry of The World'

Elizabeth Barrett was, she told Browning, in a letter six months before the Dissent confessions, a 'disciple' of Carlyle ('a devout sitter at his feet'). She'd sent Carlyle some poems and received first-hand his scorn for poetry, even for a critical, satirical poetry like hers. Why persist in ' "singing" to this perverse and froward generation', he'd replied, using fulminating words from the Old Testament. She would not give up on the poetry writing, she said, but she would heed the Carlylean scorn enough to want to do a Carlyle in verse, to write 'the poetry of the world', that is, to embrace the prose-prophet's kind of subject (*Letters*, 17 February 1845, I. 25). Browning tried to dent her attention to Carlyle's scorn for verse by, as it were, ratting on his own friend. Carlyle had recently told him he'd be 'proudest' to write a song and had quoted and explicated some 'old Scotch song'. Six months earlier Browning had even heard Carlyle 'croon' the old Jacobean song 'Charlie is my darling', and say he was moved by it. 'After saying which, he would be sure to counsel everybody to get their heads clear of all singing!' So could Elizabeth really take the old prophet's despisal of song seriously, especially when the rhetoric of his preachments to the nation showed how 'thoroughly does he love and live by' 'singing'. But she was not be persuaded.

She was, of course, already well-known as author of 'The Cry of the Children' (1843), presumably one of the poems she'd sent to Carlyle, about the plight of little kids forced to drudge in factories and mines: a poem relaying the voices of these illiterate, miserable mites as recorded in the momentous Parliamentary Children's Employment Commission report of 1842. This was one of the influential parliamentary 'Blue Books' that haunted and incited liberals in the period, not least the social-conscience

[9]   RB & EBB *Letters*, August 1846, II. 429–431.

novelists like Carlyle's friend Charles Dickens.[10] Benjamin Disraeli built his dyspeptic Condition-of-England novel *Sybil* out of materials lifted whole-sale from the 1842 Blue Book. It was researched and in great part written by Elizabeth Barrett's friend Richard Horne (later Richard Hengist Horne): devoted Shelleyan; the so-called Farthing Poet; friend of WJ Fox; temporary editor of the *The Monthly Repository* in 1836 (and so publisher of the first versions of Browning's 'Johannes Agricola in Meditation' and 'Porphyria's Lover', the 'Madhouse Cells' poems); journalist assistant to Dickens first on the *Daily News*, then on *Household Words*; author (1847) of the novel *The Dreamer and the Worker* which Horne rightly claimed was in the school of Mrs Gaskell's *Mary Barton* and Charles Kingsley's *Alton Locke*.[11] Barrett's 'The Cry of the Children' was doing the work of 1840s novels. And that's what she wanted most: to get her poems as close to the contemporary nov-el's critical realism as possible. 'Novel-poem', her word for her 'completely modern', and Carlylean, poem *Aurora Leigh* ('a sort of novel-poem'), was her coinage: a novel phrase, and notion, as novel as she hoped her new poem would be.[12]

The poem is mightily self-conscious, a polemic for the kind of 'modern' poem it seeks to be. The polemicizing is done through the struggles of its writer-heroine Aurora Leigh – plainly a mirror of Barrett Browning her-self – to become a poet of modern radical engagement, and to justify in practice that radically aesthetic ambition. Aurora is a writer with no great means (£300 a year: so she's not poor, and has enough to afford a serv-ant), determined to live by her pen, surviving by doing hack prose for the magazines and weekly papers because there's little money in poetry ('In England no one lives by verse that lives': III.307), burning to write poems, and poems that take on the modern city subject. She's up against the sneers

---

[10]   Dickens dedicated his *Hard Times* to Carlyle; in which novel the room of Thomas Gradgrind, uncaring northern factory-owner, is lined with Blue Books whose accusing contents he presumably ignores, even if he's read them.

[11]   Isobel Armstrong's *Victorian Poetry: Poetry, Poetics and Politics* does some justice to Horne's poetry and his Fox and Browning connections. Robert Dingley's entry on Horne in the *New Oxford Dictionary of National Biography* tells the Horne story with superb succinctness.

[12]   It would be (letter of February 27 1845, *Letters*, I.29ff) 'as completely modern as "Geraldine's Courtship", running into the midst of our conventions, and rushing into drawing-rooms and the like, "where angels fear to tread".' Barrett's long-ish narrative poem, 'Lady Geraldine's Courtship', late addition to, and star of, her *Poems* (1844), about the wealthy society lovely of the title, in love with a poor poet, is hardly as revolutionary as Barrett seemed to believe, for all its diatribes from the poet against aristo despisers of the 'low-born' ('Lady Geraldine', line 14) as less than human, and its theme of cross-class convention-flouting mar-riage as apt to the new Age of steam trains and electricity. Much of *Aurora Leigh* is, of course built on how traditional class consciousness gets in the way of the marriage of upper-crust Romney and servant-class Marianne.

of her wealthy philanthropist cousin Romney Leigh who thinks, like Carlyle, that poetry is a wasteful spiritualizing sideline 'In the agonizing present' (II.304), when the world cries out for social action. Women's poems are especially bad, Romney thinks, in tackling modern problems because bourgeois women are too personal, too emotionally involved with individual cases of suffering, can't take in the worldwide scene of 'universal anguish', the 'million sick' (II.209, 216). 'You weep for what you know' (213), even when writing poems like Elizabeth Barrett's 'The Cry of the Children' and 'The Runaway Slave at Pilgrim's Point':

> You gather up
> A few such cases, and when strong sometimes,
> Will write of factories and of slaves, as if
> Your father were a negro, and your son
> A spinner in the mills. All's yours and you,
> All, coloured with your blood, or otherwise
> Just nothing to you.
>
> (II.192–198)

(There's an inciting play here with 'negro' parenthood and 'coloured' blood, as if Barrett Browning is hinting that she was indeed sympathetic with the plight of black slaves because of her own inherited Afro-Caribbean-'coloured' blood.)

The world is 'Uninfluenced by you', Romney rants, because it's 'Uncomprehended by you' (II.219–220). Women's verse is anyway so girly: ' "What grace, what facile turns, what fluent sweeps / What delicate discernment" ', male readers say, expecting nothing more than 'honour to the sex' from the 'fair writer' (II.227–243). Romney recognizes that Aurora wouldn't accept such demeaning acknowledgments; which she affirms: 'Better far / Pursue a frivolous trade by serious means, / Than a sublime art frivolously' (II.257–259). She feels 'frivolous' though; fears she's in Romney's group of women playing at art and making 'thrusts with a toy-sword' III.240). She rips up her verses: city poems, alright, about London 'wiped out' by fog; poems refusing to 'despise' city reality (III.187); but, she thinks, still lacking real life: 'Just gasps of make-believe galvanic life' (III.249). (*Galvanic life*: like corpses stimulated – galvanized – into muscular activity by electricity: Carlyle's favoured word for pseudo-liveliness.) She deplores her womanly weakness in grasping the pressing social subject: she can feel the fiery seeds of divine creation burning in her hand, but will it 'open large' before the spark dies out or 'the palm' gets 'charred'? (III.251–260). But still she works on and on at her 'rhythmic thought' (III.272), burning the stinking midnight oil (III.300), making herself ill with over-work.

Not 'writing old'

Like many another young poet Aurora has tried 'writing old' – doing her own juvenile revivals of the set classical genres – the kind of pastorals written by urbanites who get scared when cows just wag their tails; epics whose trumpet calls are like babies blowing bubbles; elegies and love poems full of tepidly second-hand emotion. The genuine New Wine of a new poet of this new age will inevitably, as in Jesus's famous parable, crack and burst the old generic 'wine-skins' it's poured into (I.971–1002). Aurora speaks here, as ever, with her author's voice. Barrett was 'inclined to think that we want new *forms*, as well as thoughts. The old gods are dethroned. Why should we go back to the antique moulds, classical moulds, as they are so improperly called? If it is a necessity of Art to do so, why then those critics are right who hold that Art is exhausted and the world too worn out for poetry. I do not, for my part, believe this ... Let us all aspire rather to *Life*, and let the dead bury their dead' – momentously quoting Jesus's words to a would-be disciple who wanted to take time off to bury his father.[13] Just a few months later Barrett was upset to hear from her brother George not only that Tennyson was poorly, but that he was hard at work on a new poem 'in blank verse and a fairy tale, and called the "University", the university-members being all females'. Gossip in legal London had clearly got wind of Tennyson's 'The Princess', a poem not at all about fairies, but indeed a cross between backward-facing Milton epicity and pastoral done in Victorian-medieval dress, a scared dream-vision about a College for women involving agitated debates about women's future and role and education and the threat posed to men and traditional marriage and motherhood, all reported on the people's open-day at the grand Sir Walter's great house and garden. Barrett did not 'know what to think – it makes me open my eyes. Now isn't the world too old and fond of steam, for blank verse poems, in ever so many books, to be written on the fairies?'[14] She was wrong about the fairies, but gossip had grasped Tennyson's latest reluctance to take on a modern subject unless it could be coddled in formal cast-offs from poetry's old dressing-up box.

It was far too late, Barrett thought, now in the age of steam, for Tennysonian retroversion, the medievalizing of his *Poems* (1832), the Arthurian tendency affirmed in his *Poems* (1842) – which included Tennyson's loud shot in the direction of what became his longest poem *Idylls of the King*, namely his 'Morte d'Arthur'. Such poems were, Aurora Leigh advises with great critical verve, a dismal refusal of the epicity of the modern. She won't dictate as to the aptest poetic form for the modern subject

---

[13]   EBB and RB *Letters*, I.45–46; to Robert Browning, 20 March 1845.
[14]   Ibid, I.444; to Robert Browning, 31 January 1846.

('What form is best for poems? Let me think / Of forms less, and the external. Trust the spirit', V.223–224), but Tennyson-inspired Pre-Raphaelite fables (in turn the inspirer of William Morris's Arthurianism in *The Defence of Guenevere, And Other Poems*, 1858), are certainly not the way for poetry to render the 'times'. As Aurora puts it in these sharp, almost Robert-Browningesque lines:

> I do distrust the poet who discerns
> No character or glory in his times,
> And trundles back his soul five hundred years,
> Past moat and drawbridge, into a castle-court,
> To sing – oh, not of lizard or of toad
> Alive i' the ditch there, – 'twere excusable,
> But of some black chief, half knight, half sheep-lifter,
> Some beauteous dame, half chattel and half queen,
> As dead as must be, for the greater part,
> The poems made on their chivalric bones;
> And that's no wonder: death inherits death.
> Nay, if there's room for poets in this world
> A little overgrown, (I think there is)
> Their sole work is to represent the age,
> Their age, not Charlemagne's, – this live, throbbing age,
> That brawls, cheats, maddens, calculates, aspires,
> And spends more passion, more heroic heat,
> Betwixt the mirrors of its drawing-rooms,
> Than Roland with his knights at Roncesvalles.
> To flinch from modern varnish, coat or flounce,
> Cry out for togas and the picturesque,
> Is fatal, – and foolish too. King Arthur's self
> Was commonplace to Lady Guenever;
> And Camelot to minstrels seemed as flat
> As Fleet Street to our poets.
>   Never flinch
> But still, unscrupulously epic[15], catch

---

[15] 'Unscrupulously Epic': title of Ch 4 of Isobel Hurst, *Victorian Women Writers and the Classics: The Feminine of Homer* (Oxford University Press, Oxford, 2006), 101–129, which attempts to portray Barrett Browning as a rather superior Hellenist, doing a modern poetic epic in a sort of updated classical mode (in a poem admittedly full of Greek allusions), and thus (with Augusta Webster, who like Barrett Browning, translated Aeschylus's *Prometheus* (op cit, 184–185)) countering the general lack of classical abilities due to women's exclusion from male classical education (which Hurst is rather good at charting). But Hurst quite fails to appreciate that when Barrett Browning invokes a necessary epicity she's thinking of what contemporary novels do. (And it really is no good calling in the 14-year- old Barrett Barrett's 'Battle of Marathon', the poem 'Hector and Andromache', and 'Casa Guido Windows', as evidence of revived strong epic stuff on classical lines. That's really making a critical meal of small potatoes.)

> Upon the burning lava of a song
> The full-veined, heaving double-breasted Age:
> That, when the next shall come, the men of that
> May touch the impress with reverent hand, and say
> 'Behold, – the paps we all have sucked!
> This bosom seems to beat still, or at least
> It sets ours beating: this is living art,
> Which thus presents and thus records true life.'
>
> (V.189–222)

Tumours, Warts and Wens, and The Social Smut of Towns

We hear a lot about the poetic 'book' that Aurora writes, fired by these modernizing, and novelizing principles – a book 'organised by and implying life' Aurora tells us, by dint of its investment in 'tumours, warts and wens' (III.342–343). It wins Romney's 'soul', abolishing his old prejudices against the woman poet of social principles (VIII.261ff). But we never actually hear from it: it exists for us as all telling and no showing (to use Henry James's famous distinction). We do, though, get the strong impression that we're to take *Aurora Leigh* itself as the exemplary case of what Aurora theorizes, and allegedly practices – an unflinching epic of the modern; 'unscrupulous' in the sense of foregoing restrictive scruples about women's, and women poets', domains; the outmoded scruples by which 'The full-veined, heaving, double-breasted Age' has to don a *toga* or some other *picturesque* old bit of kit.

And usually unflinchingly, *Aurora Leigh* does give us an in-your-face fable of the harsh world, of the struggle for survival in the modern industrialized world, especially of London and Paris. The poor seamstress Marian, named as a deliberate riposte to Tennyson's medievalized heroine Mariana, daughter of a wife-beating drunk, evades her mother's attempt to trade her for sex only to be tricked into a Parisian brothel, where she's drugged and raped, and landed with a baby to nurture in near-destitution. Here, in every sense, is what Aurora's narrative voice calls 'the social smut of towns' (III.960). And presented to us with a constant showing of how sexual moral scruples are, just like top-down class distinctions, the privileged domain of the well-to-do. Marian's beloved schoolfriend, lovely laughing Rose, a motherless child, is now on the game in London (" "I heard her laugh last night in Oxford Street. / I'd pour out half my blood to stop that laugh. / Poor Rose, poor Rose!" said Marian,' III.927–929). Aurora carefully disclaims Romney's socialism and socialist action – Fourieresque social action lacks, she thinks, the individualistic soul that poetry provides

(II.475–497) – but her religiose welcome of the crowd, 'the coarse town-sights', and all that ('I would be bold and bear / To look into the swarthiest face of things, / For God's sake who has made them', VI.137–149), makes for a poetic as nearly socialist as makes no odds. The people from the grim slum of St Giles who 'ooze' into the posh church of St James, Piccadilly, for the (aborted) marriage of Romney to Marian are, to be sure, described as a 'crammed mass' of frighteningly vile, violent, degenerate ugliness ('as if you had stirred up hell / To heave its lowest dreg-fiends uppermost / In fiery swirls of slime'). But those democratically minded modern critics who have read this horrified passage (III.553–601) as unforgivably hostile to this crowd from the slums have missed its point. Barrett Browning's business is to satirize the judgement of Romney's snobby friends who see these social others as beyond the human pale. They think Romney's a lunatic for wanting to marry a woman from the lower classes. It's all very well, they think, for Prince Albert to take up 'This modern question of the poor', and build model houses for them; but 'moderation' is necessary. Otherwise society is 'dismembered'. Albert was President of the Society for Improving the Condition of the Labouring Classes; but would he 'stop his carriage in Cheapside / To shake a common fellow by the fist?' No, not even if the fellow's name were Shakespeare (*shake: Shakespeare* – a joke!). 'We draw a line', they say (IV.662–669). And the poet is drawing the line at sympathizing with *them*; and with superior Lady Waldemar, who persuades Marian to step back from marrying Romney because a lower-class wife won't do for such a rich man (Waldemar is the real 'vile', i.e. low, one, Aurora tells her: VII.292–293); and with Marian's wealthy French employer, an adulterous wife herself, who chucks Marian onto the street when she discovers the 'filthy secret' of her pregnancy (VII.74). For all she cares, Marian can throw herself into the River Seine, 'Like others of my sort' – women deemed sexually 'fallen' (VII.80–81). Aurora would 'rather take the wind-side of the stews' –, that is mix with prostitutes – 'Than touch such women with my finger-end!'. Living their lie of public respectability makes them morally inferior to the 'poor street-walker': ' "The devil's most devilish when respectable" ' (VII.92–105).

All of which was too much for a lot of contemporary critics – a set of gross matters which denied, in their view, poetry's idealizing duties. 'It is not the province of the poet to depict things as they are', said William E Aytoun, the critic and satirist of Spasmodic excess, Professor of Rhetoric and Belles Lettres at Edinburgh University (in *Blackwood's Magazine*, January 1857), 'but so to refine and purify as to purge out the grosser matter; and thus he cannot do it if he attempts to give a faithful picture of his own times, for in order to be faithful, he must necessarily include much which is abhorrent to art, and revolting to the taste, for which no exactness of delineation will be accepted as a proper excuse. All poetical characters, all poetical situations, must be idealised'.[16] In other words, poetry must flinch, girlishly. Which Barrett Browning won't do. 'What has given most offence, more than the sort of Marian – far more! – has been the reference to the condition of women in our cities, which a woman oughtn't to refer to by any manner of means, says the conventional tradition. Now I have thought deeply otherwise. If a woman ignores these wrongs, then may women as a sex continue to suffer them; there is no help for any of us – let us be dumb and die. I have spoken therefore, and in speaking have used plain words'.[17] The plain fact of London's thousands of prostitutes mustn't be flinched from: the army of poor women meeting 'libertine' males' 'gross' bodily 'need'. In Romney's words, this trade

> ... slurs our cruel streets from end to end
> With eighty thousand women in one smile,
> Who only smile at night beneath the gas.
> (VIII.409–415)

(Nobody knew the exact number. 'What of the forty-thousand wretched women in this city?', Barrett Browning asked in 1855; 'The silent writhing of them is to me more appalling than the roar of cannons', i.e. more horrifying than the scandalous losses of life in the Crimean War then raging.[18]) The poet and poem were speaking plainly and deliberately: taking up the prose-writers' subject and way. As the critical objectors knew. For Aytoun, poetic language 'is not that of common life, which belongs essentially to the domain of prose': the common genre prejudice. 'To dignify the mean, is not the province of poetry – let us rather say that there are atmospheres so tainted that in them poetry cannot live. Its course is in the empyrean or in the fresh wholesome air, but if it attempts to descend to pits and charnel-vaults, it is stifled by the noxious exhalations'. Aytoun exempted Marian from any hint of mean-ness – her presentation as 'mother of a hapless child' compared well with 'The Cry of the Children', 'one of the most pathetic and tear-stirring poems in the English Language' – but the rest was mean and prosey. And to prove the prosiness he set long segments of Barrett Browning's blank verse as continuous 'prose' – a trick also practised by John Nichol in

---

[16] Long extracts from Aytoun are given in Margaret Reynolds's wonderfully compendious Norton Critical Edition of *Aurora Leigh* (NY and London, 1996), 409–422.

[17] EBB to Mrs Martin, February 1857, *Letters of EBB*, ed Frederic Kenyon (2 vols, 1897), II.254.

[18] *Letters*, ed Kenyon, II.213. *The Return of the Number of Brothels and Prostitutes within the Metropolitan Police District, As Nearly as Can be Ascertained* (May 1857) claimed 8,600 prostitutes known to the Metropolitan Police – though that was only part of all London. Quoted in Liza Picard's lively account of prostitution in *Victorian London: The Life of a City 1840–1870* (2005; Phoenix Books, 2006), 310.

his *Westminster Review* review: 'cases in which Mrs Browning has broken loose altogether from the meshes of versification, and run riot in prose cut up into lines of ten syllables'.[19]

In The Phalarian Bull

The critics' re-formatting trick was unlikely to disconcert Carlylean Barrett Browning all that much. '[A]sk Carlyle', Aurora instructs at one point (V.156). And Barrett Browning plainly has. Her poetry is deep inside the Phalarian Bull of tormented modern society, with Carlyle. In his *Past and Present* (1843) (Book 3, Chapter 13), Carlyle took the brazen bull in which the Sicilian tyrant Phalaris imprisoned and cooked his prisoners as a metaphor for intolerable modern times. In 'no time since the beginning of Society, was the lot of those same dumb millions of toilers so entirely unbearable as it is in the days now passing over us. It is not to die, or even to die of hunger, that makes a man wretched ... it is to die slowly all our life long, imprisoned in a deaf, dead, Infinite Injustice, as in the accursed iron belly of a "Phalaris Bull!".' Romney has heard those cries, the cries

> Of tortured prisoners in the polished brass
> Of that Phalarian bull, society,
> Which seems to bellow bravely like ten bulls,
> But, if you listen, moans and cries instead
> Despairingly, like victims tossed and gored
> And trampled by their hoofs.

He heard them 'too close' he says; which turned him, 'stupid', into a socialist (VIII.385ff). They've turned Aurora Leigh and her author (more wisely we're to think) into protesting prose-poets, as it were novelists in verse. Whose fable and plot unashamedly work the novelists' territory.

The protest of Marian against the posh ladies berating for laziness the poor seamstress who has worked all through the night because she's an hour late with a frock (IV.240–250) could have come from the Christian Socialist novelist Charles Kingsley's great polemical pamphlet on the life and work of outworking dress-makers *Cheap Clothes and Nasty* (1850). Sympathy for 'fallen' women and girls is what Victorian novelists promote heavily – Dickens in *Dombey and Son* (1846–1848) and *Bleak House* (1852–1853), Mrs Gaskell in *Ruth* (1855), George Eliot in *Adam Bede* (1859), Trollope in *The Vicar of Bullhampton* (1869–1870), Hardy in *Tess of the D'Urbervilles*

---

[19] *Westminster Review* 68 (October 1857): in the Reynolds Norton edition of *Aurora Leigh*, 425–430.

(1891). *Aurora Leigh* keeps chiming strikingly with *Bleak House*. The fog that denotes Aurora's city consciousness – 'I saw / Fog only, the great tawny weltering fog, / Involve the passive city, strangle it / Alive, and draw it off into the void, / Spires, bridges, streets, and squares, as if a spunge / Had wiped out London' (III.178–183) – comes straight from the opening page of Dickens's novel. Barrett Browning shares utterly Dickens's resistance to the pious ones who would read children born out of wedlock as moral outsiders, along with their mothers. There's a strong resonance between Dickens's appearance-keeping Lady Dedlock and Barrett Browning's French lady despised for her hypocritical double life as wife and mistress. George Eliot in her January 1857 *Westminster Review* piece noticeably praises and also dispraises *Aurora Leigh* for its novelistic tendencies. The poem is good because it fits George Eliot's programme for the novel as set out in several *Westminster Review* articles and the practice which was just beginning in her own *Scenes of Clerical Life* (1856) – 'acute observation of life, its yearning sympathy with multiform human sorrow, its store of personal domestic love and joy ... given out in a delightful alternation of pathos, reflection, satire playful and pungent, and picturesque description.' It's bad because it imitates the gothicity of Charlotte Brontë's *Jane Eyre* (1847) in having its hero blinded, like Brontë's Rochester, in the fire caused caused by malevolent proles at his stately home (this 'lavish mutilation of heroes' bodies, which has become the habit of novelists ... weakens instead of strengthening tragic effect').[20] Barrett Browning said that she had forgotten *Jane Eyre*,[21] but it does rather haunt her poem. Aurora's resistance to entering marriage with Romney as a mere helpmate in his charity work smacks of Jane Eyre's refusing to go to India with St John Rivers as a missionary-wife. Barrett Browning acknowledged that the story of Marian's rape in a French brothel whilst drugged owed a lot to Samuel Richardson's novel *Clarissa* (1747–1749).[22] Margaret Reynolds points out the similarities between Marian's French fate and the innocent Fleur de Marie's in Eugène Sue's proletarian French shocker *Les Mystères de Paris* (1843).[23]

Aurora Leigh amply brings home the truth of the Barrett Browning contention that for accomplishing the modern subject of its kind the poet needed

---

[20]   *Westminster Review* (January 1857, 306–310); Reynolds' edition, 407–408.

[21]   Letter of Anna Jameson, 26 December 1856, *Letters*, edn cit, II.245–246

[22]   Letter to her sister Arabella, 4 October 1856, *The Letters of Elizabeth Barrett Browning to her Sister Arabella*, ed Scott Lewis, 2 vols (Wedgestone Press, Waco, Texas. 2002), II, 257–258.

[23]   *Aurora Leigh*, Reynolds edn, 214, fn 4. George Eliot was sceptical about the 'noxious', 'miserable fallacy' encouraged by Eugène Sue's 'idealized proletaires', 'that high morality and refined sentiment can grow out of harsh social relations, ignorance, and want'. 'The Natural History of German Life' (*Westminster Review*, July 1856, 51–79); *Selected Essays, Poems and Other Writings*, eds AS Byatt and Nicholas Warren (Penguin, Harmondsworth, 1990), 111.

the thrusts and indignations normal among the novelists and Carlyleans, the provincials and dissenters (of all stripes), the speakers from below and their familiars. The poetic familiars of *Aurora Leigh* amply confirm the position: not least *Aurora Leigh*'s poetic near-neighbour, Hood's 'The Song of the Shirt', which appeared anonymously in *Punch* at Christmas 1843, and 'The Bridge of Sighs' which came out in *Hood's Magazine*, May 1844. The implication is strong that the dead woman suicide fished out of the Thames in 'The Bridge of Sighs' was an unhappy woman of the streets and sister of the womankind who throw themselves into the Seine in *Aurora Leigh*. Of course Barrett knew of Hood and read his shortlived *Magazine*, 1843–1845, though perhaps not too closely or regularly, since she didn't seem to have come across all of Robert Browning's poems which appeared there.[24] (One also wants her to have known Dante Gabriel Rossetti's 'Jenny' with its heartbreakingly sympathetic prostitute, but that's impossible, because although it was composed in 1847–1848 it wasn't published until 1870, along with the other poems exhumed from Lizzie Siddal's grave, fourteen years after *Aurora Leigh* came out, and indeed nine years after Barrett's death.) And most revealingly for the Dissenter connection with radically disposed poetry, the mark of Barrett's co-religionist and closest poetic familiar, her husband Robert Browning, is all over *Aurora Leigh*. His wife's poem can be, in fact, almost parodically Browningesque. Take that passage where Aurora berates her contemporaries for shrinking from proletarian disfigurements, the bad bodies of 'people in the rough' (VI.202):

> How is this
> That men of science, osteologists
> And surgeons, beat some poets in respect
> For nature, – count nought common or unclean,
> Spend raptures upon perfect specimens
> Of indurated veins, distorted joints,
> Or beautiful new cases of curved spine,
> While we, we are shocked at nature's falling off,
> We dare to shrink back from her warts and blains.
>
> (VI.171–179)

The plain-speaking, the close-up bad-bodiliness, the scientific comparison (those *osteologists*) are outright *hommage* to Robert Browning's way with uglified modernity. The gentry-affronting ruined faces of *Aurora Leigh*'s poor crowding into the Piccadilly church ('such strangled fronts / Such obdurate jaws were thrown up constantly / To twit you with your race, corrupt your blood, / And grind to devilish colours all your dreams', IV.588–593), yet one more result of Barrett Browning's project to embrace the living

---

[24]   *Letters of RB & EBB* (July 21 1845), 134–135.

subject despite its 'warts and blains' (its 'tumours, warts and wens', III.342), are straight from Robert Browning democratized palette. This is the clientele of the Zion Chapel Meeting in Browning's 'Christmas-Eve', the scruffy congregation of smelly, dirty, ugly proles – the shoemaker's lad, 'With wizened face in want of soap'; 'The man with the handkerchief' who 'untied it' and 'Showed us a horrible wen inside it' (123–124; 177–178); 'these ruins of humanity, / This flesh worn out to rags and tatters' (1317–1318) – who are embraced, finally, as being and possessing truly divine (and Biblical) 'treasure' in 'the earthen vessel' ('Christmas-Eve', 1313). Robert Browning was an outsider poet exemplarily refusing to take those unprepossessing Londoners as other than children of God – mindful, as Barrett is, of God's rebuke to Jewish St Peter for wanting to treat Gentiles as untouchably taboo, 'common or unclean' (Acts 10.14–15). The Robert-Browningesque passage contrasting osteologists with poets goes on to lament the way poets dwell on lilies and roses, ignoring 'the hungry beggar-boy' staring aghast at their careless way with oranges (they throw them away half-eaten) and who has more poeticity in him than the flowers and other conventionally poetic stuff the poet prefers (181–197). And that boy is so Robert Browning: the urchin Lippo Lippi to the life, the waif whose artistic eye was schooled 'Watching folk's faces to know who will fling / The bit of half-stripped grape-bunch he desires' ('Fra Lippi Lippi', 114–115).

Conflicted Gents

The Brownings and their kind were not slumming: their sort of Dissent was indeed a religion for the social outsider which disposed them to their poetic radicalism. There were, of course, many actual poetic slummers: like William Morris, the very rich socialist, and the other radical Oxford Boys, such as Algernon Swinburne, Arthur Symons, Edward Carpenter, and Arthur Clough – the ultra-'modern' Clough. And some of the period's poetic democratism was sexually driven as theirs was. Being fleshly like Swinburne, and pederastic like Symons, and sexually rough-trading like Carpenter or Oscar Fingall O'Flahertie Wills Wilde, was inevitably socially lowering. Carpenter embraced the modern subject, socialist redemption for the modern city, with the same zest that he embraced his Sheffield metal-workers. For him it came to the same thing. Wilde's wonderfully literatured aesthetic symbolist escapist loftiness was brought down, through his rough-trading, to the very modern lower-depths of the treadmill and unknotting the old hemp ropes in Reading prison, as gloomily dwelt on in 'The Ballad of Reading Gaol'. But it is very telling just how much even the radical and radicalized gents were commonly so conflicted and contradictory in their verses and poetic careers, their poetic careers drawn now this way now that between the progressiveness of their modern politics and sexual-politics on the one hand, and the retro-gressions, the classicizings, and other escapisms on the other, which their class and education so readily sponsored.

Morris's poetic career is one long unsettled swinging between the extremes of *Jason and the Argonauts* (in *The Earthly Paradise*), of Beowulf and Guinevere, and doing socialist songs ('O ye rich men hear and tremble! for with words the sound is rife: / "Once for you and death we laboured; changed hence forward is the strife. / We are men, and we shall battle for the world of men and life; / And our host is marching on"': thus 'The March of the Workers' in his Socialist League volume *Chants for Socialists* (1885), to be sung to the tune of the American 'Battle-Hymn of the Republic', aka 'John Brown's Body'). The variant poetic turns of Swinburne, the radical who never had to do a day's work in his life, have him enthusing fraughtly and all at once over his catalogue of glamorously unhealthy mythological and literary sex-objects, Prosperpine, Hermaphroditus, Itylus, Fragoletta and the like, and (as in his *Songs Before Sunrise*, 1871) his rosters of up-to-the-minute heroes of European republican causes.[25] It would be hard to be more modern in your poetry than Clough the democrat, revolutionary, atheist, world-traveller; hard as well to be more anxious about your up-to-dateness.

Clough's big ultra-capacious poems 'The Bothie of Tober-na-Vuolich' (1848) and 'Amours de Voyage' (1858) embrace the world, like the big Victorian novels they resemble. They come crammed with quotidian stuff and Clough's reflections on the hot themes of the day. He was never not enthusiastically *engagé* – right to the end of his life when he was active not least in assisting his wife's cousin Florence Nightingale in her post-Crimean army-medicine and hospital-reforming crusades – and his poetry tracks his every current enthusiasm. 'The Bothie of Tober-na-Vuolich', story of a dem-ocratic Oxford undergraduate's proletarian love-affair, is marinaded in Clough's keenness not just on male bourgeois sexual adventuring among lower-class females (the persistent Pre-Raphaelite trope), but on the European revolutionary movements of the 1840s, as well as in his angers over the suf-ferings of the Irish peasantry in the terrible 1840s potato-famines. William Michael Rossetti had the *mot juste* for Clough: praising 'The Bothie' in the first number of the Pre-Raphaelite magazine *The Germ* (January 1850) for its 'peculiar modernness'. Peculiar modernness indeed. *Amours de Voyage*, Clough's bustling rag-bag of Italian correspondence, is a wonderfully sharp-eyed, multi-voiced visitors' tour of the whole contemporary Italian horizon, where church and politicians are watched jostling for supremacy ('George has just seen Garibaldi') in the welter of Roman ruin, ecclesiastical over-kill, and Florentine cultural over-bearing ('Galleries only oppress me'). Here was

---

[25]   Mindful discussion in Stephanie Kudick, ' "A Sword of Song": Swinburne's Republican Aesthetics in "Songs Before Sunrise" ', *Victorian Studies*, 43:2 (2001), 253–278.

the modern world done in colloquially prosey long lines that led straight to Edward Carpenter's *Towards Democracy*. Here was a flatter, plainer Robert Browning, rising (or sinking) in places to a lovely camping-up of Browning ('A gondola here, and a gondola there', as Clough's café-table poem 'Dipsychus' has it). Yet for all his engagement Clough remains a tourist, a visitor, a sort of slummer. Claude, Clough's English hero-abroad, is always somewhere else when the revolutionary trigger is pulled, sipping his *caffè-latte* as the besieging French exchange fire with the Italians (Canto II.v), always passing by, Murray's *Guide Book* in hand, *en route* to or from some tourist destination, when a man is killed ('So, I have seen a man killed!', Canto II.vii).

Matthew Reynolds pertinently invokes the contemporary spying scandal in which it was discovered that London Home Office agents were secretly opening the correspondence of the exiled Italian revolutionary Mazzini, and suggests Clough's readers are cast in the role of spies, prying into the private correspondence of Clough's people.[26] But if Clough's readers are turned into spies it's because Clough's observing travellers already are. In fact they resemble double-agents, like their author, pretending to modern political sympathies which in fact they sit rather loose to (Clough's kept-up irony, sarcasm often, is a marker of this mixed-mindedness). Like Clough, these people can, and do, always go back to England. They're only temporarily out of their safe bourgeois nest. The undergraduates of 'The Bothie' may go peasant for a while, but remain uneraseably Oxonian. Like Clough, they're never not looking over their shoulder – 'tell it not in St James's, / Whisper it not in thy courts, O Christ Church!' says Claude, unable not to think of what they might think of him back in the English corridors of power and at Oxford as he dreams for the moment of riding into revolutionary battle, and recalls some lines of the French revolutionary song the *Marseillaise* about young heroes falling and the earth bringing new ones to fight against tyranny (Canto II.iii). These characters belong, as did their author, to two worlds, the old and the new – a double agency marked by this particular modern's perpetual lookings over his poetic shoulder: revising Dryden's translation of Plutarch's *Lives* of ancient Greeks and Romans (1859), translating Homer, redoing *The Canterbury Tales* (his *Mari Magno*), even as he joins George Eliot in her undoing of the Gospels (in his poem 'Epi-Strauss-ium'), and talks up Italian liberty. In his Oxford lecture 'On Translating Homer: Last Words' (31 November 1861), Mathew Arnold emotionally singled out his late friend (dead only eighteen days before) for the 'Homeric qualities' of 'The Bothie' – 'out-of-doors freshness, life natural, buoyant rapidity'. Certain phrases from that poem 'come back now to my ear with the true Homeric ring'. What Arnold now thinks of 'oftenest, is the Homeric

---

26   Matthew Reynolds, 'Repulsive Clough', Ch 6, *The Realms of Verse*, 153–156.

simplicity of his literary life'. The most patent of moderns, Arnold wants us to think, was, in life as well as in art, a true classic. And it's a tribute that Clough would, clearly, not have been terribly upset by. After all, his favourite metre is an attempted version of Virgil's quantitative hexameter, or six-footed line. Clough was translating Homer into it as he died.

Classicists and The Modern Vortex

Here was a Janus-like double-face, the poet in a two-way poetic street. A street Matthew Arnold wished his friend weren't in. Arnold's hostility towards Clough's revolutionary enthusiasms of the 1840s was pretty clear. 'Citizen Clough' Arnold dubbed him, satirically, as if Clough were some dangerous activist in the French Revolution. 'God knows it, I am with you', Arnold's sonnet 'To a Republican Friend, 1848' assured Clough:

> The armies of the homeless and unfed –
> If these are yours, if this is what you are,
> Then am I yours, and what you feel, I share.

Two massive *if*'s. And Arnold's follow-up sonnet 'Continued' tells Clough that 'patience' is better than revolutionary action; the day of social utopia will not dawn 'at a human nod'; and 'liberated man' will still suffer from traditional sinfulness, 'Lust avarice, envy', and so still have to stand 'face to face with God'. Sin and divine judgement had better be Arnold's concern. He prefers an unworldly quietism – the subject of his poem 'The World and the Quietist' (1848?), addressed to 'Critias', ie Clough. Poetry should be for contemplation, free from the world's emotional disturbance, as Arnold puts it in his poem 'Resignation' which advocates meditativeness as the role for poet and poem. Clough thought the 'mournful rhymes' of the *Bhagavad Gita* a deplorable model for the modern poet. Arnold, though, persisted with his preference. 'The rush and roar of practical life will always have a dizzying and attracting effect upon the most collected spectator, and tend to draw him into its vortex', Arnold insisted in his notorious essay on 'The Function of Criticism at the Present Time' (*Essays in Criticism*, I, 1865). It 'is only by remaining collected, and refusing to lend himself to the point of view of the practical man, that the critic can do the practical man any service'. And what went for the Arnoldian critic would also go for Arnold the poet. So his poetry keeps turning away from the distracting annoyances of 'this iron time / Of doubts, disputes, distractions, fears', in the words, and in the manner, of his poem 'Memorial Verses' (dated April 1850).

'Memorial Verses' was written, it claims, 'by Wordsworth's tomb', in praise of the dead Goethe and Byron and the recently deceased Wordsworth – the

ic voice', now dumb. A 'triple Epicede' the radical Unitarian critic
binson called it, with little warmth (*epicede*, *epicedion*, from Greek
n, a funeral ode) in token of the poem's deliberately ancient manner
('very classical, or it would not be Matthew Arnold's'). Carefully retro in
form, this epicede invokes Wordsworth as the great escapist poet who is
embraced as the model of Arnold's desired escapist poetic retrospection, the
late poet who took Arnold back to his own pastoral childhood and the innocent pastoral childhood of the world:

> He found us when the age had bound
> Our souls in its benumbing round;
> He spoke, and loosed our heart in tears.
> He laid us as we lay at birth
> On the cool flowery lap of earth,
> Smiles broke from us and we had ease;
> The hills were round us, and the breeze
> Went o'er the sun-lit fields again;
> Our foreheads felt the wind and rain
> Our youth returned; for there was shed
> On spirits that had long been dead,
> Spirits dried up and closely furled,
> The freshness of the early world.

Modernity was, quite literally, too much for Arnold. His troubled, meander-
ing inaugural lecture as Professor of Poetry at Oxford (14 November 1857),
'On the Modern Element in Literature', spells out the problem of modernity
as an overwhelming muchness from which he, poet and critic, arguing for
all poets and critics, demands 'an intellectual deliverance':

> The demand arises, because our present age has around it a copious and com-
> plex past; it arises, because the present age exhibits to the individual man who
> contemplates it the spectacle of a vast multitude of facts awaiting and inviting
> his comprehension. The deliverance consists in man's comprehension of this
> present and past. It begins when our mind begins to enter into possession of
> the general ideas which are the law of this vast multitude of facts. It is perfect
> when we have acquired that harmonious acqiescence of mind which we feel in
> contemplating a grand spectacle that is intelligible to us; when we have lost
> that impatient irritation of mind which we feel in the presence of an immense,
> moving, confused, spectacle which, while it perpetually excites our curiosity,
> perpetually baffles our comprehension.

Greek literature, Arnold alleges, evinced this deliverance a lot; Roman
Virgil somewhat, but not much. As historiography, Sir Walter Raleigh's
History of the World is uncritical, irrational and childish compared with
Thucydides' *History of the Peloponnesian War*. For Arnold and his

contemporaries the deliverance is still to seek. They are, alas, quite unlike Sophocles, whose 'poetry' is unrivalled in its adequacy to its time, its 'unprejudiced and intelligent observation of human affairs', all 'idealized and glorified by the grace and light shed over them from the noblest poetic feeling' – Sophocles of whom 'I have ventured to say ... that he "saw life steadily, and saw it whole".' (Arnold is quoting his Sophocles-tribute sonnet of 1848, 'To a Friend' – the friend being Clough.) Victorians of Clough's type are, it's implied, unsteady and partial, more like Roman Horace.

Horace was indeed the Victorian gentleman poet's favourite imitable classical author. It was much easier (for reasons not least of length) for the classicizers to translate or imitate (and parody) an Horatian Ode than to translate or replicate a whole Homeric or Virgilian epic, and Horace in any case suited so many Victorian moods: patriotism ('Dulce et decorum est pro patria mori'), melancholy over life's transience, the elegiac, and the need for male friendship. *In Memoriam*, the great elegy for a dead friend, is full of Horatian echoes, as Norman Vance, fullest of examiners of the Victorian debt to Ancient Rome, shows.[27] Tennyson's deep Horatianism is nicely underlined by CS Calverley, lovely Horatian translator and parodist (author of the Horace-tribute 'Ode to Tobacco') whose translation of Horace's Ode I.24, the elegy for Quintilius, adopts the verse-form of *In Memoriam*, and who even took Tennyson's *In Memoriam* CVII, 'The time admits not flowers or leaves / To deck the banquet', which owes much to Horace's Ode I.9 ('Vides ut alta') and translated it into Latin, in Horatian Alcaics. Tennyson thought the four-line stanza of the Horatian Alcaic was 'the grandest of metres', which he tried to imitate 'in some measure' in 'The Daisy' (1853), and in his poems to eminent classicists – 'To Professor Jebb' (1889), preface to his poetic version of the Greek story of 'Demeter and Persephone'; and 'To the Master of Balliol' (1892), for Benjamin Jowett, father-figure of the Oxford *paiderasti*, preface to another poeticized Greek story, 'The Death of Oenone'. For his part Branwell Brontë attempted some verse translations of Horace Odes; William Gladstone, the Prime Minister, Tennyson's friend and consultant on classical metres, did so successfully; as did Bulwer Lytton of *The Last Days of Pompeii* fame (*Odes and Epodes*, 1869); and John Conington, Corpus Christi College, Oxford's first Professor of Latin, the *paiderasti*-prophet whose poetic reputation hung greatly on his generally admired verse translations of Horace

---

[27] See *The Victorians and Ancient Rome* (Blackwell, Oxford, 1997), Ch 8, 'Horace', 174–193 (early version: 'Horace and the Nineteenth Century', in *Horace Made New: Horatian Influences on British Writing from the Renaissance to the Twentieth Century*, eds Charles Martindale and David Hopkins (Cambridge University Press, Cambridge, 1993), 199–216.

in his *Satires and Epistles* (1870).[28] Clough has his hero Claude translate Horace's celebration of the pagan deities as a gesture against the Christianizing of Roman remains (*Amours de Voyage*, I.viii.156–171). Even Arnold himself couldn't resist what he called the 'Horatian Echo', in his 1847 poem 'Horatian Echo (To An Ambitious Friend)' – attentive to that echo resounding through the English tradition in its heeding of Milton's Sonnet 18, to Cyriac Skinner, itself in debt to Horace's Ode 2.11.1–4.

But this hot Victorian favourite won't do as top model for Arnold. What's up with Horace, according to Arnold, is what is up with contemporary poets who try to take in modernity but are flummoxed by it – poets like Browning, of course, who embraces the 'world's multitudinousness' but is, Arnold thinks, 'prevailed over' by it (Arnold to Clough, September 1848 – quoted in my first chapter, 'Words, Words, Words ...'). Odes to tobacco, Browning's excited curiosity over anything and everything, are all very well, but fail if, like Horace, the poet finds it 'impossible to ... rejoice in the variety, the movement of human life with the children of the world; to be serious over the depth, the significance of human life with the wise'. 'Horace warms himself before the transient fire of human animation and human pleasure while he can'. He is serious 'when he reflects that the fire must soon go out'. Such reflections can be 'exquisite', but they are not 'interpretative', and so not 'fortifying'. Arnold must have been thinking of great poems like Horace's *Songs*, 'Vitae summa brevis spem nos vetat incohare longam' (The brevity of life forbids us from going in for any far-reaching hope) and 'Non sum qualis eram bonae sub regno Cynarae' (I am no longer the man I was when ruled over by the good Cynara), done into English in the 1890s, with Horace's Latin as titles, by Oxonian Ernest Dowson, the quintessential end-of-century Decadent (friend of Aubrey Beardsley and Oscar Wilde); or of Horace's Ode IV.7 which begins 'Diffugere Nives', 'The snows are fled away', and celebrates inevitable death ('We are dust and dreams'), the poem that provoked the Shocking AE Housman Classroom Event when the rather tight-lipped Professor surprised his students by reading and translating it with unusual emotion and fleeing the room with the words 'That I regard as the most beautiful poem in ancient literature'. It was Housman's only published translation of a Latin poem. Neither Dowson nor Housman was interested in being spiritually 'fortifying'. For his own part Arnold would going on looking for that self-fortification in his beloved

---

[28] *The Victorians and Ancient Rome*, 178. Mark Pattison, though, was not a fan. Conington 'abandons himself to the laziest of all occupations with the classics, that, namely, of translating them into English; he translates Horace, I dare say, no worse and no better than the scores who have translated it before him'. Quoted in *Daphne into Laurel: Translations of Classical Poetry from Chaucer to the Present*, ed Richard Stoneman (Duckworth, London, 1982), 260.

Greeks – reposing in what the last words of his 'Modern Element' lecture called 'the absolute, the enduring interest of Greek literature and, above all, of Greek poetry.'[29]

Here, then, was a large and calculated aloofness from the perplexing modernity which Arnold encountered every day in his work as a school inspector. But which he could not, nonetheless, keep out of his poems. His 1860s poem 'East London' visits, awed, an East End Congregationalist minister, the Revd William Tyler, whom Arnold met while inspecting schools in 'squalid' Bethnal Green and Spitalfields. How, the poet asked the 'preacher', did he cope 'Ill and o'erworked', in 'this scene'? ' "Bravely!" said he; "for I of late have been / Much cheered with thoughts of Christ, the living bread" '. Being cheered like that is to make a heaven on earth; it is light in the urban, modern, 'night', setting Tyler 'Above the howling senses' ebb and flow'. Sacrament in the city; the sacrament of the city. It's not Arnold's idea of living bread. He and his poems are desperate to flee the howling realities of Bethnal Green which, vexingly, remain within earshot. There's a kind of pastoral calm in London's Kensington Gardens, a rural retreat, as 'Lines in Kensington Gardens' has it, within 'the girdling city's hum', where birds sing, and bourgeois kiddies play with their toys watched over by their nurses, and Wordsworth's Nature is to be invoked in the words of Goethe's Young Werther:

> Calm soul of all things! make it mine
> To feel, amid the city's jar,
> That there abides a peace of thine,
> Man did not make, and cannot mar.

But we never learn whether the invoked 'Calm soul of all things' answers his prayer; and still the *hum* hums and the *jar* jars the escapist poet and his would-be escapist poem.

Arnold's rather hectic search for pastoral safe-havens within the modern hum and jar is, of course, symptomatic of a whole career's escapist investment in the hoped-for reassurances of pre-modern modes and stories, manners and models: the older poet following rather monologically on in the track signposted by the Prize Poem of Rugby School's earnest little classicist, 'Alaric at Rome', on to the imitation of Antigone ('Fragment of an Antigone'), and the pseudo-Greek lyricism of the Ulysses-Circe encounter 'The Strayed Reveller', and the long pseudo-Sophoclean verse-drama

---

[29] 'On the Modern Element in Literature' (14 November 1857); not published until February 1869, in *Macmillan's Magazine*. Excluded from all of Arnold's own collections of his essays. I quote it from the best collection of Arnold's classical material, first volume in the *Collected Works* of Matthew Arnold, *On the Classical Tradition*, ed RH Super (University of Michigan Press, Ann Arbor, 1960), 20.

'Merope' (published just one month after his Oxford inaugural lecture), and the old-fiction revivals of 'Sohrab and Rustum' and 'Balder Dead', and the lengthy medievalism of the poeticized dramatics of 'Tristram and Iseult', and the ubiquitous nostalgic pastoralia peaking in 'The Scholar Gipsy' and 'Thyrsis': all of it steeped in the persistent melancholics of regret, loss, obituarizing (as described in 'Mourning and Melancholia', Chapter 8). It's a protracted exhibition of this poet's sense that present times, subjects, forms, wordings can't be managed and won't do. But still for all this escapist effort, he can't shut out the noise of modern reality, of the 'howling' city and its masses, of 'The complaining millions of men' who 'Darken in labour and pain' – the Clough stuff, the stuff of liberal and socialist consideration.

'The complaining millions' butt into Arnold's 'The Youth of Nature' (1850–1852), one more of his poems regretting Wordsworth's death. Who now can cast light on the modern matter? Arnold prefers not to try. '[D]arkness returns to our eyes'. Wordsworth the 'sacred poet' is dead and 'the age ... can rear' such 'no more'. And the poem endorses this occlusion of the modern horror in what Arnold calls Pindarics: formal homage to the old Greek modes that Arnold prefers. Rather like in, and on, 'Dover Beach' where it's Thucydides's *History of the Peloponnesian War* which provides the poem's wonderfully strong final metaphor and analogy for the perplexed modern doubter.

> And we are here as on a darkling plain
> Swept with confused alarms of struggle and flight,
> Where ignorant armies clash by night.

What, for Arnold, defines and places the noise of modern doubt ('The eternal note of sadness') is that Sophocles heard it 'long ago' on the Aegaean. (Daft, of course: recall p368 above.) For Sophocles is Arnold's supreme 'prop'. In the sonnet in the 'Friend' sequence entitled 'To a Friend', the one quoted in the 'Modern Element' lecture's tribute to Sophocles, the poet responds to Clough's enquiry about mental props in these bad modern times, 'Who prop, thou ask'st, in these bad days, my mind?' There's the 'old man', Homer, 'clearest-souled of men', who could see 'The Wide Prospect' ('Europe' in Greek, literally 'the wide prospect') even though physically blind; and the lame Stoic philosopher Epictetus whom Arnold has only recently found as a literary 'friend'; but above all there's Sophocles; to whom are offered

> My special thanks, whose even-balanced soul
> From first youth tested up to extreme old age,
> Business could not make dull, nor passion wild;
>
> Who saw life steadily, and saw it whole.

Unsteadied by modernity, Arnold turns away by preference to the Sophoclean past of poetry to be soothed by the old modes and texts which are not infected by the awful realities of modern novels. Sandwiched in the *Collected Poems* between 'Horatian Echo' – yet one more poem eschewing the modern political subject[30] – and 'Fragment of an "Antigone" ', comes the arrestingly dismissive sonnet 'To George Cruikshank: On Seeing, in the Country, His Picture of "The Bottle" '. Away in the country, far from any city's social horrors, Arnold has come across the notorious teetotal tract *The Bottle* by George Cruikshank, radical satirist, the Victorian Hogarth, Dickens's one-time illustrator turned anti-drink crusader (Cruikshank's father had died of drink). Here was the modern urban subject, and the stuff of social-conscience fiction (for all of Dickens's fall-out with Cruikshank) rudely intruding on classicizing pastoralist Arnold's pastoral retreat. And Arnold, and his poetic disposition, his aesthetic proclivities, angrily refuse these urban, lower-class, reminders, these grim images, this othering aesthetic activity, of the modern dark-side:

> Artist, whose hand, with horror winged, hath torn
> From the rank life of towns this leaf! and flung
> The prodigy of full-blown crime among
> Valleys and men to middle fortune born,
> Not innocent, indeed, yet not forlorn –
> Say, what shall calm us when such guests intrude
> Like comets on the heavenly solitude?
> Shall breathless glades, cheered by shy Dian's horn,
> Cold-bubbling springs, or caves? Not so! ...

Cruikshank is urging his case 'too fiercely', Arnold thinks. Knowing 'the worst', the truth that 'the nobleness of man / May be by man effaced', does not need this subject, these methods, this form, the taint of the hard modern prosaic. Arnold's poetry is for other measures than these. But they will not go away, for all Arnold's repugnance. They can't be stopped breaking in on his classicizing, medievalizing, pastoral enclosures. As they do even in the poem of attempted refusal. They simply refuse to heed his Keep Out signs.

The Modern Outlook and The Backward Look

And that's even truer of great Tennyson – his poetry (and his life) granted their utterly riveting interest and importance not least because built on an intense double-mindedness – past-present, public-private, and, for that

[30] Pastoral love poems about 'Eugenia' ('Philomela' in one version of the poem) and about Helen of Troy, and Shakespeare's Juliet, are more to the point of art and life than the agitations of the mass Chartist movement.

matter poetry-prose. A set of dualisms registered at large in the clashing varieties of mood and subject across his great field of texts, but also within the greatest of his individual poems. Take *Maud* as a dramatic example of these oppositions. The poem's speaker would like to enjoy peace and contentment in a garden with his beloved Maud. Pastoral delighting, anticipated, enjoyed, are the occasion of the poems's loveliest verses – the 'Birds in the high Hall-garden' section (Part I. XII); 'Go not happy day, / From the shining fields' (I.XVII); the lines contemplating 'a lovely shell' on the Breton coast (II.II); and of course the yearning 'Come into the garden, Maud' (I.XXII), the most famous pastoral lyric of the century, turned into a very popular Victorian 'parlour' song with music by the Irish composer Michael Balfe, and without doubt one of the most famous poems in the English language, securely ensconced in the tradition as the very essence of the poetic as such. A poetic Tennyson was himself massively drawn to from start to finish of his career. It's relevant to the status of *Maud*'s fundamental pastoralism that the rose-obsessions of 'Go not, happy day' ('Roses are her cheeks / And a rose her mouth') recall the splurge of early poems Tennyson addressed to his fancy, Rose Baring ('Thy rosy lips are soft and sweet', 'Early Verses of Compliment to Miss Rose Baring', and 'the Rosebud'), and that Tennyson thought of putting 'Go not, happy day' into 'The Princess', alongside, that is, the sensationally lovely pastoral dreamings of 'Now sleeps the crimson petal, now the white'. But it is most revealing for the contemporary war of the genres that *Maud*'s pastoralism should be so assaulted and broken up by the intrusions of the modern Carlylean realities that novels went in for.

The garden-intruding modern horrors that 'Maud' opens with, poverty-driven violence and crime, profiteering, the reign of 'mammon', adulteration of the bread of the poor, and so on, all the economic and social terrors, disturbances of the peace of the 'garden' of England which are allied with the failed financial speculations that have resulted in blood in the 'little wood', the ghastly death of the narrator's father, are – as Ricks's editorial notes tell – the concerns, and given to us often in the very words, of Carlyle's *Past and Present*, Charles Kingsley's *Alton Locke* and Dickens' *Oliver Twist*. Just so, the poem's late 'mad scene', in which the feet and hoofs of the street beat into the brain of the narrator as he lies in his imagined urban grave, have (rightly) reminded readers of the opening page of *The Old Curiosity Shop* where Dickens invites us to think of a bed-ridden sick man in the London slum parish of St Giles, oppressed by the 'hum and noise' of the city and feeling like someone lying 'dead but conscious, in a noisy graveyard' without 'hope of rest for centuries to come'. The pastoralizing narrator, the poem and its poet: they're each massively oppressed by the modern realities of the Novel, the *arriviste* modern subject, which cannot however be kept out of the would-be serious poem.

John Ruskin's modern-democratic (*Aurora Leigh*-like) worries over the retreatism implicit in Tennyson's investment in Camelot – 'I think I have

seen faces and heard voices by road and street side which claimed or confessed as much as ever the loveliest or saddest of Camelot' – were sound. But
he was wrong to believe Tennyson's Arthurianism was keeping him off the
street entirely. Very striking indeed is Tennyson's apparent agreement with
Elizabeth Barrett Browning's 'distrust' of the medievalizing poet who prefers Camelot to London's Fleet Street and who 'discerns / No character or
glory in his times' (*Aurora Leigh*, V.189ff). In a late note on his short poem
of 1842 'The Epic', in which the poet Everard Hall is said to have consigned
the twelve books of his retrospective epic on King Arthur to the flames,[31]
Tennyson said that Barrett Browning had 'wanted me to continue this', but
he hadn't needed to because she had 'put my answer in *Aurora Leigh*'. 'The
Epic' became the Introduction to Tennyson's 'Morte d'Arthur', allegedly the
one Arthurian Book that Everard's friend plucked from the fire. In it Everard
is said to have read aloud the 'Morte d'Arthur' in a voice resembling
Tennyson's own – 'mouthing out his hollow oes and aes, / Deep-chested
music'. Which makes the recital sound like Tennyson's response to Everard's
modern, Barrett-like, disparaging of the old epicities – a response which
turned into a torrent of practical Tennysonian rebutting in the enormous
shape of *The Idylls of the King*. And the recital is surely so. But for all that,
Tennyson did suggest that *Aurora Leigh*, the poem which lengthily sustains
Everard's charge against medievalism, answers for him. In other words,
Tennyson himself had at some point become concerned about the purpose
and efficacy of indulging in Arthurian retreats. And, to be sure, that concern
is indeed apparent rather early in his Arthurianizing career.

It's possible to read 'The Lady of Shalott' – the first of Tennyson's early
Arthurian ventures, a short cryptic pre-run of what became 'Lancelot and
Elaine' in *The Idylls* (published in 1859 as *Elaine*; known by Tennyson as
The Maid of Astolat) – as a foundational poem of doubting about
Arthurianism. In being lured away from her loom, her own weaving, her
own text-making by the mirrored reflection of Sir Lancelot – Sir Lancelot at
second-hand, romantic, chivalric lover-boy, coming out of the mirror as if
out of the old Arthurian tales, the old poems, other people's poems, Malory's
and the rest – the Lady weaver-poet embraces her own death. (Here's what
Harold Bloom calls 'the anxiety of influence' felt and presented as mortally
wounding: with the textualized meanings of things, the hold on the real of
the Lady's text, her *tissu*, her weaving – model of the poet's own text –
demonstrably precarious in their mere mirroredness: as difficult a place for
meaning-making as the recessive mirrorings of Velasquez's *Las Meninas* with
which Michel Foucault opens his textuality-challenging *Les Mots et Les*

---

[31] ' "… a truth / Looks freshest in the fashion of the day" … "Why take the style of those
heroic times? For nature brings not back the Mastodon, / Nor we those times; and why should
any man / Remodel models?" '.

Choses / The Order of Things.[32]) Camelot – it becomes the grand theme of *The Idylls of the King*, as it was of Malory – is a place of sexual unhappiness and transgression, of violence and death, and in this case death to the singer. Death to the Lady of Shalott whose song is her swan-song; and to the Maid of Astolat whose equivalent song is called by her 'The Song of Love and Death'. Love for sinful Lancelot, who is adulterously committed to Guinevere, is an infatuation for the Arthurian which contaminates, silences, kills. Compare that early Arthurian 'Fragment', 'Sir Launcelot and Queen Guinevere' (written 1830, published 1842), composed in the same stanza as 'The Lady of Shalott', in which Guinevere 'looked so lovely' that 'A man had given all other bliss, / And all his worldly worth for this, / To waste his whole heart in one kiss / Upon her perfect lips'. Here was the lure, and the kiss, of waste and ruin, and loss of all 'bliss' (which includes eternal bliss in heaven): this Guinevere is not just a close relative of Helen of Troy, and Shakespeare's Cleopatra, but a (Swinburnean / DG Rossettian) demon lover. According to Tennyson's friend John Kemble, this Fragment was part of a companion to 'Shalott', entitled 'The Ballad of Sir Lancelot', in which Lancelot makes his son the chaste Sir Galahad ('My strength is as the strength of ten / Because my heart is pure': 'Sir Galahad', 1834, pub 1842) blush for shame as his father sings the sexy verses known as 'Life of the Life Within My Blood', inviting Guinevere not to waste time wooing and being wise about eschewing sex but to 'Bathe' with him promptly 'in the fiery flood' ('a loose song' which Kemble didn't want ascribing to him as a future clergyman).[33]

It's pertinent to this early wavering about what love for the old Matter of Britain might mean and do, especially for the poet, that 'The Palace of Art' (1832, 1842) – reigned over by the Muse or Goddess of the whole known poetic tradition, eastern and western, Greek, Roman, and Christian, she who is melancholy, morbid, lonely, and guilty because her isolative art shuts

[32]   Harold Bloom, *The Anxiety of Influence: A Theory of Poetry* (Oxford University Press, NY, 1973); Michel Foucault, *Les Mots et les choses: une archéologie des sciences humaines* (Gallimard, Paris, 1966)/ *The Order of Things: an Archeology of the Human Sciences* (Tavistock Publications, 1970). Gerhard Joseph's rhapsodic 'Interweave' chapter in *Tennyson and the Text: The Weaver's Shuttle* (Cambridge University Press, Cambridge, 1992), 113ff, is àpropos in its linkage between the Lady's textual-textural work and Tennyson's own, but goes too far in suggesting the poem's move from weaving-as-work to weaver-as-text (the Lady's written name at the end) offers a parable of the move in 'recent literary history' from reading her poem as 'authored text' to a taking of it as a representation of 'free-text-making'. (Where does *free* text-making occur in the poem?)
[33]   Poems in Ricks's editions, whose headnotes supply Kemble's explanatory letter. 'Life of the Life' was not published until after Tennyson's lifetime, in Hallam Tennyson's *Memoir*, I.59. Christina Poulson is greatly informative on the Pre-Raphaelites' utter obsession with 'The Lady of Shalott' and the death of beautiful women: 'Death and the Maiden: The Lady of Shalott and the Pre-Raphaelites', in *Re-Framing the Pre-Raphaelites: Historical and Theoretic Essays*, ed Ellen Harding (Scolar Press, Aldershot, 1993), 173–194.

out 'the dully sound / Of human footsteps' – should have a whole room devoted to picturing 'mythic' Arthur lying, deeply wounded', 'dozing in the vale of Avalon, / And watched by weeping queens' ('The Palace of Art', 105–108, 275-276).[34] And poem after poem of Tennyson's is conflicted like this about the counter-attractions of the backward look and a modern outlook. Here's a poet in, as it were, Arthur's bosom (the lovely malapropism of Shakespeare's Mistress Quickly)[35], who prefers refracting modern problems through the Lady of Shalott's mirror, but who is also compelled to look at modernity head on, as he does in the many poems from his early, genuinely liberal days, writing for freedom and against oppressors. Like 'Written During the Convulsions in Spain', urging Spaniards to combat the restored monarchy of Ferdinand VII, back on his throne with French help, after the failure of Spain's liberal revolution. That poem's epigraph is from Horace's Ode, *Cantabrum indoctum juga ferre*: 'To the men of Cantabria not yet schooled to bear a yoke'. An old message to the Cantabrians updated by a modern Cantabrigian – Tennyson the Cambridge man who with other Cambridge Apostles, including Hallam, joined the ill-fated expedition of General Torrijos against Ferdinand in which their friend Boyd was shot dead by firing squad (and John Kemble was reported captured and threatened with death). Modern Cantabs and Horace's Cantabrians: here was the Janus effect in action.[36]

Dualisms Set in Wax

Early Tennyson poems cherish freedom, especially for foreigners, as in those early 1830s sonnets for the Poles in their uprising against their Russian invaders: 'Blow ye the trumpet, gather from afar / The hosts to battle: be not

---

[34] Isobel Armstrong argues that Tennyson's 1842 changes to the 1832 room in the Palace depicting a lovely pastoral scene, 'long walks and lawns and beds and bowers / Trellised with bunchy vine', all flooded in 'mild sunshine' – he substituted 'an iron coast' and 'angry waves', and added thunder and rain, and agricultural workers 'at their sultry toil' (69–80) – were a snub to John Wilson's jeery review of Tennyson's *Poems, Chiefly Lyrical* (1830) which ended with a praise of pastoral as poetry's proper subject. But this misses the point that the harder pastoral of Tennyson's revised 'Palace' is still rural and distant from towns and still scooped into Tennyson's wary repudiating of a poetry of narcissistic, escapist and retrospective loveliness. Armstrong, *Victorian Poetry: Poetry, Poetics and Politics*, 79–80.

[35] Falstaff, she says, has gone there – she meant Abraham's bosom. *Henry V*, II.ii.9–11.

[36] In the 1930s, when many Cantabs went to fight for the Republic in the Spanish Civil War, this earlier investment in the cause of Spanish democracy came to some minds, including Graham Greene's. See Graham Greene, 'Alfred Tennyson Intervenes', *Spectator* (10 December 1937); = 'The Apostles Intervene' in Graham Greene, *Collected Essays* (Bodley Head, London, 1969; Penguin, Harmondsworth, 1970), 230–234; reprinted in *Spanish Front: Writers on the Civil War*, ed Valentine Cunningham (Oxford University Press, Oxford, 1986), 67–69.

bought and sold'; and 'Poland': 'How long, O God, shall men be ridden down, / And trampled under ...?'. Democrats at home were more troubling because, as his many poems written during and after the 1832 Reform Bill agitations, like 'Hail Briton!', indicate, they were too threateningly violent and not gradualist enough – inclined to 'forge confusion from reform' and thus 'lower' than Poland's Russian oppressors ('The Cossack curst of God and man / To whom the Polish virgin cries': 'Hail Briton!', 191–192). Evidently Tennyson relished violent action for freedom, but not at home. It's no accident that the hero of *Maud* should seek salvation from all his home troubles in the Crimean War – against 'an iron [Russian] tyranny', and 'in defence of the right'. Tennyson's cult of the Duke of Wellington, champion of foreign wars against Napoleon, began early. 'We taught' Napoleon, crows the sonnet 'Buonaparte', twice but it was Wellington who was in Tennyson's mind as chief teacher in that poem of 1832 – Wellington who as Prime Minister was chief opponent of the 1832 Reform Bill.

Deep political confusions, then, and symptomatic of the larger confusions commanding this poet; but how poetically energizing! In fact it's the blending of quite opposite poetic interests, the busy swerving about, the looking all ways at once, that is so impressive. The multiplied sensitivity and impressibility of the man. It's utterly symptomatic that when the Edison Company sent Tennyson a home-recording machine he should have recorded on it his two most famous but quite opposite poems, the privately pastoral 'Come into the Garden, Maud' and the publicly engaged Crimean poem 'The Charge of the Light Brigade'. Here was his dual-facing in a nutshell. Registered for posterity in the new medium that would be modernity's latest approximation to the old desire for a memorial in something lasting (evinced classically and – yes – by Horace, whose closing Ode 30 in his Book III boasted he'd built a monument *aere perennius*, more lasting than bronze). But this was not actually in stone or bronze, only on wax cylinders – soft wax (whose survival behind a radiator at Tennyson's place on the Isle of Wight is a sort of modern miracle), impressible wax emblematic of the contradictory impressibility of this poet – so impressed, so marked, by such contradictory tendencies. The runaway Arthurian with the prickly social conscience; the medievalist (and classicist) with the anxious modern perspective.

You couldn't get more modern than the author of 'Mechanophilus (In the Time of the First Railways)' (written circa1833), a bit over the top in its celebration of nineteenth-century mechanical triumphs and thus smelling a little of irony (its MS title is even 'Aenophilus', the lover of the age), but still massively modern-conscious; or, much more importantly, 'Locksley Hall' (written 1837–1838). Of course 'Locksley Hall' finds modernity wanting. It's a prequel to *Maud*. Money triumphs in 'the jingling of the guinea'; 'Every door is barred with gold' and only opens 'to golden keys'; the narrator wonders

Maud-like whether he's mad; a marriage across the divide of class and
wealth with the girl from Locksley Hall is impossible (as in *Maud* and, for
that matter, *Aurora Leigh*); 'all things here are out of joint' (133: in Hamlet's
words); 'nature sickens' (153). There's no 'enjoyment' in modern progress,
'in this march of mind, / In the steamship, in the railway, in the thoughts that
shake mankind'; the narrator would love to escape to a Paradise island away
from contemporaneity, colonialist traders, the railway age. He looks into a
future which might perhaps be better ('Forward, forward', he urges, like
Tennyson's Ulysses, desiring to go 'seaward'), but he can only imagine the
future as a continuation of the present in railway terms. 'Let the great world
spin for ever down the ringing grooves of change'. It's a future as a rather
dismaying railway progress, and for ever. (Tennyson had thought the train he
travelled in on a dark night in 1830 from Liverpool to Manchester ran in
grooves.) The hint of irony about futurisms present in 'Mechanophilus'
seems stronger here. There's more than a touch of Carlyle's haunted vision in
Past and Present (1843) of progress (and revolution) as a speeding steam-
train bringing havoc and death (the nightmare that infects Dickens's
Carlylean *Dombey and Son*, 1846–1848). And again the point here is less
Tennyson's reactionary fears than his modern preoccupations – ones engaged
(and curiously so in the light of Barrett Browning's allegations against
Tennyson's fairiness and her notion that only a prose-poem would do to
engage the modern subject) in a kind of proximate prosiness. The regular
8-stress trochaic lines of 'Locksley Hall' arranged in jaunty end-rhyming couplets are, of course, far from prosaic. (A trochee is a metrical foot of one
stressed syllable followed by an unstressed one, – ∨. Tennyson reported that
Hallam's father 'said to me that the English people like verse trochaics, so
I wrote the poem in this metre'.) But, intriguingly, Tennyson's inspiration for
his poem of bewailing old loves was the Arabic Moâllakát in the prose
translation of the great Orientalist William Jones (1782), many of whose
prose lines fell naturally into 8-stress trochees, as Christopher Ricks's headnotes point out, suggesting that Tennyson might have in fact got this prosey
rhythm in his head.

Whatever, though, the truth of that, it's clear that this Arthurian was
closely engaged in modern problems almost from the beginning of his poetic
career, and well before his becoming Poet Laureate put such outward concerns at the heart of his poetic duties. Certainly, after his appointment as
national poet his poems go heavily public, becoming flooded with the affairs
and anxieties of nation and state: in that great swathe of monarchist, chau-
vinist, jingoist poems, beginning with 'To the Queen' (March 1851), his
first public outing as Laureate, chosen as dedicatory poem to the seventh
edition of his *Poems* (may his grandchildren speak of Her Majesty with
'reverence ... as Mother, Wife, and Queen'; 'bounds of freedom wider yet';
'people's will'; 'compassed by the inviolate sea'; all that nationalistic stuff).

And he went on beating the nationalist drum in his 1852 newspaper poems whipping up militant fervour against the French who after Louis Napoleon's coup seemed to threaten an invasion – 'The Penny-Wise' ('Arm, arm, arm'); 'Rifle Clubs!!!' (in support of Coventry Patmore's volunteer rifle-club movement); 'Britons, Guard Your Own' ('We swear to guard our own' against 'lying priests' and French 'tricks'); 'For the Penny Wise' (armed with 'super-annuated' muskets our soldiers have been beaten by 'the Kaffirs' in the Cape Colony wars; 'our glory' has been 'a little docked', that is cut like an animal's tail; we need to re-arm to 'fight the French'); and 'The Third of February, 1852' (against the House of Lords, friendly to Napoleon, hostile to a national Militia); and 'Hands All Round!' (toasting European and American friends; cursing Russians and Austrians, and worshippers of 'Ledgers' – i.e. balance-sheets); and 'Suggested by Reading an Article in a Newspaper' (calling on newspapers 'To make opinion warlike', attacking the religious press for 'unheroic pertness' and 'unchristian spite' in the pre-occupation with quarrels about 'forms' rather than truth). These newspaper poems were all anonymous (Edward FitzGerald suggested the new Laureate did not want to annoy the Queen who was on good terms with Louis Napoleon).

Arrestingly, 'The Third of February, 1852' and 'Hands All Round' were signed 'Merlin'. 'Suggested by Reading an Article in a Newspaper' is written in praise of this 'Merlin' and as from one 'Taliessin', who in an accompanying letter hopes his own poem 'has a smack of Merlin's style in it'. Merlin: the Arthurian mage, much featured in the *Idylls*, even as seduced by Vivien; Taliessin (Tennyson's spelling of Taliesin): the mythic Welsh bard who was friend to King Arthur. Taliessin: it rhymes with Tennyson. Merlin; Taliessin: the politico-satiric Tennyson finds nothing odd in assuming the bardic mantle. He'll never not be a friend of Arthur and Arthurianism. 'How much I love this writer's manly style!', the poem of 'Taliessin' for 'Merlin' begins:

> By such men led, our press had ever been
> The public conscience of our noble isle,
> Severe and quick to feel a civic sin,
> To raise the people and chastise the times
> With such a heat as lives in great creative rhymes.
> (lines 2–6)

'Great creative rhymes' are, it seems, not restricted in subject. In Tennyson's book they include 'public conscience' verses, which the Arthurian mage and poet can put their names to. And which Arthurian Tennyson would put his name to with unremitting vigour. In the manner of 'Ode on the Death of the Duke of Wellington', Tennyson's first separate publication as Laureate; and 'The Charge of the Light Brigade'; the Indian Mutiny poems ('Havelock',

1857, and 'The Defence of Lucknow', 1879); and 'The Charge of the Heavy Brigade at Balaclava: October 25, 1854' (1882); and the 1885 'Epitaph for General Gordon', killed at Khartoum ('Warrior of God ...'); and the numerous elegies for public figures; and the jubilations for the Queen, and other modern Laureate-dutiful material. Decades of it, in fact: the poet hard at his imperialist drum-beating right to the end of his career. Keep up the Nelsonian navy, or the 'mightiest ocean-power on earth' will die ('The Fleet', 1885). 'Britons, hold your own!', the late verses for the 'Opening of the Indian and Colonial Exhibition by the Queen' (May 1886) are still exhorting in the old tones of the 1852 newspaper poems. In 1862 Tennyson provides the 'Ode Sung at the Opening of the International Exhibition' (given full throat by a thousand voices). It includes some elegiac lines about Prince Albert, founder of these International Exhibitions, who died 14 December 1861. Of course it does. The Laureate was almost Victoria's family bard. In January 1864 she asks for some lines to be inscribed on the statue of her mother, the Duchess of Kent in the new Royal Mausoleum at Frogmore, whose main recumbent is Prince Albert. Naturally, the Laureate responds – with three versions, out of which the Queen chooses the one about the 'guardian mother mild' being blessed, Biblically, 'By children of the children of thy child'.

But always, alongside these attentively outward-looking, public outpourings Tennyson is producing the private, the inward and escapist, the privately troubled and doubting and grieving, and the repeated backward looks. The likes of 'Flower in the crannied wall' never disappeared from the menu, and the Arthurianism built and built and built – decades of pondering in the wake of the early Arthur poems, reading, note-taking, a research visit to Wales, a long poem in the poet's head on Lancelot and the Grail, the first public instalment of the *Idylls* in 1859, piecemeal appearances of *Idylls* volumes thereafter (1869, 1871, 1872, 1873, 1885, 1886), much rejigging and tinkering, constant preoccupation. And of course the longest-distance running of Tennyson's backward mindings and remindings, his Classicism, constantly abides.

Classicists Climbing Mount Pimplaea

Like all the big Oxbridge players – Hopkins, Swinburne, Arnold, Clough, Housman, Symonds – Tennyson begins in the Classics and like them never gets out from under the shadow of the classical heritage. The classical authors these men read in their schooldays and at university never left them. Like the narrator of Tennyson's 'Edwin Morris', who remembers Love / Amor sneezing out 'a full God-bless-you right and left', 'As in the Latin song I learnt at school' (actually, Catullus xlv.8–9). The Greek and Roman authors Tennyson read early on stayed as friends, providing him with a large echoing repertoire of ideas, moods, lines, tags, verse forms, stories, narrative moments, characters, models, for repeated plundering and recycling. His new poems live with parasitic zest on the old classical ones. You can see the many translations Tennyson did at Louth Grammar School in the great Tennyson archive at the Lincoln City Library. He was 'so over-dosed' on Horace in boyhood, he said, that it took a long time before he could like him (*Memoir*, I.16). But Horace's strong presence across Tennyson's oeuvre is characteristic of this classics-steeped Victorian. His repeated turning to the Horatian Alcaic ('grandest of metres') we've noted. Cast down in the melancholies of Hallam's death Tennyson naturally draws on the ever-ready classical menu, and on Horace not least. He remembers the appearance of Tithonus in Horace's Odes – Tithonus the death-obsessed immortal – and treats him twice, in the short 'Tithon' (1833), revised as the longer 'Tithonus' – published eventually in 1860 (in Thackeray's *Cornhill* Magazine). Tithonus speaks as one of the momentous trio of Tennyson's 1833 monologuists seriously voicing highly concerning aspects of human mortality in the wake of Hallam's death – Ulysses (out of Homer via Dante) on the necessity of carrying on after death; Tiresias (out of Euripedes's *Phoenissae*) on the courage of self-sacrificing; Horatian Tithonus on the non-blessings of immortality. The wonderfully noisy battle-episodes blind Tiresias sees and hears as he foretells the fall Thebes, draw in detail ('Tiresias', 91–93) on the tramp of the horn-footed horses in Virgil's *Aeneid* VI.590–591 (favourite lines of Tennyson, frequently recited by him 'for descriptive beauty and fine sound'),[37] as well as depending heavily on Aeschylus's *Seven Against Thebes*, another old Tennyson friend. Tennyson composed a 'Homeric book' in Greek hexameters on the *Seven Against Thebes* just before he went up to Cambridge as an undergraduate. In 1883 Mrs Tennyson wrote to Edward Lear that Tennyson was revising 'one of his old world poems' from his 'Ulysses' period. This was 'Tiresias', 'discarded', she said, because Carlyle had called it 'a dead dog'. Tennyson has come, though, to believe 'the world will receive lessons' in old world dress 'when it discards them in modern garb'.

Tiresias talks pointfully, for his intently classicizing author, on the memorialized names of Thebes' defenders. They comprise 'a song' that will be heard, influentially, down the centuries:

> Their names,
> Graven on memorial columns, are a song
> Heard in the future; few, but more than wall
> And rampart, their examples reach a hand
> Far through all years, and everywhere they meet

---

[37]   Dwelt on in the discussion of poetic noise in my 'Making Noise/Noising Truths', Ch 3, above.

And kindle generous purpose, and the strength
To mould it into action pure as theirs.

(119–125)

The reaching hand of past poems, the enlivening, encouraging, moral force
of the old heroes as memorialized in the old songs: it's a defence of the force
of old, classical writings, and an encouragement to, and defence of, their
modern imitators and revivers. Cannily, Christopher Ricks hears in these
lines, written in the aftermath of Hallam's death, an echo of that passage at
the start of *In Memoriam* asking who would 'reach a hand through time to
catch / The far-off interest of tears' – the one looked at in my 'Mourning and
Melancholia' chapter, Chapter 8) in respect of the multiplied meanings of
interest (interestingness; non-disinterestedness; accumulating value; poetic
money in the bank) for the intertextualities of the elegiac act. Here, if we're
right to hear the echo with Ricks, it's the classical texts that have such (mul-
tiplex) interest: Tennyson's oldest interest, and an interest in having the classics demonstrate their continuing interest, which Tennyson demonstrates at
every turn of his career. In the unremitting presence, in translation, quotations, epigraphs, allusions, echoes of Homer and Virgil, Pindar, Catullus,
Persius, Sappho, Euripides, Terence, Theophrastus, Theocritus, Horace of
course, and all the rest. As John Churton Collins, the extraordinarily well-
read pioneering Victorian Professor of English Literature, who seems to
have had all of classical literature in his head, made very clear in his
(astounding) series of three articles in the *Cornhill Magazine* entitled 'A New
Study of Tennyson'. Collins deep-mined Tennyson's poems for the their classical allusions, imitations, analogies, adaptations and 'simple transferen-
cies'.[38] He was on a mission to prove that notable English poetry was as
valuable in every way as the classics of Greece and Rome, that English
Literature could only be seriously read in its family relationship with those
classics, that certain poets in the family such as Virgil and Tennyson work
by imitating other poets rather than working from nature, and thus that
Tennyson could only be read, as Virgil has been read, by scholars equipped
to recognize the great classical range of his texts. (His theory and practice
are pioneers of what we now think of as the essential consideration of intertextuality, and he curiously anticipates TS Eliot's famous allegation that
whereas minor poets borrow from their predecessors great poets steal from
them.) The well-equipped scholars Collins was thinking of were, of course,
people like himself, doing analyses like his 'New Study' articles, which especially inspected *In Memoriam* and *Idylls of the King* for their much borrowed and indeed stolen classical substance. (Collins's articles were the basis

[38] 'A New Study of Tennyson', *Cornhill Magazine*, 41 (1880), 36–50; 42 (1880), 36–50; 44
(1881), 87–106.

for his great polemical book *Illustrations of Tennyson* (1891) and his 1902 edition of *In Memoriam, The Princess, and Maud).*

Stephen Harrison, in his useful article 'Virgilian Contexts' in the revealingly wide-ranging Blackwell *Companion to Classical Receptions*, rightly approves of Collins's claims in *Illustrations of Tennyson* about the Virgilianized melancholy and regrettings of *In Memoriam*, the mood music which helped make Tennyson 'the most Virgilian of modern poets'.[39] Collins was, of course, a man with an over-sensitive antenna for picking up the classical, and indeed other, echoes; an over-doer, a fanatic even. Tennyson hated the idea that he wasn't being original, and tore into Collins's manifestly bloated charge-sheet, the great lists of Tennyson's alleged debts. 'Nonsense', he kept writing on his copy of Collins's articles. '!!! nonsense' is what he typically thinks of Collins's typical suggestion that *In Memoriam* LXXVI ('Take wings of fancy ...') is like Petrarch's Sonnet 82l. Tennyson's description of Collins as 'a louse upon the locks of literature' may be apocryphal, but it fits Tennyson's scorn: Collins's scholarly criticism is lousy because parasitic on literature, and also for suggesting Tennyson's poetry is utterly parasitic on its predecessors. But Collins's principled line about massive intertextual dealings across the western tradition is, plainly, right; and he's right to notice how redolent of classical lines Tennyson's own lines can be. 'Nonsense', Tennyson wrote (again) against Collins's comparing *In Memoriam* LII, 3–4 ('My words are only words, and moved / Upon the topmost froth of thought') to Persius's *Satire* I, 104–105 (*Summa delumbe saliva / hoc natat in labris*: 'it swims on the lips, on top of loose spittle'). But, typically, the old poem was indeed much on Tennyson's mind. His *Aylmer's Field* clearly lifts its picture of 'the violet on the tyrant's grave' (line 845) from earlier in that Persius poem (I.39–40). Just 'a chance parallel' said Tennyson, but unconvincingly. And there was certainly no chance he could say that over *In Memoriam* XVIII, 'And from his ashes may be made / The violet of his native land', which is almost a direct quote from the Persius – *nunc a tumulo fortunataque favilla / nascitur violae?* ('Will not violets now be born out of the tomb and its blessed ashes?'). Undoubtedly, as Tennyson protested, the Persius came via *Hamlet*, V.i.232–241, 'Lay her i' the earth, / And from her fair and unpolluted flesh / May violets spring'. But those violets are at root Persius's, and utterly naturalized by the classicizing poet Tennyson's poetic confidants were familiar with. When Hallam quoted the Persius lines in his *Englishman's Magazine* piece on Tennyson (August 1831) at the place where he said that when

[39]   Stephen Harrison, 'Virgilian Contexts', in *A Companion to Classical Receptions*, eds Lorna Hardwick and Christopher Stray (Blackwell, Oxford, 1988), 113–126. Claims supported in Harrison's wider ranging 'Some Victorian Versions of Greco-Roman Epic', about the dealings in classical epic by Tennyson, Arnold, Clough and Morris, in *Remaking the Classics: Literature, Genre and Media in Britain 1800–2000*, ed Christopher Stray (Duckworth, London, 1007), 21–36.

Tennyson 'dies, will not the Graces and the Loves mourn over him', he was showing he knew where Tennyson was coming from, and what the appropriate classicized tribute to this classicizer would be.[40]

And how could any one think otherwise? From early on Tennyson showed himself as a huge donner of classical masks, the keen ventriloquizer of classical voices, casting and re-casting himself in classical mirrors – as the Ulysses-Tithonus-Tiphonus trio; as Oenone (in 'Oenone', from Ovid and Theocritus, and in 'The Death of Oenone' from Quintus Smyrnaenus's *The Fall of Troy*); as 'The Lotos-Eaters' (out of Homer's *Odyssey*); as 'Alexander' (out of Charles Rollin's *Ancient History*); as the ancient Greek musician 'Amphion', and as Hector and Achilles (in his *Iliad* translations); and so on. He was the classicizer's classicist. As such, he prided himself on his prowess in repeating the most finicky of classical verse forms. He could do modified *Elegiacs* (actually 'Leonine Elegiacs', as in the poem with that title – a form in which the key rhyme-words occur in the middle as well as the end of each line); and *Anacreontics* (as in 'Anacreontics') a metre based on repeated short line lengths, in this case of 7-syllables each; and Catullan *galliambics*, a rushy, jerky metre, named for the frenzied Galli, the priests of wild fertility goddess Cybele, each line consisting of two halves, each half a 'catalectic' (broken) iambic pentameter (i.e. made of four iambic feet), imitated in Tennyson's 'Boädicea', about frenzied Ancient Britons revolting against the Romans (subject got up from Tacitus's *Annals*) in the manner of, for example, Catullus's poem lxiii, about the contest of civilization and madness. No one should take at face value Tennyson's early poem about not daring to write in classic modes – ode, sonnet, satire, epic – for fear of reviewers' scorn

> I dare not write an Ode for fear Pimplaea
> Should fork me down the double-crested hill,
> And sneering say that Fancy, like Astraea,
> Has left the world to ignorance and ill –
> Should clip my wings, disgrace my wreath of laurel,
> And crown me with a withered bunch of sorrel.
>
> (1–6)
>
> ...
>
> Nor have I yet in Epics made a sally
> Since my misgiving conscience complains
> I could not sing the 'pereuntes Galli'
> In anything at all like decent strains.
> I know my laboured lines would only just go
> To wrap up sundries in the 'vico Tusco'.
>
> (19–24)

---

[40]   All these details are gleaned from Ricks's editorial footnotes.

The self-deprecation is mightily ironic; for every disclaimer he contrives a smart allusion to the great classical trove he is pretending timidity about dipping into. The opening lines about dreading Pimplaea's sneering pitchfork deftly rework Catullus's lines (*Carmina* cv) about one Mentula trying to climb the Piplean mount and getting driven down by the Muses armed with pitchforks. *Pimplaea*: Tennyson's satiric invention of a pimply-faced critic enters into the rough-tongued spirit of the Catullus in which *mentula* is the usual obscene slangy Latin word for *penis*, and that little Roman poem is as much about mounting the *mons veneris* as it is about climbing the poetic hill of Parnassus. 'Mr Penis strives to climb the Pipleian mount' is how Richard ('Dirty Dick') Burton Englished Catullus cv.[41] Tennyson would seem to be relishing the atmosphere of Catullan double-entendre, but cautiously; cutting out the *mentula* of Catullus's forking but knowing full well that every classically educated male reader would spot and enjoy what the revision (or midrash) was playing at. Knowingly too, the 'pereuntes Galli' Tennyson says he couldn't sing in 'decent' verse come from Horace's *Satires* II.i, where Horace says he can't paint ranks of armed men and Gauls falling with shattered spear-heads. The "vico Tusco' in whose shops Tennyson's 'laboured' pages would serve to wrap up odds and ends is contrived from Horace's impious crowd (*Satires* II.iii) in some quarter of a Tuscan town, a *Tuscus vicus*. 'What shall I do?' Tennyson asks in his third stanza, worried about attempting (in his first version) a Satire:

> I cannot sleep for thinking
> (Friend Flaccus made the same complaint of old),
> And having but small store of nerve and fibre,
> Though bathed in oil I could not swim the Tiber.

Flaccus is, of course, Horace, sleepless Horace, accused (*Satires* II.i) of lacking nerve, and thinking of swimming the Tiber, oiled against the cold water, as remedy for insomnia. Every Tennysonian waiver of capacity at the old generic tricks is a well-oiled intertextual trick like this one. Intertextualizing could not come more agile than this. Tennyson is not keen on being accused by critics of weakly imitating others:

> And loath I should be to be deemed as weak as
> The tribe of imitators 'Servum pecus'!
>   (29–30)

'Servum pecus': the servile herd. It's a quote from Horace's gibe in his *Epistles*, I.xix.19, *O imitatores, servum pecus*: you imitators, you herd of

---

[41]   Richard Burton was dubbed Dirty Dick after the 'filthy' footnotes of his English translation (the first ever) of *The Arabian Nights* (1885–1888).

copycat sheep or swine. Tennyson will gibingly turn the charge of imitation with a deft recall of the ancient giber in the matter.

In fact, nobody will out-do Tennyson in his canny mastery of the past. Take his late poem 'St Telemachus' about the old prophet stoned to death for protesting against Christian Rome's perpetuating gladiatorial combat, the protest which brought that pagan barbarity to an end. It's old Tennyson's protest against rival appropriators of the classical past. 'Vicisti Galilaee', says Telemachus, twice, approvingly (lines 15 and 17): 'You have conquered O Galilean', the words of Julian the famous apostate Emperor, repudiating Jesus Christ, quoted disgustedly by Swinburne in the epigraph to his 'Hymn to Prosperpine' and expanded angrily there: 'Thou hast conquered, O pale Galilean; the world has grown grey from thy breath'. Swinburne's neo-paganizing is not the way, Tennyson implies, to read Roman history. Nor is Simeon Solomon's parallel sweaty enthusiasm for the women spectators sexually aroused by a gladiator's death in his painting 'Habet!' Telemachus's shock over the 'eighty thousand Christian faces' that 'watch / Man murder man' is Tennyson's own, and a sharp rebuke to his contemporaries' continuing affection for such barbarism.

A modern barbarism as bad, perhaps, as his contemporaries' hexameters: 'lame hexameters', 'a most barbarous experiment', 'Barbarous experiment, barbarous hexameters', is Tennyson's versified thought about Sir John Herschel's translation of Book I of the *Iliad* into English hexameters in the *Cornhill Magazine*, May 1862. Tennyson's sharp hexameter lines ('When was a harsher sound ever heard, ye Muses, in England? / When did a frog croak coarser upon our Helicon?') appeared in the *Cornhill*, December 1863, in a group of his own 'Attempts at Classic Metres in Quantity'. Here was Tennyson's fusillade in a little contemporary war of classicizers, translators, imitators. Herschel's efforts had been incited by Matthew Arnold's 1860–61 Oxford lectures 'On Translating Homer', with their strong critique of most *Iliad* translators, but especially Francis Newman's effort of 1856, and by Arnold's own offering of exemplary bits of *Iliad* translation.[42] Arnold, who had for some time seen Tennyson as his big rival for ownership of the Homeric heritage[43], had swept Tennyson into his demeaning critique. In his

---

[42]   Three lectures, 'On Translating Homer', 3 November and 8 December 1860, 26 January 1861. Final lecture, 'Last Words', 30 November 1861, especially devoted to contending with Francis Newman's response to his criticism in his *Homeric Translation in Theory and Practice. A Reply to Matthew Arnold* (1861). All four lectures published as book, *On Translating Homer* (1861); now in *On the Classical Tradition*, ed RH Super (University of Michigan Press, Ann Arbor, 1960).

[43]   There's a letter to Clough (25 November 1853) implying the superiority of his 'Sohrab and Rustum' to Tennyson's 'Morte d'Arthur' in the matter of two poems, and poets, who have 'imitated Homer': *The Letters of Matthew Arnold*, ed Cecil Y Lang, I, 1829–1859 (University of Virginia Press, Charlottesville and London, 1996), 280.

third lecture he'd said that 'If blank verse is used in translating Homer ... it must not be Mr Tennyson's blank verse' – an objection expanded in his 'Last Words', in particular in response to John Spedding's defence of Tennyson's 'Homeric' qualities ('plainness of words and style, simplicity and directness of ideas') in *Fraser's Magazine* (June 1861) – one of a flurry of indignant replies to Arnold. Tennyson's thought, Arnold declared, is *sophisticated* (uncomplimentary and pejorative in Victorian times, meaning lacking proper simplicity and naturalness); his words are *distilled*: 'the most unHomeric which can possibly be conceived'. Hurtful charges which Tennyson was not inclined to take lightly. Arnold guessed the Tennyson lines about Herschel's barbarity were aimed at him. He was probably right. In Tennyson's head-note to his *Cornhill* group of 'quantitative' experiments, he said he'd 'long held by our blank verse' as instrument for Homeric translation, 'and now after having spoken so disrespectfully here of these hexameters, I venture, or rather feel bound, to subjoin a specimen, however brief and with whatever demerits, of a blank-verse translation'. And he offered a version of *Iliad* VIII 542–561 ('Specimen of a Translation of the Iliad in Blank Verse'): 'So Hector spake: the Trojans roared applause'. The lines are in iambic pentameters – Tennysonian blank verse. The choice of passage was deliberate: Arnold had included *Iliad* VIII 560–565 in his group of would-be exemplary hexameter translations of the *Iliad* in his third 'On Translating Homer' lecture, and at the end of his 'Last Words', rubbing in the dismissing of Tennyson, he reprised single lines from his own earlier translations including the first line of his *Iliad* VIII rendering. Tennyson was throwing his own pentameters back in Arnold's teeth. His blank verse will do for Homer. As Tennyson went on demonstrating. In August 1877 (in the *Nineteenth Century* maga-zine) he published a version of *Iliad* XVIII 202ff ('Achilles Over the Trench') in his own blank verse – verses actually done in the 1863 reaction against Arnold.[44] Tennyson wasn't going to let Arnold get away with disparaging his own utter at-homeness in classical modes and moods. A domestication witnessed magisterially in Tennyson's 'Lucretius'.

The Roman Modern

Lucretius quite haunted the Victorian classicizers – captivated by the way the epicurean, scientific humanism of his *De Rerum Naturae* seemed to anticipate the melancholy of a modern God-emptied universe, an existence from which confidence in an after-life was leaking away. Tennyson's friend Francis – *Golden Treasury* – Palgrave tells how Tennyson and friends sat up late one

---

[44]   A version is in the Pierpoint Morgan Library manuscripts along with other drafts of *Iliad* bits: published by Ricks in his Appendix A, 'Alternative Drafts'.

midwinter night reading 'the terrible lines in which Lucretius preaches his creed of human annihilation (Book III especially ll.912–977): and perhaps those (Book V.1194–1217) on the uselessness of prayer, and the sublime but oppressive fear inevitable to the thoughtful mind in the awful vision of the star-lighted heavens.' And, 'so carried away and overwhelmed were the readers by the poignant force of the great poet, that, next morning, when dawn and daylight had brought their blessed natural healing to morbid thoughts, it was laughingly agreed that Lucretius had left us last night all but converts to his heart-crushing atheism' (Hallam Tennyson, *Memoir*, II.500). Nervous laughter, no doubt. Tennyson, and Palgrave for that matter, cannot have been unmindful of Matthew Arnold's riff on the 'modernity' of Lucretius in his lecture 'On the Modern Element in Literature' – Lucretian modernity in the sense of troubled selfhood, not least as embraced in Arnold's memorable gloss on the 'modern problems' of his 1853 Preface: 'the dialogue of the mind with itself has begun'.

Arnold's Lucretius is a modern man, sunk in depression and ennui:

> Depression and *ennui*; these are the characteristics stamped on how many of the representative works of modern times! They are also the characteristics stamped on the poem of Lucretius.

The third book of the *De Rerum*, which so shook Tennyson and his friends, is where this Hamletian morbidity is most manifest. Arnold paraphrases it copiously. It's what, he thinks, raises Lucretius to world-class status:

> One of the most powerful, the most solemn passages of the work of Lucretius, one of the most powerful, the most solemn passages in the literature of the whole world, is the well-known conclusion of the third book. With masterly touches he exhibits the lassitude, the incurable tedium which pursue men in their amusements; with indignant irony he upbraids them for the cowardice with which they cling to a life which for most is miserable; to a life which contains, for the most fortunate, nothing but the old dull round of the same unsatisfying objects for ever presented.

The restless, unsettled, perpetually bored man of Book III: 'What a picture of ennui! of the disease of the most modern societies, the most advanced civilisations!' Lucretian man is both allured and terrified by the 'fulness and movement' of the world – the Arnoldian modern multitudinousness – which is 'too exciting a spectacle for his discomposed brain'. His only deliverance is in 'perpetually repeating his formula of disenchantment and annihilation'. In reading Lucretius 'you understand the tradition which represents him as having been driven mad by a poison administered as a love-charm by his mistress, and as having composed his great work in the intervals of madness'. Lucretius himself is obviously 'over-strained, gloom-weighted, morbid' – and shut out by his morbidity from being an 'adequate interpreter' of the modern age. Lucretius is the essence of Arnold's quintessential modern man. He encapsulates the distresses of so many Arnold ennui-driven poems and characters – the likes of Senancour and Empedocles (as featured in my Chapter 8).

All his life Arnold wanted to complete a verse Tragedy about Lucretius, and failed. ('Chew Lucretius' he advised himself in a list of poems he wanted to do in 1849.[45]) Some chewed bits were incorporated into his 'Empedocles on Etna: A Dramatic Poem'. Otherwise only toothed-over fragments remain. He was mightily miffed to hear in March 1866 that Tennyson was at work on the subject 'which I have been occupied with for some 20 years'. He suspected 'the subject was put into his [Tennyson's] head by Palgrave, who knew I was busy with it'. In the wake of the bitching over Homer translating he clearly assumed the Tennyson gang were determined to steal more of his classical thunder. Everyone 'except the few friends who have known that I had it in hand will think I borrowed the subject from him'.[46] His misgivings were probably well judged. What, though, his envy was blinding him to is the proximity of his own reading of Lucretius's melancholic modernity to Tennyson's own sense of modern subjectivity – which made no life more appropriate for Tennyson to treat, no persona more gloomily amenable for him to assume. Especially in the mythic version Arnold is so drawn to in which Lucretius was made insane by a love-potion and wrote his masterpiece in sporadic times of lucidity.

Well-practised in troubled minds, Tennyson Tennysonizes Lucretius with a terrible sense of familiarity. Tennyson's poem 'Lucretius' is, as Ricks's notes and Tennyson's classicizing investigators observe, supersaturated in Lucretian references, ideas, and means.[47] But what's most striking to the reader familiar with Tennyson's poems is how much of a fully-formed member of Tennyson's moody caste of the melancholy and mad his Lucretius is. Tennyson got his friend HAJ Munro, editor of the latest edition of Lucretius (1864) that he used (he'd been reading Lucretius since boyhood) to check his manuscript ('everything was Lucretian'). Norman Vance attractively suggests that Tennyson's 'jumbling together' of fragments of Lucretius's text 'wickedly mimes the random collision of Lucretian atoms which forms the Lucretian universe'.[48] The poem's run of iambic pentameters – Tennysonian blank verse – is cheekily spotted with some Lucretius-mimicking

---

[45]   Yale manuscript, quoted in headnote to 'Empedocles on Etna', Longmans Annotated *Poems of Matthew Arnold*, ed Kenneth Allott (1965), 147.

[46]   Letter to his mother, 17 March 1866. *The Letters of Matthew Arnold*, 6 vols, ed Cecil Y Lang (University Press of Virginia, Charlottesville and London, 1996–2001), Vol 3 (1998), 21.

[47]   The most detailed commentary is in AA Markley's otherwise over-tame *Stateliest Measures: Tennyson and the Literature of Greece and Rome* (University of Toronto Press, Toronto, 2004), Ch 6, 'Old Tales for a New Day: Lucretius, Demeter, and Oenone's Return', 140–148.

[48]   N Vance, *The Victorians and Ancient Rome*, 109.

and Arnold-annoying hexameters – including the frame narrator's tribute to Lucretius's hexameters, in a hexameter: 'Or fancy-borne perhaps upon the rise / And long roll of the Hexameter – he past' (10–11). The poem's Lucretius is as prompted into a sense of meaninglessness in a probably God-emptied universe as the Tennyson of *In Memoriam* is. The end of 'momentary man' is in sight (252); the terrifying *void* of the haunting end of *De Rerum* Book III awaits (249–258). Lucretius's master Epicurus believed in the Gods. But aren't they as dissoluble as the atoms they're made of (115)? Lucretius *meant*, he says, to lead Caius Memmius, the dedicatee of *De Rerum*, 'in a train / Of flowery clauses onward to the proof / That Gods there are, and deathless' (117–121). But any God-proof collapses as meaning and mind collapse:

> Meant? I meant?
> I have forgotten what I meant: my mind
> Stumbles, and all my faculties are lamed.
> (121–123)

Here's a self, an *I*, as fraught and demented as any of his Tennysonian predecessors, the hero of *Maud* especially. 'I hate, abhor, spit, sicken': at the sight of a classically lewd satyr pursuing a lovely Oread (199). It's a dementing vignette of 'lewdness, narrowing envy, monkey-spite / … madness of ambition, avarice' – selfish greed in action (211–212). We could be in *Maud*. And in *Maud* the 'little *Hamlet*'. Lucretius's will has been wrenched, stymied, by the 'vast and filthy hands' of 'some unseen monster' (219–221). Words fail this would-be poet. He'd like to 'shut reasons up in rhythm / Or Heliconian honey in living words, / To make a truth less harsh', but cannot. Shakespearian thoughts about the point of short-term human existence, this 'little life', weigh heavy. He could be Prospero in *The Tempest* thinking of how 'We are such stuff as dreams are made on' and how 'our little life / Is rounded with a sleep' (*The Tempest*, IV.i.156–158):

> I often grew
> Tired of so much within our little life,
> Or of so little in our little life –
> Poor little life that toddles half an hour
> Crowned with a flower or two, and there an end
> (225–229)

He becomes a Hamlet, puzzling in Hamletian words about what's human, what a man is, how merely beast-like, and whether suicide, ending himself, is not nobler than enduring life:

> And since the nobler pleasure seems to fade,
> Why should I, beastlike as I find myself,

> Not manlike end myself? – our privilege –
> What beast has heart to do it? And what man
> What Roman would be dragged in triumph thus?
>
> (230–234)

'Not I', he replies (235); but he does kill himself, this Roman Hamlet; an ancient Roman Tennysonized; his poem and his plight a triumph and manifestation of the intertextual communion Churton Collins announced as the very nature of Europe. Here are Tennyson's very modern anxieties, as man and poet, boldly refracted through this ancient life (and death). As they are, of course, *mutatis mutandis*, again and again, in the busy Victorian presentation of self and art in the mirror of earlier characters and selves classical, medieval, old fictional whatever. The grand prosopopoietic game played over and over. Modern plights and perplexities, of people and poets, which are, of course main modern*ist* issues. Or at least proto-modernist ones, in being so strongly proleptic of modernist problems and practices. The subject of my next, and final, chapter: 'Victorian Modernismus'.

10

Victorian Modernismus

The condition of Victorian poetry – its linguistics, poetics, hermeneutics, narrativity, characterologies – segues in fact rather smoothly into the dominant modernist practices of the twentieth century, practices which in turn blur and blend into so-called post-modernism. There's no clean end-of-century break. Nothing snaps cleanly just because the nineteenth century ends in 1899 (or is it 1900?) and Queen Victoria dies co-operatingly in 1901. 'Then in 1900 everybody got down off his stilts', said Yeats, wryly, in the Introduction to his *Oxford Book of Modern Verse* (1936); 'henceforth nobody drank absinthe with his black coffee; nobody went mad; nobody committed suicide; nobody joined the Catholic Church; or if they did I have forgotten'. But yes he did forget; and no everybody didn't just stop doing those late-Victorian, Decadent Nineties things.

What modernism, prevailing mode of the earlier twentieth century (and the stuff, the motor, of Theory), gets to mean is, though, pretty clear. Its narratives come shrouded in hermeneutic hesitation and doubt. 'HeCitEncy', as Joyce's coinage has it in *Finnegans Wake* – hesitancy over citing, speaking and telling – comes to reign. Narrative confidence gets squeezed out under the weight of the collapse of the old Grand Narratives, especially the Judaeo-Christian one. Impressionism takes over from realism. What's focussed in writing is presented as terribly blurred: difficult to make out, to *tell* – tell in every sense – clearly. 'The story will tell', says the narrative voice in the group awaiting the arrival of the governess's crucial papers in Henry James's early-modernist classic *The Turn of the Screw* (1898); but 'The story *won't* tell', says Douglas, who knows a thing or two about it, 'not in any literal, vulgar way'. Words fail narratives and narrators, not least because the power of

Victorian Poetry Now: Poets, Poems, Poetics, First Edition. Valentine Cunningham.
© 2011 Valentine Cunningham. Published 2011 by Blackwell Publishing Ltd.

words is felt as failing. Speakers stutter. Referring, naming, are at stake. Words run up against difficult, even impassable, stymying barriers, borders, thresholds (*aporias*, as the great deconstructive literature, after Jacques Derrida, puts the matter). Words break up, into crumbs, *apheses*, *aphaireses*, encroached on Beckettianly by silence, by the paradoxical condition of the unsaying-saying, the word without a word, the *Verbum in-fans*, the non-speaking word of TS Eliot's favourite seventeenth-century divine Lancelot Andrewes, the 'word unheard' which Eliot's poetry wrestles with from 'Gerontion' to 'Four Quartets'. It's no accident that Ferdinand de Saussure's modernist and proto-post-modernist lecture *Course in General Linguistics*, with its (extremely influential) preference for discussing the *arbitrariness* of signs (over any necessary connections with *signata*, things signified) and linguistic *difference* (rather than reference) is a close contemporary of TS Eliot's word- and hermeneutics-anorexic 'The Love Song of J Alfred Prufrock'. The modernist poet and poem are up against it verbally; as TS Eliot put it in his essay on 'The Metaphysical Poets' (*TLS*, 20 October 1921) they're having to *force* language, even to *dislocate* it, into their desired meanings. Narrators, narratives, readers 'live in the flicker', as the first narrator of Conrad's 'Heart of Darkness' (1899) puts this pervasive hermeneutic and narratological dilemma. 'Only a flicker': it's the condition of persons in Eliot's 'Burnt Norton', first of the *Four Quartets*, caught in the flickering light of the London Underground, the mazy light of early cinema films (known as the *flickers*, or *flicks*); and it's the condition of the text which contains them.

The classic realist novel is really a kind of detective story – and of course the apogee of Realism in the Victorian period coincides with the invention of the detective story – in which narration and narrators are essentially detectives, sorters out of truth from error, final arbiters of moral guilt and innocence, clearers-up of uncertainty: all parodic of the Christian God, who is to sort out all things on the Last Day of Judgement. And the modernist novel finds that old detective confidence difficult, not least because faith in the old detective deity of End Times judgement, the old model theology that sustained its confident epistemology and hermeneutic, was lapsing. Modernism's detective work gets increasingly clue-less. The clues build up, but lead nowhere much. Detective clues get their name and idea from the (original spelling) *clew*, the ball of thread that Ariadne gave Theseus to help guide him out of the Cretan labyrinth or maze after he'd successfully killed the beast-man, the Minotaur. The modernist Theseus, would-be moral hero, tries to imitate his successful maze-conquering predecessor by unravelling the clew, i.e. following the clues, and finds himself after all still stuck in the maze of moral and hermeneutic darkness. He's still *amazed* at the end of his story – and so are we. *Amazing*: it's the condition of Conrad's Africa and his story of Africa in that other classic of early-modernist fiction *Heart of Darkness* (1899). Narrator Marlow emerges physically from the jungle's maze, but morally, epistemologically, hermeneutically, he's all bemused and frustrated: *amazed*. *What Maisie Knew*, announces the title of Henry James's 1897 novel. 'I know', little Maisie keeps saying, about the adult goings-on around her, sounding like an unamazed conqueror of the moral maze; but how can she (and we) ever tell? And at the novel's end we're told there was still 'room for wonder at what Maisie knew'.

According to the first narrator of *Heart of Darkness*, the 'yarns of seamen' (*yarn*: story, named for the thread, the clew-stuff, that story-tellers traditionally manage) are known for their unreliability, but they get worse in these modernist conditions: Marlow's yarns are as hazy as 'the spectral illumination of moonshine' ('moonshine on the water': old marine expression for what's unfixed and unreadable). In other words the reader doesn't touch bottom in these narratives because the narration doesn't. The *bottom* of narrative thread – bottom is an old synonym for a ball of thread, or clew – doesn't get you to the bottom of the story matter (just as Shakespeare's Bottom the Weaver in Shakespeare's *A Midsummer Night's Dream*, so named because weavers worked with bottoms of thread, comically fails to get to the bottom of the Pyramus and Thisbe story, out of Ovid's *Metamorphoses*, home of course of the Theseus-Ariadne-Maze story, which he re-enacts ludicrously with the help of his clue-less colleagues including, we have to believe, the one playing the part of Moonshine).[1] Modernist reading becomes a matter of necessarily entrusting yourself to the 'the destructive element' of narrative waters, as Conrad's Stein advises in *Lord Jim* (1900); and this narrative element is as good, or as bad, as bottomless. The reader is left, at the end of the textual encounter, where certainties and resolutions should be in confident supply, rather bereft of sure footing – like Conrad's Razumov in *Under Western Eyes* (1911) threatened by corrupt Russian cops, 'alone like a swimmer in a deep sea'. 'Fear death by drowning' warns TS Eliot's modernist clairvoyant Madame Sosostris in the great 1922 text of modernist dilemmas *The Waste Land*, whose perturbing wateriness in a spiritual dry land pervades every aspect of that poem's selfhood and urbanism. The great cities of anglophone modernism, Eliot's London and Joyce's Dublin, are utterly deluged with the dangerous wateriness of the rivers they're built on. Dublin's River Liffey becomes the potent emblem of the fluidity of things and meanings: enigmas voiced by its watery personification in Anna Livia Plurabelle, who goes unstoppably on, round and round, in the unending verbal mish-mash of *Finnegans Wake*. The modernist text is indeed all moonshine on the water. Its reader is indeed all at sea. Or, put

---

[1]   For yarns, clues, and bottoms see Valentine Cunningham, 'Yarn', in *Glossalalia: An Alphabet of Critical Keywords*, ed Julian Wolfreys (Edinburgh University Press, Edinburgh, 2003), and 'Having a Clue … about Ovid', *Symbolism: An International Annual of Critical Aesthetics*, 5, 2005, 101–124.

another way, is stuck 'In the Cage', behind the wire of (mis)interpreting, with Henry James's hapless post-office girl mis-reading her customer's telegram messages. 'In the Cage' (1898), was later published in the same New York Edition volume of James's fiction as *What Maisie Knew*; the original subtitle of the second section of The *Waste Land* was 'In the Cage'.

And the texts of these expressive disablings are themselves threatened with disabling, ruin, even annihilation. They stutter horribly, breaking up into fragments, blanks, ellipses, *aposiopeseis*, gaps. They verge on silence. What wholeness they achieve is at best a tessellated one, the text as mosaic: 'These fragments I have shored against my ruins' says a narrative voice at the end of *The Waste Land*, summing up that poem's brokenness. Would-be presences, contents, give way to absences. Think Pound's *Cantos*, Eliot's *The Waste Land*, Beckett's plays and his novels from *Watt* on. There's a tendency for the textual container to leak meaning rather than fill up with it. Rather than a *mise en scène*, the bringing forward of a story, characters, meaning, onto the stage for the audience's benefit, there's what's been notoriously labelled a *mise en abîme*, a retreating plunge down into a kind of bottomless linguistic and epistemological plug-hole. Textuality is underpinned, but also undermined, by extensive meta-textuality – by writing about writing, self-reflecting rather than world-reflecting themes and stratagems – and by insistent intertextuality: *this* text, *your* text, looking back to its textual predecessors in an endless recessive chain of textual mirrors; like the endless receding of Velasquez's *Las Meninas* painting offered as the essence of a modern(ist) textual-epistemic by Michel Foucault in *Les Mots et Les Choses* / *The Order of Things*. Which is the text according to *Finnegans Wake* or Jorge Luis Borges and his followers such as Umberto Eco. *Multi-textuality* we might call it, a textual plenitude whose paradoxical purpose is meaning loss: like the thousands (millions?) of puns in the *Wake*, meaning doubles (portmanteaux) which radically unfix meaning in the process of multiplying it. An endless textual differing and deferring, rather than referring, as Derridean deconstruction would explain it.

And modernist character-making, the production of selves, goes the unsettling way of language, narrative, text: doling out a sequence of Doppelgänger, Double Men and Women, splitting, breaking, self-doubting. Modernist personality hides itself in adopted personae, masks, other voices. Modernist texts do the self in different voices ('He do the police in different voices', the description of Sloppy the newspaper reader in Dickens's *Our Mutual Friend*, was originally intended as the title of the first two parts of *The Waste Land*). These selves are malleable, up for remodelling. Characteristically, Eliot's Prufrock wonders who he is, and who he might become, what models for the self might be for him (John the Baptist, Lazarus, Hamlet, Polonius?). He's a leaky self, a dissolving actor, caught in a concerning fluidity of multiple self-reflections. 'All Europe contributed to the making' of *Heart of*

Darkness's Mr Kurtz: such multiplicity of the self is part of his dubiousness. Eliot tried to embrace it as a necessity and a good for the poet: who has, Eliot said momentously in his momentous piece of modernist prescription, 'Tradition and the Individual Talent',[2] no personality of his own; he's only a mouthpiece for the tradition, past writers, the 'mind of Europe', the tradition which arrives, what's more, only in pieces, as a set of ruins and rags ('O O O O that Shakespeherian rag' as Part Two of *The Waste Land*, the original 'He Do The Police in Different Voices Part Two: In the Cage' section, has it). The same went for the poem, and its human subjects. So: schizoid, even multiphrenic poet, poem, and human subject. Poetics and selfhood as neurotic disarrays. Contemporary, of course, with Freud, busily writing the self as a series of anxious Doppelgänger stories (consciousness: sub-consciousness; ego: id). Old 'narrative method', the capacity to tell a story straightforwardly, to tell yourself as something straightforward, giving way to what TSE in his famous review of Joyce's *Ulysses* called the 'mythical method' of Joyce, and Yeats, and the new anthropology and psychology: story (and self) as an amalgam of layers, myths, past stories and selves, a palaeography of being.[3]

Modernist, twentieth-century, doubtings, undoubtedly. But aren't they, or their close kin, already rather familiar to us in the Victorian poems we've been considering? And this isn't just a matter of taking into account the fact that Eliot and Pound, DH Lawrence and Virginia Woolf, Freud and Ferdinand de Saussure, were born in Victorian times, or that Conrad and James, Yeats and Freud started publishing (albeit late) in the nineteenth century and so, chronologically speaking at least, are actually Victorian writers. It is that so much of modernism is manifestly rooted in Victorianism, and continues rather than controverts so much of the Victorian operation. If the supposed border between Victorian and Modernist exists at all, it's a tumbledown, porous affair. The so modernist perplexities of hazed-over hermeneutic, tessellation of text and person, dissolution of person and text, are to be found, as we've seen, all over the scene of Victorian writing. They're the familiar components of Victorian poetry and poetics, personhood and text. Yeats brings dramatically home the way the Victorian spirit is so preludic of the modernist – playing the modernist game before modernism – when he sets Pater's notorious ekphrastic rhapsody about Leonardo's *Mona Lisa* – 'She is older that the rocks among which she sits' – as a 'revolutionary' *vers libre* poem (not free verse, of course: it's packed with rhymes, notably all the lines beginning with *And*) and offers this as the first text of his *Oxford Book*

[2] *The Egoist* (1919). In *The Sacred Wood: Essays on Poetry and Criticism* (Faber, London, 1922).
[3] TS Eliot, '*Ulysses*: Order and Myth', the *Dial* (1923). Reprinted in Frank Kermode, ed, *The Selected Prose of TS Eliot* (Faber, London, 1975).

of Modern Verse. Of course Pater's Lady metamorphoses into *The Waste Land*'s 'lady of situations', 'the Lady of the Rocks'.

Our great modernist poets, especially Ezra Pound and TS Eliot, keep proving their fructifying familiarity with their Victorian forebears. They can't help owning up to kinships and indebtednesses that their frequent rebuffings and distantiations (plain signs of the Bloomian Anxiety of Influence, of course) quite fail to erase. When Eliot began writing verses around the age of fourteen it was Edward FitzGerald's *Rubáiyát of Omar Khayyám* which 'captured my imagination' and inspired some 'very gloomy and atheistical and despairing quatrains in the same style'. These verses were suppressed, Eliot claimed, but their offspring certainly appears in the last verse of Eliot's 'The Triumph of Bullshit' (1910?) – 'And when thyself with silver foot shalt pass / Among the theories scattered on the grass / Take up my good intentions with the rest / And then for Christ's sake stick them up your ass' – plainly calqued on the concluding stanza of the FitzGerald poem ('And when Thyself with shining Foot shall pass').[4] That title 'The Triumph of Bullshit' is, of course, a nineteenth-century one – Swinburne for instance produced 'The Triumph of Time'. Eliot's 'Triumph' was published for the first time in 1996 in the collection of early and mainly unpublished Eliot poems in *Inventions of the March Hare: Poems 1909–1917*, edited by Christopher Ricks, and Ricks's notes assemble a lively roster of the Victorian poems and poets those early Eliot poems hark back to, revise, rewrite, replay and traduce – works by Tennyson (of course), Meredith, A J Symons, John Gray, Swinburne, Wilde, James Thomson (whom Eliot probably read before he read Dante; who may indeed have led Eliot to Dante), Matthew Arnold, as well as FitzGerald. There's a 'garden close' in the early 'Airs of Palestine, No.2' which clearly, if faintly, echoes 'the orchard closes' at the opening of Elizabeth Barrett Browning's 'The Lost Bower', lines which had 'always stuck in my head', said Eliot, not least as the epigraph to Kipling's ghost story 'They', which provided so many ghostly details for the opening garden encounters of Eliot's 'Burnt Norton', first of his *Four Quartets*. Eliot recommended 'The Lost Bower' to his 1916 evening class pupils for study alongside his lecture on Elizabeth Barrett Browning ('the Bardess', as he called her). He did admit that he was a bit hazy as to whether it was Kipling who led him to the Bardess, rather than the other way about;[5] but there's no hesitation about his obligation to Thomson, and Dowson and, above all, John Davidson. As he spelled it out, late in his career, in his Preface to a 1961 *Selection* of Davidson poems: he felt 'a peculiar reverence, and acknowledge[d] a

---

[4]   There's more on Eliot and FitzGerald in Vinnie-Marie D'Amrosio, *Eliot Possessed: TS Eliot and FitzGerald's Rubáiyát* (New York University Press, New York and London, 1989).

[5]   TS Eliot, *Inventions of the March Hare: Poems 1909–1917*, ed C Ricks (Faber & Faber, 1996), 289. Helen Gardner, *The Composition of Four Quartets* (Faber, London, 1978), 29,40.

particular debt, towards poets whose work impressed me deeply in my formative years between the ages of sixteen and twenty. … of these, two were Scots: the author of *The City of Deadful Night*, and the author of *Thirty Bob a Week*.' He had 'a fellow feeling with the poet who could look with a poet's eye on the Isle of Dogs and Millwall Dock'.[6]

The great modernist poet's sense of the modern city draws strongly on this good Victorian's. And of course the modernist collapsing of the Christian theological and Biblical Grand Narratives also gets strongly underway in Victorian writing, and in poetry not least of all – as we've seen. The modernist text sings joyfully from the Victorian sceptic's hymn-sheet. Like blasphemous heresy-fan Buck Mulligan in the opening pages of Joyce's *Ulysses*, who fishes a florin out of his pocket ('A miracle!') to pay the pious old milkwoman (whose invoked 'God' he's just traduced as 'the collector of prepuces'), with words from Swinburne's poem 'The Oblation' (from his 1871 volume *Songs Before Sunrise*): 'Ask nothing more of me, sweet. All I can give you I give'. As she leaves, Mulligan sings in 'tender chant' some more from the Swinburne:

> Heart of my heart, were it more,
> More would be laid at your feet.

All facetiously exaggerated enough, but also an announcement of Mulligan's (and his author's) affinity with Swinburne's blasphemous undoing of all those devout Victorian poems which offered their author's self to God, especially subverting, I'd say, Christina G Rossetti's 'Yet what I can I give Him / Give my heart' ('In the bleak mid-winter'), in a poem offering self, his *heart*, his *love*, to who knows what corrupted and corrupting beloved as a blasphemous 'Oblation' – the common label, much repeated in the Church of England's Eucharistic Service in The Book of Common Prayer, for Christ's offering of Himself as a sacrifice for sin. (We're left to guess that Mulligan is singing the words in the setting by Dante Gabriel Rossetti's chum, Theo Marzials, one of the most popular ballads of the 1880s according to the *New Oxford Dictionary of National Biography* – and presumably well known to musical Joyce.)

---

[6] 'Certainly, *Thirty Bob a Week* seems to me the only poem in which Davidson freed himself completely from the poetic diction of English verse of this time (just as *Non Sum Qualis Eram* seems to me the one poem in which by a slight shift of rhythm, Ernest Dowson freed himself). But I am sure that I found inspiriation in the content of the poem, and in the complete fitness of content and idiom, for I also had a good many dingy urban images to reveal. Davidson had a great theme, and also found an idiom which elicited the greatness of the theme, which endowed this thirty-bob-a-week clerk with a dignity that would not have appeared if a more conventional poetic diction had been employed. The personage that Davidson created in this poem has haunted me all my life, and the poem is to me a great poem for ever.' TS Eliot, Preface, *John Davidson: A Selection of His Poems*, ed Maurice Lindsay (Hutchinson, London, 1961).

Modernist doubting, its scepticism, its relativism are all, patently, nour-ished like this on Victorian precedent. What spurs modernism's pervasive impressionism, if not Pater's insistent theorizing of it in the Conclusion to *The Renaissance* (that resistance to the solidity of the world of objects as an illusion of language, because all we have are 'impressions unstable, flicker-ing, inconsistent')? Or, for example, Pater's practice of fictional ekphrasis, his close readings of invented painters and paintings in his *Imaginary Portraits* (1887). Pater was your man for the proto-modernist flicker: Victorian art criticism leading a sceptical phenomenology based in a scepti-cal aesthetics. Just so, it's only right that John Ruskin should be traced as a precursor of modernism's syncretistic formal methodology, the making of new wholes out of fragments, the Eliotic 'mythical method'; and as an inciter of certain modernists, Eliot, Yeats, TE Hulme, in finding Byzantine tessel-lated mosaic work as an inspiration and model.[7] Eliot's Burbank meditates (in 'Burbank with a Baedeker, Bleistein with a Cigar', in Eliot's *Poems*, 1920) on belated, ruinous Venice – the clipping of its emblematic lion's wings, 'Time's Ruins, and the Seven Laws' – in a brew of allusions to Ruskin's mel-ancholy over Venetian ruination and corruption, in his *Seven Lamps of Architecture* (1849), *The Stones of Venice* (1851–1853) and the 'Wings of the Lion' chapter of *Unto This Last* (1860).[8] The 'rubbishy' Venice of Clough's *Amours de Voyage*, and the lucubrations of the other Victorian ruin-bibbers, are other ghostly presences in 'Burbank'.

Eliot's intertextualized melancholy, and his sense of how a long tradition feeds it intertextually, has plenty to draw on in Victorian practice, aside from the obvious 'Maud' – and on Ruskin, again, perhaps. The Hyacinth girl in *The Waste Land* (alluded to in the hair discussion of 'Fleshly Feeling', Chapter 7 above) looks to the ancient myth that hyacinth leaves are inscribed *Ai, Ai* (alas, alas); she and her text are locked thus, as Robert Crawford nicely observes, in a nightmare world of melancholic repetition: those cries returning every spring with these spring flowers. Eliot was no doubt remembering Milton's elegy 'Lycidas' (line 107) where the bonnet of the grieving bard Camus is 'inscrib'd with woe', 'like to that sanguine flower'. As Ruskin did. 'I never read anything in spring-time (except the Ai, Ai, on the 'sanguine flower inscribed with woe')'.[9]

[7]   Dinah Birch, 'Ruskin, Myth and Modernism', and Giovanni Cianci, 'Tradition, Architecture and *Rappel à l'ordre*: Ruskin and Eliot (1917–1921)', in *Ruskin and Modernism*, eds Giovanni Cianci and Peter Nicholls (Palgrave, Basingstoke, 2001), 32–45; 133–154. Birch draws on her own *Ruskin's Myths* (Clarendon Press, Oxford, 1988).
[8]   See Giovanni Cianci, article cit.
[9]   Ruskin (1867), *Works*, 17.405. Robert Crawford, *The Savage and the City in the Work of TS Eliot* (Clarendon Press, Oxford, 1987), 149. Dinah Birch, 'Ruskin, Myth and Modernism'. article cit, 42.

Eliot's practice at large is fundamentally affected by Arthur Symons's *Symbolist Movement in Literature* (1899: very late in the nineteenth century, but still in it), with its influential heralding of Jules Laforgue's 'Disarticulated' poetry, and Mallarmé's 'deformation' of language, his and Verlaine's escape from 'the old bondage of exteriority' (reference, materialism), and Mallarmé's creation of 'the mere literature of words'.[10] And those Frenchmen are nineteenth-century poets who are close to certain Victorians, and not just the Nineties Decadents. Mallarmé, for instance, visited deep-sea swimming ('destructive element') Swinburne in 1867. He turned Tennyson's 'Mariana' into an ur-Symbolist 'prose poem'.[11] Fleshly Baudelairean, enamelling word-music maker Gautier didn't get into the *Symbolist Movement* volume until the revised edition of 1919, by which time Eliot has been introduced to his writing by Pound – and greatly indebted he was, 'for the advice to read Gautier's *Émaux et camées*, to which I had not before paid close attention'. Pound said that he and Eliot had decided around 1916–1917 that a new classicism was called for: 'general floppiness had gone too far, and ... some counter-current must be set going ... Remedy prescribed "Émaux et Camées" ... Rhyme and regular strophes.'[12] Swinburne's hermaphroditism, at least, had been running in step with *Émaux et camées* long since. (And must, not at all by the way, have infected Eliot's choice of hermaphroditic Tiresias as a main, if not *the* main, narrative persona of *The Waste Land*.)

Pound's Victorian debts are huge. The Sappho fragments, versions and translations published in Henry Thornton Wharton's *Sappho* (1885) greatly inspired what Hugh Kenner has aptly labelled Pound's 'poiesis of loss' and 'aesthetic of glimpses'.[13] (And this was to be incited by a whole anthology of Victorians poems, for the *Sappho* is dense with Symonds' – specially commissioned – verse translations, other Symonds versions, many of Swinburne's

---

[10] '... of more importance for my development than any other book'; 'I myself owe Mr Symons a great debt: but for having read his book, I should not, in the year 1908, have heard of Laforgue or Rimbaud: I should probably not have begun to read Verlaine; and but for reading Verlaine, I should not have heard of Corbière. So the Symons book is one of those which have affected the course of my life.' TS Eliot, Dublin lecture, 'Tradition and the Practice of Poetry' (1936), and review of Peter Quennell, *Baudelaire and the Symbolists*, *The Criterion*, ix (Jan 1930), 357: quoted, TS Eliot, *Inventions of the March Hare: Poems 1909–1917*, ed Christopher Ricks (Faber and Faber, 1996), 396, 402.

[11] In *La Dernière Mode*, 18 October 1874. Printed in full in Mary Ann Caws and Gerhard Joseph, 'Naming and Not Naming: Tennyson and Mallarmé', *Victorian Poetry*, 43 (i), Spring 2005, 1–18 (fn 38, pp17–18]: an important consideration of shared 'sonal repetition' and approach to 'ineffability' in these two poets.

[12] Pound, 'Harold Munro', *Criterion*, XI, no. 45 (July 1932), 590. Quoted Cianci, article cit, in *Ruskin and Modernism* (2001), 150.

[13] In his chapter on Pound's Sapphism, 'The Muse in Tatters', *The Pound Era* (University of California Press, 1971), 54–75.

Sapphic lines, versions by Charles Elton and Lord Neaves, a DG Rossetti tribute version – 'One Girl (A combination from Sappho)' – and a couple of Sapphic bits from Tennyson's *Eleänore* and *Fatima* ('in Sapphic metre').[14] Pound owes even more, of course, to Browning. Pound has been dubbed a 'rag-picker', picking his materials in the rags of poetic tradition (a not-so-kindly version of Eliot's rather high-minded vision of tradition-commerce in 'Tradition and the Individual Talent' – closer, in fact to the picking up of Victorian 'withered leaves' which Eliot admits to in sweeping up the phrase 'withered leaves' from Arnold's 'Rugby Chapel' into his 'Preludes I': as indicated in my footnote 33, 'Mourning and Melancholia', Chapter 8, p360). And Pound picks about most vigorously in Browning's poetry – doing, of course, what Browning for his part did so assiduously with earlier writings. Rag-picker son of rag-picker father.[15] Whose greatest obligation was to Browning's dramatic monologues, that key practice in the extensive Victorian literature of the fraught self. *The Men and Women* volume, Pound said, contained 'the most interesting poems in Victorian English'. This was in a review of Eliot's *Prufrock and Other Observations*.[16] Pound was hinting that Eliot's dramatic monologuizing owed much to Browning's. In his essay on 'The Three Voices of Poetry' (1953) Eliot credits 'Browning's greatest disciple, Mr Ezra Pound' with adopting 'the term "persona" to indicate the several historical characters through whom he spoke'.[17] Eliot's own play with the variable *prosopon* patently owes much to Tennyson's, and especially to Prufrock's mighty predecessor the narrator of *Maud*, but it's also obviously of the house and lineage of Browning. As is Yeats' use of the 'mask' – derived from Robert Browning, though via Wilde, in his proto-modernist dialogue-essay 'The Critic as Artist' (1891).[18] Pound (and Eliot) were evidently attending hard to what's been called Robert Browning's 'semantic stutter' – his

---

[14]   Wharton points out that *Fatima* appeared in 1832 with an epigraph from Sappho (Fragment 2 – unassigned in 1832 – which *Fatima* closely imitates, as does *Eleänore*). Wharton, *Sappho: Memoir, Text, Selected Renderings and A Literal Translation* (David Stott, London, 1885), note p.62. As Yoppie Prins, op cit, points out in her usefully informative account of Wharton, his introductory material on Sappho is mainly lifted from Symonds's *Studies of the Greek Poets* (1873). Prins does not, though, reflect on the great crowd of Victorian voices in the volume.

[15]   'Poet as Ragpicker: Browning in Pound's Early Poetry', Ch 2 of Mary Ellis Gibson, *Epic Reinvented: Ezra Pound and the Victorians* (Cornell University Press, Ithaca and London, 1995), 39–78.

[16]   In *Poetry* (1917). 'TS Eliot', in *Literary Essays of Ezra Pound*, ed and intro TS Eliot (Faber & Faber, London, 1954; 1960), 419.

[17]   'The Three Voices of Poetry', *On Poetry and Poets* (Faber & Faber, London, 1957), 95.

[18]   In Wilde, *Nineteenth Century* (July and Sept 1890), gathered in *Intentions* (James R Osgood McIlvaine & Co, London, 1891). These and other such debts are ably set out in Carol T Christ's standard account, *Victorian and Modern Poetics* (University of Chicago Press, 1984).

disjunctive syntax, his hard consonantalisms[19] – and indeed to the formal stagger, the stuttering progress, of *In Memoriam*. Just so, it's difficult to believe that Eliot's formula of the contemporary poet needing to distort and force language into his meaning, did not have Hopkins's practice, by then publicly available, much in mind – his huge semantic and syntactic deviance; his poems' stymying loss of 'syntactical ligatures' such as pronouns prepositions, conjunctions; and the gloriously fuzzy way with *-ing* words, verbs as nouns, nouns as adjectives, adjectives as nouns (as 'in his riding / Of the rolling level underneath him steady air': 'The Windhover').[20] And so on.

For encouragement in linguistic contortionism James Joyce needed to look no further than Hopkins – or, for that matter, Lewis Carroll, the most lucid explicator of 'portmanteaux' there's ever been. As Hopkins was seized on as a father for the Auden Generation, so Carroll was acclaimed as Surrealism's progenitor. He figured in the first Surrealist manifesto of 1924; Aragon translated 'The Hunting of the Snark' (1929) – he thought Carroll's fictions imagined human freedom in an age of real oppression in Ireland, in factories, and of the mirage of 'free' trade; Breton put Carroll's 'Lobster Quadrille' in his 1939 *Anthologie de l'humeur noir*.[21] Antonin Artaud, the surrealist who invented 'the theatre of cruelty', tried to translate the Jabberwocky song (he also staged a version of Shelley's *The Cenci*, whose blood, rape, incest and murder were right up his 'Cruelty' street). The surrealist 'Revolution of the Word' – Eugene Jolas's label for the linguistic doings of the quasi-surrealist *Finnegans Wake* in *Our Exagmination Round his Factification for Incamination of Work in Progress* (Faber 1929), the *Wake* celebration headed by Samuel Beckett – was eager to pay its dues to Carroll. Jorge Luis Borges absorbed the Carrollian word-gaming into his work. One of Vladimir Nabokov's early acts of literary *hommage* was translating *Alice in Wonderland* into Russian (1923).[22]

---

[19]   Stewart W Holmes, 'Browning: Semantic Stutterer', *PMLA* 60 (1945), 231–255. Effects well aired in Carol T Christ, *The Finer Optic: The Aesthetic of Particularity in Victorian Poetry* (Yale University Press, New Haven and London, 1975), Ch. 2, ' "The World's Multitudinousness": Atomism and the Grotesque', 68ff.

[20]   Hopkins's *Poems*, ed Robert Bridges, published end of 1918; Eliot's 'Metaphysical Poets', October 1921. Hopkins's linguistic distortings are sharply inspected by Carol T Christ, *The Finer Optic*, 137–139: very good, for instance, on the meaning (and perception) accumulations of those 'Windhover' lines.

[21]   Carroll releases the 'absurd' of children's games, replete with 'unconstrained morals', 'inconsistency', and 'impropriety', into the adult world, said Breton in his accompanying essay: *Anthology of Black Humour*, trans Mark Polizzotti (City Lights, San Francisco, 1997; Telegram, London, 2009, 137–138).

[22]   Much of this detail is in Michael Holquist, 'What is a Boojum? Nonsense and Modernism', *Yale French Studies*, no. 43, *The Child's Part* (1969), 145–165, which argues at length for the pure (modernist) fictionality/self-referential textuality of Nonsense: a writing that's precursive of Kafka, Borges, Nabokov in being, as Holquist has it, not reducible to something other than itself.

As for linguistic emptying and emptiness, the Victorian poetry shelf was, ironically, even more abundantly stocked – with the mere noisiness of the *bouts-rimés* merchants, the widespread loss of meaning in a Tennysonian and Christina G Rossetti-esque repetition of signifiers, the over-multiplication of names, the prevalent non-sense of Nonsense (quite literally a *verbum infans*, infant babble, the *in-fans* of small person speak). A linguistic presencing that's also an absenting; a modernist (and post-modernist, Derridean, aporetic) practice: it's what's found amply in, say, Christina G Rossetti's poems (as discussed in my Chapter 4, 'These Rhyming / Repeating Games Are Serious'); and what, of course, invites (and gets) so many enthusiastic post-Derridean readings of Victorian poems.[23] It certainly anticipates the telling / not-telling aporias of Henry James. A Jamesian anticipation which James himself recognized in his wonderfully fetching interpretative rewriting of Robert Browning's *The Ring and the Book* in his 1912 Browning Centenary lecture, 'The Novel in The Ring and the Book'.[24]

Jamesianized Browning

James's take on *The Ring and the Book* is one of the most compelling (re) readings of a poem ever, and momentous especially because it utterly Jamesianizes Browning, turning it in effect into a Henry James novel, and in so doing realizes, and releases, the copious modernist potential of this so copious poet and poem.[25]

[23]   From the likes of Gerhard Joseph, editor of the nouveau-critical Tennyson centennial number of *Victorian Poetry* (30, iii–iv, Winter 1992), singled out in my Preface as characteristic of the recent wide spread of deconstructionist readers and readings, whose post-structuralist fundamentalist *Tennyson and the Text: The Weaver's Shuttle* (1992) is mentioned, with necessary demurral, in fn 32, Ch 9, p446. And of course any reference to deconstructive readings of Victorian poetry is incomplete without including the heroic deconstructionist efforts of J Hillis Miller, Derrida's friend and sometime colleague – essays such as on Hardy's 'The Torn Letter', in *Taking Chances: Derrida, Psychoanalysis and Literature*, eds Joseph H Smith and William Kerrigan (Johns Hopkins University Press, Baltimore and London, 1984), 134—145; and 'Topography and Tropography in Thomas Hardy's "In front of the Landscape"', in A Banerjee, ed, *An Historical Evaluation of Thomas Hardy's Poetry* (Studies in British Literature 49) (Edwin Mellon Press, Lewiston, 2000), 253–274.
[24]   'The Novel in The Ring and the Book', *Transactions of the Royal Society of Literature*, 2nd Series, Vol 31, Part IV (1912), 269–298. Revised, *Quarterly Review* (July 1912). Reprinted in James, *Notes on Novelists: With Some Other Notes* (JM Dent, London, 1914). There are, of course, many handy editions of *The Ring and the Book*, but the one edited by Richard D Altick and Thomas J Collins (Radview Literary Texts, Peterborough, Ontario, 2001) has especially good General Notes and Textual Notes as well as early reviews.
[25]   Though E Warwick Slinn's important subject in the Browning section of *The Discourse of Self in Victorian Poetry* (Macmillan, Basingstoke, 1991), 118–148, is, essentially, the modernism of *The Ring and the Book* (even its post-modernism, for he invokes Derrida a lot), he quite fails to take in the force of James's (re)readings.

James has long felt, he says, 'the sense, almost the pang of the novel' that Browning's materials might have been turned into – a novel by Henry James, of course. The (necessary) 'germ', or 'donnée' of this novel-manqué was bigger than was usual in James's own case: the great collection of papers about the seventeenth-century trial of Count Guido Franchesini for the murder of his wife Pompilia and her adoptive parents, which Browning found on a Florence market stall (the 'Book of the Florentine rubbish-heap' as James calls it). Browning has developed his *donnée* in a very forceful version of the Jamesian way of slow imaginary germination, squeezing it into narrative shape. A prodigious task, quite aweing to this past-master of rather gentle germination:

> I doubt if we have a precedent for this energy of appropriation of a *deposit* of stated matter, a block of sense already in position and requiring not to be shaped and squared and caused any further to solidify, but rather to suffer disintegration, be pulled apart, melted down, hammered by the most characteristic of the poet's processes, to powder – dust of gold and silver, let us say. He was to apply to it his favourite system – that of looking at his subject from the point of view of a curiosity almost sublime in its freedom, yet almost homely in its method, and of smuggling as many more points of view together into that one as the fancy might take him to smuggle, on a scale on which he had never before applied it.

'Browning works the whole thing over – the whole thing as originally given him – and we work *him*'. James declares this twice. This is the Jamesian method, and result: the given material worked over, or *done* (favourite James metaphor, applied several times to Browning), and then handed over to the reader to be worked over. Worked over with the aid of what James called reflectors, or reflexive consciousnesses, hermeneutic leaders, characters provided through whom the story is filtered, focalized, and interpreted. James offers Giuseppe Caponsacchi of Book VI, who rescued Pompilia from the oppressive Guido, as 'the enveloping consciousness – or call it just the struggling, emerging, comparing, at last lively conscience' of this 'excellent novel'. Caponsacchi is the 'large lucid reflector' whom the mature James likes to put in charge. And Caponsacchi is indeed a lucid reflector on and of Browning's complex affair. We're even prepared to grant him his quasi-detective status when he asks us to let him 'interpret you / The mystery of this murder' (*The Ring and the Book*, VI.72–73). But offering Caponsacchi as the sole equivalent of, say, Strether of James's *The Ambassadors* (1903) ('struggling, emerging, comparing, at last lively conscience') rather depletes Browning's endeavour at the expense of this Jamesian tidying-up. For Browning gives us, in effect, a plethora of reflector characters. As James said, here is the dramatist and author of *Men and Women*, *Dramatic Lyrics* and *Dramatis Personae*, working on an unprecedented scale. *The Ring and the Book* is the dramatic monologue running riot, a large crowd scene of partial, interested narrating monologuists – Pompilia, the lawyers Hyacinthus and Bottinus, the Pope, the voices of respectable Roman public opinion pro and con Guido and Pompilia, the voice of the Roman rabble, Caponsacchi, Guido himself (twice over). Especially Guido the wife-killer, obsessed with his ancient family name and heritage (like the wife-killing Duke of 'My Last Duchess'). And Henry James, doyen of the complexly unreliable narrator, is quite awed by the amount of these on display – flawed minds at full stretch, all done from an extraordinary commanding inside perspective. What is for him magnificent here is 'the author's complexity of suggestion, to which our own thick-coming fancies respond in no less a measure'. It's a giving, and yet also a withholding of so much: the 'rich provision', as James puts it, that is 'above all a preparation for something that is not provided'. In other words, the story telling, and not telling, all at once: an 'unhusking' of truth, as Browning has it (I.989), which is never satisfactorily completed; a sharing of knowledge with the reader, which still leaves open questions of 'who' Pompilia and Guido were, 'what manner of mankind', and of how such apparent knowledge is attained, 'how you hold concerning this and that' (I.377–380). It takes, says James,

> a great mind, one of the greatest, we may at once say, to make these persons express and confess themselves to such an effect of intellectual splendour. He resorts primarily to *their* sense, their sense of themselves and of everything else they know, to exhibit them, and has for this purpose to keep them, and to keep them persistently and inexhaustibly, under the fixed lens of his prodigious vision. He thus makes out in them boundless treasures of truth – truth even when it happens to be, as in the case of Count Guido, but a shining wealth of constitutional falsity.

The truth and falsity of consciousness and narration mixed up together; the truth about the uncertainty of all witness, knowledge, self-knowledge, narration: this is the condition not just of James's mature fictions, but of modernist epistemology and hermeneutics, all told. A world of misinterpretation and misprision (Pompilia defends Caponsacchi against the people who 'misinterpret and misprise' her rescuer, VII.920). The Roman public wants certainties in the case, but they'll not get them, especially not from the Law and the Church, and certainly not from History. Browning invents a 'barefoot Augustinian' monk (XII.446) who publishes a sermon on the trial based on the text of Romans 3.4: 'Let God be true and every man / A liar' (453–454). The monk demands 'assent' to his text, reiterating it, glossing it:

> who trusts
> To human testimony for a fact
> Gets this sole fact – himself is proved a fool;
> Man's speech being false.
> (XII.601–604)

Browning beefed up the preacher's assertion by adding a line about 'earth's prerogative of lies' for his second (1872) edition. As master-narrator he urges the British Public to take away this most important 'lesson' from his poem:

> This lesson, that our human speech is naught,
> Our human testimony false, our fame
> And human estimation words and wind.
>
> (XII.834–836)

Which is of course the Cretan Liar paradox – the very human narrator Browning offering a truth that all humans are liars ('"All Cretans are liars", said the Cretan'). But it is Art's 'glory and good' that it can speak thus. Only Art can

> ... look a brother in the face and say
> 'Thy right is wrong, eyes hast thou yet art blind,
> Thine ears are stuffed and stopped, despite their length,
> And, oh, the foolishness thou countest faith!'
>
> (XII.841–844)

The reference here, apparently, is to Psalm 115.5–7, on the subject of the idols of the heathens:

> They have mouths, but they speak not: eyes have they, but they see not.
> They have ears, but they hear not: noses have they but they smell not:
> ... neither speak they through their throat.

The mendacious humanity of the poem is, then, being likened to the heathen's idols. Arrestingly, Psalm 115 is the one beginning 'Not unto us, O Lord, not unto us, but unto thy name give glory, for thy mercy, and for thy truth's sake. Wherefore should the heathen say, Where is now their God? But our God is in the heavens: he hath done whatsoever he hath pleased' (vv.1–3). These are the Biblical verses sponsoring the Browning lines in *Pippa Passes* – much scoffed-at for apparent complacency – '*God's in his heaven – / All's right with the world!*' (Pippa's song, *Pippa Passes*, 'Morning' (Part I), 227). Whatever the complacency of that, *The Ring and the Book* is indicating here that much is wrong with the world because it finds it hard to accept that God is the only one who speaks true, and that all human speech, testimony, estimation, are hollow and false; that people are as linguistically and hermeneutically disabled as the heathen idols of the Psalms; are all creatures of disabled senses and so of disabled mouths.

Which is God's truth; which only Art, says Browning, can speak. A (pre) modernist doubting, only resolvable for Christian Browning in unmodernist

Christian terms; but interrogated, in very modernist fashion, self-reflexively, in a poem constantly addressing the ways and nature of itself, of this poem and of this poet, Robert Browning, as well as the ways of poetry *per se*. Doing it directly and metatextually. Which is what Henry James and his modernist ilk regularly do: what James meant in his New York Edition Preface to *The Ambassadors* when he says that there is in the novel one's story, and then the story of one's story. What he hints at in his repeated assertion that Browning 'works the whole thing over ... and we work him': positing our reading as an encounter with the workings of the working; what James called Browning's 'poetic, esthetic' subject running alongside his 'historic, psychologic' ones. An encounter with what Schlegel called in the phrase already granted its due weight, the 'poesie der poesie'.

Poetry and the poetic are never not in question in this poem. Browning speaks to the reader in his own person, the poem's poet addressing the neglectful 'British Public', defending his poem. Sometimes he's been his only audience ('when he who praised and read and wrote / Was apt to find himself the self-same me': I.1384–1385); but his latest method will remain the old one – doing the voices, letting the voices 'sound', dramatic-monologue-wise (I.838). Poetry is not 'white lies' (I.456). In retelling this old story (as he's retold old stories before), his poem is doing God-like resurrection work, creating life from the dead. The old found Yellow Book was dead, more or less, a ruin, a crumblement, a piece of shit, ''mid the ordure, shards and weeds' (I.673, 676). He's a Resurrection Man; or a Dr Frankenstein, making new bodies out of old dead bits, 'By a moonrise through a ruin of a crypt'(I.757). You should not, though, think of Faust, but rather of the Old Testament prophet Elisha who raised a dead boy to life by lying on the corpse, mouth to mouth, eyes on eyes, hands on hands (I.760ff). 'The life in me abolished the death of things' (I.520). The work of 'resuscitation' (I.719) is salvific:

> Makes new beginning, starts the dead alive,
> Completes the incomplete and saves the thing.
> (I.733–734)

Browning's approach to the truth of things is indeed oblique (XII.856), a 'mediate word' (857), mediated as ever through these resuscitated, fictionalized others; but that's Art's way. A self-conscious way, as witnessed by all these reader-directed polemics, and by the poem's constant writerly items and textual procedures. Darkened reflections, at that. Words, the writer's only means, are necessary, but often just a pack of lies. They're a hiccup, or vomit, of hatred (II.678–679), a foaming spittle of invective (II.1041–1042). Pompilia the would-be truth-teller lacks the words ('how can I find the words?' VII.720; God will have to 'explain in time / What I feel now, but fail to find the words' VII.1760–1761); Guido the practised liar has a 'world of words' (XI.2416) at his tricky disposal over two whole Books, V and XI, the latter the longest Book in the poem. Books, the Big Book of the Bible, the secular classics, are misusable and misreadable, misused and misread. Caponsacchi – 'A brisk priest', according to Guido, 'who is versed in Ovid's art', the *Ars Amatoria*, 'More than his Summa', his theology book (V.1357–1358) – lures smart women to the Church (and Church officials?) with rude verses from Catullus and Ovid, a pander with Ovid in his 'poke' (*poke*, an aptly suggestive name for a bag), VI.391. Guido misremembers his Virgil (XI.1926). His lawyer Dominus Hyacinthus is a conscious mishandler of texts. You have, he says, to 'poke' at the adjudicating priests with Scripture (VIII.1737). For him the Bible is just a tool for rhetorical effects. Reworking his defence speech he refers to the Bible, but skews it freely, like a crazed exegete, playing interpretative games with the shoddily recalled Bible passages whizzing around the echo-chamber of his memory. Guido locks up his wife in his house; but surely Jesus said that 'Foxes have holes, and fowls o' the air their nests' and the Court would not wish her to have nowhere to lay her head (VIII.1300–1302)! Guido disguised himself for his murder attempt; but did not St Paul wrap himself in the cloak he later 'left behind at Troas' before escaping over the Damascus city wall in a basket? (VIII.1322–1330). (No he did not; Hyacinthus is luridly combining the Acts 9 escape with the Troas cloak mention in 2 Timothy 4.13.) 'Are these things writ for no example, Sirs?' he asks, rightly referring to St Paul's words in I Corinthians 10.11, but taking Samson as a farfetched model for Guido, and going on to misquote God's words in the Latin version of Isaiah 42.8 and ascribe them, what's worse, to Jesus. He invokes St Paul in I Corinthians 9.15 but makes him talk about personal *glory* rather than *glorying* in Christ (and, to boot, approving St Ambrose's fruitful comment on this text, which, however, 'I can't quite recollect') (VIII.638–681). 'Revelation old and new admits / The natural man may effervesce in ire' (VIII.683–684), he claims; but only if you wrench the Bible as he does. Protestant Browning relishes the Pope's following Hyacinthus's corrupted version of Isaiah ('...as when Christ said, – when, where? / Enough, I find it in a pleading here': X.1981–1982). The Church's top arbiter is misled by the Court's slipperiest reader. Famously, in his *Confessions*, St Augustine was urged by a divine voice to take up his Bible and read it, *tolle et lege.*' '"Surge et scribe", make a note of it! / – If I may dally with Aquinas word', says Hyacinthus, getting everything wrong: not Aquinas', and not 'Get up and *write*' (VIII.1305–6). But he would think this, because he doesn't actually read texts; he rewrites them. Here's reading as misreading as rewriting. Writings keep being made to go wrong. As they are dramatically in Guido's plottings.

The illiterate Pompilia pens a lying letter to her adoptive parents, but only by tracing over Guido's pencilled marks. Guido forges love letters between

Pompilia and Caponsacchi, to be discovered in their chamber en route to Rome by the pursuing Guido, and adduced by him in his defence (VI.1639ff). Forged epistles from Pompilia invite Caponsacchi into an affair. His early rebuttals – he's a priest; she's a wife – are freely translated by the go-between messenger maid as passionate responses. The messenger panders busily, eloquently misrepresenting each one to the other. She's thus at one with Hyacinthus as a wicked interpreter of a text. Caponsacchi has, she tells Pompilia, written her a sonnet – whose very existence, as well as its meaning, are at the mercy of the maid's say-so:

> Just hear the pretty verse he made to-day!
> A sonnet from Mirtillo. '*Peerless fair...*'
> All poetry is difficult to read,
> The sense of it is, anyhow, he seeks
> – Leave to contrive you an escape from hell,
> And for that purpose asks an interview.
> (VII.1152–1157)

(Mirtillo is a conventional poetic name for a pastoral lover.) 'All poetry is difficult to read': it's the voice of Browning's critics. Browning is swiping at the traducers of his own verses. But deeper than that is the awful link between poetry and crookery. The forged letters are, in Guido's formula, what Browning's poetry was accused of, namely a crude mixture of poetic and prosaic – 'Now, poetry in some rank blossom-burst / Now, prose' (V.1140–1141). And villainous Guido and his author Browning keep being elided like this. '[H]ere I stand', Guido says, quoting Martin Luther, as Browning liked to do (V.247). The insult Guido's ancient name has received from Pompilia's adoptive parents hitching him to a lowborn bride is like being 'stunk ... dead', pelted in the face with 'ordure', or 'fetor' (XI.1217, 1268) – which is how Browning felt about the critics' attentions. Thinking of himself as thus bemerded, Guido compares himself with the person who published a sonnet satirizing Abate Pianciatichi, one of his judges, and was sent to the galleys:

> rowing now
> Up to his waist in water, – just because
> *Pianciatic* and *lymphatic* rhymed so pat.
> (XI.1252–4)

In Browning's finest cursing style Caponsacchi wishes Guido in the lowest circle of Dante's Hell where (VI.1928ff) he'll be kissed by the Christ-betrayer Judas Iscariot and licked all over, with the verse-and-prose filth of the letters he forged, by Pietro Aretino, renowned writer of vicious epistles, but also the notorious author of lascivious sonnets:

> Lure him the lure o' the letter, Aretine!
> Lick him o'er slimy-smooth with jelly-filth
> O' the verse-and-prose pollution in love's guise.
>   (VI.1947–1949)

Guido: Aretino. Pompilia's lawyer Dr Bottinus also has Aretino on his mind when he sarcastically berates the Law for silliness in consigning Pompilia to a convent and a life of morally good-bad verse:

> Be burned, thy wicked townsman's sonnet-book!
> Welcome, mild hymnal by ... some better scribe!
>   (IX.1202–1203)

The wicked townsman is Aretino. And the Law's an aesthetic ass – like all opponents of Browning's fleshliness. And Browning seems to be endorsing Bottinus's warmth towards the censored sonneteer. Bottinus thinks of himself as a portrait painter in words. He has fifty such 'studies' in his repertoire – like Browning, for whom painters and paintings are constant analogues for poets and poetry ('We writers paint out of our heads, you see!', as the 'penman' says in 'Mr Sludge, "The Medium"', line 1467), and who in his poem 'One Word More' offered the 'fifty men and women' of the 'fifty poems' of his *Men and Women* collection to Elizabeth Barrett as so many portraits. The painter Rafael wrote sonnets, and the poet Dante wanted to paint, and Browning does both, even though, according to 'One Word More', he retreats to a 'Verse and nothing else' posture (line 114).

Guido-Aretino-Bottinus-Browning: crooked and filthy writing, reading, poetry. Which are, tellingly, the textual assumptions and anxieties of modern times according to Bottinus. The ancients 'could say anything', but an audience of priests makes him cut and curtail. 'I shall have to prune and pare and print. / This comes of being born in modern times' (IX.1575–1576). Browning, the copious resister to pruning and paring, evidently sympathizes with Bottinus's sense of 'modern' writerly plight – a modernity which includes, clearly, the demand Browning shares with Bottinus, to think and worry about what you write as you write it, the imperative of poetic self-consciousness, self-consciousness of poet as poet and poem as poem, poetic self-reflexivity, poetry about poetry, the *double* (or *doubling*) work of the poem in the phrase of Isobel Armstrong's that's entered the very grain of the discussion of Victorian poetry.[26] It's the modernist demand, in fact;

---

[26] Her *Victorian Poetry*, 13=14, etc, etc. Compare e.g. Maryon Ainsworth, *Dante Gabriel Rossetti and the Double Work of Art* (Yale University Press, 1976): it's a cliché, but nonetheless valid for all that. On the modernism and accessibility to modern Theory of *The Ring and the Book*, W David Shaw, 'Browning's Murder Mystery: *The Ring and the Book* and Modern Theory', *Victorian Poetry* 27, iii–iv, (Autumn—Winter 1989), 79—98, is usefully suggestive.

strikingly flagged, and evidenced, in *The Ring and the Book*, as it is elsewhere in Victorian poetry, in *ekphrasis*.

Victorian Ekphrasticity: Essence of its Modernism

Ekphrasis: the (ancient) literary work of describing non-written, human-made
objects (of any size, from coins to cities): analogues for the poet's own work,
mirrors of writing, surrogates for writing in any aesthetic/theoretic consideration, especially very close aesthetic analogues – statues, paintings, engravings,
drawings and books.[27] Like the Old Yellow Book at the core of Browning's
poem and the ring, Elizabeth Barrett Browning's own ring in fact, with which
the poem opens, a *sign* whose *signified* (I.32) is the Yellow Book and by extension this poem itself. What *ekphraseis* (plural) traditionally do is to reassuringly pronounce the solidity, touchability, knowability of the work of art, its
deictic *this-ness* and *there-ness*, the aweing actuality of its presence, what
ancient criticism called its *thauma*, its wonder. And, at the same time, to focus
the unknowabilities of a work of art, the difficulties of reading it, its fragility
and ruinousness, the doubtfulnes of its *this-ness* and *there-ness*.[28] The writer
addresses the object (apostrophizes it), grants it character (prosopopeia),
allows it to speak, often to some ethical or political purpose (Greek *ekphrasis*
means *speaking out*). But this avowed eloquence is always, in practice, also a
resolute muting, a silence. Ekphrasis is, as it were, modernism's most ancient
trope: a story of the aesthetic story that all at once tells and does not tell.

Nothing could be more actual and real than the old Yellow Book from which
Browning derives his vast poem and its analogous gold ring; this mass of *deixeis*: 'this square old yellow Book' (repeated: I.33 and 677); 'these letters ... veritable sheets' (691), found 'By the low railing round the fountain-source / Close
to the statue, where a step descends', read through on the way back to the Casa
Guidi, through the Florence market trash, 'through street and street / At the

27   Standard discussions are: Murray Krieger, *Ekphrasis: The Illusion of the Natural Sign*
(Johns Hopkins University Press, Baltimore and London, 1991); JAW Heffernan, 'Ekphrasis
and Representation', *New Literary History*, 22, ii (Spring 1991), 297–316, and *Museum of
Words: The Poetics of Ekphrasis from Homer to Ashbery* (University of Chicago Press, Chicago
and London, 1993); WJT Mitchell, *Picture Theory: Essays on Verbal and Visual Representation*
(University of Chicago Press, Chicago and London, 1994); G Jurkevich, *In Pursuit of the
Natural Sign: Azorín and the Poetics of Ekphrasis* (Bucknell University Press, and Associated
University Presses, Lewisburg, PA and London, 1999). See also Grant F Scott, 'The Fragile
Image: Felicia Hemans and Romantic Ekphrasis', in *Felicia Hermans: Reimagining Poetry in
the Nineteenth Century*, eds Nanora Sweet and Julia Melnyk (Palgrave, Basingstoke and NY,
2001), 36—54; and Jerome McGann, 'Medieval versus Victorian versus Modern: Rossetti's Art
of Images', *Modernism/Modernity*, 2, 1 (1995), 97–112.
28   See Valentine Cunningham, 'Why ekphrasis' in Ekphrasis Special Number of *Classical
Philology*, 102, no.1 (Jan 2007), 57–71.

Strozzi, at the Pillar, at the Bridge', at Casa Guidi, 'by Felice Church, / Under the doorway where the black begins / With the first stone-slab of the staircase cold' (I.91–116). 'The yellow thing I take and toss once more', 'this paper that I touch', with its epistles 'Here … part fresh as penned, / The sand, that dried the ink, not rubbed away / Though penned the day whereof it tells the deed' (XII.220, 226, 233–235). The old Book is as touchable as the arch-ekphrasist Browning has Lippo Lippi's fresco of the torture of St Laurence, its plaster worn through to the bricks by angry parishioners scratching and prodding the torturers' faces ('Fra Lippo Lippi', 323–332). As wondrously present as the portrait of 'My Last Duchess'. 'I call / That piece a wonder, now', says the Duke in a frenzy of *deixeis*: 'that's my Last Duchess … there she stands … that spot of joy … that spot of joy … There she stands'. The Yellow Book is almost as thaumatizing as the painting in Browning's 'Rhyme for a Child Viewing a Naked Venus in a Painting of "The Judgement of Paris"':

> He gazed and gazed and gazed and gazed,
> Amazed, amazed, amazed, amazed.

The Book's old story, its 'pure crude fact' (I.86), is resurrected and at gargantuan length. 'I … mastered the contents, knew the whole truth' (I.117). But this 'truth' is the proclamation of human untruthfulness. And like the Book, so the ring: found among old tombs, in that sense resurrected, and itself a model of repristination (I.23); a thing of pure gold, but needing gold alloy in its making into a 'ring-thing' (alloy finally got rid of by a 'spirt' of acid) – a maker's 'trick' (I.8) offered as model for Browning's own mix of fact and fiction, truth and invention. And so the aesthetic reassurance wrought, and in a measure found, in ekphrastic encounters, has this way of being diffused in modernist negativity, doubt and blur.

And Victorian ekphrasis underlines, no less, the world of worries about poetry's rights, capabilities, and achievements packed into the poets' and poems' repeated metatextuality. Christina G Rossetti, for example, exudes pleasure and confidence in her self-mirrored medium in the dedicatory sonnet of her 1881 volume *A Pageant and Other Poems*:

> Sonnets are full of love, and this my tome
> Has many sonnets: so here now shall be
> One sonnet more, a love sonnet, from me
> To her whose heart is my heart's quiet home,
> To my first love, my Mother …
>
> …
>
> And so because you love me, and because
> I love you, Mother, I have woven a wreath
> Of rhymes wherewith to crown your honoured name.

But this all-round sweetness is rare at such moments. As rare as Tennyson's wallow in Virgil's linguistic force (he's a 'lord of language').

> I salute thee, Mantovano
> I that loved thee since my day began
> Wielder of the stateliest measure
> Ever moulded by the lips of man.
> ('To Virgil. Written at the Request
> of the Mantuans for the Nineteenth
> Centenary of Virgil's Death')

Mother love, and piety induced by the Virgilian Academy of Mantua's request for something, 'however small', for a Virgil centenary, have rather carried Christina G and Tennyson away. The more usual note of these poetry- and poet-conscious moments is much more mixed. As with Clough, defining the poet as a hair- and paper-tearing madman set in a career of self-despising despair, and amusement deprivation, staying at home writing instead of going to dinners and dances ('If to write, rewrite, and write again'). The lot of the poet as represented by Tennyson's Lucretius is lifelong melancholy and ennui. Literary history holds out no promise of financial success. 'What porridge had John Keats?' And poetic failure seems even likelier. Tennyson has his old and blind Tiresias anticipate a future, after death, of renewed sight, and heroic games and battles, and heroic poetry to sing them, forever:

> while the golden lyre
> Is ever sounding in heroic ears
> Heroic hymns ....
> (172–174)

Tennyson liked to quote the last lines of his 'Tiresias' as 'a sample of his blank verse' (*Memoir*, II.318), seemingly pleased with his achievement. But what those lines announce is, like the ending of the parallel poem 'Ulysses', a merely wished-for rather than an achieved poetry: a case of 'will' and 'would' rather than *shall*.[29] The reflections on poetry's prospects are even more lugubrious in *In Memoriam*. The poet will carry on with his poem, while knowing that 'These mortal lullabies of pain' may well end up as paper stiffening the spines of books and lining trunks, or as women's curl-papers (LXXVII). His 'deepest lays are dumb', before the graveyard's yew-trees 'moulder'; his 'songs are vain' before an oak tree has reached fifty, let alone before it's been hollowed out with age (LXXVI). And we notice 'are dumb' and 'are vain': the dumbness and vanity are here and now, not in some distant future. For his part, Dante Gabriel Rossetti would try and resist such glooms

---

[29]   John Hollander reads the ending of 'Tiresias' as an attempted revival of past Miltonic glories: *Melodious Guile*, 109.

by hooking his 'Sonnet on the Sonnet', lead poem in *The House of Life* sequence, onto some of the old claims about poems being monuments resistant to time's depredations: Horace's Ode (Book III.30) *exegi monumentum aere perennius* ('I have built a monument more lasting than bronze'), and Shakespeare's sonneteering version of that claim, 'Not marble nor the gilded monuments / Of princes shall outlive this powerful rhyme':

> A Sonnet is a moment's monument, –
> Memorial from the soul's eternity
> To one dead deathless hour. Look that it be,
> Whether for lustral rite or dire portent,
> Of its own arduous fulness reverent:
> Carve it in ivory or in ebony,
> As Day or Night may rule; and let Time see
> Its flowering crest impearled and orient.
>
> A Sonnet is a coin: its face reveals
> The soul, – its converse, to what Power 'tis due:–
> Whether for tribute to the august appeals
> Of Life, or dower in Love's high retinue,
> It serve; or, 'mid the dark wharf's cavernous breath,
> In Charon's palm it pay the toll to Death.

But the old monumentalist claim is now shaking. A sonnet is still a monument, but now it's only 'a moment's monument' – monument to a moment's feeling ('I hardly ever produce a sonnet except on some basis of special momentary emotion', said Rossetti), and hovered over by the possibility that this monument lasts unmonumentally only for a moment. The sonnet's a memorial to a past hour: a *deathless* past because thus monumentalized, but still, oxymoronically, *dead*. *Dead deathless hour*: it's modernism's deconstructive paradox in a single phrase. (In Wilde's 'The Critic as Artist' his spokesman Gilbert, having praised Rossetti's ekphrastic poems for their sense that 'the ultimate art is literature', blesses the Impressionists for being beautifully 'suggestive' – which is so of the modern 'moment'; indeed they're 'the "moment's monument"', as Rossetti phrased it'.) Rossetti's crypto- modernist arduousness or intricacy of meaning (*arduous* in line 5 replaced original *intricate*) is registered as a doubleness in the sestet's trope of a sonnet as a two-faced coin: the face revelatory of soul, the obverse revealing the 'power' to which the coin is owed – life, love, or Charon the ferryman across the classical underworld's river of death. Rossetti is drawing on Jesus's use of a coin in the Gospels to answer a trick question about whether to pay 'tribute' to Caesar or not ('bring me a penny .... Whose is this image and superscription? ... Caesar's ... Render to Caesar the things that are Caesar's, and to God the things that are God's: Mark 12.14–17). And in so doing, of course, Rossetti has fallen, in the way self-reflexive poems tend to, into an ekphrasis.

John Hollander, doyen of the ekphrastic poem, has suggested that the sonnet as such may be peculiarly apt for ekphrasis, because of 'the very visual format of a printed sonnet, picture-like, rather than song-like' – especially Dante Gabriel Rossetti's sonnets, with their octave and sestet clearly demarcated, 'mimetic' of 'background/foreground, and image/interpretation'.[30] This is close to suggesting that sonnets about sonnets are ekphrastic *per se*. Be that as it may, it's certainly the case that Rossetti's sonnets keep falling into ekphrasis, like his 'Sonnet on the Sonnet'. Ekphrastic tendencies of the self-referential sonnet nicely illustrated in Eugene Lee-Hamilton's sonnet 'What the Sonnet Is' (in his *Sonnets of the Wingless Hours*, 1894), celebrating sonneteers in terms of their sonnets as jewels: the 'pure white diamond Dante brought / to Beatrice'; the sapphire Petrarch cut 'sparkling' for Laura; 'The ruby Shakespeare hewed from his heart's core'; and 'The dark deep emerald that Rossetti wrought / For his own soul, to wear for evermore'. It's almost as if there's a link between the self-conscious sonnet and ekphrasis as inevitable as the one between painter-poems and ekphrasis.

Coins have always been popular for ekphrasis. Their compactness makes them particularly attractive as textual analogues in compact poems like sonnets. It's no surprise that Charles Tennyson Turner, another sonnet-master, and, as we've seen (in Chapter 5) small-subject obsessive, should make a coin the ekphrasticized subject of a sonnet – 'On Seeing a Little Child Spin a Coin of Alexander the Great':

> This is the face of him, whose quick resource
> Of eye and hand subdued Bucephalus,
> And made the shadow of a startled horse
> A foreground for his glory. It is thus
> They hand him down; this coin of Philip's son
> Recalls his life, his glories and misdeeds,
> And that abortive court of Babylon,
> Where the world's throne was left among the reeds.
> (*Collected Sonnets, Old and New*, 1880)

Tennyson Turner's poem is defiantly deictic in the common ekphrastic way. Here is a poem reassuringly factual, actual and real, because about a real thing, this coin – a piece of history and full of story; a model of eloquence, of readability. But telling a whole set of stories. About death and absence, the perennial co-partners of life and presence: Babylon the Great is fallen, and so is Alexander the Great. As the sonnet goes on in its sestet:

---

[30]   This is in Hollander's critically superior and wide-ranging examination of ekphrastic kinds and poems, including ones by Dante Gabriel Rossetti, Swinburne, Lionel Johnson, Elizabeth Barrett Browning, James Thomson and Ford Madox Brown: *The Gazer's Spirit: Poems Speaking to Silent Works of Art* (University of Chicago Press, Chicago and London, 1997), 81.

> His dust is lost among the ancient dead,
> A coin his only presence: he is gone:
> And all but this half mythic image fled –
> A simple child may do him shame and slight;
> 'Twixt thumb and finger take the golden head,
> And spin the horns of Ammon out of sight.

The once super-powerful hand, handed down into a little child's hand. A coin, a sign of imperial power ('Whose image and superscription ...?'), and a token of commercial power, the hegemony of materialism, of trade, the power of money, grand marker of imperial commodification and the power of ownership (those issues of art and artists as commodity, as market-place fodder, of art as symbolic capital – one of the great Henry James subjects – inevitably peered at in all of poetry's dealing through ekphrasis with the materialism of the art object), whose value and values are now at stake.[31] What will the coin buy now: devalued, of no value, in the modern market place; but revalued as aesthetic object, as museum-piece?

   Aesthetic, cultural, poetic value and values are brought variously into question, like this, in ekphrastic poems (and prose, of course).

> Statues and pictures and verse may be grand,
> But they are not the Life for which they stand.

That's James Thomson in his sceptical ekphrasticizing poem 'Art' (known in draft as 'Elementary Philosophy of Love Poems'), which appeared eventually in his volume *The City of Dreadful Night and Other Poems* (1880), the volume dominated by 'The City of Dreadful Night' – not incidentally about a city dominated by an ekphrasis of the giant bronze statue of Melancholy said to be made after the 'sketch' by Dürer, his 1514 engraving of 'Melencolia', which is the subject of Thomson's ekphrastic poem 'The "Melencolia" of Albrecht Dürer'. Ekphrasis upon ekphrasis.[32]

---

[31]   For the commodification matter see Andrew Elfenbein, *Byron and the Victorians* (Cambridge University Press, Cambridge, 1995) – discussed by Kathy Alexis Psomaides, ' "The Lady of Shalott" and the critical fortunes of Victorian poetry', *The Cambridge Companion to Victorian Poetry*, ed Joseph Bristow (2000), 35–36.

[32]   John Hollander's discussion of Thomson's bronze statue in *The Gazer's Spirit*, 209ff, mentions Gautier's ekphrasis on the Dürer, his poem 'Mélancolie', and Gerard de Nerval's melancholic troubadour El Deschidado, on whose lute is the emblem 'le soleil noir de la Mélancolie': which gives Julia Kristeva's study of melancholy its title, *Soleil noir: dépression et mélancolie* (Gallimard, Paris, 1987) (*Black Sun: Depression and Melancholia*, trans Léon S Roudiez (Columbia University Press, Columbia and Oxford, 1989)) – not mentioned by Hollander, just as he doesn't at this place recall the role of Nerval's El Deschidado among the fragments at the end of *The Waste Land*.

For his part Tennyson had trouble with the projected ekphraseis of his 'The Palace of Art'. 'When I first conceived the plan of the Palace of Art, I intended to have introduced both sculptures and paintings into it; but', said Tennyson in a note to the 1832 version of the poem, 'it is the most difficult of all things to *devise* a statue in verse'. He felt the difficulty of ekphrasis as such: bearing in, perhaps, on Gotthold Lessing's old contention that the linear (writing) and the spatial (a statue or painting) make a difficult mix. But his difficulty was doubtless enhanced by the generally miserabilist nature of the art works, the tapestries, statues, and paintings which fill the poem's Palace – a collection designed to illustrate the vanity of such aesthetic labours, in the words of Ecclesiastes Chapter 2 that underlie the poem: 'Then I looked on all the works that my hands had wrought, and the labour that I had laboured to do: and, behold, all was vanity and vexation of spirit, and there was no profit under the sun … Therefore I hated life'. Actually it's art that the poem seems rather to hate. Tennyson reported his friend Richard Chenevix Trench as prompting his poem by saying 'Tennyson, we cannot live in Art'. And 'The Palace of Art' embodied, Tennyson said, 'my own belief that the Godlike life is with man and for man' (rather than with Art and for Art).[33] Tennyson's revisions to his 1832 text for its 1842 appearance cleaned out and up a lot of the aestheticized gloom. Some of the original darker segments didn't even make it in 1832, including a tapestry depicting a market-place:

> One seemed a place of mart. The seller held
> The buyer's hand, and winked and smiled,
> And pointed to his wares.

The seductions of the salesman, perennially implicit in these ekphrastic encounters, made awfully explicit. A note by Tennyson on some 'branch-work of costly sardonyx' (line 95, 1842 text) dwells on how Parisian jewellers achieve that costliness, applying heat to change the (striated white and yellow-orangey) colour of the precious stone to imitate 'among other things, bunches of grapes with green tendrils'. Doing unnatural things to make artworks for money. It's the grievous commercialization which so upsets Wilde in his ekphrastic 'Sonnet on the Sale by Auction of Keats's Love Letters' – sold, as the sonnet has it, like the garments of Jesus' that Roman soldiers gambled for before his crucifixion:

> These are the letters which Endymion wrote
> To one he loved in secret, and apart.
> And now the brawlers of the auction mart
> Bargain and bid for each poor blotted note,

---

[33]   All of these quotations come from Ricks's headnote to the poem.

Ay! for each separate pulse of passion quote
The merchant's price: I think they love not Art
Who break the crystal of a poet's heart
That small and sickly eyes may glare and gloat.[34]

Wilde's expostulatory tone anticipates the passage in *De Profundis* about the poetic love letter he'd sent to Bosie, traded among London's lowlife blackmailers, read out in court as evidence against him for 'unnatural' practices, and helping land him in gaol. Shortly after that protest in *De Profundis*, Wilde suggests that his Keats sonnet was proleptic of Bosie's scheme to make money by publishing letters sent to him from Wilde in Holloway Prison: 'Had there been nothing in your own heart to cry out against so vulgar a sacrilege you might at least have remembered the sonnet he wrote who saw with such sorrow and scorn the letters of John Keats sold by public auction and have understood at last the real meaning of my lines "I think they love not Art / Who break the crystal of a poet's heart / That small and sickly eyes may glare or gloat" '.[35] Aesthetic productions should not degenerate like this to this level of vile commodity. Where Browning's 'Old Pictures in Florence' end up, in that ekphrasis-laden poem about forgotten artists and the inevitable depredations and decay of their works, their drooping and peeling frescoes. The poem's narrator (Browning himself) hunts out these rotting works: 'Wherever an outline weakens and wanes / Till the latest life in the painting stops' (41–43). This is his *business*, where he *chaffers*, that is haggles about prices (33, 35), among the dealers in old stuff, where 'pictures are left to the mercies still / Of dealers and stealers, Jews and English' (227–228) – crooks passing off 'some clay-cold vile Carlino' as High Art (231–232). *English* rhymes with *tinglish* (226), which is how the 'tempera' felt to the painter: *tinglish* no longer because he and his work are dead. This is a bad seller's market in which Browning, ever on the look-out for some treasure among the stall-holders' trash (witness the old Yellow Book resurrected from the market rubbish), is usually frustrated. The despondency of 'Old Pictures' climaxes in Browning's failure to secure 'a certain precious little tablet / Which Buonarroti eyed like a lover' – a fabled Michelangelo 'Last Supper', missing from the San Spirito Church in Florence, which 'Turns up at last' only to be purchased by someone unknown. Browning is determined to obtain it; it's his 'Koh-i-noor', a treasure like that fabulous Indian diamond given to Queen Victoria in 1849, the 'Jewel of Giamschid', the legendary Persian king, the jewelled 'eye' of the Persian monarchs or Sofis

---

[34] Quoted from the very useful Oxford World's Classics edition of Wilde's *Complete Poetry*, ed Isobel Murray (Oxford University Press, Oxford, 1997).
[35] *De Profundis*, *Complete Works of Oscar Wilde*, Intro Vyvyan Holland, New Edition (Collins, 1966), 902. *Glare or gloat* in *De Profundis*; *and gloat* in the published poem.

). 'Detur amanti!' he cries, in Latin (244): (in English) 'it is owed [pe]rson who loves it'. But he hasn't got it, and won't get it. The [...] will fail him – like the Campanile of Giotto which the poem ends [...] [proph]esying will be completed – 'Completing Florence, as Florence Italy' (280) – but never was. A triumph of incompleteness. And Browning, failed quester for that perfect painting, can't now even remember for certain in which church he went looking for the empty place of the missing work: 'I, that have haunted the dim San Spirito / (Or was it rather the Ognissanti?) / Patient on altar-step planting a weary toe!' Missing painting; loss of memory; narrative blur.

There's some gain, of course, in the ekphrastic encounter, in this deictic aesthetic of presence and thereness, but always an accompanying experience of loss and absence such as Browning's in Florence. Or at Ancona, in eastern Italy, where Browning recalls in his 'The Guardian Angel: A Picture at Fano' looking and looking in July 1848 at 'The Guardian Angel' of Giovanni Barbieri – known as Guercino, the 'Squinter' – in Fano's Church of San Agostino, in the company of his wife. Browning's poem recalls the intensity of her attention to the painting of a sculptured angel spreading its wings over a child on a tomb. Now, in the poem, Browning gazes ('I gaze': 9) at her gazing, 'here' – 'here' in the church, here in the poem. 'My love is here' (54). She's the poet's guardian angel. He also remembers seeing a Guercino in Dulwich with his friend Alfred Domett ('Alfred, dear friend!': 37). The exercise in thereness is thus a double one; triple even, for the Fano Guercino has a healing message that 'All is beauty: / And knowing this, is love, and love is duty. / What further may be sought for or declared?' Which recalls the lesson Keats drew from the Grecian Urn in his ekphrastic poem 'Ode on a Grecian Urn', that 'Beauty is truth, truth beauty', which is 'all ye need to know'. But these strong actuals are also founded in losses. The poet would like his angel to bend low over him, like the angel in the painting, cradle his head in her 'healing hands', soothe his teeming brain and nerves. But this healing does not happen; it's a matter of what would happen if his wish for her action 'was ever granted'. The healing touch is as deferred as the rebuilding of Kubla Khan's pleasure dome in Coleridge's poem, which this one also recalls. And Browning ends with the absence of his one-time fellow-gazer Domett in far-off New Zealand:

> My love is here. Where are you, dear old friend?
> How rolls the Wairoa at your world's far end?
> This is Ancona, yonder is the sea.

So much in the poem that is deictically tangible, knowable; so much that's unreachable, and untouchable. An out-of-reachness brought even more terribly home when this poem, first published in *Men and Women* (1855), was re-published in Browning's 1863 collection two years after his wife's death. Her death underscoring the losses perpetually present in the gains of the always aporetic dualism of ekphrasis.

It's the kind of finding that's always a losing, as profoundly allegorized in Dante Gabriel Rossetti's 1881 ekphrastic sonnet on his (unfinished) painting of 1853–1854, *Found*. ' "Found" (For a Picture)' is thoroughly steeped, and characteristically for Rossetti, in aesthetic to-ings and fro-ings. The painting is a scene at a London railway bridge. Helen Rossetti Angeli, Dante Gabriel's niece, described it accurately:

> a young drover from the country, while driving a calf to market, recognizes a fallen woman on the pavement, his former sweetheart. He tries to raise her from where she crouches on the ground, but with closed eyes she turns her face from him to the wall.

The painter Ford Madox Ford modelled the Adam Bede-like countryman, in his simple smock, honest leather gaiters and sturdy leather boots. His single sheep being driven to market on a cart is an emblematic sacrifical lamb caught in a rope net. Golden-haired Fanny Cornforth modelled the painting's rather gaudily attired fallen woman. She's crouching by a brick wall, resisting the saving tugs of the good shepherd. The very detailed painted section of wall was from a cemetery at Chiswick which Rossetti had felt to be ideal not least because it was near the grave of the painter Hogarth (a good omen for his 'modern picture' Rossetti thought, especially because it was Hogarth's engravings of *The Harlot's Progress* which inspired him, his poem 'Jenny' and other Pre-Raphaelite paintings such as George Frederic Watts's *Found Drowned*, 1849–1850).[36] Friends of Rossetti thought the painting had been inspired, in an act of found-ekphrasis, by the poem 'Rosabell', by the fringe Pre-Raphaelite William Bell Scott, which Rossetti denied – unconvincingly, for he patently worked up another scene from that poem into the painting *The Gate of Memory* (1857–1864) in which a prostitute, golden-haired again, covertly spies on a group of innocent dancing girls, old and young.[37]

> 'There is a budding morrow in midnight': –
> So sang our Keats, the English nightingale.
> And here, as lamps across the bridge turn pale
> In London's smokeless resurrection-light,
> Dark breaks to dawn. But o'er the deadly blight

[36] Details from Lionel Lambourne's majestic *Victorian Painting* (Phaidon Press, 1999), 380–382.
[37] See James W Christie, 'A Pre-Raphaelite Dispute: "Rosabell", "Jenny", and Other Fallen Women', *Pre-Raphaelite Review*, I:2 (1978), 40–48.

Of love deflowered and sorrow of none avail
Which makes this man gasp and this woman quail,
Can day from darkness ever again take flight?

Ah! gave not these two hearts their mutual pledge,
Under one mantle sheltered 'neath the hedge
In gloaming courtship? And O God! to-day
He only knows he holds her; – but what part
Can life now take? She cries in her locked heart, –
'Leave me – I do not know you – go away!'

Keats sang of the morning budding at midnight in his 'Sonnet to Homer', about Jove's gift of extra sight to the blind poet, light in the darkness, a rending of the veil over his eyes, like the rending of the veil of the Jerusalem Temple at the crucifixion of Jesus, signifying salvation for sinners and enlightenment for the morally blind. And Rossetti's sonnet describes a London dawn, the painted daytime resurrection in which, however, there's no moral return – for ever. The man 'holds' the woman, as the painting does, but she's not to be re-possessed (like the boy Miles at the end of James's *The Turn of the Screw*, held by the would-be-saviour governess – 'I have you' – but he's a corpse, his little heart 'dispossessed'). The woman has been found – with echoes of the Lost Sheep found by the Good Shepherd in Jesus's parable – but she remains lost. 'Leave me – I do not know you – go away': her dismissing-disclaiming terribly blends St Peter's words to Jesus, 'Depart from me; for I am a sinful man, O Lord' (Luke 5.8) and his later denial of Jesus – 'I know him not' (Luke 22.57).

What such ekphrastic sonnets of Rossetti compel is our disconcerted gaze. They make us follow the painter's disconcerted gaze, meet the disconcerted gaze of the painting looking back at us, very often in the worrying face of a painted Other, Rossetti's roster of lovely malign females. It's an aesthetic exercise in conveying visual horrors – the painting's and the poem's. Here's Aphrodite, the subject of Rossetti's 'Venus Verticordia', with the apple for Paris and us ('for thee'), and a spear symbolic of the ruin about to come on Troy, her 'glance' 'still and coy' for a moment, but about to 'flame' with promised deadliness ('Venus Verticordia (For a Picture)'). And Prosperpine, Empress of Hell, painted holding the hellish pomegranate whose seeds she's eaten and which condemn her to eternal damnation, glancing askance at some light from the upper world she'll never regain, and at us; holding the cursed fruit, a vagina dentata, as it were, enticing us to eat; and meditating on her plight, the bit of mocking light, and the pitying voice of a lover she only imagines hearing, in the sonnet 'Prosperpina (For a Picture)'. The sonnet is inscribed on the picture's frame, an English translation of the verses in Italian which are painted in the picture's top right-hand corner. A double ekphrasis of hellish misery. (Rossetti did a third one, too, in prose.) Here, too, is Pandora, subject of more than one Rossetti creation, in 'Pandora (For a Picture)'. The picture in question is the 1874–1878 version, a chalk drawing more awful than the 1869 version, with a less clothed Pandora, more brooding, her hair more massive, surrounded by more animated 'bogies', as Rossetti called them, the evil spirits escaping from her opened box. 'What of the end?' this sonnet asks, twice, pretending not to be aware that this is a myth of evil's cosmic origin. Rossetti knows that it was not Pandora who opened the box, but husband Epimethus, but pretends not to know with another question to Pandora, 'Was it thine, / The deed that set these fiery spirits free?' Clearly painted on this version's box are the words 'Ultima Manet Spes': 'Hope Remains Finally', alluding to the story that there was a lively Hope left after all at the bottom of the box. But the poet withholds that knowledge from his Pandora: she cannot know 'If Hope still pent there be alive or dead'. Full of questions, the poet wonders why she was made 'half-divine'. Was it that her face, her gaze, might combine all the benign-malign powers of the look of Juno, Pallas Athene, Venus, Proserpina – 'and that all men might see / In Venus's eyes the gaze of Prosperpine?'

That devastating look of the ekphrastically looked-at. It's there repeatedly in these Rossetti poems for his pictures. In the 1877 sonnet 'Astarte Syriaca', of course, about his painting of this ancient semitic goddess of sex – taken by the Greeks as an earlier version of Aphrodite, outlawed for the ancient Israelites by Jahwe as a demonic moon-goddess promoting ungodly lust, modelled by Janey Morris, whose lovely face, the poem says, casts 'Love's all-penetrative spell' from 'Love-freighted lips and absolute eyes'. This is a complete 'mystery' – repeated as the sonnet's first and last words – which we are invited to behold: 'Mystery: lo!' Which is a scandalous, even blasphemous invitation, for this is the Scarlet Woman of Revelation 17.5: 'And upon her forehead was a name written, MYSTERY, BABYLON THE GREAT, THE MOTHER OF HARLOTS AND ABOMINATIONS OF THE EARTH'. Clarence Fry, the painting's purchaser, knew that all Bible-minded Victorians would catch the poem's blasphemous import (see his letter to Rossetti, 10 March 1877). A blasphemy underscored by the way in which two of Rossetti's earlier ekphrastic religious poems, 'For a Virgin and Child by Hans Memmelinck (In the Academy of Bruges)' and 'For a Marriage of St Catherine by the Same (In the Hospital of St John at Bruges)' (both of them included with other 'Sonnets for Pictures' in the *Germ* no.4, April 1850), each begin their reading of these paintings' theological paradoxes with the word 'Mystery'. 'Behold Fiammetta': so urges Rossetti's sonnet for his late painting *A Vision of Fiammetta*: a fetchingly lovely representation of Boccaccio's (probably fictional) beloved, standing against a tree bearing and shedding spring blossoms. Her eyes are 'reassuring' and 'most fair', but they presage Death – denoted by the petals falling on her arm as she shakes the tree, each petal 'like a tear'. Rossetti's painting was inspired by Boccaccio's own elegiac sonnet, 'On his last sight of Fiammetta' – the Italian version of which is inscribed on the frame of Rossetti's painting, along with Rossetti's translation of it, and his own sonnet. A triplet, then, of ekphraseis announcing death's imbrication in loveliness – a threat not assuaged by the aestheticized beauty, but rather endorsed by it. Fiammetta, 'A presage and a promise stands; as 'twere / On Death's dark storm the rainbow of the Soul'; but a rainbow not as sign of no more death-dealing rain, as it was in the apocalyptic Noah's Flood story of the Book of Genesis, but as affirmation of Death's ever-presence.

And the dismaying paradox – the aporia – of the beautiful art object, of the aesthetic as such, all at once so lovely and so unsettling, is brought home again and again like this in the period's ekphrastic encounters. Take the narrator of Robert Browning's *Pauline* pondering Andromeda in an ekphrasis of a painting by Caravaggio (656ff), an engraving of which the young Browning had above his desk. She's 'quite naked and alone', chained on her rock, 'so beautiful', her 'hair / Lifted and spread by the salt-sweeping breeze', her 'hair, such hair' stormed upon 'As she waits the snake on the wet beach / By the dark rock'. She needs a saviour. The narrator is sure 'some god' will rescue her. But meanwhile no rescuer, not even the godlike Perseus, is in sight. Later on, Browning fantasized himself as a Perseus rescuing Elizabeth Barrett from her father's grip, and he presents Caponsacchi as Perseus rescuing Pompilia from her monstrous husband in *The Ring and the Book*. But in the ekphrasticized Caravaggio the loveliest of women is poised in an aesthetic stasis of horror.[38] Or think of little Aurora Leigh staring for hours at a portrait of her dead mother, a multivalent mixture of 'Ghost, fiend, and angel, fairy, witch, and sprite' with the deadly in the ascendant: she's a Muse eyeing 'a dread fate'; a 'loving Psyche' who has lost her Cupid; a 'still Medusa' all sweaty with the slime of her snake hair; Lamia the snake-woman; the Virgin Mary stabbed with swords in the breast, 'where the Babe sucked' (I.135ff). Robert Browning thought the Florentine statue of this particular Virgin, pierced with seven swords to represent her seven sorrows, was absurdly mixed, at least as it (or an effigy like it) is carried through the streets in his 'Up At a Villa – Down in the City': 'smiling and smart / With a pink gauze gown all spangles, and seven swords stuck in her heart' (51–52). Barrett Browning's painting is introduced with what seems like a careful allusion to the portrait of the murdered Duchess in Browning's 'My Last Duchess' ('painted on the wall', all face, throat and hands and 'looking as if she were alive'): light from the maid Assunta's stoked-up fire 'made alive /

---

[38]   Richard Jenkyns's fine book about the classicism of Victorian art devotes pages to the painters' and sculptors' obsession with chained-up naked women as versions of Andromeda: *Dignity and Decadence: Victorian Art and the Classical Inheritance* (Harper Collins, London, 1991), 116–119.

That picture of my mother on the wall'. Illusory painted life, made by Robert Browning's Duke into a catalogue of alleged guilty signs. It is said that Aurora's obsessive gazing alluded to Robert Browning's own youthful fascination with the portrait by Joseph Wright of Derby of his Creole grandmother – swarthy boy face-to-face with the challengingly dark face of his ancestor. On the other hand, it's the whiteness that seems to enable Barrett Browning's acclaim of her Florentine neighbour the American sculptor Hiram Powers's statue of a young Christian woman, fetishistically dressed only in some pudenda-draping chains for the Turkish harem market, as a piece of 'passionless perfection' which the poet can egg on to preach against slavery. 'Appeal, fair stone, / From God's pure heights of beauty, against man's wrong! / ... and strike and shame the strong, / By thunders of white silence'. In truth, the American slaves whom Powers's statue is said to represent in the tribute ekphrastic sonnet, 'Hiram Powers's Greek Slave' (1850), might rather cry 'I am black, I am black' in the voice of 'The Runaway Slave at Pilgrim's Point'; but Barrett Browning's sight is protected by this allegedly desexed job ('passionless') in white Carrara marble. So the sonnet has Barrett Browning satisfyingly face-to-face with a blanking-out metaphor for colour reminders she can't face: the face of the black slaves whose inheritance has darkened her face. (Powers's title, *The Greek Slave*, seems to be cherished for its transcendent metaphoric reach: 'as if the sculptor meant her' to preach 'ideal sense' through 'Ideal Beauty'. That Browningesque *as if* again.) John Gibson's *Tinted Venus*, shown alongside Powers's *Greek Slave* at the Great Exhibition of 1851, a far more draped female nude, perturbed Barrett Browning precisely because it was coloured, painted in lifelike flesh tones, making it 'rather a grisette [a working-class French girl] than a goddess'. Barrett Browning had 'seldom' seen 'so indecent a statue'. The 'Hiram Powers's Greek Slave' sonnet looks like ekphrasis as an exercise in anxious substitution for, and evasion of, some otherwise very awkward anxiety-mongering contemplations.

John Hollander talks cannily about the poem's *awkward* verbal *loops* – 'not alone / East griefs but west'. And the awkwardness runs very deep.[39] 'Pierce to the centre / Art's fiery finger!': only someone less than aware of what she was about in this poem would talk of a seductively naked statue like that. Conversely, Swinburne, as perhaps we'd expect, rather celebrates the physical awkwardness of the Louvre's statue of Hermaphrodite and the awkwardness of the truth about his own sexuality which that statue reflects, as the conscious essence of his four-sonnet ekphrasis: *desire* and *despair* contained in one art object, this figure of *waste wedlock*, 'So dreadful, so desirable', and so on. This is the awkward attraction-repulsion too of his

---

[39] John Hollander, *The Gazer's Spirit*, 161–162. Richard Jenkyns is informative about the contrastive pairings of exhibited sculpture, *Dignity and Decadence*, 26–7; 116.

'Erotion', his ekphrasis on Simeon Solomon's painting *Damon and Aglae*, whose opening lines – in which androgynous Aglae celebrates hermaphroditic Damon, the memory of whose 'breath' lies sweet on 'lips that touch the lips of death'– were printed in the Royal Academy catalogue entry for the Simeon painting. [40]

But, whether wholly consciously or not, what gives these ekphrastic encounters their keenest edge is the way their various troublednesses reflect the deepest anxieties possible for a poet, namely concerns about poetry, about the poet's only tools, namely words, verbal signs. The verbal worries which shape, of course, the biggest category of modernist anxieties. When Dante Gabriel Rossetti in his sonnet for *A Vision of Fiammetta* reverses the 'presage' and 'promise' of the Noahic rainbow, to have it bespeak apocalyptic storm rather than the original divine forgiveness, he's not just undoing an old canonical story about God giving his word, challenging the word of God, the Bible, about the word of God, but he's challenging the stability of words, of verbal signs, as such. If this genetic sign, the rainbow of Genesis, is so unstable, what price any sign? In undoing theologocentrism, Rossetti is undoing logocentrism itself. He is in effect an ur-deconstructionist. And so it goes with his ekphrastic practice at large. Jerome McGann is quite right to suggest that 'Pandora (For a Picture)' is 'an allegory for the situation of art as Rossetti saw it', and that ' "Found" (for a Picture)' is 'as it were a commentary on Rossetti's art in general, which he felt he had prostituted for the sake of worldly success'.[41] But in raising questions about paintings and their meanings, these poems are also allegories of and commentaries on the poetry, the poems, that are the vehicle of such concerns. 'What of the end, Pandora?' The end as result, but also as the point, the purpose. What is poetry's point? The sonnet doesn't know the answer to any of its many questions. It is utterly aporetic. '[N]o r canst thou know' is a kind of musical key signature, the key the poem plays in. The painting, and the sonnet, are hermeneutically stymied; and in the matter of signs. Might Pandora's face have been half-divine, so that Juno's 'brow might stand a sign / For ever?' The painting won't tell, and neither will the poem. What is found out as lost in ' "Found" (For a Picture)' is meaning itself. It cannot be accidental that the sonnet's opening lines invoke Keats. Poetry's means and doings are at stake. These lovers' old *mutual pledges* have come to naught. The good man *holds* the woman, but has actually lost her – in an allegory of their mistake about the permanency of meaning their one-time pledges betokened. This is indeed a proleptic xerox of the end of *The Turn of the Screw*, where the governess's claim to possess the boy Miles in the face of her actual dispossession is a blatant

---

[40]   Swinburne's protracted engagement in prose as well as verse with the Simeon painting features, in relation to confused selfhood, in my Ch 6, pp249–250.

[41]   McGann, ed, Dante Gabriel Rossetti, *Collected Poetry and Prose*, Notes, 394, 396.

allegory of the nouvelle's extended drama of deluded epistemological and hermeneutic confidence in the face of apparent epistemic and hermeneutic failure. Or, put it another way: the poem's words, attempted voicings of the actual silences of paint (which is what ekphrasis of its very nature always attempts), have, in all honesty, to register the silence which their wordings purport to deny. The fallen woman's words in the poem's last line, ' "Leave me – I do not know you – go away!" ', are of course fictional, suppositious – the painted woman says nothing, because paint is utterly silent – and even in the verbal occasion arising out of the painted encounter, these words are actually supposed ones, the 'cries' of 'her locked heart'. The words of the poem – of poems – challenge silence, but are also challenged by it; and ekphrasis makes that clamantly plain. How will Hiram Powers's Greek Slave *strike* and *shame* and *overthrow* 'the strong'? 'By thunders of white silence': the paradoxical noise of silent marble, enabled by Barrett Browning's sonnet; but an enabling built on disabling thoughts about language's always fraught wrestle with very persistent silence.

Voicing white silence is what Swinburne's 'Before the Mirror (Verses Written Under a Picture) Inscribed to JA Whistler' does. The poem mirrors a woman mirrored: a mirroring within a mirroring – abysmality indeed. This triptych of verses was printed on gold paper and pasted to the frame of Whistler's *The Little White Girl*, his 1864 portrait of Jo Hiffernan, his not at all little model and mistress. The poem makes the painting's intense whiteness eloquent. The woman in white is given words in the poem's Part II – about watching her face and her 'snow-white' hand, wondering what pleasures or pains await her, and whether she or her mirrored image is 'the ghost'. Some of these words, stanzas 4 and 6 of the poem, appeared in the Royal Academy's 1865 Exhibition catalogue. This was the second of Whistler's white paintings. Perhaps inspired by Gautier's 'Symphonie en blanc majeur' (the painting Wilde singled out for praise in 'The Critic as Artist' (1891) as a key example of the 'white keynote' of the Impressionists, 'unapproachable' in its beauty, a 'flawless masterpiece of colour and music'), or maybe inspired by a critic's account of the first white painting called The *White Girl* (1861), Whistler titled his third one (1887) *Symphony in White no.3*. At which the first painting was retitled *The White Girl: Symphony in White no.1*, and the second *The Little White Girl: Symphony in White no.2*. The musicality (*symphony*) of this new title plays very well to the noise Swinburne has coming from the painting's white silences. The assigned meanings, though, are elicited from 'Behind the veil', the (Tennysonian) veil of the paintings, the as it were veiled silent pale face of the pictured woman and her less pale mirrored image, and are in consequence self-cancellingly paradoxical. They're said to bespeak love or sorrow, delight or grief; a gladness and a sadness which are both of them incomplete. The woman is 'Glad, but not flushed with gladness, / Since joys go by; / Sad, but not bent with sadness, / Since sorrows die'. Fictionalized as a speaking silence, she's further imagined as hearing impossible things – 'Dead mouths of many dreams that sing and sigh' – and as seeing impossibles too: in a reversal of St Paul in 1 Corinthians 13 who has us seeing through a 'glass' or mirror darkly, she sees 'all things', 'Deep in the gleaming glass'; sees 'Old loves and faded fears' floating 'down a stream that hears / The flowing of all men's tears beneath the sky'. It's an explosion of synaesthetics, of sights and sounds. And we're made to hear this wondrous hearer of wondrous hearings, reflected in the mirror, that thus reminds some readers of the traditional visionary mirrorings of art, 'the glass of art itself' as John Hollander has it (*The Gazer's Spirit*, 191ff). A mirroring and a hearing brought home by Swinburne's intense rhymings, the verbal repeatings, chiasmus, returns – verbal mirroring upon mirroring: verbal rhyming-mirroring which is the vehicle of this alleged speaking-hearing whiteness. A rhyming that works the meanings, whose manifest contradictory fancifulness (how *can* the poet hear this?; how can the woman?; how can the stream?) of course calls into question the very powers of the rhymings that are being worked so characteristically hard by the poet to bring them home. The phonological repeating is 'never more effective' than here, says Hollander. And, we might add, never so questionably effective.

Not unrelatedly: contemplating Botticelli's *Primavera* in the (late, 1880) 'For Spring, by Sandro Botticelli (in the Accademia of Florence)', Dante Gabriel Rossetti asks 'What mystery is read / Of homage or of hope?', and his poking at the painting's customary silences comes up with a certain line about the painting's 'masque' of the season's breakable promises ('Birth bare, not death-bare yet'). The poem ends, though, in significant retreat from its own questionings. 'But how command / Dead Springs to answer?' Dead Springs – silent because painted; and because they're dried-up, like old springs no longer yielding water. 'And how question here / These mummers of that wind-withered New-year?' The precedent *here* of the painting is overtaken by the final *here* of the poem. Ekphrasis has fallen back before the silence of the painting ('What mystery here?'); the poem gives up on the possibility of poetic questioning as such ('how question *here*?').[42]

In related vein, Rossetti's sonnet 'For "The Wine of Circe" by Edward Burne-Jones' ends with the cries of bestialized mariners, the new arrivals joining Circe's old victims, echoing the sea's roar:

> who with them in new equality
> To-night shall echo back the sea's dull roar
> With a vain wail from passion's tide-strown shore
> Where the dishevelled seaweed hates the sea.

---

[42]   John Hollander greatly thickens this poem's scene of ekphrastic and poetic failure by pointing out how the Botticelli painting itself is full of allusions to preceding poems, texts, story, and how its interpretative failures around the meaning of Spring go right back to Virgil's 3rd Eclogue. *The Gazer's Spirit*, 217ff, and notes p363.

Nobody and nothing makes a noise in painting; these echoing roars and wails are as suppositious as the (wonderful) personifying of the dishevelled and emotional seaweed. Ekphrastic convention grants the noise, as poetic convention enables the pathetic fallacy. But, once again, challengingly so, for both poem and poetry. *Echo*: that quintessence of poetry, the rhyming without with there is no verse; an echoing *back*, a to-and-fro of echo, like the repeated end-rhymes of this poem, abbaabba cdcdcd; and all 'a vain wail'. Once more, there's no answer to the poet's questions – this time about whether Helios, the Sun, and Hecate, queen of Hell, 'combine / ... to proclaim / For these thy guests all rapture in Love's name, / Till pitiless Night give Day the countersign?' McGann again thinks, and with force, that Rossetti is having dark thoughts about art.[43] But, too, he's having even darker ones about poetry. The proclaiming, like what will happen 'To-night', does not actually occur; this is all futuristic imagining. An echoing in vain, then? The poetic vanity of the merely imaginable? Apparent signing – about passion and rapture, those recurrent subjects of poetry – which is also, no less, a counter-signing – the sign that confirms but also contradicts.

It's a reflection on uncertain signing brought dramatically home as Rossetti sits in front of Leonardo's *Our Lady of the Rocks* in London in 1848 actually writing his ekphrastic sonnet about it, 'For "Our Lady of the Rocks" by Leonardo da Vinci' – the poem given pole position in the final section of Rossetti's 1870 volume, the 'Sonnets for Pictures'. The octet's questions bear in, as McGann again cogently suggests,[44] on the role of art as a difficult, occultic, dark revealer of the transcendent, 'Infinite imminent Eternity'. McGann suggests, again with force, that Rossetti is no doubt thinking (as Swinburne did) of the St Paul of 1 Corinthians seeing 'through a glass darkly' – the enigmatic mirror reflections of the Bible's Vulgate Latin version, 'per speculum in aenigmate': through a mirror in an enigma. And yet again what dominates is the silence-denying verbal activity – voices, echoes – said to be audible in the enigmatic silences of the painting, and which the ekphrastic inscription indeed purports to make audible: the 'silent prayer' of Leonardo's woman, the painting's 'Mother of grace', to the Son of God who 'silently' blesses the dead; the voices of the dead spirits *extolling* the *name* of the Lord. These souls are 'bewildered' as they 'blindly shudder' through the difficult 'pass' (between life and death), which they 'throng ... like echoes'. Voices, noises – all imagined, of course – in praise of the name of the Lord, 'whose peace' nonetheless 'abides'. These are, no less, the textual and hermeneutic paradoxes for fraught believers as spelled out in TS Eliot's 'Ash Wednesday' and 'Four Quartets' – the poet's experience of Christ the *verbum in-fans*, hearing murmurs of the Virginal 'Lady of Silences' and the 'word

---

[43] McGann, edn cit, notes p 391.
[44] McGann, notes pp 389–390.

unheard' of the allegorical garden of 'Burnt Norton'. A set of ancient, revived paradoxes which, for Eliot as for Rossetti, bear in on issues of the poet's equipment and task as much as on questions of religious knowing. Poetic questions underlined in Rossetti's pronounced difficulty with the poem's last word, with getting the rhymes right. 'Mother of grace, the pass is difficult', the sestet begins. *Difficult.* John Hollander (*The Gazer's Spirit*, 151ff) nicely suggests a self-reflexive reference here to the formal difficulty of the passage from sestet to octet; but the difficulty seems rather more to do with the words to describe the poem's harrowed intimations of mortality and immortality.

> Thy name, O Lord, each spirit's voice extols
> Whose peace abides in the dark avenue
> Amid the bitterness of things occult.

'In His will is our peace', wrote Dante, in a line perpetually haunting TS Eliot, but there's no sure poetic peace in these ekphrastic reflections; rather there's the *bitterness* of things remaining occulted and so unsayable. That last word *occult*, the one Rossetti wrote down, in front of the painting, his would-be closure of a rhyme-word, failed to satisfy him when he came back to it. *Occult* is trying to rhyme with *difficult*: a rather difficult rhyme, Rossetti realized, its difficulty overlooked in the heat of *in situ* composition. Could his brother William Michael help him amend the last line on the 1870 proofs, he wondered (letter of 27 August 1869)? He'd ask his sister Christina G's help too. But no satisfying suggestions came from either sibling. So the volume's lead ekphrastic sonnet remained as an announcement of the difficulty of getting over the enigma, the occultism of poetry's very means, of language itself.

Occultedness lasting, then, at the last (and first). So are we to think this the ekphrastic poem's ungainsayable last word in the matter of the mode's traditionally loud claim on knowability and legibility, presence and thereness, and positive hermeneutic? It's certainly not being gainsaid on the reckoning of perhaps Rossetti's most challenging of ekphrastic excursions, the sonnet 'William Blake (To Frederic Shields, on his sketch of Blake's workroom and death-room, 3 Fountain Court, Strand)'.

> This is the place. Even here the dauntless soul,
> The unflinching hand, wrought on; till in that nook,
> As on that very bed, his life partook
> New birth, and passed. Yon river's dusky shoal,
> Whereto the close-built coiling lanes unroll,
> Faced his work-window, whence his eyes would stare,
> Thought-wandering, unto nought that met them there,
> But to the unfettered irreversible goal.

This cupboard, Holy of Holies, held the cloud
Of his soul writ and limned; this other one,
His true wife's charge, full oft to their abode
Yielded for daily bread the martyr's stone,
Ere yet their food might be that Bread alone,
The words now home-speech of the mouth of God.

This is the final version of the sonnet as it appeared in Rossetti's *Ballads and Sonnets* volume of 1881. In May 1880 Frederic Shields was, apparently, inspired by Rossetti to go and sketch Blake's last residence, both outside and inside (Dante Gabriel, William Michael, and Shields had been helping Mrs Gilchrist revise Alexander Gilchrist's *Life of William Blake*). Shields made a floor plan of the small room in which the impoverished Blakes ate and slept, and he worked and died. The plan went into Volume One of the revised Gilchrist *Life* (1880). Shields also did a sketch showing the door, a bed, a cupboard, a table (probably) and the window opened onto the River Thames beyond. Dante Gabriel liked this sketch, and overnight wrote the first version of his poem about it (which Shields liked). From the earliest version on, the poem was massively deictic: 'This is the place. Even here', 'that nook', 'Yon river', 'this cupboard', 'this other one', 'that Bread', 'this very bed' (revised to 'that very bed'). No ekphrastic poem could come more deictically packed, more focussed on apparent knowables and actuals. *Here* Blake wrote and painted ('writ and limned'). The room is so small (it was 13ft 9in by 12ft, in fact) that Rossetti calls it a *cupboard*. But this cupboard is a 'Holy of Holies' – named for the inner sanctum of the ancient Israelites' Tabernacle, which contained Jahwe's most holy container, the Ark of the Covenant, the most sacred box of His presence. The *cloud* of Blake's soul was present in this box-room, just as Jahwe's presence hovered in a cloud over the ancient Tabernacle by day. The Blakes' Holy of Holies contains its box too – 'this other' cupboard, visible in Shields' sketch: a food cupboard, Mrs Blake's 'charge': so un-charged with eatables that it often contained no 'daily bread' at all, but only 'the martyr's stone'. Stone, not bread, for Blake, this holy sufferer, dying here for the sake of his art. 'Give us this day our daily bread', says the well-known 'Lord's Prayer', which Jesus told his followers to repeat. So for the Blakes the prayer evidently often failed. 'What man is there of you', Jesus asked in the Sermon on the Mount (Matthew 7), 'Whom if his son ask bread, will he give him a stone? ... If ye then being evil, know how to give good gifts unto your children, how much shall your Father which is in heaven give good things to them that ask him?' But Blake would have to wait until he got to Heaven for that food, Christ Himself, the divine Bread. Or not: 'their food *might be* that Bread'. And all the poem's cited negatives – the 'nought' of Blake's vision beyond his window; the empty food cupboard – continue into the beyond of Rossetti's imagining.

And these are negatives for artists and writers, for Blake but also for Rossetti, the artist-writer of this poem, and for his poem, and thus for poeticity itself.

'Blake's cupboard of writings' (in Jessica R Feldman's phrase[45]) and this Rossetti poem as a little cupboard packed with things, all its this and that, are fulnesses threatened by their opposite, the empty container they contain, that barren food cupboard. There's no bread there, or here in the poem, no emblematic earthly presence of the Bread of Life, which is, of course, Christ the Word, the Logos, the veriest word-stuff, just what every poet needs. And that Word, the words (capitalized in the first version), are absolutely deferred in the poem's last line to another, unworldly, place: 'The words now home-speech of the mouth of God' ('now home-heard from the mouth of God' in the first version). The nourishing words, God's home-speech, are not *now*, not in *this* sketched home-place, this cupboard of words: cruelly put out of reach, displaced from this poem, this cupboard of words about Blake's cupboard.

Which is an absenting dramatically emphasized by the fraying of the poem's importunate deictic confidences when the actual 'sketch' of the poem's title is sought. Which one actually is it? There are, apparently, five extant representations of the room, not one of them certainly the one. A warm candidate is a water-colour now in the Delaware Art Museum, signed 'Fred Shields', showing a table – cognate with Rossetti's first version which had *work-table*, rather than *work-window*; though this is a suspiciously cleaned-up scene, and might be a version of an oil painting (in Manchester City Art Gallery) signed 'F Shields' and dated (perhaps) 1882. The trouble with the rough sketch reproduced in Thomas Wright's *Life of William Blake* (1929), which is perhaps the work described in the 1911 Shields Exhibition as 'the first sketch', is not just that it has disappeared, but that it shows no table, which suggests that it dates from after the 1881 version of the poem. Two extant wash drawings, with no table, also show three ghostly figures hovering over the bed, suggestive, it's thought, of the Morning Stars in the Job engraving which Blake did at 3 Fountain Court (though they were *four*), but no doubt inspired by the poem's 'cloud / Of his soul', so anyway post-dating the poem. Unsettling for the claims of the Delaware sketch, if it is indeed a version of the Manchester painting, is that the Manchester version also has the three hovering ghosts. And, of course, most dementingly for certainty seekers, is the possibility poking through that Rossetti was first shown a sketch (like the Delaware) with a work-table; put it into his poem; but scrapped it for *work-window* when he saw a table-less version, like the

---

[45] Jessica R Feldman, in 'Arrangements: Dante Gabriel Rossetti's Victorian Modernism', Ch 3 of *Victorian Modernism: Pragmatism and the Varieties of Aesthetic Experience* (Cambridge University Press, Cambridge, 2002), 77.

Wright *Life*'s rough sketch. Whatever the case, Rossetti's confident deictics shatter terribly when you try and get close to them; a breakage only affirmed when you realize that the 'close-built coiling lanes' described as outside the poet's window – 'the steep by-way's teeming gully-hole' in the first version – are not visible at all in any of Shield's pictures, but are a purposeful fiction, endorsing the poem's afflicted sense of artists' and writers' poverty, and apparently derived from Shields's oral description of the place's miserable environs when he brought his sketch (whichever it was) round to Rossetti.[46] Squeeze the Victorian ekphrastic poem, and so to say, all modernistic hell breaks loose. But this is, after all, 1881; only a whisker in time from the appearance of those foundational modernist classics, *The Turn of the Screw* (1898) and *Heart of Darkness* (1899), and the birth of those quintessential modernist writers, Virginia Woolf in 1882, DH Lawrence, and Ezra Pound in 1885, TS Eliot in 1888. In their way, of course, Victorians – as well as post-Victorians – all.

[46]   All the details of Rossetti's dealings with Shields and the Shields picture(s) are in Robert N Essick's invaluable 'Dante Gabriel Rossetti, Frederic Shields, and the Spirit of William Blake', *Victorian Poetry*, Vol 24, no. 2 (Summer 1986), 163–172 – though Essick is not interested in the ekphrastic issue, and does not realize that the first cupboard is the room itself, and so worries that Shields doesn't show it.

Index

Poems and other works of literature are qualified with the name of the author – e.g. 'After' (Marston); names are abbreviated in cases of the major authors, e.g. *Christmas Eve and Easter Day* (RB). Abbreviations: MA (Matthew Arnold), CB (Charlotte Brontë), EB (Emily Brontë), EBB (Elizabeth Barrett Barrett/Barrett Browning), RB (Robert Browning), AHC (Arthur Hugh Clough), TH (Thomas Hardy), GMH (Gerard M Hopkins), AEH (AE Housman), CGR (Christina G Rossetti), DGR (Dante Gabriel Rossetti), RLS (Robert Louis Stevenson), AS (Algernon Swinburne), AT (Alfred Lord Tennyson), OW (Oscar Wilde).

Victorian Poetry Now: Poets, Poems, Poetics, First Edition. Valentine Cunningham.
© 2011 Valentine Cunningham. Published 2011 by Blackwell Publishing Ltd.